JOHN M. PFIFFNER, Ph.D. University of Iowa, is Professor of Public Administration at the University of Southern California, and Personnel Commissioner of the Los Angeles School District. Dr. Pfiffner was previously Professor of Political Science at the University of Wichita.

ROBERT V. PRESTHUS, Ph.D. University of Chicago, is Professor of Public Administration at Cornell University and Editor of the *Administrative Science Quarterly*. He was formerly Associate Professor of Public Administration and Political Science at the University of Southern California, Associate Professor of Political Science at Michigan State University, and did research at the University of California, Berkeley, under a Ford Foundation Grant.

PUBLIC
ADMINISTRATION

By

JOHN M. PFIFFNER

PROFESSOR OF PUBLIC ADMINISTRATION
UNIVERSITY OF SOUTHERN CALIFORNIA

and

ROBERT V. PRESTHUS

PROFESSOR OF PUBLIC ADMINISTRATION
CORNELL UNIVERSITY

FOURTH EDITION

THE RONALD PRESS COMPANY · NEW YORK

Library of Congress Catalog Card Number: 60–7771

PRINTED IN THE UNITED STATES OF AMERICA

To
GLEN *and* ANN

Preface

Remarkable progress has been made in recent years in advancing our knowledge of public administration, due in large part to our need to understand the vast expansion of activities at every level of government and its implications for democracy. This renewed interest in the study of administration has been reflected both in the work of students of public administration and in the valuable research efforts of the behavioral scientist. This text is a synthesis of these important contributions from several disciplines. As such, it attempts to achieve an integration of the descriptive-structural materials of administrative science and the behavioral analyses of administration in action.

Public Administration is designed to give university and college students a clear and interesting account of the field of administration at all levels of government. The contents are divided into five sections. The introductory chapters set the scene by reviewing the rise of the bureaucratic state, its impact on administrative theory and practice, and the nature of the new public bureaucracy. Next the tasks of the administrator and his central role of leadership are analyzed in the light of the new information revolution and its effect on improved communication and decision making. Special attention is also given to the political environment and its pressure upon the public administrator.

The next three sections of the book are devoted to the technical aspects of administration: organization, personnel, and finance. In presenting these traditional descriptive materials, we have tried to make them as meaningful as possible by including an analysis of the "why" as well as the "how" of administrative operation. Examples from all jurisdictions are used to illustrate contemporary administrative practice in these areas. The following section examines the regulatory function and administrative law as embodied in the major commissions. The formal and informal process of accommodating and controlling special interests are reviewed, as are the judicial limitations of the commissions' authority.

The final chapters tackle the thorny question of administrative responsibility. Included here is a discussion of the controls exercised on the public bureaucracy by the legislative and executive branches: appointive

v

and removal powers, the power of the purse, executive orders, Congressional hearings, and the like. We conclude with an analysis of the difficult problem of determining the public interest and weighing it against the competing demands of professional and political considerations.

The content of this fourth edition reflects the rapid changes in the "ecology" of administration. The new chapter on decision making emphasizes the impact of the information revolution in administrative fact-finding and planning. The chapter on comparative administration attests to the growing interest in this field and its contributions to an improved science of administration. And throughout we have used many of the insights and findings of recent research in group behavior, individual motivation, and leadership dynamics. In short, emphasis is placed on both the formal content of public administration and the "political" and human realities of the administrative process. For example, in the section on finance, we not only detail the various stages of budgetary planning, but also deal with the budget as a collectivity of competing social and economic value systems, all of which influence the final budgetary decisions. By doing so, the realities of a complex process are revealed, including the new approaches to systems and procedures such as performance budgeting and accountability for facts as well as fiscal control. Similarly, the chapters on organization have been entirely rewritten to recognize the cultural background of organization theory and newer developments such as the data-processing revolution. The chapters on personnel also reflect our greater understanding of the importance of the human relations approach. In sum, the book seeks to aid the student both in understanding administration as it is today and in enabling him to catch a glimpse of the likely trends in administration in the near future.

JOHN M. PFIFFNER
ROBERT V. PRESTHUS

February, 1960

Contents

vii

Part V

FINANCIAL ADMINISTRATION

Part VI

ADMINISTRATIVE LAW AND REGULATION

Part VII

ADMINISTRATIVE RESPONSIBILITY

Part I

THE ENVIRONMENT OF
PUBLIC ADMINISTRATION

CHAPTER 1

The Study of
Public Administration

The importance of public administration in our urban-indus-trial society has increased steadily in recent years, and the line between public and private activities has become more tenuous. A basic factor—perhaps *the* basic factor—in this development has been the expanding role of the United States in world affairs. The evolution of the cold war and Russia's emergence as a strong contender for global leadership in the economic and military fields have saddled government with responsi-bilities on an unprecedented scale. Within government the balance of power has also shifted, with the military now enjoying an exceptional political and administrative influence.[1] Our huge armament program has also affected government's relation with industry, further blurring the line between the public and the private sectors. In sum, this marked expansion in the scope and content of public administration has focused renewed interest on this vital area.

WHAT IS ADMINISTRATION?

Administration is an activity or process mainly concerned with the *means* for carrying out prescribed ends. Although the ends of govern-ment, business, the military, and the church are clearly different, the means of achieving them are often quite similar. Power and skill must be organized and directed. Individual expectations must be reconciled by a rough equilibrium between contributions and rewards. In every large organization one finds a hierarchy of formal and informal authority, competition between many functional units, conflict between organiza-tion and individual values, specialization of labor, and operation accord-ing to explicit rules and regulations. Ideally, administration aims at

---

[1] C. Wright Mills, *The Power Elite* (New York: Oxford University Press, 1956); Samuel P. Huntington, *The Soldier and the State* (Cambridge: Harvard University Press, 1957); John W. Masland and Laurence I. Radway, *Soldiers and Scholars* (Prince-ton: Princeton University Press, 1957).

ensuring rational, "efficient" behavior on the part of its members. These common elements permit us to define administration as a universal process.

But we are concerned primarily with *public administration*, which is a particular sector of the broader field of administration. Public administration involves the implementation of public policy which has been outlined by representative political bodies. Like most generalizations, this one must be qualified. In Chapter 3 we shall see that administrators themselves have considerable influence over policy because of their technical skill and the discretion that their legislative masters must give them.

Public administration differs in several ways from private administration. Public policy enunciated in law provides the framework within which public administration works. As a result the activities of great departments, agencies, regulatory commissions, and officials are circumscribed by legal implications. Everything the bureaucrat does must be authorized by law. This passion for accountability results in a system of "checks and balances" that gives public administration a distinctive character.

It is equally clear that government's susceptibility to public criticism —a necessary part of our democratic system, if not carried to extremes— complicates public administration and brings into play organizational forms and methods which account for many of the differences between public and private administration. An example is the public corporation which has become a halfway house between its commercial prototype and the government department. In creating such corporations, Congress intended to establish businesslike agencies that would permit government the freedom and dispatch enjoyed by industry. But because of the political milieu in which government functions, measures were introduced (aimed mainly at establishing fiscal accountability) which undercut the principal advantages of the corporation device.

Another important difference between public and private administration centers on the profit motive; its absence denies government the fairly precise standard of effectiveness and vital source of motivation found in private administration. Differences in working conditions also disadvantage the public side—among them, less prestige, fewer rights and privileges, low income ceilings, and less clearly defined career avenues. These distinctions will be discussed in detail later. In sum, although public administration shows many of the characteristics of the general field of administration, it operates in an environment which fosters a more legalistic, protective attitude on the part of administrators and generates procedures designed to ensure greater impartiality and accountability.

Organization and Administration. Public administration may be defined as the coordination of individual and group efforts to carry out public policy. It is mainly occupied with the daily work of government. To do this, it is vitally interested in organization and administration. *Organization* is the structuring of individuals and functions into productive relationships; *administration* is concerned with decision making and the direction of individuals to achieve ends that have been determined by political leaders. Organization seeks a pattern of skills and responsibilities that will ensure coordination and unity of purpose through supervision. The object of both organization and administration is the *control* of human and material resources. This concept of control, however, does not mean that final authority is neatly lodged in an executive at the top. Instead, decision making is a cumulative, pluralistic process in which the top official is like a "puppet in a puppet show with hundreds of people pulling the strings and forcing him to act in one way or another."[2] The high administrator is usually an arbitrator rather than a commander. His leadership in decision making must always be shared with subordinates because of their technical skill and their knowledge of operating problems. In this sense, to achieve "control" by organization requires a structure that will ease the flow of facts, judgments, and exhortations necessary for a group pattern of decision making.

However, there is undoubtedly an arbitrary aspect to organization viewed as control. Insofar as an individual is concerned, the administrative hierarchy is a web of supervisory relationships. Organizational limitations always condition his behavior. Through the media of status patterns, reporting devices, and sanctions, which flow roughly along formal lines of authority, individual effort is directed into desired channels. Thus, despite Pope's famous dictum[3] and the behavior of informal social groups, organization as formal structure is a vital factor in administration. There has been a tendency to underestimate its importance, mainly because of the emphasis upon human relations and small group behavior. In this book we shall try to maintain a balance between these two approaches.

The second element of public administration, *administration*, may be viewed as the activity that gives direction to the organization.[4] If or-

---

[2] Sune Carlson, *Executive Behavior* (Stockholm: Stromberg, 1951), p. 52.

[3] "For forms of government let fools contest; whate'er is best administered is best." For an analysis of organizational theory, see Philip Selznick, "Foundations of the Theory of Organization," 13, *American Sociological Review* (February, 1948), pp. 25–35; see also, C. Argyris, *Personality and Organization* (New York: Harper & Bros., 1958).

[4] While "management" is often used as a synonym for administration as defined here, we prefer to speak of "personnel administration," "financial administration," etc.; the term "management" is probably more applicable to business than to public administration.

ganization can be regarded as structure, then administration becomes process; if organization is concerned with the formal, structural aspects of public administration, administration is a directing process carried on within a given institutional framework. The nature of administration is made clearer by listing its principal tools: leadership, decision making, communication, planning, and research. These are used to increase the effectiveness of men and materials structured to express rational action. While organizations develop "irrational" patterns of behavior which reflect the vagaries of human behavior, even these patterns in time become institutionalized. Organization seeks to control them in order to keep the organization's ends in view. Thus organization (while possessing inherent ingredients of change) tends toward stability. Administration, on the other hand, concerns the lively, interpersonal aspects of public administration, involving policy making, the coordination of individual and group effort, and the maintenance of employee morale.[5]

In sum, public administration is a process concerned with carrying out public policies, encompassing innumerable skills and techniques which give order and purpose to the efforts of large numbers of people. Its importance is apparent in the fact that today one of every eight Americans works for a public agency—national, state, or local. Total government expenses amount to about one-fifth of our annual gross national product. Government is thus by far our largest enterprise and our biggest employer. It alone has a monopoly of legal and military power. Moreover the issues with which it deals are critical, involving inflation, monetary policy, and national survival.

As a discipline, public administration is concerned with all the social sciences which provide knowledge in the areas of value judgments, policy determination, and organizational behavior. There may be a separate field of "administration," but it remains descriptive and barren without the insights of political science, sociology, and psychology. Public administration can also be viewed as a social process, charged with implementing great ends. The role of government is always dynamic, often expanding, sometimes receding, reflecting changing national and international imperatives. Public administration is the instrument that carries out the new policies that result and which bridges the gap between such

---

[5] It may be useful here to define the terms "executive" and "administrator." It is common practice to differentiate them on the basis that executives occupy positions at the top of the hierarchy, and consequently make important policy decisions, while the administrator merely carries out orders. In this sense federal "executives" include the President, the several hundred persons appointed by him on a political basis, and the career civil servants at the top of the bureaucracy. This distinction is not too useful, however, because officials at every level influence policy to some extent. The differences between administrators and executives are differences of degree rather than of kind, and hence we shall use the terms interchangeably.

needs and their satisfaction. As Brooks Adams said, the function of administration is assuring social stability by facilitating change.[6] Today the most pressing issues, such as war and peace, full employment, poverty and disease, have become the responsibility of government. For these reasons the effectiveness of government administration is always worthy of study.

THREE APPROACHES TO THE STUDY OF PUBLIC ADMINISTRATION

The study of public administration is a relatively new subject. Although it can be considered a "modern" discipline, it is difficult to set any one date as marking the beginning of public administration, either as a formalized activity or as a recognized field of study. For example, some observers place its beginnings with Woodrow Wilson's essay in 1887;[7] some give credit to the writings of Frank J. Goodnow in the 1890's and early 1900's,[8] while others cite Leonard D. White, who published the first modern textbook of public administration in 1926.[9] But a century before this, de Tocqueville wrote of some of the characteristics of governmental administration as it was practiced at that time.[10] Regardless of whether the emergence of public administration as a separate discipline can be pinpointed more specifically than around the turn of the twentieth century, such a body of knowledge does exist, and it concerns all aspects of governmental operation dealing with carrying out decisions made usually by elected officials. Whether the actual making of such decisions themselves should be a part of the field of public administration is a matter of some debate, but this controversy need not be considered at the moment.

With public administration, as with administration in general, there have been numerous schools of thought directed toward how best to study the field. Scholars holding various viewpoints have written extensively, trying to document their case. Although it is impossible here to examine all these approaches, most of them can be assembled into three major types: the constitutional-legal-historical approach, the structural-

[6] Brooks Adams, *The Theory of Social Revolutions* (New York: The Macmillan Co., 1913).

[7] Woodrow Wilson, "The Study of Administration," 2, *Political Science Quarterly*, (1887), 197–222.

[8] Frank J. Goodnow, *Comparative Administrative Law*, I and II (New York: G. P. Putnam's Sons, 1893); *The Principles of the Administrative Law of the United States* (New York: G. P. Putnam's Sons, 1905); *Politics and Administration* (New York: The Macmillan Co., 1900).

[9] Leonard D. White, *Introduction to the Study of Public Administration* (New York: The Macmillan Co., 1926).

[10] Alexis de Tocqueville, *Democracy in America*, 2 vol. (New York: Alfred A. Knopf, Inc., 1945).

descriptive approach, and the socio-psychological approach. This arbi-trary categorization of the major approaches, of course, oversimplifies what is admittedly a very complicated picture.[10a] However, these three groups will serve our purpose. The first two will be discussed briefly, and the third will be dealt with at greater length because it seems to have made the most significant recent contribution to the field of public administration. It also appears to offer considerable promise for greater understanding of what administration is and how organizations actually operate.

Constitutional-Legal-Historical Approach. The constitutional-legal-historical approach, based on a framework of legal rights and obligations of government, grew out of the Constitution or precedents established by legal opinions and decisions. The role of the traditional place of admin-istration on the governmental scene is also not overlooked. This type of study is often regarded today as presenting too narrow a picture of public administration. However, during the late nineteenth century when this was the main approach, public administration was considered as an adjunct of public law rather than as the dynamic specialty it has become today. The great emphasis of the period was normative and political rather than organizational, including such issues as popular control of government and the nature of the federal union itself. In fact even civil service reform was based as much upon moral issues as upon the need for more efficient administration.

Advocates of this approach to public administration are also interested in the roles of the executive, legislative, and judicial branches of our government, their relations vis-à-vis one another, and the effects that their policies and actions will have upon the administration of govern-ment policy. An outstanding early writer in this area was W. F. Wil-loughby, who summarized the existing weaknesses in governmental ad-ministration and delineated the major areas of public administration which he felt should be included in the field.[11] The controversy over the "proper" role of the main branches of government still exists and can never be resolved to the complete satisfaction of all the advocates of the several viewpoints. Another important part of this approach is the normative consideration of the areas with which government (and there-fore public administration) "should" be concerned. In recent years this problem has been emphasized by such issues as the Dixon-Yates public vs. private power controversy in 1955, and by the current situa-

---

[10a] Dwight Waldo, *The Study of Public Administration* (Garden City, N. Y.: Doubleday & Co., Inc., 1955) surveys the scope and method of public administration, particularly the question of value conflict in the field.

[11] W. F. Willoughby, *Principles of Public Administration*, (Baltimore: The Johns Hopkins Press, 1927).

tion in the atomic energy field where the federal government has maintained control of all nuclear material and atomic energy plants under the Atomic Energy Commission.

Structural-Descriptive Approach. The structural-descriptive approach is perhaps used more than any other in public administration textbooks. Leonard D. White set the pattern for this school when he defined the components of administration as organization and personnel management combined with necessary financial and legal controls. His definition of public administration was, "the management of men and materials in the accomplishment of the purposes of the state."[12] His text discussed both organizational considerations and specific operating techniques.

Although this approach is typical of most writing in the field, it may be criticized for inadequately relating public administration to its environment and for not sufficiently considering administration as the interaction of human beings, without which the term "administration" loses much of its meaning. In addition, while the importance of techniques for the accomplishment of programs is recognized, attention must also be given to the theoretical aspects of administration and to the citizens affected by administrative activities. The structural-descriptive approach emphasizes such things as organizational structure, government personnel techniques, and financial administration. It tends to give a rather antiseptic picture of administration. These traditional areas of interest must not, of course, be overlooked, but they are not the only things to be considered. The trend among scholars using this approach tends to be in the direction of expanding their analyses into such important areas as administrative law and administrative responsibility. This is all to the good, for only by this means will public administration achieve an optimum blend of technique and theory.

Because of the origin of public administration in political science and because of its close relationship to political science as a discipline, it is difficult completely to separate these two areas. Much of the work that has been done in public administration begins with political science concepts. This fact is included in our review of the structural-descriptive approach because there is a body of writing which deals at the same time with bureaucratic structure, both as an organizational arrangement and as a theoretical concept of political science. On the one hand the bureaucracy is considered as a technical means of administering policy, and on the other, as an offshoot of our executive-legislative-judicial form of government. Of course the work done in areas such as administrative law, constitutional law, personnel management, and legislative-executive relationships has often made it difficult to distinguish where political

[12] L. D. White, *Introduction to the Study of Public Administration.*

science ends and public administration begins. Each of these disciplines is dependent upon the other. This suggests that instead of separating public administration and political science—one a theory and the other a practice—they may better be reconciled under some title such as "political administration," "public administration theory," or "political science and administration." Certainly, as the following chapter suggests, there are few areas of political science, including traditional political theory, that are not useful in understanding public administration.

The rewards made possible by combining political science with public administration are clear from such landmark studies as John M. Gaus's work on the U.S. Department of Agriculture,[13] Leonard D. White's administrative histories,[14] R. A. Cushman's analysis of the regulatory commissions,[15] H. M. Somers' study of a wartime staff agency,[16] Arthur Maass's case study of administrative irresponsibility,[17] Friedrich and Cole's essay on administrative responsibility in several countries,[18] Harold Laski's analysis of the American presidency,[19] and Gulick and Urwick's work on the nature of administration,[20] to name only a few. All these studies are of permanent value to the field of public administration, and it would be unwise if not impossible to attempt to study administration from a different focus without a thorough grounding in these kinds of analyses.

Socio-Psychological Approach. The socio-psychological approach to the study of public administration, probably the most recent of the several approaches, seems destined to enjoy greater prominence as the behavioral sciences become more established, since it is concerned with the systematic study of human behavior in an organizational context. This kind of study is much influenced by methodological considerations, and its advocates tend to be much concerned with the *means* of handling organization data and developing theoretical frameworks for the ordering of data. Whereas the older approaches often included value judgments about what public administration "should" do and what proper

[13] John M. Gaus with L. O. Wolcott, *Public Administration and the United States Department of Agriculture* (Chicago: Public Administration Service, 1949).

[14] *The Federalists* (New York: The Macmillan Co., 1948); *The Jeffersonians* (New York: The Macmillan Co., 1951); *The Jacksonians* (New York: The Macmillan Co., 1954); *The Republican Era* (New York: The Macmillan Co., 1958).

[15] *The Independent Regulatory Commissions* (New York: Oxford University Press, Inc., 1941).

[16] *Presidential Agency: the OWMR* (Cambridge: Harvard University Press, 1950).

[17] *Muddy Waters* (Cambridge: Harvard University Press, 1951).

[18] *Representative Bureaucracy* (Cambridge: Harvard University Press, 1932).

[19] *The American Presidency* (New York: Alfred A. Knopf, Inc., 1940).

[20] *Papers on the Science of Administration* (New York: Institute of Public Administration, 1937).

organizational forms "should" be, the socio-psychological approach tends to be more concerned with finding out what the actual situation "is." Generally it is concerned with the investigation of rather limited areas of inquiry. Its advocates feel we just do not know enough about the field to be very sure as to what "should" be done. Another distinction is that the newer approach consciously seeks to build up generalizations about organization and administration. It tends to believe that there is order and consistency in administrative processes, or at least in the human interaction that is at the center of administration. One could say that the hope for an administrative science is its peculiar normative value!

An obvious problem here, of course, is that decisions must still be made in the everyday world of action. For the policy-maker it is not very helpful to be told that a pressing decision requires additional research. Besides, as suggested earlier, considerations of power, prestige, and survival shape decision premises as much as objective questions of *what is* and normative questions of *what ought to be*. Such differences in perspective tend to create a gap between the student and the practitioner of administration. But we can safely say that this gap is narrowing, since administrators in our pragmatic culture always try to become more effective, and in so doing, they often bring research findings into the administration arena.

In any event the socio-psychological approach is probably most concerned with knowledge for its own sake and with applying more rigorous methods to the study of public administration. It is interested both in formal structure and in individual and group behavior in an organizational context. Perhaps more important, it digs deeper into such recurrent problems as the nature of authority, the effects of small group behavior on the organization's larger objectives, the impact of differing leadership patterns, the significance of communication as an index of power and satisfactions, and the nature and complexity of decision making. One may in all fairness say that this approach is mainly concerned with the *action process* in administration.

This is a newer view of administration resulting from the work of sociologists and social psychologists together with a relatively small number of political scientists, who are bringing to the study of administration the insights and techniques of social science, philosophy, and mathematics. The work of the Survey Research Center at the University of Michigan illustrates one of the main characteristics of this approach: the use of the theory, concepts, and methods of all the behavioral sciences (sociology, psychology, social psychology, anthropology, and political science) to analyze organizational structure and administrative processes and the way that people react to them.[21]

An example of the socio-psychological approach, or the "administrative process" approach as it may also be termed, is seen in the increased theoretical and research interest in the interaction between the typical bureaucratic structure and its individual members. This emphasis ranges broadly from normative inquiries into the harmful impact of organization demands upon individual creativity,[22] through attempts to work out broad theories of organizational behavior,[23] to attempts to set down a general theory of administration,[24] and to systematic empirical investigations of small-group interaction in operating agencies.[25] Indeed, if one searches the social science journals, he finds an embarrassing amount of data bearing upon administrative theory and behavior. Most of this material, however, is discrete and random, with little effort to develop a theory of administration or to repeat earlier studies with a view to checking upon their validity.[26]

In any event the current trend in empirical research is to move down the "abstraction ladder" to studies of limited scope that can provide generalizations upon which a broader theory of administration can some-day be built. Most of these studies are characterized by an "action" or "process" approach to administration. The individual's and the organization's structure, values, and objectives are seen as *changing* and interdependent. Obviously this lack of constancy makes for a very complicated structure of analysis, but the great gain is a closer approximation of the real world. As a consequence the generalizations that result are highly contingent; they reflect the existence of a particular combination of variables at a particular point in time. In effect they represent a snapshot of a continuous process stopped momentarily for research purposes.

In discussing the socio-psychological, or "process," approach, one also thinks of the interuniversity case program which reconstructs selected

---

[21] Leon Festinger and Daniel Katz, *Research Methods in the Behavioral Sciences* (New York: Henry Holt & Co., Inc., 1958).

[22] W. H. Whyte, Jr., *The Organization Man* (New York: Simon and Schuster, Inc., 1956); Chris Argyris, "The Individual and Organization: Some Problems of Mutual Adjustment," 2, *Administrative Science Quarterly* (June, 1957).

[23] Robert V. Presthus, "Toward a Theory of Organizational Behavior," 3, *Administrative Science Quarterly* (June, 1958), pp. 48–72.

[24] Edward H. Litchfield, "Toward a Theory of Administration," 1, *Administrative Science Quarterly* (June, 1956) p. 1.

[25] An excellent example of such research is Peter Blau, *The Dynamics of Bureaucracy* (Chicago: University of Chicago Press, 1955).

[26] A valuable exception, unfortunately rarely seen in public administration, is R. C. Hanson, "Evidence and Procedure Characteristics of Reliable Propositions in Social Science," 63, *American Journal of Sociology* (January, 1958). Such replication is rarely possible in studies of public administration, which seldom include either the methodological or the theoretical assumptions of the writer.

administrative decisions in an attempt to convey the richness and complexity of the administrative process.[27] Institutional, political, and interpersonal factors are analyzed to reveal the nature of the process of deciding. To this extent the case approach resembles the socio-psychological approach, with its efforts to isolate the many variables that press upon the administrator. However, several vital differences exist, mainly in philosophy and method. The most significant is probably that the case program has made little or no effort to build up generalizations about administration. Indeed, the conceptual framework of the case program seems to be that no generalizations are possible in an environment which is so complex, so beset by differences in politics, power, program, and level of operation. Also, in point of method, the cases are essentially individualistic and impressionistic; that is, they represent the analysis of a single observer whose theoretical, normative, and methodological assumptions are rarely made patent. This means that replication, i.e., the attempt to check the results and validity of any given case by further research, is virtually impossible. Following the categories set down earlier, we can say that the case program tends to follow the socio-psychological approach in its essentially dynamic and multifaceted conception of administration, but that theoretically and methodologically it is quite opposed.

In summing up these approaches, it should be said that each has contributed much to the study of administration and that each has played a dominant role at a given historical time. Moreover, anyone unacquainted with each approach could hardly be called knowledgeable in the field. This book draws upon each approach. Actually, as an introductory text, it attempts to offer the broadest possible interpretation of public administration. We are concerned with bureaucratic structure, its internal operations, the interpersonal side of organization, and the complexities of decision making. At the same time, what may be called the *environmental* aspects of the field are also touched upon: the political framework of administration; the normative questions of administrative responsibility and the "public interest"; the role of public administration as a social instrument; and equally, the manner in which its long-run goals and its internal structure and procedures reflect the values of the larger social system.

Now that a review of several approaches to the study of public administration has been completed, we can attempt to assess some problems that seem peculiar to research in a field whose concern with political goals, carried out through the efforts of human beings, inevitably gives it a highly normative character.

[27] A representative selection of such cases is available in H. Stein (ed.), *Public Administration and Policy Development* (New York: Harcourt, Brace and Co., 1952).

RESEARCH PROBLEMS IN ADMINISTRATION

Scientific Method. By way of introduction, something must be said of the scientific method and "science"[28] and whether the scientific method is properly adaptable to the study of public administration.[29]

It is generally agreed that a science must have certain characteristics of precision and predictability. Whereas Einstein's modification of the Newtonian theory of gravity indicates that even the formulas of the physical sciences are less precise than assumed, the physical sciences do have a relatively high degree of probability. This is to say that certain geometrical theorems can be "proved," or that certain chemical ingredients combined in exact measure will produce repeatedly the same compound. A scientific discipline has generally been held to be one in which objectively verifiable laws or principles operate in a causal sequence. This quality of predictability ensures stability of relationships; it permits us to say we "know." Thus scientists such as Kepler, Galileo, and Harvey believed that the so-called laws of nature were written in geometric lines, subject to understanding by special insight, and capable of statement in the form of principles.

Principles, in turn, rest upon facts, which have been defined as "propositions for whose truth there is considerable evidence."[30] Now, "facts" in the physical sciences have a high degree of consistency irrespective of time, place, or the emotional preferences of the observer. Strictly speaking, therefore, a scientific discipline is one in which certain firm principles exist, possessing universal validity. A "principle" in the scientific sense is not dependent upon value judgments. It is not concerned with moral precepts such as the belief that democracy is the "best" form of government. This proposition may very well be true, but there is no scientific way of proving it because objective facts are not available for classification and measurement. Democracy involves faith, while scientific principles require demonstrable evidence. However vital they are in human affairs, values have little relevance to the establishment of scientific propositions, except insofar as they motivate the scientist to do research of a certain kind.

[28] The following comments are based largely upon Morris R. Cohen's *Studies in Philosophy and Science* (New York: Henry Holt & Co., Inc., 1949); and *An Introduction to Logic and Scientific Method* (New York: Harcourt, Brace & Co., Inc., 1934); F. S. C. Northrop, *Logic of the Sciences and the Humanities* (New York: The Macmillan Co., 1947); and Gunnar Myrdal, *An American Dilemma* (New York: Harper & Bros., 1944).

[29] For a well-reasoned and reasonable essay on this question, see Kenneth E. Boulding, "Toward An Administrative Science," 3, *Administrative Science Quarterly* (June, 1958) pp. 1–22.

[30] Cohen, *An Introduction to Logic and Scientific Method*, p. 392.

To put it another way, hydrogen bombs can be made by democratic or authoritarian physicists. In deciding how the bombs will be used, however, we abandon science for ethics. We move from an area of technical rationality and high predictability to speculation based upon values that vary in time and space. Thus the nature and status of the physical sciences are bound up with the element of consistency or probability. It is comforting to be able to say that this order and consistency springs in part at least from the fact that the physical sciences are essentially much simpler than the social sciences. Today most of us would agree that social science has become more vital since control of atomic weapons has become a condition of human survival.

Something more should be said about the scientific method. It is essentially a technique of analysis involving two steps: the establishment of a hypothesis (or more properly, several hypotheses) to provide a frame of reference within which research may proceed; and the collection and verification (or nullification) of facts that relate to the hypothesis. Verification involves the act of selecting from among several hypotheses that one which is most probable, that which best explains a particular theory on the basis of the factual evidence available.[31] But the scientific method is much more than routinized procedures; it is a tentative attitude of mind, marked by the ability to suspend judgment and to avoid the development of vested intellectual interests. "Scientific method pursues the road of systematic doubt."[32]

Problem of Values. It is clear that in public administration, which is one of the social sciences where value judgments abound, the maintenance of such detachment is most difficult. Prejudice, taboos, and social controls make objective research difficult. Certain symbols are heavily charged with emotion. "Socialism," "bureaucracy," "democracy," and "politics," for example, have different connotations for persons with different social backgrounds. Currently, for example, the senior civil service plan for the federal government is being opposed on the ground that it violates democratic principles of equality. The difficulty of arriving at commonly held concepts is aggravated by the fact that human certainty seems to exist in inverse proportion to factual knowledge. Emotional conflicts are more intense in matters of religion and politics than in, say, the field of mathematics. These subjective elements are important in determining the adaptability of the scientific method to the study of administrative behavior. At first thought it would seem that the very subject matter of administration negates the use of the scientific method. How can one hope to measure, much less hold constant, the subtle varia-

[31] Cohen, *Studies in Philosophy and Science*, p. 86.
[32] Cohen, *An Introduction to Logic and Scientific Method*, p. 394.

tions of human behavior? How can one reach consensus as to the "best way" of practicing and researching administration?

Despite this, there is impressive evidence that the social sciences generally and public administration particularly can use the scientific method productively—not necessarily in the sense of establishing principles but in the sense of dealing critically with evidence. "The man who has an eye for facts, whether it be about human beings, stones, or anything else, the man who asks, 'Is it so?' and 'Can it be verified?' has the essence of all science, provided he follows the critical methods of proof and verification."[33]

If evidence is to be dealt with in this way, the problem of value judgments in research must be faced. Now value judgments are not only always present—they are often inconsistent and transitory, changing in terms of individual experience. For example, in recent decades they have been profoundly influenced by a general skepticism stemming from a series of global conflicts and the impact of an industrial civilization which has brought high material standards but neither economic nor emotional security. Such social dynamics aggravate the problem of treating data scientifically. We are aided, perhaps, by the efforts of individuals to keep their valuations in a fairly logical and consistent order. It is well known that individuals develop elaborate rationalizations to explain away evidence contrary to their beliefs. But in general, as Gunnar Myrdal has shown, values in modern society are dynamic; they change in response to changes in the material world and in the world of ideas.[34]

In sum, it has been shown that hypotheses, a form of value judgment, are necessary to give meaning to research. It is equally clear that individuals are subject to bias. The scientist himself does not operate in a moral vacuum. By the very act of selecting a certain subject for investigation, by setting down tentative conclusions about that subject, he inevitably makes subjective preferences. In brief, there is no way of avoiding the bias arising from individual beliefs and valuations about reality. The imperative obligation for the scientist then becomes that of recognizing such influences and compensating for their existence.[35] Such a statement of value premises, moreover, is helpful in laying the basis for the practical application of research findings. Conclusions reached scientifically in a value context can point the way to social change.

Now, having outlined scientific method and the difficulty of treating

---

[33] Cohen, *Studies in Philosophy and Science*, p. 86.

[34] G. Myrdal, *An American Dilemma*, pp. 1027–64.

[35] "There is no other device for excluding biases in social sciences than to face the valuations and to introduce them as explicitly stated, specific, sufficiently concretized value premises." *Ibid.*, p. 1043.

public administration according to its dictates, we can turn to a review of several research approaches to the field.

RESEARCH IN PUBLIC ADMINISTRATION

One is impressed by the tendency of writing and research in public administration to be based upon personal experience, random observation, and highly subjective claims about the virtues of a specific system or method. Vested professional interests have often resisted the introduction of more systematic research. More important, the "applied" character of public administration has encouraged teachers in the field to concern themselves with action roles, to the detriment of basic research. Again, traditional political science, the discipline in which many public administration teachers receive their training, has neither prepared nor oriented them toward the systematic field research which marks a discipline.

The Traditional Approach. Public administration research has often revealed a certain amount of uncritical thinking. As in economic theory, an unquestioned assumption of man as a rational being has run throughout the literature. The role of economic motivation has generally been exaggerated, while formal organization has been unduly emphasized at the expense of social and personal factors which greatly influence administrative behavior. Moreover, the vocabulary of the physical sciences has been applied, though rather vaguely, to public administration. The term "principle" was enlisted in reference to certain empirically determined rules for effective administrative organization and operation.[36] Organization by function, the separation of line and staff activities, and the establishment of reasonable spans of control, among others, were sometimes set down as "laws" of common applicability.

At the same time it was thought possible to exclude value judgments in favor of "scientific management" and to establish as an end some amoral precept such as "efficiency." That "efficiency" must always be defined in terms of the social objectives of a particular time was not always recognized. Only an insufficient accumulation of "facts" was held to prevent logical and "efficient" administration. That "facts" are inextricably interwoven with ideas and values was sometimes forgotten. In terms of method, pragmatism[37] and a crude empiricism[38] were

[36] For a provocative summary of traditional theory and research, see C. Dwight Waldo, *The Administrative State* (New York: The Ronald Press Co., 1948), chap. ix.

[37] Very briefly, *pragmatism* is the belief that the true measure of an idea is how it works in practice. It is based upon a distrust of speculation and reason in favor of experience.

[38] *Empiricism* is the method by which pragmatism functions: knowledge is sought through observation and experience.

accepted as the hallmarks of the scientific method. On the other hand, randomly selected facts were used as a basis for easy generalization. This, despite the knowledge that even the physical sciences must place facts within a conceptual framework if they are to provide a basis for generalization.

More Recent Methodology. Gradually, however, a more critical view developed, largely a questioning of the basic assumptions of the earlier approach. This has been part of a general effort of social scientists to achieve something of the precision and predictability of the physical sciences. The problem of method is now recognized as basic, while the need for a theoretical basis for studying public administration is widely accepted. Research tends to exhibit an awareness of limitations, in keeping with the tradition of the scientific method. The question of administrative "principles," for example, has been carefully discussed by Herbert Simon, and the qualified sense in which the term can be used is now acknowledged. It is also recognized that the objective of the scientific method in administration, as elsewhere, is *to predict*. The function of research therefore becomes the discovery of valid generalizations about human behavior in administrative situations; about the influence of different organizational structures on effectiveness; about the process of change, etc.

Perhaps the most suggestive research and theory has dealt with administrative behavior and informal organization.[39] This work is characterized by the interplay of several disciplines and a broader understanding of group behavior, leadership, and decision making. The methods and insights of sociology, social psychology, and anthropology have been helpful in determining the effect of small groups on such behavioral phenomena as loyalty, morale, and productivity. Such research has been a joint product of the universities, public and private executives, and the United States government through the Air Force, the Office of Naval Research, and contracts with quasiprivate agencies such as the Rand Corporation. The research is experimental, quantitative, and scientific in spirit. Although its results have yet to be fully assayed, much of it is immediately useful, as indicated by references throughout this book. In no previous research in administration, it seems fair to say, has there

[39] See, among others, Fritz J. Roethlisberger and William J. Dixon, *Management and the Worker* (Cambridge: Harvard University Press, 1941); Elton Mayo, *The Social Problems of an Industrial Civilization* (Boston: Harvard University Graduate School of Business Administration, 1945); Chester I. Barnard, *Organization and Management* (Cambridge: Harvard University Press, 1948); Alexander Leighton, *The Governing of Men* (Princeton: Princeton University Press, 1945); Peter Blau, *The Dynamics of Bureaucracy* (Chicago: University of Chicago Press, 1955); and Herbert A. Simon, *Administrative Behavior* (Rev. ed.; New York: The Macmillan Co., 1957); James G. March and Herbert A. Simon, *Organizations* (New York: John Wiley & Sons, Inc., 1958).

been an equal awareness of the importance of carefully delineated hypotheses and a method that can bring greater precision to the loose terminology and hazy categories which plague the social sciences.

The increasing reliance on social science in analyzing administration is also apparent in the launching of several interdisciplinary journals. Among others, *Administrative Science Quarterly*, *Behavioral Science*, *Human Relations*, and *Management Science* have brought both the concepts and the method of various social sciences to the study of administration in many contexts. In the main these journals publish systematic, research-based articles that consciously attempt to build general propositions about administrative organization and behavior, as distinguished from discrete observations based on personal experience.

The "fact-value" issue in administrative decisions has also been treated more critically.[40] That policy determination is necessarily concerned with value assumptions is clearly recognized. Public administration, like the other social sciences, is inevitably charged with normative values, for it seeks to determine what *should* be done. The importance of such questions is shown in Chapter 31 on administration and the public interest, where it is argued that whether or not the "public interest" can be defined or empirically verified, the public servant's *conception* of it will often influence his actions. In this context it is important to remember that myths as well as facts influence human behavior.

Decision making has become the focus of considerable attention in the study of public administration.[41] As we shall see in Chapter 6, the decision-making process involves a choice among several alternative courses of action, bringing into play values which in turn stem from certain attitudes. It is clear that many factors influence the administrator as policy maker, conditioning the mental set which he brings to the process. Various "external" factors, including the cultural values of society, the dominant attitudes of his client groups, and those of the public at large, influence his thinking. Competing with these for preference are "internal" factors such as his own personality structure, the power and morale of his agency, and the success with which individual goals of workers can be identified with those of the organization. Thus the process of decision making is recognized as culturally determined rather than the result of an objective analysis of facts. This view reflects the sociological approach to the law, and particularly the unexpressed

---

[40] Herbert A. Simon, *Administrative Behavior*; Wayne Leys, *Ethics for Policy Decisions* (Englewood Cliffs, N.J.: Prentice-Hall, Inc., 1952).

[41] See, for example, the special issue of 3, *Administrative Science Quarterly* (December, 1958), which is devoted to theory and research on decision making in several disciplines; Chester I. Barnard, *The Function of the Executive* (Cambridge: Harvard University Press, 1938); Herbert A. Simon, *Administrative Behavior*.

social premises of the Supreme Court justices which shape their opinions as to the "constitutionality" of given laws or executive action.

CONCLUSION

In view of what has been said, it seems clear that public administration is both an art and a science, involving the discovery and application of useful skills and techniques to implement public policies set down by representative bodies. The role of the higher administrator illustrates this point. He functions in a dynamic milieu, subject to changes and pressures which he can only hope to anticipate. He must deal with individuals, organized groups and the unorganized public, the legislature, the courts, and his colleagues at several levels. His own values demand expression. In each instance he must possess the ability to manipulate symbols and (one fears) individuals in an effort to solicit cooperation, effect compromise, inculcate loyalty, generate enthusiasm (or at least compliance), and present complicated ideas in simple form. The control factor, which in the physical sciences permits the development of principles and a context of certainty, is rarely present. Thus the administrator must be the generalist par excellence. Public administration demands of him an unusual capacity for selecting methods and maneuvers appropriate to the particular situation confronting him.

It would be remiss, however, to end on this note, since social science research is continually providing new insights into administrative behavior, propelling administration toward the "scientific" end of the continuum ranging from "folklore" to "science." Indeed, as in many fields, administration already *"knows* better than it *does,"* and the problem of putting known insights to work in operating situations is perhaps as critical as the problem of adding knowledge by further research. Certainly one of the objects of this book is to help bridge this gap.

BIBLIOGRAPHY

BARNARD, CHESTER I. *The Function of the Executive.* Cambridge: 1938.
COHEN, MORRIS R. *Introduction to Logic and Scientific Method.* New York: 1934.
DURKHEIM, EMILE. *The Division of Labor in Society.* Glencoe, Ill.: 1948.
FAYOL, HENRY. *Industrial and General Administration.* New York: 1937.
FOLLETT, MARY P. *The New State.* New York: 1918.
GULICK, LUTHER, and URWICK, L. (eds.). *Papers on the Science of Administration.* New York: 1937.
MYRDAL, GUNNAR. *An American Dilemma.* New York: 1944.
NORTHROP, F. S. C. *Logic, Science and the Humanities.* New York: 1949.
———. *Introduction to Logic and Scientific Method.* New York: 1934.
PARSONS, TALCOTT, and SHILS, E. *Toward a General Theory of Action.* Cambridge: 1944.
SELZNICK, PHILIP. "Foundation of the Theory of Organization," **13,** *American Sociological Review* (February, 1948).

Simon, Herbert. *Administrative Behavior: A Study of Decision-Making Processes in Administrative Organization.* New York: 1957.

Waldo, Dwight. *The Study of Public Administration.* Doubleday Short Studies in Political Science. New York: 1955.

Weber, Max. *The Protestant Ethic and the Spirit of Capitalism.* London: 1930.

——. *The Theory of Social and Economic Organization.* L. J. Henderson and Talcott Parsons, eds. New York: 1947.

CHAPTER 2

Why Big Government

Before turning to the traditional areas of the public administration, something must be said about the expansion of government's activity that lies behind the increased responsibilities of the civil service. Despite our tradition of voluntary, private solutions to social problems, government continues to grow. But why has government become the principal means for translating community values into action? Why have critical questions of fiscal policy, full employment, atomic energy control and development, missile research, foreign aid, and the like been placed under its aegis?

Democratic political theory suggests some of the answers to such questions. An analysis in terms of the group process in politics is also helpful, since it dramatizes the fact that expanding public programs are partly the result of interest-group demands. In addition, war, depression, and national defense provide new opportunities for government's expansion, and when the emergencies have passed, many of the new programs remain. Certain structural characteristics of our political system have also encouraged the trend toward big government. As the economy became more complex, Congress and the courts were less able to carry out the regulatory functions demanded by society. Thus the administrative branch, which had more flexibility and could act more swiftly, assumed an ever-greater role.

THE RISE OF THE ADMINISTRATIVE STATE

The following sketch reveals several reasons for government's expanding role. Technological developments and our evolution from an agrarian to an urban-industrial society provided the major framework for big government. Demands from groups which gradually came to recognize their political power added to the trend. Meanwhile, the technical complexity of government's new role brought about a transfer of power *within* our political system. Public regulation of great economic interests demanded continuous and expert surveillance, yet Congress could respond only with general statutes. Its actions, moreover, were likely to be remedial, coming only after serious problems had evolved. The courts,

22

too, were unsuited to the new environment; the judicial process was found to be too slow, too expensive, and too inflexible to meet the needs of big government. In any case, the courts themselves recognized that public policy was more properly the role of the *political* branches, Congress and the Executive.

The decline of legislative and judicial influence was counteracted by the rise of administrative power which had the flexibility and expertise now required. As Walton Hamilton put it:

> It was to correct the market that the state was called to action. A shipper cannot bargain with the railroad over the price of the haul—the Interstate Commerce Commission comes into being. The investor lacks the skills with which to judge stocks and bonds—the Securities and Exchange Commission is the answer. The law of supply and demand fails to adjust the acreage of staple crops to market demand—the Agricultural Adjustment Administration is sent to the rescue. The private sources of capital, especially in a depression, shrink from risk—the Reconstruction Finance Corporation underwrites a hesitant free enterprise. The individual wage-earner is no longer a match for the corporate employer—the National Labor Relations Board is called upon to ensure "that equality in bargaining power in which freedom of contracts begins."[1]

THE MAIN OBJECTIVES OF GOVERNMENT

Perhaps the political environment of public administration can be made clearer by an inquiry into the values that society holds. Administration does not function in a vacuum; its objectives are a reflection of the felt needs of society at a given time. In this sense government's new responsibilities are the result of changing public opinions about the "proper" role of government in making good certain basic values. For example, we have gradually come to place a high value upon equality of opportunity in education and economic affairs. When private activity has not been able to make good this claim, or in some cases has even inhibited it, most people have called upon government to secure it. In this context the study of public administration ought to begin with a review of the main objectives of our democratic government.

Ensuring Order. At the very least, government designs and enforces the rules of the social order so that human activity may proceed in a continuous, predictable way. If life is to be worth while, the individual needs the help of several institutions—the family, the village, the state, the university. As Aristotle argued, man is a political animal, bound up in a variety of institutions, ending with the state. All these institutions have accepted codes of conduct, but perhaps the most far reaching and powerful is government.

[1] Walton Hamilton, "The Smouldering Constitutional Crisis," in R. F. Harvey, *et al.*, *Government in American Society* (New York: William Sloane, Associations, Inc., 1950), p. 141.

One may assume that the obvious need for cooperation would be sufficient to ensure that individuals accept the rules of social relations. But even the slightest acquaintance with history indicates the opposite. Without accepting all of Freudian psychology, one can agree that man possesses aggressive impulses and strives for power over his fellows. Power of one kind or another is inherent in all social relations, and if such drives and the destruction that often accompanies them are not to tear society apart, some agency must have a monopoly of power and violence. This agency we know as government, or the state. Historically the centralization of power in the hands of the state has been steadily growing.

A certain utopianism in American thought has led to a neglect of the implications of power, which conflict with the pervasive optimism of Western philosophy. Also, we have often failed to recognize that power by itself is not necessarily bad, that power is a neutral instrument whose character depends upon how it is used. Political analysis in terms of group behavior reflects this power struggle, but in our society the instruments of the struggle are usually constitutional rather than violent, evolutionary rather than revolutionary. Trade associations, farm organizations, labor unions, political parties—all compete for power to influence government and the public. Our constitution and, more important, our high living standards and literacy rate ensure that such struggles will occur. The significant thing is that the struggle is usually waged peacefully and that power is subject to periodic reappraisal and redistribution.

Achieving Larger Social Purpose. This negative concept of the state as an umpire enforcing rules impartially has been changing since Colonial times. Although Herbert Spencer insisted in 1850 that poverty, starvation, and the domination of the weak by the strong were "the decrees of a far-seeing benevolence," his words were anachronistic even when he wrote them.[2] Problems of urbanization, health, and working conditions attending the Industrial Revolution had already brought in England a substantial number of remedial programs, and such "solutions by government" were only beginning. In the United States a similar pattern appeared during the last quarter of the nineteenth century, and by the end of the Depression during the 1930's, measures for health, welfare, and education equaled those of other Western industrial countries.

We can now trace briefly the way in which groups in our society have expressed and achieved their demands for a larger share of the benefits that government could provide. Obviously, no steady development of demands and satisfactions occurred; instead these fluctuated as first one group, then another, gained a temporary advantage. But the main drift

2 Herbert Spencer, *Social Statics* (New York: Appleton-Century-Crofts, Inc., 1873).

was always in the direction of big government and demands for an effective public administration.

POLITICAL THOUGHT IN COLONIAL AMERICA

The English Heritage. Early Colonial thought reflected the major values of contemporary England. During the eighteenth century, English political life was controlled by the Whigs, who had an essentially negative view of government. While they believed in freedom of discussion and the rights of man, they also insisted that government action should be limited to the advancement of commercial interests. John Locke is often referred to as the Whig's philosopher, but it was his sensitivity to the rights of property that was emphasized, rather than the more revolutionary elements of Whig philosophy. Although the triumph of Parliament in 1688 was in a sense a democratic advance, the transfer of power from king to legislature merely broadened the base of oligarchy. The rise of capitalism and the class stratification of English society brought wealth into power; the landed and commercial gentry were regarded as the proper trustees of monarchical power, and Parliament became a social oligarchy, while politics was regarded as a gentlemen's game.

Government was bent to the service of a minority. Tariff protection for domestic grain, premium payments for wheat exports, and a series of enclosure acts followed, increasing agricultural production but pauperizing the rural yeoman. The structure of land ownership was transformed, small landholders were dispossessed, and wholesale migration from country to town followed. The social costs of this economic gain were substantial. As Trevelyan put it, the radicalism of the rich was often effected at the expense of the poor.[3] Not until the reform measures of the nineteenth century was the political rule of the commercial and landed oligarchy to be threatened. In sum, as Parrington shows, the English liberal bequest to America manifested itself mainly in the fiction of the economic man and a society in which government's role was that of policeman.[4] Its basic idea was laissez faire; there was little indication of todays affirmative democracy, which provides a varied pattern of services and cushions the risks of the market for many groups.

With few exceptions the founding fathers accepted the theory of their Whig contemporaries. This was not surprising in view of the agrarian economy and the absence of the great social problems which later arose in the wake of technical and industrial change. The need for

[3] George Macaulay Trevelyan, *English Social History* (London: Longmans, Green & Co., Inc., 1944), p. 376.
[4] V. L. Parrington, *Main Currents in American Thought*, vol. I, (New York: Harcourt, Brace & Co., 1930), pp. iv–vii.

government was hardly felt. Thomas Paine's *Common Sense* warned that "society in every state is a blessing, but government even in its best state is but a necessary evil . . ." In Federalist Paper No. 10 James Madison held the principal object of government to be the protection of "the diversity in the faculties of men, from which the rights of property originate . . ."

Influence of American Theory. But if this aristocratic concept of government went unchallenged, the Whig citadel of laissez faire was strongly attacked. Alexander Hamilton, James Madison, and John Adams saw clearly that the economic policy which had served England so well was inadequate to the needs of their young nation. Hamilton shared the fears of the founding fathers in regard to majority rule, but he saw the need for a strong central government to promote commercial interests. His *Report on Manufactures* was a design for economic development under a vigorous government which would fund the national debt, establish a national bank, and encourage infant industry with a protective tariff. "Commerce like other things, had its fixed principles, according to which it ought to be regulated . . . to preserve the balance of trade in favor of a nation ought to be a leading aim of its [government's] policy."[5] As Charles A. Beard has shown, a similar property interest in strong government was shared by the Convention members at Philadelphia and reflected in the Constitution.[6]

In general, the Constitution reflected a dual intellectual climate. Our European heritage included two main philosophies: English liberalism and French romanticism. The former viewed man as a rational creature, capable of great achievements. The latter, as espoused by Rousseau, regarded man as a simple noble savage. English liberalism was divided in turn into opposing elements. On the one side was the revolutionary natural-rights doctrine of John Locke, championed by Samuel Adams and Thomas Jefferson. On the other, an aristocratic dogma, which viewed man as innately evil, manifested itself in a stratified society ordered by a negative state. Whig liberalism, largely divested of its democratic implications, was well suited to an acquisitive society and became the political theory of the influential commercial towns.[7] French romantic theory, with its emphasis upon individualism and social equality, became the ideology of the agrarian and artisan groups who supported Jefferson's Republican party. Thus, well before 1800, influences which would soon modify the dominant thought were at work.

[5] Henry Cabot Lodge (ed.), *Works of Alexander Hamilton*, vol. I, (New York: G. P. Putnam's Sons, 1904), pp. 254–55.

[6] Charles A. Beard, *An Economic Interpretation of the Constitution of the United States* (New York: The Macmillan Co., 1935), chap. v.

[7] Parrington, *Main Currents in American Thought*, vol. I, p. 13.

With few exceptions, however, the founding fathers were steeped in the negative version of English liberalism. Meanwhile the physical and economic conditions of the time, the wealth of natural resources, the endless frontier, and an expansive spirit encouraged a self-seeking individualism. Two additional tenets of Colonial thought strengthened the theory: the ingrained spirit of aristocracy and the universal acceptance of property as a criterion for political influence. Property qualifications for voting were the rule. Although there were some who opposed his view, John Adams represented majority opinion among the colonists when he said, "Property is surely a right of mankind as really as liberty . . . The moment the idea is admitted into society, that property is not as sacred as the laws of God, and that there is not a force of law and public justice to support it, anarchy and tyranny commence . . ."[8]

This attitude was reflected in the Constitution.[9] Although the colonists were committed by the Revolution itself to the ideal of democracy, their skepticism of majority rule asserted itself in a bicameral legislature dominated by an appointed Senate, and for a separation of powers reinforced by a check-and-balance system. Meanwhile a stable economic framework was ensured by giving the national government strong power in finance, taxation, foreign and domestic trade, and by providing for the supremacy of national over state legislation. The lessons of weak government under the Articles of Confederation, which had resulted in an impossible situation for commerce and finance, were well learned. The new Constitution set down an ideal economic framework for the young nation.

THE CHANGING VIEW

Challenge of the West. Yet patrician domination of political affairs was soon to end. The agrarian, artisan, and planter elements that formed the backbone of the Republican party (later to become the Democratic party) were infuriated by the Federalists, who used governmental power mainly to enhance commercial and property interests. They insisted, without avail, upon a strict interpretation of the Constitution. They sought French support to increase their domestic power. They set the claims of States' rights against national power. In the election of 1800, assisted by popular revulsion against the Alien and Sedition Act, they threw out the party of Washington and Hamilton. The triumph of Jeffersonian democracy marked the beginning of a successful attack

[8] Max Farrand (ed.), *The Records of the Federal Convention* (New Haven: Yale University Press, 1911), p. 180.

[9] "Hamilton, Madison, and John Adams stand out as the spokesmen for the rights of the commercial and propertied classes; and it was such men who wrote and secured the adoption of the Constitution." J. H. Randall, *Making of the Modern Mind* (Boston: Houghton Mifflin Co., 1940), p. 347.

against minority direction of public power. The victors were a coalition of farmers and frontiersmen, leavened somewhat by an element of planter aristocracy. Even though their leader, Jefferson, exhibited a certain *noblesse oblige*, his faith in majority rule was beyond question.[10]

The challenge of the West and the "common man" was not to be long denied. Jefferson's social and political liberalism was expanded by Andrew Jackson, and his rather paternalistic concept of government was substantially compromised. Jackson's view of the presidency as an instrument of majority will is evident in his bitter struggle with the Second Bank of the United States. The controversy reflected broadly a social and economic cleavage throughout the nation. Aligned on the one hand were the investor and commercial interests; in opposition stood the popular elements who supported Jackson—the urban worker, the farmer, and the social reformer. On both sides, of course, peripheral elements appeared. Some merchants opposed the concentration of power in the Bank. Some members of the seaboard financial community joined the representatives of state banks in support of Jackson. Both stood to gain from less central financial control.

The New Democracy. However, the main conflict was between the advocates of centralized power maintained in the interest of a powerful minority and those inclined toward States' rights, majority control of national government, and a fear of the immense power wielded by the Bank. There was some question of the good faith of the Bank, especially during the great struggle when its lending policy was modified to the disadvantage of state banks, bringing widespread financial distress. The recall of specie in 1819 and the limitation of note issues by state banks had similarly alienated members of several classes. Jackson regarded the Bank as the symbol of the union between government and the business community. His veto message, which nullified the bill to recharter the Bank, reflected this view while reaffirming his belief in the obligation of government to promote equality.

Thus began a political revolution that by the twentieth century would mean that the individualism of Jeffersonian democracy had become consistent with powerful government. The essential element was a gradual change in attitude toward government, a change from viewing government negatively to considering it a positive means of equalizing individual opportunity and reinforcing political freedom and economic security. The issue now became the location of political control. The

---

10 In his first inaugural address, for example, Jefferson maintained that "absolute acquiescence" was required "in the decisions of the majority—the vital principle of republics, from which there is no appeal but to force, the vital principle and immediate parent of despotism." Cited in Henry Adams, *The Formative Years*, vol. I (Boston: Houghton Mifflin Co., 1947), 107–8.

heritage of the Jackson era was the principle that control of government's power must rest broadly in the people and must be exercised in the general interest.[11] The period brought a democratic upheaval which set government in a new light. And it posed a serious question: How could political equality mean anything without economic equality? Although Jackson was initially committed to a strict construction of the Constitution, the pressure of events and his own personality forced an expansion of national power. His stand against Congress, the Supreme Court, the Second Bank of the United States, and the threats of southern nullification—all dramatized executive power. Henceforth democracy was to be correlated with vigorous presidential leadership.

Following the Jacksonian period, the ends of government were more broadly construed. Government, which had tended to be the spokesman of a particular interest, became increasingly a means of equalizing the strength of opposing groups in American society. As the platform of the Democratic party in 1840 declared: "Justice and sound policy forbid the federal government to foster one branch of industry to the detriment of another, or to cherish the interest of one portion to the injury of another portion of our common country." This concept of government remained paramount until the post-Civil War period. After the war the new industrialism brought a temporary return to the ideals of Hamilton and John Adams. But this move contained the seeds of a reaction which appeared in the late nineteenth century as the agrarian revolt.

THE STRUGGLE FOR EQUALITY

The development of big government was the result of many influences, including the competition among great producer groups. The changing character of economic and social life provided the milieu for the activities of such groups. The industrial revolution following the Civil War transformed almost overnight the environment of public administration, bringing into play forces which government alone could control. We learned (as England had learned a half-century before) that mass-production economy and the crowding of people into great cities brought grave problems of health, safety, and security, which demanded state intervention. Legislation regulating housing and health, wages and hours of

---

[11] "It was all very well to assume that American freedom gave every man an equal chance to enjoy the delights of success. But as a practical fact, how equal was opportunity when seaboard commercial interests were steadily bending the activities of the federal government to their own advantage? First under Jefferson, then two decades later under Jackson, the American people found a chief executive who resummoned them to the ideal that government should exercise itself to keep the avenues of opportunity open for everyone." Eric Goldman, "The Presidency as Moral Leadership," **280**, *Annals of the American Academy of Political and Social Science* (March, 1952), pp. 38–39.

work, social security, and the activities of unions followed. All reflected the change from a rural, primarily agrarian society to an urban-industrial one. The activities of great interest groups both shaped and reflected this transformation.

Although business, labor, and agriculture were the most important rivals in the struggle for power, they were not the only participants, nor did each of them constitute a unified interest. Economic interest, like the ideas of men, cannot be neatly compartmentalized. Each major sector of the economy comprises a great variety of discordant, competing interests. Big business is often opposed to small business, the small landholder or the tenant farmer has little in common with the corporation farmer, and there are conflicts between craft and industrial unions. A great diversity of interest exists and is reflected in a great number of organized groups within each major segment of the economy.

Business Hegemony. The Civil War was more than a political revolution. In destroying the economic system of the planter aristocracy, it released the industrial potential of the North. In Philadelphia alone, 180 new factories were built between 1862 and 1864. Immigration somewhat compensated for the diversion of manpower, and the introduction of labor-saving devices further eased the loss. The sewing machine changed the nature of the clothing trade. The mechanical reaper and the Homestead Act of 1862 provided the basis for an agricultural revolution. Petroleum had been discovered in Pennsylvania, and its production had increased phenomenally in the period immediately before the war. Cultural advances accompanied the conflict: Fifteen institutions of higher learning were established during the war years. And despite the absence of students who had volunteered in the Union or Confederate armies, enrollments increased.

The Civil War also marked a sharp reversal of American tariff policy. From 1833 until the war started, with minor exception, tariff rates had declined. Pressing financial need then brought an increase in rates, and after the war the high duties were continued. Until 1933 the tariff, which has been the most potent instrument of business enhancement, was to remain high. Hamilton's protectionist policy was given new life by the Republican domination of government which continued with only two interruptions until the Democratic victory of 1913. Even then World War I contrived to keep rates high. This continued until the disastrous Smoot-Hawley Act of 1930, which aggravated the disparity between industrial and agricultural prices and brought tariff retaliation around the world. Exports declined from some five billion dollars in 1929 to less than two billion in 1933. Imports fell similarly.[12] Our tariff history

[12] M. Fainsod and L. Gordon, *Government and the American Economy* (New York: W. W. Norton & Co., Inc., 1948), p. 85 *passim*; chap. iv.

illustrates clearly the demands upon government to promote a particular interest.

Agrarian Challenge. The ascendency of business continued until the third quarter of the nineteenth century, when a rising discontent among farmer and labor groups manifested itself in demands that business be regulated. If government was to be used for privilege, the farmers and artisans argued, privilege must be universalized. A competitive race for special favors began. The western farmer and small businessman were handicapped by the rate schedules of the railroads; certain restrictive practices existed, the most notorious of which was the granting of secret rebates to large concerns. The creation of the Interstate Commerce Commission in 1887 marked the beginning of an attempt to counterbalance special interests. Legislation extending regulation followed, in the form of the Sherman Antitrust Act of 1890 and the Clayton Act of 1914. An independent regulatory agency, the Federal Trade Commission, was established to administer the Acts. Similar commissions were to appear in the future, each entrusted with the regulation of an important sector of the economy.

Meanwhile, although the Republican party had been able to effect an uneasy alliance between the eastern industrialist and the western farmer, it became clear that the union functioned largely in the interest of the industrial partner. By 1875 the brief Grange movement, which reflected an indigenous radical agrarianism, had expanded its objectives from fraternal self-help to a politics of protest which demanded the control of monopoly, the regulation of railroad and warehouse rates, and other positive aids to agriculture. Two decades later, the Populist party appeared with related but more extensive objectives. The efforts of the two movements were crystallized in the regulatory legislation of the late nineteenth century. Next, although efforts to found a political party with an agricultural base were abandoned, a new development in farm strategy followed, sparked by the postwar decline of farm income. The American Farm Bureau Federation was organized to operate within the two-party system, exerting influence wherever possible in the interests of agriculture, though it drew its support largely from the more prosperous farm elements.

Following World War I, the agricultural depression, which continued through the 1920's, and the New Deal policy of vigorous action provided a fertile field for agricultural interest groups. By 1930 a crisis existed, characterized by falling prices and mounting surpluses of farm commodities both on the world market and at home, an ominous rise in foreclosures and bankruptcies, and the failure of local, state, and national relief schemes. The stage was set for sweeping changes when the New

Deal program got under way in 1933. The Agricultural Adjustment Act was pushed through in record time. In an effort to bolster prices, production control was introduced. A system of payment to participating farmers was established, financed by a processing tax on agricultural commodities. After initial adjustments, the program appeared to operate effectively. By 1935 the condition of the farmer was greatly improved.[13]

Early in 1936, however, the processing tax sections of the Act were invalidated by the Supreme Court.[14] Following this defeat, the government attempted to bolster farm income by a broadened program of soil conservation. Payments were made to farmers who introduced approved conservation practices. In general, however, this program had only limited success. Subsequently a second production control act was passed which, while retaining the objectives of the original AAA, solved the constitutional dilemma by covering the program under the commerce power.[15] Congressional appropriations amounting to over two hundred million dollars annually were provided for payments during 1938–40. The beneficial effects of the Act are indicated by the fact that annual cash farm income during this period rose to double that of 1932.

AGRICULTURAL CREDIT. The marked increase in farm credit activity was another indication of the expansion of government activities in the area of agriculture. Although no radical change occurred, the scope of farm credit was expanded enormously after 1933. A Farm Credit Administration was established to consolidate existing loan agencies. Farm mortgage debts were assumed at low interest rates by Federal Land Banks, financed in part by Reconstruction Finance Corporation funds. The Federal Farm Mortgage Corporation was established in 1934 and by 1936 had over eight hundred million dollars in loans outstanding. Meanwhile provisions were made for short-term credit through twelve Production Credit Corporations, which extended funds through local production credit associations. Disinherited agricultural elements, such as tenant farmers, sharecroppers, and farm laborers, were not forgotten. The Farm Security Administration began a wide rehabilitation program which by 1939 covered almost six hundred thousand individuals at a total loan figure of over two hundred and eighty million dollars. Finally, a system of banking for farm cooperatives was created which provided both short- and long-term loans at interest rates ranging from 1½ per

---

[13] This summary of aid to agriculture is based mainly on Fainsod and Gordon, *Government and the American Economy*, chaps. ii, v. For a study of agriculture's efforts to solve the problems of the depression following World War I, see Charles M. Hardin, *The Politics of Agriculture: Soil Conservation and the Struggle for Power in Rural America* (Glencoe, Ill.: The Free Press, 1952).

[14] *U.S.* v. *Butler* (297 U.S.I. 1936).

[15] *Currin* v. *Wallace* (306 U.S.I. 1939).

cent to 4 per cent. Some seventy-six million dollars in loans were outstanding under this program by the end of 1939.

Thus, since 1862, when the Department of Agriculture was created as a service agency for the farm community, the farmer has received a vast amount of financial aid from government. Beginning humbly in 1839 with an appropriation of one thousand dollars to provide for investigations and statistics, the farmer steadily increased his share of government largess. Agricultural education was ensured by the Morrill Act of 1862; some fifty years later the county agent was made available by the Smith-Lever Act; the agrarian protest of the late nineteenth century was reflected in regulatory functions adopted on agriculture's behalf; World War I brought an unprecedented boom, and the postwar deflation saw the emergence of the powerful farm bloc; credit facilities, largely ineffectual, were made available during the 1920's. Agrarian dissatisfaction continued until the later 1920's, but as we have seen, the advent of the New Deal brought the farmer great benefits.

Politics of Labor. Meanwhile labor began to compete for a greater share of the benefits which government could provide. The working class, those who work for wages and salaries, includes the vast majority of Americans; thus all general measures seeking to improve education and housing, as well as progressive income and inheritance taxes, have been supported by labor. The interests of organized labor and the mass of lower-income Americans tend to coalesce. A policy of expanding governmental functions is generally to the advantage of both. A late arrival in the political arena, organized labor began negatively with a demand for protective legislation. During the present century, however, public policy slowly evolved from the view that labor organizations were a criminal conspiracy,[16] through a period of relaxed restraints, into the New Deal era of positive encouragement,[17] followed during the post-World War II period by some modification, as seen in the Taft-Hartley and Griffith-Landrum legislation.

THE TRADE UNION MOVEMENT. The story of the labor movement cannot be traced here in any detail.[18] Trade union organizations appeared

---

[16] *Loewe* v. *Lawlor* (208 U.S. 274, 1908), the famous Danbury hatters' case in which union organizations were held by the Supreme Court to be combinations in restraint of trade, in violation of the Sherman Act.

[17] The change in judicial attitudes is reflected in *Hunt* v. *Crumbock* (325 U.S. 821, 1945). Union members refused to accept employment with a motor trucking firm and also refused to admit to their union anyone who did work for the firm, causing substantial loss to the latter and incurring considerable violence in the enforcement of their demands. Despite these circumstances, the Supreme Court held the union not to be a combination in restraint of trade in violation of the Sherman Act.

[18] See H. A. Millis and R. E. Montgomery, *Organized Labor* (New York: McGraw-Hill Book Co., Inc., 1945), chaps. ii–v.

near the end of the eighteenth century among certain skilled artisans in the large cities, particularly New York and Philadelphia. General antipathy, the geographical isolation of the unions, and their incongruous role as craft organizations in an emerging industrial society soon brought about their demise. Effective trade unionism awaited the industrial surge following the Civil War. From that time until the New Deal period, national craft unions composed of skilled workers dominated the scene. Representing only a fraction of American workers—the highly skilled, economic elite of labor—these organizations were allied with the conservative American Federation of Labor. The political ideology of this organization was long indistinguishable from that of the business community. In 1931, for example, at a time when several million men were jobless, the AF of L stood resolutely against compulsory unemployment insurance on the ground that employees would be "asked . . . to yield up their birthright, to practically surrender in their struggle for liberty, by enactment of legislation deliberately calculated to give the employers increased power over the workers."[19] By 1940, however, this laissez faire policy had gone by the board. Changing industrial conditions brought changes in strategy; henceforth the strike and the boycott would be augmented by political action. Affiliation with a particular party, however, was still anathema; the AF of L continued to work within the framework of the traditional two-party system.

THE NEW DEAL. Although the depression years and the Roosevelt administration brought the first positive environment for labor organization, the AF of L's craft orientation made organization of the mass production industries extremely difficult. The advocates of industrial unionism within the AF of L attempted to change this view but were obliged in 1935 to split off from the parent body to create a vigorous, politically oriented offspring, the Congress of Industrial Organizations. The junior partner grew by leaps and bounds: By 1937 it claimed 3,500,000 members; six years later the total amounted to something over 5,000,000. Meanwhile it discarded the political conservatism of the AF of L—and for good reasons. The CIO represented the easily replaced unskilled and semiskilled workers of mass-production industry. Its membership was particularly vulnerable in labor disputes and during periods of a labor surplus and thus had to rely upon a sympathetic government to protect its bargaining rights and living standard. The bitter economic conditions of the early 1930's and the support of the Roosevelt administration ensured these essentials.

---

[19] Quoted in V. O. Key, Jr., *Politics, Parties, and Pressure Groups* (New York: Thomas Y. Crowell Co., 1948), p. 68.

The demise of the National Recovery Act, which labor had viewed with high hopes, was followed immediately by a more effective substitute. Many provisions of the NRA that had given legal sanction to the principal objectives of labor were incorporated in the National Labor Relations Act of 1935. Sections 7 and 8 (a) of the Act set down a virtual bill of rights for labor. Specific unfair labor practices were prohibited; the right of labor to bargain collectively was reaffirmed; company-dominated unions, which had flourished under the NRA, were proscribed; discrimination against employees because of union membership or employee union activity was similarly outlawed; and finally, an affirmative duty was placed upon the employer to bargain collectively. Thus the New Deal brought a revolution in government's attitude toward organized labor. "A long tradition of aloofness or hostility . . . was suddenly transformed into recognition, sympathy, and, with some exceptions, open friendliness."[20] This trend was later to be modified by the Taft-Hartley Act, which reflects again both the changing currents of public attitude and government support of a particular interest.

WAR AND THE THREAT OF WAR

The expansion fostered by the depression and the group competition for an increased share of public assistance was sharply augmented by the international crises of the 1930's and the advent of World War II. The huge expenditures and the numerous alphabetical agencies of the New Deal period were vastly increased by the demands of total war.[21] Crises bring great problems which require swift and unprecedented solutions. Moreover the vast amount of capital and the grand scale of effort involved often make government the only agent competent to assume direction of the new responsibilities. When the crisis has passed, some of the emergency agencies and policies survive, for the new popular needs and expectations demand continued satisfaction.

Modern war, moreover, requires the synthesis of all elements of the economy, not only the military establishment and its needs but the civilian production system which makes total war possible. Manpower, industrial procurement, the allocation of raw materials, agriculture, transportation, the apparatus of production and consumption control—all require central direction and planning. Government, the only logical over-all director of this huge combined operation, reaches out into every sector of the community. Delegated legislative power flourishes in order that administration may have the means to meet the emergency. As a result, the

[20] Fainsod and Gordon, *Government and the American Economy*, p. 173.
[21] *Ibid.*, chap. xxii.

chief executive was authorized to allocate, through the War Production Board, scarce materials and facilities as necessary "in the public interest and to promote the national defense." The Office of Price Administration was empowered to fix fair and equitable prices as necessary to implement the purposes of the Act. Other administrators received similar increases of power and discretion. Public agencies inevitably expanded. And once again, some of them survived when the war ended.

Following World War II, for perhaps the first time the threat of war provided the essential thrust of national policy, resulting in the retention of many wartime programs and agencies. Government and the military enjoyed an unusual degree of peacetime influence. Widespread hopes of returning to normalcy were abandoned, and the nation settled down to an uneasy period of armament, heavy taxation, and international tension, the end of which no one could foresee. The inexorable expansion of governmental functions was accepted by the citizen with mixed feelings of wonder and resignation. Congress pleaded for economy and a return to legislative supremacy but was obliged to endorse Administration policy and appropriate the huge sums recommended by the chief executive. The latter, in turn, enjoyed increased power through his role as architect of foreign policy and Commander in Chief. Speed in executing policy, a vital factor in foreign affairs, further increased presidential power as Congress and the nation looked to the President for leadership and decisive action in an uncertain and swiftly changing world.

An example of the resulting expansion of executive responsibilities was clearly seen in the offer of both military and technical assistance to those countries whose security was defined as essential to our own. While Congress has resisted this program, it has been extended each year, and there seems little doubt but that it will be continued as part of our total foreign relations program. It should be noted that something over 70 per cent of the funds spent in this program are spent in the United States mainly to buy armaments, machinery, and supplies for distribution to the countries receiving technical aid. Table 1 shows expenditures in billions of dollars under the mutual security program since fiscal 1950, when military assistance spending began. The economic aid figures from 1953 to 1959 include "defense support" funds.

Perhaps the most impressive index of the expansion of governmental activities is a historical summary of the number of federal employees and the relative size of the national public budget, as shown in Tables 2 and 3. Here again, the figures reveal a secular trend upward, with depression, war, and the threat of war providing the major impetus.

A final example of government's expanded role is the Employment Act of 1946 which for the first time in our history gave the federal govern-

TABLE 1
EXPENDITURES UNDER THE MUTUAL SECURITY PROGRAM
(Billions of Dollars)

Fiscal Year	Military Aid	Economic and Technical Assistance Aid	Total
1950	$0.1	$3.4	$3.5
1951	0.9	2.8	3.7
1952	2.4	2.1	4.5
1953	4.0	1.7	5.7
1954	3.6	1.3	4.9
1955	2.3	2.0	4.3
1956	2.6	1.6	4.2
1957	2.3	1.7	4.0
1958 (est.)	2.2	1.7	3.9
1959 (est.)	2.2	1.8	4.0
Total	$22.6	$20.1	$42.7

Source: *New York Times,* January 20, 1958.

TABLE 2
FEDERAL EMPLOYMENT
(Thousands)

Year	Civil Activities	Average Military Strength	Total	Population of the U.S.	U.S. Population Employed by Fed. Govt., %
1820*	6.3	13.4	19.7	9,618	0.2
1840*	23.7	19.4	43.1	17,120	0.3
1860*	49.2	28.1	77.3	31,513	0.2
1880*	107.0	41.9	148.9	50,262	0.3
1900*	256.0	119.7	375.7	76,094	0.5
1910†	380.1	140.4	520.5	92,407	0.6
1920	686.4	422.9	1,109.3	106,466	1.0
1930	580	258	838	123,077	0.7
1940	1,034	384	1,418	131,970	1.1
1945	3,807	11,977	15,784	139,585	11.3
1950	1,949	1,537	3,486	151,683	2.3
1955	2,384	2,964	5,348	165,271	3.2
1956	2,405 (Feb. 1957)	2,836	5,241	168,091	3.1
1957	2,667	2,800	5,467	172,505	3.1
1958	2,339	2,700	5,039	175,370	2.9

* Based on figures for 1816, 1841, 1861, 1881, and 1901, respectively.
† Totals from 1910 onward are derived from U.S. Civil Service Commission revised figures.

SOURCE: M. Slade Kendrick, *A Century and a Half of Federal Expenditures* (New York: National Bureau of Economic Research, 1955); U.S. Department of Commerce, *Statistical Abstracts, 1956–57* (Washington, D.C.: U.S. Government Printing Office, 1957); U.S. Department of Commerce, *Historical Abstracts, 1789–1952* (Washington, D.C.: Government Printing Office).

TABLE 3

FEDERAL EXPENDITURES
(Millions of Dollars)

Year	Civil Activities	Military Activities	Total Fed. Expend.	Gross National Product	Total Expend. as a % of GNP
1794	$ 4.29	$ 2.70	$ 6.99	$	...
1800	4.78	6.01	10.78	....	...
1825	9.15	6.71	15.86	....	...
1850	22.42	17.12	39.54	....	...
1865	114.70	1,155.90	1,297.60	....	...
1875	217.60	57.00	274.60	7,033	3.9
1900	353.00	167.90	520.90	15,709	3.3
1910	452.00	242.00	694.00	28,783	2.4
1920	2,360.00	3,997.00	6,357.00	61,895	10.2
1930	2,366.00	734.00	3,100.00	91,105	3.4
1940	8,103.00	1,497.00	9,600.00	100,618	9.5
1945	10,615.00	84,569.00	95,184.00	213,100	44.7
1950	30,753.00	12,407.00	43,160.00	285,067	15.1
1955	25,044.00	40,626.00	65,570.00	390,860	16.8
1956	25,899.00	40,641.00	66,540.00	412,400	16.1
1957	26,170.00	45,433.00	71,603.00	440,300	16.3
1958	29,440.00	46,342.00	75,782.00	437,700	17.3

SOURCE: M. Slade Kendrick: (1) "A Century and a Half of Federal Expenditures" (New York: Nat'l. Bureau of Economic Research, 1955). (2) U.S. Dep't. of Commerce, *Statistical Abstracts*, 1956–1957. (3) U.S. Dep't. of Commerce, *Historical Abstracts*, 1789–1952. (4) Simon Kuznets, "National Product Since 1869" (New York: Nat'l. Bureau of Economic Research, 1946). (5) *Basic Economic Statistics* (Washington, D.C.: Economic Statistics Bureau, 1959).

ment the responsibility to maintain full employment.[22] While the Act was inspired in part by dire but inaccurate predictions of widespread unemployment following World War II, it symbolizes the tenor of changing public expectations. The meaning of the developments outlined in this chapter, which provided the framework for big government, can perhaps best be summed up in de Tocqueville's observation:

The passage of time constantly opens to the central government new fields of action. . . . Society, which is in the full progress of development, constantly gives birth to new needs and each one of them is for the government a source of power; for it alone is in a position to satisfy them . . . the sphere of government is mobile and never ceases to grow with civilization itself.[23]

[22] For a careful study of the legislative history of this Act, see Stephen K. Bailey, *Congress Makes A Law* (New York: Columbia University Press, 1950).
[23] Alexis de Tocqueville, *L'Ancien Regime* (Oxford: Basil Blackwell and Mott, Ltd., 1933), p. 65.

BIBLIOGRAPHY

ADAMS, HENRY. *The Formative Years.* Vol. 1. Boston, 1947.

BEARD, CHARLES A. *An Economic Interpretation of the Constitution.* New York: 1935.

DE TOQUEVILLE, ALEXIS. *Democracy in America.* 2 vols. New York: 1945.

FABRICANT, S. *Trend of Government Activity Since 1900.* New York: 1952.

FAINSOD, M., and GORDON, L. *Government and the American Economy.* New York: 1959.

GAUS, JOHN M. *Reflections on Public Administration.* University, Alabama: 1947.

KEY, V. O., JR. *Politics, Parties and Pressure Groups.* New York, 1955.

LASKI, HAROLD J. *The American Democracy.* New York: 1948.

MASON, ALPHEUS T. *Free Government in the Making.* New York: 1949.

MCIVER, ROBERT M. *The Web of Government.* New York: 1947.

PARRINGTON, VERNON L. *Main Currents in American Thought.* New York: 1930.

POLYANI, KARL. *The Great Transformation.* New York: 1944.

TREVELYAN, GEORGE M. *English Social History.* London: 1944.

CHAPTER 3

The Public Bureaucracy

The system of authority, men, offices, and methods that government uses to carry out its programs may be called the *bureaucracy*. Although the term is often used cynically, here it means only a system of complex organization, made up of a vast number of technical skills, used to carry out policies made by others, and peculiarly suited for large-scale operations. Ideally, bureaucracy demands from its members consistency, loyalty, and adaptability. Bureaucracy has existed since ancient times, and its major characteristics, both functional and dysfunctional, are the subject of this chapter.

THE RISE OF MODERN BUREAUCRACY

Modern bureaucracy developed hand in hand with the national state which assumed many functions formerly carried out by religious orders. The first modern bureaucracy was probably the army, which replaced the transitory forces of feudal times in order to ensure national survival. The mercantile policy of the early states also encouraged bureaucracy as they embarked upon various public enterprises aimed at promoting industry and commerce. The resulting accumulation of detail by the various ministers brought about one of the characteristics of public administration: the delegation of policy-making authority and discretion to the bureaucracy. The permanent subordinates of impermanent ministers gradually assumed powers which made them indispensable. This feature of bureaucracy was well established by the seventeenth and eighteenth centuries. As a French scholar noted, "The various ministers have accumulated for the century past so much detail in affairs of all kinds that it is impossible for them to attend to them directly. Thence a new kind of intermediary power has grown up between the ministers and the citizens . . . it is that of the clerks, persons absolutely unknown to the State, and who, however, speaking and writing in the name of ministers, have like them an absolute and irresistible power, and are even more than they sheltered from all investigation, since they are much less well known."[1]

---

[1] Quoted in Herman Finer, *The Theory and Practice of Modern Government*, (New York: Dial Press, 1932), p. 1234n, from de Lucay, *Les Secrétaires d'État depuis leur institution jusqu'a la mort de Louis XV* (Paris: 1881), p. 149.

Such developments gradually showed that administration was much more than merely a clerical function. Not only was the policy role of the administrator recognized but also the fact that the best of plans require loyal and expert implementation.[2] When government's role was minimal and technology was primitive, the need for a competent bureaucracy was hardly felt.[3] But the industrial state placed a premium on technical and organizational skill. As a result, the traditional criticisms of bureaucracy are often irrelevant to social reality, although they may meet psychic needs.

ECOLOGY OF AMERICAN BUREAUCRACY

If institutions are to survive, they must be able to adapt to changing conditions. History is replete with cultures and with animal life which, like the dinosaur, sank into obscurity, unable to meet the demands of change. In America the concentration of economic and political power which began after the Civil War and has become the essential fact of social life, transformed the organizational environment. The modern corporation emerged to meet the need for huge amounts of capital in the operation of big industry. The "managerial revolution" followed, bringing the ascendancy of the technician and the divorce of ownership from management.[4] Meanwhile, in agriculture, the ideal of the family-owned farm was challenged by corporation farming. Big government and big labor evolved in turn as participants in the struggle to equalize political and economic power.

This is the era of the big organization. Governments, corporations, trade unions, and political parties are characterized by vast size and scope of operation. Size alone is perhaps the basic cause of bureaucracy. General Motors and United States Steel, no less than the Department of Defense, have the essential ingredients of bureaucracy, including specialization, impersonality, routine procedures, a hierarchy of authority, and a tendency toward inertia.[5] Bureaucracy is no isolated phenomenon; it is

[2] One embryonic politician who recognized the changing role of public administration was Woodrow Wilson, "The Study of Administration," 2, *Political Science Quarterly* (June, 1887), pp. 197–222

[3] J. Donald Kingsley, *Representative Bureaucracy* (Yellow Springs, Ohio: Antioch Press, 1944).

[4] Scott Buchanan, *The Corporation and the Republic* (New York: Fund for the Republic, 1958); Adolf A. Berle and Gordon C. Means, *The Modern Corporation and Private Property* (New York: The Macmillan Co., 1933).

[5] Ernest Dale, "Contributions to Administration by Alfred Sloan, Jr., and General Motors," 1, *Administrative Science Quarterly* (June, 1956), pp. 30–62. Peter Drucker, *Concept of the Corporation* (New York: John Day Co., Inc., 1946), shows that the inertia coming from the vast size of General Motors forced devolution to promote competition between semiautonomous divisions; also Kenneth E. Boulding, *The Organizational Revolution* (New York: Harper & Bros., 1953).

a general symptom of modern life, reflecting certain needs and subject to certain tendencies. Since ancient times, technical imperatives have encouraged its growth: in Egypt, the regulation of waterways; in the late Middle Ages, effective methods of communication and tax collection; in the twentieth century, the bewildering variety of skills required to operate large enterprises.

Weber's Ideal Construct. Bureaucracy differs from nation to nation, reflecting the values and institutions of the society which it serves. Within a given society, moreover, bureaucracy is ambivalent, exhibiting both a will to power and a resistance to change. One of the most helpful theoretical models for studying large-scale organization is the ideal-type concept of bureaucracy set down by Max Weber, a German economist who wrote around the turn of the twentieth century.[6] However, his generalizations must be applied with caution. Drawn from western Europe and ancient civilizations of China, Egypt, India, and Rome, where social mobility was limited and civil service entry and advancement were closely articulated with class and educational systems, Weber's inferences are most useful in appraising the rational and structural aspects of the American bureaucracy. But they fail to emphasize adequately its "informal" character, which reflects in turn the social climate in which it developed and the demands of its members for self-expression. In this sense, although Weber's ideal model is an effective research tool and a place from which one may start to analyze bureaucracy, it must be qualified when applied to America.

Despite these qualifications, Weber is important for two reasons: he designed the first construct of twentieth-century large-scale organization; and he has had great influence on administrative thought and research in the United States.

It should be emphasized that Weber's was a construct of formal organization, and as such, parallels in many respects the integrationist model later referred to in our chapters on organization. It is impossible to consider Weber fully here; the generalizations that follow provide only a rough outline of his ideal model:

1. *Hierarchy.* Offices are organized on the hierarchical basis.
2. Bureaucracy is a term which applies to both public and private effort.
3. *Rationalized job structure.* There is a rational division of labor, and each position is accompanied by the legal authority necessary to accomplish the goals set.
4. *Formalization.* Acts, decisions, and rules are formulated and recorded in writing (red tape).

[6] Max Weber, *From Max Weber: Essays in Sociology,* trans. and ed. by H. H. Gerth and C. W. Mills (New York: Oxford University Press, 1946).

5. *Management separated from ownership.* There is a hired, professional administrative class.
6. There is no property right to office.
7. Special competence and training are required of the administrative class.
8. Members are selected competitively on the basis of competence.
9. *Legal flavor.* Weber's construct reflects the legalistic flavor attaching to administration in continental Europe. "Each office has a clearly defined sphere of competence in the legal sense."[7]

ITS APPLICATION TO AMERICAN BUREAUCRACY. As an analytical construct, Weber's theory must be modified when applied to the American scene.[8] First, it may safely be said that our public administration is characterized by considerably more "politics" than that of western Europe. This condition reflects mainly our separation of powers which, by diffusing power and responsibility among so many centers, provides many points of access into the governmental process for groups of many kinds. Thus legislators and interest-group representatives shape the administrative process in many ways. High-level bureaucrats extract concessions as the price of cooperation in such instances, building up strength with strategically placed legislators and interest-group leaders upon whom they may call for support when appropriations or statutory measures are being considered. This bargaining gives our public administration a dynamic, political character that challenges Weber's view of bureaucracy as a passive, neutral instrument. Instead, our bureaucracy tends to be actively representative of various interest groups. It tends to define the "public interest" as the interest of its major client, whether labor, business, or agriculture.

American bureaucracy also has many more career alternatives for the bureaucrat. The wealth of the nation, the positive role of government, the geographical mobility that Americans have come to accept as given—all provide more career avenues for the bureaucrat and in the process shape his image of what is possible in the bureaucratic environment. Government is often a training ground for bright young men who will transfer their skills to private industry. In general this milieu tends to increase the bureaucrat's independence and his inclination to accept the discretion provided by our separation of powers system and the growing reliance upon technical skill. While this generalization varies in terms of individual personality, the amount of lateral mobility among federal career bureaucrats is impressive. Here again, however, careful studies are needed to buttress such rule-of-thumb observations.

[7] *Ibid.*, p. 21.

[8] For sociological studies which suggest some limitations of Weber's theory when applied to the American civil service, see A. Gouldner, *Patterns of Industrial Bureaucracy* (Glencoe, Ill.: The Free Press, 1951); and Peter Blau, *The Dynamics of Bureaucracy* (Chicago: University of Chicago Press, 1955) and *Bureaucracy in Modern Society* (New York: Random House, Inc., 1956).

We may also say that mobility in the civil service is affected by the lower status that government work has in the United States as compared with that of western Europe. The bureaucrat is often the whipping boy of powerful groups, who indulge their aggressions against government servants without fear of reprisal. In our society where the organization and self-consciousness of political, economic, ethnic, and religious groups have reduced the number of relatively defenseless targets, the bureaucrat remains vulnerable. This lack of prestige means that recruitment of the best youth will be difficult and that disenchantment with the service, once entered, will result in rather high turnover rates. This mobility adds to the comparatively less structured character of our bureaucracy.

Perhaps more fundamental is the fact that no bureaucracy can function with the machine-like precision that Weber posited. Individual needs for security, power, and status will always result in efforts to "bend" the rules and regulations, as well as the program, of any organization to achieve these "extra-bureaucratic" values. This aspect of organization has been called "bureaucracy's other face," and Blau argues that catering to such needs actually makes the organization function more smoothly. Thus, instead of being viewed as disruptive forces, these subjective elements can actually be functional; they can assist the organization in achieving its goals and maintaining the equilibrium between individual contributions and rewards.[9]

THE NATURE OF BUREAUCRACY

The Search for Rationality. Having suggested some of its limitations when applied to the American bureaucracy, we can return to our analysis of Weber's bureaucratic model. Perhaps the major characteristic of the ideal type of bureaucracy is its effort to achieve rationality, i.e., planned, intelligent action. Bureaucracy is the systematic organization of tasks and individuals into a pattern which can effectively attain the ends of group effort. Individual behavior is harnessed into productive channels by rules, sanctions, and exhortation. Everywhere a "maximum calculability" of rules is sought. Predictability, standardization, and certainty are highly valued. A certain depersonalization follows in which regulations and precedents tend to become supreme and personal feelings are submerged. The discipline of the military and the attending restrictions upon individualism are an illustration. While it is obviously impossible to achieve complete predictability (as our study of informal organization will reveal), a special virtue of bureaucracy is to minimize human irrationality.

---

[9] Blau, *Bureaucracy in Modern Society,* chap. iii.

Technical Specialization. Specialization is another important condition of bureaucracy. We have seen that the origin of bureaucracy lay mainly in the need for technical skills. Trained in a certain skill, performing it again and again, and viewing his position as a career, the official develops a high degree of proficiency. Specialization is reinforced by the fact that entry and advancement are based upon technical preparation and experience in a certain type of work. In both public and private enterprise, the demand for technical expertise continues unabated. Professional societies abound; vocabularies become intelligible only to the elect; and career training becomes increasingly specialized. Thus bureaucracy is both a cause and an effect of professionalization, bringing to routine matters greater precision, disinterest (the official's loyalty is assigned mainly to competent performance), and speed of operation. But specialization and the other attributes of bureaucracy have a paradoxical effect: They encourage introversion and a limited perspective which increases the inertia of big enterprises.

Operation in a Framework of Law. Bureaucratic inflexibility is aggravated by the legal framework in which public officials work. Their conduct is bound up with the "rule of law," a principle brought to America from England, where it was developed as part of the long struggle against arbitrary government. The "rule of the law," requires that administrative actions affecting individual rights shall reflect precedents and legal sanctions rather than arbitrary, personal discretion. To insure this, Congress has included standards in most of its legislation to guide the official in his relations with the citizen. The "rule of law," it must be said, does not mean that the state cannot deprive men of life, liberty, or property but only that such action must follow certain legal guaranties. Thus the public official must be able to justify every action by law or by administrative rules and orders created under statute law. In the area of administrative discretion the citizen has certain rights. Not only is he entitled to notice and hearing in regard to the matter which the state wishes to regulate, but he has the right to appeal in a court of law against the administrative decision.

It is often maintained that the attitudes of individuals reflect their work environment. Thus salesmen tend to be hail-fellow-well-met types, while research scientists often seem rather diffident. The public official is similarly conditioned by his environment. As Weber showed, he will be oriented toward precedent; he will seek accountability through conformance with the law; he will lean toward inflexibility. The high administrator will often be dependent upon his legal and financial aides who can furnish a path through the maze of legal minutiae confronting him. The ludicrous ends to which this desire for accountability can lead are illustrated in a first Hoover Commission report. It was found that the cost of paying bills on purchase orders (half of which amounted to less than ten dollars) was more than the amount of the bill itself in nearly half of all cases.[10] Government by law requires a strict conformity to established procedures and legal regulations which necessarily reduces simplicity, dispatch, and economy.

A Value System. Administrators are conditioned also by cultural values and the dominant opinions of their colleagues.[11] Generally they develop a value system which satisfactorily identifies their role with that of the organization, and in turn, the role of the latter with the values of the society. Given the dominant free enterprise theme of our society, public servants often develop feelings of insecurity based on the common view that they have, after all, "never met a payroll." It seems fair to say that there has been a systematic derogation of government which is inevitably reflected in the status of civil servants. The official's view of his role has been influenced in turn; he seeks morale through an emphasis on professional competence. The bureaucrat's existence is bound up with his specialist role and the proper exercise of it. Bureaucratic loyalty, for example, is not conferred upon a person—the supervisor or bureau chief —but rather upon impersonal functions. In theory, at least, the bureaucrat views himself as the objective instrument of popular will. At the same time, however, loyalty to certain abstractions such as the agency "mission," the political party, or the state may exist.[12] Like other men, bureaucrats have political opinions which influence their decisions. In general, however, the public official exchanges professional expertise and competence for security and an assured income.

In European countries the official receives psychic income in the form of social approval. The United States is almost unique in its lack of respect for the public official. There are several reasons for this, including the relative lack of class differentiation in America. The social distribution of power is important too. In England, for example, the higher civil service has long represented influential social groups.[13] The

---

[10] Commission on Organization of the Executive Branch of the Government, *The Organization and Management of Federal Supply Activities* (Washington, D.C.: U.S. Government Printing Office, 1948), note 2, pp. 26–27.

[11] Paul T. David and Ross Pollock, *Executives for Government* (Washington, D.C.: Brookings Institution, 1957).

[12] Max Weber, *From Max Weber: Essays in Sociology*, trans. and ed. by H. Gerth and C. W. Mills (New York: Oxford University Press, 1946), pp. 198–99.

[13] For a provocative historical analysis of the social basis and representative function of the British civil service, see Kingsley, *Representative Bureaucracy*. However, there is evidence that change in the bases of recruitment and the status of the British administrative class is occurring; see R. K. Kelsall, *Higher Civil Servants in Britain* (London: Routledge and Paul, 1955); Frank Dunnill, *The Civil Service* (London: Allen & Unwin, 1956).

British higher public service, along with the military and politics, has been among the most honored careers. Entry has been based upon costly educational preparation which restricts the number of applicants while making for a system of "cooptation" in accepting candidates for the higher civil service. Cooptation (defined here as the control of entry by the members of a profession) is often a symptom of increasing social stratification. In the United States, on the other hand, because of its wealth and the frontier which provided unusual opportunity, class lines have been fluid and a business career has been valued more than one of public service.

The bureaucratic position involves an "office," frequently viewed as a life career, with a precise enumeration of powers. There is usually a distinction between the power exercised by the bureaucrat and his authority as a person. While deference may transfer from office to social life, there is a complete separation of power; the bureaucrat away from his job has no more authority than anyone else. His authority is the authority of the impersonal "office" in which he works. Compensation is in the form of a fixed wage, preferably in money form. Ordinarily he has no other source of income. The "offices" are arranged in an hierarchical order ensuring control over promotion, demotion, appointment, and removal. Fitness is generally determined by technical skill or academic attainment tested by examination and often requiring long periods of training. This is the general structure of bureaucracy which, as Weber points out, is the most efficient instrument of large-scale administration yet developed.

THE ROLE OF BUREAUCRACY

Having outlined the main characteristics of bureaucracy, we can now turn to its central role in the modern, industrial state. It will soon become clear that this role now includes powers and responsibilities far beyond those envisaged by the founding fathers when they proposed a separation of powers system in which policy making would be restricted to the elected "political" branches, namely, the chief executive, his high-level appointees, and the Congress. Instead, we shall find that the bureaucracy now has become a "fourth branch of government," which shares with the President and Congress the initiation and the interpretation of major policy.

Implementing Social Change. The true measure of democratic government is its ability to recognize and to meet changing social needs. We have seen how government's role expanded in response to a popular demand that public power should be directed to whatever activity seems necessary to promote the general welfare. During this century particularly, public opinion has changed in regard to the "proper" role of government. Attitudes toward the graduated income tax, the extension of social security benefits, the legitimacy of national unions, public aid to education, and government's role in the private economy have moved from sharp opposition to general acceptance.

The impact of World War II quickened the pace of this trend. The inclination toward minimizing individual risk and the acceptance of new functions by government increased among all classes of society. The industrial worker, caught between an impersonal mass production and the paternalism of his big union, has turned increasingly to government for security. Industry itself has come to depend increasingly on government contracts. In the process government has become more than the arbiter of competing interests. It has assumed the larger responsibility of achieving security and well-being for all citizens. This change has been effected through consent. But change does not implement itself. It is still easier, as Woodrow Wilson insisted, to frame a constitution than to run one. The skills and experience required to institutionalize innovation must be supplied by the public service. In this sense the bureaucracy is a social instrument, bridging the gap between legislative intent and its fulfillment.

Moreover, while the outcome of party conflict shaped by the demands and veto power of big interests determines government's broad ends, a continuous struggle for special advantage goes on regardless of which party controls our national administration. This conflict is inherent in our political system, with its lack of party discipline. Once a decision is reached at the polls or in the legislative arena, private groups turn to the alternative locus of power and discretion, the bureaucracy, which shares with Congress the task of accommodating the claims of interest groups. While the policy and programs of departments often reflect the demands of such groups, an opportunity to temper private claims in the public interest arises in the process. The better the bureaucracy becomes at developing systematic techniques of forming and implementing policy, the greater its power of resisting the claims of special interests.

Recommending Policy. We can now return to bureaucracy's role in policy determination. Congress has come to depend greatly upon the administrative expert, mainly because public policy often involves matters of technical complexity, requiring special knowledge and sustained attention. The legislator has become an amateur who must rely increasingly upon the judgment of the expert. It is painfully evident, for example, that in making military appropriations, Congress is greatly dependent upon military judgment, not only as to the relative superiority of weapons, as, say, between long-range and short-range bombers, but

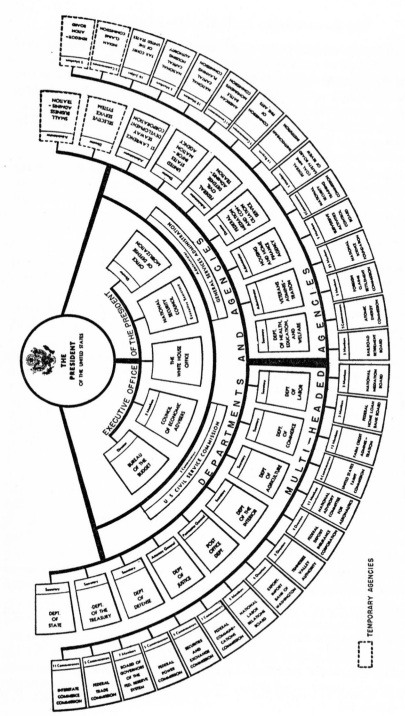

Fig. 1. Executive Branch of the Federal Government.

49

also in the more critical matters of global political strategy, insofar as these are related to military questions.[14]

As Weber insists, "It is obvious that the great modern state is absolutely dependent upon a bureaucratic basis."[15] This exchange from a committee hearing in reply to a legislator's request for information concerning the Federal Communications Commission's control of broadcasting is suggestive:

> MR. STERLING: It [interference] arose from reflections from what they call the sporadic E layer of the Ionic atmosphere and F-2 layer which would come in during the times of high sun spot activity and cause signals to be reflected in the service area of other stations from a great distance. . . .
> SENATOR BREWSTER: I think you have given me all the information I can digest. . . .[16]

The bureaucracy's influence on policy occurs during two stages of the legislative process. First, it is often called upon to initiate legislation and to offer recommendations to Congress concerning proposed measures. Second, as noted above, it enjoys some autonomy in carrying out legislation passed by Congress. The official's influence reflects his concern with action programs and his knowledge of the techniques needed to carry them out. He understands how policy works in practice. If objectives are not being attained, he is among the first to know. He can then suggest feasible alternatives.

Framing Legislation. The distinction between administration and politics begins at the point where a matter can no longer be treated according to precedent.[17] An element of discretion arises, bringing in politics. The administrator is then faced with two alternatives, each of which involves policy. He may handle the case according to his own judgment, or he may suggest, as he probably will in important matters, that the legislature adopt new methods to meet the situation. If he chooses the first alternative, the effect of the shift in administrative routine may, over time, create a new principle of action. Thus policy often limps along behind established practice, merely referending what necessity has long since demanded. If he chooses the second alternative, he will be asked to defend his recommendations. If he believes in them, he will marshall

---

[14] The critical influence of the military on national policy is set down in C. Wright Mills, *The Power Elite* (New York: Oxford University Press, 1956).

[15] Max Weber, *From Max Weber: Essays in Sociology*, p. 211.

[16] Senate Committee on Interstate and Foreign Commerce, 80th Cong., 2d. sess., *Hearings*, "Nominations of Wayne Coy and George E. Sterling to the Federal Communications Commission" (Washington, D.C.: U.S. Government Printing Office, 1948), p. 7.

[17] Karl Mannheim, *Ideology and Utopia* (New York: Harcourt, Brace & Co., Inc., 1936), pp. 99–104.

evidence to defend their rationality. In doing so, he again influences policy.

This means that a considerable amount of legislation will be initiated by the administrative branch. Actually, something over half the total legislation coming before Congress originates in the executive departments and agencies and is coordinated by the President through the Bureau of the Budget. The impetus for such measures often comes from the economic groups allied with a particular agency. Public administration has a representative function, which means that policy will reflect group interests. Legislative proposals are actually a collective product, resulting from consultation between the sponsoring agency, other administrative agencies, interest groups which support the measure, and friendly legislators who will assume responsibility for the proposal in Congress. Thus to say that a legislative measure is "initiated" by the administration often means that an expressed client need has been "formalized" by an agency for presentation to Congress.

However, another more recent development also illustrates agency participation in legislative policy making. In 1954 President Eisenhower presented in package form to Congress and the nation sixty-five proposals for new legislation covering national defense, foreign aid, farm price supports, social security, housing, etc.[18] Such an omnibus program is a post-World War II development, initiated by the Truman administration in response to domestic problems and international tension following the war. For our purposes, the main point here is the detailed preparation required to develop such a legislative program, which largely devolves upon the White House staff and the various agencies. The Bureau of the Budget, of course, plays a major role in coordinating such policy recommendation which reflect the agencies' conception of what is possible in practice and what is necessary to improve existing programs. As Neustadt concludes, the content of these suggestions "makes plain that mixed with the rethinking from on high was a good deal of educating from below."[19] In 1953–54 about three hundred major proposals were submitted by departments and agencies in response to the budget bureau's requests for legislative policy recommendations, and the Bureau took on the formidable job of clearing these for submission to its political leaders.

Much of the higher bureaucrat's time is thus spent in designing legislation that will make the job of administration easier. The work of the budget bureau's Legislative Reference Division, which acts as a clearing house for legislative proposals of the entire administrative branch,

[18] Richard E. Neustadt, "Presidency and Legislation: Planning the President's Program," 49, *American Political Science Review* (December, 1955), p. 980.
[19] *Ibid.*, p. 987.

suggests the extent of administrative policy influence. In order to avoid opposition when a measure comes before Congress, the Division consults with interested departments concerning proposed measures. Bitter struggles sometimes develop. Different agencies, of course, will have different points of view. In some cases, insuperable differences must be reconciled by the President.

The administrative branch will also discuss proposed measures with its client groups throughout the country. In departments such as agriculture and labor, which represent fairly well defined interest groups, few if any measures unsatisfactory to dominant client groups will be sent up to Congress. Administrators also consult with their friends in Congress. Most agencies have sympathetic legislators who protect their interests and in turn receive certain favors from the agency. Such consultation insures that the chances of congressional approval are as bright as possible.

Influencing Congress. Bureaucratic influence on policy also occurs during the consideration of legislation by Congress. Here again, the indispensability of the expert enhances bureaucracy's role. Administrators frequently appear in public hearings to give evidence on proposed legislation. Written statements are often requested by congressional committees concerning such measures. Administrators will also appear in the executive (secret) sessions where the major decisions are reached. The departments and agencies meanwhile provide committee members with data for speeches in support of the legislation. Finally, administrators sit in on conference committees to offer advice on measures affecting their departments.

Charles M. Hardin's analyses of agricultural policy formation suggest such administrative policy influence.[20] His study of the Hope and Aiken bills, introduced in the Eightieth Congress in an unsuccessful attempt to modify existing agricultural programs, indicates that the differences between the bills were reflections of policy differences between Department of Agriculture agencies and their respective alliances in agriculture.[21] The influence of the Production Marketing Association (formerly AAA) and the Soil Conservation Service on the measures was emphasized: "the Hope and Aiken field hearings in 1947 were full of planned testimony in support of particular agencies, especially PMA and SCS."

[20] Among others, see Charles M. Hardin, "Reflections on Agricultural Policy Formation," **42**, *American Political Science Review* (October, 1948), pp. 881–905; "The Bureau of Agricultural Economics Under Fire: A Study in Beliefs and Valuation Conflicts," **28**, *Journal of Farm Economics* (August, 1946), pp. 653–68.

[21] Charles M. Hardin, "Conservation and Land-Use Programs in Agriculture," **30**, *Journal of Farm Economics* (November, 1948), pp. 641, 619–44.

In conclusion, Hardin asks: Does realism compel us to accept as inevitable the monopolization of the policy-forming process by public agencies and their allied private associations? This question emphasizes administration's central role in policy determination and the extent to which the dichotomy between politics and administration is unreal.

It must be remembered that bureaucracy functions in a highly competitive milieu. There is a constant struggle for power, prestige, and survival. More action programs mean a larger share of public funds and the means of solidifying the agency's position with groups that benefit from such programs. Under our political system, with its lack of party cohesion, the bureaucracy not only has a large share in policy formation, but it must also organize the political strength necessary to implement policy. Agencies such as the International Cooperation Administration or the U.S. Information Service, which lack disciplined support in important interest groups, have little chance of satisfactory operation. Administrators must either have a firm base of public support or they must go out and develop such support. Clearly many motives are involved in such efforts. The public receives needed services, while the bureaucracy derives status and power. Such reciprocal advantages result in a unity between public agencies and their client groups which is often irresistible. In the process, executive control and responsibility are sometimes sadly impaired.[22]

The bureaucracy has other means of swaying Congress. Some "buttonholing" or obvious lobbying occurs; administrators approach powerful legislators informally, requesting support for measures which affect their agency. Legislation is also influenced through the manufacture of grassroots support in favor of a certain measure. The network of field offices which some agencies maintain provides an effective mechanism for such demonstrations. The activities of the Extension Service of the Department of Agriculture, which sponsors the county agent program, are germane. Its strength is increased by an alliance with the Farm Bureau Federation, the most powerful farm lobby.[23] The effectiveness of the National Rivers and Harbors Congress, a strong water lobby, in promoting the objectives of the Corps of Army Engineers is of similar interest.[24]

[22] For an excellent analysis of such irresponsibility, see Charles McKinley, "Federal Administrative Pathology and the Separation of Powers," 11, *Public Administration Review* (Winter, 1951), pp. 17–25.

[23] See Grant McConnell, *The Decline of Agrarian Democracy* (Berkeley: University of California Press, 1953).

[24] A. Maass, *Muddy Waters: The Army Engineers and the Nation's Rivers* (Cambridge: Harvard University Press, 1951).

Weighing Competing Interests. In carrying out legislation, the bureaucracy also has discretion which greatly expands its power. It becomes, in effect, a partner in policy determination. (The resulting threat to democratic processes and the popular control of the bureaucracy will be considered elsewhere). Note again that this influence is a by-product of big government, modern technology, and the attending demand for expertise.

The administrator sometimes adopts a "public interest" rationale which broadens his discretion. This rationale assumes an area of general interest which transcends particular group interest and is therefore properly subject to administrative influence. The bureaucrat may leaven both the substance of legislation and the pressure of special interest with his own personal criterion of the "public interest."[25] This practice, however, is limited by certain political realities. The official often regards his agency as the agent of a particular interest, in conflict with other particular interests, represented in turn by other agencies. Thus he may view the "public interest" as a by-product or the net result of the competition between a number of special interests. This rather crude rationalization has historical substance, for most departments were in fact established to promote the interests of a certain sector of the economy. The bureaucrat who interprets the "public interest" too broadly may find that the dominant client groups of his agency have to remove him.[26]

Thus one must recognize that the high-level administrator often uses his discretion to promote the most powerful groups served by his agency. In every case he must weigh several "political" factors before he acts. He must balance the rival claims of public interest, client demands, organizational needs, and personal value preferences. In this sense administrative agencies have an interest and existence apart from that of Congress and the President who seek to control them. They are often self-sufficient, and their primary loyalty is often to great feudal economic interests which persist regardless of the outcome of party conflict.[27] Thus the bureaucrat cannot always afford to support (assuming that he wants to) the program of the President, the cabinet member, or the department, or to cooperate with other public agencies in seeking the "public interest." If he is to survive, he must constantly evaluate his

---

25 For a detailed analysis of the "public interest" and its operational effect, see Chapter 31.

26 For a striking example, see Joseph P. Harris, *The Advice and Consent of the Senate* (Berkeley: University of California Press, 1955), pp. 178–93.

27 For an interesting statement of the power of farm interest groups in the Department of Agriculture, see W. McCune, *The Farm Block* (New York: Doubleday & Co., Inc., 1943).

position in terms of political realities and act accordingly.[28] The nature of this process of adjustment is suggested in the following example:

The Farm Security Administration operated under one unchanged law, under one President, but under four different administrators; it changed substantially in each case and very greatly under its fourth administrator. All of the policy changes were administrative. Some involved substantial changes in clientele, attention swinging from very low income to moderately low income farmers. All of the changes were made below the level of Presidential direction, and below the level of Congressional determination. In part they reflected an accompanying shift from more liberal to more conservative administrative leadership. In part they reflected and anticipated changes in Congressional sentiment later crystallized in a new law.[29]

Implementing Legislation. Bureaucratic influence over policy implementation is also significant, ranging from virtual nullification of some legislation to the limited discretion involved in administering a detailed statute. But in every case discretion is involved. Nullification, the power of officials to ignore or half-heartedly carry out legislation, is an extreme example of bureaucratic policy making. Examples include prosecuting officials who have the authority to decide if a particular case will be acted upon. Thus an intelligence officer in the Bureau of Internal Revenue will recommend whether or not an individual charged with tax evasion should be indicted. Similarly, officials of the Antitrust Division of the Department of Justice enjoy considerable latitude in deciding whether a vigorous enforcement policy will be adopted, and specifically what kinds of cases will be emphasized. There are also several types of laws in which enforcement has been practically nullified by administrative discretion, largely because of an adverse public opinion which would not support enforcement.

Nullification, however, is of less practical importance than the discretion which officials enjoy in the implementation of broad policy adumbrated by the legislature. The rule-making power is a case in point. This permits administrative officials to prescribe rules and regulations which interpret or extend basic statutes. Such prescriptions have legal effect and may extend to private individuals or to agencies and employees of the government. Although the power has been resisted, industrialization and the growth of regulatory functions now mean that over

[28] A useful way of defining such dilemmas is as "role conflicts" which characterize all organizations; for empirical studies in this context, see Oscar Grusky, "Role Conflict in Organizations: Study of Prison Camp Officials," 3, *Administrative Science Quarterly* (March, 1959), pp. 452–72; A. Etzioni, "Authority Structure and Organizational Effectiveness," *ibid.* (June, 1959), pp. 43–67.

[29] Paul Appleby, *Policy And Administration* (University, Alabama: University of Alabama Press, 1949), p. 133.

one hundred federal departments and agencies exercise rule-making power. Although their discretion is always subject to the requirements of impartiality, conformity with legislative standards, and the rule of law, officials have considerable latitude in using this power.

The Federal Trade Commission, for example, is directed under the Sherman and the Clayton Acts to prohibit "unreasonable" restraints of trade and "unfair" methods of competition. Clearly these are subjective criteria. What is "unreasonable" and "unfair" is a function of time, place, and the dominant attitudes of Federal Trade Commissioners. Similarly, when members of the Federal Communications Commission hold hearings to consider license applications or to revoke a license because a broadcasting station has failed to fulfill its "public interest" obligation, they exercise discretion while making policy.[30] Their decisions are not fashioned in a vacuum; rather they represent a compromise among a complex of value judgments reflecting social and economic assumptions, the "public interest," the conflicting demands of economic rivals, and in general the influence of what Justice Holmes called "inarticulate major premises."

Balancing Professional and Ethical Considerations. The experience of a foreign service officer in Indonesia indicates the value context within which administration occurs.[31] In this instance, the officer, an economist by profession, found himself involved in a conflict between his personal and professional ethics and loyalty to his administrative superior. The issue concerned negotiation with officials of the Republic of Indonesia (in revolt against the Dutch after World War II) in regard to some economic surveys to be submitted to Washington. The other element of conflict was provided by the young official's superior, the consul general. An "old school product," with a long background in overseas administration and a marked sympathy for the Dutch, the latter was extremely reluctant to permit official discussions with the Indonesians. After considerable soul-searching, influenced by his sympathy for Indonesian independence ("my study of the pre-war pattern of colonialism in Indonesia left me with marked sympathy for the nationalist cause"), the vice-consul decided that his professional standards and the State Department's need for the most complete information warranted consultation with the Indonesians.

The instructive elements here include the role of personal ethics and value judgments, as well as professional standards, in influencing the

---

30 For an example of the problems involved, see the *New York Times,* January 25, 1958, p. 14; also "Investigations" in *Congressional Quarterly,* 1958.

31 Charles Wolf, Jr., "Indonesian Assignment," Harold Stein (ed.), *Public Administration and Policy Development* (New York: Harcourt, Brace & Co., Inc., 1952), pp. 55–61.

young official's decision. He knew that strained personal relationships would follow the unpopular alternative, that his future career rested upon the consul general's good will, and that no criticism of the easier decision would reflect upon him from Washington. Despite this, he chose the difficult alternative, suggesting the role of values and the "zones of discretion" that exist in any organization.

Carrying Out the Routine Work of Government. Our emphasis upon the policy influence of officials should not obscure the fact that they are mainly concerned with carrying out the ordinary tasks of government. These tasks include a bewildering number of activities. The ownership of an automobile, for example, suggests some of them. Involved at one time or another are licensing and inspection, traffic control and law enforcement, construction and maintenance of highways, national and state regulation of petroleum policy, state and national taxation of gasoline, as well as government regulations concerning wages, working conditions, and prices involved in the manufacture and sale of automobiles. More broadly, education, essential public utility services, the whole range of social security benefits, the police and judicial systems, the military establishment, and the intricate patterns of taxation—all influence the daily life of the citizen. And all involve routine tasks, whose importance becomes apparent only when they are disrupted.

CRITICISMS OF BUREAUCRACY

In our society with its dominant values of free enterprise and a fear of centralized political power, the growth of a huge federal bureaucracy has brought many criticisms, even predictions of national decline, because of the loss of individual freedom, initiative, and reliance as government assumes more and more responsibilities for ensuring security. The remainder of the chapter will be concerned with the nature and the validity of such criticisms.

The criticisms of bureaucracy include the charge that bureaucracy is unresponsive to popular demands; that bureaucrats have a lust for power; and perhaps most important, that the bureaucracy is usurping the policy-making role which traditionally has been the prerogative of the legislative branch or the President.[32] The critics of bureaucracy proceed upon the Hobbesian assumption that men thirst for power, that power corrupts and power once delegated is impossible to control. The basic idea is often fear of government. Allied with this is a belief, of eighteenth-

[32] Among others, see Ludwig von Mises, *Bureaucracy* (New Haven: Yale University Press, 1944); Fredrich Hayek, *Road to Serfdom* (Chicago: University of Chicago Press, 1944); James Burnham, *The Managerial Revolution* (New York: John Day Co., Inc., 1941).

century liberal origin, that big government necessarily subverts individual political and civil liberties. On the other hand there is the "twentieth-century" liberal doctrine which, stemming from a happier view of the nature of man, would invest government with great power in the firm belief that public power alone can mitigate social and economic inequity. Of late, however, this group too has become more concerned with the potential dangers of big government, particularly in the area of civil liberties. Although these conflicting ideologies are not watertight, they represent roughly the dominant split in regard to the "proper" role of government.

The Charge of Unresponsiveness. "Responsiveness" here refers to the speed and the attitude with which the bureaucracy reacts to changes in the political climate. We are not now concerned with responsibility viewed as legal or moral accountability, a problem which will be discussed in the concluding chapters. The claim that the bureaucracy is unresponsive has some basis in fact. The factor of size is relevant, for bigness brings about standardized procedures which make change difficult. Face-to-face contacts are minimized, and when they occur, officials often seem unduly impersonal. This frustrates the human desire for personal recognition, if not for preference. Actually the very attributes of bureaucracy that make for effectiveness and popular control tend to move toward extremes which destroy their initial advantage. Routine procedures breed inflexibility, while a passion for accountability fosters legalism and delay.[33] The official becomes a specialist, intellectually isolated, oriented toward techniques rather than people who may appear as vexing inconsistencies in an otherwise rational system.

The bureaucracy, moreover, is an institution with a certain self-sufficiency; it has its own hierarchy of values and its drives for status and power. Like other institutions, it resists change when change threatens its interests. The precedents and procedures, the "official secrets," the social values of individual officials, and the innate inflexibility of big organizations—all tend to slow down the reaction time of the bureaucracy. Thus it is not surprising that the civil service, which is often regarded as radical, is often conservative. Many examples can be cited: the counterrevolutionary view of the German service under the Weimar Republic; the resistance of certain elements in the British civil service to the economic policy of the Labour government; the opposition of the old-line agencies to the New Deal. More recently, the Eisenhower adminis-

---

[33] A well-known essay on this theme is Robert K. Merton, "Bureaucratic Structure and Personality," 17, *Social Forces* (1940), pp. 560–68; this essay is also available in Merton *et al.* (eds.), *Reader in Bureaucracy* (Glencoe, Ill.: The Free Press, 1952), pp. 361–71.

tration soon learned that radicalism was hardly a flourishing quality among federal civil servants.

Despite this, the democratic civil service has been responsive to great changes in public policy during this century. It is in this large context, rather than in the area of random individual contacts with reluctant officials, that responsiveness is meaningful. In both the United States and Britain the social programs of the New Deal and the Labour government were carried through. There was inevitably some resistance, but the protests of those who opposed the programs suggest the extent to which change *was* effected. The political neutrality of the British civil service is surely exaggerated, but the British system of party government ensures majority rule. In the United States, a much greater opportunity for official resistance exists, but here, too, the experience of the recent past indicates that the bureaucracy, like the Supreme Court, will follow the election returns.

The reconciliation of responsibility and the official's need for initiative is perhaps the basic problem of democratic administration. The expanding role of government has brought a greater need for topnotch personnel. The casual acceptance of indifferent performance and the uninformed criticism of government which have been part of our ideology are luxuries we can no longer afford. The solution may require more faith in the good intentions of government rather than the corrosive attitude that often exists. To strew the bureaucrat's path with every conceivable obstacle, seeking accountability, while condemning him for failing to act decisively, is unfair. Private management has usually tried to get good men, make their authority and responsibility clear, and then leave them alone. We fail to follow this policy in government. Obviously the final control must rest with elected representatives, but if the reaction time of the bureaucracy is to be quickened, there is a need for the positive attitude reflected, for example, in the policy of transferring the hiring responsibility from the Civil Service Commission to the line agencies.

The Will to Power. That there are power-hungry bureaucrats, no one can doubt. The struggles between the Army Corps of Engineers and the Bureau of Reclamation or between the Soil Conservation Service and the Extension Service furnish illustrations. But to assume that big government results from the personal ambition of officials is a great oversimplification. This view also underestimates the final authority of Congress as keeper of the purse. The executive branch has a big advantage in preparing the national budget, framing political issues, and presenting them to the country. But if government is to expand, large appropriations are needed, and these in the last analysis must come from Congress.

Moreover, if Congress is now unable to control the executive budget because of inadequate staff aid, this too is a condition which the legislators could improve. In sum, it is interest group demands, war, depression, and the threat of war that have brought big government.

Usurpation of Policy Determination. A more significant criticism of bureaucracy is the claim that too much policy determination has been wrested from the President and the Congress. This is a reasonable claim. In the past we have had a philosophical ideal (and a useful teaching device) which called for a nice distinction between policy and administration. This doctrine holds that "politics" and policy determination must be reserved to the legislature and chief executive and that the administrative branch must limit itself to carrying out policy. Democratic responsibility can be achieved only if the broad outlines of public policy are determined by a representative Congress. The appointed bureaucracy is obviously less responsible to the citizen and henceforth should have no part in determining what government should do. Like Aristotle's slave, the bureaucracy is merely an animated instrument, requiring the guidance of a rational master, the legislature.

The extent to which such traditional beliefs persist is suggested by the Second Hoover Commission, which included among its recommendations a "clear delineation between career and noncareer posts. More noncareer executives at the departmental level to take over all political and partisan tasks, including work of that nature which many career executives now are forced to handle." Similarly the words of Philip Young, former chairman of the United States Civil Service Commission, indicate that the old dichotomy between policy and administration remains seductive; with respect to the personnel policy of the Eisenhower administration, Young maintained, "the policy means that we are making a clear distinction for the first time between the political appointment area and the career service area. We are providing an orderly logical means of placing in policy-making positions persons who are sympathetic to the policies of the administration. At the same time, we are removing the career service as far as possible from political interference."

This thesis is tenable; it is good democratic theory. But it does not fit either the needs or the realities of government today.

This is because our public administration functions in a political context. The separation of powers system, local election of Congressmen, the competition among bureaucrats for new programs, the efforts of political parties to effect change once they achieve control of government, and the exceptional influence of big interests groups (which reflects the separation of powers and the localism of American politics)—

all tend to make ours a highly political administrative system.[34] Zones of discretion that grow increasingly "political" as one ascends the hierarchy exist throughout civil service. The policeman chooses between a ticket and a reprimand; the foreign service officer "makes policy on the cables." The political nature of administration and the need for the delegation of legislative authority blur the line between policy making and the execution of policy; the technical character of government forces the legislator to lean upon the official.

The activities of the regulatory commissions are illustrative. Congress was obliged to create expert bodies to handle the complicated task of regulating important economic interests. The general framework for such regulation was set down by Congress, but in implementing that policy and meeting the bewildering variety of special conditions arising therein, considerable policy discretion had to be delegated to the commissions. In England, similarly, it has been shown that the administrative class exercises a sustained influence on policy. Indeed some observers claim that only the most accomplished minister can avoid becoming an instrument of career officials.[35] J. Donald Kingsley has pointed out similarly that the development of technology and the increasing complexity of social relations have fundamentally altered the traditional relationship between politician and administrator.

Some Conclusions. In reviewing the principal criticism of bureaucracy, it seems possible to temper the claim that the administrative machine is unresponsive to changing popular demands. While routine matters are often time consuming and exasperating, in the vital area of broad policy change the bureaucracy is responsive. Within the past thirty years, minor social revolutions have been carried out under the New Deal in the United States and in Britain with the cooperation of the bureaucracy. The official apparatus is often legalistic and bound up in red tape; yet much of this comes from the passion for accountability which the public brings to government. Here, perhaps, a change in the external environment is the main requirement for improvement. That public servants sometimes have a lust for power, or at any rate, for survival, is undoubtedly true. This is a universal attribute of men; but government service is a poor place to indulge it. Both the nature of our

---

[34] Among others, see "Unofficial Government: Pressure Groups and Lobbies," **319**, *Annals of the American Academy of Political and Social Science* (September, 1958).

[35] Sydney and Beatrice Webb, *Constitution for the Socialist Commonwealth of Great Britain* (New York: Longmans, Green & Co., Inc., 1920); "the Government of Great Britain is in fact carried on, not by the Cabinet, nor even by the individual ministers, but by the Civil Service," p. 67. See also Harold Laski, *Parliamentary Government in England* (New York: The Viking Press, 1938).

federal system and of bureaucracy thwart vigorous action: power and responsibility are too broadly shared. The expansion of public power is largely due to depression, war, and world revolution rather than to aggressive officials.

That these officials now have a major role in policy determination cannot be denied. In the light of its implications for democratic control, this development is of crucial significance. In view of the political and technical nature of administration, however, it seems unrealistic to advocate that the official restrict himself to a purely advisory role. Delegation will continue; alternatives will present themselves; differences in value judgments will abound; and technical expertise will command respect. Perhaps more adequate control of administrative discretion is necessary but this must be done without hamstringing the bureaucrat.

BIBLIOGRAPHY

ARGYRIS, CHRIS. *Personality and Organization*. New York: 1957.

BENDIX, R. *Work and Authority in Industry*. New York: 1956.

BLAU, P. M. *Bureaucracy in Modern Society*. New York: 1956.

MERTON, R. *et al.* (eds.). *Reader in Bureaucracy*. Glencoe, Ill.: 1952.

MICHELS, R. *Political Parties*. Glencoe, Ill.: 1949.

PFIFFNER, JOHN M. *The Supervision of Personnel*. New York: 1958.

ROETHLISBERGER, FRITZ J., and DIXON, W. *Management and the Worker*. Cambridge: 1941.

WEBER, MAX. *From Max Weber: Essays in Sociology*. trans. and ed. by H. H. GERTH and C. WRIGHT MILLS. New York: 1946.

——. *The Theory of Social and Economic Organization*. New York: 1947.

WHYTE, W. H. *The Organization Man*. New York: 1956.

CHAPTER 4

Comparative Administration

As the preceding chapter suggests, the study of bureaucracy has often been comparative, showing differences and similarities among the administrative systems of Western countries. This chapter will continue that tradition by analyzing public administration in Britain and France. However, since World War II, comparative administration has been transformed by the United States government's expanding role in world affairs and by its technical and military assistance programs for underdeveloped countries. In turn, new research and teaching programs have been adopted in the universities. Non-Western societies have received the greatest attention because their demands for political freedom and economic security are the most important social force at this stage in history, and we know very little about their people, history, or governmental systems. Both in politics and economics, considerable thought is being given to the cultural factors that determine the degree to which Western administrative theory and practice can be introduced in long-neglected areas of Africa, Southeast Asia, the Far East, and the Middle East. After an introductory survey of selected aspects of British and French public administration, we shall outline some of these developments in the Middle East.

BUREAUCRACY IN WESTERN EUROPE

The study of comparative administration by American political scientists centered for the most part on western Europe and particularly on England, for like ourselves, these nations shared a common cultural heritage. In the case of England, even the language was essentially the same, so that research was relatively easy. The sharing of common values also made the emphasis on Western bureaucratic systems understandable, since it meant less adjustment for the American scholar trying to understand the system at work. Similar literacy rates, educational standards, institutional forms, advanced industrial systems, a reliance upon government for ensuring security and easing the risks of the market place, all encouraged an emphasis on western Europe in the study of comparative administration. Moreover, differences in governmental structure and educational values made for interesting differences in several aspects of administration. It is these differences with which the following analysis will be mainly concerned.

The British Administrative System. British administrative practice seems to have been mainly influenced by the cultural homogeneity of the nation, the cabinet system of government, and the dominant attitudes toward education and recruitment for the civil service. Each of these factors will be discussed in an effort to show that administrative systems are not isolated islands existing apart from the mainstream of a society but are closely interwoven with its institutional and value fabric. This lesson needs especially to be learned by Americans, since we have often been taught that "government" is some alien institution, foisted upon us by sinister, or at least misled, individuals, and is a necessary evil at best. An important comparative factor is that this fear of government is much less apparent in western Europe.

CULTURAL HOMOGENEITY. A major reason for the effectiveness of the British civil service is found in the long tradition of public consensus upon major social values, including the governmental system and the role of the bureaucracy. The sense of history and of national solidarity, based in good part upon common ethnic origins, seems to result in a pride and trust in public institutions, which in turn invigorates those who man such institutions.

Many examples of this respect for tradition and agreement upon common values exist. There is the well-known British love of pomp and ceremony, signalized by the Coronation, carried out in accord with centuries-old ritual. There is the fact that, despite the operational weakness of the monarchy, in the eyes of the law the sovereign's powers are still exactly the same as in the days of absolute monarchy.[1] All laws are still made in the name of the Queen. Every policeman is exercising powers that belong to the Crown, even though the Crown now has only symbolic value.[2] Again, Parliament did not come into being as the result of a revolution, as in many countries, but instead is the result of a history dating back to the middle thirteenth century.[3] Finally, as a French commentator says, "it is typical of the British respect for tradition that when they came to rebuild their House of Commons after it had been destroyed in an air raid on the night of 10-11th May 1941, it was decided . . . to build the new chamber on the same site and on exactly the same plan as the old."[4]

In sociological terms we can conclude that the social roles of politi-

---

[1] Andre Mathiot, *The British Political System* (London: Hogarth Press, 1958), p. 29.
[2] *Ibid.*
[3] *Ibid.*, p. 24.
[4] *Ibid.*, p. 25.

cian, bureaucrat, and policeman are not only *legitimated* by the society but that they are also highly valued. Psychologically, of course, the knowledge that the public respects one's role pays high dividends in morale.

THE CABINET SYSTEM. As mentioned earlier, the American separation-of-powers system complicates governmental operations by diffusing power and responsibility among too many centers. This structural feature of our system makes public administration difficult for various reasons, including the absence of a strong Cabinet to aid the chief executive and the interference in administration by the legislature through its powers of appointment, law making, investigation, and appropriation.[5] In the British system these effects are minimized by the fusion of the executive and the legislative arms of government in the office of the Cabinet, which is the directing and coordinating instrument of the entire governmental system.[6] The Cabinet is composed of approximately twenty heads of the major departments; these officials are also members of the Parliament. In most cases they have had long experience in political and administrative affairs. The vital feature here, however, is that the separatism and the power struggle between executive and legislature, characteristic of the United States system, are minimized by this device; and therefore government is capable of action.[7] As De Tolme once said, "Parliament can do everything but make a woman of a man." By refusing to support major Cabinet policy, the Parliament can force the Government of the day to "go to the country" for a new election. But this occurs only rarely because, given the British tradition of extreme party discipline, the party in power is unlikely to defect from its leaders who make up the Cabinet.

What effect does this system have upon the bureaucracy? Since the Minister is rarely chosen on the basis of expertise in the work of the department which he heads, he must rely heavily upon the advice of his permanent assistants. While the Minister has one or two politically appointed undersecretaries, they too lack special knowledge. Therefore the Minister will turn mainly to the permanent secretary of the department who is a career civil servant, member of an administrative class of about four thousand carefully selected career officials, including about two hundred women.[8] As Herman Finer shows, this relationship between

[5] Charles McKinley, "Federal Administrative Pathology and the Separation of Powers," 11, *Public Administration Review* (Winter, 1951), pp. 17–25.

[6] For details of Cabinet government, see Herman Finer, *Theory and Practice of Modern Government* (Rev. ed.; New York: Henry Holt & Co. Inc., 1950), pp. 575–621.

[7] Cited in W. I. Jennings, *Parliament* (London: Cambridge University Press, 1939), p. 2.

[8] A good, brief description of the administrative and other classes may be found in *Royal Commission on the Civil Service, Report*, (London: HMSO, 1955), *chaps.* ix, x, xi, xii, xiii.

the Minister and the permanent secretary (as well as the latter's top assistants) rests mainly on two bases: the *neutrality* and *anonymity* of the career servant.

The career official must be anonymous so that he can give the Minister full and disinterested advice about proposed policy matters, without fear of public criticism or approval of his role; nor should he become personally associated with particular views in the public's mind, since this would disqualify him for future service with politicians whose policies were different. Neutrality requires that he serve his successive political masters with equal loyalty and energy. He must be prepared to offer alternative plans to the Minister and to present each plan objectively. Obviously the entire system rests upon this expectation of neutrality by incoming Ministers; if this confidence were lost, the system could not function, and the Minister would feel obliged to bring in with him trusted political aides to ensure that his political program would be carried out. This is where tradition is important since the weight of this tradition and practice of neutrality inspires both incoming politicians and members of the administrative class with confidence that the system works in practice and that they can and should perpetuate it.[9]

There are, of course, differing views as to the effect of this relationship. Some critics argue that only the most astute and independent Minister can avoid becoming a pawn in the hands of the permanent officials who have the great advantage of technical skill and long experience in administrative affairs. On the other hand there is evidence that the *neutrality* of this administrative elite enables them to carry out policies which by virtue of their training and social position one might expect them to resist. This was shown, for example, in 1945 when a Labour government came to power in England, pledged to nationalize basic industry and to introduce far-reaching social security programs.[10]

A more frequent criticism of the administrative class has been that its members represent a social and intellectual elite and that this affects their ability to carry out social programs of a welfare state in which the major elements of production are nationalized. And it is true that before World War II, the base of recruitment to the administrative class was a limited one, regarded by many as a violation of democratic principles

[9] J. B. Christoph, "Political Rights and Neutrality in the British Civil Service," **51**, *American Political Science Review* (March, 1957), pp. 67–87.

[10] For a survey of two of these programs, with parenthetical comments on the administrative class reaction to them, see Robert V. Presthus, "British Public Administration: The National Coal Board," **10**, *Public Administration Review* (Summer, 1949), pp. 200–10; Presthus, "British Town and Country Planning: Local Participation," **45**, *American Political Science Review* (June, 1950), pp. 756–69; Presthus, "A Note on British Town Planning Coordination," **14**, *Journal of Politics* (1952), pp. 208–19.

of equal opportunity. For the most part, university training, a prerequisite to entry, was limited to those of upper and middle-class origin.[11] However, since World War II there has been considerable liberalization of entry, with promotions from the executive class (the civil service category just below the administrative class) amounting in 1950 to about 40 per cent, and open competition amounting to about 50 per cent of the total number in the administrative class.[12] This broadening of the recruitment base represents an impressive, almost revolutionary, change from the pre-war era.[13] Certainly the situation in 1937, when over 60 per cent of the class came from a few of the famous public schools, Oxford, Cambridge, and Edinburgh, is past history. Also, the creation of a "dual hierarchy" of scientific and professional positions has provided for recognition of the inadequacy of a purely liberal education to provide all the skills necessary for administration in a complex, scientific world. However, as we have already noted, privileged social origin does not by itself prevent the administrative class civil servant from carrying out policies which, were he to decide them personally, might be incongenial.

But the main benefit to the bureaucracy of the Cabinet system is that the warfare between the executive and the legislative branches is eased because the Minister comes to know and to trust the civil servants from whom he receives expert disinterested advice and counsel. The individual legislator approaches the bureaucracy through the Cabinet member, using the question period in Parliament. The morale and independence of the civil service is thus protected against legislative onslaughts by investigating committees and the like. At the same time the fact that there are only three political appointments to be made in each department when a new Government takes office protects the civil service from demands for patronage and the bargaining that goes along with such concessions by the civil service. All this obviously rests upon the confidence that Parliament and the public have developed in the neutrality and competence of the civil service.

Even the Eisenhower administration, after an initial period of suspicion, increasingly came to rely on the permanent career officials because the career administrator provided policy continuity and often proved to be effective in dealing with Congress, as well as in under-

[11] As late as 1950 Kelsall shows that the highest social class "...I which only accounts for 3.4 per cent of the adult male population of working age, has hitherto included a third of the fathers of senior members of the Higher Civil Service, and even now includes 29.3% of them. Classes I and II together form only 18.4 per cent of the census sample, but accounts for nearly 70% of higher civil servants in the 1950 group." R. K. Kelsall, *Higher Civil Servants in Britain* (London: Routledge, Kegan Paul, Ltd., 1955), p. 156.

[12] *Ibid.*, pp. 52–58.

[13] *Ibid.*, p. 53.

standing the peculiar character of government operations in which major programs necessarily require coordination and consultation among departments and agencies.[14] As a political commentator of the day observed, the President's continuing difficulty in finding and keeping key men with the attending danger of a lack of continuity resulted in "some talk here about the need for strengthening and evaluating the professional corps, and of introducing a system of permanent undersecretaries of all the departments who, as in Britain and the other parliamentary democracies, can give continuity from one Administration to another, and help carry the burdens in time of personal illness to the top political leaders."[15]

Undoubtedly an important reason for this tendency to trust the higher official is the difficulty of obtaining qualified men to serve in the appointive positions of assistant secretary, undersecretary, commissioner, and the like. Moreover the turnover rate among these people, once appointed, is extremely high; according to the second Hoover Commission, the average tenure for undersecretaries from 1948–52 was 23 months, with assistant secretaries serving 28 months.[16] "Too frequently, political appointees come to their posts without any prior federal experience and depart in a year or two without having served in more than one position."[17] According to the Commission, there are several reasons for this situation: scarcity of qualified people; lack of systematic development or training programs for such posts; disadvantages to the individual's private career; and psychological and financial barriers raised by the insecurity and limited salaries of appointive positions.[18] Under the Eisenhower administration the problem was aggravated by the definition of "necessary qualifications," which seems to have been largely one of business success, which may have relevance to operations in a government milieu and then again may not. Certainly the Strauss case, in which the Senate refused to confirm the President's nominee as Secretary of Commerce, indicated a sharp difference in assumptions about the quali-

---

[14] "With all deference to the political executive, who comes and goes, he does not have the same familiarity with program as his career staff. Congress knows this and wants to get at the fellow who has the facts," cited in M. Bernstein, *The Job of the Federal Executive* (Washington, D.C.: Brookings Institution, 1958), p. 45, pp. 40–62, *passim.*

[15] *New York Times,* March 4, 1959.

[16] Commission on Organization of the Executive Branch of the Government, *Personnel and Civil Service* (Washington, D.C.: U.S. Government Printing Office, 1955), p. 26.

[17] P. T. David and R. Pollock, *Executives for Government* (Washington, D.C.: Brookings Institution, 1957), pp. 9–10.

[18] Commission on Organization and the Executive Branch of the Government, *Task Force Report on Personnel and Civil Service* (Washington, D.C.: U.S. Government Printing Office, 1955), pp. 40–42.

ties needed for a high federal position. The President insisted that Strauss was qualified in every way by business success, loyalty, and government experience, but a majority of the Senate refused to accept these qualifications, mainly on the basis of Strauss' evasive tactics before the Joint Atomic Energy Commission and the Senate Committee considering his confirmation, as well as his role in the Dixon-Yates case.[19]

In any case a recent "round table" on the problem concluded that the first of "three deterrents" to businessmen taking government jobs was "the reluctance of younger executives in their thirties and forties to leave the corporation ladder for fear of losing places or sacrificing their pension rights."[20] One possible conclusion to be drawn here is that the sense of a "public service" obligation is inadequate in our competitive society.

RECRUITMENT IN THE BRITISH ADMINISTRATIVE CLASS. Public confidence in the top, policy-influencing class of officials rests in good part upon their training and recruitment. This in turn reflects dominant social values about education, which are most dramatically illustrated in the difference between British and American conceptions of education, especially at the university level. Members of the British administrative class are recruited in two general ways: through special examinations given upon graduation from university and by appointment from other sources, mainly from the executive class of the civil service, or from private industry, and university faculties or administrations.

Those recruited through examination upon university graduation have often had a liberal education, in which mathematics, literature, ancient and modern history were prominent. The essential factor here is that no specific training in administration or technical subjects is regarded as essential for administrative posts at the higher levels. Brains are the main requirement. This is in some contrast to our own philosophy with regard to career preparation at the university level. Our educational programs are highly specialized; we tend to believe that individuals can and should be trained to perform certain technical skills, such as budgeting, personnel classification, and organizational surveys. There is also a basic difference in regard to method of instruction: in the United States the lecture system is the common method; in Britain the tutorial system is favored.[21] This latter method tends to force the individual to grapple with problems by himself, and perhaps more important, it enables him to have a personal relationship with his instructors. The attending emphasis upon the preparation of seminar papers and the oral presentation and defense of them is invaluable in developing writing and rhetorical

[19] *New York Times,* June 21, 1959.
[20] Bernstein, *The Job of the Federal Executive,* p. 161.
[21] Finer, *Theory and Practice of Modern Government,* pp. 768–73.

skills that the administrator will need for his work. This difference marks a basic conflict in educational philosophy, which reflects itself in the civil service of the two countries. As to the final evaluation of the product and performance of administrators trained under these divergent systems, no final or conclusive answer can be found. Value judgments, national pride, and professional commitment will skew one's answer. Apparently there is some political influence in appointments, and the British have often been less candid about self-criticism than we have in the United States.[22]

In the main, however, it is generally agreed that the British civil service is an excellent one, and acquaintance with members of its administrative class leaves one with considerable respect for their competence and high morale. Security-loyalty programs, legislative investigations, limited prestige, and a high turnover rate make it difficult for our own civil service to achieve a similar continuity and élan.[23]

In sum, even this brief analysis suggests that three factors are in some measure responsible for differences in American and British administrative practices, namely, the respective governmental systems; the great difference in the weight of tradition and agreement on major social values, reflecting in turn the relative youth of the United States and its cultural and ethnic diversity over against the age and homogeneity of Britain; and finally, the respective attitudes of the two societies toward higher education and the most desirable kind of preparation for an administrative career. Thus, even in two countries which in point of language, law, and political institutions are among the most similar in the world, quite important differences in administration exist. In the subsequent sections we shall see that differences are even more pronounced when one turns to other Western societies.

The French Bureaucracy. A recent essay on the French political system begins with a section on "The Diversity of France," enumerating the following elements: race, geography, ideology, economy, France before 1789, and France after the revolution.[24] The French administrative system reflects the impact of these factors.

---

[22] J. L. Roberts, "Political Influence in Appointments to the Public Service," **21**, *New Zealand Journal of Public Administration* (Spring, 1958), pp. 37–57.

[23] For documentation, see Herman M. Somers, "The Federal Bureaucracy and the Change of Administration," **58**, *American Political Science Review* (March, 1954); *Washington Post* September 29, 1953, quoted the Under Secretary of Interior as follows, "I have got rid of a group of Ph.D.'s from Harvard and Columbia"; Herbert Hollander, *Crisis in the Civil Service* (Washington, D.C.: Current Issues Publishers, 1955).

[24] Maurice Duverger, *The French Political System* (Chicago: University of Chicago Press, 1958), pp. 3–12.

The structure of French government is superficially somewhat like that of England. It is a parliamentary regime with a Cabinet that exercises the main share of governmental power. The Parliament is divided into two houses, the Council of the Republic (formerly the Senate) and the National Assembly (formerly the Chamber of Deputies). Since World War II, political power in France has shifted toward the Right, signalized by the advent of De Gaulle as President of the Fifth Republic (October 4, 1958) with new and far-reaching powers, including the authority to dissolve Parliament and apparently (Article 16) to suspend the Constitution, to act as chief executive, to appoint the Prime Minister, preside over the Council of Ministers, negotiate and ratify treaties, and command the armed forces.[25]

However, in terms of actual operation, the systems are quite different. The British Cabinet system ensures strong, responsible government; the French system results in weak, diffused government. In France the Member of Parliament must resign when he becomes a Cabinet minister; in England, as we have seen, he will normally be a member of Parliament and remain so during his term as head of a department. In England there is collective leadership through the Cabinet; in France, under the Fifth Republic, the President holds many vital powers in his own hands, although it is significant that Parliament reserves the right to declare war.[26] It is perhaps symbolic of this executive supremacy that, unlike our own Constitution, the powers and duties of the President are set down *before* those of the Parliament.

In England there are no permanent Parliamentary committees dealing with special substantive areas, finance, commerce, armed forces, etc. The French Parliament has such committees, and they affect administration, since high-ranking civil servants are frequently called before them for questioning and explanations, thus undercutting the Cabinet Minister concerned.[27] In England, legislators question the departments through the appropriate Minister during a special period set aside for such activity during parliamentary sessions. Equally important, whereas the Cabinet Minister is in many ways superior to Parliament in the British system, under French practice he is obliged, politically at least, to appear before the committees when summoned and to explain his actions or to indicate his opinion of proposed legislation. As Duverger says, "committees exercise a strict control over the government."[28] Thus there is a ·

[25] For an American commentary on the new Constitution, see K. Loewenstein, "The Constitution of the Fifth Republic: A Preliminary Report," 21, *Journal of Politics* (May, 1959), pp. 211–33.

[26] Article 35.

[27] Duverger, *The French Political System*, pp. 24–25.

[28] *Ibid.*, p. 24.

legislative influence over French administration that is quite absent in Britain, although quite comparable with United States experience.

The political parties are another source of influence over administration, providing as they do a uniquely unstable and discontinuous political environment. Whereas England has three viable parties, Labour, Conservative, and Liberal, France has at least six distinct parties; these must be distinguished from Parliamentary political "groups," however, of which there are about twenty-five, each of which must be political in nature, i.e., not the representative of some specific economic interest, and have at least fourteen members. Not only is the number of organized parties greater than in England or the United States, but the ideological values of the French parties range even more widely: from extreme rightist groups such as the French People's Party (De Gaulle) and the monarchist and Poujadist groups through middle-of-the-road parties like the Socialists and the Christian–Democrat MRP, to extreme left parties such as the Communists.

The diversity of parties and their sharp ideological conflicts reflect the French social environment. For centuries there have been deep cleavages between monarchists and republicans; clericals and anticlericals; radicals of the right and the left against those who desired a liberal democracy; business and the conservative peasants versus labor; and more recently, the conflict between the advocates of colonialism (or, as the Fifth Republic's new constitution puts it, "Community") and those who advocate freedom for Algiers, Morocco, and other French possessions. In France these diverse social and political values are institutionalized in political parties and groups. By contrast, in England and the United States, there is a basic agreement upon most social and economic questions, plus a desire and a talent for compromise. In the United States, we have what may be called a pseudo-party system in that there are no important policy differences between the two major parties. The resulting consensus makes for stable government and in some ways for less reliance upon the civil service for impartial, skilled, and continuous service.

As is well known, it is extremely difficult to form a consistent majority among French parties, so that continuity in political leadership and in major policy matters is lacking. In Britain such continuity is assured at least through the common five-year term of each Government, which provides the bureaucracy with some permanency both in ministerial leadership and in major programs.

French administration is complicated by the turnover among ministers that reflects the inability to form persistent majorities among the several parties, resulting in turn in the frequent overthrow of governments. As Finer notes, ministers lose control over their departments simply because they are not in office long enough to become acquainted with the problems or the thinking of their high-level career assistants.[29] This turnover partly explains legislative intervention in administration: Since the Minister is temporary and necessarily uninformed of departmental affairs, the legislature goes around him to the high-ranking, permanent official. A certain amount of this practice exists in all political systems, but in France the practice is institutionalized to a greater degree than in other Western systems. As Duverger concludes, "ministerial instability is a deep-seated evil."[30] However, one must always add that turnover among Ministers is less pronounced than generally assumed, and many Ministers serve in several cabinets; thus some of the disadvantages of this problem are eased.

Also, the French system takes special measures to insulate the bureaucracy against ministerial instability. Promotion by seniority is one of these safeguards. Discipline may be administered only according to a fairly elaborate due-process procedure in which the civil servant must have prior notice of the complaint against him, and may appeal disciplinary decisions. The high administrative court, the *Conseil d'État,* helps enforce such procedural guaranties. Also, the civil servant may belong to a union, and the government cannot deny him the right to strike. No entry may be made upon his service record of his political affiliation, and there are joint committees that officially represent civil servants before their superiors. In a sense, then, we can conclude that (like the British service) the French bureaucracy is more isolated from politics than the American; and that it tends to provide continuity in government affairs, despite the volatile and changing character of French politics and political leadership. However, whereas we can say that the French bureaucracy has learned to operate without sustained political direction, the British and the United States bureaucracies are highly subject and sensitive to their political masters. The analysis of President Eisenhower's role in the Dixon-Yates case, Chapter 5, suggests the weight of such direction in our system.

Yet another vital structural feature of French government is that, like England, it is a unitary state in which power is centralized at the national level. Each of the one hundred departments of France is under the direction of a *prefect* who represents the central government and acts as executive officer of the department. The departments are miniatures of the central ministerial system, organized into divisions handling the major substantive tasks of government. One conflict arises here in that the various division heads find themselves torn between their natu-

[29] Finer, *Theory and Practice of Modern Government,* p. 628.
[30] Duverger, *The French Political System,* p. 138.

ral desire to communicate directly with their opposite numbers in Paris and their legal obligation to function through the *prefect*.[31] Countries such as Turkey, which have adopted the French department system, have the same problem. In the United States, with our federal-state system, the problems of administration are quite different, and a whole battery of problems in authority, duplication, and cooperation arise from federal-state and federal-municipal relations.

As Finer shows, the French system of centralization has many influences upon administration. Generally it results in a deep-seated suspicion of the whole executive branch by Parliament.[32] (This attitude, which is also characteristic of our American separation-of-powers system, apparently does not depend only upon governmental forms but may also reflect historical experience.) Centralization means that the department is not really a geographical community but a "framework within which state services function."[33] Any stimulus to activity and morale that may come from local autonomy and from the civil servant's identification with a local area seems to be lost. The *prefect*, moreover, is responsible directly to the Minister of Interior, which means that he will tend to make decisions with central rather than local considerations in mind. Even in the communes, which are political subdivisions enjoying limited delegation, with locally elected officials, "the controlling powers of the higher authorities are quite extensive."[34] Apparently it is again a matter of financial imbalance. The commune is dependent upon state taxes; it may not levy its own, and therefore it must turn to Paris for financial aid, which usually brings with it control.

THE EDUCATION AND RECRUITMENT OF FRENCH CIVIL SERVANTS. Here again we shall confine our generalizations to the higher civil service. We observed previously that World War II marked a revolution in British practices with regard to recruitment and promotion to the higher service. The same is true for France. Before that time, recruitment for the upper service was largely by competitive examination open to those who had served a certain minimum time in lower service grades and to those possessing diplomas from advanced high schools or higher. All candidates had to be between twenty-one and thirty years of age. Tests were both written and oral; and unlike the British tests, the written tests were technical and specific in nature, concerned with the substantive fields of

[31] For a current summary of French administration, see A. Diamant, "The French Administrative System," in William J. Siffin (ed.), *Toward the Comparative Study of Public Administration* (Bloomington: Indiana University Press, 1957), pp. 182–218.
[32] Finer, *Theory and Practice of Modern Government,* p. 750.
[33] Duverger, *The French Political System,* p. 167.
[34] *Ibid.,* pp. 164–66.

interest of the various Ministeries.[35] Again, whereas the British tests were general and the successful candidate might be put into any one of several departments, the French candidate was required to express his preference for service in a particular department and was tested on materials specifically related to that department.

Before World War II little criticism of this system appeared, but after the War, at least one aspect of it came in for sharp criticism. This was the same question raised about the British administrative class: whether the civil servants were not representative of too narrow a socio-economic stratum of French society and whether a group selected on such a basis could carry out the liberal reforms demanded after the war. There is considerable evidence that, unlike the British higher service, which seemed able to carry out policies that may have seemed repugnant to them, the French higher service was antidemocratic and out of sympathy with the aspirations of the French people. There was little doubt but that they were indeed selected from a narrow social stratum and that the École Libre des Sciences Politiques, in which many of them were trained, was "a school for the wealthy," "inclined to laissez faire in economics and the legalistic approach in constitutional and public law."[36] In discussing the character of this group, one French commentator said that the two or three thousand persons in the higher bureaucracy "were recruited from the ruling classes by a system of co-option and in a spirit of caste; they were reactionary and full of contempt for the mass of French people. They subordinate . . . the public interest to the interest of their caste and of the social class with which they were closely connected."[37] David Thompson wrote of the French higher service: "In so far as it is authoritarian, and attracts or breeds a narrow, rigid, over-traditionalist unimaginative type of personality, it lends itself to eager canvassing by totalitarian and undemocratic political movements which seek to overthrow the parliamentary system from within. . . . [Its] betrayal came to light . . . in the willing response given to the experiment of Vichy in 1940."[38] And Finer concludes, "the double fault of the higher administration was that the officials were authoritarian and that the disjointed structure of the departments ruined the usefulness of such professional competence . . . and loyalty to the nation."[39]

Partly as a result of such views, laws were passed in 1945 establishing for the higher grades a single system of competitive entry to the newly

[35] Finer, *Theory and Practice of Modern Government*, pp. 816–21, *passim*; Diamant, "The French Administration System," pp. 193–94.

[36] Finer, *Theory and Practice of Modern Government*, p. 820.

[37] Andre Ferrat, cited in T. Feyzioglu, "The Reforms of the French Higher Civil Service Since 1945," 33, *Public Administration* (Spring, 1955), pp. 76–77.

[38] Cited in Feyzioglu, *ibid.*, pp. 77–78.

[39] Finer, *Theory and Practice of Modern Government*, p. 821.

created National School of Administration.[40] In effect, the recruitment system was unified and democratized. Before, as Duverger put it, "the individual selection panels composed of members of the recruiting service had been influenced by considerations of social prestige. In practice, the only candidates who had any chance of success were those who had prepared by following courses at the École Libre des Sciences Politiques, a private institution of somewhat conservative tendency."[41] A major step was the nationalization of the École Libre des Sciences Politiques, which had been supported by rather high tuition fees paid by its students who were usually from bourgeoisie Parisian families. To break the monopoly of positions long enjoyed by Parisians, the resulting National School of Administration included regional institutes of ·administrative studies. Scholarships were provided to permit qualified but unpropertied youth to attend.[42] Recruitment was democratized by organizing for promotion to the higher service from lower ranks. An effort was made to provide a defined career avenue from the bottom to the top of the civil service. Finally, it was decided that those selected for the highest posts were to be equally divided between those promoted from within the service and those who had graduated from the National School of Administration. In generalizing about the effect of these measures, Feyzioglu concludes:

1. It is not possible to claim that there has been as yet considerable progress toward the "democratization" of the higher civil service, insofar as the social origins of higher civil servants are concerned: (from 1945 to 1950, of students entering the Institute of Political Studies in Paris, only 2 per cent came from farm families, who represent 25 per cent of the French adult male population; only 0.3 per cent came from families of skilled workers, who represent 22 per cent of French male population; unskilled and agricultural workers were not represented at all).[43]
2. The most noticeable influence has been equal recruitment in the upper grades from the ENA and from junior civil servants.
3. The reforms may have enhanced the opportunities of lower and middle bourgeoisie, even though the chances of farmers, industrial, and agricultural workers have not been considerably increased.
4. Although the social structure of the higher service as a whole may not have been changed, the distribution of people from different social classes inside the civil service has "probably" been changed.
5. The fact that very few candidates come from numerically important social groups such as farmers, skilled and unskilled workers, and agri-

[40] For a general appraisal of post-war developments see Roy Jumper, "Recruitment Problems in the French Higher Civil Service," 10, *Western Political Quarterly* (March, 1957), pp. 38–48.

[41] Duverger, *The French Political System*, p. 170.

[42] For a most sympathetic appraisal of post-war reforms by a member of the French Civil Service Commission, see Jean Trouve, "The French Civil Service Office," 11, *Public Administration Review* (Summer, 1951), pp. 180–86, 181–95.

[43] *Ibid.*, p. 186.

cultural groups reflects deeper social causes than those removed by the reformers in 1945.

6. Finally, the way to reconcile equality of opportunity with efficiency and competence in the civil service is through democratization of the entire educational system; "reforms which affect only some institutions at the apex of this system are bound to remain superficial."[44]

Similarly, Brown found that the type of academic training of candidates for admission to the ENA was not much different in 1954 than it had been during the period from 1947–51.[45] Legal training was still most common. However, training in political science was becoming more characteristic of candidates for the higher posts. In 1954 "political science degrees were held by 70 per cent of the 1954 class who entered by way of the First (student) Examination, [and] these candidates will fill '85 to 90 per cent' of openings in the grands corps."[46] Before concluding that this means a great liberalization in training, one would have to know more about the actual content of the political science course. Given the French educational tradition, one would suspect that the courses were still heavy on the legal, historical, and philosophical side and light on the behavioral and political dynamics side.

Once again then, we note that changes in the civil service require changes in the underlying social values and institutions of a country, and that efforts to overcome such social forces by legal and procedural innovation are often disappointing. This point reinforces the major theme of this chapter: that bureaucracy is not some alien intruder isolated from the main social values of a given society but instead reflects these values and can rarely rise above them even when its administrative structure has been imposed upon it by some foreign power. This formulation can be documented further by a résumé of administrative problems in so-called underdeveloped societies, to which we now turn.

THE NEW COMPARATIVE ADMINISTRATION

As noted earlier, before World War II the term "comparative administration" had a rather narrow connotation, referring to the public administration system of a country without much concern for its social context. Administration, moreover, was just one of several categories of study that included constitutional and public law, political parties, governmental structure, and interest groups. Today comparative public administration is developing a much broader scope, reflecting the experiences of our government and various international agencies with technical

---

[44] Ibid.

[45] John C. Brown, "Education of the New French Administrative Class," 16, Public Personnel Review (January, 1955), pp. 17–27.

[46] Ibid., p. 18.

and military aid programs. These programs dramatized the uniqueness of Western administrative norms and structure and emphasized the relationship between a bureaucracy and the kind of culture in which it exists. This new conception of the field was often forced upon us by the frustration and painful slowness of our attempts to superimpose American technology and administrative forms upon non-Western cultures whose history and values are quite different.[47]

In its new context, comparative administration now includes overseas or technical aid administration, international administration (involving the UN and other international bodies), as well as the analysis of the major institutions of foreign societies. Precisely speaking, studies in "comparative administration" in non-Western societies should probably include a conscious attempt to compare their institutions with those of the Western model. However, at this stage, we are content to include studies that confine themselves to a given country. The amount of basic data about non-Western systems, defined broadly to include their major institutions, is very limited. In many of these countries accurate statistics about production, employment, capital formation, public health, rainfall, and agricultural productivity are simply not available, and comparative administration thus remains at a rather abstract level, awaiting more rigorous field studies.

The Need for Theory. Comparative administration dramatizes the need for a working theory because one finds himself confronted by so much data and so many cultural forms that he could easily spend a lifetime on any given country, yet not develop any generalizations about its administrative system simply because he had failed to test his findings against some organizing theory.[48] "Theory" here means a statement of assumed causal relations between two or more variables. Causation is vital because, without the discovery of interrelationships among different sets of such assumed uniformities, the collection of evidence can go on indefinitely without advancing us along the road to social "laws."[49]

Such theory needs to be limited in scope. Social science has turned away from the universal systems of Pareto and Marx because conceptualization at such levels has not provided a basis for empirical research. Most social scientists are now content to analyze smaller chunks of reality, using as their guide "middle range" theory which attempts to

[47] Robert V. Presthus, "The Social Bases of Bureaucratic Organization," 38, *Social Forces* (December, 1959), pp. 103–9.

[48] Much of which follows is a revision of Robert V. Presthus, "Behavior and Bureaucracy in Many Cultures," 19, *Public Administration Review* (Winter, 1959), pp. 25–35; see also in the same issue, Fred J. Tickner, "A Survey and Evaluation of Comparative Research," pp. 19–24.

[49] Robert Merton, *Social Theory and Social Structure* (Glencoe, Ill.: The Free Press, 1957), pp. 95–99.

abstract from the whole social context some limited but meaningful part for analysis. "Middle-range" theory attempts to explain a limited set of relationships, as opposed to theory which attempts to comprehend and to explain an entire social system. A middle-range theory concerns such things as the relationship between a given economic system and its public administration system. Such abstraction is arbitrary and artificial, but its segments are manageable and provide us with findings that are more precise and cumulative.

The need for middle-range theory and systematic "public" research, in which theories, working hypotheses, definitions, and findings are explicitly stated so that the research can be built upon by others, is aggravated in comparative administration because agreement about the impact of cultural values upon administrative systems is otherwise almost unobtainable.[50] Overcoming the private tradition of comparative research requires the use of middle-range theory so that bases for comparability can be more precisely stated and kept in view throughout. It would also seem that the application of such theory would have to be limited for some time to small blocs of similar countries. Fruitful studies along these lines have been done with several Middle East states that have similar subsistence economies, underemployment, low per capita income, low literacy rates, dependence upon government for social services, economic development, a common religion, stratified class systems, and so on. Such regional groupings are useful, but they have to be handled with care.[51]

Analyzing Variables in Administrative Development. Another problem in comparative administration is to isolate the variables that are critical for bureaucratic development. A greater challenge, however, is

[50] For example, at a recent Council on Foreign Relations seminar on human factors affecting economic development in the Middle East, social scientists, several oil company executives, and two or three UN economists were unable to agree about such factors as religious values, the impact of fatalism upon motivation and change, concepts of time and the universe, the relation of low per capita income to industrial development, the impact of class on bureaucratic recruitment, and so on. It soon became apparent that the conferees were often unable to agree upon either the existence or the operational effect of these values. Some were not prepared to say that there were significant differences between the West and the Middle East insofar as several noneconomic factors were concerned, including fatalism, which one might have thought were among the most striking of Moslem characteristics. What was occurring was the clash of essentially *private* views of these societies, undisciplined by any theoretical framework or system for weighting such variables.

[51] The term "Middle East" must be used with care, since important ethnic, religious, and linguistic differences characterize those nations usually subsumed under this geographical category. Turkey, Iran, and the Arab states are different ethnically. While the dominant religion of the area is Moslem, a large Christian minority exists in Lebanon. Moreover, Lebanon is more literate, more commercial and industrial than its neighbors. However, despite such differences, it is convenient to speak of the area roughly bordering the Eastern Mediterranean as the Middle East.

to evolve a theory and a research design that will bring out the "consistent relationships" between them and a given bureaucratic system. Certainly, as our analysis of Britain and France shows, the class system is related to bureaucratic norms and behavior; in the Middle East, as we shall see, analysis is eased by the monolithic elite structure because recruitment sources, loyalties, and patterns of communication are less diversified than in Western societies. Aligned with class is the question of social power, and here again, analysis is in some ways easier because of the highly structured power relationships that exist in underdeveloped societies.

As we have seen, the educational system also affects the competence and values of the bureaucracy. Unlike much of the statistics and data available in underdeveloped countries, elite biographical data that include educational information are adequate. To "know" privately that educational systems have not prepared bureaucrats in underdeveloped countries for their technical role, however, is different from "knowing" this in a scientific sense. Even if it should turn out that one's personal notions are correct, prior research is necessary to give them validity. This is needed because private judgments are inadequate to evaluate a true comparative administration, which requires comparability in terms of public evidence.

Family structure and personality (including such elements as child-raising patterns and attitudes toward authority) are also among the research areas now available to social scientists. Psychologists agree that national cultures tend to produce typical personality structures. It seems clear that personality structures are not discarded like snakes' skins when one becomes a bureaucrat; the patterns of bureaucratic authority and deference are reflections of values acquired in prebureaucratic institutions, primarily in the family. Several "ordering constructs" are now accepted by psychologists, including self, ego-ideal, superego, and the concepts of socialization, identification, social role, and values. All are available as instruments of analysis in comparative administration.[52]

One may ask, what have personality patterns and family relationships to do with bureaucratic organization and behavior? But one has only to consider the fact that the nepotism and subjectivity seen in underdeveloped bureaucratic systems is a reflection of existing preindustrial family relations in which family loyalties outweigh the demands of technical skill and objective recruitment. (Here we should note that even in highly developed societies such as Britain and France, objective recruitment has not been wholly achieved, nor has elite control of the

---

[52] Alexander H. Leighton et al., Explorations in Social Psychiatry (New York: Basic Books, 1957), pp. 17–28.

higher civil service been entirely dissipated.) Without some theory that clues one into such relationships between social values and administration, this condition will be explained in irrelevant moral terms.

The nexus between economic systems and bureaucracy is another important variable. As Weber says, "the development of a money economy, insofar as the pecuniary compensation of officials is concerned, is a presupposition of bureaucracy,"[53] While payment in kind was used in the early bureaucracies of Egypt, Rome, China, and the Roman Catholic Church, a "certain measure of a developed money economy is the normal precondition for the unchanged and continued existence, if not for the establishment, of pure bureaucratic administrations."[54] Thus the economic system is useful for analyzing bureaucracies and for explaining differences among them. The subsistence economy, as well as the extended family system, are closely associated with the present stage of bureaucratic development in underdeveloped countries.[55]

RECENT THEORY AND RESEARCH IN COMPARATIVE ADMINISTRATION

Having outlined some problems of theory and research in comparative administration in poor countries, let us now examine some research studies that illustrate what is being done. Three studies will be used to illustrate two approaches to the study of comparative administration: the broad conceptual approach and the tight, rigorous field survey. Both approaches are needed, although in the past the historical, far-ranging kind of analysis has been far more common.

Riggs' "Agraria and Industria." The broad, conceptual approach is seen in Riggs' "Agraria and Industria: Toward a Typology of Comparative Administration."[56] Administration is defined in a broad way, and societies are divided into "agraria" and "industria," two ideal types against which actual societies can be analyzed.[57] Several variables are analyzed in each model, and their consequences for public administration are suggested. *Agraria's* economic base, for example, rests upon a predominantly rural population living on a subsistence basis. Government officials are often the most powerful social group, and they extract from the villages "large

[53] Max Weber, *From Max Weber, Essays in Sociology,* trans. and ed. by H. Gerth and C. W. Mills (Oxford University Press, New York, 1946), p. 204.
[54] *Ibid.*
[55] See, for example, Thomas C. Cochran, *The Puerto Rican Businessman* (Philadelphia: University of Pennsylvania Press, 1959).
[56] In William J. Siffin (ed.), *Toward the Comparative Study of Administration* (Bloomington: Indiana University Press, 1957).
[57] For a detailed critique of Riggs's work, see Robert V. Presthus, "Behavior and Bureaucracy in Many Cultures."

amounts of consumer goods to maintain their high social status." However, there are compensations, for the villages neither ask for nor need much from the government, which remains as "abstraction symbolized chiefly by the periodic appearance of a hated tax collector." *Agraria* is poor, and government's power, which rests upon its ability to collect taxes from a productive economy, is necessarily limited.

Another critical variable is social power, which in *agraria* often rests upon a monarchical, religious, or "sacral" basis. The official thus views his power as of "royal" origin, which in turn encourages him to expect deference from the public with whom he deals. In *industria,* on the other hand, power and authority come from the people; bureaucrats are "public servants"; and their behavior toward the public is democratic. However, Riggs adds, the technical skill and power of modern bureaucracy in *industria* gives it considerable leverage in dealing with the public.

Recruitment in the public service is analyzed, with *agraria* using "particularistic" criteria of birth, wealth, education, and class in selecting its public servants, whereas *industria* recruits on a more objective, competitive "universalistic" basis. In *agraria,* widespread illiteracy means that the bureaucracy must be recruited from restricted sources. Also, there are few other vocational alternatives for the educated minority. The character of educational systems in *agraria* further shapes the attitudes and competence of its public service. Since education is usually historical, legal, and philosophic in character, civil servants will not always be prepared to meet the technical demands of modern government. At the same time, as noted above, their loyalties are attached to family and community rather than to impersonal procedures and abstractions such as the "public interest."

The Egyptian Civil Service. The more rigorous field approach in comparative administration is exemplified by Berger's survey of the Egyptian higher civil service.[58] This is a rigorous sociological study which attempts to measure the behavior of Egyptian civil servants against certain standards derived from the typical Western model of bureaucracy, with its demands for objectivity, technical skill, and professional standards. Following a historical introduction, Berger turn to the attitudes of Egyptian higher civil servants on several critical variables. He assumes that the degree to which Egypt will achieve its economic aspirations is a function of its ability to adopt the Western bureaucratic model. The following qualities of bureaucracy and professionalism are "distilled" from this model:

[58] M. Berger, *Bureaucracy and Society in Modern Egypt* (Princeton: Princeton University Press, 1957).

BUREAUCRATIC SCALE:

Rationality and universalism: emphasis upon efficiency; recruitment based upon competence rather than upon family, religion, and so on.

Hierarchy: emphasis upon the prerogatives of position, upon authority and obedience.

Discretion: emphasis upon personal judgment and initiative, acceptance of responsibility, and full use of discretionary power within the rules.

PROFESSIONALISM INDEX:

Skill: emphasis upon technical competence as the chief characteristic of an organized group and upon self-discipline and self-regulation within the group to maintain its standards of skill.

Self-protection: emphasis upon the self-interest of the professional group through monopoly, exclusion, and secrecy.

Services: emphasis upon service to clientele groups and public as the main feature of professional activity.

These are the criteria used to determine how closely the Egyptian bureaucracy matches the ideal model. In addition, there are an "exposure" scale, designed to measure an official's degree of exposure to Western influences such as education, reading, and travel, and a job-satisfaction index.

What are the findings? Concerning adherence to bureaucratic norms, the most significant factors are age, grade, function, mobility, and degree of satisfaction with one's job. No significant relationship between exposure and degree of bureaucratic tendency was found. As would be expected, grade and age are similar in effect; older, higher ranking officials tend to be more bureaucratic than technical workers. Those who are upwardly mobile (i.e., occupy a post having higher status and prestige than their fathers' occupations) tend to be higher in bureaucratic orientation. Among younger workers, the more satisfied tend also to be more bureaucratic; however, this factor has no effect among older officials who, as we have seen, are more bureaucratic in general.

Regarding professionalism, neither age nor exposure is significant. Grade makes little difference. Social mobility is not significant and the influence of job satisfaction is very limited. But when one turns to function, a sharp distinction is found: "Among the technical workers, the proportion of 'high professionals' is much greater than among the administrative workers; the two proportions are 36 per cent and 8 per cent, respectively." Here, then, some clustering occurs: exposure, age, grade, social mobility, and job satisfaction are all closely related to bureaucratic orientations, but none has much effect upon professionalism.

The status of the civil service is generally higher in Egypt than in the West, yet officials are ambivalent. While 82 per cent of them answered "Yes" to the question, "Does the man in the street respect the civil servant?" their doubts are reflected in replies to questions such as: "What sort of a career would you advise him [a young cousin] to follow?" (only 4 per cent recommended government service); "What do you think of the civil service as a career for an intelligent man?" (only 9 per cent were favorable); "Do you think you might leave the civil service entirely for some reason?" (56 per cent said, "Yes"); and among younger civil servants asked the same question (two-thirds replied, "Yes").

Another index reveals the same ambivalence. When asked to appraise occupations in terms of selected criteria, ranked by the officials as "chance to serve the state," "good salary and working conditions," "skill," and "chance to serve the public," the following scale resulted:

> doctor
> bank director
> lawyer
> factory owner
> landowner
> government bureau chief
> government clerk
> small merchant
> factory worker
> peasant

A. T. J. Matthews asked Turkish administrators the same question, with the following results:[59]

> provincial governor (Vali)
> national legislator
> engineer
> general
> doctor
> judge
> diplomat
> professor
> big businessman
> government department chief
> lawyer

This would indicate that government employment fares much better in Turkey than in Egypt, since six of the eleven occupations involve the public service, whereas in the Egyptian case only two out of ten are government positions and these are ranked lower. Yet, in defining the most important basis of occupational prestige, both Egyptian and Turkish officials ranked "serving the state" and "holding a political office" first.

[59] A. T. J. Matthews, *Emergent Turkish Administrators* (Ankara: Institute of Administrative Sciences, University of Ankara, 1955), p. 21.

Civil servants' loyalties in Egypt were also analyzed. The tension here is between the bureaucrat's loyalty to the public, the state, and his profession, and competing demands of self-protection, hierarchy, and clientele groups. As noted earlier, age, exposure, grade, social mobility, and job satisfaction were not significant insofar as professionalism was concerned. Function was the only factor distinguishing high from low professionalism. Skill and public service, two of the professionalism items, are not rated highly, but self-protection, the third element in the index, is rated high.

In addition to its relevance to professionalism, the following illustration suggests the difficulties of interpreting research data. The question concerns a government economist who is directed to prepare a memorandum that he knows will contradict the views of professional economists. Should he yield to his superior or should he stand on his professional loyalty and refuse to prepare the memorandum? Of the 247 officials who replied, 129 said that he should not prepare the memorandum. This suggests that more than half the respondents are dedicated to "professionalism." However, when asked the *reasons* for their view, one-half said that the economist should follow his conscience, and the other half said he should refuse because otherwise he would contradict his professional economics colleagues. The question here is whether the latter rationale is an index of professionalism and self-protection, or whether "professionalism" is really evidenced by conformity with the 'conventional wisdom."

Berger finds that more technicians consistently, although usually by small margins, (1) believe that the official will be disciplined by his superior when his judgment turns out to be wrong, (2) believe that he *ought* to be punished for assuming the initiative, (3) are less prepared to defend him when his judgment proved to be wrong. In sum, greater initiative, as measured by the bureaucratic scale, characterizes older administrators in higher grades who are upwardly mobile and more satisfied with their jobs—"in short those longer exposed to Western patterns of attitude and behavior and to Western bureaucracies. . . ."

Insofar as the entire study is concerned, several unexpected results appear. Berger assumed initially that the relations between his bureaucratic scale and professionalism index and selected variables would be uniform, i.e., that the components of each would be found together when set against characteristics such as age, exposure, mobility, and so on. However, the findings are inconsistent. For example, exposure to Western influences affects the three indexes of professionalism differently. Egyptian officials highly exposed to the West tended to emphasize the skill factor and minimize the self-interest factor. Insofar as the third component, public service, was concerned, results were inconclusive.

Also, while it was assumed that those most exposed to the West would score highest on all elements of professionalism, it was actually those "only moderately exposed" who so scored.

Concerning bureaucratic orientations, similar disparities occurred. High exposure to the West did correlate highly with rationality, one of the bureaucratic indexes, but was low vis-à-vis another index, hierarchy. Similarly with age and higher education, neither yields uniformly high or low scores against the three elements in the bureaucratic scale.

From these findings Berger concludes that his "study of bureaucracy in a non-Western setting points to the limitations of current bureaucratic theory, developed mainly in the West." This is especially significant because it raises serious questions about the validity for comparative purposes of a model that has proved most useful for teaching and research in the West.

The Turkish *Conseil d'Etat*. A third study illustrates the adaptation of statistical methods to comparative administration in a society where this type of study was virtually unknown.[60] Random sampling methods were applied to 87,640 cases treated during the period 1947–54 by the Turkish *Devlet Surasi*, the highest administrative court and patterned after the French *Conseil d'État*. The resulting sample of 2,131 cases provided a statistically valid basis for generalizing about the kinds and the relative proportions of cases handled by the Court. Records of decisions had been kept chronologically and included the essential facts of the case, such as the parties, their occupation, the nature of the issue, the geographical area in which the issue occurred, and the decision. To order these data, a framework or code of seven factors was prepared. When the sample was analyzed, the research revealed several characteristics of administrative law and government in Turkey. Many of these were "known" in an impressionistic fashion, as, for example, the fact that the Court dealt mainly (over half its cases) with income tax cases involving merchants in the large cities. However, such things as the proportion of types of cases treated by the Court, as well as the kinds of decisions which were normally handed down in cases of a certain kind, were not known.

One interesting finding was the fact that procedural errors, reflecting mistakes in drafting a complaint or meeting time limits for submitting a case, were causing the Court to reject an extremely high proportion of cases (over 18 per cent). This denial to citizens of their "day in court" brought out the need to teach the public the legal requirements of appealing to the Court. The situation also suggested the corrosive effect

[60] Robert V. Presthus with Sevda Erem, *Statistical Method in Comparative Administration: The Turkish Conseil d'État* (Ithaca: Cornell University Press, 1958).

of having so many substantive conflicts go unresolved. It was also found that civil servants usually fared badly before the Court, since the Administration's side was upheld in the following impressive majorities (in terms of number of cases):

	Administration Upheld	Denied
Dismissals of Civil Servants	24%	10%
Promotions of Civil Servants	31	9
Salary Disputes	16	8
Compulsory Retirements	23	3

However, in the areas of determining years of service for pension rights, travel expenses, and recoveries of overpayments to civil servants, the Court was more sympathetic.

Concerning the noted centralization of Turkish government, which is patterned after the French system with departments (Vilayets) and provincial governors (Vali) performing the same role as the *prefects,* the study provided further documentation. The agencies of central government were involved in an overwhelming majority of cases: 1,822 of the total sample of 2,131. Most of these involve tax officials in major cities. In all, only 337 cases concerned local government jurisdiction, which suggests the extent of centralized government's involving most if not all major functions such as taxation, customs, and regulation of military service and of civil servants. This picture of centralization is supported by statistics on the Court's rulings in cases involving decisions by local boards and commissions. In the case of the provincial local board, its findings were denied in 36 cases and affirmed in only 24, with 12 cases being rejected for procedural errors of one kind or another. The smaller jurisdictions within the provinces (Kazas) fared even worse, being denied in 26 cases, affirmed in only 12, and rejected in 19 for procedural errors.

The kinds of raw data provided by the two studies on Egypt and Turkey are most helpful in the development of comparative theory that must build upon a substratum of basic information which is often not yet available. On the other hand, the kind of theoretical framework set down by Riggs is also most useful because it helps us decide what kinds of questions are worth asking about public administration in poorer countries. A constant interplay between these two kinds of work is required if a discipline of comparative administration is to be built.

BIBLIOGRAPHY

BERGER, M. *Bureaucracy and Society in Modern Egypt: A Study of the Higher Civil Service.* Princeton: 1957.

FRIEDRICH, CARL J., and COLE, TAYLOR. *Responsible Bureaucracy.* Cambridge, 1932.

HEADY, FERREL. "Bureaucratic Theory and Comparative Administration," 3, *Administrative Science Quarterly* (March, 1959).

Human Relations Area Files, "Country Survey Series," "Behavior Science Bibliographies," *et al.* New Haven: 1956–.

KELSALL, R. A. *Higher Civil Servants in Britain, from 1870 to the Present Day.* London: 1955.

KINGSLEY, J. DONALD. *Representative Bureaucracy.* Yellow Springs, Ohio: 1944.

LERNER, D., and WIENER, A. J. (eds.). "Attitude Research in Modernizing Areas," 22, *Public Opinion Quarterly* (Fall, 1959).

LERNER, D., *et al. The Passing of Traditional Society.* Glencoe: 1958.

MEYER, PAUL. *Administrative Organization: A Comparative Study of the Organization of Public Administration.* London and Copenhagen: 1957.

MORSTEIN-MARX, FRITZ. *The Administrative State.* Chicago: 1957.

PRESTHUS, ROBERT V. "Behavior and Bureaucracy in Many Cultures," 19, *Public Administration Review* (Winter, 1959).

——. "The Social Bases of Bureaucratic Organization," *Social Forces* (December, 1959).

PRESTHUS, ROBERT V., with EREM, SEVDA. *Statistical Method in Comparative Administration: The Turkish Conseil d'État.* Ithaca: 1958.

SELLIN, T., and LAMBERT, R. D. (eds.). "Partnership for Progress: International Technical Cooperation," 323, *Annals of the American Academy of Political and Social Science* (May, 1959).

——. *Asia and Future World Leadership,* 320, *Annuals of the American Academy of Political and Social Science* (July, 1958).

SIFFIN, WILLIAM. J. (ed.). *Toward the Comparative Study of Public Administration.* Bloomington, Indiana: 1957.

Part II

THE FUNCTIONS OF
THE ADMINISTRATOR

CHAPTER 5

Administrative Leadership

As we have seen, the size and specialization of modern organizations increased their efficiency and objectivity. But bureaucracy was a two-edged sword; the very factors that made for competence and predictability tended to become harmful as the logic of organization was pushed to an extreme. Size brought inertia, expertise brought introversion, specialization encouraged impersonality, and the problem of coordinating functional and geographical units became more difficult. As a result, unusual qualities of inspiration and direction were required to weld giant organizations into self-conscious, purposeful alliances. A new emphasis upon leadership as an administrative skill followed. Meanwhile the expansion of executive power became the outstanding fact of modern government, reflecting, perhaps, Robert Michels' theory, which holds that the larger organizations become, the greater the tendency for control to center in a few hands.[1]

BUREAUCRATIC LEADERSHIP

Although leadership occurs in all group life, leadership in big organizations is our principal concern. While indigenous or natural leadership asserts itself throughout the organization, it is exercised mainly by executives occupying strategic positions at the top. In a democratic society where interest groups are articulate, where employee morale is reflected in productivity, and where a rich economy provides many vocational alternatives, the executive's task is far more complex than the simple command relationships of the past. It requires a facility for control of interpersonal relations, for bringing together the many diverse views and interests that make up the organization.

Broadly, we may say that command is being replaced by manipulation as the primary tactic of leadership. Administrative behavior is group behavior; thus persuasion, compromise, and coordination assume a new importance. New demands for technical skill and specialization have

[1] Robert Michels, *Political Parties: A Sociological Study of the Oligarchical Tendencies of Modern Democracy* (Glencoe, Ill.: The Free Press, 1949).

also contributed to the change from command to manipulation, even in such typical bureaucratic structures as the military, where the technical complexity of modern arms and the fluidity of battlefield situations force delegation.[2] At the moment, moreover, a concern with preserving the individual from excessive organizational demands for conformity is probably having a similar effect on the conditions of leadership.

In this chapter we shall analyze changing definitions of leadership and the role of bureaucratic leaders. Once again public administration's dependence upon the social sciences is illustrated by the research studies upon which the chapter draws. The universal character of bureaucracy and the administrative art is reaffirmed by the similarity of leadership in public and private enterprise. However, a word of caution is in order: The executive's role is similar mainly in the *internal* aspects of administration. These include interpersonal relations in organization, group participation in decision making, and the delegation of authority that accompanies size and technical specialization. While the *conditions* of bureaucratic leadership have changed and have become similar in various kinds of organizations, the leadership function is modified greatly by the different *external* environments of government and business, particularly differences in public attitudes, accountability, the "service" orientation of public administration, and the separation of powers system under which it labors.

NATURE OF LEADERSHIP

Leadership is the art of coordinating and motivating individuals and groups to achieve desired ends. It is mainly concerned with verbal, intellectual, and social skills. Leadership is often contrasted with command; the former requires intuitive judgment and exhortation, whereas the latter involves authority[3] and the securing of consent by virtue of formal power and sanctions. This point is probably well taken, for ideally, leadership is freely accepted in recognition of the leader's knowledge and his moral right to lead. However, it is difficult to separate these qualities from the influence of the leader's formal role. Perhaps the two may best be regarded as constituent parts of leadership. With the exception of indigenous leaders who function without any formal sanction, leaders usually have an institutional position, and the status and authority associated with this position becomes a part of their leadership role. At the very least, the mere recognition of legitimate authority disposes most men to obey. But this is a rather negative conception of the leader's role.

---

2 M. Janowitz, "Changes in Organizational Authority: the Military Establishment," 3, *Administrative Science Quarterly* (March, 1959), pp. 473–93.

3 See W. G. Bennis, "Leadership Theory and Administrative Behavior," 4 *Administrative Science Quarterly* (December, 1959).

Although power is an essential part of leadership involving the ability to secure compliance by persuasion or command, formal authority or position cannot by itself ensure leadership. Any study of the United States Presidency reveals that the powers of the office have been used very differently, largely on the basis of the chief executive's personal qualities and the demands of the time.[4] But the "halo effect" is always present. It is clear, for example that the greater the social distance between the individual and the leader, the more "prominent" the leader seems to be.[5]

Situational Nature of Leadership. Traditional concepts of leadership have been sharply modified by research in sociology and social psychology, particularly the notion that leadership is a somewhat authoritarian, individualistic, and general quality exercised over a passive group. Increasingly, leadership is viewed as *situational*: Its requirements and manifestations vary greatly in time and place. For example, although the United States and England are similar in values, language, and political institutions, their views in regard to leadership are quite opposed. In England the politician, the churchman, the educator, and the soldier enjoy the greatest prestige. In America, on the other hand, it is generally true that the big business executive, the medical doctor, and the physical scientist have the highest status.[6] Also in America, leadership seems more often to be correlated with aggressive and emotional characteristics. Certainly, with regard to politics and the public service the views of the two countries are polar. In a broader context, the spiritualism of Gandhi's leadership was practically incomprehensible to the Western world, where leadership has a connotation of aggressive power. Leadership thus varies with the values of a particular group or society.

This means that the popular view of leadership as a complex of personal aptitudes of general applicability must be revised. Instead, certain patterns of leadership behavior are required in certain situations. For example, campus political leaders have been found to be socially adaptable but intellectually mediocre; campus editors, bright and self-confident

[4] An excellent documentation here is Harold J. Laski, *The American Presidency* (New York: Alfred A. Knopf, Inc., 1940), particularly chap. v.

[5] A. W. Gouldner, *Studies in Leadership* (New York: Harper & Bros., 1950), pp. 201–5. For more recent collections of empirical studies of leadership see: Dorwin Cartwright and Alvin Zander, *Group Dynamics: Research and Theory* (Evanston: Row, Peterson & Co., 1953), pp. 535–628; Ralph M. Stogdill and Alvin E. Coons (eds.), *Leader Behavior: Its Description and Measurement* ("Ohio Studies in Personnel," Research Monograph No. 88), (Columbus, Ohio: Bureau of Business Research, Ohio State University, 1957).

[6] For a study of the social backgrounds of 8,000 United States business leaders, see W. L. Warner and J. C. Abegglen, *Big Business Leaders in America* (New York: Harper & Bros., 1955).

but ill-adjusted socially; university debaters, exceptionally intelligent but very insecure emotionally.[7] Now, each of these types is a "leader," but each possesses specific qualities required for leadership in a particular setting. If there is such a person as a "born leader," it would seem that he must appear in the proper place at the moment when his particular aptitudes are needed.

Perhaps the validity of the situational thesis is shown in the experience of President Eisenhower, whose demonstrated leadership qualities in the military arena proved generally less impressive in his political role as chief executive. Certainly, his attempt to use a chief-of-staff method of operation ran against the political demand for a responsible chief executive. Apparently, too, as revealed in several press conferences, his dependence for current information upon his personal staff often left him without essential information about current affairs. In effect it would seem that the political role demands a capacity for extemporaneous judgments on a broad range of affairs, to the extent that staff aides can never provide the required information in depth.[8]

In sum, the situational concept differs sharply from the traditional view of leadership, emanating from Aristotle and Machiavelli, with its highly individualistic and autocratic bias. This view assumed that certain exceptionally gifted leaders appear in crisis periods to direct a mindless mass of followers. It assumed that leaders possess a set of attitudes or traits of general validity. This concept, moreover, had a self-confirming effect: Its very acceptance caused men to act as though it was actually a valid explanation.

Group Character of Leadership. Leadership is now seen as a function in which the leader is primarily a *coordinator* of group effort rather than a man apart using extraordinary powers of insight and dominance to manipulate the group. Democratic leadership, especially, is a group phenomenon in which the qualities of leadership are defined by group values.[9] These values provide a pattern to which the leader must conform. He cannot inflict leadership upon the group; instead he must possess those particular aptitudes which it already regards as essential. This point is implicit in the fact that leaders emerge only after an

---

[7] Ralph M. Stogdill, "Personal Factors Associated with Leadership: A Survey of the Literature," 25, *Journal of Psychology* (January, 1948), pp. 60–62.

[8] For a commentary on this subject, see Marian D. Irish, "The Organization Man in the Presidency," 20, *Journal of Politics* (May, 1958), pp. 259–77. However, we shall see later in this chapter that President Eisenhower did assume leadership in certain policy matters, particularly in the Dixon-Yates case.

[9] Ralph M. Stogdill, *Leadership and Structures of Personal Interaction* ("Ohio Studies in Personnel," Research Monograph No. 84) (Columbus, Ohio: Bureau of Business Research, Ohio State University, 1957).

exploratory period of interpersonal contact during which they identify themselves as potential leaders by their ability to guide group affairs with a minimum of friction. In every case the personal objectives and qualities of the leader must have a positive relation to the characteristics and goals of the followers. Leadership is apparently less a function of status and exceptional aptitudes than a matter of reciprocal social relationships in which the leader acquires recognition and confidence because of his ability to guide group activity toward group objectives.

Studies of group dynamics provide further insight into the reciprocal and interpersonal nature of leadership. The characteristics of weak and strong leadership, as reflected in group reactions, have been established.[10] With some exceptions, morale, cooperation, productivity, and resourcefulness have been found to increase under responsive, democratic leadership. Contrary to what one may presume, quick response and high productivity are best secured by persuasive methods and the use of the "human relations" approach. The leader attains these ends by a peculiar sensitivity to individual needs and differences.[11] He emphasizes direct communication to workers, maximum delegation of authority, and clear definitions of authority and responsibility. As a result the measurement of leadership has become concerned with the temperament of the executive, how he leads, and the morale of employees under him because these are apparently related to his employees' attitudes and productivity. For example, Donald Campbell found that naval officers who described themselves as "high on organizational behavior" had units with low morale.[12] That is, those officers who stressed operations "by the book" actually inhibited participation and the achievement of the unit's goals. An interesting paradox here is that the very traits that make for success in administration seem to correlate negatively with those qualities that stress personal worth and human interest.[13]

[10] Among others, see Kurt Lewin, *Resolving Social Conflicts* (New York: Harper & Bros., 1948).

[11] For an empirical study that focuses on the leader's perceptions of the follower, see James K. Dent, *Managerial Leadership Styles: Some Dimensions, Determinants and Behavioral Correlates* (Ann Arbor University Microfilms, Inc., 1957).

[12] Donald T. Campbell, *Leadership and Its Effects Upon the Group* ("Ohio Studies in Personnel," Research Monograph No. 83) (Columbus, Ohio: Bureau of Business Research, Ohio State University, 1956), p. 60–62; see also H. Baumgartel, "Leadership Style as a Variable in Research Administration, 2, *Administrative Science Quarterly* (December, 1957).

[13] John M. Pfiffner, *The Supervision of Personnel* (2d ed.; Englewood Cliffs, N. J.: Prentice-Hall, Inc., 1958), pp. 335–36; B. Gardner, "Successful and Unsuccessful Executives," 13, *Advanced Management* (September, 1948); Rensis Likert and Samuel P. Hayes, Jr., *Some Applications of Behavioral Research* (New York: UNESCO, 1957); Ronald Lippett, Jeanne Watson, and Bruce Westley, *The Dynamics of Planned Change* (New York: Harcourt, Brace & Co., 1958).

Similar generalizations were obtained from studies of group behavior in military organizations by Shils, Janowitz, and Stouffer.[14] Group morale and motivation were found to be based primarily upon personal factors associated with loyalty to immediate companions and group-established standards of conduct rather than upon generalized loyalties to the state or political ideals. In every case, face-to-face or primary group association was the critical factor in determining individual attitudes. The implications of such findings for executive leadership seem compelling. The leader must recognize that human motivation rests upon immediate, social values, rather than upon economic or individual appeals. Group sanctions are more effective in channelizing behavior than administrative decrees. In a sense the irrationality of much individual behavior is again underscored. The motives of individuals in group situations are evidently less self-conscious and calculated than we have assumed.

A pioneer study which suggests the new demands upon leadership is that by Likert and Katz for the Prudential Life Insurance Company.[15] Their survey of two large departments revealed that productivity was positively correlated with the quality of supervisory practices. Differences in productivity and morale between the highest and the lowest units were found to be due to the methods of supervisors. In the most proficient units these methods included less direct control of supervisors by their superiors, more emphasis on employee interests than on production goals, and conscious efforts by supervisors to increase worker participation in decision making. In sum, individuals seem to be more effectively motivated when they have some freedom in determining how their work should be done. They respond more fully when treated as individuals. And they do better when they have a part in decision making. Apparently the effective leader does a minimum of "leading" in the traditional sense of the word.

Leadership Traits and Types. Social psychologists have generally been reluctant to suggest that types of leaders or generalized leadership traits exist. Sociologists, however, have established types by differentiating among situations. Although they agree with psychologists that different social structures require different kinds of leadership behavior, generally, they posit an ideal type of social or organizational structure, such as

---

[14] E. Shils and M. Janowitz, "Cohesion and Disintegration in the Wehrmacht," **12**, *Public Opinion Quarterly* (Summer, 1948), pp. 280–315; Samuel Stouffer *et al., The American Soldier*, vol. I (Princeton: Princeton University Press, 1949), 410–20. Also, see R. M. Stogdill, *Leadership and Structures of Personal Interaction.*

[15] Rensis Likert and Daniel Katz, *Supervisory Practices as They Affect Employee Production and Morale* (New York: American Management Association, 1948). See also *Productivity, Supervision, and Employee Morale* ("*Human Relations Series*"), (Ann Arbor: Survey Research Center, University of Michigan, 1948).

"bureaucratic." This is then used as a criterion for measuring actual organizations. Similar models are used to delimit leadership type studies. Finally, types have been proposed that are not specifically related to a certain environment or social structure. This suggests that a central core of social characteristics may be shared by leaders, despite the current view that leadership is a situational phenomenon.

Some interesting work has been done in this trait approach. The group concept has been combined with a psychoanalytic approach to personality in an attempt to bring together some common elements of leadership.[16] It has been shown that the leader requires a certain intellectual flexibility which enables him to coordinate the group. This capacity is essential because the conflicting needs of individual members cause strong separatist tendencies. The needs of self fly in the face of the need for cooperation. The leader must provide the focal point about which group activity centers. This requires not only an unusual sensitivity to individual differences of temperament and opinion but also the ability to formulate the compromise which will ensure solidarity. Thus the leader is coordinator, planner, and spokesman for the group. In this context, Redl suggests that the symbol "leader" is anachronistic and should be replaced by the terms "central" or "focal" person.

Freud, too, expressed a suggestive opinion of the leader-group relationship.[17] He saw it as a continuation of the early family situation in which the leader's role is similar to that of the patriarchal father who personifies the values of the family and is its major catalyst. Leaders, as a result, appear as a succession of "father images" who evoke the whole battery of dependency attitudes inculcated during the individual's formative years. The use of the term "father" to designate leaders in various kinds of organizations suggests the validity of Freud's hypothesis. In the Indonesian army, for example, the officers are addressed as "bakap," which means father.[18] In any case, there seems little doubt that some individuals find psychic comfort in submission to organizational leaders, who may be viewed as protectors. Such postures may also have career utility, since deference and submission are valued by most leaders.

Certain aggressive tendencies seem necessary for leadership in our society, regardless of the particular context. The contemplative and withdrawing individual has little chance for leadership. Leaders have also been found to excel the average members of their group in intelli-

[16] Fritz Redl, "Group Emotions and Leadership," 5, *Psychiatry* (November, 1942), pp. 576–80.

[17] E. Jones, *The Life and Work of Sigmund Freud*, vol. III, (New York: Basic Books, 1957).

[18] S. Soemerdjan, "Bureaucratic Organization in a Time of Revolution," 2, *Administrative Science Quarterly* (September, 1957), pp. 182–99.

gence, scholarship, dependability, social participation, and socio-economic status.[19] Again, intellectual integrity and courage have been found essential to leadership in maturity, while physical strength and athletic skill are required during adolescence. Appearance, weight, age, and energy similarly have a low but positive correlation with leadership. Bertrand Russell insists that the leader must excel in those qualities which confer authority: self-confidence, skill, and quickness in selecting among alternatives.[20] Robert Michels suggests similar qualities, including exceptional strength of conviction, force of will, and relatively wide knowledge.[21] Common-sense or impressionistic views of leadership such as these have induced many observers to seek leadership traits of general validity.

It would certainly seem that the successful leader must be able to identify very closely with the organization as a whole. He must be able to accept the legitimacy and rationality of its objectives and its means. Such a posture will enable him to make decisions in terms of organizational imperatives, as opposed to competing values that may harm the organization. As Mishler points out, there seem to be two distinct premises for making decisions: *universalistic* and *particularistic*. The former refer to "tough-minded" premises that reflect the needs of the organization, whereas the latter concern "tender-minded" premises such as friendship and a preference for subjective values. Particularism is "associated with the rejection of authority, a permissive view of dissent, an acceptance of one's own impulses, and an objective appraisal of one's parents."[22] In the context of leadership these values seem dysfunctional, since they interfere with the capacity to make the "tough" decisions that organizational leaders must often make. Thus we may assume that the "upward-mobile" organization man[23] has "universalistic" values, which as Burleigh Gardner found in a study of several hundred executives, include an idealization of one's father, a detached view of one's subordinates, and the ability to perceive one's superiors as friendly models of appropriate behavior.[24] Warner found a similar complex of attitudes in his study of business executives.[25]

19 Ralph M. Stogdill, "Personal Factors Associated with Leadership: A Survey of the Literature," p. 63–66.

20 Bertrand Russell, *Power: A New Social Analysis* (New York: W. W. Norton & Co., Inc., 1938), chap. ii.

21 Michels, *Political Parties*, p. 64.

22 E. G. Mishler, "Personality Characteristics and the Resolution of Role Conflicts," 17, *Public Opinion Quarterly* (Spring, 1953).

23 For a discussion of organizational role types, see Robert V. Presthus, "Toward a Theory of Organizational Behavior," 3, *Administrative Science Quarterly*, (June, 1958), pp. 48–72.

24 B. Gardner, "Successful and Unsuccessful Executives," 13, *Advanced Management* (September, 1948), pp. 116–25.

25 W. Lloyd Warner, *American Life: Dream and Reality* (Chicago: University of Chicago Press, 1953), pp. 184–90.

This trait approach, however, is questionable. It is mainly concerned with description rather than analysis; it fails to show which traits are most important; and it is based upon the notion that an individual's personality is the sum of its parts. Actually, personality seems to depend upon the position or arrangement of traits, which function accordingly.[26] The situational and group concepts avoid some of these pitfalls by recognizing that the same trait functions differently in different persons as well as in different group situations. While size, for example, is probably a critical factor in football success, lack of it does not prevent small men like Hitler, Napoleon, or Stalin from attaining political leadership. Even though the psychologists themselves occasionally suggest that certain traits have a common leadership value, the earlier view of general traits and leadership types has been seriously modified. In sum, "leadership resides not exclusively in the individual but in his functional relationship with other members of his group."[27]

THE BUREAUCRATIC LEADER

An analysis of the bureaucratic leader as a deviation from Weber's ideal types provides suggestive generalizations.[28] We have seen that modern government requires a huge administrative branch, reflecting the expansion of private enterprise and the increasing demand for services by the "customers" of government. At the same time there has been a similar pressure toward the bureaucratization of leadership. The charismatic or natural leader who possesses a personal, revolutionary appeal, opposed to tradition and above institutional routine, is soon brought under control as his dogmas are modified to meet the need of organizational routine.[29] Friedrich traced the development of administration in western Europe and the United States and found a recurrent pattern of growth, including centralization of control and supervision, division of labor, and the development of qualifications for office such as objectivity, precision, continuity, and discretion in policy determination.[30] Such trends brought a structural and psychological framework that required

[26] Gouldner, *Studies in Leadership*, pp. 23–25.

[27] Cecil A. Gibb, "The Principles and Traits of Leadership," **42**, *Journal of Abnormal and Social Psychology* (Summer, 1947), p. 231.

[28] Max Weber, *From Max Weber: Essays in Sociology*, trans. and ed. by H. H. Gerth and C. Wright Mills (New York: Oxford University Press, 1946), pp. 51–55, 245–48. It must be said that in Weber's view, a "bureaucratic leader" is probably a contradiction in terms in the sense that the primary function of bureaucracy, as he saw it, was the elimination of those personal, intuitive, factors upon which leadership thrives.

[29] Max Weber, *The Theory of Social and Economic Organization* (New York: Oxford University Press, 1947), pp. 364–73.

[30] Carl J. Friedrich, *Constitutional Government and Democracy* (Boston: Ginn & Co., 1946).

executive leaders with certain distinct attitudes and skills. The following survey of the changing role of the executive in private industry illustrates this development.

The Managerial Revolution. Thorstein Veblen first analyzed the transfer of power in modern industrial systems from the owner to the manager.[31] This trend came about partially as a reflection of the separation of ownership from management which began late in the nineteenth century when the modern corporation appeared to provide capital for the development of big industry. Although realization of the change lagged behind, business and government were rapidly transformed. Size, scope, and technicality became the hallmarks of largescale enterprise. The atomization of corporate ownership provided the impetus for that divorce of ownership and management which has been called the "managerial revolution." The art of leadership became of signal importance as a means of combatting the inertia and impersonality brought by big organizations and the weakening of the Protestant Ethic of personal success and striving.

Professionalization of Bureaucratic Leadership. In business and government alike, size and specialization fostered bureaucracy and reduced the differences between private and public executives. The maturing of economic institutions demanded a new type of leadership. The dynamic, risk-taking, promotional, owner-leader of private enterprise was replaced by a "hired hand"; the professional executive doing a management job of coordinating specialists and approving decisions but initiating less and less policy.[32] The executive's incentive to undertake risk was correspondingly less. The lure of large income was increasingly challenged by status and security incentives. The new executive was better educated and more scientific than the entrepreneur, as evidenced by his increasing reliance on research staff, planning, conferences, and human relations techniques. Since risk-taking no longer offered the prospect of personal profit and might well entail the onus of failure, he tended to play it safe.[33]

This trend was associated with an increase in group policy making. Size and specialization encouraged group participation by substituting collective for individual wisdom *and* responsibility in decisions involving high stakes. Consultation among many specialists was required in major

[31] Thorstein Veblen, *Absentee Ownership and Business Enterprise in Recent Times* (New York: B. W. Huebsch, Inc., 1938).

[32] R. A. Gordon, *Business Leadership in the Large Corporation* (Washington, D.C.: Brookings Institution, 1945), p. 71; C. Wright Mills, *The Power Elite* (New York: Oxford University Press, 1956), pp. 118–46; William H. Whyte, Jr., and the editors of *Fortune, Is Anybody Listening?* (New York: Simon and Schuster, Inc., 1952).

[33] Gordon, *Business Leadership in the Large Corporation.* pp. 324–27, chap. xiv.

decisions. Such action was both formal, as in the case of management committees, and informal, as in *ad hoc* meetings.[34] Meanwhile, functional specialization brought increased delegation of operating decisions. Policy often originated among sales managers and production experts at operational levels. Decentralization was also encouraged to combat the inertia of size, and here again decision making was delegated on both a functional and a geographic basis.

Some Conclusions. The results of these trends for leadership are clear. The top executive becomes responsible for coordination as much as for direction and initiation, and his principal means of operation is through groups. As we have seen, this requires qualities of tact, personal relations skill, and intuition somewhat different from the traditional demands upon leadership. Manipulation replaces command. Policy making becomes a continuous and collective process, diffused throughout the higher levels of organization. Selection among several alternative policies, rather than initiation of a single policy, becomes routine. Education, training, and the scientific approach tend to encourage certainty and caution at the expense of flexibility.[35] There is also a reliance upon directors and bankers, which again tends to narrow the scope of executive discretion. (The importance of this factor is lessening as corporations rely increasingly upon their own profits as the source of new capital.) Finally, the "hired hand" status of the executive reduces the profit-making appeal while strengthening certain nonfinancial incentives which the large corporation can offer.[36] Power, prestige, the satisfaction of the creative urge, and security are not entirely dependent upon personal income or profits.[37]

[34] Temporary National Economic Committee, *Bureaucracy and Trusteeship in Large Corporations*, Monograph II (Washington, D.C.: U.S. Government Printing Office, 1940), p. 26.

[35] *Ibid.*, p. 324; also see M. Newcomer, *The Big Business Executive* (New York: Columbia University Press, 1955); *Fortune* (February, 1940) summarized the educational backgrounds of one hundred corporation presidents; William H. Whyte, *The Organization Man* (New York: Simon and Schuster, Inc., 1956).

[36] P. S. Florence, *The Logic of Industrial Organization* (London: Routledge & Kegan Paul, Ltd., 1933), pp. 224–25.

[37] Chester I. Barnard, for example, says, "Notwithstanding the great emphasis upon material incentives in modern times and especially in current affairs, there is no doubt in my mind that, unaided by other motives, they constitute weak incentives beyond the level of the bare physiological necessities." *Functions of the Executives* (Cambridge: Harvard University Press, 1938), p. 143, 142–48. Compare also, "The management has an interest in the business different from that of any investor. That interest is the management status which is significant in terms of control. Control is all-important. It means salaries and prestige. It means power to dispense normal business patronage to affiliated interests. It has been likened to a feudal tenure with rich incidents accruing to it." Securities and Exchange Commission, *Report on the Study and Investigation . . . of Protective and Reorganization Committees* (Washington, D.C.: U.S. Government Printing Office, 1937), Part 7, p. 11.

"The result of these tendencies seems to be very much what we should expect—greater caution, frequently more red tape, but often also more rational handling of management problems and better coordination at the lower levels of authority."[38] Like big government, then, big business suffers from a bureaucratic stiffening of the joints. Size, technology, the maturing of business and political institutions, and an inclination to avoid risks are visible in both. As a result the leadership qualifications, methods, and incentives of the business executive have become similar to those of his government counterpart.

THE PUBLIC EXECUTIVE: POLITICS AND ADMINISTRATION

We now turn to the obligations and responsibilities of public executives. As has been indicated previously, it is the external environment that marks the most important distinction between government and business executives. For the public executive this external environment is the public, interest groups, legislatures, and the courts. In our system, as we have tried to show in earlier chapters, the higher civil service is enmeshed in politics; its activities are carried out with one eye on legislatures and interest groups who, under the separation-of-powers system, have many points of access to administration. Perhaps the most political of our administrators is the President, and while both his power and his responsibility are far greater than that of other high political or career executives, his activities are similar enough in kind to make a detailed analysis of his political-administrative role worthwhile.

The President as Chief Administrator: the Dixon-Yates Case. Rather than generalize about the President's role in administration, we will trace through a recent case in which Presidential influence both on policy and administration is sharply defined and documented by volumes of testimony. This is the Dixon-Yates case, which concerns national policy of far-reaching consequences, involves great political and economic interests, and suggests emphatically the leadership that the chief executive can exert when he so desires.[39] The background and a brief synopsis of the case follow.

Eisenhower come to the Presidency in 1953, dedicated to checking the role of public power in the development of the natural resources of the country and increasing the role of private power. On June 17, 1953, referring to an earlier speech in South Dakota, he associated the Ten-

---

[38] Gordon, *Business Leadership in the Large Corporation*, p. 105.

[39] For a detailed analysis of this case, see Robert V. Presthus and L. Vaughn Blankenship, "Dixon-Yates: A Study in Political Behavior" (Unpublished ms., Cornell University, 1960).

nessee Valley Authority with socialism and deplored this "curious thing in the socialist theory" that the nation should provide cheap power for one region of the country at the expense of other regions.[40] On May 13, 1953, in his budget message, the President had announced that he was reducing the TVA appropriation; and the budget completely eliminated a $30 million dollar appropriation for a proposed steam plant at Fulton, Tennessee.[41] On June 16, 1954, Rowland R. Hughes, then Director of the Bureau of the Budget, received a letter from the White House directing him to proceed with a contract with the Dixon-Yates utility interests to build a power plant at West Memphis, Arkansas, which would provide "replacement" power to the TVA for power it was presently selling to the Atomic Energy Commission at Paducah, Kentucky.[42] Five months later the AEC signed the contract for the plant, which was to cost about $120,000,000 and to have a capacity of 650,000 kilowatts of electricity.

Although this contract was rationalized in the name of free enterprise, its conditions were calculated to remove all risk for the Dixon-Yates interests.[43] Not only was the Dixon-Yates combine providing only $5,500,000 of the estimated $120,000,000 required to build the plant but the Mississippi Valley Generating Company (as the Dixon-Yates operating company was named) was to receive at a wholesale rate any excess power produced above the needs of the city of Memphis, to whom the power was going, and was to be entitled to sell this excess power. Since the existing load factor for Memphis was only 68 per cent of the proposed plant's capacity, the Company would be receiving something like 200,000 kilowatts per day for resale at commercial rates.

Beyond this, the Dixon-Yates interests were to be reimbursed, indirectly, for all local, state, and federal income taxes. The Company was further guaranteed a minimum return of 9 per cent per year on its $5,500,000 of invested capital. Moreover, if the government canceled the proposed contract, it was liable for damages up to a maximum of $50,000,000. However, in order to build transmission lines that would carry the new power into Tennessee from the middle of the Mississippi, which was the furthermost eastern point that the Company was obligated by the contract to transmit the power, the TVA would be obliged to spend $6,500,000. And, using this alternative to the TVA steam plant at Fulton would cost the federal government $100,000,000 more than the

[40] *New York Times,* June 18, 1953.

[41] *Ibid.,* May 14, 1953.

[42] Bureau of the Budget, *Record of Procedure and Development of AEC Power Contract,* August 21, 1954, Attachment B-16, p. 1.

[43] Joint Committee on Atomic Energy, 83rd Cong., 2d sess. *Hearings.* Exercise of Statutory Requirement of sec. 164, Atomic Energy Act, 1954, (Washington, D.C.: U.S. Government Printing Office, 1954).

proposed steam plant, calculated over the 25-year term of the contract (at which time the plant would become the property of the Company).

The case was further complicated by the dual role of one Adolphe H. Wenzell, a vice-president of the First Boston Company. Mr. G. D. Woods, president of First Boston, had informed Joseph M. Dodge, Hughes' predecessor as Director of the Bureau of the Budget, that he "was in sympathy with the published desires . . ." of the Administration to "get the government out of the power business,"[44] and was therefore recommending Mr. Wenzell as a man who could help achieve this objective, since he was experienced in the financing of utilities projects. Wenzell thereupon became a consultant to the Bureau of the Budget, charged with carrying out a study of the TVA. His recommendations, which must have surprised no one, included the establishment of a new corporation to take over TVA operations and the organization of private, special generating companies to meet TVA power needs.[45] This report was part of the basis upon which the Dixon-Yates contract was proposed and signed. Equally interesting, First Boston Company was to handle the sale of the securities to finance all but the $5,500,000 put up by Dixon-Yates.

On November 4, 1954, the Joint Committee on Atomic Energy began hearings on the proposed contract, as required by section 164 of the Atomic Energy Act.[46] The administration came before the Committee, recommending that the normal 30-day waiting period be waived, since everyone concerned was anxious to get the project underway so that power could begin to flow as soon as possible. However, by this time, Congressional supporters of TVA, public power interest groups, Congressional opponents of the Administration, politicians and the press had begun a counterattack. Their arguments were varied, long, and versatile. The conditions of the contract itself, as outlined above, provided the main target. The fact that Lewis Strauss, chairman of the AEC, had pushed the contract through without the knowledge and against the wishes of two AEC Commissioners added fuel to the fire.[47] The apparent effort to undercut TVA inspired southern senators and governors to appear before the Committee.

[44] Senate Subcommittee on Antitrust and Monopoly, Committee on the Judiciary, 84th Cong., 1st sess., *Hearings* (Washington, D.C.: U.S. Government Printing Office, 1956) pp. 515–16.

[45] These recommendations were similar to those later proposed by the second Hoover Commission in the organization of the executive branch.

[46] Senate Subcommittee on Antitrust and Monopoly Committee on the Judiciary, 84th Cong., 1st sess., *Hearings* (Washington, D.C.: U.S. Government Printing Office, 1956).

[47] *Ibid.*, Bureau of the Budget Record, Attachment B-6.

Although the Joint Committee waived the waiting period, so that the contract was finally consummated on November 11, 1954, subsequent hearings before the Securities and Exchange Commission brought new charges by Senator Lister Hill of Alabama that "conflicts of interests" were involved because of Wenzell's simultaneous affiliation with the Bureau of the Budget and the First Boston Company. (This charge was later substantiated by the Attorney-General who, in breaking the contract in November, 1955, charged among other things that a "conflict of interest" had occurred.)

On January 28, 1955, the Joint Committee on Atomic Energy rescinded its earlier resolution authorizing the AEC to proceed with the contract, and said, ". . . it is the sense of the Joint Committee that the said contract is not in the public interest, and the Committee recommends that the Atomic Energy Commission take steps to cancel the Dixon-Yates contract."[48] On June 25, 1955, the Senate Subcommittee on Antitrust and Monopoly began hearings, with Director Hughes as the first of many reluctant witnesses. Chairman Strauss of the AEC and Chairman Demmler of the Securities and Exchange Commission continually pleaded "executive privilege" to avoid testifying. Meanwhile the Memphis City Commission, which had not been informed of the Dixon-Yates project until quite late in the negotiations even though the city was immediately affected, passed a resolution authorizing their utilities department to build a steam plant which would provide power for the city. TVA was notified simultaneously that Memphis would not renew its contract for TVA power when it expired in June, 1958. Shortly thereafter, Chairman Vogel of the TVA, which had also been by-passed during the AEC–Dixon-Yates negotiations,[49] recommended that the contract be "reconsidered."

As a result of these developments, on June 30, 1955, the President ordered the AEC, the Bureau of the Budget, and TVA to determine ". . . whether it is in the interest of the people of the area now to continue or cancel the Dixon-Yates contract."[50] On October 3, 1955, Assistant Comptroller-General Frank Weitzel notified the AEC that there was reasonable doubt about the legality of the contract, and a month later, AEC announced that the contract had been canceled. One month later the Dixon-Yates interests brought suit against the government for $3,500,000 damages. In the Government's brief, the main basis for voiding the contract was ". . . the activities of one Adolphe H. Wenzell,"

[48] Hereafter cited as *Staff Report.*
[49] Senate Subcommittee on Antitrust and Monopoly, Committee on the Judiciary, 83d Cong., 2d sess., *Interim Report* (Washington, D.C.: U.S. Government Printing office, 1955), p. 67.
[50] *New York Times,* July 1, 1955.

who had been working at the same time for both the Bureau of the Budget and the First Boston Company.[51] The matter was finally settled in July, 1959, when Dixon-Yates were awarded $1,500,000 in damages by the United States Court of Claims.

The case has significant implications for administrative leadership at the highest level. As Director Hughes of the Bureau of the Budget said in his memo to the AEC on June 16, 1954: "The President has asked me to instruct the Atomic Energy Commission to proceed with negotiations with the sponsors of the proposal made by Messrs. Dixon and Yates, with a view to signing a definitive contract . . ."[52] Once the President had made his pro-private power policy clear to his major political and career aides, they did everything possible to carry out this policy. Strauss's behavior, his loyalty to the President, his protestations that the contract was clearly in the public interest—all suggest the weight he attached to the Presidential imperative. Dodge and Hughes of the Bureau of the Budget clearly felt the same way. As Hughes said before the Joint Committee on Atomic Energy, "The contractor's ability and willingness to meet such needs and to assume a share of the risks involved is the very essence of our free enterprise system. I unreservedly recommend to the committee this contract which is a splendid example of the way that system works."[53] In view of the virtually riskless character of the proposed contract, this statement is explicable mainly in terms of intense identification with the President's policy of promoting private power development. The testimony of AEC Commissioner Thomas Murray is also suggestive. After complaining to the Committee that he had learned about the contract only in the newspapers, when Murray was asked whether he felt the contract should be authorized, he replied, "Yes."

Not only the AEC was eager to comply with White House policy; the Securities and Exchange Commission also took unusual steps to expedite the contract. Following the resolution by the Joint Committee on Atomic Energy, declaring their opposition to the contract, its chairman, Senator Clinton P. Anderson, sent the resolution with an explanatory letter to the SEC, requesting that he be allowed to appear before the Commission. Similarly, Joseph Volpe, counsel for the state of Tennessee, asked the Commission to reconvene to hear additional testimony. Both these requests were denied. Also, whereas the Commission usually requires that operating companies put up approximately 60 per cent of the capital required for a project, in this case, as noted earlier, Dixon-Yates was providing only 4.5 per cent. Moreover, in its earlier hearings on the

[51] "Answer Filed July 12, 1956, by the United States to Dixon-Yates suit in Court of Claims," in *Staff Report*, pp. 167–68.
[52] Senate, BOB Record, Attachment B-16, p. 2.
[53] Joint Committee on Atomic Energy, 83rd Cong., 2d sess. *Hearings, op. cit.*, p. 19.

equity financing of the Mississippi Valley Generating Company, the Commission dispensed with its customary procedure of having an examiner hear the case and present his findings to the Commission. Instead, the Committee met as a whole. Later, its chairman, Ralph Demmler, testified that during his two years with it he knew of no other case in which the SEC has sat "en banc."[54] In other words, the SEC was doing what it could to expedite the contract, which could not be signed without SEC approval for its financing provisions.

The Federal Power Commission was similarly cooperative. After an initial judgment that the costs were too high, its Chief, Bureau of Power, Mr. Francis L. Adams, reviewed and supported a revised proposal. We have also seen that TVA went along, although reluctantly, with the AEC. Thus five important federal agencies (three of them independent regulatory Commissions) including the Bureau of the Budget, the AEC, FPC, SEC, and TVA, united in an effort to carry out Presidential policy by a contract that a disinterested observer must surely regard as unduly favorable to the private utility interests concerned. This case suggests two conclusions, one at odds with traditional opinion in administration, the other reinforcing it. The first conclusion is that, despite their expertise, experience, and their partial insulation against undue pressure by the President, the legislature, and, presumably, interest groups, the independent regulatory commissions are quite receptive to Presidential influence in cases when the President feels strongly about a policy matter, as in the Dixon-Yates case. Secondly, it is often maintained that the federal bureaucracy is too large, self-conscious, entrenched and powerful to be mobilized for quick, joint action in support of Administration policy. This may be so, but in this case at least, the bureaucracy, both at the political and the career levels, moved with loyalty and dispatch to carry out White House policy.

THE ROLE OF THE PUBLIC EXECUTIVE

By the term "public executive" we mean the so-called policy-making civil servants, including chief executives, department heads, their assistants, and staff aides, as well as bureau chiefs, division and section heads, and housekeeping staff, including officials in personnel, finance, purchasing, and public relations. Given the similarity of roles between those at the under-secretary level and their immediate career subordinates, our analysis covers both politically appointed and permanent administrators. While top administrators are clearly more occupied with the legislature, party matters, and over-all policy, those at the upper levels of middle

---

[54] Senate Subcommittee on Antitrust and Monopoly, Committee of the Judiciary, 84th Cong., 1st sess., *Hearings on Power Policy: Dixon-Yates*, pp. 667, 1271.

management require a similar generalizing capacity in order to recommend new policy which often arises from their work with specialists at the operating level.

Defining the Organization's Purpose. While legislators set the broad objectives of government, we have seen that administrators have some latitude in interpreting the legislature's will and in shaping the directions that the organization will take over time. In some cases the organization may enjoy such prestige and public support that its dependence upon the legislature for support is more apparent than real. Social conditions may provide an environment in which the organization's skills are so badly needed that its power and discretion go relatively unchallenged. At present, the professional military, the FBI, and the Atomic Energy Commission enjoy this kind of influence, although the prestige of the AEC has probably suffered from the Dixon-Yates affair.

But even among less favored organizations, the administrators can expect influence by a careful evaluation of the organization's mission and by the anticipation of changes in its social and economic environment. This process of reappraising the organization's role and adjusting it to change seems to be among the administrator's most vital functions. It requires a detachment from routine administration and an ability to forecast the future. It requires inspirational or charismatic qualities of leadership, since change is usually resisted and its necessity is not always clearly apparent. Here the administrator must often be able to evoke consent on the basis of the confidence he inspires rather than upon demonstrable evidence of the need for change.

The administrator's task is eased by the authority which his formal position gives him, and by the opportunities for forecasting which his external relationships with the community provide. Such associations enable him to see the organization in larger perspective, to keep abreast of changing community expectations in a way that the rank and file members of the organizations cannot. If clientele groups become restive, he is among the first to know. In a word, his role of interpreting the organization to the outside world provides him with the information necessary to keep the organization abreast of changing conditions. By defining the organization's purpose in line with such conditions, the executive can to some extent shape and control its environment. By making clear the organization's contributions to the community, he can ensure reciprocal support from the groups affected by its program.

But even aside from this, the executive's redefinition of the organization's purposes is vital because large organizations have a way of losing sight of their mission. They tend to become an instrument for serving their members; developing an internal life of their own, which persists without much regard for their main reason for existence. This is particularly so when the organization's work is intrinsically satisfying and rewarding. In this situation, both public and clientele groups may be viewed as a necessary evil, and the organizational mission then becomes a vague symbol for manipulation rather than a viable guide to its conduct.

The executive's function is to keep the organization's sense of collective purpose alive, to weld the members together in seeking it, and to adapt this purpose to changes that may otherwise render it anachronistic. Since he alone has the power and the vantage point to do so, the top executive must be held responsible when the organization falters. If he is to succeed, he requires a philosophic ability to think in long-run terms and to select appropriate means. He must struggle always against the tendency of the means to become paramount or to distort the ends of the organization.[55] In a democratic society this role is difficult because the means available to the top executive are circumscribed; he must often persuade the members to accept his leadership; and he will never be able to control more than a few of the *external* conditions that affect his organization. Yet, as Michels shows in his classic study, leaders have many advantages in carrying out their will.[56] Their tenure is relatively stable; they are more experienced and older than the rank and file; they have greater oratorical skill, knowledge, and political acumen; they can define the terms and the time for raising major issues; they have access to the funds and the organizational apparatus. Beyond this, in large organizations, "effective power is . . . in inverse ratio to the number of those who exercise it."[57]

Leadership by Compromise, Not by Command. The executive is frequently, though quite wrongly, regarded as an omnipotent individual at the top of an organization who initiates policy and issues orders. The real fact is that policy making is a collective process which the top executive influences only by formally endorsing a decision rationalized by his subordinates. He may command and he may appeal to legal authority. But in most cases, his formal position is only the beginning, not the end, of his leadership. He must rely on persuasion and inspiration. As W. J. M. Mackenzie has said:

There is perhaps a peculiar and specialized activity called "command" which takes up a small percentage of the "commander's" time; but when one looks at it closely, the nearest parallel to his work is the work of the arbitrator,

[55] On this problem of organization, see Kenneth E. Boulding, *The Organizational Revolution* (New York: Harper & Bros., 1953).

[56] Michels, *Political Parties*, pp. 31, 33, 58, 84, 85.

[57] *Ibid.*, p. 58.

not that of the drill sergeant. One might almost say that he is paid to spin a coin for the organization, when it has exhausted other means of decision. From another point of view, that of the outer world, it is true that the "Commander" in some sense "is" the organization; but if he is to be successful he must represent it . . . acting for the most part as spokesman. It is only occasionally, and only if his "subordinates" fully trust him, that he can give a lead on the issues which he himself in virtue of his position understands best, *the issues which relate to the place of the organization in a social structure bigger than itself.*[58]

It seems clear also that governmental executives, like their business counterparts, are not distinct types, nor do they operate in identical environments. There are newly established organizations without a tradition. There are mature and dignified establishments in which a new executive's influence is limited. There are service organizations such as the post office. There are financial or businesslike agencies, such as the International Bank. There are organizations with high morale and those with low. Requirements are different in each, depending on a variety of circumstances. In addition, each executive will bring to his task a different personality and method of operation and a different concept of his role.

Public Spokesman for the Organization. The governmental executive has a dual role as politician and administrator. The higher he ascends in the hierarchy, the more his task becomes that of political generalist and the less that of administrative specialist. This is true of executive behavior everywhere. From 65 to 90 per cent of the executive's time is spent in interpersonal contacts, not only within the organization, but with client groups, his counterparts in other agencies, and the public generally. Communication between an organization and the public must be a two-way affair. This is because "an administrative body is always part of the pattern of leadership and authority in the social organization in which it operates."[59] The executive should know not only what the supporters of his program think but also how its opponents feel.

There is actually a conflict between these dual roles, for the more proficient the executive becomes as a specialist charged with a particular program with a particular clientele, the more difficult it is for him to develop the required generalizing qualities. This is a common problem. Increasingly, however, it appears that the limiting effect of specialization upon potential leadership is being recognized; hence the development of executive talent is being encouraged by pushing decision making as far down as possible, while emphasizing the organization's

---

[58] W. J. M. Mackenzie, "The Study of Public Administration in the United States," **29**, *Public Administration* (Summer, 1951), p. 134. [Italics added.]

[59] Alexander Leighton, *The Governing of Men* (Princeton: Princeton University Press, 1945) p. 343.

place in the larger community. If the organization is to prosper, the executive must maintain contact with the external world by conferences with interest-group representatives, appearances before the public and clientele groups, and association with persons outside his own social class. In this way the executive correlates his organization with the outside world.

The Executive as Coordinator. Having outlined several major activities of the executive and some of the skills and personality attributes which seem required for his success, we can now turn to what is probably his central task in the big, complex organizations with which we are concerned. This is the art of coordination. Organization is mainly concerned with creating a rational structure of operating units, based on special functions and skills. A separatist tendency follows as the various fragments become preoccupied with their respective purposes. Expertise breeds introversion and the specialist often magnifies his own role. He cannot always be convinced that he should participate as a coequal team member. This aggravates the splintering tendency which colors organization on a functional basis. Coordination seeks to overcome this tendency.

Coordination, then, is a technique for drawing together a number of conflicting skills and interests and leading them toward a common end. It is the centripetal force in administration. While there is a hierarchy of coordination including every individual responsible for the work of others, and while various devices are used to promote coordination, we are concerned here with the personal, charismatic means available to those who direct the organization.

Coordination's importance as a measure of leadership is implicit in Barnard's comment, "The executive art is nine-tenths *inducing* those who have authority to use it in taking pertinent action."[60] Given the many activities of large organizations, this is an imposing task. The problem is complicated, moreover, by the common reliance upon technical skill in executive selection, as well as a tendency to pay mere lip service or to reject the human relations element so critical in coordination. Clearly the individual must be made to feel a part of the group before he will identify with organizational objectives and values. Coordination often requires the acceptance of objectives which are inconsistent, if not in conflict, with the immediate, personal values of the individual. Thus essentially emotional appeals are necessary to evoke individual loyalty.

[60] Chester I. Barnard, for example, insists that coordination, which is attained through leadership, is the most vital factor in organizational survival. Leadership, in turn, is defined as the quality of morality and responsibility which can bind the wills of men to accomplish purposes beyond their immediate interest; *Functions of the Executive*, p. 283.

It appears that an organization, like a nation, must possess a system of commonly shared values and objectives.

The implicit conflict between the individual and the organization is not conclusive, however, for men have a psychological need for identification with some entity greater than themselves. Erich Fromm has shown that modern man has never been so free; yet he feels a compelling urge to "escape from freedom." We are not referring here to the authoritarian personality thesis which explains the "escape" in terms of a need to submit to a father-leader to overcome feelings of anxiety and isolation. Rather we are concerned with a facet of modern society wherein structural rationalization fosters anxiety and alienation. The dynamics here include alienation from work, the differences between theory and practice in human relations, and the promise of political influence and its frustration by the existing power structure.[61] These conditions nourish a need for personal identification with groups and organizations which can provide permanent values in an unstable world.[62]

In this context, a means of achieving coordination through leadership is by an inspirational appeal which instills in its members an understanding and acceptance of the organization's larger goals, as well as the importance of the role which each individual plays in achieving them. Yet this hypothesis is in conflict with the conclusions of the group behavior studies in military organizations which place a premium on primary or immediate values as motivating factors. The final answer is not clear. The executive must, of course, be able to inspire individuals to cooperate in attaining goals which are beyond their immediate interest.[63] The question again is *how* and under what conditions the executive can do this. To say that he must be vigorous, imaginative, statesmanlike, and have psychosexual appeal is hardly adequate. Nor is it enough to generalize by incident; to say, for example, that particular executives have these qualities while others do not. Perhaps we can only conclude that leadership is situational, that certain traits appear to ensure success in certain group situations. Certainly we are dealing with an intangible quality which is hard to analyze and perhaps impossible to teach. Nevertheless, those who aspire to leadership can safely assume that coordina-

---

[61] Karl Mannheim, *Man and Society in an Age of Reconstruction* (New York: Harcourt, Brace & Co., Inc., 1940).

[62] Among others, see Eric Hoffer, *The True Believer* (New York: Harper & Bros., 1951); David Reisman, *The Lonely Crowd* (New Haven: Yale University Press, 1951).

[63] Yet, leadership always depends greatly upon the condition and quality of those to be lead; for impressive documentation that some individuals are immune to either organizational or individual leadership, see Eli Ginzberg *et al.*, *The Ineffective Soldier*, 3 vols., (New York: Columbia University Press, 1959), particularly vol. III, "Patterns of Performance." For a fascinating novel on military leadership and administration, see C. S. Forester, *The General* (Boston: Little, Brown & Co., 1947).

tion is best achieved by identifying the individual with the organization's larger values because this appeals to deep-seated psychological needs.

BIBLIOGRAPHY

BARNARD, CHESTER I. *Functions of the Executive.* Cambridge: 1947.

BENNIS, W. G. "Leadership Theory and Administrative Behavior," 4, *Administrative Science Quarterly* (December, 1959).

CARTWRIGHT, D. (ed.). *Studies in Social Power.* Ann Arbor: 1959.

GIBB, CECIL A. "Leadership," in GARDNER and LINDZEY (eds.). *Handbook of Social Psychology.* Cambridge: 1954, Chapter 24.

GOULDNER, A. W. *Studies in Leadership.* New York: 1952.

HUNTER, FLOYD. *Top Leadership: USA.* Chapel Hill: 1959.

KEESING, FELIX. *Elite Communication in Samoa.* Stanford: 1956.

MERTON, ROBERT K. *et al.* (eds.). *Reader in Bureaucracy.* Glencoe, Ill.: 1952.

MILLS, C. WRIGHT. *The Power Elite.* New York: 1956.

STOGDILL, RALPH M., SCOTT, ELLIS L. and JAYNES, WILLIAM E. *Leadership and Role Expectations,* Research Monograph, No. 86. Columbus, Ohio: 1956.

CHAPTER 6

Decision Making

In a behavioral context, the main activity of the administrator consists in making decisions, that is, selecting from among certain alternatives both the goals of the organization and the assumed best way of achieving them.[1] While this is a complex process involving facts, values, and unanticipated consequences, the decision maker always oversimplifies the matter by abstracting only selected parts of the total environment that impinge upon the decision. We usually regard decision making as an intellectual process, the product of an individual mind. However, we must emphasize that organizational decision making is an *institutionalized process*. Any ultimate decision is the end product of the combined efforts of many individuals at many different levels in the hierarchy. Organizational decisions, then, must be looked upon as a collective product rather than the result of any given official's unilateral choice.

What really occurs in organizations is that the administrator often *referends* decisions that have been submitted to him by line and staff members who have already traced through several alternatives, marshalled the supporting evidence, and indicated with varying degrees of precision the probable consequences of each alternative. It is clear enough that technical skill and the possession of relevant information give those concerned a considerable influence in determining what the formal leader's choice will be. And in highly technical matters, involving, for example, atomic weapons and missiles, such influence must be exceptionally compelling. Here we can see how technology and the specialization of our society have decentralized and diffused decision making. It is such conditions that underlie Mills' conception of big organizations as systems of "organized irresponsibility."[2]

---

[1] The conception of administration as essentially a process of decision making is Herbert A. Simon's; for an excellent review of decision-making theory and research, see his "Theories of Decision Making in Economics," 49, *American Economic Review* (June, 1959), pp. 253–83.

[2] C. Wright Mills, *The Power Elite* (New York: Oxford University Press, 1956).

THE DECISION-MAKING PROCESS

In this chapter we are concerned with rational choice and with the barriers to such choice stemming from lack of information, value conflicts between the several participants in a decision, the failure to assign priorities to the values or goals we seek, and the problem of a "contingent universe" in which we can never anticipate or account for all the possible consequences of our actions, so that decision making must be highly tentative.

Some inroads have been made into this tentative setting by the development of machines which can quantify and manipulate the factors relevant to a decision and thereby increase its rationality by increasing both the number of variables that can be considered and by tracing through the effect of a larger number of alternative choices. However, due to the great number of variables involved in most real-life decisions and also due to the complications involved in setting up "hierarchies of strategies" or models for solving various kinds of problems, much work remains to be done before computing machines can be coded in a way "that approach[es] the sophistication of the experienced scholar."[3] The "information revolution" cannot replace individual judgments because humans must still program the data handled by the machines. However, their impact on routine decisions has already been great, and they will undoubtedly be developed to handle more sophisticated decision situations.[4]

In this chapter we shall focus upon two aspects of decision making: some theoretical aspects of choice, and the manner in which the decision process occurs in large organizations. There is, of course, a disparity between the theory and the manner in which such choices are "really" made, but as time passes, this gap is continually narrowing. At the theoretical level, it must be stressed that decision making requires a constant oversimplification of reality. That is, the verbal and quantitative symbols (the models) that are used to define a given decision situation are abstractions from a total universe, and as such they encompass only a small number of the variables that impinge upon any given decision. While decision-makers try to ensure that their models include the most critical variables, it is probably impossible always to do so. Moreover it is even more difficult in such hypothetical exercises to assign weights

[3] "Comment on Explorations in the Realm of Organization Theory," 3, *Behavioral Science* (January, 1958), pp. 78, 68–78.

[4] For a recent survey of literature on this approach to decision making, see William J. Gore and Fred S. Silander. "A Bibliographical Essay on Decision Making," 4, *Administrative Science Quarterly* (June, 1959).

to relevant variables, including the goals the individual or the organization desires. As Simon has shown, we do not usually know which of several values is the most important to us, and as a result our decisions must be in some measure unrational.[5] What we are saying here is that the real social situation is always untidy and complex, whereas the decisional model is usually precise.

Another vital theoretical aspect of decision making is the concept of rationality, by which is meant the capacity of man to make choices based upon conscious deliberation about the means selected to achieve specified ends. Both democratic political theory and classical economic theory have dramatized and reinforced the image of man as a rational creature. The first premise of democratic self-government is a knowledgeable, interested, calculating citizen who, through discussion, thought, and the conflict of ideas and policies in the market place, will emerge with a reasonable conclusion. Insofar as economic theory is concerned, the demands of a consistent, watertight theory of economic behavior apparently demanded a rational man who would save his money, spend wisely, and generally exhibit predictable behavior in the arena of economic choice.[6] Consumers were supposed to maximize utility, but no one ever showed how they did so or, indeed, what utility actually was.

This model has been subjected to a merciless attack by Simon and others, mainly on the ground that it posits a man who never existed. The reasons for this critique are many. "The capacity of the human mind for formulating and solving complex problems is very small compared with the size of the problems whose solution is required for objectively rational behavior in the real world—or even for a reasonable approximation to such objective rationality."[7] As a result Simon concludes that human behavior is "intendedly rational," and adds that what men really seek are reasonable decisions rather than perfect ones. As George Katona showed several years ago, the typical business firm seeks a "fair profit," a "reasonable share of the market," etc., rather than maximization of profits and market.[8]

Some economists complain that "economic man" has been used as a straw man, set up for easy demolition by critics of conventional economic

[5] Herbert A. Simon, "Recent Advances in Organization Theory," in Research Frontiers in Politics and Government, S. Bailey (ed.) (Washington, D.C.: Brookings Institution, 1955), pp. 32–35.

[6] S. Schoeffler, The Failures of Economics (Cambridge: Harvard University Press, 1955); see also, for an experimental refutation of classical value theory, D. Davidson et al., Decision Making: An Experimental Approach (Stanford: Stanford University Press, 1957).

[7] Herbert A. Simon, Models of Man—Social and Rational (New York: John Wiley & Sons, 1957), p. 198.

[8] George Katona, Psychological Analysis of Economic Behavior (New York: McGraw-Hill Book Co., Inc., 1951).

wisdom. Yet, economic theory did build upon such rather astringent concepts of human behavior, and as Galbraith has recently shown, basic assumptions about demand and production were not subjected to critical inquiry but were defended in some cases *because* the conventional definitions were necessary to support the logical structure of economic analysis and explanation of economic behavior.[9] Thus the common-sense notions that demand is subject to a law of diminishing returns and that there are probably normative differences among various kinds of demands were resisted.[10] Decision-making man was thus too often presented as a calculating machine, and the present emphasis upon his limited rationality is probably a necessary counterpoise.

BARRIERS TO RATIONAL CHOICE

In discussing decision making, then, we necessarily spend considerable time on the barriers to rational behavior. These include ignorance, prejudice, lack of information, unanticipated consequences, the impact of "sunk costs" which limit our flexibility in future decisions in the sense that a given decision discounts the future, and our inability to conceptualize and trace through the consequences of *various* alternative means to a desired end. Here empirical research suggests that decision making is often characterized by a shutting out of alternatives, once a means is found that meets the criterion, "will this enable us to do better than we are now doing?"[11] We do not know definitely what factors account for this limiting tendency. Perhaps the psychological rewards of having made *any* decision, which relieves one from the strain associated with an unresolved problem, is involved. Certainly there is considerable resistance to "intellectualizing" decision making among "practical" executives, both in business and government, as suggested by one businessman who said in response to questions as to how he made decisions, "Every time I think, I lose money."[12] More significant, most of his brethren in the same survey tended to conclude that they didn't really know how they decided.[13] The role of "hunch," "feel," speculation was large.

Subjective Factors. It is clear that value judgments play a vital role in decision making. Even when conflicting data are presented and when information tracing out several alternatives is available, the individual sometimes disregards or "skews" the data in order to justify the choice

[9] J. K. Galbraith, *The Affluent Society* (Boston: Houghton Mifflin Co., 1958), chap. ii.

[10] *Ibid.*, pp. 143–52.

[11] R. Cyert, W. Dill, and J. March, "The Role of Expectations in Business Decision Making," 3, *Administrative Science Quarterly* (December, 1958) pp. 307–40.

[12] "How Businessmen Make Decisions," *Fortune* (August, 1955).

[13] *Ibid.*

that he initially preferred on normative grounds.[14] In administration, as well as law, one suspects that expertise is often manipulated to validate subjective claims. As the old quatrain goes:

> The proper skill of expertise
> Is to arrange the premises
> So that the most foregone conclusion
> Will fit therein without confusion.

In the political arena, one finds that congressional committees often have preconceived views about bills or subjects under consideration. This is indicated by the questions they ask, the attitudes they reveal toward witnesses, and the conclusions they reach about policy matters. A look at the hearings cited in Chapters 21 and 29 illustrates this. At the administrative level, several cases suggest the same tendency. The decision of the young foreign service reserve officer in Indonesia, cited in Chapter 3, exemplifies the role of values in decision making. Parenthetically, such influences indicate the limitations of decision making by machines: They can handle only the data that is "programmed" into them, and this programming is subject to many of the subjective factors mentioned here. It is important in understanding administration to remember that the organization's goals of "efficiency" are always challenged by "latent" functions of power, security, and survival. These compete sharply with manifest program goals.

Problem of Sunk Costs. The factor of "sunk costs" also conditions decision making. Essentially this concept refers to the fact that one's commitments at any one time inevitably limit the range of his future alternatives. In choosing a vocation, for example, it is quite clear that the long preparation and money required for most professional jobs make it highly improbable that one will shift into some other kind of work. One's mobility is limited by the high "sunk costs" expended in preparing for the vocation. Similarly a business enterprise that invests millions in capital equipment, specialized personnel, and organizational structure in order to carry on a certain type of operation has sharply reduced its future decisional maneuverability. An automobile plant cannot readily be modified to produce aircraft.

But the clearest example of "sunk costs" exists in public administration in the context of budget determinations. Each new Administration comes into office determined to reduce or to redirect the main drift of government expenditures and activities. Yet with monotonous regularity we see that previous commitments have made this virtually impossible. The Eisenhower Administration is perhaps outstanding here, since its

---

[14] Cyert, Dill, March, "The Role of Expectations in Business Decision Making." p. 318.

intentions were more widely broadcast and perhaps less rational. Despite his announced intention of limiting federal spending, in 1957 the President gave to Congress the largest budget in peace-time history; by 1959 the limit on the national debt had to be raised. In this context we can say that the "sunk costs" of military expenditures, interest on the national debt, social welfare programs, and veterans benefits had so structured the decision situation that very little latitude for modification was left to the new Administration; similarly with any given department. Obligations in the form of programs and personnel mean that each year's decisions are likely to be much like those of the previous year.

Unanticipated Consequences. The making of decisions is also structured by unanticipated consequences, which by definition cannot be included in the rational calculus of alternatives. Here, as Merton has shown, the very fact of committing ourselves to one objective tends to shape that objective.[15] Thus Marx's prediction of the progressive concentration of wealth and the increasing misery of the masses influenced the very process predicted by encouraging unionization, which slowed down the predicted development.[16] This raises the idea of the "self-fulfilling prophecy," whereby an expressed preference tends to influence the outcome of the desired end. Some observers deplore election polls on this basis, and while we know of no evidence to support this claim, it does seem that such predictions may influence behavior, if only in terms of the well-known popular desire to back a winner.

Merton also shows that the realization of certain values may lead to their devaluation; once something is attained, it often seems less desirable than before. The effort is often more satisfying than the realization of the goal itself. Some people say this is true of marriage, and divorce statistics appear to support their view. As Weber shows, the ascetic self-denial associated with the Protestant Ethic led to its own decline through the accumulation of wealth and material goods made possible by the saving and intense productive activity stimulated by the prevailing deification of sacrifice and hard work. Clearly, if the ends achieved by decisions turn out to be different from those sought, or are unsatisfying once achieved, decision making can be only partially rational, since we can measure its rationality, as Simon argues, only in terms of how effectively its means achieve certain ends.[17] Rationality cannot be determined *in vacuo*, but only in terms of means, which by themselves are meaningless until attached to certain desired consequences or goals.

[15] Robert K. Merton, "The Unanticipated Consequences of Purposive Social Action," 1, *American Sociological Review* (December, 1936), pp. 894–904.
[16] *Ibid.*

[17] Herbert A. Simon, *Administrative Behavior* (Rev. ed.; New York: The Macmillan Co., 1957), chap. iii.

In sum, since decision making by its very nature must always deal with expectations of the future, which can never be fully known or anticipated, the process is inherently unable to achieve complete rationality. However, given these several barriers to rational decision making, there are still varying degrees of rationality, and it is these differences that often account for success or failure. The administrator and the organization have certain techniques and guides that increase the rationality of their decisions. We now turn to these.

ORGANIZATIONAL DECISION MAKING

At the outset, let it be clear that the organization itself is an important aid to rationality. It can be described as a system for limiting and prescribing decisions.

Effect of Organizational Goals. In the first place, organizational goals, policies, and rules are formulated and made known to members. In a broad way these structure the behavior of individuals and the factors that they will take into consideration in deciding what to do in particular cases. Individuals throughout the hierarchy will know (in a very general way, to be sure) that certain decisions are in line with organization policy and that certain other decisions probably do not meet this criterion.

Secondly, the organization always seeks to convince its members that such goals are legitimate and rational and that they "should" be accepted on these grounds. Thus the organization's values often provide the ethical premises for individual decisions. Perhaps this factor operates something like one's "conscience," which results from the internalization of social values and guides one's conduct accordingly. The organizational conscience exercises a similar control, but its effectiveness varies, of course, in terms of the individual's identification with the organization's main goals.

Here the sociological concept of latent and manifest functions is helpful. *Manifest* goals are the formal goals of the organization. In government these goals are to provide services, protect our natural resources, preserve national security, etc. In education they include teaching the young, providing an intelligent labor force, and the like. In business they include making a profit and providing goods and services to the community.

But these are only part of what the organization and its members devote their energies and loyalties to: The other aspects may be called *latent* functions. They include the drives of the individual for security, income, power, and deference. They also include the organization's drive for survival, for greater programs, for a larger share of the budget or the market. The existence of manifest and latent goals obviously distorts the neat picture of individuals acting in terms of formal, organizational goals. Instead, of course, the individual's decisional premises also include highly personalized values, which sometimes (although not always or necessarily) compete with those of the organization as a whole.[18]

Another obvious organizational means of ensuring rationality is by setting up a structure in which tasks, functions, and responsibilities are precisely assigned to certain individuals and subunits, all of which are peculiarly competent in such areas. Similarly, authority is structured to ensure that appropriate decisions are made at appropriate levels. Organizational structure, then, by itself, is a system for ensuring that problems will be handled at the place where the probabilities of getting an effective decision are greatest.

The Communication Network. Equally important is the process by which *information* is secured, routed, and used. Negatively, one can conceive of organization as a means of limiting information to executive and supervisory groups. This denies to other members the capacity for deciding, and in some cases, for evaluating decisions even after they are made. However, it seems preferable to conceive of the organization as a great communication net in which information is acquired, sorted, and directed to the various functional decision centers, making rational decisions more probable.[19] Many observers define the organization in these terms, and for our immediate purposes this is most helpful. Certainly we know that decisions cannot be made without some information; at the very least, one must be aware of the existence of the problem to be dealt with. We also know that incoming information must be directed to appropriate places in the hierarchy where the skill and experience necessary to use it are found. Thus most organizations have a common receiving center for incoming communications, from which they are so routed. This conception is obviously quite formal and, for the moment, does not take into account informal communication of all kinds.

[18] Questions may be raised here as to the propriety of viewing the organization as *an organic* whole, distinct in some ways from its members. Perhaps logically, this is not possible, yet I have concluded that *the organization* as a continuing entity is distinct. Like the corporation, it exists permanently, it is a *collective* reality whose rights and authority are different from those of its individual members, and certainly there are many cases when its "good" demands the sacrifice of its members. See, among others, Donald Calhoun, "The Illusion of Rationality" in *Life, Language, Law: Essays in Honor of Arthur F. Bentley*, R. W. Taylor (ed.) (Yellow Springs: Antioch Press, 1957); Chris Argyris, "The Individual and the Organization: Some Problems of Mutual Adjustment," 2, *Administrative Science Quarterly* (June, 1957), pp. 1–24.

[19] Among others, see John Dorsey, "A Communication Model for Administration," 2, *Administrative Science Quarterly* (December, 1957), pp. 307–24.

CYBERNETICS AND FEEDBACK. It is in the over-all organizational communication structure that cybernetics theory and data processing machines are having their greatest impact. Cybernetics is a relatively new discipline, developed in the United States by Norbert Wiener.[20] It is concerned with the transmission of information and with the way that the structure of organisms, machines, and organizations affects their capacity to send, receive, and retain information. Cybernetics (a word coined by Wiener from the Greek symbol kubernētēs or "steersman") is therefore concerned with learning and essentially with the role of "feedback" in the learning process. Feedback is defined as a "method of controlling a system by reinserting into it the results of its past performance."[21] A simple illustration is the way an automobile is kept to the right of the center line. If the car moves too near the white line, or perhaps even to the left of it, this information is transmitted through the brain and the muscles and an immediate correction occurs. Information inserted into the organism as a result of its experience or performance has changed our behavior, and we can say that learning has occurred.

The idea of feedback is particularly helpful in analyzing the way the organization "learns," by reinserting into its system the information provided by its operation, thus enabling the organization to modify the system as required. Data processing machines are vital here because, like the human brain, they provide reservoirs for storing and manipulating information that can be brought into play when decisions must be made.

Perhaps one or two additional examples of feedback and the use of data processing machines will make their utility clearer.[22] While feedback is usually explained in mechanical or engineering contexts, such as the operation of a thermostat which automatically regulates one's furnace in response to the information "fed back" into the system from the environment, other analogies are more germane for our purposes. The administration of a course in a university provides instances of the use of feedback. The "system" here may be roughly viewed as the process and conditions involved in getting across certain materials to a student group. Lectures, readings, and discussions are prescribed as the ap-

---

[20] Norbert Wiener, *The Human Use of Human Beings* (Boston: Houghton Mifflin Co., 1954).

[21] *Ibid.*, p. 61. A dramatic account of "feedback" as used by the captain of a destroyer on antisubmarine patrol in the Atlantic during World War II is C. S. Forester, *The Good Shepherd* (Boston: Little, Brown & Co., 1956).

[22] The current emphasis upon data processing and systematic decision making is suggested by the appearance of new journals such as *Behavioral Science, Operations Research,* and *Management Science.* The administrative generalist should be acquainted with these developments and their implications for his own role during the next few decades.

propriate means of achieving this major goal. Yet we are not content merely to assume that all is going well; therefore controls are used in the form of tests that provide information as to the effectiveness of the system. The results of such tests are *reinserted* into the teaching process, which is modified to overcome any revealed disutilities. An essential point here is that feedback is the information coming from the operation of the system itself; it is not information brought in from some external source.

DATA PROCESSING MACHINES. The main use of data processing machines has so far been in rather stereotyped activities of a clerical or record-keeping nature, such as maintaining store accounts, personnel records, and payrolls. Perhaps the biggest program of this kind is in the Bureau of Old Age and Survivors' Insurance in Baltimore, where the earnings records of 120 million people are maintained. The Bureau estimates that it is saving $1,000,000 per year and about 350 staff persons in using the computer to locate misquoted social security numbers. The storing or memory function of the computers is shown by the transfer of data from punched cards to magnetic tapes, which now comprise some 8,000 reels.[23] A similar although smaller program in California illustrates the use of the tapes: When claims are received by the Department of Employment for compensation, they are processed automatically by running a "claims" tape along with the master tape; the machine identifies and extracts the necessary information from the master tape, which enables the claim to be checked and the amount of benefit to be calculated. This Department estimates that it is saving $15,000 per month and the work of one hundred people by this application of the computer.

Gathering information about the environment is thus one way of increasing rationality by controlling or discounting the future, or at least by avoiding decisions that seem to run against environmental trends. The activities of business firms are suggestive here. In order to insulate themselves against risk, the larger firms engage in such activities as market research, product diversification, price agreements, high investments in research for new or better products, and advertising. These activities may also be viewed as efforts to decrease the probability of ill-fated decision making by gaining as much information as possible about the market. These hedges against the future are built-in parts of the organization whose function is to produce signals that will guide the administrators toward more rational choice.

[23] H. S. Jordan, Electronic Data Processing in the United States, *O and M Bulletin* (December, 1956), p. 12; also L. H. Hattery, "Automatic Character Reading for Data Processing Systems," **17**, *Public Administration Review* (Summer, 1957), pp. 159–63.

BASES OF ADMINISTRATIVE AUTHORITY

Like many aspects of administration, the concept of authority may logically be treated in several contexts. Here we shall consider it in terms of its implications for decision making. Certainly one of the premises impinging directly upon the administrator's decision-making role is the character of the authority (defined as the ability to influence decisions) which resides in his position and in his person. This condition is a premise both for himself and for those affected by his decisions. In the first case, his own estimation of the authority he commands is always a variable in the choices he makes. Equally, the image that subordinates have of his authority is a vital factor in *their* responses to his directives and influences.[24] Needless to say, in this kind of reciprocal evaluation there are many opportunities for error. But it is important to stress immediately that "authority," as used here, encompasses various kinds and degrees of ability to influence decisions.

Formal Authority. Perhaps the most patent kind of authority is the "formal" authority associated with a given position, such as that of division head, bureau chief, or sales manager. Such authority may be defined as the influence and sanctions available to any incumbent of the position regardless of personal characteristics of the individual who may occupy the position at any given moment. Clearly this is a somewhat abstract definition, since in practice it is always impossible to separate the individual's own personality from the position. Yet, for analytical purposes, such a separation is valid and germane, as one can quickly see by considering the broad range of influence and initiative exercised by the various Presidents of the United States, all of whom operated under similar legal prescriptions although, of course, the historical demands pressing upon each were dissimilar.

In any event it seems that individuals can "go a long way" on formal authority by itself, particularly in big organizations where size and impersonality shelter the leaders from the organization's rank and file. Undoubtedly one of the main weapons in the formal category of authority is the ability to use sanctions to achieve compliance. While sanctions of various kinds are available to individuals throughout the hierarchy,[25] those available to the administrator in the upper reaches are more de-

---

24 For an analysis of authority in this "transactional" context, see Robert V. Presthus, "Authority in Organizations," in S. Mailick (ed.), *Organizational Theory and Research* (Englewood Cliffs, N.J.: Prentice-Hall, Inc., 1960).

25 Simon refers to sanctions as "factors which induce the acceptance of authority in an organization," and lists several kinds, including social disapproval, alienation from leaders, acceptance of authority because one believes in the organization's values, acceptance through hope of economic and prestige gains, and desire or fear of additional responsibility. *Administrative Behavior*, pp. 123–53.

cisive and dramatic. Although this is a fundamentally negative and latent weapon, it is probably ever present in interpersonal relations in the organization. A more important effect of formal authority is its role in legitimating authority. Formal symbols and rituals are vital in ensuring desired reactions in organizations of all kinds. Official stamps, seals, and signatures serve this function in matters of state. Upon succeeding to office, the high official swears an oath on the Bible to carry out his duties faithfully. In many state universities, professors swear that they have no unorthodox political views and that they will do their jobs well. The English monarchs are crowned with impressive ceremony and solemnity. As a result individuals accept directives (i.e., deem them legitimate) merely because they come from above. In the business milieu, the subordinate will often say "I don't agree with the boss, but it's his money and he can do what he wishes with it."

However, like most organizational variables, authority varies with the size and character of the organization. In a small group where interpersonal relations are intimate or where crisis demands unusual measures, as in an army patrol, formal authority has definite limitations. There, it seems, the administrator or leader must reinforce his formal authority with qualities of skill, judgment, wisdom, and experience that provide additional legitimations for group acceptance of his claims for dominance on a formal basis.

The Permissive Factor. This leads us to Barnard's concept of a "zone of indifference," which emphasizes the permissive nature of authority by stating that commands will be obeyed only as long as they fall within an undefined, and perhaps undefinable, area of unquestioned acceptance insofar as the receiver is concerned.[26] Here again, variations occur according to the type of organization. Where the organization's goals are clear and unquestioned, where its role is regarded as essential and legitimate, the "zone of indifference" will be broader than in organizations which are segmented, highly stratified, and divided by conflicting definitions of what the organization's "real" goals and "proper" behaviors ought to be. This condition explains why organizational goals are often verbalized in extremely general terms (for example, political party platforms), which permit greater attachment or at least tend to discourage critical inquiry into the exact meaning of organizational objectives.

We think Barnard's "indifference" concept is a helpful generalization but one that fails to note adequately the psychological and social forces that tend to make acceptance of authority almost automatic. This means that the reciprocal, active role of the rank and file implied by Barnard's

[26] Chester I. Barnard, *Functions of the Executive*, (Cambridge: Harvard University Press, 1947), pp. 131.

concept is somewhat overstated. Clearly, authority relations are never entirely "one-way"; the anticipated reactions of his subjects conditions even a dictator's behavior. But obedience is often more of a conditioned reaction than a thoughtful response.[27]

Technical Skill. Nevertheless it is clear that however conformity-minded a society is, authority must usually rest upon more than mere formal position or upon automatic responses. Technical skill is another basis of authority.[28] In our society specialized skills compete strongly with formal position for recognition. Democratic values are at work here, urging that employment and rewards be based upon objective standards of performance and ability rather than upon subjective bases of race, religion, color, "old school tie," or the various other criteria that often persist. The influence of democratic values is reinforced by a national disposition toward efficiency and specialization which honors the claims of special skill and training. The Russian scientific and educational challenge will undoubtedly increase this influence, making investment in the training of our youth as acceptable as investment in capital plant and equipment. The whole paraphernalia of public personnel systems, recruitment, testing, evaluation, and so on, follow naturally from this national ethos which values objectivity, skill, and measureable performance.

As a result the administrator with exceptional skill and training can reinforce his formal authority and enhance his influence in organizational decision making. His influence is strengthened by the opportunity it gives the specialist to argue from an *objective basis:* it is the "law of the situation," the technical demands of the issue at hand that shape his recommendations. If these recommendations happen to enhance his power or the program of his agency, this is only a fortuitous by-product of overriding skill considerations. Needless to say, there are endless examples of specialists being influenced by power and program as well as pure science. The arguments among the military branches concerning the kinds of weapons and strategy essential to national survival are illustrative.

However, it is clear enough that the main drift in administration is toward technical supremacy, reflecting the complexities of modern industrial society, the armament race and its basis in scientific knowledge, the willingness of the universities to supply specialized courses whenever

---

[27] For a discussion of this "condition" of authority in our society, see Robert V. Presthus, "Toward a Theory of Organizational Behavior," 3, *Administrative Science Quarterly* (June, 1958), pp. 48–72.

[28] Herbert A. Simon calls this type of authority one of *confidence,* "Authority" in C. M. Arensberg, (ed.) *Research in Industrial Human Relations* (New York: Harper & Bros., 1957), p. 106.

the market appears sufficient, and the resulting creation of special vocabularies, special clienteles, special professional associations, and related special interests. All this reinforces technical skill as a critical
variable in decision making throughout the organization.

Social Class. In older societies, and in the United States as it gets older,
other less objective bases of authority may be seen. Class and wealth are
among these. In Eastern societies, recruitment to the public service is a
virtual monopoly of the educated, upper strata which comprise about
15 to 25 per cent of the population. If one thinks of authority as a continuum with objective skill at one end and class or birth at the other,
such societies would be placed toward the class-birth end, and some of
them, as in central and East Africa still have a theistic-monarchical base
for authority. In the United States, in politics and political appointments
at the top reaches of the civil service, wealth and family often compete
strongly with ability, training, and experience. Obviously all these qualities may appear together in the same individual, but the careful passing
along of family advantage through education at prestigeful universities
and the personal contacts derived there blurs objectivity somewhat.[29] As
university training, which has been the greatest instrument of mobility
in the past two or three decades, becomes universalized, distinctions
among universities become more significant as selection devices. Thus,
as Baltzall shows, a preponderance of those in *Who's Who* and in positions of influence come from the Ivy League universities. But even
within this group there is a tacitly recognized scale which ranks certain
schools at the top, others in the "middle," and some at the bottom; indeed, a few of them are not always included in the Ivy League spectrum.

Seniority and Experience. Age, seniority, and experience are other
bases of authority that carry weight in organizational decision making.
In all societies the old men of the tribe have long enjoyed superordinate
influence, based upon a combination of objective and subjective qualifications including social skill, achieved formal position, the knowledge
that comes from experience, and considerable effectiveness at bureaucratic infighting. Even in the United States, which is among the most
"objective" societies in terms of the bases of authority, positions of status
and influence are dominated by age: the most respected and presumably
the most influential positions according to research are Supreme Court
justices, bankers, senators, and big business executives. In all these cases,
the incumbents tend to be old. No doubt this is partially the reflection
of the obvious fact that it takes time to get through the various hierarchies, but in both politics and the Supreme Court, neither long train-

[29] For a careful study of this phenomenon, see G. E. Baltzall, *Philadelphia Gentle-*
men: The Making of a National Upper Class (Glencoe, Ill.: The Free Press, 1958).

ing nor experience has traditionally been required for election or selection.

One is on firmer ground when discussing the impact of seniority as a basis of authority. Here for many reasons, many of which are subjective, seniority has become the main criterion for promotion in big organizations.[30] The subjective reasons are clear: Seniority is the most widely accepted criterion within the organization and validates an old American folk belief that "there's no substitute for experience." Equally important, the honoring of seniority is an important organizational weapon, demonstrating in the most visible way that the organization rewards those who have been loyal, and suggesting in the process that loyalty is a functional behavior for all members of the organization. For these reasons, bringing in an outsider to fill a high-level position is usually the result of failure to reconcile extreme internal friction among several contenders for the vacancy. On the other hand, of course, seniority often has objective bases, including long experience with the problems of a given organization, demonstrated ability over time, and the development of a battery of interpersonal alliances and associations that ease the carrying out of work. However, it seems fair to conclude that seniority is often suspect when used as the primary index of promotability.

Social Mandate. All these bases of authority may be looked upon as resources that can be used in influencing decisions, both in shaping them and carrying them out. One other aspect of organizational authority is worth analyzing. This is the view of authority as a resource that is given to the organization in the form of a social mandate from society itself. In this context, authority is not so much something that an individual or an organization imposes upon others as it is something granted willingly to them by society and subject to revocation should the bases upon which it is granted fail. An example will make this clearer. Medical doctors in our society enjoy a great measure of authority; they write their own laws governing training, and they have a large measure of independence and autonomy in treating their patients; they are not obliged to testify in court; they enjoy high social status and income; and in an immediate administrative context, in several states their automobiles bear identification tags that make it difficult for them to get traffic citations.

This degree of authority and the resulting influence it gives the profession in medical and other matters is a resource that society has granted to the profession because it believes in the excellence of the technical

[30] For an analysis of the bureaucratization of seniority, see T. Caplow, *Sociology of Occupations* (Minneapolis: University of Minnesota Press, 1957).

skill, training, and performance of the doctor. Here we see the technical basis of authority at work. But this authority is also granted because the doctor is a *professional* man, with the connotation of service, ethics, and pecuniary restraint symbolized by this concept. As long as a majority of the public believes that the profession is operating in professional terms of adequate care, ethical behavior, and the like, society will continue to give the profession its mandate of authority. Here the technical basis of authority is reinforced by status authority based upon the viability of *professionalism* as an honorific vocational value. This suggests, then, that authority will rarely be based upon only one index but that effective authority is usually the result of several indexes, none of which by itself is effective over time. That the authority enjoyed by the medical profession is not irrevocable is shown by the case of England, where majority opinion came to believe that (1) the profession was not offering adequate care, mainly in terms of volume and (2) the ordinary person was unable to afford adequate medical care under the existing system. The result, of course, was that the profession was socialized.

Organizations of all kinds depend for their authority and survival upon a similar social mandate. In the federal government, certain agencies such as the FBI and the Passport Division of the State Department apparently enjoy this mandate, since Congress, which is assumed to represent majority opinion, faithfully accepts their appropriation requests and even at times insists upon increasing the amounts they ask for. On the other hand, the Department of Labor has long suffered from the absence of a positive social mandate, and its experience with appropriations committees has been much less satisfactory. Other agencies that have suffered include the U.S. Information Agency and the International Cooperation Administration. We may conclude that society has usually been unwilling to grant them the measure of authority required to carry out their programs at the level desired by their administrators.

AN EMPIRICAL STUDY OF DECISION MAKING

Although there are very few empirical studies of decision making in public organizations, we do have some that are helpful in suggesting what the process seems to consist of. One of these is a study by William Gore of decisions by federal field offices.[31] The study consists of locating and analyzing thirty-three case histories of important policy decisions among eighteen federal field offices in the state of Washington. Gore concludes that the following stages characterized decision making.

[31] "Decision Making in Federal Field Offices," **16,** *Public Administration Review* (Autumn, 1956), pp. 281–91.

1. *Perception:* This initial stage consisted of the realization of the need for policy change. An important consideration here was the amount of support for the agency and its programs and the impact upon such support that failure to make the policy change implied. At this stage a great deal of information came in from external sources, and its use within the organization varied considerably according to the agency directors and those most directly concerned with its information system. In evaluating information, the agencies relied a great deal upon a body of doctrine or values that it had learned and adhered to in the past. It seems that this doctrine acted as a theory does in research, determining what information would be accepted and acted upon, and vice versa. The doctrine apparently acted as a filter, shaping the perception of the agency's members.

2. *Interpretation:* In this stage the "initial objectives behind which the power and the influence of the field office will be mobilized" are determined. This seemed to involve the "consideration of alternatives" which is part of the stereotyped decision-making sequence. Alternative decisions were interpreted against the doctrine and objectives of the field office concerned. The agencies seemed to see themselves as in a state of war with external groups, competing agencies, competing private interests. Within the agency, leadership was exercised by groups, with each member bringing some special knowledge to the decision-making process. Such groups monopolized the interpretation process, monitoring the activities of external groups, sending up trial balloons, seeking advice from all interested groups, and discussing the implications of the proposed decisions. Gore concludes that leadership cliques are motivated by power, the perpetuation of agency doctrine, the agency's mission, and the reduction of future demands for change.

3. *Struggle for Power:* Here the scene shifts to the external power centers with which the leadership cliques negotiate to get support for their proposed action. Gore found that most administrators felt embarrassed about such negotiations, probably because they increase tension during the initial stages. This was because the clique's suggestions seemed to evoke from outside interests a whole battery of "incompatible demands . . . which had apparently been lying dormant." However, most leaders recognized the need to build support for their decisions and were willing to make the compromises necessary to get it. In every case, leaders found themselves in a dilemma brought by demands for concessions that conflicted with the agency's policy or with other concessions demanded by other external groups. Several patterns of support building appeared, most of which involved the leadership in a cooperative role, reconciling the claims of the several external interests while

trying to keep paramount the agency's goal. These were shifting alliances that changed with the issues and the groups involved in them. Also, "this intangible and usually invisible *ad hoc* support seem[ed] to be the material from which power was developed."

4. *Formalization:* Once the alliances have been built and the policy negotiations effected, a formal policy statement is drawn up. Gore found that many administrators "equated decision making with formalization," rather than seeing it as merely the last stage in a longer process. Some of the issues involved here included: securing formal authorization for the proposed policy change; securing the funds necessary to carry it out; providing for new personnel or for transferring others.

Perhaps the vital conclusion here is that "decision making" involves a great number of contingent elements and processes, including the external environment of the organization. As suggested at the beginning of the chapter, decision making is not the product of a single leader's mind, carried out in a highly intellectual fashion, but rather it is an *institutionalized process* involving many individuals and interests within and outside the organization; many interpretations of what the organization "should" be doing and what it "is" doing; and many sources of information and diverse skills. Also, as Gore concludes, decision making seems to be a rough model of *organizational change,* a facet of organizations about which little is known. This emphasis upon change illustrates one of the main difficulties in our attempts to generalize about administration: so often the phenomenon under analysis (decision making, for example) is subject to so many peculiar and changing conditions that the generalization becomes submerged by the "givens" of any one situation. That is, our generalizations become so limited in scope that their usefulness is impaired. However, at this early stage in the development of administrative science, there is no need for despair.

BIBLIOGRAPHY

CARTWRIGHT, D. (ed.). *Studies in Social Power.* Ann Arbor: 1959.

GORE, WILLIAM J. "Decision Making in Federal Field Offices," 16, *Public Administration Review* (Autumn, 1956).

GORE, WILLIAM J. and SILANDER, FRED S. "A Bibliographical Essay in Decision Making," 4, *Administrative Science Quarterly* (June, 1959), pp. 97–121.

HUNTER, FLOYD. *Community Decision Making: A Study of Decision Makers.* Chapel Hill: 1953.

MARCH, JAMES G., and SIMON, HERBERT A. *Organizations.* New York and London: 1958.

MATTHEWS, DONALD R. *The Social Background of Political Decision-Makers.* Doubleday Short Studies in Political Science. Garden City, N. Y.: 1954.

MILLS, C. WRIGHT. *The Power Elite.* New York: 1956.

PRESTHUS, ROBERT V., and BLANKENSHIP, L. V. "Dixon-Yates: A Study in Political Behavior," (Unpublished ms., Cornell University, 1960).

SIMON, HERBERT A. *Administrative Behavior*. 2d ed.; New York: 1957.
——. "Theories of Decision Making in Economics," 49, *American Economic Review* (June, 1959), pp. 253–83.
SPECIAL ISSUE ON DECISION MAKING, 3, *Administrative Science Quarterly* (December, 1958).
STEIN, HAROLD (ed.). *Public Administration and Policy Development*. New York: 1952.

CHAPTER 7

Communication

Communication provides the thread that binds an organization together by ensuring common understanding. Organization values and objectives must be made known. Clear assignments of authority and function are required for success in large operations. Supervisors at every level have a special responsibility for encouraging a two-way communication pattern in which policies and directives are interpreted to the worker and his reactions are brought back to management. Employees want to know what is going on. Without a broad sharing of information, their morale will be low and the agency's task will be more difficult.

This chapter will attempt to explain why communication in organizations is so often inadequate. We shall see that many factors are involved and that the human factor is as important as the structural factors in determining the quality of communication. By way of introduction, several structural factors may be mentioned, including size, specialization, and hierarchy. Although it is impossible to separate these factors from the psychological behaviors that arise from them, for purposes of analysis we can treat them as though they were independent.

Size is an important factor in any organization. While one would hesitate to suggest that a *law* of increasing size governs governmental agencies, it is certainly clear that they do tend to grow in response to public demands and internal power struggles. This growth in number of employees and in scope of operations complicates communication, if only because of the sheer physical task involved in transmitting information to the large numbers of subunits and individuals who need such information. Specialization is another characteristic of modern organization, particularly in the United States, where our educational system (partly as a result of the demand for specialists) is geared to producing specialists. Here, the barriers to communication reflect different ways of thinking, different vocational interests, and the introversion that tends to accompany specialization. Finally, there is the problem of hierarchy which is related to both size and specialization and results in a horizontal stratification of the organization in terms of function, power, authority, status, and responsibility. While the figure may be overdrawn, it seems valid to view each level in the hierarchy as a semi-pervious membrane that restricts the flow of information both upward and downward. Certainly, at the very least, any given communication is subtly changed in transmission from one level to the other. We may assume that the parts of it which coincide with the interests of those at a given level are reinforced, while threatening elements are toned down or even deleted.

Communication is thus an extremely complicated process. The larger and more specialized an agency becomes, the greater the need for planned methods of communication which can cut through the barriers of specialization and span the gap between center and periphery. But much more than a rational system for distributing information is required. Communication is a subtle and complex process involving psychological and cultural factors that create barriers between individuals whose experience and values are different. It is not enough merely to recognize these obstacles; a special effort must be made to overcome them. This is not easy, for many reflect deep-seated social values that are difficult if not impossible to change. In this chapter the "why" of communication is emphasized rather than the "how," simply because the major barriers are psychological as well as structural and technical. Indeed, the extent of poor communication despite the excellent technical media of transmission is one of the great ironies of our time. Finally, the recent developments in data processing, cybernetics, and such concepts as feedback will be treated only in passing, since they are fully covered in later chapters.

THE COMMUNICATION PROCESS

Communication may be defined as the process of transmitting cues in order to modify human behavior. Communication seems to occur roughly as follows.[1] Some event occurs which stimulates Mr. X through sight, hearing, or other sense perception. The nervous impulses that result travel to his glands and muscles, producing tensions which are translated into thoughts and words according to his background of experience and the attitudes which come from it. He then forms certain verbal patterns and transmits them to Mr. Y, who goes through a similar process except that Y's selection of words to express his reaction to X's statements is

---

[1] Wendell Johnson, "Speech and Personality," in Lyman Bryson (ed.), *The Communication of Ideas* (New York: Harper & Bros., 1948), pp. 55–58; also Wendell Johnson, *People in Quandaries: the Semantics of Personal Adjustment* (New York: Harper & Bros., 1946), pp. 469–81; John T. Dorsey, Jr., "A Communications Model for Administration," 2, *Administrative Science Quarterly* (December, 1957); Norbert Wiener, *Cybernetics* (New York: John Wiley & Sons, 1948).

probably different. Once he arranges his patterns of expression, however, he too speaks, and his words again become the stimulation for X or some third party. It is clear that many opportunities for misunderstanding arise during this complex series of events, especially at the point where X translates the stimulus into words. For here his entire cultural background together with his personal point of view about the immediate subject provides a frame of reference that will color his perception. Communication is strongly affected by the personal values of the listener. We must recognize the role of personal experience in determining meaning.

Sociocultural Influences. The cultural nature of communication must be emphasized. Although the term covers a wide field of human action, communication is grounded in the interchange of ideas. Communication makes living together possible. This requires, in turn, common skills, expectations, and understandings which can be transmitted by the written or spoken word. Communication is also a cultural process in the sense that individuals and groups develop certain commonly shared beliefs about the nature of things and the meaning of words.[2] A complex set of values as to "right" and "wrong" is created and enforced by group approval. It is an exceptional individual who will flaunt established ways of thought or behavior. Insofar as these values and meanings are really common, communication is made easier. A common substratum of beliefs makes for certainty and sympathy in human relations.

At the same time it is clear that the store of common meanings is limited. Society is composed of a variety of different groups, many of which hold opposing views as to eternal truth or the proper distribution of the national income. This complexity makes it difficult to weigh the impact of the mass media upon the various groups. Very few generalizations are possible, and the present state of mind among both public and specialists has recently been described as "pessimistic."[3] In spite of favorable economic circumstances and a democratic environment which increase tolerance, separatism seems to be increasing as powerful, self-conscious groups become better organized and wiser in the ways of public opinion manipulation. This suggests again that values reflect

---

[2] An excellent source here is F. Keesing and M. Keesing, *Elite Communication in Samoa: A Study of Leadership* (Stanford: University of Stanford Press, 1956); for a sophisticated analysis of major aspects of communication, see C. Cherry, *On Human Communication: A Review, A Survey, and A Criticism* (Cambridge, Mass.: The Technology Press, 1957), particularly chapters i, ii, and iii.

[3] Some of the difficulties of conceptualization and research in communication reflecting this complexity are considered in J. T. Klapper, "What We Know About the Effects of Mass Communication," 21, *Public Opinion Quarterly* (Winter 1957–58). This article contains a good research bibliography on the effects of mass communication.

personal and cultural conditions which vary considerably within and between nations. At the international level, for example, the term "democracy" is used frequently by the United States, Britain, and Russia. In each country, however, the word has a different meaning. In America "democracy" has meant a maximum of opportunity in a highly individualistic and primarily economic sense, with a minimum of political interference. In Britain it has long had a similar connotation of political freedom and equality, but it has also provided a much greater scope for collective public action to bring this about. In Russia, on the other hand, the term has little suggestion of individualism, implying instead the opportunity to work and sacrifice for a monolithic state. As the United Nations debates reveal, international communications suffer greatly from the varied connotations of this honorific symbol, which tends to become an instrument of manipulation.

Such differing concepts shape and determine thought so that reasonable people often reach opposing conclusions about the same set of facts. Communication is inhibited accordingly. The fact that the physical media of transmission—radio, television, telegraph, cheap newsprint, and motion pictures—have achieved a high degree of technical efficiency only makes the failure more of a paradox. As Hayakawa puts it, "the better the communications, the bloodier the quarrels."[4] However, there is a real question whether international order and understanding depend only upon a commonly understood language. It must be remembered that individuals in the same family and community can have extreme and bitter differences of opinion. Competition is as common an element in human relations as cooperation, and there are undoubtedly some basic differences of interest which understanding alone cannot solve.

THE ORGANIZATION AS A COMMUNICATION SYSTEM

So far we have been concerned with communication as an individual process, affected by sociocultural values. We can now turn to another view of communication, the concept of the organization itself as an elaborate communication system or network.[5] In this view the effectiveness of an organization depends upon the volume and quality of information that the organization is able to get from its environment, and its means of transmitting it throughout the organization to the centers where such information is needed if rational decisions are to be made.

---

[4] S. I. Hayakawa, *Language in Action* (New York: Harcourt, Brace & Co., Inc., 1947), p. 27.

[5] Among others, see A. Bavelas and D. Barrett, "An Experimental Approach to Organizational Communication," 27, *Personnel* (1951); E. Jacobson and S. E. Seashore, "Communication Practices in Complex Organizations," 7, *Journal of Social Issues* (1951).

In this context, communication is not some secondary activity, as it has been traditionally viewed, but instead it is the essence of organization. "Administration can be viewed as a configuration of communication patterns relating individuals and collectivities (groups) of varying size, shapes, and degree of cohesion and stability . . . administration appears as a patterned swirl and flow of communications, many of them channeled through transactional 'circuits' between persons and persons, persons and groups, and groups and other groups."[6] An integral part of this concept is the self-correcting character of the organization, which depends upon its ability to feed back into its decisions and behavior the information which comes not only from the environment generally but, more important, also from the *results* of the organization's decisions as these are put into effect. Thus through feedback decisional errors can be corrected.

This view of organization as a communication system is theoretically appealing for several reasons. First, it defines organization as an active, changing entity, instead of as a structured, superrational system. In terms of our three approaches to the study of administration, it falls in the "sociopsychological" area. Second, this concept seems to meet the test of common sense or experience in that it is clear that our ability to act rationally depends critically upon the information we have about the problem at hand. This necessity is dramatically illustrated in warfare where intelligence as to the strength, location, morale, strategy, as well as the information potential, of the enemy is so vital. Also, for research purposes and conceptualization, the organization as a communication system model gives us a theoretical framework, a way of defining organization and giving order to empirical data.

The communication system concept also permits one to incorporate into administrative theory some useful concepts from the biological and physical sciences, such as homeostasis, or equilibrium, which defines the tendency of all systems to seek a satisfactory balance between input and output. In terms of the individual and organization, for example, it is convenient to speak of the individual as seeking to reach a satisfactory balance between what he puts into the organization in terms of energy, skill, and loyalty and what he receives from the organization in return. If a rough equilibrium between these elements is not achieved, we can predict that the individual will leave the organization or at least that his morale will be lower than it would otherwise be.

Among the uses of communication so viewed is the opportunity to increase our understanding of interpersonal relations and the power structure in a given organization. For example, since communication

[6] Dorsey, "A Communications Model for Administration," p. 310.

between individuals is rarely spontaneous, inasmuch as individuals tend to select certain figures with whom to share information, communication between individuals becomes an index of their interpersonal values and their self-images, insofar as individuals usually associate with those whom they respect and like.[7] The same index can also reveal something about the distribution of power in an organization, since access to information ("who talks to whom about what") is the essence of influence. Here, the differences between the formal authority structure (between the way communications "should" flow) and the informal authority structure (the way they actually do flow) can often be quantitatively demonstrated. Patterns of contact usually develop between and among influential people, and these patterns are not necessarily along hierarchical lines. Again, for those who are interested in such problems, the degree of centralization-decentralization can be measured by the analysis of the scope and content of communication in an organization. How far "down" the hierarchy does participation occur and in what kinds of decisions? What is the relative influence of administrators vs. functional specialists in selected kinds of decisions? The answers to such questions could tell us more than we now know about decision making.

But both the individual and the "communication system" approaches to communication are valuable in the study of organization, and indeed they are closely related in the sense that the same variables that affect communications among individuals in relatively unstructured social situations are present in the organizational environment, if in an aggravated degree. For this reason it seems appropriate to turn now to a general consideration of the role of communication, and the main barriers to it in large organizations. We begin with a consideration of the psychological impact that communication has upon the individual.

THE IMPORTANCE OF COMMUNICATION

In large organizations that are highly specialized and depend on written communications and authoritative relationships, individuals often feel unimportant and ineffectual. This is especially so when the individual knows that decisions which affect him personally are made without consultation and appear as a *fait accompli*. This lack of a sense of participation and belongingness has been called *anomie* by Emile Durkheim, a French sociologist who noted that the worker had become a mere appendage to a machine in the industries of western Europe. This alienation is now even more widely apparent. Newspapers, the radio, and motion pictures have made a single community out of a nation of 170

---

[7] Among others see, O. N. Larsen and R. J. Hill, "Social Structure and Interpersonal Communication," 33, *American Journal of Sociology* (March, 1958), pp. 497–505.

million people. However, largely because of technical advance and concentration of ownership, control of the mass media is in relatively few hands. As a result, millions listen to a single voice, and millions of voices are unheard. Magazines read by millions are edited by a few individuals who exercise a selective judgment among a vast potential of information. This situation exists on a smaller scale in large organizations. Both through chance and design, much information is stifled or limited. It is difficult for the rank and file to be heard. This reflects not only the size of organizations but also the increasing concern of organizations with "public relations." Most ideas and opinions that reach the outside world are filtered through a central unit which ensures that they are consistent with the larger objectives of the organization. Yet individuals at every level need and want recognition and an opportunity for self-expression. As one worker put it:

You know there is something more important to work for than money. I'll work as hard as any man as long as I am interested in the job, as long as it seems worth while. But I'll spit in the face of any man, no matter how much he wants to pay me, if he expects me to work *blind* to plug ahead like a machine at something unimportant and uninteresting.[8]

In this context, communication can be a process that meets an important psychological need. Man does not live by bread alone. He needs to associate himself with great ends. For example, the superior morale of individuals in highly self-conscious occupations such as the medical profession seems to come from the pride in achievement which these professions systematically instill in their members. Standards of entrance are high, and the individual is protected by the group. He knows he can depend upon the organization and derives personal strength from its unity of purpose. In large organizations generally, morale and productivity go hand in hand. Both are associated with individual and group participation in decision making and the realization that management looks upon the worker as a responsible individual. Informing workers about personnel, procedure, and policy has a therapeutic effect. It lets the individual know where he stands and dispels rumor mongering which reflects uncertainty. Unfortunately, however obvious this need may seem, it is violated with monotonous regularity in large organizations, often through oversight rather than by design.

COMMUNICATION BARRIERS IN ORGANIZATIONS

Psychological and Semantic Barriers. We can now outline a number of specific obstacles to communication in large organizations. Communi-

[8] Cited in John J. Corson, "Management—Tongue-tied, Deaf, and Blind?" 11, *Advanced Management* (September, 1946), p. 101.

cation functions through language. But the use of language is extremely complicated because words are merely symbols or abstractions for some real object or process. Their meaning is determined by the ideas and experiences they evoke in the reader's mind. Actually, words are rather inadequate substitutes for the things they represent. They are at best extreme oversimplifications of complex ideas and concepts. There are only about six hundred thousand words in the English language (of which the average individual knows and uses about 10 per cent), but they must be used to symbolize billions of individual facts, experiences, and relationships. As a result, words are very abstract and are often used imprecisely.

We have seen that the word "democracy" must be carefully defined before it can be used meaningfully. The word "liberal" is even more slippery. It is often used to describe one who believes in big government as a means of promoting economic and educational equality. Yet the eighteenth-century theorists who popularized the term regarded a minimum of government action as the basic requisite of social progress. True, they believed in civil liberties, as do many contemporary "liberals," but this only illustrates again the elusiveness of symbols. In England today the word "liberal" can refer to a political party, an eighteenth-century philosophy, or a general point of view which encourages or at least tolerates social and political heterodoxy. Thus, when the term is used, its meaning is determined to a larger extent not by the word itself but by the meaning which the user and his audience give it. The latter is a product of their cultural backgrounds.

Thus, although communication depends upon generalizations expressed through words, language is a rather awkward tool. Real events are dynamic and changing, whereas language is static and rather inflexible. Popular connotations of words often continue long after the situation which they once described has changed. Nor are words always used to convey meaning; often they are used deliberately to mislead or confuse. There is also the tendency to confuse a word with the thing it represents, rather than realizing that it is only a symbol. Many words are taboo simply because they are regarded as identical with the object or process they suggest. The fact that we must take many things for granted similarly complicates communication. We cannot personally check many important facts. We "know," for example, that there is a hydrogen bomb, not through experience but from news reports which "establish" its existence.

Meaning and communication are further hampered by the tendency toward reification, or rendering of facts or abstractions overly concrete and personal. The "state," for example, is often personalized and given qualities of reason and behavior that make it seem a living, concrete reality. Thus we say that the "state" takes the life of criminals, rewards its heroes, grows old, etc. Similarly, great and catastrophic events are personalized and attributed to some individual. Hoover's Depression, Roosevelt's New Deal, and Hitler's World War II are examples of over-simplifications which are almost meaningless but are used to give an unwarranted degree of certainty to what one says.[9] Stereotypes serve the same purpose. "Republicans" or "Democrats," "Jews" or "Catholics" are lumped together indiscriminately, with little regard for the fact that each category includes "liberals" and "conservatives," rich and poor, highly educated and uneducated, businessmen, professional, and blue-collar workers. Stereotypes not only make abstractions seem more concrete to the user; they also are helpful in avoiding thought, which is at best a painful process.

Ideological and Status Barriers. Differences in background, education, and expectation result in different social and political values. These are probably the greatest handicaps to effective communication and the most difficult to overcome. In large organizations, for example, the executive and the rank-and-file worker differ in many ways. Executives have more distinguishable social backgrounds. They are generally highly educated. They live in the more fashionable part of town, have their own group of friends. They are more competitive and more motivated by economic gain than the workers. By contrast, the average worker, as Elton Mayo and others have shown, desires psychological security, group recognition, and the achievement of immediate and personal ends rather than organ-ization objectives. Such ideological differences cannot be overcome by public relations campaigns or lip service to democracy and equality. There is indeed little evidence that they can be overcome at all.

Differences in educational level also inhibit communication. In administration, as noted earlier, communications are often written in a legalistic style which defeats understanding. This is due in part to the negative, legal origin of public administration which fosters a labored definition of terms in an attempt to cover all contingencies. In measuring communication, word difficulty, length of sentences, and the number of prepositional phrases are the chief indexes to reading difficulty. The average American adult has about eight years of education, and his reading level is seventh grade. Popular magazines are nicely tuned to this level. But agency communications often fail to meet the reading level of their employees, and understanding lags accordingly. This failure, however, is not confined to government. Business, too, often fails to communicate, both in its efforts to sell free enterprise and to streamline

[9] Daniel Katz, "Psychological Barriers to Communication," in Wilbur L. Schramm (ed.), *Mass Communications* (Urbana, Ill.: University of Illinois Press, 1949), pp. 281–85.

internal correspondence and verbal communication. "A businessman who castigates government bureaucrats, for example, is at the same time apt to be activating, expediting, implementing, effectuating, optimizing, minimizing, and maximizing—and at all levels within the framework of broad policy areas."[10]

Status differences also affect communication in organizations. Although the military has the most obvious system of distinction through rank and its perquisites, all organizations in all societies tend to establish systems of rewards which motivate and discipline their members. In the Washington milieu, for example, there is an extreme consciousness of job level. Certain obvious status symbols characterize high-level positions. Separate dining rooms, official cars (with or without chauffeur), a private office of a certain size, equipped with varying examples of conspicuous consumption, such as a rug, an extra-size desk, a private secretary—all denote a certain level of achievement and status. In addition, individuals at this level often treasure the "official secret." They apparently deal mainly with important policy matters, which they may discuss freely with equals but are reluctant to reveal elsewhere.

Despite these status differences, it is often assumed that employees are free to talk frankly with their supervisors. Indeed, the theory even holds that the employee may short-circuit his supervisor and talk directly with top management. Several factors, however, make this assumption rather farfetched. Workers are apprehensive of authority generally, and short-circuiting is inhibited by the obvious fact that one's immediate supervisor is likely to misunderstand the worker's motives. A status gulf thus divides management and the worker. As Stouffer has shown, a similar lack of understanding exists between officers and men in the army.[11] Large organizations inevitably develop status barriers which impede the exchange of ideas and reflect the wide differences in technical skill, value assumptions, and personal motivation found in any big organization.

Barriers of Size, Hierarchy, and Specialization. Communication failure in organization has other specific causes. The sheer number of employees and levels in the organization creates problems. Information must percolate through several levels, each of which may include empire builders

---

[10] *Fortune*, November, 1950, p. 115; W. H. Whyte, Jr., *Is Anybody Listening?* (New York: Simon and Schuster, 1952).

[11] "Although the Army's social system was such that officers with the best will in the world would find it difficult to bridge the gulf which separated them from the thoughts and feelings of the men under their command, one of the surprises experienced by the observant social scientist in the Army was the number of officers who assumed, apparently quite sincerely, that they succeeded in so doing." Samuel Stouffer, "Barriers to Understanding Between Officers and Men," in Robert K. Merton *et al.* (eds.), *Reader in Bureaucracy* (Glencoe, Ill.: Free Press, 1952), p. 265.

who consciously modify or subvert higher authority. Furthermore individuals interpret facts differently and tend to color them in transmission. As information descends, those responsible seem to transmit less and less.[12] They tend to convey only the bare essentials; moreover they may fail to transmit certain information for reasons of strategy or power. Geographical dispersion of administrative agencies also increases the difficulty of communication. Some 90 per cent of all federal employees are scattered about the country. This means that communication between the center and the field services must usually be written; this is less effective than verbal communication, which permits more intensive discussion. Understanding is facilitated through gestures and voice inflexions, and ideas that are poorly phrased or only partially understood can be clarified immediately.

It seems clear, moreover, that the desire to communicate is not always present. Executives may be indifferent to or unaware of the need for a widespread sharing of information. "What they don't know won't hurt them," is a persistent attitude. The "official secret" is also useful as a means of reinforcing the ego of insecure supervisors. In upward communication it is widely known, moreover, that line supervisors sometimes withhold information that is unpleasant and may put them in an unfavorable light. Thus information is filtered to give the executive only what those below think he wants to hear. Burleigh Gardner has immortalized a foreman who kept two sets of production records, one for the boss and one for his own information.

The specialization that characterizes modern bureaucracy also inhibits communication. Line and staff personnel, for example, have some difficulty in understanding each other. The reason for this lies in part in the nature of their respective organizational roles. "Line" activities are usually concerned with the basic program or function of the organization. "Staff" activities are somewhat different, being concerned with the co-ordination, control, and "service" needs of the organization. For example, forest service or soil conservation are program bureaus in the Department of Agriculture, while finance and personnel are not. In a university, the faculty is the line or program element, while administrators play a staff role of service and advice to the faculty.[13] Staff specialists usually

---

[12] A clear statement of hierarchy's stifling impact on communication is available in B. Gardner and D. A. Moore, *Human Relations in Industry* (Homewood, Ill.: Richard C. Irwin, Inc., 1955), pp. 89–101.

[13] For a differentiation between line and staff roles in various kinds of organizations, see Amitai Etzioni, "Authority Structure and Organizational Effectiveness," 4, *Administrative Science Quarterly* (June, 1959), pp. 43–67; for the difficulties that the research administrator has as a result of his unusual staff role, see Norman Kaplan, "The Role of the Research Administrator," 4, *Administrative Science Quarterly* (June, 1959), pp. 20–42.

have easier access to higher executives, which enhances their status and often makes the line operator suspicious and resentful. As a result, procedures originated by staff are sometimes watered down or subverted by line units. Central and field services of the same department have difficulty in communicating because of geographical diffusion and special interests. Communication between field services representing different bureaus is almost nonexistent, although here the problem is not always a matter of specialization but may be one of intent. Within a particular agency the various functional specialists find communication difficult because of terminology, background of training, and varying sociopolitical beliefs. Certain professions, very generally speaking, seem to develop distinct beliefs about the nature of man and government. As de Tocqueville and others have noted, lawyers (who have long dominated public administration) tend to have a rather conservative social view.[14] Again, those trained in the physical sciences are often less concerned with social and political developments than those trained in the humanities.

These opposing points of view impede communication. One need only consider the elaborate terminology which the various professions have developed to appreciate the problem. Modern bureaucracy undoubtedly requires specialization for maximum technical competence, but it is equally clear that the transmission of ideas suffers accordingly. Also, written communications are subject to interpretation by each group in the light of its particular set of attitudes. Ideas are sometimes distorted and redirected in the light of group expectations and values. Thus group experiences as well as those of individuals influence meaning. The resistance encountered in the attempt to unify the armed forces indicates the strength of group *esprit de corps* in defeating coordination and communication.

FORMAL COMMUNICATION

By formal communication we mean the rational, planned system of procedures and channels by which information flows through an organization, roughly along the lines of formal authority. Formal communication has three broad objectives: (1) to transmit policy decisions and instructions throughout the hierarchy (this is sometimes called the "flow of command"), (2) to bring back to management the suggestions, reports, and reactions of employees, and (3) to inform the rank and file of the over-all objectives of the organization. Despite the delay that results,

---

[14] Alexis de Tocqueville, *Democracy in America*, vol. I (New York: Alfred A. Knopf, Inc., 1945), pp. 272–80. See also Karl Mannheim, *Ideology and Utopia* (New York: Harcourt, Brace & Co., Inc., 1936), for an analysis of the impact of social influences on thought.

most observers agree that directives from the top should go through every level of the hierarchy. Bypassing the head of any subunit by giving orders directly to one of his subordinates encourages conflict and also keeps him in the dark as to activities within his own jurisdiction. Morale is probably hurt, since bypassing may be interpreted as a reflection upon the ability, discretion, and loyalty of those bypassed.[15] The extent of formal communication varies from agency to agency, depending upon such variables as size, age, and tradition. In the military, one finds extremely elaborate provisions that tend to restrict communication to formal channels. Information and orders closely follow the "chain of command." Procedural manuals enumerate in great detail the style, form, and routing of letters and directives. Communication and control are also increased by periodic reports from subordinates to their superiors throughout the hierarchy. Standardized forms and procedures exist for recruitment, discharge, physical examination, pay, and promotion. This standardization makes for thoroughness and a reasonable degree of efficiency but suffers necessarily from inflexibility. Other agencies, because of relatively small size, newness, or sustained effort by management, may be able to operate with a less detailed formal plan.

But all large organizations must provide some formal system for transmitting information and instructions. Usually information passes along the formal levels of authority. Obviously the amount of information that will be circulated is influenced greatly by the views of top and middle executives. Although decisions are influenced by individuals at every level, the important ones are usually formalized and released at the top. If executives feel that decisions should be made widely known, they are in a position to do so. This assumes, of course, that they can overcome the psychological and cultural obstacles mentioned previously. If they can, communication occurs through written directives sent along formal channels, in supervisory conferences, announcements at mass meetings, agency publications, and annual reports. Other formal media include organization manuals, the "paper flow" along designed channels, periodic reports, memoranda which are designed to provide a record of decisions, and oral communication at every level. Although oral communication often occurs between individuals in supervisory positions and is "formal" to that extent, it is more often a means of informal communication, cutting across lines of authority both vertically and horizontally.

[15] The various techniques of communication have been set down nicely in several texts and need not be summarized here. A competent source for such information is Charles Redfield's *Communication in Management* (2d ed.; Chicago: University of Chicago Press, 1958). Redfield's book also contains a comprehensive bibliography on various aspects of formal communication, most of which are at the practical, operating level.

The greatest problems in formal communication in federal administration probably arise between central and field offices. Opportunities for personal contacts are necessarily limited. There is sometimes friction between offices, based on an alleged lack of understanding of each other's problems. The proper division of authority is difficult to establish. Usually it is agreed that the center must make policy, but the problem of how much authority and discretion field units should assume in carrying out policy remains, and differences in the organization's mission, historical background, and the personalities concerned make generalization impossible.

INFORMAL COMMUNICATION

The information descending from the top and that brought back to management through what we have called "formal" channels is only a part, and probably not the most important part, of communication in organization. The nature of individual and group behavior means that informal communication will occur at every level. Informal media include the complete web of interpersonal contacts as well as the personal relationships occurring under the formal media. Communication on the basis of friendship, mutual confidence, and off-the-job associations always cuts across formal lines of command. Officials often rely upon personal friends in other agencies for information required to make decisions affecting their own organization. Decision making often involves drawing upon informal sources for information before a final judgment is made. The ability to short-circuit formal channels is thus a necessary and valuable art. This is why "knowing one's way about Washington" (or other government centers) is an important basic requirement for higher posts. At a lower level the suggestion-box system is used for bypassing official lines of communication, indicating that these lines are to some extent inhibitory. In sum, although informal communication may reflect inadequate information and may subvert decision making at identifiable "proper" levels, it also plays a necessary role in administration.

Government by Telephone. One of the characteristics of administration is the great dependence upon the telephone and personal communication to make decisions and to carry on the routine business of government. The following comment by General Vaughan, military aide to President Truman, is illustrative:

I suppose that if I have done this once I have done it 5,000 times in the Senator's office, and in the White House. A man will come to me and say, "Now, you don't know me, but I am a friend of so and so," and he'll mention a mutual acquaintance. "I don't want to bother you, but John Smith told me if

I got in a jam that you'd help me out. I've been here a week and I haven't seen anything but 15 receptionists and 47 assistant clerks."

Then I ask him what he wants and he says that he wants to see so and so. I think that looks like the Department of Commerce, so I call up somebody I know in Commerce and say, "There's a gentleman in my office who wants some information on such and such. Is that in your alley?" He'll say, "No, that's in Jones's office." I'll say, "Put him on," or I'll call Mr. Jones, and ask, "Could you see Mr. So and So?" "Why, sure, send him on up."[16]

When a specialist in the Department of State calls a friend in Commerce for estimates of the cost of packing plants and tanneries to transform cattle herds into a meat industry, informal coordination and communication have occurred. If he calls someone in Agriculture to get information on the potential markets for frozen meat, then calls someone in Commerce about the construction of a quick-freeze and storage plant and the facts about refrigerated transportation, coordination has again taken place.[17] Recently the hearings by the Subcommittee on Legislative Oversight on the federal regulatory agencies revealed that telephone calls and similar informal communications are among the common media used by business groups to influence commission decisions. The usual procedure is for the interest concerned to contact high officials, often at the Presidential level, to call commissioners directly on their behalf.[18] (For a detailed survey of this Subcommittee's findings, see Chapter 29.) The extent of such informal coordination is unlimited; its benefits in speed and more complete decision making are obvious, and despite any ethical implications, it is difficult to see how government could function without such practices.

Other Informal Media. Government by telephone illustrates both the functioning of informal communication and the many social needs it meets. Although it is often assumed that agency decisions are made in consultation among those in formal positions of authority and skill, these channels are often ignored or bypassed. Individuals build up associations over a period of time with officials in other agencies. Although these may begin on an official basis, they are continued and strengthened largely because of mutual respect and similar social attitudes. Individuals also bypass channels because of personal dislikes or lack of confidence in a particular administrator. There is no way of completely controlling individual behavior, regardless of the hierarchical system in organizations. Individuals will communicate horizontally, so to speak, across

[16] *U.S. News and World Report*, October 26, 1951, p. 25.

[17] James L. McCamy, *The Administration of American Foreign Affairs* (New York: Alfred A. Knopf, Inc., 1950), p. 136.

[18] Among others, see the *New York Times* at random during January, February, and June, 1958.

agency and authority lines to exchange information and opinions. This is inevitable because administration requires not only technical knowledge but also a "feel" for administration and personal relations. Experience in the general, informal way that policy is made, completely apart from the substantive questions involved, is a valuable asset.

It is important to recognize also that formal announcements of policy are merely the end product of considerable preliminary discussion, often carried on over lunch, or by telephone, or through *ad hoc* meetings. Official memoranda are usually written after a decision has been hammered out informally. They are prepared and distributed to participants mainly for the record. This informal incubation period is characteristic of most administrative behavior. Public offers of high positions in Washington, for example, are rarely made until the person sought has indicated his willingness to accept if asked. These rather obvious points suggest again that the common picture of decisions being arrived at formally by top-level conference is somewhat out of focus.

Informal communication serves many ends in addition to providing information. It enables an individual to bypass those he dislikes or whose judgment he questions. It may enable him to build a private empire in which he becomes powerful as a result of his informal role. Information can be deliberately "leaked" to press and radio to achieve desired results.[19] He can indulge his need for social relationships with persons of common interest. Administrators, after all, have all the problems, fears, and expectations that others have, and they meet them in similar ways. Thus certain modes of group behavior exist in organizations of all kinds. One of these is the custom of seeking assistance from personal friends in whom one has confidence. Formal channels of authority, even those as rigidly enforced as in the military, are unable to overcome this social characteristic.

COMMUNICATION AND COORDINATION

Communication and coordination are inseparable parts of administration. One may say that coordination is the end product of effective communication. Communication by itself is only an intermediate goal whose final end is the successful carrying out of programs. The number of units that an individual can coordinate (his so-called span of control) is determined in part by his ability to maintain communication with them.[20]

---

[19] For documentation on this and related techniques, see Douglas Cater, *The Fourth Branch of Government* (Boston: Houghton Mifflin Co., 1959).

[20] Some change has occurred here in that some firms, notably Sears, Roebuck and Co., have structured organization so that the executive's span of control is broadened, thereby increasing, it is assumed, the development of independence and initiative on the part of his subordinates

Similarly the size of subdivisions is greatly influenced by the limits of effective communication. The effectiveness of hierarchy, periodic conferences, staff agencies, and the other physical means of achieving coordination similarly depends upon achieving communication with those whom the administrator seeks to influence. For these reasons a word about coordination is in order.

Obviously the fact that most agencies are organized on a functional basis causes strong separatist tendencies in administration. Each agency tends to become immersed in the task for which it alone is responsible. It will work hard to enhance its own program through bigger appropriations and legislative sanctions. This means that conflict will exist between agencies. As James L. McCamy says, "Washington is a bear pit in which agencies spend much time gaining and protecting their claims to certain fields or work."

In addition, as we have seen, whirlpools of interest composed of client groups, legislative friends, and the public develop around certain agencies. These alignments aggravate the problem of coordination, placing a premium on temporary, minority-oriented solutions to complex problems. The great appeal of a central planning agency rests upon this facet of our national administrative system. A disinterested body with the resources and the power to formulate basic goals and integrate the entire administrative branch is a compelling prospect.[21] However, this is an extremely rational approach to public policy which neglects the fundamentally "political" character of administration. It flies in the face of competing values and interests held by individual agencies, Congress, interest groups, and many citizens: freedom from government controls, decentralization, the separation of powers dogma, and the belief that the problems facing a central planning agency are too complicated for the human mind to handle.

The problems of coordination remain. Size and specialization provide the greatest obstacles. Size and geographic dispersion make necessary written media which cannot achieve the precision of face-to-face communication. Size aggravates the problem by the sheer number of individuals and activities which must be focused toward a common end. In large organizations there is always someone who doesn't get the word. Size also breeds inertia because the individual often feels ineffectual and unimportant. He may regard organizational objectives with cynicism because of his remoteness and relative unimportance in the larger scheme. The inspirational quality that ideas had when created at the top is gone by the time they reach him. Meanwhile the specialist often acquires a vested interest in established procedures which reduces his

[21] W. Robert Parks, "Political and Administrative Guide-Lines in Developing Public Agricultural Policy," 33, *Journal of Farm Economics* (May, 1951), pp. 157–68.

willingness and ability to accept change. What, then, are the main ways of overcoming these problems?

Methods of Coordination. Major programs always involve relationships with different departments as well as various subdivisions within each department. They often cut across several levels of government, as do the foreign aid programs of the State Department. If the individuals and activities involved in such dissimilar programs are to work together, their efforts and skills must be synchronized. A willingness on the part of participating units to accept their assigned roles and the objectives of the over-all program is also required. A variety of inducements and sanctions is available to encourage this acceptance. The basic sanction is the authority of supervisors to discipline or dismiss those who fail to comply. Communications from the top carry *authority* as well as information. Subtle measures are also available. Generally, positive appeals are relied upon. Loyalty to the agency "mission," to one's professional standards and his moral responsibility to do a good job, as well as promotion and pay are the usual internal incentives to compliance. External sanctions also exist. These include client pressure, executive or congressional influence, and public attitudes. The maximum success of formal means of coordination and control, however, will probably be achieved by creating a widespread understanding of the "why" of the program. If all concerned know the personal, legal, and practical bases for major policy decisions and programs, they will inspire greater sensitivity and cooperation.

Several other means of coordination exist. Perhaps the basic one is organization itself and the lines of authority and responsibility which flow within its confines. The organization's structure, by placing skills, authority, and responsibility in certain patterns, limits and prescribes the decisions of all its members. Authority, as we have suggested, is the ultimate means of coordination. As military command organization illustrates, authority makes possible a centralization of decision making and a general scheme of operations which binds all members of an organization. Although lacking the degree of control enjoyed by the military, public agencies similarly concentrate authority, decision making, and planning toward the top in order to guide the efforts of their members toward agency goals. The smaller an agency is and the more clearly defined its principal objective, the more effectively authority can be used for coordination. On the other hand, competition for power and the diversity of functions existing within departments and bureaus make authority correspondingly more difficult to assert. The role of formal organization in achieving control will be discussed more fully in the chapters immediately following.

COORDINATION BY CONSENSUS. A more positive basis for coordination and control in big organizations is sometimes achieved by instilling in the organization's members a sense of common purpose. Psychologically the organization achieves something of the character of a *family*, closely knit, with a strong in-group feeling. (Attempts to achieve this condition are apparent in the use of the word "family" to describe organizations.) The resulting consensus as to the legitimacy and rationality of the organization's goals and methods results in high morale and motivation. While this climate is difficult to achieve, we all know organizations that have it; through a combination of tradition, accomplishment, in-group protective devices, shared values, exhortation and the like, the organization becomes a meaningful entity to its members, who identify with it and define their own participation in terms of its values.

The most effective way of achieving consensus is through a system of reciprocity in which an equilibrium between the individual's contributions and rewards is consciously sought by those who direct the organization. At the same time there are organizations, such as hospitals, churches, and perhaps most universities, where a sharp dysequilibrium between institutional demands and tangible individual rewards exists. In such cases the appeal to and the satisfaction of the individual's sense of service may be said to become part of his income. Such bases of motivation are too often underestimated, often by those who direct the organization and are themselves not always motivated and rewarded by such idealistic considerations.

COORDINATION BY CONFERENCE. At higher levels the principal centers of coordination include the Bureau of the Budget, personal assistants to the President, central staff agencies including the Council of Economic Advisers, the President's Cabinet, the Central Intelligence Agency, and powerful committees like the National Security Council. Within a particular department a variety of measures is used, but the primary avenue of coordination is the conference, which brings together the individuals and interests affected by a particular problem. The term "conference" means administrative or staff meetings called by executives to consider operating problems, to make decisions, and to integrate multiple-interest programs. The use of collective, expert judgment in administration has reduced considerably the role of any given individual in decision making. As a result the conference technique has become of considerable interest to research scientists.[22] Conference duties, for example, are said to take from one-quarter to one-half of the executive's time. This makes it worth while to analyze and improve the conference method.

[22] Martin Kriesberg and Harold Guetzkow, "The Use of Conferences in the Administrative Process," **10**, *Public Administration Review* (Spring, 1950), pp. 93–98.

Regular conferences are apparently helpful in encouraging subordinates to bring bad news to the top. We have seen that such information is often muzzled at lower levels. The informal nature of conferences seems to stimulate freedom of expression as individuals come to understand that their problems and mistakes are seen as neither unique nor a sign of personal inadequacy. This is perhaps another way of saying that personal, verbal communication is superior to written. Meanwhile, decision making is made more rational by bringing in the views of operating persons and other experts who know what is technically possible. The fact that collective responsibility is achieved seems another important advantage of the conference method. In critical decisions the person formally responsible (for example, President Truman in the case of the decision to use United States troops in Korea) probably finds a varying amount of psychological comfort in sharing morally, if not legally, his responsibility with others. In private management, as noted previously, the importance of top-level decisions that often involve long-range commitments and huge amounts of money has brought a similar dependence on group decisions. Furthermore, there is some evidence that groups are superior to individuals in solving complex and unusual problems.[23] Certainly, bringing to bear the best judgment of several experts—and rationality compels one to believe that there are experts—on a difficult problem such as, say, the methods of easing the 1957–58 recession, would seem to ensure a more intelligent policy solution.[24]

The execution of policy is also eased by the conference technique, which brings into the decision process those responsible for execution. Individuals generally cooperate more willingly in programs which they have helped shape. Meanwhile the over-all purposes of an agency are more easily kept in view by the conference method. A collective view tends to submerge partial goals. Motivation, too, is apparently increased by conferences. There are, of course, several levels of motivation, ranging from reluctant compliance to positive support for a program, each of which is probably sufficient to get the job done. But conferences evidently increase the chances of enthusiastic participation. This conclusion is supported by the discovery that morale and productivity are highest in units whose supervisors encouraged a maximum of participa-

---

[23] H. H. Kelley and J. W. Thibaut, "Experimental Studies of Group Problem Solving and Process," in G. Lindzey (ed.), *Handbook of Social Psychology*, Cambridge: Addison-Wesley Publishing Co., Inc., 1954, chap. xxi. However, for a rigorous study which concludes that group decision making via brainstorming *inhibits* effective thinking, see D. W. Taylor, "Does Group Participation When Using Brainstorming Facilitate or Inhibit Creative Thinking?" 3, *Administrative Science Quarterly* (June, 1958), pp. 23–47.

[24] This judgment must be qualified, for many of the criticisms of the "organization man" theme also apply to decision making by committee: Harry A. Kissinger, "The Policymaker and the Intellectual," 20, *The Reporter* (March 5, 1959), pp. 30–35.

tion in decision making. In sum, the conference technique is clearly superior to written communication in promoting coordination. Command or authority has by comparison several negative implications. Command generates only a minimal sense of responsibility. People prefer to be asked rather than be told to do things. Either will probably work; it is a matter of relative effectiveness. While organizational structure itself is also an instrument of coordination, something more is needed to galvanize organizations into action. The communication of agency objectives, policy decisions, and the means of carrying them out seems to supply this need.

BIBLIOGRAPHY

CARNAP, RUDOLF. *The Logical Syntax of Language.* New York: 1946.

CHERRY, COLIN. *On Human Communication.* Cambridge: 1957.

"Communications and Social Action," **25**, *Annals of the American Academy of Political and Social Science* (March, 1947).

DORSEY, JOHN T. "A Communications Model for Administration," **2**, *Administrative Science Quarterly* (December, 1957).

KATZ, ELIHU. *Personal Influence: The Part Played by People in the Flow of Mass Communication.* Glencoe, Ill.: 1955.

HAYAKAWA, S. I. *Language in Action.* New York: 1947.

LASSWELL, HAROLD D., CASEY, RALPH D., and SMITH, BRUCE L. *Propaganda, Communications, and Public Opinion.* Princeton: 1946.

MORRIS, CHARLES W. *Sign Language and Behavior.* New York: 1946.

REDFIELD, CHARLES E. *Communication in Management.* Chicago: 1958.

SCHRAMM, WILBUR LANG. *Responsibility in Mass Communication.* New York: 1957.

SHEPARD, C. "The Relation Between Selected Interpersonal Variables and Communication Effectiveness," **18**, *Sociometry* (May, 1955).

CHAPTER 8

The Political Role of Higher Administrators

At the higher levels the administrator has a vital role of inter-action with the several publics that affect and are affected by his agency. This political role pays off in terms of agency appropriations, programs, popular support, and survival probabilities. Administrators must build support among their various publics, and this is a continuing process, since popular good will and legislative support require sustained cultivation. This political aspect of administration is often neglected, partly in deference to the assumed separation of administration and politics, partly because it raises questions about the folklore of democratic government, and partly, one suspects, because of a tendency to confine ourselves mainly to descriptive analyses of administration. All this notwithstanding, it is clear enough that administration demands certain political skills that are no less vital than the traditional areas of finance, personnel and organization analysis. In this chapter we shall analyze this aspect of public administration.

It is well to note that we are not concerned here with normative judgments about the propriety of the political activities discussed. One man's Picasso is another man's poison, and each of us tends to feel that some agencies and interest groups are "good" and others "bad," in terms of certain subjective value premises. In this chapter we are only concerned with suggesting characteristic kinds of "political" behavior of higher administrators. The examples are chosen at random, for illustrations showing similar activities on the part of other administrators and agencies could equally well have been used. The other point is that high officials must play a political role in marshalling support for their programs. A "good" administrator is one who gets things done, and such political, support-building activity is a necessary means to this end.

POLITICS IN ADMINISTRATION

As noted earlier, there is a tendency in our separation-of-powers system for agencies to build alliances with various groups within and outside government. Such alliances strengthen the agency's bargaining position and give it the base of popular support necessary to carry out its programs. They enable the agency to escape control by the chief executive and in some cases, by the department secretary and even their bureau chief. At the federal level this condition is encouraged by the fact that departments and bureaus are largely staffed by permanent officials, whereas legislatures, chief executives, department secretaries, and some bureau chiefs are subject to removal as political fortunes change. This means that some agencies actually do not "need" their political chiefs; they prefer instead to place their faith in legislative committees and interest groups whose tenure is more secure and whose interests tend to remain stable despite changing Administrations.

This political role is evident at state and local levels as well. The city manager, for example, is an executive whose job uniquely depends upon maintaining rapport with his council. Turnover among managers results mainly from poor relations with councilmen.[1] It is equally clear that the manager must play a political role insofar as interest groups in his city are concerned. There is some disagreement as to whether he should play an active role in promoting policy programs, but at least one highly successful manager believes that the manager has a responsibility, based upon his special knowledge and his responsibility for public service, to provide such leadership.[2] The extent of the political activity of city managers in larger cities is apparent in the Cambridge city manager case, where the manager is shown to function in a great variety of institutional and political alliances, all of which affect his own administrative role.[3]

MAINTAINING RELATIONS WITH LEGISLATORS

Career administrators at the higher level have the job of maintaining good relationships with strategically placed legislators, particularly those who sit on committees that consider either the appropriations requests of the agency or substantive measures that, if passed, will fall within the agency's program area. What are some of the ways that such relationships are maintained? Personnel appointments are important, since appointments are the basis of the legislator's political machine. Political "pros" do not usually work for the mere satisfaction of seeing their candidate

[1] George K. Floro, "Continuity in City-Manager Careers," 61, *American Journal of Sociology* (November, 1955), pp. 240–46.

[2] C. A. Harrell and D. G. Weiford, "The City Manager and the Policy Process," 19, *Public Administration Review* (Spring, 1959), pp. 101–7.

[3] Frank C. Abbott, "The Cambridge City Manager," in H. Stein (ed.), *Public Administration and Policy Development* (New York: Harcourt, Brace & Co., 1952), pp. 573–620.

put into office; they seek more tangible rewards. This is sometimes done by securing positions for them in the unclassified service. If this service is not large enough, it can sometimes be expanded. For example, on December 1, 1954, the Eisenhower administration removed all deputy marshal positions from the classified, "merit" system, placing them in the excepted Schedule B category.

Obviously it is difficult to draw a line between high level positions of a "political" character and those which are "career." The second Hoover Commission set down six types of positions as properly in the "political" executive group:[4]

1. Heads of departments and agencies and deputy heads.
2. Assistant secretaries and assistant heads of agencies.
3. Department solicitors or general counsels.
4. Heads of departmental staff offices concerned with policy.
5. Heads of departmental information offices.
6. Political aides and assistants to political executives.

Insofar as "career" executives were concerned, the Commission set down the following categories:[5]

1. Administrative assistant secretaries and equivalent positions.
2. Heads and members of departmental staff offices concerned with organic matters.
3. Deputy heads and other members of departmental staff offices concerned with substantive policy.
4. Chiefs of line (or operating) bureaus.
5. Assistant bureau chiefs, division chiefs, and others at lower levels.
6. Heads of regional or district field offices.
7. Professional (career) aides and assistants.

While such categories leave many questions unanswered, they are helpful for our immediate purpose of analyzing the "political" role of the higher civil servants. These are the general types of positions, both "political" and "career," that seem to require quite similar political skills and behaviors.[6] The Hoover Commission's findings on the number of such positions in the federal system are shown in Table 4.[7]

According to the estimates of the second Hoover Commission, there are approximately 755 high-level "political" administrative positions at

[4] Commission on Organization of the Executive Branch of the Government, *Task Force Report on Personnel and Civil Service* (Washington, D.C.: U.S. Government Printing Office, 1955), pp. 15–19.

[5] *Ibid.*, pp. 20–25.

[6] *Ibid.*, p. 16.

[7] Among others, see M. Bernstein (ed.), *The Job of the Federal Executive* (Washington, D.C.: Brookings Institution, 1958), chaps. viii, ix; P. T. David and Ross Pollock, *Executives for Government* (Washington, D.C.: Brookings Institution, 1957), pp. 121–31.

TABLE 4

POLITICAL, EXECUTIVE, AND CAREER ADMINISTRATOR GROUPS
IN THE FEDERAL GOVERNMENT
(APPROXIMATE IN ALL AGENCIES)

Political Executives

1. Heads and deputy heads of departments and agencies	230
2. Assistant heads of agencies (except administrative assistant secretaries)	125
3. Heads of "substantive" staff units	40
4. Heads of departmental information offices	50
5. Political aides and assistants to political executives	300
6. General managers of boards and commissions	10
Total	755

Career Executives

1. Administrative secretaries (or equivalent positions)	60
2. Heads and deputy heads of "organic" staff offices	250
3. Deputy heads of "substantive" staff offices	40
4. Chiefs of bureaus	350
5. Assistant bureau chiefs and division chiefs	2000
6. Regional and district office directors	1000
7. Career civil servants, aides, and assistants	300
Total	4000

SOURCE: Commission on Organization of the Executive Branch of the Government, *Personnel and Civil Service* (Washington, D.C.: U.S. Government Printing Office, 1955).

the federal level. These are the strategic positions, which not only enable the victorious party to effect its policies but also amply reward the incumbent for the support given the party or the legislator concerned. In addition, there are the patronage appointments, including such jobs as positions on the independent regulatory commissions, minor judgeships, federal marshalcies, postmasterships of a certain level, ambassadorships, ministerships, and staff positions on *ad hoc* committees. By consulting with legislators and appointing men whom they recommend, the department concerned is able to repay past favors and create obligations for future ones.

Legislators need publicity to keep their names before their constituents and to signalize their efforts on behalf of their state or district. This political necessity provides another avenue for administrators to mend their political fences. This is often done by tacit agreement that important news releases concerning department or agency affairs will be released through the relevant legislator's office. This not only gives the latter publicity but also enables him to share in the achievement announced by the news release. Cordell Hull remarked on his efforts to ensure that legislators got all the information they wished; "I made it a rule at the State Department that, when requests from Congressmen presented difficult questions, I should be informed. I then got in personal contact with the Members of Congress immediately interested."[8] He adds, "in other instances where the questions involved technical subjects, I sent the Department experts to the Congressional committees concerned, generally accompanied by such key men as an Assistant Secretary or the head of a division."[9]

Since legislators find it difficult to get the information necessary to make informed judgments on many aspects of government policy, they are dependent upon and grateful for information provided by the administrators. As suggested in Chapter 29 on legislative scrutiny of administration, they are often frustrated and somewhat helpless in trying to oversee such activities. Nevertheless, when they do select an issue and worry it sufficiently, the legislators can dig out information.

Harold Ickes, Secretary of Interior for thirteen years during the Roosevelt administration, shows that higher administrators are very sensitive to legislative wishes:

Most of the Cabinet meeting today was taken up with a discussion of the complaints of the Congressmen covering their treatment in the various departments, especially in the matter of patronage. A Committee appointed by the recent Democratic House caucus spent an hour or more with the President just before Cabinet meeting relating the woes of themselves and their colleagues. They complained of harsh treatment at the hands of the executives, of being shoved from pillar to post, of brusque and irresponsive letters, and, of course, of lack of consideration in the matter of appointments. . . . I suppose that all of us become overstrained at times and are brusque and lacking in courtesy. In the matter of letters, however, I do think that this Department has a good record. Except for a few form letters I sign all communications to Senators, Congressmen, and governors, and other important public persons."[10]

Occasionally some career official, because of special personal qualities and experience, becomes in effect his department's liaison man with Congress and other influential interests. In the Truman administration, then Assistant Secretary of Interior Oscar Chapman became a "salesman" for the Department's policies both with Congress and the public.[11]

---

[8] *The Memoirs of Cordell Hull* (New York: The Macmillan Co., 1948), pp. 214–15.

[9] *Ibid.*, p. 215.

[10] *The Secret Diary of Harold L. Ickes* (New York: Simon & Schuster, Inc., 1953), pp. 143–44.

[11] "Triumph of the Empire Builders," *Fortune* (February, 1952), p. 179. While alarmist and highly selective, this article gives one a broad picture of public administration's scope and significance. The following example is taken from the magazine's evaluation of Interior activities: "The Geological Service's performance in cartography, particularly in rapid reconnaissance mapping, has been first rate; the Bureau of Mines has done exemplary work in safety and in the development of mineral and fuel substitutes; and new legions of hunters can thank the Fish and

His ability to conciliate Congressmen hostile to the Department's public lands program and its public power projects proved invaluable, and Interior's appropriations and influence grew steadily, culminating in the Department's active (although unsuccessful) role in the Tidelands issue involving the exploitation and conservation of vital oil resources.

State Department Example. About 1950 the State Department, whose relations with Congress have rarely been cordial, took steps to establish better liaison with the legislators. Some time before this, a new position was established in the Department, that of Assistant Secretary for Congressional Relations. Such a post had been recommended by the first Hoover Commission, which mentioned the need for better communication in view of "recent events [which] have changed the situation and made the Congress a much more significant and regular participant in foreign affairs." A series of meetings was held for selected Congressmen during which Department officials briefed them on foreign policy. Although this irritated certain legislators and resulted in criticism in the press, it did have useful results. In reply to the Chairman of the House Committee on Lobbying Activities, the first incumbent of the new position, Mr. Jack K. McFall, outlined several of the Department's "new approaches:"[12]

1. A program was instituted by my office to have the Assistant Secretaries of the State Department and their principal assistants call on the 165 Members of Congress who traveled abroad during the 1949 recess.
2. On the opening day of the present session I personally wrote to every Member of Congress placing the services of my office and, of course, myself at the complete disposal of the Congressmen and their staffs.
4. (*Sic.*) There is now in progress a program of visits and discussions between members of Congress and their Foreign Service officer constituents which, from the Department's point of view, we regard as a most healthy relationship. Foreign Service personnel from all corners of the earth are now making the Hill a port of call between assignments abroad and their Congressmen are discovering the great majority of them are still good examples of people back home. Of course, "back home" is where we recruit Foreign Service personnel, but if we hadn't done something by way of proving it the rumor might persist indefinitely that we grew them on some enchanted island.

Wildlife Service for a game population that has kept up with their own numbers. But on the vital matters of water, land, and electricity—areas where decisions must be made and maintained in the furnace heat of controversy—a hundred examples of greed, indecisions, and anarchy arise. These shortcomings, rather than its more passive functions, reveal the true character and influence of the Department of the Interior today."

[12] House Select Committee on Lobbying Activities, 81st Cong., 2d sess., *Hearings*. Part 10: "Legislative Activities of Executive Agencies," (Washington, D.C.: U.S. Government Printing Office, 1950), pp. 450–57.

5. The Department has endeavored at all times to render the greatest possible service and assistance to the Committees and the individual Congressmen in the preparation for their travel and their movement in foreign countries.

6. We have presented . . . a series of briefings on current world problems to which we have invited as many of the administrative assistants and secretarial assistants of the Members of Congress as time would permit—both our time and their own—during the present session. . . . Altogether, about 150 staff assistants to Members of Congress have attended one of the types of functions indicated.

7. On the Senate side our Senate liaison officer, Horace Smith, has staged, at his personal expense, a series of briefing luncheons for smaller groups of Senators and State Department officials throughout the session.

8. We started a program this session, and would hope to extend it considerably next session, of briefings for the congressional delegations of the various States, thus enabling us to concentrate on the clarification and consideration of many local and regional problems which stem from the implementation of our foreign policies.

Last named, but not least in import, of the new programs my office has initiated, is the series of informal gatherings of State Department officials held at Prospect House in Georgetown with Members of Congress and staff assistants to congressional committees as our guests. Four of these "get-acquainted" meetings have been held to date. . . .

It should be made clear that all of these described activities are in a sense incidental to, but an important incident of the primary function of my office, which is to assume responsibility for, and management of the legislative program of the President and the State Department in the field of foreign affairs. When it is considered that during the past session of Congress the State Department had some degree of interest, running from remote to vital, in 48 per cent of the total of 10,600 bills, public and private, introduced in that session, some idea is conveyed of the nature and volume of this managerial responsibility.

We have seen how the administrator's knowledge and experience is helpful to legislators in policy making. Such influence is exerted in many ways, most common of which is probably before committees when bills are considered. Here again, mutual interests, experiences, and knowledge permits the administrator and the legislative committee to develop alliances which the administrator can use to further his agency's program and to build good will for its future activities.

It is also possible for agencies with nationally organized field units to mobilize popular support for a particular measure. The Extension Service in the Department of Agriculture has such a network of offices, which enables it to bring pressure upon Congress when this seems necessary. Agencies with mass constituencies, such as the Veterans Administration and the Post Office Department have a large "electorate" of their own, which can subject Congress to pressure when services are curtailed. Some agencies, such as the FBI and the Passport Division of the

State Department, apparently have no need for such patent devices, since Congress tends to treat them most considerately without such influence. On the other hand, agencies such as the State Department or the U.S. Information Services, which have neither a mass constituency nor a reservoir of congressional good will, do not always fare well before Congress. Sometimes this is a result of the political ineptitude of their leaders, as seems to have been the case in USIS when Arthur Larsen was Director. Although Larsen was unable to secure congressional support, while his successor George V. Allen was able to do so, Allen apparently had more of the "political" qualities that ensure successful relations with Congress.

There is evidence that administrators carry on considerable lobbying before Congress, and that they are expected to. For example, the Chairman of the House Select Committee on Lobbying Activities stated, "the executive agencies have a definite requirement to express views to Congress, to make suggestions, to request needed legislation, to draft proposed bills or amendments, and so on."[13] His approval of such activity is implied by his dictum, "It is very easy to talk about . . . 'flagrant lobbying' by Government agencies, but I hope we will not be making such statements here unless we can document them fully."[14]

A most interesting example of administrative lobbying on an intergovernmental level is the New York State Power Authority's activities before Congress in a successful effort to obtain a license to develop the Niagara River's power potential.[15] For six years following a treaty between the United States and Canada in 1950 for the joint development of the Niagara site, Congress held hearings in an effort to decide between the advocates of public and private power. Some unusual alliances appeared, including one between the Authority and Governor Dewey, a staunch Republican, who appeared before Congress advocating public development of the site. John Burton, Dewey's appointee as Chairman of the Authority, also appeared in favor of public construction, although he believed that this should be under state rather than federal aegis as proposed by President Truman, who felt that the Corps of Engineers should handle the project.[16] Robert Moses, Burton's

[13] House Select Committee on Lobbying Activities, 81st Cong., 2d sess., *Hearings.* Part 10: "Legislative Activities of Executive Agencies," p. 2.

[14] *Ibid.*, p. 3.

[15] The following data are from an unpublished seminar paper by S. Kenneth Howard, "The Politics of the New York State Power Authority," Cornell University, 1959.

[16] Senate Subcommittee of the Committee on Public Works, 82nd Cong., 1st sess., *Hearings*, "Niagara Falls and The Niagara River, New York" (Washington, D.C.: U.S. Government Printing Office, 1951); House Subcommittee on Rivers and Harbors, Committee on Public Works, 82nd Cong., 1st sess., *Hearings*, "Niagara Power Development" (Washington, D.C.: U.S. Government Printing Office, 1951).

successor as Chairman of the Authority, also appeared before Congress, advocating public development and quick Congressional action. Moses deplored the "page advertisements and misrepresentations . . ." sponsored by five New York private utility companies.[17] Moses also censured the McGraw-Hill Publishing Company who, he argued, had put pressure on one of their vice-presidents to refuse reappointment to the Power Authority because of the firm's close financial ties with the five utility companies.[18] Meanwhile a vigorous campaign for private development was carried on by the five private utility firms in New York, supported by local chambers of commerce and some citizen groups.

Finally, fate entered to accomplish what neither Washington nor Albany seemed able to do. On June 7, 1956, a rockslide demolished the Niagara-Mohawk Company's power plant at Niagara Falls. Power was available only at higher rates from Canadian plants, with the result that local groups began to demand a solution to the extended controversy. Niagara–Mohawk, which had previously been the spokesman for the five utilities, came to terms with the Power Authority, which agreed in return to supply the private company with power equal to its commercial needs in the area. Finally, on August 2, 1957, after considerable legal wrangling, a compromise bill was passed which authorized the Power Authority to build the Niagara power plant. However, power produced at Niagara was to be divided equally between public and private consumers, and private utilities were to buy the power at the switchboard for resale at commercial rates.[19]

MAINTAINING RELATIONS WITH INTEREST GROUPS

Broadly speaking, most federal departments are established on a functional basis which gives them a built-in representative character for the interests concerned. This means that the higher officials of such departments and agencies are appointed by the dominant interest groups in the economic sector represented. It may be more accurate to say that such officials will rarely be appointed without the approval of such interest groups. Thus higher administrators are the spokesmen for a peculiar constituency, and their behavior and the programs of their agency must be analyzed in this context. In Labor, for example, no Cabinet member, and presumably none of his top career aides, will be assigned without the participation of the AFL–CIO. In the so-called independent regulatory commissions, the industries concerned have a

17 *Ibid.*, 83d Cong., 1st sess. *Hearings* (Washington, D.C.: U.S. Government Printing Office, 1953).

18 Senate Committee on Public Works, 83d Cong., 2d sess., *Hearings*, "Niagara Falls Power Development" (Washington, D.C.: U.S. Government Printing Office, 1954).

19 "Niagara Goes to Work at Last," *Business Week* (August 17, 1957).

hand in the appointment of Commissioners. The extent of their influence in such appointments is sometimes all too clearly revealed, as for example, when a recent Presidential nominee for Director of the Bureau of Mines testified before a Congressional Committee that he was against mine safety legislation. Further, as we shall see, members of the Federal Communications Commission have felt no compunction about accepting travel expenses, honoraria, and hotel accommodations from the broadcasting industry.

Alliance of Interests. Such conditions suggest the close relations that exist between the bureaucracy and the major organized groups in society. As a result, important legislation sponsored by the agency will reflect and may often be drafted by the interests which the agency represents. Some observers believe that out of the attending competition among such groups, an equilibrium results which reflects as closely as possible in an imperfect world the "public interest." This view is influenced by classical economic theory, which holds that unrestricted individual competition culminates in the public interest. Whatever the validity of such a view, it is clear that this process of bargaining for a share of public funds and programs describes the reality fairly well. Although the greatest pressure is probably exerted upon legislators, the bureaucrats who share public power are also the target of group efforts at persuasion.

In the promotion of legislation we often see an alliance between the administrative agency concerned and various private groups whose interests coincide with that of the agency.[20] This fusion between private and public interests is so pervasive and complete that it is difficult to differentiate one from the other. In some cases, of course, the differences in interest between and among the groups within any given sector are so great or diverse that mobilization by the agency is a difficult process. Business and agriculture, for example, are splintered into many conflicting groups, making unified action or cooperation difficult. On the other hand, such groups and interests as veterans, mass communications, stockbrokers and investment houses, labor and public health are more self-conscious and cohesive. They may be called "clientele" groups in that they become the major group serviced by the administrative agency.[21]

The instruments of alliance between the agency and its clientele are varied and complex. They include the mobilization of support for a par-

[20] This general theme is developed in J. L. Freeman, "The Bureaucracy in Pressure Politics," in D. C. Blaisdell (ed.), "Unofficial Government: Pressure Groups and Lobbies," 319, *Annals of the American Academy of Political and Social Science* (September, 1958), pp. 10–19. See also, D. C. Blaisdell, *American Democracy Under Pressure* (New York: The Ronald Press Co., 1957).

[21] For an excellent selection of readings concerning such groups, see Henry A. Turner, *Politics in the United States* (New York: McGraw-Hill Book Co., Inc., 1955), pp. 73–208.

ticular program, exercised vis-à-vis Congress; agency sponsorship and participation in meetings and conferences that discuss proposed policy directions in a given sector; articles and speeches by agency officials seeking support of such policies; and obtaining Presidential approval, publicly expressed, for proposals in which the agency and its clientele groups are interested. As noted earlier, clientele groups participate in the selection of high officials in their respective service agencies, and this ensures over time a sympathetic posture toward their problems and interests. Continuity is given such alliances by the fact that while administrations and political figures come and go, the essential economic interests of the various groups remain consistent, so that the bulk of the agency's personnel are clear as to its major mission and reservoirs of public support.

A good example of the kinds of liaison between public agencies and groups interested in a given policy is the case of the Federal Security Administration (now part of the Department of Health, Education, and Welfare) and its cooperation with a private organization, the National Health Assembly, Inc. An outgrowth of this cooperation was a conference sponsored by the Assembly to promote a ten-year plan for health in the United States, prepared by the FSA at the request of President Truman. In testifying before the House Committee on Lobbying Activities, Oscar R. Ewing, Federal Security Administrator, said in this regard:

What that [National Health Assembly, Inc.] was formed for, Mr. [Congressman] Brown, was the President in the spring of 1948 asked me to develop a 10-year program for health in the United States, research, hospitals, diagnostic clinics, medical education, all of that. I decided that the best way to get that going was to have a conference at which the experts would be called in to do it. We had that conference here. Now, there were not— we could not finance a great part of that. The amount that would have been proper Federal expenditure was very small. So we organized that as a charitable corporation to pay the expenses of that conference. That was done, there were to be contributions made to it, of, I believe, around $45,000 . . .[22]

Mr. Ewing's reception was something less than cordial, since he was advocating a form of "national health insurance" which the legislators insisted upon calling "socialized medicine." He was subjected to sharp questioning about an official trip to England to study "socialized medicine" and about the then pending Murray–Wagner–Dingell bill which would have considerably increased the federal government's role in health care. Another tactic of public agencies was also apparent in the National Health Assembly's contract with Harper Brothers to publish a book, *America's Health—A Report to the Nation by the National Health*

---

[22] House Select Committee on Lobbying Activities, 81st Cong., 2d sess., *Hearings.* Part 10: "Legislative Activities of Executive Agencies," pp. 356–57.

Assembly. This publication comprised the proceedings of the conference mentioned above, and was designed to ensure widespread dissemination of the debates, meetings and recommendations of the Conference.

American agriculture, too, has usually maintained close public-private relations. Although there is a split between the so-called conservative, prosperous large-farm group membership of the Farm Bureau Federation and the liberal, family-farm, group symbolized by the Farmers Union, each has had "representatives" within the Department of Agriculture. Perhaps the best illustration of agency relations with a private interest is the alliance between the Extension Service of the Department and the Farm Bureau Federation. Again, as Grant McConnell shows, the TVA has been heavily influenced by the Farm Bureau, particularly during the term of Harcourt Morgan, one of the governors of the corporation, who "had a free hand with the agricultural program [and] as the former president of a land grant college . . . made the greatest possible use of the extension services and enforced the fullest possible decentralization."[23] The "cooptation" of the TVA that followed has been documented by others.[24] The Farm Bureau Federation's support of the extension services administered through the land grant state universities includes defining and supporting extension's role, as well as bringing pressure to curtail the programs and appropriations of other agricultural agencies that threaten the extension services, such as New Deal agencies like AAA.[25] As Edward A. O'Neal, long-time president of the FBF told assembled county agents of the extension service, "Why break up a good team; I used to fight your battles in Washington when you didn't have another damned fool to fight them for you."[26]

MAINTAINING RELATIONS WITH THE UNORGANIZED PUBLIC

The building of popular support is a constant element in the administrative drama. This is because, as James Forrestal remarked to a friend, "the difficulty of government work is that it not only has to be well done, but the public has to be convinced that it is being well done. In other words, there is a necessity for both competence and exposition. . . ."[27] Administrative agencies live in a precarious environment in

[23] *The Decline of Agrarian Democracy* (Berkeley: University of California Press, 1953), p. 124.

[24] Philip Selznick, *TVA and the Grass Roots* (Berkeley: University of California Press, 1949).

[25] Charles M. Hardin, *The Politics of Agriculture* (Glencoe, Ill.: The Free Press, 1952), chaps. iii, ix, xv.

[26] *Ibid.*, p. 37.

[27] Walter Millis and E. S. Duffield (eds.), *Forrestal Diaries* (New York: The Viking Press, 1951), p. 300.

which the currents of public favor are ever changing. The strength of clientele groups may decline; powerful friends in the legislature may be defeated; a new party may come to power, motivated by values which threaten existing programs; worst of all, perhaps, the objective conditions of depression, emergency, or war which ensured agency survival may change, to be followed by circumstances in which its skills are no longer needed. An effective counterpoise is a viable base of popular support which can provide strength in a moment of crisis.

The Administrative Lobby. The New Deal marked the beginning of a trend in which public agencies devoted systematic efforts to increasing popular knowledge and understanding of their far-flung activities. Perhaps for the first time there existed a favorable psychological climate for the selling of government services. Public administration took the offensive, and the new agencies established information sections and hired newspaper men in unprecedented number. Old line agencies, meanwhile, began to see the advantages of support building. The State Department, particularly, adopted a more positive attitude toward public relations. In general the impetus was provided by new functions which required, in turn, the development of new public attitudes and understandings. The strains and insecurity of the depression era made the acceptance of change relatively easy. The National Recovery Administration, under the direction of General Hugh Johnson, initiated the largest "selling" campaign in recent history. A Senate investigating committee, alarmed by the trend, in 1936 found the following publicity activity in the executive branch: 4,900 news releases from public offices, 7,000,000 copies of printed materials, mailing lists of over 2,000,000 names, and 533 films available for public distribution. The materials ranged from unobjectionable releases of an informational nature to self-laudatory blurbs designed to make up people's minds for them or to picture an agency as perfect. The Brookings Institution estimated that the annual cost of publicity activities in the federal government was approximately $1,000,000.

By 1948, mainly because of the phenomenal expansion of government's role, the Bureau of the Budget estimated that 45,000 persons were engaged directly or indirectly in dispensing publicity and information. Their salaries amounted to $13,043,452 annually. The Government Printing Office issued some 60,000,000 copies of government literature at a cost of $50,000,000 a year. In 1951 a subcommittee of the House Committee on Expenditures in the Executive Departments reported on an investigation of publicity activities in agriculture, housing, universal military service, federal housing, and reclamation. After fifteen months of study, the Committee chairman, Representative Harness, concluded that the most influential lobby in Washington was the administrative lobby. He warned, moreover, that "whether the immediate purpose of Government propaganda is good or bad, the fact remains that individual liberty and free institutions cannot long survive when the vast power of the Government may be marshaled against the people to perpetuate a given policy or a particular group of office holders."[28]

Other observers were less pessimistic. In 1950 the House Committee on Lobbying Activities devoted four days to the activities of the federal government and concluded that "the existing law in this field . . . provide[s] adequate means for ascertaining and checking any abuses of the executive role in the legislative process."[29] The majority report of the Committee held, furthermore, that Congress needed information from the administrative side, and justified agency lobbying by maintaining that "government cannot be captive to the narrow force of private interest, that responsible public policy cannot be the product of willy-nilly submission to the demands of whatever group has the largest material resources at its disposal."[30]

The rationale of public agencies is that their role in policy determination requires that the executive branch must consult and advise Congress on legislative considerations of many kinds. In addition, departments and agencies have an obligation to keep the public informed of their programs and to provide extensive information services through all possible channels. This obligation is specifically recognized by Congress in several acts. For example, "there shall be at the seat of the Government a Department of Agriculture, the general design and duties of which shall be to acquire and to diffuse among the people of the United States useful information on subjects of agriculture, in the most general and comprehensive sense of that word . . ."[31] Again, "the administration of Civil Aeronautics is empowered to collect and disseminate information relative to civil aeronautics . . ."[32]

Administrative Public Relations. Both government and private industry have in recent times become increasingly conscious of the need for public support. The public relations man has become an accepted part of every organization. His objective is to create an attitude of public respect, confidence, and approval toward his organization. Government's task is usually difficult, especially in a period of prosperity such as that of the past decade. Although the development of atomic energy, the threat of a third world war, and the greater demand for economic se-

[28] Cited in *Congressional Digest*, May, 1951, p. 142.
[29] *Ibid.*, pp. 139–40.
[30] *Ibid.*, p. 140.
[31] 5 U.S.C. 511.
[32] 49 U.S.C. 456.

curity following World War II have increased popular dependence upon government, depression and unemployment, which made government's expanding role during the 1930's virtually unquestioned, are absent. Public administration, as a result, must fight a continual battle with the legislative branch for funds to maintain its information program. Congress tends to regard official publicity as somehow immoral and unjustifiable. But despite the resistance of Congress and state legislatures, administrative public relations continue to flourish.

THE STATE DEPARTMENT'S PROGRAM. Formal public relations systems are illustrated by the Department's Press Relations Office and Office of Public Affairs. The practices of such agencies are not unusual. In every department, one finds an "information" division in which the news that is released is often prepared by those who release it. News items are not only carefully selected and written, but they are timed to achieve the maximum strategic advantage, and almost never will they reveal information detrimental to the agency concerned unless that news is thought bound to come out in any event. The publicity function, moreover, is centralized so that conflicting statements are kept to a minimum. While the deliberate "leaking" of information to gain public support for a particular policy is not uncommon, in the main it is recognized that a consistent public image requires systematic control of news releases.

In the Department of State, the Special Assistant to the Secretary of State for Press Relations distributes about one thousand releases a year, makes available the speeches and statements of departmental officials, advises these officials on what questions they may anticipate from the press, and arranges conferences for them with Washington correspondents.[33] More broadly, his function is to prepare the public mind for the announcement of United States foreign policy. The nature of policy determination is such that new policies will often come as a surprise to the public. This is because foreign policy usually cannot follow popular opinion but must lead it. As McCamy says, "for the conduct of foreign relations, the executive officials of the Federal Government, together with the organized groups that take an interest and the members of Congress . . . form an elite that makes the decisions in the name of the sovereign masses."[34] This means that the Department's public relations officials will often be concerned with preparing the public for the announcement of a new policy and then building up popular support after it has been enunciated.

---

[33] W. P. Davison, "More than Diplomacy," in Lester Markel *et al., Public Opinion and Foreign Policy* (New York: Harper & Bros., 1949), p. 132.

[34] James McCamy, *The Administration of American Foreign Affairs* (New York: Alfred A. Knopf, Inc., 1951), p. 319.

To do this, the Department's Public Liaison Division maintains contact with over six hundred citizens' groups whose members presumably accept and spread its policies. Printed materials are provided these organizations, speakers are recommended, and subjects are made available for discussion. A series of *Pocket Pamphlets and Foreign Affairs Outlines*, which summarize the United States' position on vital questions such as land reform or German rearmament, are issued to promote understanding and support. The Division also answers inquiries from individuals, provides general information for scholars, and encourages organizations of several kinds to promote the reading of departmental publications.

Meanwhile the Office of Public Affairs holds conferences twice a year, to which representatives of selected groups are invited.[35] High officials of the department discuss specific world problems and the Department's policies and programs in regard to them. Expert discussion of specific topics is carried on through a series of panels. The conferences serve a dual purpose: They not only enable the Department to inform and enlist the support of selected "opinion leaders," but they also provide an opportunity for evaluation and suggestions by individuals who have a particular interest in foreign affairs. The round-table procedure and the discussion periods that follow the remarks of major officials provide an informal atmosphere which encourages frank statements of opinion. Sustained relations with the interest groups who keep a watchful eye on departmental activity are maintained. The government bureaucracy works hand in hand with the private bureaucracy. Staff members of groups such as the Foreign Policy Committee, the National Association of Manufacturers, and the Farm Bureau Federation collaborate with the State Department and Congress in drafting proposals for foreign policy.

In this way a community of purpose is maintained in which "the constant, informed, and friendly exchange between government officials and pressure group officials . . . provides the most effective collaboration."[36] Any realistic appraisal of administration must recognize such working relationships between high officials, legislators, and interest groups. It seems fair to say, however, that this interchange of ideas occurs between select groups only, without participation by the unorganized public.

[35] See, for example, Department of State *Program of the National Conference on the United Nations*, January, 1949. These conferences have been severely criticized by Congress, allegedly because the press is barred, information of a confidential nature is revealed, and the Department's policies are systematically "sold" to opinion leaders. Subcommittee of the Senate Committee on Appropriations, 82nd Cong., 2d sess., *Hearings* [on the appropriation for the Department of State] (Washington, D.C.: U.S. Government Printing Office, 1952), pp. 363–70.

[36] McCamy, *The Administration of American Foreign Affairs*, p. 325.

But this is perhaps an inescapable facet of organization and decision making in our complex society, reflecting again the tendency in group organization for a minority to determine policy and exercise power. This dominance is made possible by various factors, including the intelligence, discipline, and resourcefulness of the elite as well as the apathy of the rank and file. In government this elite is composed of persons who first of all are interested enough to concern themselves with political matters. They must also be informed as to the conditions under which policy is made. And, finally, they must be on the scene, prepared to contribute their time and energy to work with other interested individuals and groups.

To build popular support, the State Department tries to find out what the public thinks about foreign policy through its division of Public Studies. The various media of communication are analyzed, including editorial comments in the press, the attitudes of newspaper and radio commentators, the views of congressmen, and the public statements of opinion leaders in several areas. Public opinion polls are also scrutinized, but apparently these are not accorded much weight: "Public opinion aspects of policy receive in practice far less attention than political, economic, and legal considerations"[37] Officials are evidently keyed to special organized publics, rather than to the public at large.[38] Face-to-face contacts, it should be remembered, are the most effective communications vehicle. Organization groups also provide a labor-saving device; they have funds and a staff which can often be bent to the use of an agency. They have an "organized opinion," professionally dedicated to influencing public behavior, upon which the agency's message can be superimposed. Officials are, moreover, extremely sensitive to such public opinion because an unfavorable opinion will often be reflected in losses of power and money. Thus public agencies will spend considerable time and energy cultivating the good will of the social groups who benefit

---

[37] Davison, *More than Diplomacy*, p. 129.

[38] This orientation is well illustrated by the remarks of H. H. Sargeant, Deputy Assistant for Public Affairs, before the Senate Subcommittee on Appropriations, "They [public studies] first of all review editorials in some 88 daily newspapers. They look at the columns that are written by about 43 writers and commentators. They have about 100 magazines which they skim through to see what opinions are being expressed on foreign-policy issues. They look at the transcripts of radio broadcasts by some 40 commentators and perhaps 5 or 6 public-opinion forums of the type of the American Town Meeting of the Air or the University of Chicago Round Table. They also have available the normal results of public opinion polling organizations which are published in the newspapers. They also get what we call leadership opinion. We get bulletins from as many as 60 or 70 of the national private organizations which would include the American Legion or the General Federation of Women's Clubs, and so forth; and they analyze those bulletins to see what opinions are being expressed by the leadership and the membership." Subcommittee of the Senate Committtee on Appropriations, 82nd Cong., 1st sess., *Hearings*, p. 168.

directly from their services and consequently can be expected to support them before Congress and the general public.

THE POLITICAL ROLE OF THE MILITARY. The remarkable ascendancy of the armed forces since World War II and the movement toward the "garrison state" have brought new developments in the political role and power potential of the military.[39] Not only has there been an unprecedented influx of professional army officers into civilian government agencies, but the armament program has fostered closer relations between large corporations and the Defense Department which negotiates the contracts for military hardware. This influx of military men into government posts was not unopposed, and several of Truman's appointees were rejected by the Senate.[40] The nexus between business and the military was also encouraged after the War by the hiring of retired generals and admirals by industrial concerns, who assumed that their experience in military administration was transferable to business, and perhaps more important, that the officers' previous contacts in Washington were useful in both the corporations' business and public relations.

The impact of such alliances is suggested by President Eisenhower's statement about the pernicious influence of the "munitions lobby."[41] Big defense contractors, the President said, were bringing improper pressure to bear upon Congress and the Defense Department in their attempts to decide what kinds of weapons ought to be manufactured. General James M. Gavin, who retired in 1958 as Army Chief of Research and Development, also stated that industrial pressure was causing decisions to be made in favor of weapons that were already obsolete.[42] Certainly the impact upon aircraft manufacturers of missile developments suggests the kind of problem raised here. As a result of the President's comment, the House Armed Services subcommittee began hearings on July 1, 1959, on the hiring of retired military leaders by defense contractors.

Various organizational ties define and cement such contacts. The Air Force Association, for example, provides valuable links between the aviation companies and the military departments. The establishment of the Air Force Academy was encouraged by the Air Force Association. In 1944 James Forrestal organized the National Security Industrial Asso-

---

[39] Among others, see A. E. Ekirch, Jr., *The Civilian and the Military* (New York: Oxford University Press, 1956), particularly chap. xvii "Toward the Garrison State"; Charles E. Merriam, "Security Without Militarism," in J. Kerwin (ed.), *Civil-Military Relations in American Life* (Chicago: University of Chicago Press, 1948).

[40] S. Huntington, *The Soldier and the State* (Cambridge: Harvard University Press, 1957), p. 360.

[41] *New York Times*, June 10, 1959.

[42] James M. Gavin, *War and Peace in the Space Age* (New York: Harper & Bros., 1958), pp. 255-56.

ciation "to insure that American business will remain close to the services."[43] This organization in 1954 had 600 members, "virtually all of whom had significant defense contracts."[44] As Huntington concludes, "in general, the defense businesses supported for economic reasons the same military policies which the officers supported for professional reasons."[45] This commingling of public and private interests and influence characterizes public administration generally and is often viewed as its "representative" function. Reciprocal benefits flow to both parties. The agency receives interest group support when its appropriations and its programs are being reviewed. The interests concerned receive government contracts, federal legitimation for their activities, and services of many kinds.

Something must also be said of the support-building activities of the armed forces who are among the most sedulous promoters of publicity seeking to build and maintain the prestige of the military. Here again, international tension has provided a fruitful environment.

This condition emphasizes a critical aspect of public relations: Successful external communication depends principally upon conditions of war, depression, international stress, and popular expectations of governmental service. The prevailing notion that effective public rapport can be conjured up, like the proverbial rabbit from the magician's hat, through a public relations campaign seems highly superficial. It is because the armed forces today enjoy such a propitious climate that their influence on national opinion is probably greater than ever before. For perhaps the first time, military opinion has become the most compelling factor in foreign and domestic policy. Despite the United Nations and the Point Four Program, the hard fact remains that the overwhelming majority of our public budget is being spent for war materials and a huge armed force. The National Security Council, which is probably the most important high-level planning and decision-making agency in our government, is in essence a coordinating mechanism for military, economic, and foreign policy.

Military tactics of persuasion are well illustrated by postwar efforts of the Army to secure Congressional and public approval for Universal Military Training. Provided with unlimited funds, enjoying the advantage of ultimate authority in defense affairs, and using every technique of private pressure groups, the department launched a nation-wide publicity campaign "without parallel in our history," in the words of Oswald Garrison Villard.[46] The comprehensiveness of method and effort which

43 *Ibid.*, p. 365.
44 *Ibid.*
45 *Ibid.*, p. 366.
46 Oswald Garrison Villard, *The New Leader*, January 11, 1947, p. 1.

characterized the campaign was revealed in hearings during 1947 before a subcommittee of the House Committee on Expenditures in the Executive Departments.[47] "Consultants" were hired from universities to tour the nation, arranging forums and delivering lectures on behalf of UMT.[48] Citizen Committees were organized, headed by distinguished Americans, including Justice Owen Roberts of the Supreme Court. A Women's Interest Unit was established in an effort to overcome the well-known opposition of women to UMT. An advisory council to the unit soon appeared, comprising thirty-six leaders of national women's organizations, providing ready-made channels through which the Department could disseminate information and propaganda for UMT. The cooptation of established organizations is, of course, a venerable labor-saving technique in promotional campaigns. Two films supporting the proposed program were produced, "Plan for Peace" and "A Pictorial Report of UMT at Fort Knox, Kentucky." These were widely distributed; the Department estimated that some 680,000 persons saw "Plan for Peace." Meanwile, transcriptions of programs concerning UMT were prepared and sent to radio stations in several states.

But the most spectacular of the Department's tactics was the establishment at Fort Knox, Kentucky, of an experimental training center for UMT. Here was a program to stagger the imagination of any former soldier. Barracks had varnished interiors, single-deck bunk beds (with bed lamps), and chintz curtains. Attendance at church and morality lectures was compulsory for the first month of training; profanity, gambling, and liquor were prohibited. A system of "self-government" was outlined, in which trainees served on juries which dealt with violators of these proscriptions. The training staff and cadre was almost equal in number to the trainees: 560 officers and enlisted instructors to 664 trainees.[49] Although the department admitted that these conditions could not be duplicated on a national scale, the center was used as a demonstration unit to which opinion leaders were flown by the Army to acquaint them with the type of training which could be offered under UMT.

As far as public opinion in general is concerned, the Army, Navy, and Air Force maintain publicity offices in Washington which have daily contact with the various communication media. Each public relations chief is directly responsible to his respective Secretary and each is supposedly accountable to the Director of Public Information of the Sec-

[47] Subcommittee on Publicity and Propaganda of House Committee on Expenditures in the Executive Departments, 80th Cong., 1st sess., *Hearings* (Washington, D.C.: U.S. Government Printing Office, 1947).

[48] *New York Times*, July 24, 1947.

[49] Alexander Stewart, "Is UMT the Answer?" **64**, *Christian Century*, May 28, 1947, p. 681.

retary of Defense. However, as the bitter internecine conflict during the unification controversy indicated, coordination among the three branches is far from complete. Each command in the respective branches also has its special public information section, which formulates stories of local interest and restructures unsavory information.

In the case of the military, as in other public agencies, the central problem is one of maintaining a judicious balance between information and propaganda. Promotional activities are undoubtedly proper, but the use of slanted and misleading statistics and "scare stories" to bludgeon Congress and the nation into larger military appropriations is improper and has caused concern among thoughtful observers. The Air Force, for example, in attempting to secure support for a larger air force, informed newspapermen that the Russians were operating some 14,000 combat planes and producing 40,000 to 50,000 planes per year. The best intelligence later revealed, however, that only some 8,000 of these operating planes were combat aircraft, and the figures for annual plane production referred to Russia's maximum *wartime* production.[50] While information of many kinds from the armed forces is undoubtedly necessary, publicity staffs are too large, and the pervasive emphasis upon force as the principal ingredient of foreign policy seems both alarming and negative.

As pointed out earlier, one's evaluation of these relationships is largely a function of one's value premises. Some individuals argue that the public interest gets lost in the interplay of the more powerful and vocal private interests, while others maintain that the public interest, or the most operational facsimile of it, can be achieved only by competition and compromise among such groups.

CONCLUSION: EFFECTIVE PUBLIC RELATIONS

A final issue concerns the validity of the assumption that popular support can be built by exhortation without much consideration of the substantive conditions involved. It seems clear that much support building at present is based upon this misconception. But individuals cannot be conditioned to accept information unless it conforms to their experience. As Sir Stephen Tallents put it, "There is no more tiresome heresy in this field than the idea that publicity can be applied like an eyeshade to hide, but not to heal, defects in organizations."[51] Just as social change requires objective dynamics such as war and depression, effective public

---

[50] Hanson Baldwin, "When the Big Guns Speak," in Lester Markel, *Public Opinion and Foreign Policy*, pp. 111–14.
[51] Sir Stephen Tallents, "Public Relations and Publicity," 27, *Public Administration* (Autumn, 1949), p. 218.

relations must rest upon a foundation of actual needs and effective service. Clearly public relations programs can stimulate interest and awareness, but they cannot create a point of view which is at odds with individual experience.

The fact seems to be that effective support building is a substantive line function, in which every member of an organization participates. It is not an isolated staff function. Favorable public opinion is molded by the character of government services. Indeed, when citizen satisfactions are at odds with agency promises, formalized public relations programs may be harmful. Internally also, such programs may lead employees to assume that responsibility for effective public relations can be delegated to some auxiliary division. But public relations is not a function of brochures, news releases, luncheon speeches, or exhortations based on vague generalities. Instead, it is the sum of public reactions generated by government services. It is the way a policeman makes an arrest, the receptionist treats a visitor, the tax clerk handles a disenchanted citizen. It is the veteran receiving his GI subsistence check on time, the post-office clerk binding up the torn package, the cleanliness of city streets, and the availability of parks and playgrounds.

BIBLIOGRAPHY

APPLEBY, PAUL H. *Policy and Administration.* University, Alabama: 1949.

CATER, DOUGLAS. *The Fourth Branch of Government.* New York: 1959.

DAVID, P. T., and POLLOCK, ROSS. *Executives for Government.* Washington, D.C.: 1957.

EULAU, H., ELDERSVELD, S. J., and JANOWITZ, M. (eds.). Political Behavior. Glencoe, Ill.: 1956.

HARRELL, C. H., and WEIFORD, D. G. "The City Manager and the Policy Process," **19**, *Public Administration Review* (Spring, 1959).

HOUSE SELECT COMMITTEE ON LOBBYING ACTIVITIES, 81st Cong., 2nd sess., *Hearings,* Part 10: "Legislative Activities of Executive Agenies," Washington, D.C.: 1950.

LONG, NORTON E. "Bureaucracy and Power," **9**, *Public Administration Review* (Autumn, 1949).

MCCAMY, JAMES. *Government Publicity.* Chicago: 1939.

MCKINLEY, CHARLES. "Federal Administrative Pathology and the Separation of Powers," **11**, *Public Administration Review* (Winter, 1951).

RUBIN, B. *Public Relations in the Empire State.* New Brunswick, N. J.: 1958.

"Unofficial Government: Pressure Groups and Lobbies," **319**, *Annals, American Academy of Political and Social Science* (September, 1958).

Part III

ORGANIZATION

CHAPTER 9

Organization Theory: Historical and Cultural Background

Our concepts of administrative organization are a strange mixture of democratic political thought, on the one hand, and a rather authoritarian approach to bureaucratic and management theory and practice on the other. These are a product of the diverse historical and cultural influences which have shaped our political system. The two strongest forces involved have probably been Anglo-American concepts of political democracy and the influence of our business culture with its overriding drive for organizational arrangements making for productive efficiency. The two are not always compatible because the business community has traditionally mistrusted government, whereas democratic thought often suspects the assumed authoritarian flavor of business management. However, it would be wrong to overemphasize the divergence of the two groups because democratic reformers have often advocated structural reorganization as an instrument of popular control.

OUR DEMOCRATIC TRADITION

Born in an era of revolt against royal influence both here and in Europe, it is little wonder that our organization concepts should reflect a strong democratic bent, tempered by the fear of executive power. The world revolutions of 1776 and 1789 were followed a half-century later in America by Jacksonian equalitarianism, which regarded one man not only as good but as competent as another, and embraced the popular election of administrative officials. The twentieth century brought a curious reversal of democratic theory in which reformers sought to fight corrupt political machines by *abolishing* all elective officers except the governor or mayor and concentrating administrative authority in the latter. The "Short Ballot" advocates hoped to break the machine by concentrating attention on a single responsible individual, in contrast to the "invisible government" created by a system of numerous elective officers.

While the structural reform movement reflected this democratic bias, there is little doubt that it was also influenced by the effectiveness of industrial institutions. Bringing "business into government" appealed to the participants in the original "economy and efficiency" movement early in this century. The same was true of the governmental research movement, the reorganization movement, and those who wanted to adapt scientific management to government. Note also that the terminology of orthodox organization theory smacks strongly of a military flavor, with such expressions as "line of command."

Some understanding of these two diverse and conflicting trends— democratic political institutions and authoritarian management institutions—is vital to much of the discussion in the chapters following. The agnosticism of younger political scientists springs in part from a wholesome respect for the political process, combined with apprehension that administration is fundamentally antidemocratic in nature. Anthropologists, sociologists, social psychologists, and other social scientists also tend to have an antiadministration bias because they sense it to be production-centered and insensitive to human needs. This attitude is also influenced by a feeling that administration is an applied, technical discipline in contrast to the older studies of man based on the humanities and liberal education.

The democratic tradition is so ingrained in American culture that it not only profoundly affects governmental organization but also influences the somewhat authoritarian business community, as suggested by the trend toward group decision making and by current writings about the demands for conformity on the part of big organizations.[1] It now seems desirable to examine in greater detail those forces which have the greatest bearing on administrative organization.

Fear of Executive Power. The grandest drama in Anglo-Saxon history is the harnessing of the royal prerogative by Magna Charta, Lord Coke's assertion of judicial independence against the Stuart kings, the Bill of Rights of 1689, the emergence of a ministry responsible to Parliament, and the American Revolution. It may be that American school books, in a patriotic fervor, have blinded us to the fact that our democratic political fabric was inherited from an English background of bloodshed and revolt, that the American Revolution was the culmination of cen-

---

[1] The editors of *Fortune* have apprehensions about what they call "group think." William H. Whyte, Jr., *Is Anybody Listening?* (New York: Simon and Schuster, Inc., 1952), p. 224; also Whyte, *The Organization Man* (New York: Simon and Schuster, Inc., 1956).

turies of resistance to royal prerogative, and that a parallel revolt against arbitrary power was going on in England.

Our attitude toward executive power illustrates how our ideas about administrative organization are not governed by clear-cut national dogmas. They pose themselves in terms of conflicting issues and dichotomies, perhaps the most enduring of which is the Hamilton-Jefferson disagreement over the powers of the chief executive. The constitution established the Hamiltonian interpretation of a strong executive which continued not only among the Jacksonian presidents but has persisted until our own day.[2] This development, however, was in direct contrast to the administrative position of governors and mayors who could be accurately classified as "weak executives." The latter were "weakened" by the Jacksonian trend toward electing the chief administrative officers, thus removing them from the control of the chief executive. This movement toward elective officials might have invaded federal structure had the constitution permitted it.

In spite of the fact that we seem generally to approve a strong Presidency, the mistrust of executive power is still a pervasive factor on the state and local levels. Fifty years of campaigning for the short ballot has made little headway in abolishing elective offices in the states.[3] The cry of "dictatorship" is still raised against proposals to adopt the council-manager plan, although it must be admitted that the movement toward a strong administrative officer has secured widespread popular approval. Nevertheless a city manager who would survive must seem not to act officiously.

Jacksonian Democracy. The administrative process was influenced in three specific ways by Jacksonian democracy: (1) the multiplication of elective offices; (2) the modification of personnel administration through spoils appointments and rotation in office; and (3) the equalitarian philosophy exemplified in the credo of the common man. Although elective offices existed in Colonial municipalities,[4] the practice was greatly accentuated during the Jacksonian era.[5] The administration of government was in the hands of aristocrats and gentlemen during the Federalist years and continued so under the Jeffersonians.[6] However, the Jacksonian era coincided with two developments that were to have profound effects on the political scene for at least a hundred years: the impact of European

[2] Leonard D. White, *The Jacksonians* (New York: The Macmillan Co., 1954), pp. 20–49.

[3] Richard S. Childs, *Civic Victories* (New York: Harper & Bros., 1952), p. 115.

[4] Ernest S. Griffith, *History of American City Government* (New York: Oxford University Press, 1938), p. 184.

[5] Arthur W. Bromage, Introduction to *Municipal Government and Administration* (New York: Appleton-Century-Crofts, Inc., 1950).

[6] White, *The Jacksonians*, p. 419.

immigration on the urban voting population and the influence of the agrarian frontier.[7]

The extremes of Jacksonian democracy should be remembered in connection with the Civil Service Reform Movement of a half-century later and the demand for experts at the opening of this century. The latter brought an attempt to distinguish between politics and administration, which was in many respects a reaction against the influence of Jacksonian democracy. From the standpoint of organization the most profound effects of Jacksonian theory were to come from 1883 onward in the form of the independent civil service commission. The administration of civil service was sealed off from political machination (or at least so it was thought) by placing it under an autonomous commission. This tended to divorce personnel administration from line management, a development deplored today by many who regard the two as logically inseparable. Here is still another example of the conflict between democratic political theory and administrative orthodoxy.

Legislative Supremacy. It has been said that the executive and legislative branches are natural enemies.[8] Certainly a cornerstone of the American system has been legislative surveillance of the executive branch. But legislators have not been content to stop at mere surveillance; they have often seemed to desire to take over administrative functions. A prime example is offered in the history of the General Accounting Office, headed by the Comptroller General, where for a quarter-century the administrative and legislative functions were mingled in what many thought to be a false concept of organization.[9] Today a workable distribution of activities has been reached by agreement without altering the law. This is a social science lesson in organizational change: Face has been saved while accomplishing desirable functional objectives.

The main question in executive-legislative relationships relates to the balance of power between the two. Some fear that emphasis on streamlined administrative structure, the creation of a professional class of civil servants, and concentration on administrative detail will tend to skew the balance undemocratically toward the executive branch. Others resist the concept of administrative hierarchy with the chief executive at the head, as postulated in the reorganization movement, and as embodied in Willoughby's concept of the President as "general manager."[10]

[7] Thomas H. Reed, *Municipal Government in the United States* (New York: Appleton-Century-Crofts, Inc., 1934), p. 78.

[8] Attributed to John Adams by White, *The Jacksonians*, p. 104.

[9] Harvey C. Mansfield, *The Comptroller General* (New Haven: Yale University Press, 1939).

[10] W. F. Willoughby, *Principles of Public Administration* (Baltimore: Johns Hopkins Press, 1927), p. 36.

The fear of bureaucratic power is always present.[11] Strong administrators want a wide area of discretion in decision making, just as industrial managers insist upon "management prerogative." The former want freedom from legislatures, while the latter regard the labor unions and government as their natural opponents. Those who are afraid of administrative discretion tend to favor tipping the scales toward the legislators.

The Rule of Law. The underlying objective of democratic reform movements throughout history has been to limit administrative discretion. In the thousand-year struggle to harness the British monarchy, one finds fundamental recurring themes, and many of these were restated in our own constitutions.[12] Parliament was to be called regularly; no taxes were to be levied without the consent of Parliament; every citizen was to have his "day in court" before a judge not answerable to the king for his acts, and before a jury of his peers. Our modern law of arrest, dating back hundreds of years, restricts the discretion of police officers by requiring a warrant before entering private premises, prescribing the conditions of taking a suspect into custody, and requiring bail and habeas corpus hearings.

The industrial viewpoint is perhaps best typified in the phrase "management prerogative" by which the business man usually means his right to make decisions free from government regulation and restrictions imposed by labor unions. Strong and creative men do not like to be restricted, whether they are administrative heads or artists and writers. The administrative empire builder is often a creator who is contributing much to society and for that very reason is impatient of legal restraints.

One frequently hears it said that "ours is a government of laws and not of men," by which is meant, of course, that administrative officials must act within the law. This fact has served to enhance the importance of the lawyer on all levels of government. He is an interpreter of the law, and the need to consult him before taking action has brought him also into deliberations on policy.[13] In some local governments the city or county attorney seems to have as much influence on the course of administration as the chief administrative officer.

In general two broad loci at each end of a continuum represent popular viewpoints toward administrative discretion. This division does not represent a democracy-despotism dichotomy, for the advocates of

[11] Charles S. Hyneman, *Bureaucracy in a Democracy* (New York: Harper & Bros., 1950), pp. 20–37.

[12] See Roscoe Pound, *The Development of Constitutional Guarantees of Liberty* (New Haven: Yale University Press, 1957).

[13] For an analysis of the lawyer's role in the federal government, see Esther Brown, *Lawyers, Law Schools, and the Public Service* (New York: Russell Sage Foundation, 1948).

either viewpoint regard themselves as democratic. At one end are those who would write into the law broad general directives and goals, giving administration the discretion to select the means but leaving administration accountable for the results. In general those representing the professional administrative viewpoint tend toward this pole. Those toward the other pole would write detailed directions and controls into the law, leaving a minimum of discretion to the administrator. The federal and state constitutions are often cited as representative of these two loci, the former containing practically no administrative detail, whereas the latter are believed by many students of government to be excessively packed with it.

The problem of administrative discretion not only involves management decisions but also embraces the area of regulation, which raises two broad problems of organization, each reflecting the "rule of law." The organized bar has long opposed the growth of administrative regulation and the tendency to give administrative agencies and officers more power to make decisions in areas affecting personal and property rights. This viewpoint was implicit in the Brownlow Commission's recommendation in 1937 that the great regulatory commissions, such as Interstate Commerce, be at least partially integrated into existing executive departments.[14] Those who opposed such a move felt that it would violate the separation-of-powers principle by undercutting the independence of these agencies and subjecting them to undue executive influence in their quasijudicial and quasilegislative functions.

The other problem embraced both structure and procedure. The organized bar objected to subordinate department officials, for instance in Agriculture, making decisions and rendering judgments which were essentially judicial. The Administrative Procedure Act of 1946 required that heads of agencies either hear the evidence personally or read the transcript when the hearing takes place before subordinate officials. It also introduced procedural changes requiring the administrative officers to observe some aspects of the rules of evidence and formal court procedure in conducting the hearings. This development is discussed in detail in subsequent chapters; it is mentioned here only to set it in the framework of "democracy versus administration." When the lawyer talks about the "administrative process," he is not referring to management problems but rather to the exercise of administrative discretion in regulating the behavior of people and the use of property.

Checks and Balances. The American concept of separation of powers has been explained. Here our emphasis is on its corollary of checks and balances which is often mentioned in relation to organization reform.

[14] President's Committee on Administrative Management, *Report with Special Studies* (Washington, D.C.: U.S. Government Printing Office, 1937), p. 229.

The concept of checks and balances is often advanced to defend the elective status of the chief accounting officer, whereas the structural reformers would place accounting under the chief administrative officer. This issue is common to all levels of government. It is found in the long-standing controversy over the functions of the federal Comptroller General, the elective state auditor versus the governor's budget and finance office, and the elective city or county auditor versus the manager's staff aides. The idea of checks and balances also underlies the philosophy of the independent civil service commission which is now under criticism from the structural reformers as well as those who see personnel administration as a line prerogative.

Checks and balances are regarded as safeguards against corruption, misfeasance, and malfeasance. It is thought that independence from the chief executive will enable the elective auditor to detect or prevent the mishandling of funds. Advocates of civil service reform see the independent commission as a bulwark against the spoils politician, while employee groups regard the commission as the main protector of job security.

Future chapters will deal at greater length with this issue, but it should be said here that the advocates of structural reform have impressive counterarguments. They view finance and personnel as phases of an integrated administrative process which should be under the direct supervision of the chief administrative officer. Democratic control would be preserved by several devices, including: (1) legislative investigation and audit; (2) post-audit by an independent agency; (3) internal checks built into the management process itself; and (4) "visible" government, to be attained by concentrating administrative authority in one democratically responsible officer.

The use of boards as department heads is directly related to the issue of checks and balances, but they are dealt with separately in the subsequent paragraphs because of the representation issue.

Boards and Commissions as Department Heads. The demand for boards as department heads comes from at least three sources: (1) the desire for citizen representation in administration, (2) the pressure of functional groups for autonomy, and (3) the belief that such boards are a logical part of the check-and-balance network. Those who seek structural reform tend to deplore the use of boards as department heads, primarily because in at least two ways they interfere with unity of command. They constitute a collegial head for the department itself, and they also fracture the chain of command by placing a collegial supervisor between the chief executive and the main body of departmental personnel.

Evaluation depends on the values of the one who views the situation. Professional managers on the generalist side, such as city managers, do not like it. However, the professionals representing functional specialties, such as parks and recreation, schools, and waterworks, tend to prefer autonomous boards. Although this is a complicated problem which merits a treatise rather than a paragraph, here we are concerned mainly with the issue of democracy versus a possibly arbitrary exercise of authority. But even that issue is not clear-cut. Some of the arguments in favor of boards are based upon prodemocratic precepts, on the assumption that hierarchy inevitably has authoritarian tendencies. On the other hand the advocates of streamlined structural reform argue that democratic responsibility will be promoted by focusing the spotlight of accountability on a recognizable line of command.

ADMINISTRATIVE REFORM

The Era of Corruption. Improvements in the moral and ethical level of the American political scene mean that contemporary observers may not fully appreciate the impact of political corruption on administrative reform. Federal administration has been relatively free of corrupting influences except during the Presidencies of Grant and Harding. On the municipal level, however, the period from 1850 to 1950 was characterized by the corrupt machine and boss.[15] As late as the 1930's Los Angeles had its Shaw, Memphis its Crump, New Jersey its Hague, Chicago its Kelly, and Boston its Curley.[16] But the situation has improved in recent years. Philadelphia, New Orleans, and Los Angeles have achieved a rather high level of municipal purity, and even Chicago and New York are displaying evidences of respectability.

How does all this pertain to an understanding of administrative organization? Part of the answer lies in the tendency of the electorate to cure its own ills and guard against their recurrence. But how much of the improved tone of our civic life during recent years can be attributed to moral regeneration and how much to structural reforms combined with procedural improvements? This raises the old philosophical question of form versus spirit, and the answer cannot be found in absolute terms. Certainly no case for the superiority of structure over civic spirit is intended in what follows. The objective is merely to present the record, which clearly shows that from 1900 to 1950 there were a

---

[15] The corrupt political machine has been well researched. For a popular muckraking and journalistic approach, see Lincoln Steffens, *The Shame of the Cities* (New York, 1905), now available in paperback.

[16] On the colorful career of Boss Curley, see his autobiography, *I'd Do It Again* (Englewood Cliffs, N.J.: Prentice-Hall, Inc., 1957); for a novel based upon Curley, see Edwin O'Connor, *The Last Hurrah* (Boston: Little, Brown & Co., 1956).

number of reform movements which envisaged structural change as a part of their programs.

The Governmental Research Movement. The movements that emphasized organization change had their original impetus during the first decade of the twentieth century. Although civil service reform started a quarter-century earlier and the National Municipal League appeared during the 1890's, it was not until 1906 that the New York Bureau of Municipal Research began the research movement which in turn brought the reorganization and the economy and efficiency crusades.

Early efforts to end corruption were based upon the belief that the solution was to elect "good men" to office. But the results of this approach were disappointing. "Even the good men measurably failed to deliver good government, and as soon as the wave of civic enthusiasm receded, the old forces came back into power with their old ways and their old mismanagement . . ."[17] The New York Bureau of Municipal Research, subsequently known as the Institute of Public Administration, was organized by a group of private citizens to adopt a new approach. In Gulick's words: "In place of platforms, conventions, and politics, it substituted the painstaking research methods of natural science; in place of intuitive and rationalized programs of reform, it insisted upon an unbiased observation of facts; in place of personal attacks upon public officials, it devoted its time to analysis of 'the system' which controlled those officials. . . ."[18] William H. Allen stated the Institute's philosophy as follows: "Inefficiency of government is primarily due to badness of methods rather than to badness of men. Efforts to correct misgovernment have too frequently failed, or have had only passing success, because men not methods were changed or attacked."[19]

Thus the heart of the movement was fact finding and the publicizing of such facts. The staffs of the Bureau consisted of full-time specialists in government organization, public management, finance, engineering, public safety, health, welfare, and educational administration. Its work struck a responsive chord in the minds of reformers everywhere. As a result the Bureau made "efficiency" surveys in a large number of states and cities, and local research bureaus were established in many cities.

Many of the founders of the research movement—Frederick A. Cleveland, William H. Allen, and Frederick Bruere (first director of the New York Bureau)—were men associated with philanthropy or settlement work. They were interested in getting the maximum dollar's worth of

[17] Luther Gulick, *The National Institute of Public Administration: A Progress Report* (New York: The National Institute of Public Administration, 1928), p. 9.
[18] *Ibid*, p. 13.
[19] *Proceedings of the Pittsburgh Conference for Good City Government and the Fourteenth Annual Meeting of the National Municipal League,* 1908, p. 127.

public health, education, and social welfare. To ascertain community needs, they conducted social surveys.[20] The original funds came from Rockefeller and Carnegie, whose interest seems to have been altruistic rather than economic. However, other bureaus founded elsewhere in the country tended over the years to take on a taxpayers' economy viewpoint. In fact, the emphasis on economy and efficiency stemmed in all these reform movements from both welfare and tax-cutting motivations.[21] It will be shown below that the scientific management movement also attracted both profit maximizers and persons who saw productive efficiency as a boon to human welfare.

Economy, Efficiency, and Reorganization. The words "economy and efficiency," particularly the latter, have acquired a certain opprobrium. While the reasons may be very complex, certainly an important factor was the great emphasis on the economic gains of reform and the comparative neglect of its contributions to improved civic welfare, at least in the minds of some critics. This may be due in part to the fact that the American culture of 1910 was responsive to the cry of "economy and efficiency." The reformers of that era were civic- and socially minded. They were searching for solutions that would eliminate graft and corruption and thus permit better program development. In addition to the same kind of citizens found on the boards of social welfare agencies today, professors of political science were also active in the structural reform movement.

Beginning about 1910 there was a rash of "efficiency and economy" commissions in the states and cities, largely triggered by the governmental research movement and surveys conducted by the New York Bureau of Municipal Research. Together with the "Municipal Program" of the National Municipal League,[22] this was the origin of the reorganization movement which continues today. Basically it called for: (1) concentration of administrative authority in the hands of a single responsible officer, whether governor, mayor, or manager; (2) the grouping of offices in a small number of departments with functionally germane activities; (3) the department heads appointed by and responsible to the chief administrative officer; (4) the executive budget; and (5) staff agencies to assist the chief administrative officer.

The Taft Economy and Efficiency Commission, authorized by Congress in 1910 and reporting in 1912 and 1913, symbolized the impact

20 Henry Bruere, *The New City Government* (New York: D. Appleton and Company, 1912), p. 107.
21 See discussion of research bureau support in Norman N. Gill, *Municipal Research Bureaus* (Washington, D.C.: American Council on Public Affairs, 1944), pp. 134–46.
22 Frank M. Stewart, *Half Century of Municipal Reform* (Berkeley and Los Angeles: University of California Press, 1950), p. 28.

of the spirit of the times on federal administration. However, the Taft Commission did not emphasize structural change. It did make the first comprehensive set of organization charts of the federal administrative system, but its efforts were mainly confined to recommendations for improved procedures and methods. It recommended some shifting of functions and activities among the bureaus, but the reports today give the impression that attention was directed primarily toward such matters as the filing of correspondence, electric lighting costs, record keeping, indexing, and the handling of mail.[23] It did not present a grand plan for structural reform as did the Brownlow Commission in 1937 or the first Hoover Commission in 1949.

The Industrial Model. The demand for structural reform in government was to a considerable extent based upon the alleged effectiveness of the business corporation, the slogan often being to "put business methods into government." Thus the Mayor of Baltimore told the National Municipal League in 1896 that a municipal corporation was similar to a profit-making corporation. Both "use the same methods and both pay dividends, the only difference being that in the one case they are in the form of cash while in the other they are in the form of better government, better school houses, more efficient teachers, better pavements, better sewers, a more cleanly condition of the city, and eventually, lower taxes."[24] In 1902 the League program again carried a paper entitled, "The City as a Business Corporation."

The council-manager plan in particular has been postulated as a prototype of the corporation. Thomas H. Reed has said that "such a plan is usually employed in the private corporation—the stockholders choose the directors, the directors select a manager. The directors settle questions of policy, and the manager carries out the decisions. The circumstance that the manager may have recommended the policy to the board does not diminish the fact that the board adopts the policy and is responsible to the stockholders for its success or failure."[25] The old commission form of municipal government was originally advanced as a business approach toward cleaning up corruption and

[23] Some of the reports are to be found in *Economy and Efficiency of the Government Service*, 62nd Cong., House Doc. No. 670, April 4, 1912; also *House Documents*, Vol. 104, 62nd Cong., 3rd sess., 1913. The latter document stated that this "vast organization has never been studied in detail as one piece of administrative mechanism. Never have the foundations been laid for a thorough consideration of the relations of all its parts. No comprehensive effort has been made to list its multifarious activities or to group them in such a way as to present a clear picture of what the government is doing . . ."

[24] *Proceedings of the Second Annual Meeting of the National Municipal League* at Baltimore, 4 (May, 1896), p. 291.

[25] Reed, *Municipal Government in the United States*, p. 202.

waste; but in 1910 Richard S. Childs, long a crusader for structural reform, insisted that "there would have to be a manager put under the board to resemble a corporation."[26] Reference to the industrial model in the literature of the council-manager plan is more implicit than explicit, but there is little doubt that men like Childs had it in mind, especially when they pointed out that the failure of the earlier commission plan lay in the need for concentrating administrative leadership in a single responsible officer.[27]

Willoughby's use of the terminology of corporate management in advocating administrative reforms in the federal government has already been noted. The point was made that the constitution vests administrative power in Congress rather than the President; that Congress should act as a "board of directors." Willoughby recognized a separate and fourth branch of government called "administration." All its powers would come from Congress which, acting as a board of directors, would supervise the President in his capacity as "general manager" of administration. The analogy is strained by the fact that the general manager of a corporation is chosen by and answerable to the board, which the President would not be. The point is interesting because it shows that the pioneers in public administration were conscious of the industrial model and were in varying degrees influenced by it.[28]

The Scientific Management Movement. The scientific management movement is of concern to structural reform as a *symbol* rather than as a process or a discipline. The original scientific managers were primarily interested in the study of task rather than structure. They measured work and also directed their attention to system and procedures but gave scant attention to hierachy and structure in its over-all form. Taylor's concept of functional supervision was, of course, structural in nature, but it did not receive acceptance until long after his death. Scientific management was related to structure principally because it was interested in the study of *task* or *job,* the latter constituting in many respects the molecule of organization.

The early scientific management movement attracted a strange combination of economizers, and efficiency experts, and social reformers. To all of them Taylor took on an aura of infallibility; scientific management became a crusade if not a religion.[29] Members of the original apostolic in-group sometimes found themselves apologizing for, or explaining

---

[26] Richard S. Childs, *Civic Victories* (New York: Harper & Bros., 1952), p. 144.
[27] Harold A. Stone, Don K. Price, and Kathryn H. Stone, *City Manager Government in the United States* (Chicago: Public Administration Service, 1940), pp. 5–14.
[28] Willoughby, *Principles of Public Administration*, pp. 9, 36.
[29] Dwight Waldo, *The Administrative State* (New York: The Ronald Press Co., 1948), pp. 159–91.

away, antisocial impressions created by Taylor himself, perhaps un-wittingly.[30] Among Taylor's disciples were persons also engaged in the governmental reform movements of that day, the most notable being Morris Lewellyn Cooke, Director of Public Works under a Philadelphia reform administration in 1911 and one of the four disciples authorized by Taylor to install his principles.[31]

Taylor himself had a low opinion of the productivity of government employees as evidenced in an article published posthumously in 1916, in which he stated that, ". . . the average government employee does not do more than one-third to one-half of a proper day's work."[32] Taylor may have been smarting under the sting of the Congressional investiga-tion which resulted in the law prohibiting stop watches in government arsenals, a prohibition annually reenacted into appropriation bills until World War II. The introduction of the Taylor system into the govern-ment arsenals in 1909–11 is described by General Crozier, Chief of Ordnance, as consisting of two parts: (1) the systemization of the process of manufacture, and (2) the stimulus offered by establishing the quan-tity of output expected from workmen.[33]

The most revealing record of the Taylorites' attitudes toward struc-tural reform is contained in the record of the Taylor Society meeting in Washington on December 8, 1917. Many members were in Washington on wartime assignment, and the proceedings reveal some of the frus-trations they experienced, particularly in the War Department.[34] Em-phasis was placed on definite assignments of authority and responsibility. The leading paper by Henry P. Kendall advocated that every "depart-ment ought to be organized, from the bottom up, as perfectly as is pos-sible under functional management, built into a general scheme of things where there is no duplication, no overlapping, where responsibility is defined and backed up by authority, where men must make good or be removed quickly, where there are staff organizations and boards for advisory purposes; for while we know that an effective administrator is a man, we recognize also that an effective advisor is a board . . ."[35] This

---

[30] See for instance, Robert G. Valentine, "The Progressive Relation between Effi-ciency and Consent," 2, *Bulletin of the Taylor Society* (July, 1916), p. 7.

[31] Kenneth E. Trombley, *The Life and Times of a Happy Liberal* (New York: Harper & Bros., 1954), p. 19.

[32] Frederick Winslow Taylor, "Government Efficiency," 2, *Bulletin of the Taylor Society* (December, 1916), pp. 7–13.

[33] William Crozier, "Scientific Management in Government Establishments," 1, No. 5, *Bulletin of the Society to Promote the Science of Management* (October, 1915), pp. 1–8.

[34] Henry P. Kendall, "Centralization of Administrative Authority," 4, *Bulletin of the Taylor Society* (April, 1919), pp. 2–4.

[35] *Ibid.*

early statement of the concepts of structural reform appeared repeatedly in the literature of public administration.

The Military Model. The terminology of administrative organization has a strong military flavor, but tracing the source of this influence is not easy. Perhaps the influence may spring from the fact that so many of our public figures have been either professional military men or citizen soldiers during war. On the other hand the military and industrial models are entirely congenial. Leaders in both fields tend to be men of action conditioned to "command" rather than to "lead" in the sociological sense. C. Wright Mills has characterized the military as one of the three components—along with corporate management and corporate ownership—of the power structure in contemporary American society.[36] Both the industrial and military cultures have traditionally relied upon an authority structure and system characterized by command from the top, although both are now undergoing a metamorphosis toward more democratic practices.

But regardless of origins, the argot of public administrative organization has borrowed from the military many designations which have a markedly authoritarian flavor. Such expressions include "line of command," "chain of command," "communication through channels," "control," and "echelon." These designations have the advantage of being expressive; one usually grasps the meanings intuitively. On the other hand they have the disadvantage of sounding harsher than warranted and of being inconsistent with many of the research findings of modern social science.

Such research has often been sponsored by the military itself. For instance, the Ohio State studies in naval and industrial organization show that even in healthy units, contacts and communications do not always follow the line of command. Sociometric charts show a variety of cross-contacts in which the immediate superior-subordinate relationship is not involved.[37] Furthermore the word "control" has come to have a technical meaning more democratic than authoritarian in essence. Thus "control" today embodies the concept of feedback, information, and communication of achievement data. The planning of the goals tends increasingly to be a group process based upon joint consent.

The "staff" concept is usually attributed to German military sources going back perhaps to Frederick the Great.[38] The "general staff" for the American army was established during the War of 1812, but it was com-

---

[36] C. Wright Mills, *The Power Elite* (New York: Oxford University Press, 1956).

[37] Ralph M. Stogdill and Carroll L. Shartle, *Patterns of Administrative Performance*; Ralph M. Stogdill, Ellis L. Scott, and William E. Jaynes, *Leadership and Role Expectations* (Columbus: Bureau of Business Research, Ohio State University, 1956).

[38] Walter Gorlitz, *History of the German General Staff, 1657-1945* (New York: Frederick A. Praeger, Inc., 1953).

posed of heads of bureaus independent of each other and not engaged in over-all planning but in furnishing supplies and auxiliary services.[39] This situation continued into the twentieth century, when in 1904 Secretary of War Elihu Root pushed through, against opposition from top army brass, a plan for a modern general staff.[40] For many years thereafter the general staff mixed administrative and planning functions, and it was not until after World War I that the general staff's function as a planning agency became finally established.

One gets the impression that the staff concept is a military contribution and that civilian administration has something to learn from the military in this respect. Dwight D. Eisenhower told Ernest Dale that "business has overlooked an important opportunity to increase the effectiveness of the chief executive through a larger and abler staff of assistants to reduce his load, making it possible for him to devote himself to broader issues and closer contact with his men and with others. The experience of businessmen with the armed forces seems to show that this is the principal lesson they have learned from the military."[41] Certainly President Eisenhower followed this policy during his tenure. The size of the White House staff was increased by fifteen hundred persons between 1952 and 1959.[42] However, there are real doubts as to whether the military concept of the staff system is suitable to a high political office which demands responsibility from the top man and not from anonymous, appointed assistants. In President Eisenhower's case, moreover, there is evidence that information was kept from him by his top staff aides. Furthermore these assistants did not always understand that while Presidential *power* can be delegated, the President's political *responsibility* can never be.

Civil Service Reform. Civil service reform has been mentioned in passing, but here it seems appropriate to review the ways in which it has affected organization theory. The history of the spoils system is well documented and its effect upon the public service well known.[43] Organization theory was influenced in at least two important ways: (1)

---

[39] White, *The Jacksonians*, p. 190 ff.

[40] Otto L. Nelson, Jr., *National Security and the General Staff* (Washington, D.C.: Infantry Journal Press, 1946); also Willoughby, *Principles of Public Administration*, p. 146.

[41] Ernest Dale, *Planning and Developing the Company Organization Structure* (New York: American Management Assn., 1952), p. 65.

[42] Douglas Cater, "Loneliest Job in a Crowded White House," *The Reporter* (June 25, 1959), p. 12.

[43] Carl Russell Fish, *The Civil Service and the Patronage* (Cambridge: Harvard University Press, 1920); Frank M. Stewart, *The National Civil Service Reform League* (Austin: University of Texas, 1929); William Dudley Foulke, *Fighting the Spoilsmen* (New York: G. P. Putnam's Sons, 1919); White, *The Jacksonians*, pp. 174–78, 220.

the separation of personnel administration from line management, and
(2) the demand for an expert official class.

The original civil service reformers mistrusted line management because its members were either elected or appointed by political patronage. Mayors, governors, and Presidents, together with their department
heads and bureau chiefs, as well as their subordinates were bound up
in patronage. In order to counteract this unhappy aspect of politics, the
reformers set up a separate hierarchy in the form of a civil service commission, among whose chief duties was to act as a watch dog to frus-
trate the spoils politician.

As American public administration has become more mature, some
observers have questioned the concept of an independent civil service
commission. Perhaps the most important consideration is the growing
realization that personnel administration is really a phase of line management and that the independent commission setup tends to divorce
the two. This trend has been bolstered by two developments, one the
rise of a professional administrative group, such as the city managers,
who became irked at what they regard as needless restrictions, delays,
and obstructionism of civil service. The other is the emerging pattern
of research that illumines the relationship between group leadership and
work motivation. All this is leading to new concepts of personnel administration emphasizing training, placement, and development, with
the line supervisor as the key figure. Organizationally, this results in
placing the personnel function under the chief administrative officer, as
recommended by the *Model City Charter*,[44] and in the extension of the
personnel hierarchy into the operating departments by establishing
personnel directors and supervisors who are answerable to department
heads and even to foremen.

The other respect in which the reform movement influenced organization theory was the early emphasis on the need for experts in government. Today we recognize that a clear-cut separation between politics
and administration is neither possible nor advisable. Nevertheless our
criticism of Goodnow and others of his generation should be tempered
by some understanding of contemporary influences which led them to
advocate this dichotomy. Among these were the Jacksonian view that
any citizen could fill public office; the difficulty of securing technical and
professional competence under the patronage system; and the absence
of a career system due to frequent spoils turnover. Thus A. Lawrence
Lowell argued that, ". . . positions must be independent of political
change." The expert in government "must keep entirely out of politics,
both national and local. He must take no part in political campaigns,

44 National Municipal League, 1941.

although the issues may be ones that affect his department or his plans. Nor must he in a democracy strive for political notoriety or public applause. A truly ambitious and worthy permanent official is abundantly satisfied by recognition from his employers and the members of the profession to which he belongs."[45]

Invisible Government and the Short Ballot. A striking characteristic of state and local government during the opening decades of this century was what Munro called "invisible government" and Key termed the "plural executive."[46] They were referring to the proliferation of elective officers uncoordinated, independent of each other, and subject to no central leadership. Another factor in making administration "invisible" was the tendency to place activities such as schools, asylums, and parks under administrative boards not subject to coordination by the governor or mayor. Thus a given state might have as many as a hundred separate administrative agencies, only a handful of which were under direct gubernatorial supervision.

The adjective "invisible" referred to the belief that the complexity of administrative organization resulted in obscuring the activities of the officers and agencies. Thus citizens could not discern the lines of responsibility, and unethical and corrupt acts could be hidden behind a facade of complexity. The political machine could hide behind the diffusion of responsibility created by the organizational system.

Here again the remedy advanced by both political and administrative reformers was the same. The short-ballot movement sought to bring these elective officers into the spotlight by making them appointive, by the mayor or governor. Invisibility would be curbed by making them satellites of their chief executive so that they would share in the reflection of the publicity concentrated upon him.[47] The same means would bring about a coordinated and integrated administrative machine. The main reason for mentioning these developments at this point is to emphasize the fact that structural reform often had political origins. This seems a necessary preliminary to a more thorough discussion of structural reform in Chapter 10.

BIBLIOGRAPHY

BROWNLOW, LOUIS. *A Passion for Anonymity.* Chicago: 1958.
BUCK, A. E. *The Reorganization of State Governments in the United States.* New York, 1938.

[45] A. Lawrence Lowell, "Experts in Government," in Clinton Rogers Woodruff (ed.), *A New Municipal Program* (New York: D. Appleton and Company, 1919).

[46] William Bennett Munro, *The Invisible Government* (New York: The Macmillan Co., 1928); V. O. Key, Jr., *American State Politics* (New York: Alfred A. Knopf, Inc., 1956), p. 197.

[47] Childs, *Civic Victories.*

CAPE, WILLIAM H. *Constitutional Revision in Kansas.* University of Kansas Governmental Research Series, No. 17. Lawrence, Kansas: 1958.

COKER, FRANCIS W. "Dogmas of Administrative Reform," **16**, *American Political Science Review* (August, 1922), pp. 399–411.

FESLER, JAMES W. "Administrative Literature and the Second Hoover Report," **51**, *American Political Science Review* (March, 1957), pp. 135–57.

GAUS, JOHN M., WHITE, LEONARD E., and DIMOCK, MARSHALL E. *The Frontiers of Public Administration.* Chicago: 1936.

GULICK, LUTHER. *The National Institute of Public Administration.* New York: 1928.

GULICK, LUTHER, and URWICK, LYNDALL (eds.). *Papers in the Science of Administration.* New York: 1937.

KAUFMAN, HERBERT. "Emerging Conflicts in the Doctrines of Public Administration," **50**, *American Political Science Review* (December, 1956), 1057–73.

KRAINES, O. *Congress and the Challenge of Big Government.* New York: 1958.

MILLER, ERNEST G. "Farewell Town Meeting," **47**, *National Municipal Review* (April, 1958), pp. 162–65.

REDFORD, EMMETTE S. *Ideal and Practice in Public Administration.* Alabama: 1958.

ROURKE, FRANCIS E. "The Politics of Administrative Organization: A Case History," **19**, *The Journal of Politics* (August, 1957), pp. 461–78.

SAYWELL, JOHN T. *The Office of Lieutenant Governor: A Study in Canadian Government and Politics.* Toronto: 1957.

WEAVER, ROBERT H. *Administrative Reorganization in Louisiana.* Baton Rouge, 1951.

WHITE, LEONARD D. *The Federalists 1789–1801; The Jeffersonians 1801–1829; The Jacksonians 1829–1861; The Republican Era 1869–1901. Four separate volumes.* New York: 1958.

CHAPTER 10

The Basic Models

The study of organization can be an exciting adventure which opens new vistas of an emerging world in which man is becoming ever more dependent upon large-scale organizations as a way of life. Here we hope to study organization as both a technical and a human problem in a nuclear and electronic era. Later attention will be directed toward the social science aspects of organization, including anthropology, sociology, and social psychology. More than passing notice will also be accorded Herbert Simon and his many followers, who see decision making as the key to organization theory and structure. Every student of public administration should be aware of these several approaches to organization, but he must first understand the ideological underpinnings of his own discipline. This chapter will therefore present the traditional models of public administrative organization and discuss the prevailing orthodoxy. The treatment will be, like the one it follows, largely historical and descriptive.

At present there is no such thing as an administrative "science" in the sense of a body of principles that have been tested experimentally. However, there is an orthodox organizational model, called the "integrationist" model, which has the approval of a wide segment of professional students of administration.

THE INTEGRATIONIST MODEL

Administrative integration refers to an organizational structure in which authority and responsibility are centered in a single, elected chief administrator and his immediate aides. All units within the organization are departmentalized by major purpose and arranged in a hierarchy that is coordinated from the top by lines of authority and communication which run throughout its various levels. Within the organization this system ensures control by the official at the top, while citizen control is enhanced by centering responsibility in a single head. Staff units and such elements as a reasonable span of control, clear-cut assignments of authority and function are provided to assist the head in directing the organization. By these means, the proliferation of independent agencies, the attending duplication of work, and the diffusion of authority and responsibility are reduced.

As James Fesler says, "This ideal structure continues to command the respect of all official commissions and committees that have made major investigations of the administrative needs of national, state, and municipal governments."[1] The integrationist model may be better understood by an examination of the so-called weak executive model, which preceded it on the state and municipal level and still exists in about half the states as well as many cities.

The Weak Executive Model. The weak executive model, which may be viewed as the first step toward integration, came into existence primarily because of three influences: (1) the historical dominance of the city council in municipal administration; (2) reaction against the arbitrary exercise of executive power by Colonial governors; and (3) the Jacksonian impetus to the election of administrative officers. It should be repeated in passing that the federal constitution, as implemented by Hamilton and interpreted by Justice Marshall, established a strong executive in the Presidency. However, from the beginning Congress has not been happy about Presidential domination of federal administration.[2]

Under the weak executive form of organization, a mayor or governor is elected by the people for a term of two or four years, and has little actual summary control over the administrative agencies, which are largely independent. The only supervision over elected officials consists of repudiation at the polls, judicial action, or recall—all nonadministrative controls. Since many areas do not have the recall, even this remedy is sometimes unavailable. Those offices headed by elective officers or by administrative boards often act independently of and even contrary to the will of the mayor or governor. The latter's influence in agency decision making is exercised by informal, political, social, and personal means rather than by the authority of formal hierarchy. The integrationists would give him more of the latter.

Under the weak executive organization, where the governor or mayor is given authority to appoint certain administrative officials, he must usually consult the senate or council for approval. His power of controlling these appointees from an administrative standpoint is impaired because he does not have a free hand in directing their work, owing to fear of alienating their political friends and because of the difficulty of removing them. The authority of the governor or mayor is further im-

[1] James W. Fesler, "Administrative Literature and the Second Hoover Commission Reports," 51, *American Political Science Review* (March, 1957), pp. 135–36.
[2] Leonard D. White, *The Federalists* (New York: The Macmillan Co., 1947), pp. 13–115.

paired by council appointment of certain officers and by the establishment of boards with overlapping terms as department heads.

In summary, the weak executive's administrative authority, if he has any, is personal and informal rather than institutional. A recent study of the governor's powers in the states says that, "The concept of the governor being primarily responsible for the management of the executive branch has not yet gained a firm foothold in most states in spite of some rather substantial reorganization."[3]

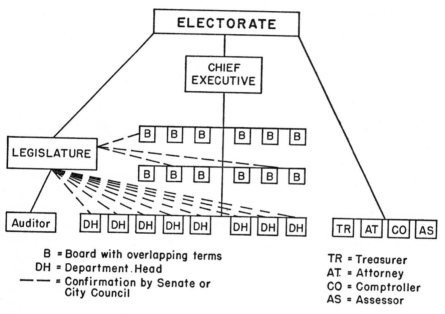

FIG. 2. Weak Executive Model.

Greater inroads have been made on the weak executive model in the cities, primarily because of the widespread adoption of the council-manager plan. However, many cities both large and small have a mayor who is essentially a weak executive. The Inter-University Case Program has done a study of the way that the weak mayor operates in a New England city of 30,000. In the first place, he is elected on a partisan basis and must therefore make his decisions with party considerations in mind, often as the result of conference and collaboration with party

[3] Coleman B. Ransome, Jr., *The Office of Governor in the United States* (University, Alabama: University of Alabama Press, 1956), pp. 222 ff.

officials.[4] Although focused on the mayor's appointments of other officials, the study reveals the following pattern relative to the mayor's role: (1) decisions were made after consultation with the local party boss; (2) there were many boards with overlapping terms who nominated individuals for appointment to administrative posts; (3) the mayor could exert influence on program but mainly through personal influence and political negotiation rather than in an administrative sense,[5] and (4) the technical trappings of professional personnel and budget administration seemed to be lacking.

Advocates of integration criticize the weak executive plan primarily because of its lack of hierarchical arrangements which make for coordination. We shall now consider what the true integrationist model embraces. There are roughly three submodels: the strong executive, the council-manager, and the elected executive plus chief administrative officer. All have one characteristic in common: The departments are organized in a manner that ensures a unified line of command; all subdivisions are answerable to the supervision of a single responsible officer, known variously as president, governor, city or county manager, or chief administrative officer. The difference lies in the manner of organizing for direct political responsibility at the top.

The Strong Executive Model. Under the strong executive model, administrative authority is centralized in the hands of an elected executive who appoints the heads of departments without legislative confirmation and who may remove them without restriction. Lines of authority run from the bottom upward and inward, converging in the mayor or governor. Activities are departmentalized on a unifunctional basis as nearly as possible. Civil servants become administratively responsible to the elective chief executive who can be held politically responsible for his acts. By combining power and responsibility in a single person responsible to the electorate, the strong executive organization aims to bring political leadership out into the open instead of leaving it in the hands of bosses and machines.

The proponents of this plan argue that, contrary to the reaction of the average citizen, the old weak form of organization favored control of administration by machine politicians. It gave government a touch of mystery which barred attempts at further insight on the part of most people. This permitted the political organization to carry on its plunder, shielded by a veil of complexity impenetrable by the workaday voter.

[4] While this is fairly common in most parts of the country, it seems strange to the senior author from California where municipal elections are nonpartisan and most administrative personnel are chosen by civil service.

[5] William N. Kinnard, Jr., *Appointed by the Mayor* (University, Alabama: University of Alabama Press, ICP Case No. 36, 1956).

The advocates of integration would meet this situation by simplifying government through placing administration in the hands of a single leader who is compelled to act in the open and upon whom the influence of popular sentiment can readily be brought to bear. As a means of controlling arbitrary and dishonest acts and preventing administration from falling into the hands of political machines, there would exist the recall, the legislative audit of administration, citizen advisory committees, and a rigorous merit system for personnel.

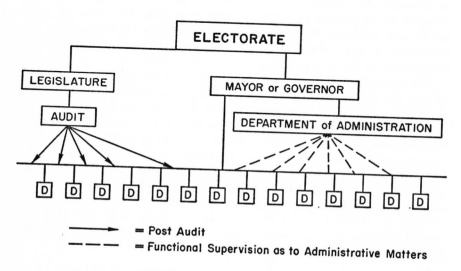

= Post Audit

= Functional Supervision as to Administrative Matters

FIG. 3. Strong Executive Model.

The reorganization movement, now about fifty years old, has not produced many examples of thorough-going integration on the state level, but it has succeeded in emphasizing and expanding the administrative role of the governor.[6] In the smaller and medium-sized cities, the reform movement has embraced the council-manager model, which tends to minimize the administrative role of the mayor. In the larger cities, on the other hand, the move toward integration has produced a variant model characterized by a chief administrative officer (CAO) responsible to the mayor. Variations of this model exist in Los Angeles, New York, and San Francisco.[7]

[6] Unsigned, *Reorganizing State Government* (Chicago: Council of State Governments, 1950), p. 9.

[7] John M. Selig, "The San Francisco Idea," **46**, *National Municipal Review* (June, 1957), pp. 290–95.

The CAO-strong executive variant is an attempt to give the elected chief executive administrative authority by furnishing him with professional assistance by placing certain departments under the line management of the CAO. In Los Angeles the latter functions wholly in a staff capacity and is equally responsible to mayor and council. New York would seem to be the only one of the three where the "city administrator" is a genuine staff and management arm of the mayor.[8]

The model state constitution provides that the "governor shall appoint an administrative manager of state affairs" to whom the governor may delegate broad powers to supervise administration. The states of Minnesota and Michigan have moved in this direction by establishing departments of administration under the governor, and the California Department of Finance functions in much the same way.

The trend toward structural reform in large cities has been influenced by two related considerations. The first is a widespread feeling that the council-manager model is not applicable to large municipalities.[9] This is because of the alleged inability of one man to master the complexities involved and its alleged failure to provide adequate political leadership. The second objection is really an elaboration of the latter, namely, the fear that a mayor without administrative authority would also be ineffective as a political leader and that democratic concepts would be compromised by the tendency of the professional administrator to fill the vacuum in political leadership. Certain observers have felt that the council-manager model possesses this underlying weakness of not institutionalizing political leadership.

The Council-Manager Model. The council-manager model calls for an elected city council which appoints an administrative officer responsible to the council for the operation of city departments. The orthodox theory of council-manager government, as stated in the National Municipal League's *Model City Charter*, calls for a clear distinction between the powers of the elective council and the professional manager. For instance, the manager is given complete authority to appoint and remove department heads and to administer a personnel program. Members of the city council are prohibited by law from influencing appointments and from giving direct orders to subordinates of the manager, violations thereof being a misdemeanor. Of course this extreme dichotomy is not ordinarily observed in practice.

The council-manager model resembles the industrial model mentioned earlier and the traditional organization of many local governmental activi-

---

[8] For a survey of the progress of the CAO idea in cities, see Wallace S. Sayre, "The General Manager Idea for Cities," **14**, *Public Administration Review* (Autumn, 1954), pp. 253–58.

[9] This is not necessarily the view of the authors.

ties such as school districts. Its structure consists essentially of a demo-cratically responsible board of lay citizens who choose a professional administrator to direct operations. This industrial model may not be an exact prototype of the council-manager setup because in many corpora-tions the management selects and controls the board of directors. More often than not, responsibility of the board to the stockholders would seem to be merely nominal. Furthermore most successful corporations have two executive officers, the chairman of the board and the president, both

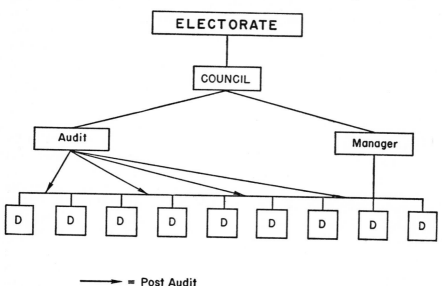

Fig. 4. Council-Manager Model.

of whom may have a rather active role. Perhaps council-manager theory has overlooked the significance of these dual roles in solving one of the knottiest problems that has arisen in council-manager cities, that is, the proper roles of mayor and manager.

Orthodox theory provides that the mayor shall be elected by the council from its own members, although there are a few cities where the mayor is elected by the voters. The Model City Charter provides that he shall preside at meetings of the council, act as head of the city for ceremonial purposes, but that he "shall have no regular administra-tive duties."[10] Several problems flow from this arrangement, most sig-nificantly its failure to provide a structural role of political leadership.

[10] National Municipal League, *Model City Charter* (5th ed.; New York: 1941), Sec. 7.

The chief areas of conflict in the actual operation of the council-manager model center around the roles of mayor and manager. A vigorous mayor tends to become impatient with his circumscribed powers and soon finds himself invading the area of administration. If the manager also happens to be an aggressive person, he will resent the mayor's invasion of his own sphere of action. If, on the other hand, the mayor is content to play a rather passive role, the manager inevitably finds himself called upon for guidance on matters of community policy. Indeed, many managers believe that they should play a leadership role in arriving at policy, provided they avoid backing particular candidates at election. These are not hypothetical issues; situations of this kind are constantly arising. Some observers believe that one solution would be to spell out the political role of the mayor with greater specificity, but the theorists have thus far been content to deal in generalities.[11]

ADMINISTRATIVE LEADERSHIP
IN THE INTEGRATED MODEL

Kaufman has suggested that three different values have dominated our quest for solutions to the problem of administrative organization: representativeness, neutral competence, and executive leadership.[12] The Jacksonian devices of elective officers, rotation in office, and boards as department heads were attempts to secure representativeness. The unforeseen consequences in ineffective service led to the civil service reform movement and the demand for "neutral competence." The failure of civil service reform to produce the desired results led in turn to a demand for executive leadership in administration. As pointed out earlier in this chapter, the quest for executive leadership took two forms: one the strong political executive, president, governor, or mayor; and the other, the professional administrator responsible to the governing body—the council-manager model.

The concept of executive leadership in the integrationist model was to be carried out by the organizational arrangements outlined here and followed by fuller subsequent discussion:

1. A planned "hierarchy," as expressed in such terms as unity of command, communication through channels, the "scalar process," and chain of command.

11 This problem is the subject of a long-range research project at the University of Southern California; see John M. Pfiffner and Frank P. Sherwood, *Prospectus for an Empirical Analysis of Leadership in Council-Manager Government in a Metropolitan Area* (Los Angeles: mimeo., 1957).

12 Herbert Kaufman, "Emerging Conflicts in the Doctrines of Public Administration," **50**, *American Political Science Review* (December, 1956), p. 1057.

2. Administrative activities grouped on the basis of function into a small number of activities under the direct supervison of the executive.
3. A small span of control; meaning that the number of department heads should be small enough so that the executive will be able to give sufficient personal attention to each.
4. An executive with complete authority to appoint and remove department heads.
5. Boards functioning in an advisory capacity, not as administrative agencies.
6. Staff services to enable the executive to carry out his duties to supervise and direct the administrative departments.
7. A merit system of personnel administration.[13]
8. The executive budget, bolstered by systematic management practices.

The Ideal Concept of Hierarchy. The administrator is to be at the apex of a hierarchy where he can exert both personal and management leadership upon the entire organization. The activities that people perform are grouped into jobs or positions, a position consisting of the tasks to which one person devotes his full time. These positions in turn comprise supervisory groups, which in turn are combined to make up units, divisions, bureaus, and finally departments. The chief administrator exercises his leadership upon the occupants of every "position" through the "chain of command." He and his supervisors have "unity of command," which is a military way of saying that everyone has a single superior who is the only one who can give him orders. Every leader is a member of three "echelons," which means that he is a member of the work group that he supervises; he has horizontal relationships with supervisors on his own level; and he is a member of his own supervisor's staff.

DELEGATION. The formal concept of hierarchy involves the corollary of delegation, by which is meant that basic authority is vested in the individual at the top of the hierarchy but delegated by him to his subordinate leaders. There is an interlocking chain of superior-subordinate relationships from top to bottom. Each subordinate has delegated to him by his immediate superior a sphere of discretion in which he may make decisions, but he is always responsible to his superior for his acts. This is in line with Appleby's concept of a policy continuum, which again contradicts the traditional view that all policy is made at the top.[14]

[13] In general the professionals have tended toward the pole of neutral competence and have drawn some line of distinction between political and administrative activity, but this is one area where theory is in a state of flux. As indicated in the next chapter, many professors of political science would abolish the so-called dichotomy, and there is indication that some of the professionals now lean in that direction.

[14] Paul H. Appleby, *Policy and Administration* (University, Alabama: University of Alabama Press, 1949), p. 15.

It must be said that we are dealing here with the formal theory of hierarchy because in government there are two forces operating to defeat the concept of delegation. One is the practice of the legislature and charter-makers to give specific grants of authority to particular department heads, which they may exercise without reference to the chief executive. The other is the tendency in practice for power centers to develop, using the term "power" in the sociological sense, meaning informal power not dependent upon formal hierarchical authority. Then, too, the degree to which delegation is actually carried out is related to the personal desires and capacities of individuals: Some will not delegate, others will not accept responsibility. Nevertheless the concept of a policy continuum and the delegation of authority to subordinates is consonant with the modern theory of hierarchy.

Departmentalization by Function. The next "prevailing hypothesis" is that the departments reporting to the executive should be organized on the basis of major purpose, such as agriculture, defense, or foreign affairs at the national level. Examples at the state level may be corrections and penology, highways, mental institutions, and education; and at the municipal level one may find departments of health, public works and parks. Departmentalization by major purpose is referred to as functionalization, and a major-purpose department may be referred to as unifunctional. The word "function" has a variety of meanings, but it is used here to indicate activities which may be grouped upon the basis of similarity either as to purpose or process.

As a general proposition, Gulick's discussion of grouping of tasks, although now over twenty years old, remains applicable today:[15]

In building the organization from the bottom up we are confronted by the task of analyzing everything that has to be done and determining in what grouping it can be placed without violating the principle of homogeneity. This is not a simple matter, either practically or theoretically. It will be found that each worker in each position must be characterized by:

1. The major *purpose* he is serving, such as furnishing water, controlling crime, or conducting education;
2. The *process* he is using, such as engineering, medicine, carpentry, stenography, statistics, accounting;
3. The *persons* or *things* dealt with or served, such as immigrants, veterans, Indians, forests, mines, parks, orphans, farmers, automobiles, or the poor;
4. The *place* where he renders his service, such as Hawaii, Boston, Washington, the Dust Bowl, Alabama, or central High School.

[15] Luther Gulick, "Notes on the Theory of Organization," in Gulick and Urwick, *Papers on the Science of Administration* (New York: Institute of Public Administration, 1937). p. 15.

However, the problem of establishing unifunctional departments is difficult because certain functions seem logically to fit into more than one department. For instance, a matter of controversy for decades has been whether the United States Forest Service belongs in Agriculture, where it is now, or in the Department of the Interior where some related activities are located. Moreover there are inevitably some activities that do not fit too comfortably into any department. To give them separate departmental status would create too many departments; the usual alternative is to group unlike activities in uneasy federation in a "holding company" department. An example is the Federal Department of Health, Education, and Welfare. The educationists have always wanted their own department with cabinet status, as illustrated by their resistance to having their library integrated into a department-wide library.[16] Another example of a holding-company department is the United States Department of Commerce, which comprises such disparate activities as patents, civil aeronautics, public roads, and census.

Span of Control. The concept of "span of control" is based upon the idea that there is a psychological limit to an individual's span of attention. As applied to organization theory, it assumes that there is a psychological as well as a physical limit to the number of immediate subordinates one person can supervise. Older organization theory assumed that top executives should have a great deal of personal interaction with each immediate subordinate. This in turn resulted in a widespread assumption that an executive's span of control should be relatively small, perhaps as little as five or six persons. Today we realize that this may not be realistic; some industrial thought and practice even favors a wide span of control in order to force delegation, on the theory that it may be a good thing for management to leave subordinates more to themselves, especially in decision making. Certainly there are many variables that influence how many persons a given executive should supervise.

In government, however, most professional opinion agrees that the span of control for the President, governors, and mayors has been too large. The Brownlow Committee in 1937 and the Hoover Commissions in 1949 and 1955 criticized the huge span of control of the President. The former found upward of one hundred separate agencies "presumably reporting to the President," while the latter listed sixty-five, not including the independent regulatory agencies, which partly accounts for the discrepancy. Both reports insisted that the President could not possibly give proper attention to this number of agencies even if he had legal

---

[16] Harold Stein, (ed.), *Public Administration and Policy Development* (New York: Harcourt, Brace & Co., 1952), p. 33.

authority to do so. In many instances the agencies were not legally amenable to his supervision or to anybody else's.

The Brownlow Committee recommended the regrouping of these agencies into twelve major departments, each headed by a cabinet officer responsible to the President, each independent regulatory commission to be attached to a department for housekeeping convenience but the commissions to remain autonomous. The first Hoover Commission contented itself with a recommendation that "these various agencies be consolidated into about one third the present number," which would amount to something over twenty, not including the independent regulatory agencies.[17]

The Model State Constitution of the Council of State Governments limits the number of executive departments to twenty; yet most states have over fifty separate administrative agencies (Colorado, Connecticut, Minnesota, and Oregon having over a hundred each).[18] George C. S. Benson states that in military organization, the span of control rarely exceeds five or six and is not likely to run higher than ten or fifteen.[19] It seems unrealistic, however, to expect a governmental jurisdiction to meet these standards because the problems may not be the same. More to the point would be to consider the analogy between a governmental jurisdiction and the holding-company type of corporation, such as the Standard Oil Company (New Jersey) with as many as fifty or sixty wholly or partially owned affiliates and subsidiaries.[20]

Public administration theory has not yet embraced one relatively new aspect in the evolution of the industrial model. This is the distinction between the functions of management at the corporate level and at the operating level. At the corporate level the function of executives is to plan, formulate policy, conduct public relations, raise money, and evaluate operations, all the while staying out of daily operations. At the operating level, management's task is to carry on manufacturing, procurement, sales, and transportation. The corporate level can probably

[17] President's Committee on Administrative Management, *Report with Special Studies* (Washington, D.C.: U.S. Government Printing Office, 1937), p. 32. Commission on Organization of the Executive Branch of the Government, *General Management of the Executive Branch* (Washington, D.C.: U.S. Government Printing Office, 1949), pp. 35, 47. For a recent sophisticated summing up of the span of control issue see Chris Argyris, "The Individual and Organization," **2**, *Administrative Science Quarterly* (June, 1957), p. 16.

[18] Unsigned, *Reorganizing State Government* (Chicago: Council of State Governments, 1950), p. 12.

[19] National Municipal League, *The Model State Constitution* (5th ed.; New York, 1948), p. 32.

[20] The 75th Anniversary edition of *The Lamp* (Standard Oil Company, New Jersey, 1957, no month or volume designated), the company house organ, listed over 60 associated, affiliated, or subsidiary companies.

supervise a relatively large number of operating units if adequately provided with staff services. But this supervision will not be of an order-giving nature. It would seem that the answer may consist of proper staffing and rethinking the duties of the governmental executive to make a clearer distinction between his "corporate" and his "operating" functions.

This distinction between corporate and operating levels appeared recently in connection with the reorganization of the Department of Defense concerning a proposal to make the Joint Chiefs of Staff strategic planners and evaluators, relieving them of the command and operating duties which they have exercised in the past. This problem is not new, Willoughby having deplored the General Staff's proclivity to issue orders immediately after its establishment in 1903.[21] However, one should not rush to the conclusion that the distinction between the corporate and operating levels is primarily based on a line-and-staff dichotomy. The true distinction is that the corporate level *does* have authority to issue orders and direct, but it refrains from doing so on a day-to-day basis. Its very real authority is exercised by broad policy directives and by follow up which evaluates the over-all accomplishments of operating units. The meaningful distinction is in the behavior of the leaders at the various levels.

Operating leaders have difficulty in adjusting to the new role when they are promoted to become corporate leaders. It is in essence a change from action and order giving to planning, reflecting, conferring, and reading. This may be at least partially responsible for the fact that the Defense Reorganization Act of 1958 was a compromise in that the Joint Chiefs' level retained more operating authority than may be theoretically desirable. Nevertheless some observers feel that it may have made some progress toward taking the Department of Defense out of operations, leaving the latter to the subdepartments of Army, Navy, and Air Force.

Appointive Power. Orthodox administrative theory assumes that complete authority to appoint and remove department heads is essential to the executive's ability to control the hierarchy. This is basic to the belief system of industrial executives who cling to the right to "hire and fire" as essential to management prerogative, especially when the unions want to "organize" the lower supervisors. The Model City Charter of the National Municipal League gives the city manager (or the mayor in strong mayor cities) the power to appoint and remove department heads

[21] W. F. Willoughby, *Principles of Public Administration* (Baltimore: The Johns Hopkins Press, 1927), p. 146; for recent events in Defense reorganization, see Paul Y. Hammond, "Effects of Structure on Policy," 18, *Public Administration Review* (September, 1958), p. 175.

without council approval, exempt from civil service. The governor is given the same powers in the Model State Constitution. It is well known that the federal constitution requires senate confirmation of important officials, but that Congress may vest in the President alone the power to appoint designated "inferior officers." However, here again there is a wide gap between theory and practice. Governors and mayors do not usually have a broad and unrestricted power of appointment and removal.[22] City managers, on the other hand, are given rather broad authority to appoint and remove department heads.

Boards and Commissions. Integrationist theory strongly opposes plural department heads, that is, boards and commissions with administrative power. The principal argument in favor of boards is that by overlapping terms, they will "keep politics out of administration" and provide continuity in jurisdictions where the political executive changes frequently, especially where the governor or mayor are elected for only two years at a time. Functional specialists in such areas as parks and recreation, welfare, and education want their own boards for an additional reason, namely, to secure administrative and budgetary autonomy and to develop a group of laymen aggressively loyal to their programs.

The orthodox administrative viewpoint opposes boards as department heads because: (1) they interfere with administrative direction and coordination by the executive; (2) they make for separatism and autonomy rather than over-all administrative cooperation and unity; (3) boards with separate taxing power violate the concept of the executive budget and therefore make economy difficult to achieve.[23]

A strong consideration in favor of boards is that they tend to satisfy the value of "representativeness" as posed by Kaufman. This factor motivated the Los Angeles Charter Commission—to cite a typical example—to place virtually every department under a five-member board, with overlapping terms, the members of which were appointed by the mayor with council confirmation. The administrative management school would agree that citizen boards can serve a very useful purpose in vitalizing the democratic process, but they would confine the boards to an advisory role. *Ad hoc* citizen boards have also been used rather extensively in federal administration, that is, boards appointed as commissions of inquiry on the British model, to inquire into a particular problem, render a report, and then disband.[24]

---

[22] *Reorganizing State Government*, pp. 21–27.

[23] A chapter was devoted to this subject in the first edition of this book. See John M. Pfiffner, *Public Administration* (New York: The Ronald Press Co., 1935).

[24] See David S. Brown, *The Public Advisory Board and the Tariff Study* (University, Alabama: University of Alabama Press, ICP Case Series No. 30, 1956).

Relatively little experience with permanent advisory boards has been reported in the literature of public administration, but anecdotal evidence points toward two problems. One is the difficulty of spelling out meaningful activities which would be advisory as distinct from administrative; the other is the problem of keeping board members interested when they are confined to giving advice only. It would seem that the lay citizen is often not content to play a passive advisory role. Consequently, advisory boards either become rubber stamps for decisions made by administrators or develop their own areas of extra-legal but genuine dominance and autonomy.

Staff Services. The traditional literature on organization often assumed a doctrinaire distinction between line and staff. While it is still important to recognize this distinction in some circumstances, the growing sophistication of organization theory has introduced at least two new emphases. The first is the necessity to get staff work done; in other words, the need to secure the facts, formulate plans of action from them, and present these to the administrator for decision. The other is a recognition that the staff function is not an ivory tower role, but that it can be successful only when carried on in a group or team relationship with the line people who have to arrive at decisions and put them into effect.

The administrative integration model would furnish the executive with staff services and agencies. The early theory placed considerable emphasis upon the passive advisory role of staff agencies, but today we are assigning the staff more of an action role in executive decision making, and it is an important factor in aiding the executive to coordinate, supervise, and direct the organization. The tendency now is to furnish executives with staff aid, particularly in the field of budgeting and administrative management. The Executive Office of the President was set up in 1939, and while it is staffed to furnish some leadership and surveillance in all areas of federal administration, its Bureau of the Budget has developed into the staff arm of the President for administrative management. The division of the budget of the state of New York operates in a similar capacity for the governor; and this practice is growing in other states.[25]

The management staff services needed for assisting the executive include budget and finance, personnel, procurement, and administrative analysis. Indeed, a point could be made with considerable justification that a management-minded governor or mayor under a weak-executive law could exert considerable control over administration through his budget power. This he would do in two ways: by making decisions

---

[25] Lynton K. Caldwell, *The Government and Administration of New York* (New York: Thomas Y. Crowell Co., 1954), p. 233 ff.; Ransome, *The Office of Governor in the United States*, pp. 323 ff.

about the allocation of expenditures, and by requiring the introduction of good management practices as a prerequisite to including particular projects in the budget.

The division of the budget in New York, the departments of administration in Michigan and Minnesota, and the department of finance in California are really the governor's staff arms for administrative management. The maturity of administration in any particular jurisdiction can be measured by the extent to which the budget process is linked up with administrative management processes. Are there administrative analysts who devote their time to studying organization problems throughout the entire structure? Does the executive have the power to make budgetary decisions, and if so, does he use the services of staff assistants in arriving at such decisions? Staff services of this kind are now available on the departmental level in the more mature jurisdictions.

Personnel Administration. The integration model embraces the concept of a merit system and a professional civil service. There has been a reaction, however, against the old reform idea of removing personnel administration from line management and placing it under an independent civil service commission. But the pendulum moved too far in the attempt to eliminate the spoils system; in the effort to combat political appointments, it was forgotten that the motivation of people is affected by those who supervise them in their daily tasks. Hence reform proposals now attempt to integrate the two reform movements by having a civil service commission to make rules, classify positions and hear appeals, on the one hand, and a personnel director under the administrator on the other.

The Model City Charter places responsibility for personnel administration under a personnel director appointed by the city manager. A three-member personnel board appointed by the city council would have only advisory, investigatory, and appellate functions. The Model County Charter, drafted fifteen years later (1956 as against 1941), eliminated the board idea entirely; the county manager would serve as personnel officer, or designate someone to act in that capacity for him, and the elective governing board would be the rule-making authority, providing by rules for a method for hearing appeals from dismissal. The general tenor of the Brownlow Commission (1937), the first Hoover Commission (1949), and the second Hoover Commission (1955) was that personnel administration should be brought closer to executive direction and that the Civil Service Commission should operate as a central personnel agency without giving up its "watch dog" activities.

There is also some apprehension about the expanding power of a professional civil service. The quest for "neutral competence," some observers say, has brought the danger of placing the power of decision making in a bureaucracy only indirectly subject to democratic control. Some professors and most federal bureaucrats opposed it, but for different reasons. The former saw it as a means for structuring the federal service in the direction of fortifying bureaucratic power centers while setting up an elite group in the European tradition. The latter felt that it would weaken their individual statuses by transforming them from career specialists into politically controlled generalists. Since these matters will be discussed later in Chapter 20 in connection with the second Hoover Commission proposals for a senior civil service, we shall conclude here with the generalization that advocates of the integrationist model favor a professional civil service, free from party politics and characterized by "neutral competence."

The Executive Budget. The proponents of the ideal model also support the concept of the executive budget which started out as a reform measure fifty years ago but which has since gone through considerable change. In the beginning it merely implied that the executive should submit a budget plan to the legislature to replace the existing lack of planning and uncoordinated scramble for appropriations. To this was subsequently added the planning of revenues, the governor's item veto, executive control of spending to keep within appropriations, the concept of pre- and post-audit, and budgetary accounting.

The executive budget has become an instrument of executive supremacy at all levels of government. It has become a coordinated plan of administrative operation for the entire governmental unit. On the federal level it has become the means of coordinating the President's general legislative program through the Bureau of the Budget. In states where the governor is well staffed, such as New York and California, the budget becomes the master plan for operations and control. The same is true for strong-mayor and council-manager cities, especially where the executive enjoys the item veto and there are safeguards against legislative attempts to secure appropriations not provided for in the budget.

BIBLIOGRAPHY

AMERICAN ASSEMBLY. *The Forty-eight States.* New York: 1955.

AUMANN, FRANCIS R., and WALKER, HARVEY. *The Government and Administration of Ohio.* New York: 1956.

BROWNLOW, LOUIS. *A Passion for Anonymity.* Chicago: 1958.

INTERNATIONAL CITY MANAGER'S ASSOCIATION, COMMITTEE REPORT. *City-Management—A Growing Profession.* Chicago: 1957.

DALAND, ROBERT T., and WICKHAM, RAYMOND. "States Seek Efficiency," **47**, *National Municipal Review* (April, 1958), pp. 166–70.

HIGHSAW, ROBERT B. "The Southern Governor—Challenge to the Strong Executive Theme," **19**, *Public Administration Review* (Spring, 1959), pp. 7–11.

HYNEMANN, CHARLES S. "Administrative Reorganization: an Adventure into Science and Theology," 1, *Journal of Politics* (February, 1939), pp. 62–75.

RANSOME, COLEMAN B., JR. *The Office of Governor in the United States.* University, Alabama: 1956.

RICH, BENNETT M. *The Government and Administration of New Jersey.* New York: 1957.

ROSS, RUSSELL M. *The Government and Administration of Iowa.* New York: 1957.

SECKLER-HUDSON, CATHERYN. *Organization and Management: Theory and Practice.* Washington, D.C.: 1955.

SHERWOOD, FRANK P., and MARKEY, BEATRICE. *The Mayor and the Fire Chief.* IUCP No. 43, University, Alabama: 1959.

SOMMERS, WILLIAM A. "Council-Manager Government: A Review," 11, *The Western Political Quarterly* (March, 1958), pp. 137–48.

WALL, HUGO. "The Changing Role of the City Manager," 41, *Public Management* (January, 1959), pp. 2–4.

CHAPTER 11

Contemporary
Organizational Theory

During the past two decades traditional organizational theory has been subjected to extensive criticism by a new generation of scholars who have raised searching questions about its premises. Perhaps their most provocative question has been whether public administration is really a separate discipline or, on the other hand, whether it is not merely one aspect of the study of government; or, again, whether it is not merely an applied element of the social sciences.[1] Questions have also been raised about the validity of the traditional doctrines and principles of public administration. For example, what proof is there that the integrationist model described in Chapter 10 is really superior to rule-of-thumb methods? Finally, the critics, who are mainly social scientists, have argued that the integrationist model is inherently antidemocratic, since it attempts to submerge individual self-realization by organizational demands for loyalty, predictability, and "efficiency." These questions must be touched upon before we turn to the main object of this chapter, which is to examine the state of contemporary organizational theory.

CRITICISM OF TRADITIONAL THEORY

Certainly, as suggested by our introductory chapters, public administration would be a barren field without the insights provided by political theory and behavior dynamics. The whole administrative machine exists to achieve certain normative ends, and to neglect these or subordinate them to concepts of efficiency and economy surely leaves out much of the picture. Similarly, to neglect the highly political environment of public administration, including such factors as the struggle for power between executive and legislature and the influence of great interest groups, is to reduce administration to a bundle of techniques, presumably

[1] This last issue is nicely discussed in James W. Fesler, "Administrative Literature and the Second Hoover Commission Reports," **51**, *American Political Science Review* (March, 1957), pp. 137–43.

operating in a social vacuum. Finally, to conceptualize administration as some superrational instrument that functions with machine-like precision according to official prescription is to present a dehumanized view of a process that is carried out by *individuals* and shaped by them in their efforts to achieve many ends other than those set down by the organization.

Critics have argued that traditional scholars have at one time or another and in varying degree committed all these acts. Waldo argued that public administration was lacking any explicit theory and that its premises reflected inapposite analogies from business organization and scientific management.[2] Sociologists have argued that public administration has neglected the "bureaucratic" aspects of administration, the impact of small-group behavior upon the organization, the struggle for power among agencies, the efforts to bend the organization to meet personal and political objectives as opposed to organizational ones. In the area of method and theory, sociologists and some political scientists have been especially critical, maintaining that public administration substituted exhortation for careful analysis and that its principles were really proverbs.[3] Finally, social scientists have criticized the highly normative approach that most public administrators, trained in traditional political science, brought to the study of administration. Democratic theory held that politics and administration must be separate because policy was made by legislators or elected officials who could be controlled by the citizen. Bureaucrats, on the other hand, could not make policy because they were appointed, beyond the reach of their legislative and citizen masters. Thus, they contended, an unreal dichotomy was strong-armed into administrative theory, mainly to meet the demands of democratic ideology.

Although most of these criticisms were somewhat overdrawn, each had enough validity to inspire a healthy self-analysis in the field of public administration, with the result that one can argue that it has been

[2] Dwight Waldo, *The Administrative State* (New York: The Ronald Press Co., 1948), chaps. iii and iv.

[3] Among others, see Francis W. Coker, "Dogmas of Administrative Reform," **16**, *American Political Science Review* (August, 1955), pp. 399–411; Charles S. Hyneman, "Administrative Reorganization: An Adventure Into Science and Theology," **1**, *Journal of Politics* (February, 1939), pp. 62–75; Herbert A. Simon, "The Proverbs of Public Administration," **6**, *Public Administration Review* (Winter, 1946), pp. 53–57; Earl H. Latham, "Hierarchy and Hieratics," Dwight Waldo (ed.), *Ideas and Issues in Public Administration* (New York: The McGraw-Hill Book Co., 1953); Glendon A. Schubert, Jr., "The Study of Judicial Decision-Making As An Aspect of Political Behavior," **52**, *American Political Science Review* (December, 1958), p. 1008; Schubert, "The Public Interest in Administrative Decision-Making: Theorem, Theosophy or Theory," **51**, *American Political Science Review* (June, 1957), pp. 346–68; L. J. R. Herson, "The Lost World of Municipal Government," **51**, *American Political Science Review* (June, 1957), pp. 330–45.

the most lively, research-oriented aspect of political science during the past decade. The results of the research and theory stimulated by these criticisms are apparent in the following analysis of current organizational theory.

THE NEW ORGANIZATIONAL THEORY

The main ingredients of the new approach to organization include the following: (1) A more explicit recognition of the place of *values;* (2) much more attention to *methodology;* (3) a changed conception of *jobs* or *positions;* (4) a recognition that civil servants are *individuals* who work (a) as members of a *group* and (b) in an organization that must be defined as a *social institution.* The emphasis upon decision making as the heart of administration could also be included here, but since it has been discussed in detail in Chapter 6, it will be mentioned only in passing. Several of these elements will now be discussed briefly.

The Role of Values. Perhaps the most apparent example of the role of values in the study of administration was the attempt to divorce policy making from administration. This has already been discussed.[4] We also saw earlier that the civil service reformers were motivated by scientific management values of economy and efficiency, and at least in part by the notion that man is motivated mainly if not exclusively by economic values. The problem in such cases was that these normative premises were never made explicit, so that their role in shaping research and recommendations remained beneath the surface. In addition, values such as those of scientific management tended to obscure the fact that business and government are different; the methods, motivations, and assumptions that characterize one are not necessarily applicable to the other. But the early administrative theory was a misconception of the nature of man and his place in the administrative operation. The formal theory of administration has been too logical and rational; the fiction that jobs or positions are separate from the individuals who fill them is a good example of this rationale. As we saw earlier, there was a tendency to view man as one among many kinds of physical resources, equally amenable to scientific organization and direction. For this reason, we shall devote most of this chapter to the new social theory which re-examines this perception of man.

Method: The Problem of Validation. The critics maintain that the concepts of the administrative management model lacked verification in the scientific sense. Some insist that they do not even enjoy "face validity," that is, they are not even supported by the evidence obtain-

---

[4] For a detailed analysis of this question, see pp. 48–57.

able through casual observation, logic, and common sense. It may be said that they have not been proved even empirically, using that word in the pragmatic sense of operational effectiveness. Indeed, there is no denying that the body of ideas that currently defines the administrative management model must be taken largely upon faith supported by pragmatic observation and trust in professional opinion. But this is not enough in an era of scientific method and behavioral science.

EXPERIMENTAL METHOD. The word "validation" necessarily brings up the question of how to establish validity, which in turn raises the matter of research methodology.[5] Political science, the discipline which is the home base for public administration, has not been experimentally oriented in its research. Indeed, there exists among political scientists considerable skepticism toward scientific method, springing from the belief that the important facets of human behavior cannot be measured statistically. This attitude also reflects the political philosopher's preoccupation with social values and his knowledge that values are relative and subjective; that is, by definition not subject to empirical validation. (This, of course, neglects the fact that the values held by an individual can indeed be measured, which is, however, a different question from the one posed above.)

In spite of these strictures, the fact remains that social science is undergoing a great metamorphosis. Inasmuch as public administration draws from all the social sciences, its students should have some insight into existing developments. In the main, there is greater insistence upon observing *actual behavior* than upon speculating about how people "should" behave or are thought to behave, as has been done in the past. This necessitates the gathering of field data and the orderly processing of such data so that their meaning can be interpreted. There is more than one way of doing this, but no student will be sophisticated in this area unless he has some understanding of "classic research design." One is more likely to encounter these conditions in the literature of psychology and sociology than in political science, but the latter is making some forays in this direction.

Experimental Research Design. The heart of experimental design is the premise that there should be a comparison between goodness and badness, measured statistically. Hence the main problem is that of obtaining an *objective* criterion of goodness and badness, that is, a standard

[5] For valuable discussion of methodological problems in administration, see Herbert A. Simon, *Administrative Behavior* (2d ed.; New York: The Macmillan Co., 1959), pp. xiv–xxxvi; for a general analysis of method, see L. Festinger and D. Katz (eds.), *Research Methods in the Behavioral Sciences* (New York: Henry Holt & Co., Inc., 1953).

that is free from the errors introduced by man's value judgments. We know that this desideratum is not always possible, that it is a matter of degree. However, experimenters are always struggling toward some objective criterion, such as productivity, which is measurable.[6]

The classical research design also requires clear hypotheses about the behavior to be measured. These hypotheses can be framed deductively or inductively, and in practice they consist of elements of both approaches. Deduction means that the hypotheses are based upon preconceived ideas about what behavior may be, whereas induction implies the forming of hypotheses only after preliminary exploration and the gathering of some data. For instance, in a study of the forest service it was suggested by a preliminary investigation that the better district rangers were strong at planning and public relations.[7] Hypotheses were framed, data collected from all rangers in the region, and the behavior of the higher-rated rangers was correlated with the lower-rated ones.[8]

Perhaps the distinguishing feature of the classical research design is the use of an experimental group and a control group. The former has usually received some special research treatment, whereas the control group has not. For instance, one may measure the effectiveness of training by obtaining data from a group which has received training and one which has not. Where a productivity or rating criterion is used, all subjects are ranked along a continuum from high to low, and the behavior of those on each end is compared.

Another feature of experimental method is statistical measurement. The data from the control group are compared with those from the experimental group by means of the statistical procedure of correlation: Coefficients of correlation are prepared. Then an attempt is made to establish the degree of significance of any differences between the two groups. Are the differences large enough to really matter, to be dependent on more than chance? There are statistical indexes such as significance, often referred to as "significant at the 1 per cent level" or at the "5 per cent level." The former implies very high significance because the results could have happened by chance only once in a hundred times; 5 per cent level is considered a very satisfactory significance. Research results that fall within these ranges strongly support

---

[6] Experiments in which productivity was used as a criterion are: Daniel Katz, Nathan Maccoby, and Nancy C. Morse, *Productivity, Supervision and Morale in an Office Situation* (Ann Arbor: Survey Research Center, 1950); Andrew Comrey *et al.*, "A Survey of Aircraft Supervisors," 8, *Personnel Psychology* (Summer, 1955), pp. 245–57.

[7] John M. Pfiffner and Frank P. Sherwood, "The 90% of Public Relations," 17, *Personnel Administration* (July, 1954), p. 2.

[8] A. L. Comrey, John M. Pfiffner, and W. S. High, "A Survey of District Rangers," 7, *Personnel Psychology*, (Winter, 1954), p. 533.

the validity of the hypothesis. An experimental study of this type is referred to as a "validation" study.

APPLICATION TO ADMINISTRATION. Can the concepts underlying the ideal administrative model be tested by experimental research of this kind? The answer is that it is just beginning to be tried and that some research groups are encouraged by their results. The chief difficulties are the size of group and size of sample required. Many relatively successful experiments have been conducted with small groups but not with large hierarchies.[9] It can be stated with confidence, however, that research directed at small groups has thrown light upon hierarchical relationships. Indeed, one can predict with confidence that the next quarter-century will see a much more sophisticated body of knowledge about administration and that the source for such knowledge will be the social science journals that specialize in reports of research results.

The following examples of group research having some bearing on administration suggest the type of inquiry that may be expected in the years to come. A study of clerical workers, using group productivity as a criterion, revealed that close supervision was more characteristic of the supervisors of the low groups than the high,[10] suggesting among other things that a short span of control may not be desirable at the lower levels. Studies in the U.S. Forest Service, using rank-order rating of forests and rangers by the regional office as criteria, showed that the better staff people do not arrogate line authority. The higher-rated hierarchical leaders paid more attention to formal organization; they used job descriptions, organization charts, and written work orders and schedules. They also planned and organized their work; workers knew what to do and conflicting orders were rare.[11]

The Swedish national telephone system practiced a form of functional supervision at the switchboard level, in which supervisors directed and inspected operators on various aspects of their work. In order to find whether line supervision might not be more effective, an experimental group was set up under line conditions. After a comparison of several months with the control group, results indicated that line super-

[9] For an article that links small group research with the larger organization, see N. J. Demerath and J. W. Thibaut, "Small Groups and Administrative Organizations," 1, *Administrative Science Quarterly* (September, 1956), pp. 139–54.

[10] Katz, Maccoby, and Morse. *Productivity, Supervision, and Morale in an Office Situation.*

[11] See Comrey, Pfiffner, and High, "A Survey of District Rangers"; A. L. Comrey, J. M. Pfiffner, and H. P. Beem, "The U.S. Forest Survey," 5, *Personnel Psychology* (Winter, 1952), pp. 307–28; for reports of other experiments, see D. Cartwright and A. Zander, *Group Dynamics Research and Theory* (Evanston: Row, Peterson and Co., 1953).

vision was more effective than functional supervision.[12] Behavioral research of this kind is becoming much more common, much of it done by interdisciplinary groups in the leading universities.[13]

Jobs, Tasks, and Positions. Organizations are established to accomplish specific ends; they are functional structures. As we have seen, early organization theory focused on the work to be done, assuming that the individual should adjust to the work situation. Individuals entered an organization to perform specific tasks which they were competent to perform; if they failed, the organization fired them and got someone else who could do the work. In sum, organizational ideology was almost exclusively task-centered, to the exclusion of the idea of the worker as an individual.

A more precise designation of organization jobs is the term "position," which defines the group of tasks or responsibilities requiring the full time of one person. "Job" is used in industry to indicate roughly the same thing, although it sometimes has a broader meaning, covering the activities of several people, e.g., the "personnel job" or "the management job." The important thing is that when one looks at an organization chart, he is seeing a structure whose basic units are composed of the work performed by one full-time worker. The grouping of these "jobs" or positions into hierarchical relationships provides the basic ingredient of the orthodox structural approach.

Another point which should be emphasized is that the new criticism has not made this job technology obsolete; the work that people do still is and always will be the indispensable ingredient of organization. The new criticism does not abandon work analysis; rather it acknowledges that work is done by people who are human beings first and workers second, and that they are better workers when administrators recognize this. Hence our new construct of organization theory will have the analysis of work, the grouping of tasks into jobs, and the grouping of jobs into hierarchies as an essential element. It differs from past approaches in that it will not be the only approach; it will be combined with the others to be discussed in this chapter.

People as Individuals. It is important to restate this conflict in organization theory concerning the role of the individual. This is the conflict between those who regard the organization's values and objectives as supreme and those who insist that the organization is properly used as a means of fulfilling individual needs for self-realization. These

---

[12] G. Westerlund, *Behavior in A Work Situation with Functional Supervision and with Group Leaders* (Stockholm: Nordisk Rotogravyr, 1952).

[13] For a comprehensive bibliography of such research, see James G. March and Herbert A. Simon, *Organizations* (New York: John Wiley & Sons, Inc., 1958), pp. 213–48.

could be called the "hard" and the "soft" schools of organizational theory. In general the "hard" school accepts the concepts of scientific management, "efficiency," measured production, and the necessity of making tough decisions for "the good of the organization." Individual goals are recognized, but the organization's objectives are necessarily prior to them.

On the other hand the "soft" school, composed mainly of social scientists, rejects the view that administrators must manipulate individuals (along with other kinds of resources) to achieve organizational ends. They fear that social science research will be used to dehumanize and to control human behavior, as motivational research tends to do.[14] Particularly they reject the view that "human relations" is properly defined as a manipulative device, that "happy workers produce more," and therefore human relations is just another technique. Willam H. Whyte's *Organization Man* symbolizes this "soft" point of view in deploring the conformity fostered by big organizations.[15] However, it is important to note that conformity is not deplored only on ethical grounds. It is also resisted on the basis that it destroys the capacity of an organization and a society to meet the demands of change by inhibiting criticism of existing institutions and values. Thus this conflict involves much more than an ethical question of the individual's right to self-realization. The following analysis should be read with this in mind.

The fourth organizational ingredient thus consists of viewing people as human beings. It is a truism, of cause, that people are different. No two persons have ever been alike, not even identical twins. Among the ways that people differ are several that are important to the study of organization: (1) differences in work pace; (2) differences in natural aptitudes; and (3) differences in acquired skills.

The importance of this concept is best seen when set against traditional organizational theory. The rationalized job structure expects the individual to adapt to it; it does not expect the organization to adjust to the idiosyncracies of the individual. In this sense organization is a standardizing process, which further accounts for the social scientists' resistance to orthodox theory. The pressures of organization tend to suppress individuality; the individual must surrender some aspects of his freedom and conform to the behavioral norms of the organization. The old structural approach did not concern itself with this matter very much because the individual was expected to conform or get out. However, the democracy of our political life is now being extended into

[14] For a suggestive, although mildly hysterical interpretation, see Vance Packard, *The Hidden Persuaders* (New York: David McKay Co., Inc., 1957).

[15] See also, Chris Argyris, *Personality and Organization* (New York: Harper & Bros., 1957); and his "The Individual and Organization: Some Problems of Mutual Adjustment," **2**, *Administrative Science Quarterly* (June, 1957), pp. 1–24.

the world of administration, even into the authority-structured industrial corporation.

One of the problems of organization theory today is to seek a reconciliation of these basic approaches which will retain the best elements of each. We need solutions that will recognize not only that individuals do differ from the standpoint of science but also that ethically they have the right to differ and that such differences are often essential to the organization's well-being. The latter would involve some sort of fundamental declaration of rights, and this is being partially achieved, at least in embryo, by means of civil service laws and collective bargaining. And, in fact, an entirely new concept of authority and motivation is being applied to organization theory. It has stemmed from two sources, each of which is treated later in this chapter: group theory and the sociological approach to authority and motivation.

APPLYING THE NEW ORGANIZATIONAL THEORY

The new approach involves a new departure in bringing the individual and the organization together. Instead of assuming that the individual must make all the adjustments, personnel administration now works toward building a more positive environment that will integrate his needs with those of the organization. Barnard and Simon have treated this development under the heading of "organizational equilibrium: the conditions of organizational survival."[16] The idea of equilibrium suggests a balance between what the individual contributes to the organization in energy, skill, and loyalty, and what he receives in return by way of recognition, pay, and security. March and Simon have recently called this concept the "general theory of organizational equilibrium," and have centered it on the individual's "decision to participate."[17] Behavioral research indicates (with some recent exceptions) that this accommodation will be more than a marriage of convenience because a positive social environment tends to increase productivity.[18] Once the individual accepts the existing balance between himself and the organization, we may assume that he can work more constructively, without the emotional strain and insecurity that come from an unsatisfactory work bargain.[19]

[16] Chester I. Barnard, *Functions of the Executive,* (Cambridge: Technology Press, 1947), pp. 56–59, chaps. xi and xv; Simon, *Administrative Behavior,* pp. 110–17.

[17] March and Simon, *Organizations,* pp. 83–110.

[18] For a summary and critique of such research, see John M. Pfiffner, *Supervision of Personnel* (Rev. ed.; Englewood Cliffs, N.J.: Prentice-Hall, Inc., 1958).

[19] Interpersonal theory of psychiatry is helpful here in understanding how the individual's ability to accommodate to his work and interpersonal relations is correlated with his effectiveness; see Harry Stack Sullivan, *The Interpersonal Theory of Psychiatry* (New York: W. W. Norton, Inc., 1953); for research dealing in part with executive behavior, see Timothy Leary, *Interpersonal Diagnosis of Personality* (New York: The Ronald Press Co., 1957).

Improved supervisory practices and "developmental personnel administration" are being used to achieve this equilibrium.

Improved Supervision. Supervision must obviously be more personalized if it is to fit such concepts of motivation and authority; a new style of individual-centered guidance will have to replace the traditional "driving," command-centered approach. This calls for individualized contacts and motivation by leadership rather than by sanctions. The supervisor must recognize that people are different and that they have to be dealt with as such, but this will be accomplished without sacrificing organizational needs and objectives. People who fail to measure up to organization needs are to be helped in every possible way to correct their deficiencies, but they will be expected to reciprocate by putting forth the proper effort.

Far from being a mollycoddling approach in dealing with people, this is a realistic one. It simply acknowledges that certain persons are superior workers and others are deficient in certain skills and aptitudes, both vocational and social. It attempts to secure the facts about each individual, to diagnose his skills and aptitudes, and to fit him into the organization on the basis of such diagnosis. If an individual's deficiencies can be remedied, and the organization has the proper facilities to do so, it will provide help in the form of coaching by immediate supervision, counseling by the personnel department, or treatment by the medical staff.[20]

In the new supervision, as in the old, a decision will sometimes have to be made to take disciplinary action, perhaps involving dismissal. Here, the public service needs to be toned up because one of the problems of public administration is the belief that "you cannot fire anyone under civil service." While there is an element of truth in this, experience indicates that the problem is not insuperable. The remedies lie in several directions, but the most likely avenue consists of a "clinical" approach to supervision which involves (1) getting the facts, (2) diagnosing the facts, (3) trying to strengthen the individual, and (4) taking disciplinary action only as a last step. Civil service appeal boards will ordinarily uphold disciplinary action when the evidence shows that this procedure was followed.

Developmental Personnel Management. This concept is based upon the proposition that the organization must try to help the individual acquire those skills which will be beneficial to the organization, as well as improve existing skills. The organization will attempt to do this by means of several procedures, the chief of which will be diagnosis and evaluation, placement, counseling, and training. Traditional public per-

[20] Pfiffner, *Supervision of Personnel.*

sonnel administration has emphasized examining, classification of positions, and pay. These techniques have all been *job-centered* rather than people-centered, including examining which has been interested only in the degree to which an individual possesses the skill requirements at the time of examination.

In the future the evaluation of employees will be concerned with their potential as well as their immediate attainments. Such evaluation in the past has consisted of the traditional competitive ranking by efficiency or service ratings. Based on concepts of efficiency and motivation advanced by economists and engineers, it has tended to minimize the human factor. These ratings have proved to be universally unsatisfactory, and their results have been a flat curve which rates everyone as superior. The new systems of personnel evaluation retain group and individual norms of desirable performance, and some elements of competition persist. But the evaluation of an employee is now a clinical procedure taking place between an employee and his supervisor, in which the latter tries to help the employee improve himself rather than conduct a punitive interview.[21]

Placement and counseling are taking on a new importance because of the need to halt high turnover in a full employment economy. For twenty years personnel agencies have been competing for the more competent people, but now we find that these individuals are changing jobs so rapidly that turnover is becoming very costly. A reorientation of basic personnel philosophy based upon two premises is needed: (1) making people happy in their work and associations; and (2) encouraging people to develop their potential skills. The diagnostic approach will attempt to place people in jobs which most closely suit their social and vocational aptitudes. One should not be surprised to find a sociometric score in every personnel folder. The aversion to transfer, because it often means accepting incompetents, will recede in the face of scientific placement based upon facts about people.

There is some evidence, interlarded with considerable hope, that problem employees such as alcoholics, hypochondriacs, neurotics, and just plain "screwballs" will in time be dealt with clinically by a team consisting of the supervisor, the personnel department, and the medical department. Administrators will work in a team relationship with psychologists, social workers, physicians, and nurses. Their aim will be to rehabilitate and to help people help themselves, the object being to make the individual better able to perform the duties expected of him.

Skeptics may see this as an attempt to manipulate the worker and mould him to organizational ends and purposes. Indeed, the interest

[21] Douglas McGregor, "An Uneasy Look at Performance Appraisal," **35**, *Harvard Business Review* (May–June, 1957), pp. 89–94.

of behavioral science research in worker motivation has been referred to by at least one scholar as neo-Taylorism, by which he intended to be uncomplimentary. These matters are all relative, as is the "manipulation" issue which is often raised when social science concepts are applied to increasing organizational productivity. All that can be said in rebuttal is that the new approach to personnel springs from two sources: (1) the democratic value systems of most social scientists, and (2) the democratic revolution in administration brought about by social legislation and the penetration of the collective bargaining process into authoritarian industrial management.

THE USES OF SOCIAL THEORY

The study of public administration has largely ignored social theory. Perhaps this is due to the fact that political science sprang from history and law, but part of the blame must be attributed to those who embraced the industrial model with its mechanistic concepts. Furthermore social theory is a rather new field. Sociology, social psychology, and anthropology are relatively new parts of most university curricula. Whatever the cause, study of organization can no longer ignore these disciplines because their concepts and their research methods are essential to an understanding of why organization man behaves as he does. These disciplines provide the foundation of organization theory.

Here we shall be concerned primarily with four social phenomena which are central to the study of organization. These are: (1) role and status, (2) small group behavior, (3) authority and leadership, and (4) the organization as a social institution.

Role and Status. Social *role* consists of the behavior expected of an individual by the social group, whereas *status* is the valuation put upon the importance of that role by the group.[22] Role and status have parallels in position classification and job analysis where the objective is to define and classify the duties and tasks performed by individuals. This suggests the chief point of difference between organization as conceived by the integration model and by the sociologists; and this difference goes to the heart of the misunderstandings between orthodox management people and their critics among the social scientists.

As we have seen, traditional theory requires that the organization itself lay down the law as to what tasks individuals are to perform. The rationale of organization demands that there be an *official version* of the duties attaching to positions and the grouping of their positions into

[22] A most useful source for sociological concepts is Robert K. Merton, *Social Theory and Social Structure* (Rev. ed.; Glencoe, Ill.: The Free Press, 1958).

organization subunits. This official version of job roles is to be found in organization charts, manuals, and job descriptions.

JOB ROLE VERSUS SOCIAL ROLE. It becomes necessary at this point to distinguish between job role and social role, but it should first be emphasized that they may be identical under certain circumstances. In other words, the job behavior of an individual may conform both to the official version and the expectations of the social group. It seems desirable to emphasize this point because of a tendency to assume that so-called informal organization is necessarily antimanagement in its orientation. We can hypothesize that an organization is healthier when its official leaders play roles which have the approval of the rank and file.

The deeper ones goes into this matter, the more essential it becomes to have some insight into group theory, which is the keystone to the understanding of the social process. The group dynamics movement is based upon the concept of the primary group as the basic unit in organization; in a sense it is regarded as the atom for the study of organization. That is why so much basic research in sociology and social psychology is directed toward the behavior of people as members of groups.[23] The assumption is that the key to the understanding of human behavior is knowledge about how people react to each other in their intimate work contacts; not their behavior in prescribed job roles alone, but what they think and do as social beings. Group theory is interested in the natural, intuitive, and uninhibited reactions of people to each other. This does not exclude their relation to prescribed job roles because it is quite possible that people will naturally behave in the officially desired way— but often they do not.

ROLE CONFLICT. This suggests the idea of role conflict, which is helpful in understanding individual behavior in organizations. While certain expectations are usually attached to a given organizational role, a problem often arises because one's superiors or his peers have conflicting expectations of one's role. Often these conflicts are the results of contradictory directives issued by those in higher posts. For example, in prison administration there is a deep-seated conflict in regard to the proper objective of the prison as a social institution. On the one hand, some observers say that its main objective should be to punish criminals by keeping them in custody. Others insist that the prison's proper role is to rehabilitate the offender, to help him find a place in society. Here again

---

[23] Dorwin Cartwright and Alvin Zander, *Group Dynamics, Research and Theory* (Evanston: Row, Peterson & Company, 1953); Herbert A. Thelen, *Dynamics of Groups at Work* (Chicago: University of Chicago Press, 1954); Hubert Bonner, *Group Dynamics—Principles and Applications*, (New York: The Ronald Press Co., 1959).

we have a dichotomy between the "hard" and the "soft" attitudes toward organizational theory.

Research indicates that prison administration is characterized by role conflict, particularly among the guards who deal directly with the prisoners.[24] On the one hand they are directed to be "tough" with the inmates; on the other, they are directed to try to understand their problems, to avoid friction by easing the impact of the many rules and regulations for governing inmate behavior. The resulting problem for guards is apparent in the following comment by one of them:

I think the big problem in here is the problem of counselors. You hear in the schoolroom [in-service] training that we are supposed to be counselors to these men . . . , you have to help them and such things as that. But if you get caught talking to an inmate, it's murder. They see you talking to an inmate and they think that you're trying to help him get over the wall or smuggle in whiskey or something like that. Now that just isn't right.[25]

As another guard said, "The number one problem is the dual role of counselor and guard that I play. This is in terms of getting a positive feeling toward me so they will upon their own choosing come to see me."[26]

Contradictory roles exist in most organizations, as do conflicting expectations of the "proper" way to play a given organizational role. Does one identify with his fellow workers or with his superiors in the organization? Does he make decisions that reflect the organization's welfare or his own? Role conflict theory provides a way of looking at organizational behavior that helps us understand it.

Small Group Behavior. A basic procedure in scientific method is to set up a "construct," a way of conceptualizing a unit for study, followed by a hypothesis about its behavior. Constructs are usually designed as possible explanations of phenomena that are only partially known or sensed. Thus much of the behavior and composition of the atom has never been observed, yet physicists know a great deal about its behavior. They made their discoveries through educated guesses, followed by experiments which tested these theories. In the study of organization, the idea of the social group is a major construct: indeed, the primary group is the basic unit in applied social theory.

A primary social group is an aggregation of "socialized" individuals, that is, its members share a number of similar behavioral norms and values, which govern their conduct toward each other and toward out-

[24] Donald R. Cressey, "Contradictory Directives in Complex Organizations," 4, *Administrative Science Quarterly* (June, 1959), pp. 1–19.

[25] *Ibid.*, p. 10.

[26] Oscar Grusky, "Role Conflict in Organizations," 3, *Administrative Science Quarterly* (March, 1959), p. 462.

siders.[27] The number of individuals in such a group does not usually exceed the limits set by face-to-face interaction among all members. It may be "open" or "closed" in the sense that membership may be easy or difficult to achieve. It may be highly structured or relatively fluid, that is, there may be a rigid hierarchy based upon seniority, strength, expertise, wealth, and the like, or authority and influence may be randomly distributed. Adherence to its norms or expected kinds of behavior may be rigidly enforced or, on the other hand, the group may be relatively permissive.[28]

An aggregation of individuals becomes a social group when there is social interaction. Thus, on an automobile assembly line, people work in rather close proximity to each other, but social groups are not formed there because the work process inhibits social interaction. On the other hand social groups do form among the people working in the service units that supply the assemby line because their work permits social interaction.[29]

Group research has shown that individual behavior is deeply affected by membership in a social group. The group is characterized by various degrees of empathy, understanding, solidarity, and identity of values and goals. One should not make too much of the latter, however, because a social group can have considerable internal dissension and yet act as a group. This suggests one of the main characteristics of small group behavior, namely, the group will proceed intuitively as a unit in sizing up certain situations and in taking action. A common example is that of an outsider intervening when he sees a man beating his wife, only to have both man and wife turn upon the interloper in spontaneous defense of family solidarity. Similarly, a social group will present a unified front in defense of group goals and values, and the action will often be prompt and decisive, arising from spontaneous understanding of particular situations without the need for overt communication and deliberation.

THE USES OF GROUP THEORY. What are some of the implications of group theory for understanding organization? First, it throws new light upon the nature of authority, showing clearly that there are many alternative forces competing with formal hierarchy for individual loyalty and allegiance. Take, for example, the idea of "reference theory," which suggests that in some types of organizations individuals and small groups look *outside* the organization for the guides and norms of their organ-

---

[27] For theory and research in small groups, see Merton, *Social Theory and Social Structure*; W. F. Whyte, *Street Corner Society* (Rev. ed.; Chicago: University of Chicago Press, 1958).

[28] Merton, *Social Theory and Social Structure*, pp. 299–326.

[29] Charles R. Walker and Robert H. Gnest, *The Man on the Assembly Line* (Cambridge: Harvard University Press, 1952), p. 56 ff.

izational conduct. Some, for example, look to long-established codes of professional conduct and achievement. These codes may conflict with the bases of hierarchical authority within a given organization.[30]

Group research shows also that an organization is really a system of competing values in which the norms and objectives of the small group may conflict with the formal goals as defined by the organization as a whole. All large organizations are composed of a variety of groups, but these groups are not necessarily "social groups," that is, they may be merely work groups and not be characterized by the intimate sharing of social attitudes and empathy that would make them social groups. This has significant implications for the organization in terms of their motivation, work satisfaction, morale, and again, the acceptance of hierarchical or formal authority. For organizational effectiveness, this suggests that social groups should actually be encouraged, since they often help members adjust to the organization. Such findings also help to modify the traditional assumption that workers are dominated by economic incentive alone, which is a lesson that still needs to be learned by organizational leaders.

Authority and Leadership. Another characteristic of a social group which has organizational implications is that the leaders are designated by the group, that is, they emerge naturally and people follow them intuitively. Such leaders, often referred to as natural, indigenous, or charismatic leaders, do not achieve their positions by appointment or by formal election, as do official leaders. They emerge through the social process itself because they initiate action which is socially approved, because they command the confidence of group members, and they have an ability to get things done.

One should not fall into the trap of believing that an essential quality for indigenous leadership is personal popularity. A group will accept strong but unpopular leadership when its survival is threatened. A thoroughgoing study of group behavior conducted at Harvard found that two indigenous leaders are likely to emerge in a task-centered group. One is a popular social leader who will be looked to for diversion and the lightening of task. The other is a methodical individual who constantly motivates the group toward task accomplishment; when activity strays toward play and diversion he puts them on the track directed toward work goals.[31]

In social theory, authority springs from the group rather than from the top down, a view essentially similar to the Barnard-Simon "permissive"

[30] Alvin V. Gouldner, "Cosmopolitans and Locals," 2, *Administrative Science Quarterly* (March, 1958), pp. 444–80.

[31] Robert F. Bales, "In Conference," 32, *Harvard Business Review* (March–April, 1954), pp. 44–50.

concept of authority, which suggests that "authority" is *granted* to supervisors by their subordinates, rather than imposed from above. An understanding of this social process becomes exceedingly helpful to the administrator in understanding resistance to authority manifested by slowdown of work pace and reluctance to accept change. The subtle nuances of most organized resistance to orders from above are essentially social phenomena. That is why the problems of authority and motivation are so largely social in nature.[32]

The importance to the administrator of understanding the group process lies in part in this area of motivation, especially today, when full employment is responsible for labor shortages and high turnover particularly at the federal level. The times call for a type of supervision in which leadership will predominate over force. As we have suggested, the group process can be either a negative agent or a positive motivator. What is new is the fact that democratic concepts for the organization of work are now being accepted in administration, not because of altruism but because (1) cultural change is forcing it; and (2) from a purely pragmatic view, we are beginning to realize that permissive work processes often pay off in organizational effectiveness.

More important for the student is the fact that an important sector of social science sees group process as the most useful construct for studying human behavior, whether in the work situation or other walks of life. In this chapter and the next we are primarily concerned with appraising where the theory of organization stands, now that it is clear that some modification of orthodox approaches has occurred.

The Organization as a Social Institution. One shortcoming of the emphasis on small groups has been that complex organizations are composed of large groups, or rather hierarchies, which are an aggregation of many small groups. In economic terms the small-group approach is through *microanalysis,* whereas organizations seem in addition to require analysis in-the-round, or *macroanalysis.* The informality of the small group no doubt appeals to the values and interests of the behavioral scientist, but this is only part of the organizational picture.[33] The problem is one of the validity of generalizing from the small group to the larger organizational context. Most of the approaches to the study of organization mentioned in this chapter, other than the primary group, are concerned with hierarchy. This is certainly true of the traditional management model and the decision-making process.

[32] William Foote Whyte *et al., Money and Motivation* (New York: Harper & Bros., 1955).

[33] For an analysis at the *macro* level, see Robert V. Presthus, "Toward a Theory of Organizational Behavior," 3, *Administrative Science Quarterly* (June, 1958), pp. 48–72.

The concept of the social institution as applied to a bureaucratic organization may be very old, but it has only recently been rationalized into the body of theory. One of the major discoveries by the landmark Hawthorne study was the importance of social organization in the motivation and morale of the work force.[34] In this case the social organization was determined by the sentiments of members toward the roles performed by the various individuals in the organization, particularly supervisory roles. Subsequent studies have confirmed this, especially as applied to the inculcation of new patterns of behavior in human relations. Thus training, which aims to change supervisory behavior from authoritarian to democratic, will not be effective unless the broader organizational climate is altered to permit supervisors to behave in the same manner. Their own superiors must also behave permissively, and their subordinates must learn to expect to be treated similarly. In this sense the organization consists of the attitudes, sentiments, and evaluations placed by its members on the roles played by each of them but more particularly by the supervisors.

This coincides with Talcott Parsons' concept of a social institution as a system composed basically of the roles which the members play. This system consists of "patterned expectations defining the *proper* behavior of persons playing certain roles, informed by the incumbents' own positive motives for conformity and by the sanctions of others."[35]

Another approach to organization stems from the so-called functional anthropologists, the most precise definition coming from Malinowski, who describes an institution (read organization) as "a group of people united in a common task or tasks, bound to a determined portion of the environment, wielding together some technical apparatus, and obeying a body of rules."[36] Malinowski's ideas evolved gradually and were left to be applied by others. In a manuscript published after his death, he elaborated more specifically a framework for institutional analysis, the main points of which were: (1) charter, (2) personnel, (3) norms, (4) material apparatus, (5) activities, and (6) function.[37]

It is neither necessary nor desirable for us to go into the details of institutional analysis at this point because our only purpose in citing it

[34] F. J. Roethlisberger and W. J. Dickson, *Management and the Worker* (Cambridge: Harvard University Press, 1939), pp. 358–64.

[35] Talcott Parsons, *Essays in Sociological Theory* (Rev. ed.; Glencoe, Ill.: The Free Press, 1954), p. 231: for applications of social theory to administration, see Parsons, "Sociological Approach to the Theory of Organizations," 1, *Administrative Science Quarterly* (June and September, 1956), pp. 63–85, 225–39.

[36] Bronislaw Malinowski, Introduction to H. Ian Hogbin, *Law and Order in Polynesia* (New York: Harcourt, Brace & Co., 1934), p. xxxiii; also Malinowski, *A Scientific Theory of Culture and Other Essays* (Chapel Hill: University of North Carolina Press, 1944), pp. 43–51.

[37] *Ibid.*, p. 52 ff.

is to suggest again that organizations are actually social institutions, composed of a culture complex instead of a mere hierarchy of jobs. The principal work based directly on Malinowski's concepts was conducted in a New England factory[38] and is important to students of public administration because it is a *case study* using anthropological methods of analysis.[39]

To sum up, the importance of this institutional concept is the realization that bureaucratic organizations are social institutions. This is true of a tax collection office, a public works department, the U.S. Forest Service, a military post, a hospital, a state university, or a fire department. A theory of administration that fails to recognize this fact is necessarily sterile. Malinowski's approach to institutional analysis is not cited here as the final answer but merely as a starting point for the development of a method of analysis that will be useful in the future study of administration. Moreover, institutional analysis is only one of several approaches to organization research, as indicated by the other approaches treated in this chapter. The imperative is that the study of administration shall take more notice of social phenomena than it has in the past.

BIBLIOGRAPHY

ARGYRIS, CHRIS. *Personality and Organization.* New York: 1957.

BECKER, JOSEPH M., S.J. *Shared Government in Employment Security: a Study of Advisory Councils.* New York: 1959.

BELKNAP, IVAN. *Human Problems of a State Mental Hospital.* New York: 1956.

BENDIX, REINHARD, and LIPSET, SEYMOUR M. (eds.). *Class, Status and Power: a Reader in Social Stratification.* Glencoe, Illinois: 1953.

CARTWRIGHT, DORWIN, and ZANDER, ALVIN. *Group Dynamics: Research and Theory.* Evanston, Ill.: 1953.

COSER, ROSE LAUB. "Authority and Decision-Making in a Hospital: a Comparative Analysis," 23, *American Sociological Review* (February, 1958), pp. 56–63.

CONSTAS, HELEN. "Max Weber's Two Conceptions of Bureaucracy," 63, *The American Journal of Sociology* (January, 1958), pp. 400–409.

ELLSWORTH, JOHN S., JR. *Factory Folkways: A Study of Institutional Structure and Change.* New Haven: 1952.

GORE, WILLIAM J., and SHIPMAN, EVELYN. *Commuters vs. the Black Ball Line,* ICP No. 42. University, Alabama: 1959.

LASSWELL, HAROLD K., and KAPLAN, ABRAHAM. *Power and Society.* New Haven: 1950.

MACKENZIE, W. J. M., and GROVE, J. W. *Central Administration in Britain.* London: 1957.

McCLEERY, RICHARD H. *Policy Change in Prison Management.* East Lansing, Mich.: 1957.

MARCH, JAMES G., and SIMON, HERBERT A. *Organizations.* New York: 1958.

[38] John S. Ellsworth, *Factory Folkways* (New Haven: Yale University Press, 1952).

[39] Another interesting approach to institutional analysis has been developed by the Yale Labor and Management Center. See E. Wight Bakke, *Bonds of Organization* (New York: Harper & Bros., 1950).

MILLS, C. WRIGHT. *The Power Elite.* New York: 1956.

PARKINSON, C. NORTHCOTE. *Parkinson's Law.* Boston: 1957.

RIESMAN, DAVID, *et al. The Lonely Crowd.* Garden City: 1955.

SHIPMAN, GEORGE A. "The Policy Process: an Emerging Perspective," **12,** *The Western Political Quarterly* (June, 1959), pp. 535–47.

SIMON, HERBERT A. *Administrative Behavior.* Rev. ed.; New York: 1957.

STANTON, ALFRED H., and SCHWARTZ, MORRIS F. *The Mental Hospital.* New York: 1954.

STOGDILL, RALPH M. *Individual Behavior and Group Achievement.* New York: 1959.

THOMPSON, JAMES D., and BATES, FREDERICK L. "Technology, Organization, and Administration," **2,** *Administrative Science Quarterly* (December, 1957), pp. 325–343.

WEISS, ROBERT S. *Processes of Organization.* Ann Arbor: 1956.

CHAPTER 12

Staff, Feedback, and Control

A technological revolution is occurring, and its impact on organization theory and behavior is only beginning to be felt or understood.[1] Certainly it has touched only the periphery of administrative literature. It comprises the great technological changes in the communication of information and the mathematical analysis of what such information means. Its theoretical basis lies in what has been referred to as cybernetics and "feed-back."

The devices for ensuring feedback are furnished by the new electronic data processing machines. Here public administration can refute the claim that private enterprise is more creative because the idea for electronic data processing began in the U.S. Bureau of the Census in the nineteenth century when Hollerith conceived the idea for the punched card. Moreover the major impetus for the contemporary electronic revolution came out of World War II, and the military phase of this development resulted from a team effort by industry, government, and the universities. This is mentioned here because the present chapter deals with subject matter not ordinarily touched upon in the literature of public administration.

THE ELECTRONIC REVOLUTION

A primary need in large-scale organization is to know what is happening in the remote corners and recesses of the organism. A nineteenth-century enterprise could be coordinated by one man who kept most of

[1] For a glimpse of what may happen to the study and teaching of political science, note the emphasis on empirical method in the following two publications: V. O. Key, Jr., in a presidential address at St. Louis in 1958, 52, *American Political Science Review* (December, 1958); (presidential address, St. Louis meeting of the American Political Science Association, September, 1958). Also *Report to the Carnegie Corporation on the Curriculum Revision Project, 1955–1957* (Evanston: Northwestern University, Department of Political Science, July, 1958).

the information in his head.[2] But there comes a time in the growth of all organizations when control by records must replace control by personal contact.[3] The income tax forced the introduction of the kind of record keeping that yields over-all fiscal results periodically, but today such rudimentary information is not sufficient. The large-scale organization of today needs, and is beginning to get, continuous information on how things are going in every subordinate division, information pertaining not only to the situation at the close of the last fiscal year but at the close of the previous day's operations. Such information includes both fiscal or cost information and data about productivity and achievements against planned goals. It permits "feedback" because these reports themselves yield information which enables executives to take remedial action at once.

Information Feedback. An example of "feedback" familiar to viewers of television programs is the police *modus operandi* report (MO), which reveals the trade-mark or characteristic behavior pattern of individuals in committing a crime. The feedback element allows the statisticians to punch MO's on cards so that the sorting machine can select the persons with a record of a particular behavior. This information "feeds back" to the investigating officers the names and other information about suspects who have that MO. There is nothing new about this because Chief August Vollmer introduced it in the Los Angeles department in the early 1920's, but it took a long time to gain acceptance by old-time detectives. This is an example of feedback of information to line workers, but ordinarily we think of the principle as applying to information furnished to administrators.

The electronic feedback principle is now used in public administration in connection with military maintenance and supply. For instance, the Air Force and the Navy now operate huge establishments for the repair of planes and ships. When a ship or a plane comes in for overhaul, an estimate is made of the nature of the work required and its cost, similar to the bid in private contracting. This estimate becomes the target and the goal against which administrators can judge the progress of the job. The time of workmen is budgeted and reported daily on mark sense cards. The commanding officer gets a daily report on the

---

[2] An example in public administration is the role once played by Third Assistant Secretary of State Adee, a career diplomat of the old school who maintained a tight control over departmental correspondence of subordinates. All outgoing correspondence went through his hands, and his standards of editorial composition and English style were so exacting as to confound his subordinates.

[3] A study of manufacturing enterprises indicated that about 150 employees may be the dividing line. Paul F. Lawler, *Records for the Control of Manufacturing Enterprises* (Boston: Harvard Business School, 1947).

progress and status of each job, which enables him to act in case achievement does not match planned goals.

Electronic feedback is also used to control inventory in the huge military supply bases. As items are checked in and checked out, records are made on cards so that the "permanent inventory" shows at a glance exactly how much of every item is on hand. When combined with operations research, the inventory is maintained by a purchasing schedule related to time of need. This prevents overbuying and understocking.

A recent development in military supply is electronic feedback relative to the costs and productive performance of those who manufacture airplanes for the government. Contracts are now negotiated on an incentive-cost basis; a stated price is the basic target, but the profit allowed to the manufacturer varies according to whether his costs are over or under this target. If he beats the negotiated cost, his profit is larger, and vice versa. This has meant that suppliers install detailed costing systems which periodically feed back the status of costs as compared with negotiated prices. This is accomplished, of course, by mark sense cards, electronic tape, and computing machines.

Data Processing Tools. Now for the first time man is solving the technical problems of recording, collating, and communicating mass data that are pertinent to the moment of immediate decision. In other words it is now becoming possible to know a great deal about the course of events and the factors affecting them at all points in a large-scale organization. Of course many factors have brought this about, but only the principal technical developments can be outlined here.

THE PUNCH CARD. For decades the punch card was used principally as a means of collating post-statistical information, that is, for purposes of historical record rather than for day-to-day control. The card was punched manually and then fed into a tabulating machine. The machine was activated by an electrical impulse transmitted through the hole punched in the card. These cards were punched by girls specially trained for the purpose, who took the data from original records, often handwritten. These girls, who were known as key punchers, were in short supply after the increase in punched-card accounting during World War II. Thus it is easy to see how a shortage of key punchers could cause a bottleneck in data processing or tabulation, as the machine accounting process came to be known.

THE MARK SENSE CARD. The punch card is still, and will perhaps continue to be, the basic record for electronic data processing, but the "mark sense" card promises to replace it for reporting current production data. This card records the same kind of data as the punch card, but instead of punching a hole, a mark is made by a graphite pencil which delivers an electric impulse in the same manner as the punched hole on the older card.

The advantage of the mark sense card is that it can be made out in the shop or at the point of production by the supervisor or a shop clerk. It eliminates the key puncher. Thus data on operations for a particular day can be sent to the tabulating unit at the end of that day, processed through the machines by a night shift, and be on the administrator's desk by the next morning. This meets the objection to a great deal of data processing in the past, namely, that the tabulations arrived too late to be useful for decisions. Up-to-the-minute data can now become a key factor in the process of hour-to-hour decision making. That is why later in this chapter much stress is laid upon the team nature of the staff function. Today the mark sense card is widely used in military maintenance operations such as shipyards and airplane repair stations.

THE COMPUTING MACHINE. Computing machines are essentially devices for speeding up recording, tabulating, and analysis processes which could be done by hand if one had enough trained people and sufficient time. The machines eliminate the drudgery of hand computation and render almost instantaneous solutions to problems too arduous for manual computation or requiring too much time and labor. The machines are not mechanical "brains" in the sense that they do creative or abstract thinking, although it should be noted in passing that the vacuum tubes or transistors that constitute the heart of the machines do perform a "brain" function of recognizing signals and issuing "orders" in response to them. The machines also perform the function of memory by storing data which can be recalled as needed. But essentially, the machines will perform only those tasks that man has laid out, or programmed for them.

THE INFORMATION REVOLUTION

The new technology outlined above and the wealth of data it provides will have profound influence on administration in three important areas: automation, feedback in management control, and research.

Automation and Its Uses. Automation refers to the substitution of machine processes for human effort, ordinarily consisting of operations in which the machine can correct its own errors. Automation substitutes machine control for human control, and this is ordinarily accomplished by means of the principle of "feedback." Most American homes have two instruments that demonstrate the feedback principle; one is the thermostat on the furnace and the other the automatic control on the water heater. These will operate indefinitely without human intervention because they contain a communication network wherein messages relative to temperature are flashed to a control point where a mechanical impulse adjusts the fire to the range of tolerance, say 65° to 75° F. room temperature.[4] This concept of a range of tolerance constitutes a phase of automation systems because the limits of tolerance furnish the signal for the machine to correct itself; the furnace is turned off when the temperature reaches 75° and turned on when it gets back to 65°.

Most automatic production systems today were made possible by the invention of the vacuum tube (and recently by the transistor), the same tube used in our television and radio sets. These also constitute the heart of the computing machines. Automatic production is made possible by the fact that these tubes receive and transmit signals which correct errors without human intervention. The machine is set for certain tolerances, and when these are exceeded, the signals either stop the machine and make corrections or make corrections before the error exceeds the tolerance. Developments using this principle have been going on apace in manufacturing industry, an example being the drilling of automobile engine blocks without human participation.

Automation is also coming to the office, and this is probably where its first major impact on public administration will take place. Los Angeles County, for example, has installed a machine that will record and store records of two million taxpayers, compute the individual tax bills, print the statements, and address the envelopes. In addition it will render accounts of the amounts due some sixty cities for which the County collects taxes. While automation in government is being applied to mass clerical and bookkeeping operations such as tax collecting, social security, and motor vehicle license administration, it is too early to know how it will be used in the nonclerical functions. However, the element of feedback and communication networks will find very wide application.

Administrative Feedback. Feedback involves the communication of information to a control point which then issues instructions to take any corrective action called for by the information. In automation the control point is a mechanical instrument, say, a vacuum tube or a series of them; but in administration the control point is usually manned by human decision-makers. Perhaps the most familiar example lies in the area of budget control, where the ideal setup has all the elements of feedback. The limits of expenditure are known, and these become the goals, targets, or tolerances. The administrator receives constant messages about the status of the various expenditure accounts and also information on actual revenue as compared with expectations. If expenditures or rev-

---

[4] For a discussion of mechanical feedback intended for the lay reader, see Symposium, *Automatic Control* (New York: Simon and Schuster, Inc., 1955), pp. 10 ff.

enues are at variance with the tolerances for any particular period, he takes compensatory action. For example, perhaps the tolerances have been exceeded in program rather than revenues for, say, an unexpected street repair cost caused by abnormal rain and floods. Then the communication network buzzes between control and performance points. Performance says, "we need more money," and control says, "we do not have it in your account, but we shall see if we can get it from some other source."

This is a good example of what goes on in the biological analogy postulated by Wiener.[5] Messages from the body are constantly sent to the brain, and these bear information that evoke messages from the brain, directing parts of the body to take action. Thus there is constant communication throughout the nervous system symbolized by goal messages and achievement messages. Continuous adjustments take place as a result of precise and up-to-the-minute information. This physical principle applies to the proper operation of an organization, the difference being that the human nervous system is a highly perfected communications network, whereas until now organizational communication has been primitive. As a result of the new technical developments in data processing and the ability to communicate, it is now possible for the first time to build feedback systems approximating the biological analogy.[6] However, it may be that man is not yet psychologically prepared to take full advantage of this technology.

In 1958 the Comptroller General reported to Congress the results of his study on the use of automatic data processing machines in federal administration. They are being used extensively and increasingly for purposes of bookkeeping, statistical routines, inventory control, and the automation of clerical operations. However, the development of administration-by-exception techniques for the over-all control of departmental, bureau, or project operations has not yet been realized. Nevertheless feedback control systems are now being used in a growing number of organizations, and it is expected that integrated systems will be forthcoming; these will furnish decision-makers with up-to-date information comparing achievements with goals.[7]

An understanding of the profound implications of these developments should include the importance of their impact upon decision

---

[5] Norbert Wiener, *The Human Use of Human Beings* (Rev. ed.; New York: Doubleday & Co., Inc., 1954).

[6] A research study showing the impact of a 650 computer on the internal administrative system of the Detroit Edison Company is underway at Michigan's Survey Research Center, under the direction of Floyd Mann.

[7] *Survey of Progress and Trend of Development and Use of Automatic Data Processing, etc.* (Washington, D.C.: Comptroller General, mimeo., 1958).

making and, in turn, on organizational theory. Feedback becomes the cornerstone of decision making. Decisions can now be based upon precise, current information, whereas in the past they had to rely more on outdated information or hunch. Moreover the sheer burden of recording, analyzing, and communicating stood in the way of getting the desired information at the proper time. Now the machine can do this rather easily. Although this development will not eliminate the mature judgment of the administrator, it should serve to sharpen his hunches. Certainly the control function can be carried out with greater precision.

New Research Horizons. The third factor in the information revolution is the expansion of research horizons. The machines not only record and store information but they will also conduct mathematical analyses which once required many laborious man-days of manual calculation even though a desk calculator was used. These same analyses today require at the most only a few hours of machine time. Indeed, it is now possible to undertake problems that formerly could not be tackled at all, not only because of cost but also because of the problems of housing and supervising the army of pencil-pushers required with hand calculators.

The significance of this development lies in the resulting ability to handle an almost unlimited number of variables. This means that mathematical analyses can be conducted of the relationship to each other of a vast number of categories of data, a feat which could not be done before because of the limitations mentioned above. To give an example, in planning a long-term study of leadership in council-manager cities, a limited experiment was designed to try to measure such leadership variables as the manager's participation in policy making and the council's participation in operations. The problem of criterion posed an obstacle because it would require the grading of cities on some standard of goodness or badness. About this time it was decided to add to the research team a psychologist experienced in working with big computers. He proposed that the concept of criterion be abandoned as such and that each of a larger number of variables be correlated with each other. He suggested as many as three hundred variables from one hundred cities. The object would be to discover significant relationships between such variables as number of traffic citations issued and aggressive leadership by the mayor. There was no attempt to pair these variables on a logical basis, the objective being to let the analysis reveal the relationships among them.

No claim is made here for the quality of this research design; it is merely an illustration of what is now possible, given the new machines. In the past the cost of this design would have been prohibitive, but now the machine time involved can be met by a thousand-dollar budget. The main problem will be to obtain the data. Fifty years from now, cities will have data processing equipment with ready-to-use data for studies of this kind, but today's researchers still have to dig them out for themselves.

Intellectualization of Administration. For several decades the part of the work force engaged in so-called direct labor has declined while that in "indirect" or staff kinds of work has increased.[8] In this period productivity has risen. Automation will undoubtedly accelerate this trend. One significant implication of data processing, feedback, and automation is the increasing demand for highly trained, methodologically sophisticated people in public administration. And the economic and social problems attending automation will themselves require solutions based on objective data, collected and evaluated by research groups composed of members from government, industry, and the universities.

A current example of this kind of collaboration is the Purdue-Calumet project, in which several interested groups are attempting to ease some of the problems in the steel industry on the south shore of Lake Michigan. A basic reason for the project was that "automation was increasing slowly but steadily, and more and more technical men were needed to guide it. Their skills were well paid, and they demanded better homes than East Chicago could offer for their wives and children."[9] Steel management tried to buy a farm in the area for a traditional housing development, but Purdue University, which owned the tract, wanted a systematic analysis made of the people and the area before committing itself. As a result a vast "combined operation" was launched to handle a question that would probably have been handled casually in the past.

The point here is that man is now using that greatest of social science gifts, problem solving, to attack the problems of his living together with others in a world that is becoming increasingly complex. He is using his brain and the power of abstract thought. Furthermore, in the United States, this is happening to both public administration and private management; the two are learning to live together and to cooperate in solving social problems that can be solved in no other way. But apart from any implications of social philosophy, the important fact for students of administration is that the "staff" function is coming into its own; the decisions of today tend to be based more and more on staff work, and this staff work pertains not only to production problems but also to social strategy involving the entire community.

---

[8] Unsigned, "Nonproduction Workers in Factories, 1919–1956," **80**, *Monthly Labor Review* (April, 1957), pp. 435–40.

[9] John Lear, "Science in the Slums," **40**, *Saturday Review* (August 3, 1957), pp. 31–32.

STAFF WORK—ITS NATURE AND IMPORTANCE

The staff concept seems to have developed in the military and only recently to have been emphasized in civilian administration. Teachers and students of administration formerly spent considerable time discussing the minute differences between staff and line, in much the same manner that scholastics of the Middle Ages debated how many angels could sit on the head of a pin. While the distinction between line and staff is still important, discussion of whether particular jobs are line or staff may lead to minimizing the really important question—that of getting the staff work done. What Is Staff Work? Staff work is really the institutionalization of the intellectual function as evident in legal, planning, personnel, and budgeting services. This division of labor is necessary in organizations for several reasons. First, the action, or "line," people who are chosen as hierarchical leaders are often not intellectually inclined and hence take a defensive attitude against the fact-finding approach, although this was more true in the past than today. Second, the resistance to change, present in all organizations, leads people to resent scrutiny of their job performance; staff work often threatens security. Third, thinking is the most difficult thing that most of us do, especially if it involves arduous and patient collection of facts. The result is that the staff work will not get done unless we organize for it by creating jobs and groups of jobs charged only with staff work.

The change in the nature of administration, especially the growing importance of information in decision making, is also bringing about certain changes in attitudes toward the staff function. The staff man is becoming more of a team worker because the line must increasingly recognize the need for his work. He is getting closer to production, and hence participates more and more in team decisions. The notion of the staff man as an isolated dreamer is certainly outdated now, if there ever was any truth in it. Of course there is an infinite variety of staff positions, but in general, staff work is getting nearer to operations.

Effect of the Electronic Revolution. The information revolution discussed earlier has enlivened staff work because it has placed a premium on the intellectual approach; the overriding need for facts in decision making will require consultation with those who either have the facts or know how to obtain them.[10] Although there will always be jobs whose duties are essentially staff in nature, the important consideration does not

---

[10] Robert C. Sampson, *The Staff Role in Management* (New York: Harper & Bros., 1955), pp. 11–23.

lie in abstract distinctions between staff and line but in getting staff work done.

An Air Force directive tells the story effectively:

COMPLETED STAFF WORK

Study a problem and present its solution in such a form that only approval or disapproval of the completed action is required.

1. Work out all details.
2. Consult other staff offices.
3. Study, write, restudy, rewrite.
4. Advise the Chief what to do. Do not ask him.
5. Present a single coordinated proposed action. Do not equivocate.
6. Do not make long explanations or memoranda. Correct solutions are usually recognizable.

If you were the Chief, would you sign the paper you have prepared and thus stake your professional reputation on its being right? If not, it is not yet completed staff work; take it back and work it over.

The Chief-of-Staff Concept. A related facet of military organization is the chief-of-staff position, often referred to on the lower echelons as the "executive officer." This individual usually ranks immediately under the commanding officer and is supposed to act as his alter ego by attending to those matters which, under the exception principle, need not require the CO's attention. Under the military premise that an officer is a generalist trained in command but who may have subordinates more proficient as specialists, it is assumed that a mass of detailed business will be transacted over his signature, but the signature may be added virtually after the decision has been made through completed staff work.

The question arises as to how far the chief-of-staff principle can be used by a political executive. To what extent is it possible or advisable for him to insulate himself from the stream of detail, familiarity with which may be vital to making decisions on major policies? President Eisenhower has been widely criticized for relying upon the White House staff for actually making decisions which properly should be made by the President himself.[11] Critics have charged that the President delegated power to make decisions on matters of delicate national interest; that he carried the "clean desk" principle to the point where it caused him to be uninformed, as demonstrated by his replies to questions during news conferences. His partisan critics compared this aspect of his role

[11] Marian D. Irish, "The Organization Man in the Presidency," 20, *The Journal of Politics* (May, 1958), pp. 259–79.

unfavorably with Presidents Franklin D. Roosevelt and Truman who were avid newspaper readers and had personal knowledge of events equal to that possessed by members of their staffs. Perhaps the public was inclined to indulge the frequent absences and vacations of a President who had suffered two major illnesses during his incumbency. But some doubt must arise in the minds of objective observers as to the extent to which a political executive should rely on completed staff work to keep him informed.

Classification of Staff Work. An important distinction between line and staff in the past has been whether one gives orders, the assumption being that staff personnel only advise. But the chief of a staff unit gives orders to his own people, and staff units also exercise authority over line agencies. In recent years there has been a tendency to use the term "program" as synonymous with line. The word "program" refers to the cardinal general-purpose functions of an agency, while staff activities involve advisory or "housekeeping" functions such as research, personnel, finance, and planning that service the major line or program functions of the agency. But even such an obvious distinction has its difficulties because program bureaus have their own staff activities with many persons engaged in indirect labor. One will find personnel doing staff work in any federal field organization, thus it seems that an organization of any size has a number of persons doing staff work.

Despite these qualifications, we believe that the classification of staff work set forth in an earlier edition of this book is still generally valid and helpful. There it was said that three types existed: general staff, technical staff, and auxiliary staff. The general staff consists of those who assist the chief and whose time is spent for the most part in strategic planning and deliberation on high policy. Department heads may spend part of their time in general staff work, especially when the chief calls them into conferences on policy. That is why it is often more accurate to refer to staff work rather than to staff agency. Some persons who do staff work actually spend part of their time in performing operating, line, or production activities.[12]

The second type, technical staff, consists of specialized activities, including laboratory research, engineering design, and functional supervision of direct workers. Thus factories usually have safety supervisors,

[12] For discussion of the general staff concept, see Otto L. Nelson, Jr., *National Security and the General Staff* (Washington, D.C.: Infantry Journal Press, 1946), pp. 1–9; John M. Gaus and Leon P. Wolcott, *Public Administration and the United States Department of Agriculture* (Chicago: Public Administration Service, 1940), p. 289. For the three-way division, see Arthur W. Macmahon, John D. Millett, and Gladys Ogden, *The Administration of Federal Work Relief* (Chicago: Public Administration Service, 1941), p. 245.

forests have fire assistants, and school systems have reading and spelling supervisors. These persons give the line advice, training, trouble-shooting, counseling, standardization of practice, and inspection. Theoretically they have no authority to give orders to production workers, but if they handle themselves properly, their word and presence are authoritative. Theirs is the authority of specialized knowledge and whatever personal respect they can command. The fact that they usually come from a higher echelon tends to give them a status that calls for respect. Indeed, functional supervision is a widely used tool for coordination and control, although those engaged in it may not recognize it as such.

The third type, auxiliary staff, is the one that gives students the most trouble because it seems to contradict the saying that staff people should not command or give orders. Perhaps it would be better to call these "auxiliary services." They include personnel, finance, supply, industrial engineering, or administrative analysis. On a more pedestrian level one finds central mailing, maintenance of buildings and equipment, control of transportation, archives and record keeping, real estate management, and communication facilities. These are all activities that must be performed in any large organization; yet for the most part they serve direct labor or program activities. Personnel, finance, and administrative analysis can be high-level professional activities worthy of the term "staff." Some of the others, such as building maintenance, are performed by low-status laborers. Hence, if it satisfies the reader's desire for consistency, it is quite all right to call the latter merely "auxiliary" activities.

Some difficulty occurs when personnel, finance, budget, and supply are called staff units because they seem to have considerable influence over the line or program people. Thus personnel officials tell the line supervisor whom he can employ, how much he can pay his people, and whether his best worker can be promoted. Finance can deny his budget requests, force him to buy one kind of tire when he wants another, and require him to move from the third floor to the tenth. This practice has been rationalized as being consistent with the advisory staff concept because control is exercised in the name of the program chief who in reality is making the decisions. Such a rationalization falls down in those cases where personnel and finance are given such control by law, independent of the chief. The fact remains that finance and personnel do exercise control power without obtaining the decision of the chief on each item.

Objectives of Staff Work. Staff work, then, consists of high-level general program planning, technical and specialist planning and supervision, and the planning and supervision of auxiliary or establishment services. Such work, by its very nature, must be performed by persons of high intellectual capacity and specialized training. This often results in conflict between staff personnel and the line. Staff workers are usually younger, more ambitious, and socially mobile. The great mass of workers in most organizations is composed of low-status persons who reinforce their personal security and pride by setting up certain defenses. The most important of these is the demand that seniority be the sole basis for preferment. They build up job status by pressing for long apprenticeships and giving excessive credit for experience. This is the universal defense of low-status and unschooled persons against the inroads of brains and technical competence.[13]

The objective of all staff work is the improvement of both product and production methods. In general staff work such as that performed by a budget bureau, economy and efficiency are important objectives. The result is that staff work constitutes a latent threat to line security. The staff studies line operations, looking for ways of improvement; this constitutes a threat to the security and equanimity of the line. The line supervisor will feel that his chief will wonder why he did not discover the need for improvements himself. As a defense measure, he will fall back on certain universal adjectives such as "impractical," "theoretical," and "bookish."[14] The young engineer, accountant, or public administration graduate is frustrated by this experience because he has been taught the logic of administrative improvement but not the illogic of human nature. Staff workers need to know that every improvement in procedures must be accompanied by social and psychological change. Machines, desks, chairs, benches, and assembly lines are activated by individuals. When work flow and layout are changed, there must be an accompanying adaptation of the human element; otherwise workers will resist technical change.

Staff work is accomplished through friendly cooperation with the line, especially when the objective is to secure acceptance of change. When staff work is done on a hit-and-run basis, the percentage of acceptance is much smaller than when the recommendations for change are developed in cooperation with the line people who have to live with the new methods. That is why many administrative analysts have an aversion to writing elaborate survey reports. They have discovered from painful experience that such reports, while they may enhance professional status on the outside, actually impede acceptance of change within. The most successful staff work is done by persons who can work well with pro-

---

[13] For a description of the rift between staff and line in factories, see Melville Dalton, "Conflicts Between Staff and Line Managerial Officers," 15, *American Sociological Review* (June, 1950), pp. 342–51.

[14] Delbert C. Miller and William H. Form, *Industrial Sociology* (New York: Harper & Bros., 1951), p. 201.

gram people, persuading them to make changes, even encouraging them to believe that they originated the ideas. But the analyst must take care that his social integration with the program departments does not deprive him of objectivity. He cannot become so sympathetic with the aims of particular agencies that he becomes their advocate.

BIBLIOGRAPHY

BELL, JAMES R. *Coordinating California's Governmental Programs.* Berkeley: 1959.

BRIGHT, JAMES R. *Automation and Management.* Boston: 1958.

EDMUNDS, STAHRL. "The Reach of an Executive," 37, *Harvard Business Review* (January–February, 1959), pp. 87–96.

FRIEDMAN, BURTON DEAN. *Punched Card Primer.* Chicago: 1955.

GAUS, JOHN M., and WALCOTT, LEON P. *Public Administration and the United States Department of Agriculture.* Chicago: 1940.

GLASER, COMSTOCK. *Administrative Procedure.* Washington, D.C.: 1941.

GORLITZ, WALTER. *History of the German General Staff, 1657–1945.* New York: 1953.

HITTLE, JAMES DONALD. *The Military Staff: Its History and Development.* Harrisburg, Pennsylvania: 1952.

HOBBS, EDWARD H. "The President and Administration—Eisenhower," 18, *Public Administration Review* (Autumn, 1958), pp. 306–13.

IRISH, MARIAN D. "The Organization Man in the Presidency," 20, *The Journal of Politics* (May, 1958), pp. 259–77.

NELSON, OTTO L., JR. *National Security and the General Staff.* Washington, D.C.: 1946.

RANSOME, COLEMAN B., JR. *The Office of Governor in the United States.* University, Alabama: 1956.

REDFIELD, CHARLES E. *Communication in Management.* Rev. ed.; Chicago: 1958.

SAMPSON, ROBERT C. *The Staff Role in Management.* New York: 1955.

SYMPOSIUM. *Automatic Control, a Scientific American Book.* New York: 1955.

UNSIGNED. *Improving Staff and Line Relationships.* Studies in Personnel Policy No. 153. New York: 1956.

WIENER, NORBERT. *The Human Use of Human Beings.* Rev. ed.; New York: 1954.

CHAPTER 13

Patterns of Organization

Power in administrative hierarchies is structured both legally and sociologically, that is, there is both a formal organization and an informal organization. But this dichotomy should not be overemphasized because an effective organization is one in which the sociological and legal structuring of power tend to coalesce. In this chapter we want to deal with some general problems of the over-all structuring of the formal hierarchy, including such matters as centralization versus decentralization, the struggle between generalist and specialist, the mechanical problems of coordination, organization planning, and the difference in the nature of authority wielded by executives at the top of the hierarchy and those at the operating level. We shall also deal with the concept of administration as an entity to be organized for accomplishing its own ends, exemplified by the White House staff and the department of administration in state governments.

TWO MAJOR MODELS

Most large scale hierarchies are organized on the basis of either one or both of two models. One is known as the staff and line model; the other, as the functional model. However, most organizations are a composite of each rather than pure types, and the following definitions are generally applicable. The functional model (see Figure 5) is one in which bureaus representing each major specialized area of work are set up at headquarters. Thus metropolitan police departments will have headquarters bureaus covering traffic, criminal records, juvenile officers, and detectives. In a government factory the functional bureaus will usually include design and engineering, product research, and production. Each of these bureaus will have its own auxiliary staff services embracing accounting, budgeting, personnel, and maintenance. A major problem here is the relationships between the functional headquarters bureaus and the individuals doing the program job in the shop or in the field. Usually, continuous direction and control runs from each functional headquarters unit to its production unit in the field.

The line and staff model (see Figure 6) is one in which there is a single line of command running from the chief administrative officers through their subordinates to the field or the shop. The functional bureaus are entirely subordinate to this chain of command. Thus, while functional supervision refers to the direction, control, and authority exercised by the functional bureau at headquarters, line supervision refers to the direction, control, and authority exercised by individuals in

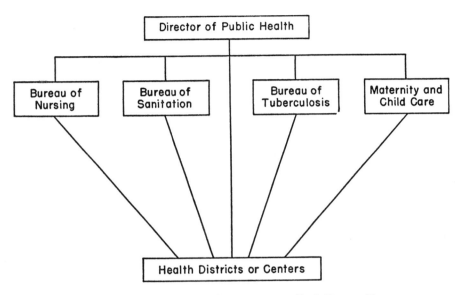

FIG. 5. Functional Type of Organization. Each Bureau Has
Line Authority to Field.

the chain of command, regardless of hierarchical level. The following discussion and illustrations will make the two models and their problems clearer.

The organizational problem presented here is really one phase of the perpetual struggle between generalist and specialist, to be found in most big organizations where specialists or a specialist type of production are represented. Today that includes practically all organizations. The problem is very well posed in an Inter-University Case Program study involving practically a half-century of attempts to reorganize the health department of New York City.[1] Large public health departments usually have a bureau structure at headquarters with each of the principal

_____

[1] Herbert Kaufman, *The New York City Health Centers* (University, Alabama: University of Alabama Press, ICP Case Series No. 9, 1952).

specialties having a bureau of its own, e.g., tuberculosis, communicable diseases, sanitation, vital statistics, maternity and child care, and public health education. Historically, the establishment of these headquarters bureaus usually precedes the introduction of decentralization through the creation of health centers in the outlying areas. In New York the bureaus established their own field offices, each separated from the other without any coordination in the field. The result was that the bureaus

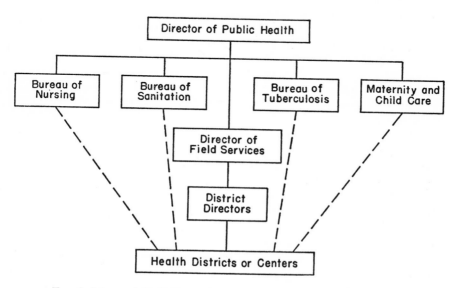

FIG. 6. Line and Staff Type of Organization. Headquarters Bureaus Have Only Staff Relationship to Field.

became largely autonomous; one commentator called them "a series of kingdoms." This represents a functional type of organization under our two major models postulated above.

Beginning in 1915, attempts were made to establish a line-and-staff type of field organization as represented by the other major model. Under this type New York would be divided into a number of health districts, each administered by a health center. From then on the specialized bureaus at headquarters would act purely in a staff capacity. Each decentralized district would have a single district director who would be administratively responsible for all health activities in that district. The public health nurses, the sanitary inspectors, and those working in the other specialties would be responsible to him. What actually happened was that the specialists in the districts continued to look to the specialized bureaus at headquarters for supervision and leadership. The district health director had difficulty in asserting administrative leadership, and the representatives of the bureaus did everything to undermine his power and to retain it for themselves. Over the years attempts were made to impose a line-and-staff type of organization, but most of them failed. As things now stand, the department has a line-and-staff type of field organization in name, but the conflict between the functional bureaus and generalist administrators continues. This is one of the foremost problems in the structuring of hierarchy. Those who advocate the ideal administrative model usually favor the staff-and-line type of organization because it promotes coordination.

DUAL SUPERVISION

A candid recognition of dual supervision has been urged by Arthur W. Macmahon and John D. Millett.[2] They do not argue in favor of functional autonomy but for a balance in which line and function recognize the contribution of the other, working together in harmony. Under this arrangement the line administrator would coordinate. Specifically he would be concerned about the amount of staff services required, seeing that there was no unnecessary duplication of effort; he would manage the staff agencies so that they could give the maximum service to the specialties; and he would lead them to cooperate, settling internecine strife and easing interfunctional maladjustments. In so doing he would observe the natural limitations of the generalist by not substituting his judgment for that of a specialist in areas where the latter is presumed to have extraordinary competence.[3] These authors do not seem to be arguing for any great change from orthodox theories of organization; instead, they merely desire a frank recognition that functional authority may exist alongside the line of command, if not actually in the bonds of matrimony, at least with enough platonic respect to ensure effective operation.[4]

Macmahon and Millett are not the first since Taylor to advocate a dual type of supervision, for Mary Parker Follett advocated something similar. To her, "command" was merely one of a number of functions, its purpose being primarily that of coordinating all the specialties. If coordination consists mainly of securing voluntary cooperation and syn-

[2] Arthur W. Macmahon, John D. Millett, and Gladys Ogden, *The Administration of Federal Relief* (Chicago: Public Administration Service, 1941), pp. 244–68; John D. Millett, "Field Organization and Staff Supervision," in *New Horizons in Public Administration* (University, Ala.: University of Alabama Press, 1945), pp. 96–118.

[3] John D. Millett, *New Horizons in Public Administration*, pp. 113–15.

[4] Fesler takes issue with Millett's concept of dual supervision. James W. Fesler, *Area and Supervision* (University, Ala.: University of Alabama Press, 1949), pp. 82–83.

thesis, the hierarchy may be regarded as a servant rather than a master. In discussing "the illusion of final authority," "the law of the situation," "constructive conflict," and "power with" versus "power over," Follett develops such a viewpoint. Authority is not based upon formal position but on the capacity to act in accordance with the "law of the situation," a pattern of behavior associated not only with personal ability but with specialty or function.[5] In making a final decision, an executive is merely completing a process which included a series of preliminary decisions made by technically qualified subordinates. In a large share of decisions he is bound by the demands of function. Indeed, line supervisors in any large-scale organization are subject to many such functional limitations which cut across hierarchical lines.

Some agencies openly recognize the different types of functional authority, and it is not uncommon to see functional charts with broken lines indicating the paths which the formal organization expects such authority to follow. In some county health departments, for example, the organization chart depicts the headquarters' functional units and minimizes the field organization where the health work actually takes place. A distinction is made officially between "technical control" exercised by the headquarters' bureaus and "administrative control" by the district health officers.

SOME KEY PROPOSITIONS

As a result of these observations, our key proposition suggests that *a good organization recognizes functional interests without departing from the essential supremacy of the line of command.* This requires an arrangement in which relationships are spontaneous and mutual and where teamwork prevents the rise of issues over prerogative.

SUBPROPOSITION 1. The line supervisor formally controls all the activities and people in his jurisdiction, but he must also observe certain standardized functional controls which operate uniformly throughout the entire line organization; these controls are usually in writing and are issued under the authority of the chief administrative officer.

SUBPROPOSITION 2. The line supervisor has been delegated a maximum of latitude in decision making. He observes the standard functional regulations; he seeks the advice of functional specialists; but he has the authority to act in a wide variety of situations where he must use his own judgment.

[5] Henry C. Metcalf and L. Urwick (eds.), *Dynamic Administration, The Collected Papers of Mary Parker Follett* (New York: Harper & Bros., 1942), pp. 147–286.

SUBPROPOSITION 3. The line supervisor is a coordinator, but he is more than a mere housekeeper. To be sure, he should see that people are at work on time, give them their pay checks, have good physical working conditions, and make sure that records are properly kept. But if he stops there, he is not a coordinator, for coordination involves leadership. He should not let the functionalists steal his show; he must coordinate by positive means rather than by fencing off his domain.

SUBPROPOSITION 4. The normal relationships are those of staff functionalism rather than line functionalism; and variations from this rule should be justified by a demonstration of unusual circumstances.

SUBPROPOSITION 5. Functional specialists gain acceptance of their ideas through persuasion rather than command. Their *modus operandi* emphasizes advice, training, research, conference, inspection, installation, and collaborative trouble-shooting. They are conditioned to avoid command and order giving.

SUBPROPOSITION 6. When contacting line workers, the functionalist should observe hierarchical courtesy. Thus he will call first on the line supervisor when visiting field or shop; and he will give orders to line workers only in exceptional circumstances.

DECENTRALIZATION

The last quarter-century has been characterized by the expansion of most organizations, both governmental and industrial. When organizations are relatively small, the tendency is to concentrate decision-making power at headquarters. Very often this means placing power in the hands of a single individual. Strong men usually prefer to operate this way; they like to make decisions themselves. And some observers believe that decisions are best reached in this way; they contend that the industrial leaders of the nineteenth century were uncommon men with a rare genius for coordination. These critics feel that the new emphasis upon group decision making, decentralization, and delegation will prevent such individuals from emerging in the future because the new group approach to corporate life cramps their style.[6]

But as organizations expand, it becomes physically impossible for one person to make all the decisions or to supervise the details of operations personally. Usually the persons who have grown up with the organization and who have been close to operations find it difficult to decentralize and to delegate, to push decision power down to appropri-

---

[6] William H. Whyte, Jr., *Is Anybody Listening?* (New York: Simon and Schuster, Inc., 1952).

ate operating levels. As a result new managers are brought in and a new pattern of structuring formal hierarchies begins to emerge.

Concentration of Power to Organize. The power to organize should reside at the top of the hierarchy, and by the power to organize is meant the authority to prescribe the functions, duties, responsibilities, and decision-making limits, both of positions occupied by individuals and the organizational subunits. In public administration the legislature may designate by law the distribution of functions and activities by departments, although some advocates of the integrated model would give the chief executive the power to do this.

Only during the last decade have large industrial corporations set up specialized units for organizational planning, often under the executive vice-president or the vice-president for administration. The duty of this unit is to keep an eye on the over-all organization structure and to recommend proper hierarchical relationships. The organization planning people comprise a part of the staff team which is in on the discussion of changes affecting future plans for product, plant, sales, and employees. Inasmuch as proposals for change inevitably affect structure, the planners are expected to present proposed organization changes to go along with the plans.

Organization planning is not so well structured in public administration, but the administrative analyst in the bureau of the budget does some organization planning on all levels of government. Usually the over-all pattern of organization is set forth in state constitutions and city charters to the extent that organization planners must confine their studies to changes of internal organization within particular departments.

Delegation of Decision Making. Paul Appleby once insisted that much of the discussion of decentralization fails to recognize the fact that it is impossible to decentralize until administrative power has been centralized. This concept is in line with the distinction between the power to make decisions and the function of decision making. It also fits into both Appleby's idea of a vertical continuum of decision making and Simon's vertical structuring of decisions. The point is that concentrating the power to make decisions at the top of the hierarchy is not at all inconsistent with the concept of decentralization and delegation. Before power can be rationally allocated throughout the organization, it must first be pulled together at the center. Indeed, there is a central unity between decision making, the job-structured organization, and the concept of decentralization. When these are combined with the concepts of feedback, control, and communication networks, the over-all pattern of organization begins to make sense and to hold together.

As we have seen, under traditional concepts an administrative hierarchy consisted of jobs structured both horizontally and vertically. The principal basis for structuring was the duties performed, the functions, the service, or the product. Decision theory does not destroy this; it merely adds to the job description a statement relative to the individual's authority, that is, his power to make decisions. This neatly points up the distinction between the power to make decisions and the function of decision making. For the power to make decisions is at the top of the hierarchy, but those who have such power have delegated a portion of it to subordinates at all levels.

Decision making is assigned to people along this vertical continuum in line with what Mary Follett called "the law of the situation." By this she meant that people at the several hierarchical levels are assigned decision-making authority in accord with the needs of operations. Elton Mayo said the same thing in a different way when he stated that the locus of decision should be at the lowest appropriate level. The advantages of such delegation are clear: The top administrator is relieved of part of his burden; things are accomplished quicker; psychologically, a feeling of involvement is achieved by the individual who makes the decision; rationality is fostered by encouraging those who know most about the technical requirements of the decision to make it.

OBSTACLES TO DELEGATION. A common problem of decentralizing decision making in most organizations is that two forces are working in opposite directions—the one, centrifugal, the other centripetal. First, there is a constant struggle among specialized subunits to become autonomous, to be free of central administrative control, and to resist coordination, as evidenced in the bureau structure of federal departments. It has long been known, for instance, that the bureau structure in the Navy has hampered effective coordination.[7] Similar centrifugal tendencies are found in the Department of Defense, with each of the armed services wanting to go its separate way. This problem is also related to the span of control when, in an attempt to keep the number of departments down, activities only remotely related to each other are grouped together in the same department. These are sometimes referred to as "holding-company" departments, a leading example being the federal Department of Health, Education, and Welfare.

The opposite tendency, to retain at headquarters the power to make decisions which should be made at subordinate levels, is also at work in most organizations. There can be empire building at headquarters as well as on subordinate levels. In federal administration this frequently occurs in relations between Washington and the field. At the beginning

[7] Herbert Emmerich, *Essays on Federal Reorganization* (University, Alabama: University of Alabama Press, 1950), p. 41.

of World War II housekeeping functions such as finance and personnel in the War Department were highly centralized in Washington. This created a problem not only of processing an avalanche of paperwork which could just as well be done in the field but also of crowding Washington with thousands of people who did not need to be there. The old-time bureaucrats who grew up with the system were unwilling to change, thus it was necessary to bring to the key spots administrative-minded people from the outside.

Psychological and political considerations also inhibit delegation. One of the main reasons for failure to decentralize decision-making authority is the fear that subordinates will make mistakes. This is particularly true in the case of public administration because of the political implications of many decisions. For instance, it is said that personnel actions such as appointment, dismissal, and transfer are centralized in bureau or departmental offices in Washington because of the interest of Congressmen in these actions. But another reason for failure to push decision making down is the lack of understanding or lack of confidence in the new techniques that ease delegation and control. The most important of these is the communication of information about performance and achievement at subordinate levels as compared to planned targets. The other is the administrative audit, a device which was used to decentralize personnel during World War II. The power to take action on civilian personnel was decentralized to the post and field commands, but auditing teams from headquarters conducted periodical examinations of the way that decision-making power had been exercised. This procedure survived and today has become a pattern for organizing a vertical structure of decision making in federal personnel work.

Decentralized Industrial Management. The concept of decentralization is made clearer by the distinction between corporate and operating levels developed in industry. It was pointed out in Chapter 9 that industrial and military models had tremendous influence upon the development of the public administrative model, including the concepts of hierarchy, unity of command, staff-and-line organization, and general staff. While public administration reform dates roughly from 1910, the great developments in the internal management of our industrial corporations have evolved more recently. The history and rationalization of these developments is just beginning to be studied. This is evidenced by Ernest Dale's account of the structural evolution in General Motors and du Pont, which is typical of the distribution of decision making in all expanding organizations, whether public or private. What usually happens is that a strong executive who is both creative and aggressive has made the original decisions which were responsible for the organization becoming large and prosperous, but as it becomes larger, he finds himself incapable of relinquishing either power or decision making to subordinates. He continues to play the game close to his vest, often to the great annoyance and anxiety of his subordinates. There comes a time when he must leave because of internal crisis, superannuation, or death. Group management succeeds personal management, and the decentralization of decision making results.

In General Motors the aggressive organizer was W. C. Durant, whose strength was in financial manipulation rather than internal management. While maintaining corporate offices in New York, he nevertheless interfered in decisions at the operating level. Durant was eventually forced out because the corporation was going broke under this type of management. He was ultimately followed by Alfred P. Sloan, Jr., who introduced decentralized management and is sometimes regarded as the father of the idea which we are emphasizing at this point, namely, the distinction between corporate and operating levels.[8]

Sloan's idea was that the corporate level should not concern itself with operating decisions and details but with high policy on matters which affected all divisions of the corporation. In addition, the corporate level should conduct over-all planning, research, supply technical help to the subordinate divisions, and maintain supervision over the operating units by means of communication and feedback, in line with concepts set forth above as basic to decision making.

One particular development at du Pont illustrates very aptly this distinction between the corporate level and the operating level. Members of the du Pont executive committee have no operating responsibilities. They spend their time planning and keeping in touch with what is going on in all departments of the company as it affects the whole organization. While these individuals are specialists who have had production experience, they are not individually responsible for the results obtained in any plant or specialized activity. This is quite important because it was found that when the head of a plant or an operating division became a member of the executive committee, his decisions tended to be colored by how they would affect his own operations.[9]

In public administration an outstanding example of how the distinction between corporate and operating level is violated is seen in the tendency of state constitutions to set up numerous boards with elected constitutional officers such as secretary of state, attorney general, auditor, and treasurer serving as ex officio members. In addition to being a

[8] Ernest Dale, "Contributions to Administration by Alfred P. Sloan, Jr., and GM," 1, *Administrative Science Quarterly* (June, 1956), pp. 30–62.

[9] Ernest Dale, "Du Pont: Pioneer in Systematic Management," 2, *Administrative Science Quarterly* (June, 1957), pp. 25, 47, 51.

burdensome task for these men who already have full-time jobs, the concept violates the distinction between operating and corporate level. Many observers believe that this concept of corporate level may be usefully applied to the span of control concept at the top levels of a governmental hierarchy.

THE SPAN OF CONTROL

As indicated earlier, the span of control idea is based upon the psychological concept of span of attention, which in turn springs from the belief that an individual's ability to direct subordinates is limited to a certain number. As applied to organization theory, there has been a belief that a top executive should have only a small number of persons, perhaps three, five, or seven, reporting to him. This belief reflected the conviction that an executive should have constant interaction with his principal subordinates and that he should be constantly accessible to them. Consequently, practically all the "boiler-plate" reports on organization recommend a smaller span of control for the President, governors, mayors, and city managers.

Practically all governmental jurisdictions have a large number of units or departments when arranged horizontally on the top echelon, ranging from seventy-five for the federal government into hundreds for state government and as many as forty or fifty for large cities. This condition is regarded as undesirable by the administrative experts—they would reduce it to twenty or so.

A running controversy has been going on between Lyndall F. Urwick and Herbert A. Simon, the former defending the concept of span of control, and Simon adopting a questioning attitude.[10] Urwick advocates a rather small span of control, whereas Simon insists that the smaller the span of control, the greater the number of vertical echelons which are necessary, in turn making vertical communication difficult. Administrative practice here varies greatly, of course. For example, Sears, Roebuck and Company deliberately uses a flat type of organization in which there is a long span of control at the top. This is said to force executives to delegate, thus giving greater autonomy in decision making to field offices and store managers.[11]

The span of control concept as applied to governmental organization needs to be reexamined in the light of the information revolution dis-

[10] Herbert A. Simon, "The Span of Control, A Reply," **21**, *Advanced Management* (April, 1957), p. 14; Lyndall F. Urwick, "The Span of Control, Some Facts about the Fables," **21**, *Advanced Management* (November, 1956), pp. 5–14.

[11] James C. Worthy, "Organizational Structure and Employee Morale," **15**, *American Sociological Review* (April, 1950), pp. 169–79.

cussed in Chapter 12. The short span of control is based upon the belief that a top executive must have intimate and frequent personal contact with his immediate subordinates, and that the power to hire and fire is essential to control. We now know that communication and feedback information about planned production goals are perhaps just as important as intimate personal contact in maintaining supervision over subordinates. Here the governmental chief executive is operating at the corporate level rather than the operating level. Industrial corporations often have a span of control at the top just as great as those of the big governmental units. They are able to maintain supervision over this multiplicity of units by means of highly organized staff work on the corporate level, and by organizing the flow of information from the production worker on up through the board of directors. Hence the solution to improvement of administration in a state which has over a hundred departments may not be to reduce their number to fifteen or twenty but to inaugurate a flow of goal-centered information and feedback.

In any case, the span of control should be adjusted to the needs at the particular point in the hierarchy under consideration; there is no constant number applicable to every situation. It therefore seems wiser to substitute the concept of "supervision needed" for the much-abused span of control concept. This means simply that as many variables as can be isolated should be studied in each particular situation to ascertain how many persons should be reporting to a particular supervisor.

EXECUTIVE COORDINATION

The most outstanding development in the last quarter-century has been the attempt to institutionalize the office of the President and of the governors. On the national level this has given rise to the Executive Office of the President and the White House staff. On the state level it is exemplified in the department of administration or the department of finance under the governor. These agencies operate almost entirely in a staff capacity with the exception of certain budget and housekeeping activities where some element of control over the operating agencies is involved.

Presidential Staff Aids. The Executive Office of the President was established in 1939. Today it includes the Bureau of the Budget, the Council of Economic Advisors, the National Security Council, the Office of Defense Mobilization, and the President's Advisory Committee on government organization. Significantly these staffs have all grown up in the last twenty-five years to meet the needs arising from: (1) the depression of the 1930's; (2) World War II; (3) the needs of the post-war economy; (4) the build-up for Korea; and (5) the fight against Communism.[12]

The President really has two staffs, the Executive Office and the White House Staff. The Executive Office is not located in the White House, and under the Eisenhower administration was not so close to Presidential policy and decision making as the White House staff.[13] The White House staff consists of the people who actually work in the White House and who have daily access to the President. During much of the Eisenhower administration the group was headed by a chief of staff, Sherman Adams, to whom was delegated a great deal of hour-to-hour decision making. This arrangement was said to be in keeping with military precedent, which is to rely upon staff to relieve the commander of the burden of operating decisions. This is in line with the principle of delegation, which says that only exceptional matters outside of routine shall be taken to the chief, widely known as the "exception principle."

It should be noted that many of the activities in the President's staff relate to policy matters particularly in the area of foreign affairs and economic development; moreover the Bureau of the Budget coordinates proposals for legislation originating in the agencies. This is mentioned here because at the state and local level such executive staffs are more concerned with budgetary control, housekeeping, and auxiliary services. The federal Bureau of the Budget has some control functions such as the quarterly allotment of expenditures under the budget, and during the 1940's, Congress authorized the Bureau to set ceilings on personnel to be hired by the nondefense agencies. From the standpoint of day-to-day coordination of operations, perhaps the Budget Bureau is the most important of the President's staffs. The power to prepare the annual estimates and to explain them to the Congressional committees places the Bureau at the center of power as far as administration is concerned.

There are certain coordinating activities that are sometimes referred to as business functions, housekeeping services, auxiliary services, and by the British as establishment services. On the federal level these are placed in the General Services Administration, an agency not in the Executive Office of the White House but nevertheless under an administrator appointed by the President. Its jurisdiction includes such activities as purchasing, supply, buildings, transportation, and public utilities,

---

[12] A discerning history and comment on the development of the president's staffs is contained in: Richard E. Neustadt, "Presidency and Legislation: Planning the President's Program," 49, *American Political Science Review* (December, 1955), pp. 980–1021; Neustadt, "Presidency and Legislation: The Growth of Central Clearance," *American Political Science Review*, 48, (September, 1954), pp. 641–71.

[13] John R. Steelman and H. Dewayne Kreager, "The Executive Office as Administrative Coordinator," 21, *Law and Contemporary Problems* (Autumn, 1956), pp. 688–709.

national archives, and records. The governors of the states are less
generously supplied with staff help than the President, although we may
expect that social and technical developments will force strengthening
of the governor's role and therefore necessitate better staffing of his
office.[14] States are going to have to deal realistically with problems of
population, natural resources, land use, and public works, and in doing
so, each state will require central coordination agencies. It seems quite
natural that these will head up in the governor's office.

The Department of Administration. Survey reports are beginning to
advocate the establishment of an office of administration in the governor's
office. Minnesota and Michigan have adopted proposals along this line.
In Michigan, structural and political obstacles have prevented complete
fulfillment of the objectives of this agency.[15] In general, administrative
departments deal with such matters as budget, purchasing, supply,
auxiliary services, accounting, and administrative surveys. The latter is
sometimes referred to in the vernacular of administration as "O and M,"
meaning organization and methods. Members of such an organization are
administrative analysts who make reorganization studies of the agencies,
evaluate administrative methods, devise new methods, forms and systems,
and conduct analyses of the use of buildings and space.[16]

BIBLIOGRAPHY

APPLEBY, PAUL H. *Big Democracy.* New York: 1945.
DUBIN, ROBERT. *The World of Work.* Englewood Cliffs, New Jersey: 1958.
GAUS, JOHN M. *Reflections on Public Administration.* University, Alabama: 1947.
HEADY, FERREL, and PEALY, ROBERT H. "The Michigan Department of Administra-
    tion," 16, *Public Administration Review* (Spring, 1956), pp. 82–89.
KAUFMAN, HERBERT. *The New York City Health Centers* ICP Case. Rev. ed.; Uni-
    versity, Alabama: 1959.
LAWRENCE, PAUL R. *The Changing of Organizational Behavior Patterns.* Boston: 1958.
MACMAHON, ARTHUR W., MILLETT, JOHN D., and OGDEN, GLADYS. *The Administra-
    tion of Federal Work Relief.* Chicago: 1941.
MARTIN, ROSCOE C. (ed.) *TVA The First Twenty Years: a Staff Report.* University,
    Alabama: 1956.
MORSTEIN, MARX, FRITZ. *The Administrative State.* Chicago: 1957.
SIMON, HERBERT A., *et al. Centralization vs. Decentralization in Organizing the
    Controller's Department.* New York: 1954.
SOUJANEN, WAINO W. "Is Military Organization *Really* Better?" 23, *Advanced Man-
    agement* (September, 1958), pp. 10–14.
UNSIGNED. *A State Department of Administration.* Chicago: 1957.

[14] Coleman B. Ransome, Jr., *The Office of Governor in the United States* (University, Ala.: University of Alabama Press, 1956), p. 302 ff.

[15] Ferrel Heady and Robert H. Pealy, "The Michigan Department of Administration," 16, *Public Administration Review* (Spring, 1956), p. 89.

[16] Unsigned, *A State Department of Administration* (Chicago: Council of State
Governments, 1957); unsigned, *Reorganizing State Government* (Chicago: The Council
of State Governments, 1950), pp. 103–7.

Part IV

PERSONNEL ADMINISTRATION

CHAPTER 14

What Is Personnel Administration?

As we have just seen, the new organizational theory stresses the human aspects of administration. Instead of assuming that man is made for the organization, the new theory seeks an equilibrium between organizational demands and individual self-realization. This trend is apparent in attempts to conceptualize the individual-organizational bargain as a fusion process, in which neither element can be understood apart from the other.[1] In this chapter we turn directly to this human element in administration and to the various concepts and procedures that have evolved for handling the individuals in the bureaucratic apparatus.

Most large-scale organizations have a certain number of people assigned to what is known as personnel administration.[2] Until quite recently most governmental personnel specialists worked in a central staff agency known as the Civil Service Commission. In the last few years, however, there has been a tendency to decentralize personnel work, so that today many specialists are employed in line or operating agencies. In this chapter we shall outline some of the major problems and trends in personnel, followed in succeeding chapters by a consideration of its major operational aspects.

THE FUNCTIONS OF PERSONNEL ADMINISTRATION

By way of introduction, it may be helpful to outline the major activities covered by the term "personnel administration." These vary in emphasis from place to place, but they consist of a body of duties or services which must be performed by someone in every big organization.

[1] Among others, see Chris Argyris, "The Individual and Organization: An Empirical Test," 4, *Administrative Science Quarterly* (September, 1959), pp. 145–67; also, E. D. Bakke, *The Fusion Process* (New Haven: Yale University Press, 1955); Felix Nigro, "The Modern Concept of Personnel Administration," 18, *Public Personnel Administration* (July, 1957), pp. 160–66.

[2] Current personnel ratios for government and industry have been prepared by Dale Yoder and appear annually in the July-August issue of *Personnel*.

1. Job analysis and position classification: the description of the work to be performed in a given job which becomes the basis for effective recruitment.
2. Recruitment and placement: the process of matching individual skills and aptitudes with job or class specifications.
3. Evaluation, promotion and transfer: the procedures used to recognize accomplishment and to use individual abilities to greatest advantage.
4. Compensation scales: plan for assuring equal pay for equal work, with salary gradations based on individual skills required by the job.
5. Training, counseling, and improvement of working conditions: the most important of a variety of services designed to motivate employees.
6. Relations with employee organizations and unions: handling relationships with these groups.
7. Disciplinary action: the supervision of individual suspension and dismissal cases.
8. Personnel records: maintaining such employee records as rosters, time cards, sick and vacation leave records, eligible lists, payrolls, and employee folders.

These methods and their underlying assumptions have evolved over a long period of time, and they are constantly subject to change in the light of changing national conditions and the new insights into organizational behavior afforded by research and experience. For this reason our analysis begins with a consideration of several cultural and historical influences that have shaped modern personnel administration.

CULTURAL INFLUENCES ON PERSONNEL PRACTICE

In both England and the United States public personnel administration has suffered from negative popular attitudes and manipulation for political purposes. Government jobs have sometimes been held by individuals not qualified for work in the private sector of the economy. In England during the eighteenth and nineteenth centuries, the children of upper class families (other than the oldest son whose role as head of the family was cut out for him) were taken care of through government jobs.[3] Class attitudes toward work severely limited vocational choice, but a career in Whitehall was quite acceptable socially. Even today a high-level civil service appointment has greater prestige than a business career. In the middle of the nineteenth century, laws appeared that formalized class privilege by making entrance to the higher civil service dependent upon an education which only the upper class could secure. On the whole, the result was healthy because it gave the British civil service at the top a high degree of competence. The virtues of the British "administrative class" have been extolled for decades by American

[3] See J. D. Kingsley, *Representative Bureaucracy* (Yellow Springs, Ohio: Antioch Press, 1944), chaps. ii, iii.

observers. Today, partly because of democratic ideology and partly because the old preparation did not meet all the needs of a technological age, this elite is being democratized by providing avenues of entrance other than the university honors course.

The development of personnel administration in the United States has been subject to a different set of influences.[4] The equalitarian philosophy of the young republic fostered the concept that one man was as good as another, legally, if not by natural endowment. Moreover, it was felt that the work of government was so simple that any citizen was qualified to perform it. Thus arose the famous spoils system so familiar to Americans. In brief it consisted of passing out government jobs to the followers of those who won elections. This resulted in considerable turnover when a new party came to power. As a result competent people tended to avoid public employment. Government jobs were filled by party workers, their friends, and relatives. A public job was a reward for political service or a haven for those who had not found their niche in the private economy.

During the last half of the nineteenth century the abuses of such a system called forth considerable protest.[5] Following the assassination of President Garfield by a disappointed office seeker, Congress passed the Pendleton Act of 1883, which has been the basic civil service legislation up to now. Since that time the civil service movement has made constant gains—particularly during the last quarter-century—until almost all federal employees (over 90 per cent) are now under some form of civil service or merit system. All states have some kind of merit system for those social security services that are partly financed from federal funds, and three-quarters of the states have civil service systems covering other positions.[6] Furthermore, patronage has been substantially reduced in cities and counties. Nevertheless there are huge areas in some states and in local government which are still subject to patronage.[7] The battle against the spoilsman must continue on at least two fronts. The first entails pushing back the patronage boundaries through new merit sys-

---

[4] For a survey of historical trends in personnel administration, see John M. Pfiffner, "The Personnel Function in Government," 17, *Public Personnel Review* (October, 1956), pp. 181–88.

[5] Civil service reform was sponsored by the Civil Service Reform League, still existing under the name of the National Civil Service League with offices in New York City. See Frank M. Stewart, *The National Civil Service Reform League, Activities and Problems* (Austin: University of Texas, 1929).

[6] "Civil Service Progress in the States," 68, *Good Government* (January-February, 1951), pp. 1–6. The same issue shows that 92.7 per cent of federal positions were in the competitive civil service on September 30, 1950.

[7] See H. O. Waldby, *The Patronage System in Oklahoma* (Norman, Okla.: The Transcript Co., 1950); also reports on patronage in Indiana and Pennsylvania in 74, *Good Government* (September-October, 1957), pp. 45 ff.

tem laws. The second requires the policing of civil service to see that merit system laws are not perverted to permit patronage in day-to-day administration.

CHANGING PHILOSOPHIES

The terms "civil service" and "merit system" have so far been used interchangeably. They do, for all practical purposes, mean the same thing, but the growing use of "merit system" is to a considerable extent symbolic of a basic change in philosophy. The original civil service laws were written as a protest against the abuses of spoils and patronage; but the existence of these laws did not assure their observance. The result was that the first several decades of civil service administration were characterized by a negative attitude; civil service commissions were cast in the role of protecting the virtuous against the wolves of patronage. This resulted in the centralization of personnel administration in a control agency usually called the "civil service commission." The politicians were not the only culprits to be fended off by the defenders of purity; the operating departments were also suspect, sometimes justifiably because they were headed by political appointees.

Public personnel philosophy has turned almost full cycle since those early reform days. At that time personnel administration was highly centralized. Appointments, promotions, dismissals, recruiting, and position classification were either performed directly by the civil service agency or had to be approved by it. Central personnel agencies were jealous of their prerogatives and suspicious of operating officials. This suspicion was partly justified because of the empire building and protective mentality characteristic of those who have entrenched authority. Those in central personnel agencies also like to wield authority; so they rationalized that it was part of the inexorable order of nature that they should approve all personnel actions. No one else could be trusted to do so.

The progress of public personnel administration in the last century can be described in three broad phases.[8] These followed each other quite naturally, although the rate of change varied among the several governmental jurisdictions. The first phase was that of civil service reform, which began around 1850 for the nation as a whole and is still going on in many regions. The second phase consisted of the introduction and widespread adoption of technical improvements in such areas as psychological testing, job analysis, and the mechanization of procedures, and record keeping. The third phase is characterized by decentralization and the focus of attention upon the motivation of workers. This phase of the

[8] A recent history on the national level is: Paul P. Van Riper, *History of the United States Civil Service* (Evanston, Ill.: Row, Peterson and Co., 1958).

cycle is just beginning, and more and more public personnel jurisdictions are embracing its tenets.

It is now apparent that there were certain defects in the early approaches to public personnel administration which actually impeded the most important factor, namely, getting the job done with the minimum application of manpower. In other words, both citizens and governmental officials often concluded that workers protected by civil service did not work hard enough and that they put security and job protection ahead of creativeness and productiveness. It is alleged that they are perhaps more concerned with rights and perquisites than with their obligations. And it is widely thought that protective laws make it difficult to discipline governmental workers because it is almost impossible to dismiss them.

The net result has been what Wallace Sayre called "the triumph of techniques over purpose."[9] We have eliminated party patronage by law, guaranteed equality of treatment, introduced the cold logic of scientific management, and established an elaborate system of protectionism. But all this has failed to produce a highly motivated working force. By and large, the man who pays the bill believes that civil servants are obsessed with security, grasping for ever-greater rights and perquisites, and committed to a slower work pace than their counterparts in industry. Many civil service administrators feel similarly, as evidenced by their frustration at their inability to motivate their subordinates. Parenthetically, many managers in private industry react in the same manner about their own employees. Regardless of the validity of this indictment, the important thing is that the man on the street and even some public administrators tend to feel that public employees as a group are somewhat inferior in terms of competence and motivation, and that they do not put forth maximum effort.

These attitudes have caused a considerable amount of soul-searching among those who believe that a competent public service is an essential part of our democracy. The result has been a certain reaction against what has gone before, a tendency to wholesale condemnation of classic civil service reform. Indeed, some observers believe we have failed to achieve a first-class public service because of these reforms: (1) civil service protectionism, (2) the emphasis of personnel administration on techniques, (3) the negative, policing attitude of civil service reformers, (4) the extreme centralization of personnel actions, and (5) the failure to recognize as a human being the man who does the work. They argue that the remedy consists in complete decentralization of personnel administration to the

---

[9] Wallace Sayre, "The Triumph of Techniques over Purpose," 8, *Public Administration Review* (Spring, 1948), pp. 134–41.

responsible heads of agencies.[10] This should be accompanied by a philosophy of personnel administration that fulfills the needs of line management instead of the prerogatives of central control. Emphasis would be placed upon developing leadership and motivation to ensure that people perform up to their capabilities. Advocates of such a program have confidence in the human relations approach, which will be discussed at greater length in the following chapter.

PROBLEM OF PROTECTIONISM

By civil service protectionism we mean the efforts of employee groups to write into law a great many safeguards against arbitrary treatment. These include the right to hearing and legal redress on discipline and dismissal, an open channel of communication for grievances, and promotion and layoff according to seniority. The emphasis is upon job security, personal rights, and perquisites which, critics say, results in a corresponding indifference to work achievement, Indeed, highly motivated management often feels frustrated by its inability to motivate the rank-and-file civil service worker. It often compares civil service unfavorably with private industry, overlooking the fact that industrial managers react in the same manner to industrial unionism. In a sense, top management in any large impersonal hierarchy is engaged in a constant struggle with the rank-and-file employee. Management wants productivity in the form of measured accomplishment. It tends to be mobile and ambitious and expects others to be likewise. Ambitious, competent, and competitive persons gravitate naturally to positions of responsible leadership; but nature has provided a relatively small percentage of them in its normal distribution of human abilities. Most men yearn for certainty, security, stability. Throughout human history leaders have by and large exhibited considerable indifference to the welfare, sentiments, and yearnings of the ordinary man. Now in the twentieth century, he is rising up and presenting a united front against management indifference. His weapons are, on the one hand, industrial unionism and collective bargaining, and civil service legalism on the other. But, as in almost every human controversy, there are two sides.[11]

Restrictions on Executive Discretion. Management insists with some justification that it must have maximum discretion in making decisions

---

[10] Commission on Organization of the Executive Branch of the Government, *Personnel Management* (Washington, D.C.: U.S. Government Printing Office, 1949), pp. 49–50.

[11] For example, in one area, the loyalty-security program, the civil servant found himself extremely vulnerable to "management prerogative." This subject is discussed in detail in Chapter 17.

if it is to do a good job. This discretion includes freedom in making decisions about people. Management wants to hire people on its own evaluation without being required to take employees off civil service lists. Management wants to discipline and dismiss employees without having to defend its action before an appeal body. It wants to promote workers on the basis of its own standards of merit, instead of being forced to do so according to seniority or civil service lists. Management wants a flexible working force which can be expanded or contracted according to work load, with layoffs based on merit. Management wants to pay individuals on the basis of its own assessment of their merit and not according to a uniform plan which rewards everyone alike. These elements are all part of "management prerogative."

Civil service protectionism has also tended to color personnel administration with the brush of legalism. The emphasis upon "rights" has created a personnel jurisprudence providing due process of law for the aggrieved employee. Thus the governmental supervisor who would discipline or dismiss an erring employee must be prepared to establish his case in court much in the manner of the plaintiff in a criminal trial. He must present documentary evidence that the employee committed wrongful acts or is incompetent. It must be shown that the waywardness was continuous over time rather than an isolated event. The supervisor must show that he tried to assist and develop the employee and that dereliction nevertheless continued. Every effort must be made to impress the hearing agency that the supervisor is not being vindictive and is not motivated by personal dislike.

Hearings of this kind often take several days, during which the dismissing officer is under considerable stress, in addition to losing time from regular work. The result is that administrators avoid this experience whenever possible, often refusing to take disciplinary action when needed. Furthermore the need to protect both the taxpayer and administrative officers against expensive lawsuits causes excessive reliance upon the attorney. The total effect is to instill in executives an attitude of caution which operates against the decentralization and generally positive attitude advocated by modern personnel administration.

PERSONNEL VERSUS OPERATING UNITS

No one can be in contact long with a line organization without hearing uncomplimentary expressions about the personnel agency. This feeling even prevails among other staff agencies such as finance and management improvement. What is the reason for this widespread antipathy toward a unit whose purpose is to facilitate the work of others? The answer is not easy because the reasons are complex and obscure. One can offer certain speculations because the main weaknesses of federal personnel administration have been set down succinctly in reports such as those of the first Hoover and Brownlow Commissions.[12] In the first place, it should be recognized that much of this problem is inherent in auxiliary staff control. A great deal of the resentment toward central personnel agencies springs from the irksomeness of controls and the seemingly endless burden of paper work which they require.

Operating executives want greater latitude in making decisions and taking action in personnel matters. They do not want to be restricted to the top of an eligible list in hiring; they want to assign people to work where needed without being hampered by what they believe to be an artificial classification of jobs. They want to be able to discipline and dismiss without being subject to protracted hearings. They want to promote individuals and give them pay increases without having to justify such actions to a personnel technician. Much of the line's resentment against personnel administration arises naturally from the control process itself. That is why reformers would go a long way to lessen the extent of such controls. It also explains why the decentralizers would send personable envoys down where direct labor works. They would woo the line by giving the line supervisor the principal voice in personnel actions.

Much lack of understanding springs from the crusading spirit of civil service reform. The need for vigilance against patronage is always present, even in those jurisdictions which have a long history of merit personnel administration. The memory of a raid by the marauders is always in the minds of defenders of the merit system, and their defense remains the independent civil service commission manned by laymen. It matters not to them that these civil service commissioners are often politically appointed; as between two evils, the reformer would chose the autonomous civil service commissioner as against the line department head. The latter has been too often identified with partisan politics. This situation explains why personnel administration has been regarded as a control activity administered in an atmosphere of suspicion by a central agency. The line departments are policed as potential delinquents, which partially explains why they often regard personnel administration as a deadening force.

Technical Introversion. The technical character of personal administration also raises problems about the internal relations of personnel staffs. Perhaps the core of the matter concerns the development of several

[12] Commission on Organization of the Executive Branch of the Government, *Personnel Management;* President's Committee on Administrative Management, *Report with Special Studies* (Washington, D.C.: U.S. Government Printing Office, 1937).

personnel specialists: examiners, classifiers, wage analysts, and trainers. Specialists, as we have seen, tend to become empire builders. The result was that instead of putting up a united front, several different specialists from personnel began telling the line what to do. Now, there are many very charming people who are personnel technicians; yet it must be admitted that the term "technician" has acquired a certain opprobrium. Persons who style themselves as "practical" delight in making whipping boys out of specialists. Although one suspects that this uncomplimentary use of the word "technician" is more a symbol of resentment than a fair appraisal, there is nevertheless a tendency for all specialists to assume a certain abruptness and impatience toward the layman who questions them.

The specialist also tends to seek the companionship, and hence the sympathy and security, of his own kind. The technical specialist, one often finds, is not likely to be hail-fellow-well-met; he is more likely to be introverted. Because he has devoted so much time to specific skills, he attaches high value to the symbols of his calling; they may even assume the stature of a moral crusade to a personnel technician. Thus the line supervisor fails to understand why the position classifier cannot interpret borderline data in favor of an employee; nor can he see why the examiner refuses to let him contribute to an examination. Yet the technicians in these cases know that if they yield in one instance, they will probably have to yield in another. It is not easy for one human being to say "no" to another in matters of intimate personal concern.

BACK TO THE LINE

Progressive personnel administrators have now become quite conscious that all is not well with their relations to legislatures and the line, and they are trying to do something about them. Their efforts provide the subject matter for the remainder of this chapter. Before World War II those engaged in public personnel administration usually worked in a central control agency called the Civil Service Commission. To be sure, there were in the line agencies a number of clerks who kept records, who routed and filed papers having to do with personnel actions, but they were regarded as clerks rather than professional personnel workers. Personnel philosophy then frowned upon having any personnel work, such as classifying or recruiting, done in the departments. This was due partly to empire building and partly to the situation described above.

The Civil Service Commission. Civil service commissions are organized in several ways; they vary considerably from place to place, but there is a certain thread of uniformity. The members are usually appointed by the political chief executive: President, governor, or mayor.

They are appointed for overlapping terms, and their appointments must often be approved by the Senate or city council. In some jurisdictions both major political parties must be represented. The orthodox commission also has administrative powers: It is the head of the civil service department, with power to appoint the staff and direct its work. Until recently the title of the commission's chief administrative officer was "secretary and chief examiner," but now the usual title is "director of personnel."

This evolution in titles is symbolic of the change in philosophy which personnel administration has undergone in recent years. Emphasis once centered upon the lay commission, and giving examinations was the principal activity. Now the focus of attention is on the professional staff, and examining is merely one of several activities. Civil service commissioners give but a part of their time to official duties, with the exception of a few large jurisdictions such as the federal and New York City commissioners. For the most part, the commissioners have equal status, electing their own chairman; but here again the federal setup is the exception, with the chairman, designated by the President, acting as chief administrative officer. Under the director of personnel, there are usually several divisions performing activities such as classification, examination, training, and employee relations.

Positive Personnel Administration. Recent years have brought a revolt among personnel administrators against the supremacy of the independent and autonomous commission. This is due partly to the quality of the commissioners, who have often been political hacks. Even when a successful businessman becomes a commissioner, he often undergoes a strange transformation, assuming a protective attitude which he would not display toward employees in his own business. Sometimes particular commissioners take greater than ordinary interest in technical details which are more properly matters for professionals to decide. In other instances the line agencies become irked at the delay and paper work necessitated by routing a mass of detail through the commission for approval. Again, commissioners have been known to manipulate civil service procedures to serve political interests.

Perhaps the greatest indictment of the administrative commission was that it failed to foster a creative personnel administration. The emphasis on protection placed a premium on conformity and discouraged innovation. Personnel administration settled into a comfortable routine of paper pushing in which one did not get hurt if he did not step out of line. But the new professionals who began to come into personnel administration with the expansion of governmental activities in the 1930's wanted to work in a more satisfying atmosphere.

The result has been that the newer civil service laws have trimmed the sails of the commission and have given the personnel director administrative powers in his own right.[13] Today the trend is toward eliminating the commission entirely or taking away its administrative powers. This does not mean that civil service commissions are rapidly disappearing in the United States—they are too deeply implanted in the American culture —but their powers are being limited. Federal practice now makes the chairman the executive officer of the commission and definitely limits the powers of the other two commissioners. Elsewhere the tendency is to confine the commission to hearing appeals from grievance and disciplinary actions, approving general policy, and playing a watchdog role. The new philosophy holds that the commission should abandon its former habit of making day-to-day administrative decisions and take on a positive role of promoting a superior brand of personnel administration. This would include selling government career service to schools and civic bodies. The commission would also shoulder the responsibility of dealing with the chief executive and the legislature in improving the law and developing a better service. In other words, the desirable functions of a lay civil service commission could be classified as follows: (1) appeals, (2) relations with political officers and bodies, and (3) relations with citizens and citizen groups.[14]

The survival of the commission form is due to an ingrained notion that somehow or other the lay commission is more likely to resist corruption than would a single administrator. This reflects an American belief system which runs somewhat as follows: (1) The political process is inherently amenable to corruption. (2) The best way to counteract corruption is to divide power among several officers and agencies. (3) The independent civil service commission is the best guarantee of purity in personnel matters.

Professional groups in public administration, however, are beginning to challenge traditional theory. They believe in checks and balances as fundamental to the Anglo-American concept of constitutional limitations. They believe that there is a role for the lay citizen to play in democratic government. This role, however, does not include carrying on day-to-day administration. Commissioner Pollock signalized the opinions of this group when he stated that substitution of a single administrator for the commission would not weaken its protective functions.[15] He added that sufficient protection would be provided by a statute outlawing political

[13] Joseph Schechter, "Personnel Management in the City of New York," 18, *Public Personnel Review* (October 1957), pp. 203–12.

[14] *Ibid.*

[15] Commission on Organization of the Executive Branch of the Government, *Personnel Management*, pp. 54–55.

favoritism in appointments and by developing enlightened personnel administration in the agencies.

PROBLEMS OF DECENTRALIZING

Decentralization is fundamentally the process of making decisions at the place where the work is done. Thus if a district ranger of the forest service has the power to hire, fire, or discipline an employee without consulting someone higher up, there is complete decentralization. Furthermore, if he can add a new position or buy a wheelbarrow without higher approval, decentralization exists. Decentralization took place when the U.S. Civil Service Commission allowed the line agencies to classify positions during World War II (a procedure made permanent by law). But transferring the power to make certain decisions from the Commission to departmental headquarters in Washington is only partial decentralization. At the beginning of World War II, many personnel actions had to go from the field to Washington for approval. The result was that Washington tended to become a bottleneck, unnecessarily delaying actions; too many people were employed in Washington for clerical work that could just as well have been done in Omaha or Atlanta.

Factors Encouraging Centralization. There are several reasons why it is difficult to decentralize personnel administration to the point where the work is done. First, administrators in Washington are extremely sensitive to political repercussions because of their proximity to the Hill; because they have had their fingers burned by personnel blunders in the field, they require that such actions be approved in Washington. Second, decisions about classification, promotion, and pay are intimately related to budgetary considerations. Washington is afraid that field officials will be too generous in making pay decisions; therefore it again requires that they be referred to headquarters for approval. Third, and perhaps most important, the central personnel agencies want to make the decisions.

Advantages of Decentralization. A central personnel agency performs differently under a decentralized regime than one that is centralized. The decentralization that took place in federal personnel matters during and after World War II demanded a new pattern of behavior on the part of civil service commission employees. Instead of making personnel decisions on such matters as classification and recruiting, they became functional supervisors of the departments. It was, and is, the Commission's job to prepare general standards for the departments to follow and then post-audit on a sampling basis to see whether the departments are conforming. Instead of being a policeman, the central personnel agency assumes a role of leadership and motivation; its job is to persuade others to do better. This is a difficult role which requires a special type of person. Instead of being artful at devising systems, pushing papers, and wielding the scepter of authority, the new pattern calls for skills in persuading, influencing, and creating. Personnel administration's principal task, then, is developing men, inspiring them to rise in stature. There are relatively few persons in any population group who have this ability. It is not strange that central personnel agencies find it difficult to alter their behavior overnight.

Under decentralized personnel administration, inspection becomes an important task for the central agency. Thus the regional offices of the U.S. Civil Service Commission have inspection teams calling upon field agencies. Some of the larger operating agencies, such as the Department of Defense, have their own personnel inspectors in the field. They go into a field unit and observe the conduct of personnel administration in all its aspects.[16] There has been some criticism that these inspections have degenerated to mere auditing of papers to see that employee records are in good order. Critics say that the inspectors should pay more attention to the developmental aspects of personnel instead of concentrating on routine. They should attempt to evaluate the qualitative and man-building functions of training, recruiting, morale, and leadership. But this again is much more difficult than poring through employee folders to see that papers are in order.

Need for Personnel Generalists. Frequent reference has been made to the need for a new type of personnel administration to replace the paper-pushing and hypertechnical approach. What is needed is someone who can get along with line officials and induce them to observe good personnel practice, not because it is required but because such practices are intrinsically beneficial. Kenneth O. Warner feels that too many personnel specialists have been dealing with the line. Thus in a single day a supervisor might be confronted by a position classifier, an examiner, a trainer, and a counselor. Such specialization at the contact level makes difficult the friendliness, understanding, and acceptance needed to make personnel management an integral part of line management. Warner would decentralize, but he would have only one person, a personnel "generalist," do most of the contact work. This generalist would be reasonably competent in all technical phases of personnel. If he ran into technical difficulties, he could seek advice from specialists in the personnel department. For all practical purposes, this generalist

[16] F. W. Luikart, "An Inspection Program to Improve Personnel Administration," **10,** *Public Personnel Review* (April, 1949), pp. 72–78.

would be on the staff of the appropriate line supervisor. He would seek to gain the line's acceptance of good personnel practices.[17]

Since Warner initiated his idea in 1946, the principle has been widely adopted in the federal service.[18] On the whole the effort has been successful, although there is some criticism that in federal administration the generalists attached to the line must devote too much time to paper work and not enough to constructive and developmental activities. In some cases the line supervisors shift some of their own paper work to personnel men. One also suspects that personnel generalists who are highly motivated in the beginning eventually settle down to making a career out of routine activities.

Some central personnel agencies have experimented with making generalists out of their own technicians. Instead of having separate subdivisions dealing with examining, classification, and pay, the work is reorganized so that the same people deal with all these matters. The assumed benefits from this arrangement fall into two categories. First, the line agencies have to deal with only one person instead of several and thus come to know the personnel technician more intimately. This also brings the latter into closer contact with the operating problems of the agency, thus reducing the tensions caused by the old standoffish approach. Second, the personnel specialists are forced in a sense to "de-specialize"; the examiners must learn classification and pay, and vice versa.[19] However, it should be said in passing that this argument has a less favorable side, that is, by spreading his attention, the technician may lose some of the skills accruing from narrower specialization. At the present time the personnel generalist movement is regarded as a progressive step, but this view may be modified or even reversed as a result of experience.

The Personnel Council. The idea of the personnel council originated in the federal government in 1939 as a result of the decentralization of personnel administration. Some instrument was needed for bringing agency personnel people together for the purpose of discussing and coordinating common problems. Although originally semiautonomous, the federal unit now operates as an integral part of the Civil Service Commission under the name of the Interagency Advisory Group. Fundamentally it is an interdepartmental committee composed of personnel

[17] Kenneth O. Warner and Donovan Q. Zook, "The Role of the Generalist in Personnel Management," 7, *Public Personnel Review* (July, 1946), pp. 117–25; Lyman H. Cozad and Kenneth O. Warner, "Personnel Generalist: Experience and Advice," **60,** *Public Personnel Review* (July, 1955), pp. 131–38.

[18] Harold L. Dickinson, "Some Problems in Establishing a Generalist Personnel Office," 12, *Personnel Administration* (July, 1950), pp. 19–22.

[19] Frederick C. Mosher, *The Reorganization of the California State Personnel Board* (University, Alabama, University of Alabama Press, ICP Case No. 32, 1956).

directors or their representatives, meeting under the sponsorship of a central personnel agency. It serves as a clearing house where personnel directors meet on a service-wide basis to discuss their problems. It has weekly meetings of the entire body in addition to meetings of special committees to deal with particular problems that affect a number of agencies. A number of Field Personnel Advisory Groups now operate locally in the same manner. Such large jurisdictions as New York and Los Angeles have established advisory groups composed of representatives of the operating departments.

RELATION TO OTHER STAFF ACTIVITIES

There are several points at which personnel administration touches other staff activities, such as budgeting and administrative analysis. Thus the question often arises as to whether position classification and wage analysis are properly personnel or financial activities. Both are obviously intertwined with administrative analysis because each is based upon job analysis procedure and each has to study organizations. There are instances where the management improvement function is an integral part of the personnel office. Perhaps the best solution is to organize each principal level of leadership in such a way that the auxiliary staff and control activities will be coordinated into a team approach, as in the Army G-1, G-2, etc. Under such an arrangement, personnel becomes a component part of the leadership (command) staff organization at each echelon. It would be in close contact with budgeting, supply, management improvement, and production. In other words, personnel people would no longer be an isolated guild of empire builders but would become members of an administrative team. They would be socially integrated into the family, where their principal objective would be to maintain morale.

BIBLIOGRAPHY

ABRAMOVITZ, MOSES, and ELIASBERG, VERA. *The Growth of Public Employment in Great Britain*. Princeton, New Jersey: 1957.

CAMPBELL, G. A. *The Civil Service in Britain*. London: 1955.

CAPE, WILLIAM H., and STENE, EDWIN O. *State Civil Service in Kansas*. Lawrence: 1954.

CROUCH, WINSTON W., and JAMISON, JUDITH NORVELL. *The Work of Civil Service Commissions*, Report No. 553. No date.

KAPLAN, H. ELIOT. *The Law of Civil Service*. Albany: 1958.

KINGSLEY, J. DONALD. *Representative Bureaucracy*. Yellow Springs, Ohio: 1944.

LINDSAY, DAVID R. *What's Ahead for Civil Service?* New York: 1957.

NOLTING, ORIN F. (ed.). "Municipal Personnel," *Municipal Yearbook*. Chicago: Consult current volume.

RICH, BENNETT M. *The Government and Administration of New Jersey*. New York: 1957.

ROSENBERG, MORRIS. *Occupations and Values.* Chicago: 1957.

STAHL, O. GLENN. *Public Personnel Administration.* 4th ed.; New York: 1956.

SUBNAMANIAM, V. "Graduates in the Public Services—A Comparative Study of Attitudes," 35, *Journal of the Royal Institute of Public Administration* (Winter, 1957), pp. 373–93.

TEJERA-PARIS, ENRIQUE. "Observations on Personnel Management in Latin America," 17, *Public Personnel Review* (October, 1956), 295–301.

UNSIGNED. *Municipal Personnel Administration.* Chicago: Consult currently revised edition.

CHAPTER 15

The Federal Personnel System

The central personnel agency for the federal government is the Civil Service Commission composed of three members appointed by the President and subject to Senate confirmation. They serve for overlapping terms of six years, one being appointed every two years; there must be one member from the minority political party. The President designates one member as chairman and another as vice-chairman to serve as chairman in the former's absence. The chairman has administrative powers in his own right and acts as the administrative head of the agency.[1]

There are about two and one-half million federal civilian employees, about 10 per cent of whom work overseas. (This does not include the more than three hundred thousand foreign nationals employed in various countries who are on the federal payroll). Over 90 per cent of the two and one-half million are under civil service in the sense that they are subject to some statute administered by the Civil Service Commission and are regarded as having either complete or limited civil service status, that is, their appointment and tenure is not subject to political and patronage influences.

THE CHANGING ROLE OF THE COMMISSION

The Civil Service Commission is responsible for the administration of the major personnel functions, but in the last two decades its role has changed considerably. Prior to the early 1940's the Commission recruited, examined, and classified on a centralized operating basis, that is, the Commission did the work itself. Since then, the actual operating activity has been performed on a decentralized basis by the line agencies them-

---

[1] Two recent works on federal personnel administration are: Paul P. Van Riper, *History of the United States Civil Service* (Evanston, Ill.: Row, Peterson and Co., 1958); Wallace S. Sayre (ed.), *The Federal Government Service: Its Character, Prestige and Problems* (New York: Columbia University, The American Assembly, 1954).

selves and by the decentralized components of the Commission in the field. These latter include its regional offices and the hundreds of boards of examiners stationed in the line agencies. The examiners are composed of agency personnel authorized to administer examinations under Commission supervision.

The Commission still has primary responsibility to ensure that such personnel activities as examining, classifying, and training are properly carried out. But now, instead of performing these activities itself, it functions as catalyst, mentor, and friendly counselor to help the agencies develop and administer their own personnel programs. To be sure, the Commission still administers such programs as retirement, security investigations, and appellate functions; and it also handles various tests such as the Federal Service Entrance Examination. But by and large it has changed its operating philosophy from "we must do it ourselves or it will not be well done" to one of helping the agencies administer their own personnel programs.

The devices used by the Commission to facilitate decentralization are those referred to earlier in the chapters on organization, namely, central determination of broad policy, centralized setting of standards and goals, and feedback to the Commission of information about how well the programs are being administered by the agencies. The functions of two of the Commission's bureaus will illustrate its current role. The Bureau of Programs and Standards has a Program Planning Division which acts as a broker for ideas on the improvement of personnel administration. The term "broker" is used to emphasize the Bureau's role as a catalyst to stimulate progressive thinking throughout the service rather than posing as the sole source of ideas itself. In addition to concerning itself with improvement of personnel administration in general, the Bureau has the more specific tasks of developing job standards to guide the agencies in classification decisions; and it also conducts research in test development.

The information feedback function is accomplished by sending into the agencies inspection teams from the Commission's regional offices. These activities are carried on by the Bureau of Inspections and Classification Audits. Whereas inspectors once focused their attention upon compliance with classification and pay standards, recently there has been more attention toward the developmental aspects of personnel administration. The inspectors provide liaison between the Commission and the agencies, and one of their duties is to advise the agencies on how to improve operations.

There have been two main streams of criticism of the inspection program, one having to do with the manner in which the inspectors operate in the field; the other, with the Commission's alleged failure to keep its job standards up to date. In the past it has often been charged that the inspectors are principally concerned with the examination of papers to establish compliance with regulations. The Commission is aware of this charge and is increasingly directing its attention toward major facets of personnel administration. Moreover, criticism has been directed at the classification standards program on the bases that the Commission has never developed standards for thousands of positions and that many of the existing standards are obsolete and unusable.[2] Special attention is now being directed toward this problem.

ISSUES SURROUNDING FEDERAL PERSONNEL ADMINISTRATION

There are a number of unsettled controversial issues dealing with federal personnel administration which should be posed and discussed at this point. They deal with such matters as the eternal conflict of interest between the President and the Congress, the nature of the career service, how to deal with the patronage issue, the fusion of the career service with the policy echelons, and the nature of personnel administration itself. Inasmuch as many of these are intertwined, we shall deal with them jointly.

The Nature of Personnel Administration. As we have seen, there has been a tremendous shift in attitudes toward the personnel function. These new attitudes have in general been embraced by professional personnel people. This metamorphosis has been characterized by a swing away from the old negative, protective approach to one which views personnel administration as part of line management, providing stimulus toward more effective results. The present staff of the Commission has adopted this new approach, and the Commission has reorganized and restaffed with people who believe in it. Nevertheless, as in all cases of organization change, there have been some retarding influences. First and foremost the public, and to some extent the Congress as a reflector of public opinion, still retains the classical picture of civil service as a device for resisting spoils and patronage. Moreover, employees and their organizations tend to look toward the independent civil service commission as a protective buffer against the threat of arbitrary administration. Consequently this whole issue is related to the eternal conflict between the President and the Congress over control of the bureaucracy.

The President Versus Congress. The new philosophy calls for a close alliance between personnel and line administration. The Brownlow Com-

[2] Consult the Watson report: *Report of the Committee on Post Office and Civil Service.* U.S. Senate, 85th Cong., 1st sess. (Washington, D.C.: U.S. Government Printing Office, 1957), pp. 56–63. Hereafter cited as Watson Report.

mission of 1937, which set forth what is perhaps the classic statement of the new philosophy,[3] called for a new kind of central personnel agency closely associated with the President, with a member of the White House staff acting as liaison officer between the President and the central personnel agency. Both Hoover Commissions[4] supported the new approach to personnel administration. President Eisenhower implemented this trend by making Philip Young, Chairman of the Civil Service Commission, a member of his cabinet as well as a member of the White House staff for personnel liaison.

There is difference of opinion as to the success of this venture, some saying that it gave a prestige to the personnel function which it never had before, and that it enabled Young to get action on personnel matters which otherwise might not have happened. On the other hand, there were apprehensions that this could bring the Chairman of the Commission into the patronage realm, although it seems agreed that Mr. Young was able to steer clear of such embroilments. Nevertheless, when his successor was appointed, the policy of his attending cabinet meetings was discontinued, and a new position of personnel liaison man was set up in the White House staff.

One of the main reasons for discontinuing the dual role of the Chairman was undoubtedly the view, widely held in Congress, that the Civil Service Commission is an independent agency rather than an instrumentality of the President. Willoughby's concept of the President as a general manager of the administrative machine has not received complete acceptance on Capitol Hill. Moreover, it has been reported that some of the former Congressmen who have been appointed to the Commission in recent years find the Congressional concept of the Commission's role to be more congenial. The patronage issue will be discussed below, but it may be suggested here that fear of increasing Presidential patronage influenced those who did not want to place personnel administration closer to the White House.

The Patronage Issue. The President of the United States is at once nominal head of his political party and chief administrative officer of the federal government. These roles inevitably conflict because in the former he must deal with patronage, while in the latter he will feel an obligation to preserve a politically neutral career service. This can be a very ex-

[3] President's Commission on Administrative Management, *Report with Special Studies* (Washington, D.C.: U.S. Government Printing Office, 1937).

[4] Commission on Organization of the Executive Branch of the Government (first Hoover Commission) *Personnel Management* (Washington, D.C.: U.S. Government Printing Office, 1949); Commission on Organization of the Executive Branch of the Government (second Hoover Commission), *Personnel and Civil Service* (Washington, D.C.: U.S. Government Printing Office, 1955).

plosive issue, as illustrated by the Harding administration's tampering with certain positions in the Bureau of Engraving during the early 1920's. More recently, during the first Eisenhower administration, the same issue was raised over the career service by the so-called Willis plan. The plan called for political clearance of all appointments to positions in grades GS-14 to GS-16 inclusive, by submitting both vacancies and the names of proposed appointees to the Republican National Committee. Flamboyantly labeled "Operation People's Mandate," it was justified on the basis that the new administration's landslide election indicated a popular demand for Republican appointments to top jobs. This argument was coupled with the fact that the outgoing administration had been in power for twenty years and that presumably top bureaucrats would be unfriendly to Eisenhower policies.

Two practical factors seem to have rendered the Willis plan largely unworkable, although James R. Watson noted in 1957 that the order had not been officially rescinded.[5] One of the factors was the administration's difficulty in securing competent persons via the political route and the resulting necessity to rely on the permanent civil service for competent administrators. Then there was the further consideration that it gradually became evident that career service people were not wild-eyed New Dealers, that many were in fact Republicans, and that they could be relied upon to subordinate personal views to loyalty to superiors. In other words the American career administrator evinced in practice a neutrality comparable to that of his British counterpart. A second important factor was the displeasure of Eisenhower's own agency heads at the necessity for political clearance.[6] Many had been corporation executives and were accustomed to merit-system procedure in choosing higher personnel.

Fusing the Political and Career Service. The American governmental system has not yet succeeded in making a neat distinction between political positions and those appropriate for career service.[7] Gradually, throughout the twenty years of the Roosevelt-Truman regimes the career service was successively broadened until many top jobs had been placed under civil service. As a result the Eisenhower administration found many positions which it considered to be politically sensitive manned by career status appointees. The result was the establishment of Schedule C, which consisted of a number of positions of a "policy-making nature." The number of positions put under Schedule C has been small when compared with the entire service; and over half of the appointees had

[5] Watson Report.
[6] Watson Report, p. 34.
[7] Paul T. David and Ross Pollock, *Executives for Government* (Washington, D.C.: Brookings Institution, 1957), p. 115 ff.

been in the government prior to 1953.[8] Nevertheless the move caused apprehensiveness out of proportion to the actual threat and may have been at least a minor factor in the exodus of people from the federal service during the 1950's.

The second Hoover Commission also attempted to set up certain standards for positions in the "noncareer" category. In addition to positions subject to direct Presidential appointment, this group would include positions where the incumbents are required by law to "make final decisions in the establishment of governing policies, programs, objectives, and in the enunciation of principles which would control the action of subordinates" in these matters. In this category would also fall those positions requiring the incumbents to enter into public controversy while advocating or defending "governing politics or the basic principles or philosophy" upon which agency action or decision is based. The Commission's related recommendation for a Senior Civil Service will be examined in Chapter 20.

THE FEDERAL SERVICE ENTRANCE EXAMINATION

Since the mid-1930's the federal government has been interested in recruiting college graduates for careers. For several years prior to 1955 this recruitment was carried on through a series of specialized examinations, usually given once a year. The principal vehicle for recruiting future administrators was the Junior Management Assistant (JMA) test which covered the subject matter of administration, and resulted in a high casualty ratio. The competition with industrial recruiting, particularly government's poorer competitive position in salary, prestige, and fringe benefits, and the decrease in available applicants, owing to the declining birth rate of the 1930's; the impact of the loyalty-security programs; and the Eisenhower administration's lukewarm attitude toward the civil service—all led to a drop-off in applicants for the JMA test during the 1950's. This challenge was met by the inauguration of the Federal Service Entrance Examination (FSEE) in 1955.[9]

The FSEE changed the basis of recruiting and examining from one of a series of rather specialized tests to that of a single test based on general knowledge over which a college graduate could be assumed to have

[8] Watson Report, p. 36; also Herman M. Somers, "The Federal Bureaucracy and the Change of Administration," 48, *American Political Science Review* (March, 1954), p. 143.

[9] During the second term of the Eisenhower administration, when the difficulty of finding and retaining talented executives had become more apparent, high officials attempted to encourage recruitment by speeches and articles. Among others, see Rocco C. Siciliano, "Uncle Sam Wants You," 48, *Management Review* (June, 1959), pp. 20–24, 80–84.

gained some mastery. Thus the emphasis on recruiting for specialized knowledge gave way to a somewhat greater stress upon a general liberal arts background. Students interested in becoming administrators could indicate a desire to become management interns, the idea being that administrative skills would be developed after entering the job rather than through preservice college instruction. The new method simplified the examining process by substituting a single examination for the dozen or more then being given. Selective certification for specialized backgrounds was retained, however. The FSEE had several immediate advantages. It opened up federal service to thousands of graduates who had not previously been either attracted or eligible. Another favorable feature was continuous recruitment, since the tests were administered throughout the year. Previously, if one had failed to file at the specified time, he had to wait a year.[10]

The experience with the FSEE during the first years was spotty. It is true that it was successful in attracting thousands of applicants who formerly did not apply. However, the response was not uniform as to geographical sections of the country, and there was a surplus of applicants in the Northeast and a dearth in California and the Midwest. One agency had to appoint people in New England and then transfer them to shortage areas. Certain other developments also will bear watching. In the first place one need not be a college graduate to take the test, and there is no age limit. Those already in the service may take the FSEE and must receive primary consideration for appointment. This, coupled with the fact that the test is not too rigorous, has resulted in the certification of persons in the middle and upper age groups, a fact that has drawn some critical comment from appointing officers. Furthermore those who favor some sort of administrative orientation in the undergraduate curriculum complain that the test does not examine such subject matter. The defenders of FSEE answer this complaint by noting that those who choose the management intern option get an opportunity to grow along these lines. And it does seem agreed that a very fine type of candidate has appeared among the latter group,[11] although not always in the numbers that may be desired. For in addition to competing against industry, the attractions of federal service must vie with the state and local services in such states as New York and California which offer career opportunities along similar lines.[12]

[10] Philip Young, "The Federal Service Entrance Examination," 16, *Public Administration Review* (Winter, 1956), pp. 1–5.

[11] For a critique based upon early experience, see Henry Reining, Jr., "The FSEE: The University Point of View," 16, *Public Administration Review* (Winter, 1956), pp. 11–14.

[12] Henry Reining, Jr., "JMA *versus* Jobs at Home," 18, *Personnel Administration* (March, 1955), pp. 5–11.

DEPARTMENTAL PERSONNEL SERVICES

Executive departments have a formal personnel organization which follows the line of command throughout all levels of the hierarchy. The units at the top have subdivisions for specialties such as recruiting and placement, classification, training, and employee relations, As one goes down the hierarchy and into the field, one finds a tendency to combine these functions until at the direct labor level a generalist becomes the personnel supervisor. One of the principal problems in the departmental setup is in securing adequate recognition for personnel administration from the Chief and his immediate associates. Personnel people naturally feel that the director of personnel should be a member of the Chief's general staff and his intimate adviser, instead of a person on a subordinate level reporting through one or more assistant chiefs or through a finance man. In general it would seem desirable that every personnel director be able to report directly to the line or program Chief.

OTHER PERSONNEL AGENCIES

Interagency Advisory Group. The establishment of departmental personnel units in 1938 signaled the need for coordination at that level. The constant stream of problems having service-wide implications could best be solved by joint deliberation of agency representatives. This is now accomplished by the Interagency Advisory Group in Washington and almost fifty Field Personnel Advisory Groups. The former is composed of agency personnel directors and is chaired by the Executive Director of the Commission. In addition to the bi-weekly meetings of the parent group, numerous *ad hoc* committees are constantly studying and reporting on current personnel problems. In a real sense the Interagency Advisory Group with its committee system serves as the vehicle for establishing personnel policy that affects all agencies.

The White House Personnel Advisor. As a result of a recommendation of the Brownlow Commission, the Liaison Office for Personnel Management was created in the White House in 1939. During the first Eisenhower administration the functions of this office were performed by the Chairman of the Civil Service Commission who also attended cabinet meetings. For reasons already discussed, the two jobs were separated in 1957 when Philip Young left, and an Executive Order established the position of Special Assistant to the President for Personnel Management. The duties of the latter include advising the President on over-all personnel policy, and it is understood that he has nothing to do with patronage matters. He is to represent the President before the Commission, a very important duty because many of the Commission's actions require authentication by the President. He also cooperates with the Bureau of the Budget, especially with a view toward coordinating the several personnel systems not coming within the purview of the Civil Service Commission, such as the Foreign Service, the FBI, and the Tennessee Valley Authority.

The Budget Bureau. No discussion of federal personnel agencies would be complete without some mention of the Bureau of the Budget. Most of the impetus for the more effective use of civil servants has come from this agency. While the Bureau has always been interested in management improvement, an exceptional opportunity was given it by Congress in the early days of World War II. Congress was impatient with the failure of civilian peace-time agencies to curtail activities, and it ordered the Bureau to set limits on the number of employees each agency could hire. Although regarding itself as a staff agency, which ordinarily should not exercise controls of this nature, the Bureau nevertheless had no alternative but to comply. The result has been a series of manuals on work measurement and work simplification that have been widely used in supervisory and management training and as aids in telling the agencies how to tone up their administration. All this is directly related to positive personnel administration and the motivation of workers. Of course the Bureau also exercises tremendous influence through its recommendations on appropriations for personnel work. Here again it has been forced into the area of personnel ratios because of Congressional criticism of personnel costs.

Influence of Congress. It is unrealistic to discuss public personnel administration without considering Congress. Legislative bodies tend to be critical of the civil service system for at least three reasons. First, even thought they may not care to admit it, many legislators want to retain their influence in appointments; they regard personnel administration as their natural enemy in this respect. Second, the Civil Service Commission is an executive agency and hence is regarded by Congress as being on the President's side during those frequent periods when the President and Congress are at odds. Third, members of Congress tend to reflect the layman's stereotype about the inefficiency of civil servants and associate all their shortcomings with some sinister entity known as "civil service."

The legislative agency that has had most influence on personnel matters is the House Committee on Post Office and Civil Service, particularly its subcommittee on civil service. The student who wishes to investigate the legislative history of civil service reform will find valuable source material in the transcripts of the hearings before these committees as well as those before the subcommittee of the Appropriations Committee which handles civil service matters.[13]

The Boards of Civil Service Examiners. The Commission has several hundred boards of examiners which act on a decentralized basis as little civil service commissions but under the supervision of the Commission. They are stationed in the agencies and are composed of agency personnel. They exist mainly in units such as naval shore establishments and veterans' installations where a considerable number of blue-collar workers are employed. Such establishments, which employ large numbers of people in categories where examining has been routinized, are usually in communities where the local labor market is unique, where job seekers do not care to leave the area, and where recruiting from a nationwide list would be impractical. Stocks of examination papers prepared by the Commission are kept on hand, and the Commission trains specified agency people to conduct the examinations.

THE SEVERAL FEDERAL SERVICES

Lack of Uniformity. It is not accurate to speak of a single federal service under a uniform set of rules, for in reality there are several such services operating under different arrangements. When referring to the officers and employees under civil service, one ordinarily has in mind those under the examining and classifying jurisdiction of the Civil Service Commission. Yet several hundred thousand craftsmen and semiskilled workers in shipyards, arsenals, and in construction and maintenance work are not under the classification laws. Their wages are set by area wage boards, which base their determinations upon local wage surveys. Such employees are referred to in the federal vernacular as "ungraded." Also the postal field service has its own separate pay schedules set by Congress. For examination and other purposes, however, they fall under normal civil service law.[14] The Office of Foreign Service Administration in the State Department operates under its own law and rules covering recruitment, advancement, and pay. The same is true of the TVA, the Atomic Energy Commission, the Central Intelligence Agency, and the military. However, in the subsequent discussion we shall deal only with

---

[13] Consult particularly, *Report of the Committee on Post Office and Civil Service,* 84th Cong. 2d sess., Union Calendar No. 648, House Report No. 1844, March 1, 1956. Particularly p. 11 where the Commission is criticized for being uncooperative in carrying out the intent of the Whitten Amendment.

[14] Joseph P. Goldberg, "The Government's Industrial Employees," **77**, *Monthly Labor Review* (January, 1954), pp. 1–6; *ibid.* (March, 1954), pp. 249–56.

those departments and agencies which are under the examining and classifying jurisdiction of the Civil Service Commission. Civil service jurisdiction has been so expanded in recent years (with the exceptions noted) that this includes almost everyone except the military. The latter, moreover, has always employed large numbers of civilians who are under civil service. Every domestic military installation, as well as many abroad, has a civilian personnel setup similar to those in purely civilian agencies.

The General Schedule. Specific rates of pay are set by Congress, but the agencies are delegated the power to determine where specific positions are to be placed on the scale. They do this by classification of positions under delegation from the Civil Service Commission, which may and sometimes does alter the agencies' allocations after post-audit. The basic legislation relative to classification and pay is contained in the Classification Act of 1949[15] as amended by the Pay Act of 1958. The Civil Service Commission prepares standards for placing positions in their proper classes and grades.[16] These standards take the form of job descriptions specific enough to constitute guides but sufficiently broad to apply to a variety of departments. The departments then make their own classifications, following the Commission's standards. The Commission post-audits the allocation of the departments and may order a change. Furthermore, whenever the Commission finds that an agency is not obeying the classification laws or observing the Commission's standards, it may suspend the department's power to classify and take over this function.

The General Schedule is divided into eighteen grades of responsibility, which the law spells out in broad general terms. Appointments to Grades 16 and 17 are limited specifically in number and require prior approval of the Civil Service Commission. Grade 18 requires the approval of the President. The following schedule from the Act of 1958 lists only the minimum and maximum. Each grade, except 18, has several intervening pay steps.

GS-1	$2,960 to $3,530		GS-10	$ 6,505 to $ 7,405
GS-2	3,255 to 3,825		GS-11	7,030 to 8,230
GS-3	3,495 to 4,065		GS-12	8,330 to 9,530
GS-4	3,755 to 4,325		GS-13	9,890 to 11,090
GS-5	4,040 to 4,940		GS-14	11,355 to 13,555
GS-6	4,490 to 5,390		GS-15	13,770 to 13,970
GS-7	4,980 to 5,880		GS-16	14,190 to 15,150
GS-8	5,470 to 6,370		GS-17	15,375 to 16,335
GS-9	5,985 to 6,885		GS-18	17,500 to .....

[15] 63 Statutes-at-Large 954 (5 USCA 1071).
[16] 5 USCA 1113.

TWO PERSONNEL PROBLEMS

Traditionally the federal service has been regarded as having an "open back door," meaning that an employee could be dismissed without the right of appeal to the Commission except on grounds involving political, religious, or racial discrimination. Theoretically this door is still "open" for all except veterans, but it has been gradually closing. For instance, nonveteran employees may now appeal to the Commission on the grounds that the procedure regarding dismissal was irregular.

The Commission has a Board of Appeals and Review which carries a rather heavy load involving issues relative to veterans' preference, loyalty-security, postal classification, reduction in force, Hatch Act matters, questions involving examinations, and classification. Each regional office of the Commission has an appeals examiner, and most field appeals are settled there. The two most significant of these issues will be discussed in more detail.

The Loyalty-Security Program. The events of the last two decades have added to personnel administration a function as old as the ages although rather foreign to our traditions. This involves the investigation of both incumbent and prospective employees to determine whether they are "loyal" and whether they have manifested any "subversive" tendencies. These investigations were originally conducted by the FBI but were made the Commission's responsibility after World War II. "Full field" investigations are now required for appointment to positions which are "sensitive" in terms of national security. This type of investigation may be requested by any agency, but most such investigations involve positions in the Atomic Energy Commission, the Department of the Army, International Cooperation Administration, and the U.S. Information Agency. Furthermore the Commission conducts loyalty investigations of American citizens employed, or being considered for employment, by the United Nations and other public international organizations in which the United States participates.

The impact of the loyalty-security program upon American public administration warrants several observations. At bottom, it illustrates well the politicization of the civil service at all levels of government, since it is clear that politicians have systematically used the issue to gain publicity and the support that comes from personal identification with the symbols of patriotism and nationalism. The impact of the separation of powers upon public administration is also illuminated, since in most cases it has been legislators who have pressed for security legislation and procedures. Chief executives and their political and career aides have sometimes been powerless to defend their administrative bureaucracy against invasion by publicity-seeking politicians such as the late Senator Joseph McCarthy and others of similar view in both state and municipal legislatures.

The detrimental effects of the security programs upon the civil servant seem clear enough. As Robert K. Carr says of the federal program, "that few disloyal employees have been found under it is clearly proved by the facts of its operation. That it has excluded any truly dangerous agents of espionage or subversion from the federal service is exceedingly unlikely. But that it has had an unfortunate effect upon the morale and caliber of the federal civil service has been indicated over and over again.[17] Not only were they treated as a special group whose loyalty was presumably less well established than bankers, legislators, or gamblers, but the program was extended far beyond the needs of national security by covering under it the most lowly and powerless of civil servants. The lengths to which this policy overreached itself were revealed in 1951 when it was shown that of some three million federal employees investigated, only about three hundred were found to be guilty of any security breach or inadequacy.[18] Another unhappy facet of the program was the violation of the due process guaranties of those accused. While the technical rationalization for abrogating such fundamental rights as cross-examination, confrontation of witnesses, and knowledge of one's accuser was that the hearings were not really judicial but administrative in character, the individuals concerned were, of course, suffering grave personal and property damage, including the rather basic right to make a living. The impact of such procedures and their underlying psychological effect upon the whole civil service system was undoubtedly to make it even more difficult to attract first-rate people into government work,[19] to depress the morale and prestige of those in the service, and to create an atmosphere of suspicion which made the job of administration even more difficult than it normally is.[20]

---

[17] As Carr concludes, the House Un-American Activities Committee ". . . has played a part in the demoralization of the federal service brought about by the emphasis of recent years upon loyalty testing," *The House Committee on Un-American Activities* (Ithaca: Cornell University Press, 1952), p. 456.

[18] *Report,* Loyalty Review Board, April 29, 1951. In addition to the 308 persons dismissed, some 3,000 others who were under investigation quit their jobs before their cases were concluded. It would be wrong to assume that they were all security risks.

[19] This is particularly true of scientists; see Walter Gellhorn, *Security, Loyalty,* and *Science* (Ithaca: Cornell University Press, 1950), pp. 55–62, 157–74; and for the denouement in the celebrated Service Case, see David Fellman, "Constitutional Law in 1956–57," **52**, *American Political Science Review* (March, 1958), pp. 144–46.

[20] Carr, House Committee on Un-American Activities, pp. 455–58: Eleanor Bontecou, *The Federal Loyalty-Security Program* (Ithaca: Cornell University Press, 1953); for documentation of the character and impact of the programs at the state level, which, according to Carr, copied the "disgraceful" methods of the Committee, see Walter Gellhorn, *The States and Subversion* (Ithaca: Cornell University Press, 1952).

Veterans' Preference. Most administrators and personnel technicians deplore preferential civil service treatment for veterans on the ground that it violates the merit principle and further reduces the "management prerogatives" which are believed necessary for an effective public service. On the other hand, the problem is eased by the great and growing number of veterans among the general population, as well as by recent modifications of preference laws. Some of these provisions will now be outlined.

Veterans' preference laws require that a veteran be favored over a nonveteran in many types of personnel action, including appointment, reinstatement, layoff, and retention. For certain purposes the law makes a distinction between five-point and ten-point veterans, on the basis of the number of points added to their earned scores on examination. Prior to 1954 the disabled veteran went automatically to the head of the list if his earned score plus the ten point bonus added up to the minimum passing score of 70. This has now been changed so that both five- and ten-point veterans must earn a passing score before qualifying for the list; his bonus points are then added to his earned score to determine his total score.

Another change enacted at the same time required that one could claim disability status only when certified for 10 per cent or more disability by the Veterans Administration. Able veterans receive five points, while the following receive ten points:

1. Disabled ex-service men and women.
2. Wives of disabled veterans who are themselves unable to qualify for appointment.
3. Widows of servicemen not remarried.
4. Widowed mothers of ex-servicemen, subject to certain qualifications relative to current marital status.

An appointing officer still has a choice of three from the eligible list, but if he passes over a veteran who is number one to appoint a nonveteran who is number two, he must send his reasons in writing to the Civil Service Commission, which then investigates and makes a decision on the propriety of the action. Veterans who are removed, suspended for more than thirty days, or reduced in rank may appeal to the Commission, which has power to overrule and reinstate. Furthermore, a veteran who resigns, was furloughed, or was separated may ask the Commission to place his name on the appropriate eligible or reemployment list.[21]

[21] 5 USCA 861-865.

BIBLIOGRAPHY

BERNSTEIN, MARVER H. *The Job of the Federal Executive.* Washington, D.C.: 1958.

BONTECOU, ELEANOR. *The Federal Loyalty Security Program.* Ithaca: 1953.

BROWN, RALPH S., JR. *Loyalty and Security, Employment Tests in the United States.* New Haven: 1958.

CASE, HARRY L. *Personnel Policy in a Public Agency.* New York: 1955.

COOKE, CHARLES. *Biography of an Ideal: The Diamond Anniversary History of the Federal Civil Service.* Washington, D.C.: 1959.

DAVID, PAUL T., and POLLOCK, ROSS. *Executives for Government.* Washington, D.C.: 1957.

HARVARD BUSINESS SCHOOL CLUB OF WASHINGTON, D.C. *Businessmen in Government.* Boston: 1958.

KAUFMAN, HERBERT. "The Growth of the Federal Personnel System," *The Federal Government Service.* New York: 1954.

MOSHER, FREDERICK and EDITH. "Distinguishing Marks of the Federal Government Service," *The Federal Government Service.* New York: 1954.

PRESIDENT'S (BROWNLOW) COMMITTEE ON ADMINISTRATIVE MANAGEMENT. *Report with Special Studies.* Washington, D.C.: 1937.

SENATE COMMITTEE ON FOREIGN RELATIONS. Staff Study. 85th Cong., 2d sess. *Recruitment and Training for the Foreign Service of the United States.* Washington, D.C.: Doc. No. 91, 1958.

SOMERS, HERMAN MILES. "The Federal Bureaucracy and the Change of Administration," 48, *American Political Science Review* (March, 1954), pp. 131–151.

——. "The President, the Congress, and the Federal Government Service," *The Federal Government Service.* New York: 1954.

UNITED STATES CIVIL SERVICE COMMISSION. *Annual Report.* Washington, D.C.: Annually.

UNITED STATES CIVIL SERVICE COMMISSION. *Federal Careers.* Washington, D.C.: 1956.

UNITED STATES DEPARTMENT OF INTERIOR. *Career Profiles.* Washington, D.C.: 1959.

VAN RIPER, PAUL P. *History of the United States Civil Service.* Evanston, Ill.: 1958.

YARMOLINSKY, A. *Case Studies in Personnel Security.* Washington, D.C.: 1955.

CHAPTER 16

Recruiting, Examining, Evaluation, and Promotion

Cultural attitudes have played an important role in shaping our civil service. An earlier edition of this book emphasized the influence of certain pervasive attitudes here: our egalitarian political philosophy as a bar to testing for educational achievement; popular demands for "practical" civil service tests; and the contrast between our system and the British program of general testing. However, in the last two decades these views have undergone important modification, though the change has been so gradual that the observer has scarcely been aware of it. It can be seen clearly, nonetheless, in several areas of personnel practice. Today, college graduation or some equivalent is usually required in tests for higher positions. Aptitude testing is also now quite generally accepted, and standardized commercial tests are used by many jurisdictions. Recruiting in America, as in Britain, tends increasingly to be geared to superior achievement in the nation's school system. We have not yet, of course, evolved a single formula such as the Oxford honors course for discovering exceptional talent, but our FSEE is an aptitude test conforming to our own higher education. The traditional assumption that European practice is necessarily preferable is no longer valid. This view may have been appropriate at the turn of the century before the rise of the "new management" and the subsequent exploration of the "human relations" aspects of American personnel administration. It is no longer apposite.

REASONS FOR THE PRESENT VIEW

What has caused this change in American attitudes? Why are Americans now willing to accept educational qualifications and aptitude testing? An initial word of caution is in order. First, the last two decades have been an era of virtual full employment. If one did not get the civil service job he desired, he could get another job elsewhere. One can only guess as to what would happen to current standards in case of widespread unemployment. Second, we fail to realize the profound culture change brought about in recent decades when almost every able-bodied man has gone through military training. There he has been trained, tested, and examined. In order to progress, he has had to use his head and demonstrate his technical skill. Furthermore, in a great many cases the ex-serviceman attended college under the G.I. Bill of Rights, raising the intellectual tone of many campuses. As a result, he is less apprehensive about being tested for educational and intellectual achivement than was his father after World War I.

We sometimes fail to realize, moreover, how closely the normal processes of life have become intertwined with technology and science. Those of us who were raised on the Model T knew that if the motor started jerking, the trouble was caused by pumping oil in the front cylinder. So we got out and cleaned the front spark plug. Today the modern service garage has a dialed gadget which, attached to the motor, acts like a stethoscope, electrocardiograph, and blood-pressure gauge. Radar and electronics are forcing the skilled craftsman to become a theorist whether he wants to or not. Our productive processes are becoming so complex that we have virtually abandoned the term "unskilled labor." The Ph.D. has become a rock-bottom requirement for chemists and physicists. Industry is demanding that engineers have a certain minimum of graduate study. For the men who organize and lead others, the managers and executives, the Master's degree is beginning to have increasing importance. The foreman's job is becoming so complex that industry is having difficulty in finding qualified persons in the worker group.

The point is the obvious one that we are living in a world different from that of the turn of the century. The implication for civil service recruitment is that it must not be bound by the past. As we tried to show in the introductory chapters, our world is one of scientific research, large-scale enterprise, interdependence of peoples, and mutual security of nations. Living and working in this world requires skills different from those of previous eras. From now on emphasis will be placed increasingly on intellectual skills and aptitudes. These will cover the whole spectrum of human knowledge. In the administration of both industrial and governmental enterprises, research and operations will be combined somewhat along the lines of "operations research" developed by the British during World War II. Administrative decisions will be based upon quantitative measurement, and the applied social sciences will more and more adopt mathematical methodology.

The import of this for public personnel recruitment is that the leaders must have broad vision. Personnel recruitment for the second half of the twentieth century will have to be geared to a nuclear world in which the solution of human problems will demand the utmost in competence. The emphasis will be not only on finding but on building men who are capable of performing the complex task of coordinating institutions growing ever more complex. Clearly, in such a world, emphasis will fall less upon "keeping the rascals out," than on how to induce the best to serve the state.

CIVIL SERVICE OPPORTUNITIES

Not long ago it was a truism that America did not have a career civil service. What was meant was that there was no well-defined career ladder with a hierarchy of grades, which one could mount at an early age and gradually climb. It must be remembered that the foreign service, which has such a career ladder, was established as late as 1925. While civil service classification laws do establish salary levels tied to definitions of responsibility, their primary objective is salary administration; their function in demarcating career ladders is incidental. Furthermore the original classification law was enacted in 1923. The acceptance by Congress and the nation of the concept of a professional civil service is a product of the last quarter-century. It is sometimes difficult to realize that it is only in the last few decades that qualified young people have been able to enter governmental career service and spend there a rewarding and satisfying life.

The most marked changes have occurred in the recruitment of college graduates for careers in public administration. In the 1930's and before, it was necessary to "sell" appointing officers on the recent graduate with a general training. Recruiting emphasis was placed on employing persons with specific skills ready for use, such as accounting, engineering, and economics. Existing internship programs were designed to (1) provide induction training; (2) sell the graduate to the agencies; and (3) sell the agencies to the graduates. While these internship programs have been continued, and even expanded, they have more and more tended to fulfill the function of supplying the new recruit with administrative skills.

Today the recent graduate, male or female, is not only accepted but eagerly sought after. The college student who has any inclination to spend a lifetime in government service should have no hesitancy on any score other than the financial one. There is a myriad of challenging, interesting, and even romantic careers on all levels of government. Those who choose such careers will be amply paid with a middle class income supplemented by adequate provisions for retirement. As substitutes for lack of opportunity to amass personal fortunes, they will discover other rewards: (1) a sense of community service; (2) the sense of being close to the seats of power where decisions are made, whether international, national, state, or local; (3) the intellectual satisfaction of dealing with the issues and problems that challenge society; and (4) the spiritual rewards that come from working for mankind rather than for one's self. In this latter sense, the government bureaucrat shares many of the rewards of the missionary abroad. His work may entail service at any of the several levels of government. In federal service he may find himself helping to raise the standard of living in lands less favored than his own. Or he may be conserving forests or studying how to prevent labor-management strife. As a staff member of a state budget bureau he may be devising means to rehabilitate criminals. In local government he may be dealing with the problems of urban renewal or welfare programs, or he may be serving as city manager.

ADMINISTRATIVE GENERALISTS

A liberal arts education with a major in political science, including special courses on public administration, prepares one to be an administrative generalist. This means that he is equipped with a certain flexibility of mind, an ability to think objectively, to be at home in a wide variety of problems. He is skilled at dealing with human beings engaged in a constellation of businesses and professions, from banker to labor leader. Above all, he has some basic knowledge about how to coordinate the efforts of many diverse people, groups, and projects. In general the work that he does divides itself into action (line) jobs and research (staff) jobs. But we should not make too much of this distinction because many jobs have an element of each. A sampling of some of these career avenues will show more clearly what a generalist does.

Staff Jobs. Administrative generalists often work for staff agencies, and many spend rewarding careers in the budget and personnel field. They will often be found doing administrative research and budget analysis in a budget bureau. Many go into personnel administration, where they become position classifiers, wage analysts, trainers, and, eventually, personnel directors. Others become assistants to department heads, administrators of auxiliary services, management consultants, superintendents of institutions, and managers of special programs. As they grow more mature and capable, they will assume all types of responsibility, some in active program or line administration, others in staff jobs with duties essentially investigative in nature.

Organization Work. The public administration graduate's skill is essentially that of an organizer and coordinator. The first few years will usually tell whether he is fitted to exercise these skills in one of two broad ways. If he is cut out for staff work, he will spend most of his career as an analyst, either in personnel or budget. Here he will be suggesting how to organize and coordinate; he will be essentially a consultant to those who make administrative decisions. As such he will enjoy considerable status and be comparatively well paid. If he demonstrates exceptional abilities and personal qualities, he may become a budget director, a personnel director, or a chief of administrative services.

Assisting a Line Executive. On the other hand, if he is originally placed as an administrative assistant to a program executive, his career pattern will probably be different. If he is able to establish confidential relationships with his chief, the latter will unload many duties on him. These will include the reading of certain types of correspondence and composing replies; interviewing many people whom the chief cannot see personally; investigating problems and suggesting possible solutions. If he manifests considerable ability to get along with people, the chief will use him as a trouble shooter to ease conflicts. He will also tend to become the chief's repository for facts, having at his fingertips a wide variety of data about production, condition of the budget, personnel quotas, program planning, and accomplishments. He thus relieves the chief of a great mass of detail; yet he is not essentially a researcher, but a coordinator of detail. With this kind of experience he is likely some day to become a program chief himself.

City Management. The city-manager profession has a romantic appeal to many college students. Although graduates in public administration have always been among those chosen to be managers, the trend at present is unusually favorable to the generalist. In a recent typical year, two-thirds of the new manager appointees were nonresidents, one-third had formerly been managers, and approximately three-fourths had other public administration experience. The turnover of city managers is still fairly high, but it is a prestige factor to have been a city manager. Managers do not as a rule remain involuntarily unemployed. They were formerly chosen from such occupations as engineer, accountant, or chamber of commerce secretary, but today there is a trend toward selecting generalists with college training in public administration. Over one-third come from other city administrative positions, divided equally between those promoted from within their own city and those who come from other cities. There are now over fifteen hundred city managers.[1] Those in cities of over one hundred thousand are paid around $20,000 per year, which is better than the top federal pay of GS-18. Young men who so desire should be encouraged to prepare themselves for city management; each city (or county) has in addition other jobs that need the training and skill of the generalist.

[1] Consult latest issue of *The Municipal Year Book* (Chicago: International City Managers' Association).

Service Abroad. Formerly there were very few Americans working abroad except those in the foreign service, missionaries, and military personnel. This has changed vastly as a result of world turmoil in which we have had to assume a reluctant leadership. Now every ICA mission has public administration specialists whose duty is to aid underdeveloped countries to improve their administration.[2] In addition there are many desirable administrative civilian jobs in connection with our military efforts. A considerable proportion of the American teachers of public administration have served hitches abroad in efforts to introduce American education in that field. Moreover, the foreign service has been reorganized to give greater recognition and prestige to those trained in administration. In a sense, we are now sending secular missionaries to undertake the very important mission of showing people of other lands how to organize themselves to create a better life. As a result, the United States is becoming the handmaiden of material progress in many areas of the world.

Assessing Career Service. The main conclusion from these remarks is that America now offers a career in public administration. It is not a stratified ladder based upon rank, as in Europe, but this is perhaps a point in its favor. While encouraging a professional outlook and approach, the disadvantages of class structure are avoided. The variety of positions and preparation bolsters American social democracy. The virtues of American pragmatism are retained; new problems are tackled without the inhibitions of precedent. This is the pragmatism of democratic co-operation and objective problem solving. The pioneer of the mid-nineteenth century could settle the West aided only by the art of the plow and the science of gun powder. The pioneer of the mid-twentieth century is living in a world of science and teeming urban crowds from which he cannot escape. America must have trained administrators who know how to build and manage large-scale hierarchies in a world dominated by the laboratory spirit—a world of atomic reactors, supersonic speed, and slide rules. Competent young Americans should be encouraged to enter a career of public administration. All except bureau chiefs and similar high officials will be paid as well as their counterparts in private industry. Those who have a natural civic motivation will also enjoy a substantial psychic income.

THE EXAMINATION PROCESS

The normal method of entering the federal civil service is through competitive examination. In most state and local jurisdictions promotions

[2] Harlan Cleveland and Gerald J. Mangone, *The Art of Overseasmanship* (Syracuse: Syracuse University Press, 1957).

are also based upon competitive examination, restricted, however, to agency employees. The examination procedure is fairly uniform throughout the country. Examinations are usually publicized through an announcement containing statement of duties, minimum requirements as to education and experience, and compensation. As a result of the manpower shortage in recent years, examinations have often been publicized in newspapers and other more aggressive recruiting media. Prerequisites as to experience and education are evaluated, and those who qualify are usually brought together for a written examination, sometimes called an "assembled" examination in contrast to the unassembled which consists of evaluating candidates individually, largely on the bases of education and experience. The federal government uses the latter method for higher posts.

Civil Service Examinations. A civil service examination usually consists of several parts, each of which is weighted.[3] Thus the written portion may have a weight of forty points, the oral, fifty points, training and experience, ten points. Those who fail the written test, which is given first, are usually not permitted to take the oral. The written tests of today are almost exclusively of the short-answer type, with multiple-choice questions being preferred. Essay or free-answer questions are still used occasionally when the field of competition is small, the preparation of a short-answer test is uneconomical, or the subject matter does not lend itself to short answers.

The multiple-choice items are preferred for two reasons: they are less vulnerable to criticism, and research has shown that they have higher reliability. The two measures used in judging the effectiveness of a test are validity and reliability. A test is valid when it measures what it purports to measure; it is reliable when it does so regularly during repeated use. Another advantage of the short-answer test is ease of scoring. Most civil service departments are harassed by a backbreaking load of examinations. The test-scoring machine has been a boon in this respect.

Tests can, in general, be divided into two varieties, achievement tests and aptitude tests. The popular insistence, frequently written into law, that tests be "practical" has led to considerable emphasis upon achievement tests. This means testing for job knowledge, job content, and immediate ability to perform. Aptitude tests, on the other hand, attempt to discover innate abilities and potential capacity for development. Thus there are tests that attempt to measure mechanical aptitude, verbal facility, vocational interests, and intelligence.

[3] The current status of testing is reviewed in Dorothy C. Adkins, "Selecting Public Employees," 19, *Public Personnel Review* (October, 1956), pp. 259–67.

Many aptitude tests have been "standardized" and marketed commercially. By "standardized" is meant that they have been administered to persons thought to have the desired abilities and those who have not. For instance, a mechanical aptitude test would be standardized by trying it out on selected groups of skilled craftsmen. Until fairly recently, civil service agencies hesitated to use commercial aptitude tests for two reasons. First, they could often be purchased and studied by candidates in advance. Second, there was a certain political hazard involved because these tests do not have "face" validity to many practical laymen. To a layman who is inclined to be critical, the items often seem unrelated to job knowledge and sometimes even nonsensical. However, criticism is lessening, perhaps because the public is becoming more familiar with testing as the result of experience with tests in the armed service and the school system. Nevertheless, civil service testing must still be prepared to defend itself upon pragmatic grounds.

Construction and Validation of Tests. In the larger agencies examining is a profession or career to which many persons devote their lives. Examiners tend to specialize in particular functional areas such as engineering, law enforcement, skilled trades, and clerical work. Most civil service agencies prepare their own tests. Card files containing thousands of test items are built up so that in preparing a test, one need not start entirely anew. Some agencies that have adequate staff analyze the results of test items on the basis of difficulty. These data are entered on the cards containing the items, with the result that an examiner will have some indication of difficulty when choosing items for a new test. Other agencies analyze a test item by item as a part of the scoring process, eliminating from the final score those items shown to be defective. This procedure is referred to as "item analysis." Ideally it would perhaps be desirable to validate all civil service tests in the same manner that commercial tests are standardized, that is, by administering them to groups of persons known to have the desired achievement or aptitude. Although this is a practical impossibility in most instances, the U.S. Civil Service Commission is still conducting an interesting program of validating tests for supervisors.[4]

The fact that civil service tests are not formally validated does not mean that they are invalid. As a matter of fact, testing is subject to constant practical scrutiny from a variety of sources. In the first place, there is the pragmatic experience of the testers themselves, who, through experience, acquire a know-how worthy of respect. Second, many agencies submit the questions and intended answers to persons in the line depart-

---

[4] Milton Mandell, "Validation of Group Oral Performance Test," 3, *Personnel Psychology* (Summer, 1950), pp. 179–85.

ments after the test has been given but before it has been scored. (Experience has shown that it is usually inadvisable to submit it to the departments in advance.) Third, outside subject-matter experts are often brought in to aid in the preparation and scoring of tests in specialized fields. Finally, the examinees are allowed to inspect their own corrected papers and are permitted to make formal protests. In New York City, for example, the answers are published after the test has been given, subjecting the examiners to widespread criticism. Gotham culture has evidently evolved a fireside pastime of baiting civil service testers. The honors go to the person who can prove the examiners wrong. Proponents of the system argue that it has the noteworthy advantage of keeping the examiners alert.

Civil service testers are often called upon to defend themselves from political and legal attack. Examinations are from time to time taken into court upon the ground that they are not "practical." In addition the newer type of testing sometimes utilizes a statistical system of scoring which is not readily understood by laymen. Not long ago the scoring of oral examinations was questioned in a series of New York suits; consequently, many jurisdictions now record these tests verbatim. The end result of such litigation, however, has been to uphold the exercise of discretion by testing agencies.

It would seem that the time may soon be at hand when the American public will both tolerate and finance a program of thoroughgoing test research such as that carried on by the military. This will require not only sympathetic legislative bodies but also the development of professional maturity in the public personnel profession. It seems a safe prediction that its leaders will look increasingly to research for the solutions to problems that cannot be answered by experience alone. This is what happens in all budding professions. Ultimately the basic testing research now conducted in the universities will find its way into the operating arena. A generation from now, test research will be an accepted phase of operation in the larger agencies. Meanwhile some progressive agencies have applied test research in the form of "item analysis."[5] This consists of a statistical treatment of each test item to ascertain how often it was correctly and incorrectly answered, and how it was answered by examinees in the upper, lower, and middle quartiles.

PROBLEM OF PERSONALITY

Appointing officers tend to question civil service tests because they lack confidence in their ability to measure personal qualities. This is

[5] David M. Earl, "Item Analysis in Public Personnel Testing," 10, *Public Personnel Review* (April, 1949), pp. 79–85. See also Ira E. McConnell, "An Application of Test Item Analysis," 8, *Public Personnel Review* (October, 1947), pp. 205–10.

perhaps the primary reason for the "rule of three," which prevails in most jurisdictions, according to which the appointing officer has a choice of three names from the top of the list. Supervisors want to employ persons who will satisfy at least two requisites of effective human relations: (1) They must handle the public without creating antagonism toward the agency, and (2) they must fit into a working team. Recent management research has shown the second to be especially important. Appointing officers are afraid that examining procedures will fail to give proper attention to such qualifications. The result is that they often feel they could do a better job of selection using only the personal interview. There are at least two reasons why this cannot be allowed. The first relates to the protective tendency of civil service: appointing officers may appoint brothers-in-law or personal favorites. In addition, psychological research has shown that the interview is of questionable validity, even in the hands of an experienced executive.

Methods of Testing Personal Qualities. Pencil-and-paper tests that measure some aspects of personality are now available. Notable among these are the so-called temperament or personality inventories. These consist of questions in which the applicant is asked to evaluate himself relative to certain aspects of psychiatry and abnormal psychology. Such tests are subject to a great deal of controversy, however, and there is a school of experimental psychologists which condemns them, mainly on two grounds. First, individuals will not give honest answers in a competitive test that asks them to describe their abnormal and intimate behavior or beliefs. Second, it is maintained that the value of these tests lies in their use as therapeutic or clinical aids rather than as vehicles for competition. Nevertheless claims have been made that one of these tests has predicted failure among industrial executives,[6] while another has been used for many years as a guide for placement in a metropolitan police department.[7]

Milton Mandell, who conducts test development for administrative and supervisory positions for the U.S. Civil Service Commission, insists that it is possible for tests to appraise personal factors. He lists, for example, several areas in which tests have been demonstrated to have some validity in measuring administrative ability:

1. Ability to appraise people.
2. Interest in theoretical and abstract matters.

[6] Burleigh B. Gardner, "What Makes Successful and Unsuccessful Executives," 13, *Advanced Management* (September, 1948), pp. 116–25; and William E. Henry and Burleigh B. Gardner, "Personnel Evaluation in the Selection of Executive Personnel," 10, *Public Personnel Review* (April, 1949), pp. 67–71.

[7] Such testing is now gaining acceptance in recruiting policemen; see Thomas W. Oglesby, "Use of Emotional Screening in the Selection of Police Applicants," 18, *Public Personnel Review* (October, 1957), pp. 228–31.

3. Administrative judgment.
4. Performance or behavior in a group.
5. Intelligence.
6. Respect for people.
7. Interest in and aptitude for the work supervised.
8. Supervisory judgment in interpersonal relationships.[8]

Another device for discovering personal qualities and predicting behavior under stress was developed by the British and used by our Office of Strategic Services during World War II. It consisted of inviting candidates for sensitive and hazardous foreign posts to a country house where they could be observed under a variety of conditions. Pencil-and-paper tests were administered, social decorum was observed, and candidates were exposed to several forms of stress. The British have subjected the results to vigorous statistical validation, revealing validity coefficients of .5 and .6, thought to be good when it is considered that the subjects were in the top 2 per cent of the nation intellectually.[9] Our OSS program was not similarly validated, but there are pragmatic reasons to believe that it would have been worthwhile.[10]

The most common method for assessing personal qualities is the oral interview in which the candidate is questioned in a manner designed to reveal his personality. Usually this interview is only incidentally related to vocational subject matter. The main idea is (1) to obtain a look at the candidate, and (2) to detect positive or negative qualities. The candidates are usually graded competitively. The oral score is combined with the other parts of the test. Special rating forms are often used as a result of court decisions which have held that these ratings must be objective! Many jurisdictions also record the conversation mechanically to provide a record in case of appeal. The oral interviews are usually conducted by personnel examiners assisted by outside specialists. Sometimes representatives of the employing departments sit on an oral board, but this is frowned upon by some who believe that the procedure results in bias, especially in promotional tests.

[8] Milton Mandell, "Research Findings in the Field of Supervisory and Executive Selection," **27**, *Personnel* (November, 1950), pp. 215–16, and his "Testing for Administrative and Supervisory Positions," **9**, *Public Personnel Review* (October, 1948), pp. 190–93; U.S. Civil Service Commission, *Selecting Supervisors* (Washington, D.C.: U.S. Government Printing Office, 1951), pp. 15–18.

[9] P. E. Vernon, "The Validation of Civil Service Selection Board Procedures," **24**, *Occupational Psychology* (April, 1950), pp. 75–95. A ten-year evaluation published in 1958 recommended continuation of this program and revealed that about half of the new recruits for the administrative class come from that source. See Sir Percival Waterfield, "Civil Service Recruitment," **36**, *Journal of Public Administration* (Spring, 1958), pp. 3–8.

[10] Office of Strategic Services, Assessment Staff, *Assessment of Men* (New York: Rinehart & Co., 1948); "A Good Man is Hard to Find," *Fortune.* March, 1946, pp. 92–96, 217–19, 233.

One of the newest approaches to testing is the group oral, wherein a half-dozen applicants are observed in a group situation. They are given a topic to discuss while examiners observe their behavior. The examiners do not participate beyond giving the necessary beginning instructions. Every opportunity is used to stimulate participation. Whereas the traditional individual oral test takes only 15 minutes, the group oral gives the examiners an hour and a half or more to witness each individual's conduct. In order to counteract the possibility of a single candidate doing all the talking, the test may be divided into two sessions. In the first, each candidate is called upon to make a statement on the assigned topic; the second phase consists of free discussion.[11] This group device is said to help in appraising personality traits more effectively than is possible with individual interviews.

Civil service practice usually observes the "rule of three," according to which an appointing officer can choose among the top three individuals certified to him. The purpose of this rule has been, at least in part, to overcome the objection that written tests cannot adequately appraise personality factors. Another objective has been to appease the selecting officer by giving him some discretion in the selection process. But perhaps the fundamental reason for the "rule of three" has been the unexpressed but genuine feeling that the normal examining process may provide individuals who qualify intellectually but have grave personal defects. Despite these considerations, the Hoover Commission recommended that the "rule of three" be abandoned. Under its proposal, applicants would be grouped into categories such as "outstanding," "well qualified," "qualified," and "unqualified." Veterans would be placed at the top of each category to which they had been rated. Appointing officers would make their selections successively in the higher categories, going to the next lower as a higher bracket is exhausted.

SCORING AND CERTIFICATION

The scoring of civil service tests and the ranking of candidates raise many problems. Early civil service laws usually set a passing mark of .70 or .75, based upon the familiar grading system of the public school. This was in the day of the essay test and comparatively small numbers of candidates. The advent of the short-answer test, machine-scoring, and a multitude of applicants has made the absolute pass mark somewhat obsolete. The written tests of today may have several hundred items divided into sections that can be separately scored and weighted. When

[11] Harold Fields, "The Group Interview Test: Its Strength," 11, *Public Personnel Review* (July, 1950), pp. 139–46; Rufus C. Browning *et al.*, "Self-Selection of Personnel," 12, *Public Personnel Review* (January, 1951), pp. 9–12.

a large number of successful candidates have to be marked on the basis of a percentage pass mark, it often becomes necessary to rank them to the hundredth or thousandth decimal point, for instance: 87.99, 87.98, 87.97, etc.

Many test administrators prefer to establish a separate pass mark for each test, based upon the probable number to be employed. Instead of stigmatizing failures, the eligible list consists of those at the top of the list, the cutoff being based on the probable number needed in that class during the life of the list. The others are informed that their passing score was not high enough to qualify them for the eligible list.

This also has certain budgetary advantages in eliminating unneeded individuals before the more expensive oral test is administered. In times of unemployment, many agencies are overwhelmed with candidates and are obliged to put large numbers of unneeded applicants through the examining machinery. However, high cutoffs sometimes encounter opposition because of alleged violation of civil rights. The frontier concept that one man is as good as another still pervades our culture. The Jacksonian doctrine, which held that any citizen could hold a government post adequately, is still strong enough politically to challenge discrimination on intellectual or educational grounds. It is sometimes difficult to reconcile natural rights with civil service needs.

Establishing the Register. Test results are used to establish an eligible list or register. This is merely a list of the successful examinees, usually issued by the Civil Service Commission. Upon the request of an appointing officer, the personnel agency certifies the top three names on the eligible list. After interviewing all three, the officer makes a probationary appointment, the remaining two going back to their respective positions on the list to be certified again at the next request. An eligible list expires after a specified period, usually one or two years.

A favorite method of avoiding the merit system is to cut the appropriations of the personnel agency so that it cannot conduct enough examinations to keep its eligible lists up to date. If no eligible list is available, the appointing officer may make a *temporary* appointment of someone who has not yet taken the examination. Usually the law limits such appointments to a specific period, such as ninety days, but formerly such appointments could be continued indefinitely in the absence of an eligible list. It was not uncommon to find as many as a quarter or a half of the employees in some cities or states in the status of "permanent temporary," meaning that they had served for years without being tested. The newer laws combat this by providing that no person can serve more than one temporary appointment in the same position and that no position shall be filled by two successive temporary appointees.

A rough index of the quality of personnel work in an agency is its percentage of temporaries.

The pressure of an emergency is often required to bring about reform in human institutions, and this was certainly true of personnel administration in World War II. The shortage of manpower, both among applicants and among the personnel technicians needed to process them, necessitated the streamlining and speeding up of many procedures. Eligible lists were frequently outdated before they were promulgated because the applicants had obtained jobs elsewhere. The examining process was too slow. One by-product of this problem is continuous testing for those classes that have a large turnover and are therefore always in short supply. These included during the 1940's, as well as today, occupations such as clerical, stenographic, engineering, skilled trades, and custodial. The examinations are given on the spot, and those who pass are fitted into places on the eligible list. In the past it was customary to give those low on a list a chance for appointment, but under continuous examining this may not be so.

PROBATION

Most jurisdictions provide that a new employee must serve a probation period for a stated time, usually six months. During this time the supervisor is supposed to give him special attention in matters of instruction, indoctrination, and general adjustment to the job. Personnel theory now views probation as the last phase of the testing process, for at this time the neophyte may be discharged without right of appeal and reinstatement. Personnel people often become highly emotional about the failure of supervisors to live up to their obligation to conduct rigorous probationary appraisals. Ordinarily there are very few dismissals during probation. The fact is that there has been little systematic research on probation. The general concensus is that it is not living up to its possibilities as a testing opportunity.

Various measures have been used to encourage supervisors to pass judgment on probationers. Perhaps the most common is to require frequent ratings, often three during the six months. One rating will be made at the end of one or two months, another after three or four months, and a third just before the end of probation. Sometimes a special rating form for probationers is used, containing a question asking the supervisor whether he recommends retention of the employee. Supervisors, however, do not like to evaluate people; whenever possible they avoid unpleasant personal judgment.[12]

[12] John M. Pfiffner, *The Supervision of Personnel* (Rev. ed.; Englewood Cliffs, N. J.: Prentice-Hall, Inc., 1958).

At least one local jurisdiction is tackling this problem through the so-called field review method.[13] Here a personnel technician visits the supervisor just before the end of a particular employee's probation. Through informal conversation with the supervisor, the personnel man attempts to put him in a frame of mind that will permit an uninhibited response. Specific questions from the rating form are woven into the conversation in an effort to avoid the stereotyped responses that often result from filling out a form. The principal objection to the field review method seems to be the cost involved in the time of the personnel technician. However, it could be argued that an expenditure of this kind may more than offset training costs, turnover, and reduced productivity by eliminating misfits at the beginning.

EMPLOYEE EVALUATION

The folklore of our competitive culture demands that workers be rated on the basis of their worth to the organization. Most civil service laws require that workers be given efficiency ratings once or twice a year. Because of the reaction against the term, such devices are no longer called "efficiency ratings"; instead some less offensive term such as "merit rating" or "performance report," is used. The average citizen feels that such ratings motivate people to put forth their best efforts. Hence, provision for such rating is usually written into civil service laws. But it should be pointed out that the rating of personal efficiency is not limited to government work, but is also widespread in private industry, especially for managerial positions.

It is well known that supervisors hesitate to rank workers on the basis of performance. Workers ordinarily resent not only a low rating but also one that is not commendatory. Thus the story is told about the employee who complained: "I simply cannot understand why I should receive a rating as bad as 'Good.' "[14] In this case, "good" was the lowest of three possible grades, below "excellent" and "very good." The resulting tendency to place everyone in the two top categories usually is self-defeating.

Recent Developments in Evaluation. There is an increasing tendency to overhaul the entire philosophy of superior-subordinate relationships. The reasons for this are twofold. The well-known failure of rating in practice, and recent social research findings on motivation.

The punitive philosophy of motivation characterized by punishment for failure to do one's part has been at least partially modified to embrace

---

[13] Glendale, California.
[14] Charles H. Bentley, "Performance Ratings—What Next?" 11, *Public Personnel Review* (July, 1950), p. 119.

what has been called a "clinical" approach to supervision.[15] Under the clinical approach the supervisor is regarded as a teacher, counselor, and helper to his subordinates. It is readily evident that this role is inconsistent with the traditional concept of the punitive, driving, task master. Employee evaluation under this new philosophy is directed primarily at helping the employee adjust himself to the organization and to his role therein.[16] Employee evaluation in this sense becomes one very important phase of contemporary personnel administration which emphasizes placement, employee development, and face-to-face dealing with disciplinary problems.

There is a certain inconsistency in the role prescribed for the supervisor under this new dispensation in that on one hand he is supposed to be the trusted confidante of the employee and on the other the one who administers discipline. However, this inconsistency may be more apparent than real because the employee-supervisor relationship may range from complete laissez-faire to rigid, arbitrary authority. While supervisors occasionally have to take disciplinary action, this is not at all inconsistent with their being counselors.

Our chapters on organization indicated that much of the philosophy and practice of public administration was taken from the industrial model. It is interesting that the pattern in industry seems to be shaping up along the developmental lines indicated above. Evaluation of personnel is carried on along with the management development program, which is itself closely associated with organization planning. Evaluations are conducted by immediate supervisors in a clinical manner designed to make the subordinate more valuable to the organization. The movement is away from percentage ratings, the evaluation records being worded in cryptic phrases framed by the supervisor himself. Emphasis is upon the future development of the individual and what both he and the organization will have to do in order fully to realize his abilities.[17] Judgments may be stated in such categories as "promotable," "not promotable," "satisfactory in the present job," or "due for early retirement." These evaluations are confidential and are usually in the files of the

[15] Donald R. Schoen, "Human Relations: Boon or Doggle?" 35, *Harvard Business Review* (November-December, 1957), pp. 41–43; John M. Pfiffner, *The Supervision of Personnel.*

[16] See recent views advanced by public personnel people: Philip B. Haggerty; "Why not take the Rating out of Performance Rating?," 16, *Public Personnel Review* (January, 1955), pp. 39–44; E. W. Chopson, "Service Rating Won't Serve Two Masters," 15, *Public Personnel Review* (October, 1954), pp. 171–75.

[17] However, writings such as William H. Whyte's *The Organization Man,* which includes a chapter on how to outwit psychological tests, and which generally advances the theme that the organization demands too much from the individual, suggest that industry, too, has a long way to go in achieving a truly developmental kind of personnel administration.

organization planning department rather than in the personnel folders of the individual.

It would seem that public personnel administration may soon abandon the punitive, competitive type of rating in favor of a new clinical and developmental approach to the superior-subordinate relationship. Inasmuch as old ideas and practices die hard, progress in this regard will be slow; however, one sees increasing evidence of the fact that competitive public rating has failed to serve any useful purpose. Evaluation in the future will be a continuous clinical process of interaction between supervisor and supervisee. For this, a new generation of supervisors will have to be trained and conditioned because such a process calls for a pattern of behavior which in many respects is contrary to the present state of our culture. It is to be expected that competitive evaluations for purposes of promotion will continue to be used, but they will be directed toward a specific purpose at a particular time.

An important objective of evaluation, of course, is to determine who is qualified for promotion and higher pay. This is another aspect of public administration to which the concept of a career service is germane. Talented individuals are reluctant to commit themselves to careers in which the avenues of advancement are not clearly defined. They are also concerned that advancement be based upon performance; but traditionally the civil service has not been characterized by rapid advancement or competitive promotional examinations. We now turn to this subject.

COMPETITIVE PROMOTIONAL EXAMINATIONS

Most state and local jurisdictions require a civil service examination for promotion, but this is not true of the federal government except in isolated instances such as naval shipyards. Even there the practice applies only to the lower supervisors. In the federal service there is a certain aversion toward competitive promotion which is not present in better state and local jurisdictions. Indeed, in some of these, promotion by competitive examination for higher supervisors and even department heads has prevailed for many years. It is our contention that competitive promotional examination should be the rule for all positions recruited by promotion. We are living in an age when a high order of intelligence is required for the proper filling of administrative posts. Both industry and the public service want individuals from the top of the class. There are those who object that administration is different because it deals with people. There is some truth in this, but the objection is becoming dated as administration becomes more professional. There is sufficient flexibility in most civil service examining systems to shut out the educated fool.

The great advantage of open competitive promotion is the factor of motivation. People are put upon their mettle to study and prepare for higher jobs and more responsibility. Included in their studies are such subjects as general administration, personnel, industrial psychology, and various allied fields. Thus individuals develop ideas for improving administration, ideas that eventually become accepted practice. This process sometimes makes higher-ups uncomfortable because new ideas necessarily imply some criticism of accepted methods. Supervisors are also afraid that competitive promotion will force upon them associates who are not personally acceptable. But this may be a good thing for the public service. Our contention is that *promotion by open competitive examination energizes an organization,* helping it to combat the inertia and time serving that too often characterize big institutions. This proposition can be validated by scrutinizing the operation of those jurisdictions where such a system has been in operation for many decades.

BIBLIOGRAPHY

ADKINS, DOROTHY C. "Selecting Public Employees," **17,** *Public Personnel Review* (October, 1956), pp. 259–267.

BONTECOU, ELEANOR. *The Federal Loyalty Security Program.* Ithaca: 1953.

CLEVELAND, HARLAN, and MANGONE, GERALD J. *The Art of Overseasmanship.* Syracuse, New York: 1957.

GINZBERG, ELI, and ANDERSON, JAMES K. *Manpower for Government: a Decade's Forecast.* Chicago: 1958.

GOODE, CECIL E. *Personnel Research Frontiers.* Chicago: 1958.

LIKERT, RENSIS, and HAYES, SAMUEL P., JR. (eds.). *Some Applications of Behavioral Research.* New York: 1957.

McCANN, FORBES E. *et al. Physical Condition Tests in the Selection of Public Employees.* Chicago: 1957.

MAIER, NORMAN R. F. *The Appraisal Interview.* New York: 1958.

MANSFIELD, HARVEY C. "The Dilemma of Party Patronage and the Public Service," *The Federal Government Service.* New York: 1954.

NIGRO, FELIX. *Public Personnel Administration.* New York: 1959.

OGLESBY, THOMAS W. "Use of Emotional Screening in the Selection of Police Applicants," **18,** *Public Personnel Review* (October, 1957), pp. 228–31.

OSS ASSESSMENT STAFF. *Assessment of Men.* New York: 1948.

SHERWOOD, FRANK P., and BEST, WALLACE H. *Supervisory Methods in Municipal Administration.* Chicago: 1958.

SHILS, EDWARD A. *The Torment of Secrecy.* Glencoe, Ill.: 1956.

TOYNBEE, ARNOLD J. "Thinking Ahead: Will Businessmen be Civil Servants?" *Harvard Business Review,* **36,** (September-October, 1958), pp. 23–38.

TYLER, LEONA E. *The Psychology of Human Differences.* Rev. ed. New York: 1956.

YOUNG, TIEN-CHENG. *International Civil Service: Principles and Problems.* Chicago: 1959.

CHAPTER 17

Jobs and Pay

Every human organization is composed of two basic elements: people and their functional tasks. This is true of primitive societies as well as of huge governmental hierarchies. When administrative institutions grow to the point where they must formalize their organizations, they study, analyze, and write down what persons in the various posts are supposed to do, the tasks they are expected to perform. The social scientists who study organization are doing much the same thing when they study what they call *role* and *status*.[1] While the industrial engineer is more likely to use the term "job evaluation," the public personnel man will usually speak of "position classification." They are both referring to the analysis, description, and evaluation of the tasks which people perform.

MYTHS OF JOB CLASSIFICATION

An organization chart, together with the organizational manual, is a visual presentation of the roles to be performed in an organization. If the charting is broken down in sufficient detail, the book of charts will contain a box for every individual role in the organization. Each of these is referred to as a "job" or a "position," the latter term being preferred in public personnel circles. "Position" denotes the duties performed by a single person during his tour of duty, usually at a particular place. The term "job" is not as precise, although management people will usually know what is meant when they use the term.

Separation of Positions from Persons. It seems that every area of social science—and personnel administration is applied social science—must have its fictions and myths. The social scientist does not use these terms in the popular sense to indicate something of doubtful validity but to explain a rule of action which is thought to be desirable, yet is difficult to achieve, owing to human frailty. Perhaps the leading fiction of personnel administration is that position classification and job evalua-

---

[1] For a discussion of job and status systems, see Robert Dubin, *The World of Work* (Englewood Cliffs, N.J.: Prentice-Hall, Inc., 1958), pp. 54, 85.

tion should be carried on without consideration of the persons who are incumbents at the moment. The personal characteristics, desires, ambitions, and skills of those occupying the positions studied, it is held, should not influence the decision of the position classifier. To him a particular position is a combination of duties and tasks to be performed by one person having specialized qualifications. The analyst must ignore "impertinent" data such as the fact that this job is virtually the private domain of John Doe who has occupied it for twenty years and who does almost as he pleases. To the analyst the job could just as well be filled by any qualified person who meets its specifications.

Now this is not so bad as it may seem to those who rebel against the depersonalization of the individual. As a matter of fact, analysts do pay attention to the individual and sentiment when studying jobs; they cannot avoid doing so. The pressure for the reclassification of positions upward is so great that there is little danger that they will ignore human sentiments and human values. From an over-all organization standpoint, the hazard probably lies in the other direction, namely, that they will be unable to resist these pressures and therefore will not be objective about their recommendations. Thus the rule that the job analyst studies duties and tasks instead of people is a useful fiction.

Separation of Position from Pay. Every organization has a job hierarchy and a pay hierarchy. In public administration the former is referred to as the classification plan and the latter as the compensation plan. Here again one encounters a myth, namely, that position classification is carried on separately from the determination of pay. There are several reasons for this, perhaps the most persuasive being that the classification plan is used for many purposes other than setting pay. Indeed, as is quite obvious, the formalized job hierarchy provides the basis for almost all personnel activities. People are recruited as carpenters, stenographers, and engineers. The same applies to placement, training, layoff, promotion, and job accounting. As a matter of fact, all organization and management decisions hinge upon job analysis—who does what, when, and how.

The separation of classification from pay sometimes results from a private vendetta between the budgeting and personnel authorities. If the budget agency has virile leadership, it will probably conduct the salary surveys and studies and make the pay recommendations. However, many personnel administrators feel that this is a personnel function and that the budget bureau should not recommend pay rates for individual classes. It is generally conceded that classification is a personnel activity, with the result that budget personnel often make pay recommendations on the basis of a classification scheme established by the personnel staff. The proper approach is to regard personnel and budget staff work as phases of an integrated management process. In other words, they should live next door to each other, both under an administrative chief, and they should work closely together.

CONSTRUCTING THE JOB HIERARCHY

There are several methods of analyzing and grading jobs so they will fit into a systematic hierarchy. By and large, civil service jurisdictions use a position classification procedure, whereas industry uses either factor comparison or point rating, or a combination of the latter two. A special navy study of twenty-five representative industrial firms showed that two firms used job classification; five, job ranking; nine, point rating; four, factor comparison; and five, a combination of the last two.[2] The report recommended that the navy adopt a point-rating (or modified factor comparison) system as its basic tool of evaluation. It concluded that such "systems are demonstrably superior—faster, simpler, more precise, and more understandable—than present methods of evaluation based upon narrative standards."

Factor Comparison. Industrial systems differ mainly from public classification procedures in that they use statistical methods. They grade positions just as in classification, but they attempt to be precise—to measure—whereas classification functions through logic, subjective judgment, and verbal standards. In the federal system, position classification becomes a torrent of words, with job descriptions at three levels: (1) each employee writes what he does, and this description is then fitted into (2) departmental job specifications, which in turn must conform to (3) detailed standards issued by the civil service commission.

Public personnel people have assumed that position classification systems are more suitable for government because of the greater variety of jobs.[3] Students of personnel administration should nevertheless be familiar with the general nature of industrial job evaluation systems. In the first place, this technique is used in some jurisdictions. Twenty per cent of state and local jurisdictions responding to a questionnaire indicated that they were using some form of point evaluation system.[4]

---

[2] Navexos (Executive Office of the Secretary of the Navy) P-261, *Job Evaluation, A Comparison of Practices in Industry and in the Departmental Service of the Navy* (Washington, D.C.: Department of the Navy, 1949).

[3] The most authoritative work on public personnel administration, for example, gives point and factor systems a mere paragraph in a forty-page chapter on job evaluation; O. Glenn Stahl, *Public Personnel Administration* (4th ed.; New York: Harper & Bros., 1956).

[4] Samuel Gruver, "Job Evaluation and Wage Setting in the Public Service" (Unpublished Master's thesis, University of Southern California Library, 1949).

Moreover, when industrial management firms make job studies in public jurisdictions, they tend to use the job evaluation methods with which they are familiar. In government activities of an industrial nature, there is also a tendency to adopt industrial management methods.

Factor comparison procedure involves three broad steps. First, one selects the factors to be used. These commonly include "mental requirement," "skill requirements," "physical requirements," and "working conditions." Experience and experiment have indicated that increasing the number of factors beyond three to five will not yield substantial refinement of results. The second step consists of the selection of "key" or "benchmark" jobs. These are representative jobs existing in the job hierarchy that are thought to have some characteristics which make them comparable to other jobs. For instance, "stenographer" is first related to the clerical and stenographic hierarchy. The third step occurs when a job evaluation committee fits these jobs into the pay scale by evaluating each factor in terms of pay. When the key jobs have been evaluated, the other jobs are fitted into the appropriate relationship. In a word, each factor for each job has a money value which adds up to the total pay for the job. For example, a key job might be evaluated as follows:

Mental Requirements	68.00
Skill Requirements	108.00
Physical Requirements	68.00
Responsibility Requirements	100.00
Working Conditions	44.00
Total	388.00

The main difference between the factor comparison and point evaluation systems is that the latter provides numerical points instead of dollars and cents. The points can be, and usually are, converted into money. In those governmental jurisdictions where the personnel agency does not recommend compensation rates, the point system is naturally to be preferred. Thus a comparison between a junior clerk and a laborer might run as follows:

	Junior Clerk	Laborer
Mental Requirements	3	1
Skill Requirements	2	1
Physical Requirements	2	5
Responsibility Requirements	2	1
Working Conditions	2	2
Total	11	10

One of the main arguments in favor of the point or factor comparison approaches is that they provide for the participation of the line supervisors and operating personnel in the process of evaluation. A committee composed of such persons actually makes the evaluation.

This is said to result in greater line acceptance of the job evaluation process, minimizing the tension in a classification program that often exists between supervisors and classifiers.[5]

The experimental studies that have measured the effectiveness of the two techniques conclude that nonquantitative classification and job ranking achieve substantially the same results as the quantitative factor and point systems, with about the same cost.[6] Even if one breaks down jobs in statistical detail, the final evaluation reflects the experienced analyst's judgment of the whole job.

Position Classification. We can now discuss orthodox governmental job evaluation procedure, properly referred to as "position classification." It is essentially nonquantitative until it becomes tied in with the setting of wages, when simple statistical devices such as averages and quartiles are used. Position classification developed as a phase of the reform movement to combat pay inequity resulting from political favoritism. It was not at all uncommon to find a secretary in one part of the Capitol building receiving $4,500 while another on the next floor got $2,100. Thus the object of the reformers, "equal pay for equal work," was sought by establishing a "classified service," whose positions were to be graded into classes based on similarity in duties, responsibilities, and qualifications. Each class had a single pay rate which was uniform throughout the service. By and large, this objective has now been achieved throughout the federal service and in those state and local jurisdictions that have mature personnel systems. Today the question is not whether to have job evaluation but what to do to improve traditional classification procedures.

THE GENERAL SURVEY. Classification has two phases: the general survey of all positions and continuous maintenance. The survey usually takes place at the time a jurisdiction initiates systematic job evaluation, often when a new civil service law appears. It may occur when a new department or bureau is launched. Sometimes private consulting firms are engaged to do the classification survey. The procedure has been fairly well standardized and corresponds roughly to the steps taken in an organization study. After all, the basic component of organization is jobs. The job analyst and organization analyst both study jobs, although for different purposes. Ideally, the organization staff should do its work before the classification staff appears. The former should decide the

---

[5] Francis E. McGilvery, "The Problem of Position Evaluation," 13, *Public Personnel Review* (January, 1952), pp. 12–17.

[6] Nesta Gallas, among others, found this to be true in her comparative study of the use of the two systems in the building materials industry, "An Experimental Study in the Application of Wage and Salary Data to a Classification Plan" (Unpublished Master's thesis, University of Southern California Library, 1951).

organizational pattern; the latter should grade or classify jobs on the basis of what management says it wants done. The position classifier is out of place as a designer of organizations. If a new job is involved, he takes management's job description and indicates what class it should go into. If the job is an existing one, he does not accept management's judgment entirely but decides for himself what duties are actually being performed. The classifier must constantly resist pressure to classify positions upward. It is his business to call the shots objectively. He is out of his area, however, when he tells management how to organize.

THE DUTIES QUESTIONNAIRE. The basic instrument in a classification survey is the duties questionnaire in which every employee describes the duties and tasks he performs. The form usually contains a space for the supervisor to comment upon the job without altering the employee's version. The questionnaires are then sorted into broad general categories. When the job data are insufficient, ambiguous, or inconsistent, the analysts go into the organization and interview and observe those concerned. Sometimes the surveyors follow the policy of conducting such "desk audits," as they are called, on a random sample of positions. It is too expensive to observe every job and interview all incumbents. Additional face-to-face contact between incumbent and analyst takes place in maintenance work after the survey recommendations have been carried out. Having the employee describe his own job not only gives him a feeling of participation but also a sense that his own statement may serve as useful evidence if he should later appeal his allocation.

The classification staff divides the completed questionnaire into rough categories in terms of an over-all classification scheme. This is done on the basis of preponderance of duties, their difficulty and complexity. Numerous refinements follow. When the scheme has been crystallized and the positions allocated, it is time to write the class specifications, which, when legitimated, become the official record for the class. The "specs," as they are called, contain the official class title, the write-up of duties, responsibilities, and job relationships, a list of typical tasks, qualifications of incumbents, and usual avenues of promotion. A class specification need not and often does not contain the amount of pay except when used as a recruiting bulletin.

PROBLEMS IN CLASSIFICATION. Public administration tends toward what has been termed "pigeonhole" classification. It springs at least in part from the same source as jurisdictional disputes in unionized industry. Workers try to build up their jobs, to make them seem unique and important. They like to emphasize experience and seniority, even for simple jobs. As a result, there are relatively few "common labor" jobs, for now everyone is "semiskilled" even though he is a neophyte. This is partially due to mechanization and the production control which goes with it. But also present is the individual's ego, his desire to make his job seem important, and his drive to secure social as well as monetary recognition for his specialty. The result is that most classification plans tend to have a large and increasing number of classes. Some look upon this with dismay mainly on the ground that it restricts flexibility in job assignment. Observers have compared unfavorably American pigeonhole classification with the British broad and general categories. American personnel experts reply that this is an unfair comparison because it excludes the great mass of British craftsmen, technicians, and laborers among whom the classes are much the same as ours.

Another problem is to determine who should have the power to approve the classification scheme and the allocation of individual positions to the classes set up in the scheme. In the federal setup Congress establishes a broad general classification scheme; the Civil Service Commission breaks it down into class standards; and the operating agencies set up their own classification schemes within this framework. But federal departments are now so large that overcentralization still exists. Relations between the classifiers and the supervisors can become the focus of considerable tension. The pressure upon the supervisors for the upgrading of positions can be powerful; furthermore a given supervisor may have his own official status improved if those under him are upgraded. There is a feeling among Congressmen, certain taxpayers, and management consultants that the organizational tendency toward empire building is exaggerated in government, where the competitive pressures for economy are largely absent. Supervisors are accused of overstaffing and upgrading in order to inflate their own jobs.

Federal practice delegates the power to classify to the heads of executive agencies, and usually this means further delegation by the heads to subordinates in the line of command. Personnel workers, of course, are advisory to line executives who make the actual decisions. There is a school, however, which maintains that decisions should be made by the classifiers themselves, independent of the line of command. It is claimed that the operating personnel, in doing their own classifying, will allow subjective personal considerations to enter into a procedure which "should" be objective.[7]

[7] In 1956 the Navy abandoned its long-standing practice of lodging the power to reclassify with the classification people themselves and transferred it to commanding officers of field installations. This ha' long been a matter of controversy and represents a triumph of the line management viewpoint, although there are die-hards among the personnel fraternity. See H. Donald McInnis, "Death of a Program," 18. *Public Personnel Review* (October, 1957), pp. 222–27.

In most state and local jurisdictions the power to classify resides with the civil service commission. There has been comparatively little delegation to the operating personnel.

THE COMPENSATION PLAN

The salaries and wages paid to public servants are set in a variety of ways, among which the following are the most important:

1. By legislatures, spelled out in detail in the law. This method applies in those states and local jurisdictions which do not have mature personnel systems.
2. By legislatures in broad schematic outline, but with the detail left to administrative determination. This applies to the federal classified service.
3. By collective bargaining, as in the U.S. Government Printing Office and Tennessee Valley Authority.
4. By local or area wage determinations based upon periodic study of prevailing rates, as with "nongraded" federal employees.
5. By haphazard or unplanned determination, also characteristic of immature personnel setups.

Problems in Pay Determination. It has long been customary to begin a discussion of employee compensation with a somewhat metaphysical exercise in such concepts as ability to pay and the ingredients of a living wage. While these dimensions are important, it is now felt that at least on all but the top levels compensation is adequately reflected in the prevailing rate. For wage scales are partially based on the prevailing wages paid by private industry in the area concerned. This is another example of the growing maturity of personnel administration, evident in its attempt to base decisions on fact finding. Salary surveys based upon the statistical analyses of comparative data are not new, but their use has multiplied in the last twenty years. Furthermore, such surveys have in that time emerged as a special vocation whose methodology has been considerably refined.

Despite efforts to base pay upon existing community rates, one of the most vexing problems is still the disparity between compensation in the public service and that in industry. This disparity is especially marked for the higher level jobs with which we are mainly concerned. Indeed, at the lower and middle levels, government pay compares very favorably with pay in private industry. Government pay also suffers from a general tendency, brought about by union efforts and bureaucratization in both government and industry, for salaries to cluster around a central range; the income pyramid has flattened out, and the range between entry salaries and those at the top is being narrowed. One survey shows that high-ranking private executives are paid four times as much as their governmental opposites.[8] When one compares the size and scope of program and responsibility of a bureau Chief who works for around $18,000 a year with a private executive who may administer a single department in a small corporation, the disparity in income is striking. Another study indicates that whereas the salary mean for industrial relations officials in 1957 in government was $9,268, the mean for all industry groups was higher—with banking, which is notoriously low-salaried, having a mean of $10,866, or about $1,600 per year more than government salary.[9] Still another example of the disparity in pay is shown in the following statistic: Engineers who work for industry received in 1958 an average annual salary of $8,400; those in the field of education received $7,100; while those in government received $6,600.[10]

Recent raises have improved the picture somewhat, but the differentials at the higher levels continue. As noted, there is an increasing trend toward flattening out the salary pyramid; for example, from 1939 to 1956 the rise in average salaries for the lowest grades in the federal service, 1 and 2, amounted to 140 and 112 per cent, respectively, but the increase for those in Grade 15 was only 42 per cent.[11] The second Hoover Commission recommended that the pay of assistant secretaries in large departments like Defense be raised from $15,000 to $25,000, although the Commission recognized that salaries in government could never compete with those offered for top jobs in industry. There is plenty of evidence that high-level civil servants are often forced out of government by economic pressure, and as we saw earlier, one of the barriers to recruiting executives from industry is the low pay of even the highest federal jobs. One basic problem here, rarely mentioned, is that Congress is extremely reluctant to provide higher pay for civil servants than it provides for itself. Nevertheless, since Congressmen receive $25,000 per year plus many perquisites, there is still some room for increasing administrative pay without upsetting Congressional superiority in this respect.

Establishing Area Rates. Statistical studies of basic rates paid in the community are not scientific wage determinations; they merely try to ascertain the average rate in particular occupational categories. The basic determination has already been made by social and economic forces over which the wage analyst has no control; he is merely trying

[8] J. Rosnow, "Executive Compensation in the Federal Government," 30, *Personnel* (1953).

[9] Dale Yoder and Roberta J. Nelson, "Salaries and Staffing Ratios in Industrial Relations, 1957," 34, *Personnel* (July–August, 1957), pp. 16–22.

[10] S. E. Harris, "Who Gets Paid What," 201, *Atlantic Monthly* (May, 1958), p. 37.

[11] Ruth W. Benny, "Federal Classified Employees Salary Changes, 1954–56," 80, *Monthly Labor Review* (July, 1957), pp. 816–20.

to measure what exists. Here he is confronted with two statistical problems: how to secure a representative sample of jobs and employers, and how to establish norms of central tendency or averages. He must first decide which jobs are to be studied. If a general salary survey covering all classes in a governmental jurisdiction is sought, the task is naturally more complex than if only blue-collar jobs are involved. The area wage boards that study nongraded federal jobs cover only the area of skilled trades and related vocations such as machinists and helpers. When the survey must cover the entire hierarchy, it is customary to select certain representative or "benchmark" jobs, such as "typist," "general clerk," "structural engineer," "janitor." The data on these classes are projected by both mathematical formula and expert judgment to set rates for related classes.

Next, brief job descriptions must be prepared, short enough so that other employers are willing to take the time to read them. The analyst then calls upon the sample of employers furnishing information. Here the survey people often have a selling job in order to secure cooperation. The pay schedules of public agencies are matters of public record, but private employers tend to be secretive about their pay. Among other things, private employers must be assured that the data will be treated confidentially. Sometimes the study staffs refuse to disclose the names of cooperating firms. Some unions and groups of employees object to such secrecy, charging that low-paid, nonunion firms are favored and unionized firms are slighted. Many unions are suspicious of this whole approach to wage setting, ostensibly because they question the fairness of the studies, but more basically because they believe that the union's role as bargaining agent will be undermined. As a result, unions have sometimes gone to court to force the personnel agency to reveal the sources of its data.

Constructing the Pay Scheme. When all the data have been collected, they are analyzed and fitted to the salary scheme of the particular jurisdiction. A step plan, usually with five levels, seems to be preferred for several reasons. In studying a community rate, one finds a wide range in virtually all categories, even in those trades where unions predominate. Furthermore, clerical salaries are commonly paid on a step basis by private employers. Very often the step plan is regarded as an incentive, with advances being based upon meritorious service. It is also thought that in most jobs there is a learning period during which the employee is not worth as much as he will be later. Another consideration is turnover; the employee about to receive a step increase may be less inclined to leave or to sacrifice the increase once it is attained. There are also solid administrative reasons for having a schedule with orderly statistical relationships. For instance, it is general practice to set the median (or range of the medians) discovered in the survey at the middle step of the salary schedule. Thus the recommended rate will be obtained by matching the middle figure obtained in the survey with the middle step of the appropriate schedule.

Under a step plan, newcomers are usually hired at the first step and advanced at specific time intervals, say a step a year, until the maximum is reached. This plan offers some difficulties, however. In times of labor scarcity good workers are unwilling to sacrifice immediate gain for ultimate security. This is especially true in classes where labor is scarce. After World War II these included skilled trades, structural engineers, and operators of certain types of office machines. Some jurisdictions met this emergency by hiring at the middle or higher steps. Also there is a strong tendency for step increases to become automatic, even when they are geared to efficiency ratings. In the latter event, the raters will be subject to so much pressure for pay raises that they will mark everyone high enough to receive the step. This results in the flat curve, referred to earlier, which largely vitiates a rating system. The theory of within-grade salary increases based upon merit is very sound, but it is difficult to enforce in public administration.

A feature of a pay plan ordinarily acceptable to employee groups is the longevity increase. The Federal Classification Act of 1949 provided that an employee who had completed ten years of service at the maximum of his grade, and whose status was below Grade GS-10, was entitled to a one-step advance for three years' service, with a maximum of three such advances.[12] Employee organizations tend to look upon such an arrangement with favor because it recognizes stability of employment and security. Management has mixed feelings for another reason, namely, that it constitutes official recognition and approval of seniority and inertia. What will be the effect upon the motivation of workers to provide by law that one who remains for ten years on the same status shall have three successive boosts if he stays there? This, they feel, may be a structuring influence that will discourage initiative.

Determination of Pay. Who should make ultimate pay decisions? Should it be the legislature or some administrative body? It is obvious that Congress cannot set individual salaries for millions of federal positions or even for the ten thousand classes for which the Civil Service Commission has issued standards. The Classification Act of 1923 established the principle that individual salaries would be set administratively in line with broad guides established by Congress. With certain exceptions, this policy is followed today. In local government the council

12 63 Statutes-at-Large 954; 5 USCA 1071.

usually approves the pay for each class, sometimes in a salary ordinance enacted annually at budget time. In some cities this power is scattered among several independent agencies. It is often argued that the legislative body should also set the pay for each position because it is the elected representative of the people. In the authors' opinion the following procedures for states and cities are the most desirable:

1. The central personnel agency classifies positions.
2. The personnel agency or the budget bureau conducts the community salary studies and recommends the pay scale for each class.
3. The final pay schedule for each class is determined administratively, either by the Civil Service Commission or some other designated single central body.
4. The elected governing body determines how much is available for salary purposes in each department.
5. The departments adjust their payroll totals to fit the limitations placed upon them by the appropriation ordinance.
6. If money is not available to pay prevailing rates for all positions in the budget, the number of positions should be reduced accordingly.

The preceding plan would be as objective a method of setting pay rates as is possible in an imperfect world. Specialists would study the wage structure of employers in the community. They would advise a centralized administrative body as to their findings. That body would determine the prevailing rate in the community for each class in the job hierarchy. The mayor or city manager would, through his annual budget, inform the council of the total amount needed for each department or program. The council would then pass the appropriation ordinance, setting limits on total amounts to be spent by departments or programs. The mayor or manager would then approve the departmental programs or budgets that would pay personnel at the prevailing community rate. The departments would have to trim their personnel budgets to the amounts allotted. The council would retain democratic control of expenditure and program without making decisions that are essentially administrative.

RETIREMENT

Most public employees in jurisdictions having a formal personnel setup are under a retirement plan based upon an actuarial reserve fund. This is a fairly recent development. Not long ago retirement plans were enacted without thorough study, as a result of pressure by employee groups. Inadequate provision was made to finance them, usually a specific tax levy on the assessed valuation. As employees retired, the burden became too great, with the result that pensioners faced loss of payments. This situation happened often enough to point up the necessity to plan for reserve funds that would be adequate to pay anticipated costs as they accrued. This is now accomplished by having actuaries determine life expectancies, just as in life insurance companies. If it is determined that the average employee lives eight years beyond the retirement age, the problem will be to have enough money on hand, plus the interest it will earn, to pay each employee's pension for that time. Contributions are made to this fund during the employee's working life, in part by pay check deductions and in part by the government. This money is invested in securities considered suitable for trust funds.

Impact of Inflation. Actuarial retirement systems, like most of us, have been caught in the scissors of low interest and inflation. The two most important variables are interest earnings and longevity of pensioners. After 1929 the average interest rate on trust funds of this nature fell from $3\frac{1}{2}$–$4\frac{1}{2}$ per cent to 2–3 per cent, although it began to rise again in the late 1950's. At the same time pensioners have come to live longer. The result has been that the contributions from payroll have increased while interest earnings have decreased. A serious problem often arises because employees cannot understand why 4 to 8 per cent payroll deductions bring such small retirement incomes. This is especially so among those who have entered the system at middle age and for whom interest has not had long to work.

In the past, standard practice favored the investment of retirement reserve funds in conservative, liquid bonds such as those favored by insurance companies and private trust funds. Government bonds—federal, state, and local—constitute a large proportion of such investment. Although such a program provides the maximum protection against the loss of principal as measured in dollars, it does not hedge against the dollar's loss of purchasing power, which has always been the pensioner's worst enemy. The laws governing insurance companies, college endowment funds, and private trust funds have been amended in many states to permit investment in common stocks, since their yield increases during periods of inflation. The trouble is that they also decline during periods of deflation. To meet this situation the Teachers' Insurance and Annuity Association of America, which provides actuarial annuities for most of the nation's college professors, has established an equity fund alongside its orthodox setup. Half the contributions go into what amounts to an open-end investment fund, devoted to common stocks. In any long-run period, the price curve has always gone up, but there have been fairly long deflationary periods like the 1930's. The public employee who retired at such times would get a smaller pension, but the price level would also be lower.

Retirement in the Federal System. Many changes have occurred recently in the federal retirement system, which was established in 1920 to furnish retirement, death, and disability benefits to its employees. Although the act has been amended many times in good part as a result of the pleas of employees to their Congressmen, inequities have developed over the years. In addition, the inadequacy of federal provisions compared with those in industry was becoming an important factor in recruitment and turnover. In 1952 Congress authorized a committee on retirement policy to study the problem carefully and report to Congress. Early in 1956, hearings were held on Senate bills 2875 and 3041 to revise civil service retirement provisions.[13] The House also held hearings on similar legislation, and as a result, on July 26, 1956, Public Law 854 was signed by the President. The new legislation included the following major changes:[14]

1. An increase in employees' deductions for retirement.
2. A more liberal formula for computing annuities for retired employees.
3. Higher children's annuities.
4. Survivor annuities for dependent widows. (Previously, if one had been a federal employee for less than five years before he died, his dependents received no annuities.)
5. Refunds were made available to separated employees with twenty or more years service.
6. A minimum disability allowance was set down.

The major improvements over previous terms included the more favorable formula for computing the employees annuities, brought about by increasing the percentage of the employee's salary used in determining retirement pay; the establishment of a minimum payment for disabled employees; and greatly liberalized payments to the dependents of deceased employees.[15]

Social Security. In state and local systems, since 1954 all employees have been eligible for participation in the federal social security system. Congress made it a policy of such coverage not to reduce the amounts due the employees from their own state retirement systems. A referendum vote by the employees is also required before the state may enter the federal program. Approximately half of the states now participate. However, there is some resistance. In December, 1955, state employees in California rejected the proposal that they come under the federal plan. Apparently some civil service union leaders have resisted joint coverage

[13] Subcommittee, Senate Committee on Post Office and Civil Service, 84th Cong. 2d sess., *Hearings,* "Civil Service Retirement" (Washington, D.C.: U.S. Government Printing Office, 1956).

[14] U.S. Civil Service Commission, *News Release* (Washington, D.C.: August 1, 1956).

[15] Committee on Post Office and Civil Service, *Improvements in Federal Civil Service Retirement Benefits Contained in Public Law,* 854 (H.R. 7619), (Washington, D.C.: U.S. Government Printing Office, 1956).

because the appeal of their own union retirement systems would suffer accordingly. State systems vary considerably with regard to their social security participation. In some, payments are made regardless of the amount the employee receives in retirement benefits; in others, the amount of social security benefit is deducted from the retirement pay; while in still others, the retirement benefit is reduced somewhat, but the combined income is still more than that from the retirement system alone.[16]

The federal system differs in that employees are not eligible for coverage under the social security system. Although combined retirement and social security benefits were recommended in a 1956 proposal (Senate 3041, the Johnson bill), they were not included in the final act. Under the 1956 law as passed, an employee who had an average salary of $4,700 (which, by the way, in 1956 was the average for all federal employees), was sixty years of age and had thirty-five years of service, qualified for an annual benefit of $2,880, about $480 more than he would have received under the earlier legislation.[17]

Fringe Benefits. Federal employees receive a number of fringe benefits which will be reviewed in concluding this chapter. These may be considered under four categories:[18]

1. Payment for time spent away from work, such as annual leave, vacations, sick leave, military leave, educational opportunities.
2. Overtime payments.
3. Payments for health and security benefits, such as group life insurance, life insurance, hospitalization, etc.
4. Payments for special services provided employees, such as medical and health services, cafeteria, etc.

Government employees receive many of these benefits, although the advantages that public employees once had over those in industry no longer exist. For example, the generous annual leave provision of twenty-six working days that federal employees once received was changed in 1951 to a graduated system whereby employees with less than three years service now receive thirteen days; those with service between three and fifteen years receive twenty days; while only those with more than fifteen years get a twenty-six day vacation.[19] These provisions are not much different than those current in industry. In sum, while government employees still compare favorably with industry in terms of fringe bene-

---

[16] H. Eliot Kaplan, *The Law of the Civil Service* (New York: M. Bender and Co., 1958), p. 363.

[17] Committee on Post Office and Civil Service, p. 4.

[18] Edith B. Kidney, *Fringe Benefits for Salaried Employees in Government and Industry* (Chicago: Civil Service Assembly, 1954), p. 1.

[19] *Ibid.*, pp. 6–7.

fits, superior benefits which were once regarded as a surrogate for higher pay, have disappeared. This factor must be considered when one contemplates such problems as high turnover in government service. When added to low pay and restrictions upon political autonomy,[20] the reduction, or at least the equalization of fringe benefits with those in industry, must account for much of the vexing tenure problem.

BIBLIOGRAPHY

BARUCH, ISMAR (ed.). *Position Classification in the Public Service.* Chicago: 1941.

BATSON, ROBERT J. *Employee Evaluation: a Review of Current Methods and a New Approach.* Chicago: 1957.

BELCHER, DAVID W. *Wage and Salary Administration.* Englewood Cliffs, N.J.: 1955.

BELL, JAMES R., and STEEDMAN, LYNWOOD B. *Personnel Problems in Converting to Automation,* IUCP No. 44. University, Alabama: 1959.

BENNET, C. L. *Defining the Manager's Job,* Research Study No. 33. New York: 1958.

BIBLIOGRAPHY. "Retirement Policies in the Public Service," **19,** *Public Personnel Review* (January, 1958), pp. 68–71.

COMMITTEE REPORT, INTERNATIONAL CITY MANAGERS' ASSOCIATION. *City Management—a Growing Profession.* Chicago: 1957.

DREW, FRANKLIN E., and HALL, GEORGE LAWRENCE (eds.). *The Management Guide.* Rev. ed. San Francisco: 1956.

FORDYCE, J. K. "Officer-Civilian Relationships in Semi-Military Technical Organizations," **65,** *Journal of the American Society of Naval Engineers, Inc.* (February, 1953), pp. 9–22.

HELDEN, KARL. *Mr. Bureaucrat, a True Inside Story of the Federal Civil Service, etc.* New York: 1958.

PCHELTREE, KEITH. *How to Prepare a Sound Pay Plan.* Chicago: 1957.

ROBINSON, CARL W. "New Price Tags for Government Managers," **36,** *Harvard Business Review* (September–October, 1958), pp. 81–86.

STAFF REPORT, PUBLIC PERSONNEL ASSOCIATION. *Pay Rates in the Public Service.* Chicago: Revised and reissued annually.

UNSIGNED. *Trends in Salaries of City Managers.* Chicago: 1957.

---

[20] See, for example, Arch Dotson, "The Emerging Doctrine of Privilege in Public Employment," **15,** *Public Administration Review* (Winter, 1955), pp. 77–88; Adam Yarmolinsky, *Case Studies in Personnel Security* (Washington, D.C.: Bureau of National Affairs, 1955).

CHAPTER 18

Employee Relations

Perhaps the foremost problem in administration today is how to motivate the rank and file of large-scale organizations. Those who plan and administer these institutions are themselves highly motivated, and sometimes they naïvely expect the other nine-tenths of the staff to be equally inspired. Furthermore, since the time a hirsute hyperthyroid clubbed the first army private into line, the leaders of the world hierarchies have been peculiarly indifferent to the sentiments and welfare of the common man. Any modern reader who doubts this should review the social history of the Industrial Revolution, particularly the exploitation of child labor in the nineteenth century. By and large, the conditions of employment have been determined unilaterally, as evidenced by the fact that the basic law is referred to in the legal digests under the heading of "Master and Servant." Labor was until recently regarded as a commodity, to be bought and sold in the market place in the same manner as wood or steel. This is attested to by eminent authority, including the late Elton Mayo, who referred to the nineteenth-century attitude toward labor as the "rabble hypothesis."[1]

COLLECTIVE BARGAINING IN INDUSTRY

The scientific management movement, now scarcely more than a half-century old, had as its main technique the motivation of people by establishing production standards. Through time-and-motion study, the alignment of machines to simplify work flow, and a minute division of labor, productivity skyrocketed, and is continuing to do so. But labor has always resisted work measurement and still does. Indeed, Congress passed laws, now superseded, which prevented the use of stop watches in government establishments. Even with the demonstrated effectiveness of industrial engineering, labor has not become motivated in the manner expected by management. As a result, a pattern of bilateral cooperation has evolved, assisted by government through the national labor laws.

[1] Elton Mayo, *The Social Problems of an Industrial Civilization* (Boston: Harvard School of Business Administration, 1945), pp. 34–56; also R. Bendix, *Work and Authority in Industry* (New York: Wiley and Co., 1956).

Relationships between employers and employees in industry now follow a fairly uniform procedure. The basic features of this process, known under the generic term of "collective bargaining," are as follows:

1. An independent employee organization, officially recognized by management as having the power to speak for employees on certain matters.
2. The periodic settlement, through negotiation, of disputes over policy matters affecting the whole range of employer-employee relationships, formalized in a written agreement called the "contract."
3. The settlement of current disputes under the contract through a grievance system in which union officers deal directly with supervisors.
4. The establishment at the shop level of an area of freedom of speech and freedom of petition rather similar to civil liberties on the political level.
5. Official recognition by the employer that one of his own employees, the shop steward, will transact union business on company time.

This brief decription of industrial collective bargaining precedes a discussion of governmental employee relations because similar issues prevail in each area and similar bargaining procedures are being introduced. However, it has been assumed that the legal protection and security of civil service provide an adequate if not superior substitute for unionism. Is this necessarily so?

PUBLIC EMPLOYEE ORGANIZATIONS

Blue-Collar Unions. Although there are local variations, the organization of public employees conforms to a certain pattern. In the first place, wherever skilled craftsmen—printers, carpenters, machinists, or plumbers—work for a governmental unit, they usually belong to their own traditional unions. These artisans often represent the conservative branch of trade unionism. Any given jurisdiction is likely to have locals of both or either of the craft and industrial unions set up by the American Federation of Labor and the Congress of Industrial Organizations for government employees. An "industrial" union is one that takes in all the employees of a given employer or industry without regard to their occupations or jobs. Thus a janitor, a laboratory assistant, and a clerk would all be eligible for the same industrial union.

So far we have referred only to those unions that are "affiliated with the labor movement"—that is, with the AFL-CIO. However, in many places there are also organizations that are independent but which are very similar to traditional unions. Historically they were affiliated either with the AFL-CIO, or they were often organized by persons who were once labor leaders. It is difficult to establish a standard that will distinguish a union from other employee organizations, but the criteria would relate to militancy, type of work, and occupational level of membership. The Public Workers of America was formerly in the CIO, and the American Federation of Federal Employees in the AF of L. The postal unions were for the most part affiliated with the AF of L.[2]

White-Collar Associations. Professional, semiprofessional, and clerical workers are often antiunion in their social views. They are culturally and emotionally more closely allied to management than to labor. This attitude persisted even during the 1940's and 1950's when the blue-collar worker tended to be considerably better paid than the lower categories among the white-collarites. This is perhaps the principal reason for the multiplicity of employee organizations that are not affiliated with the labor movement and which differ in certain respects from the independent unions. The generic title for them runs somewhat as follows: the "___ State Employees Association," "the Administrative Employees' Council," etc. These organizations, while open to the rank and file, tend to be led by high-status personnel rather than by those of humble occupation.

The picture, then, is one of great number and variety. There are few places where a single union covers all the employees in a particular unit or office. The union shop is the exception. A given industry often deals with several unions. Thus the bartenders will be in one union, the teamsters in another, and the window washers in yet another. In a given government office, people working side by side in substantially related occupations will belong either to no union or to different unions. To meet a similar situation, the British have developed the Whitley Councils, which represent the unions on the one side and management on the other. They give a united front to the employees while preserving the integrity of various unions.[3]

British Experience. The Whitley Councils were established in 1919 to answer a need highlighted by the experience of World War I.[4] The membership of the National Whitley Council is divided equally between representatives of the government or "official" side and representatives of the workers or "staff" side. There are also decentralized Whitley Councils to deal with departmental matters. Experience indicates that Whitleyism has been fairly successful, but more so in recent years than in the beginning. It originated at a time when persons on the official side tended to be rather aloof toward employees, while labor

[2] Sterling D. Spero, *Government as Employer* (New York: Remsen Press, 1948), p. 163. While the AFL and CIO are now united, each still retains its essential flavor of craft, on the one hand, and industrial on the other.

[3] Leo D. Cagan, "Recent Transformation in Civil Service Whitleyism," 12, *Public Personnel Review* (January, 1951), pp. 25–30.

[4] See Glynn Picton, "Whitley Councils in the Health Service," 35, *Journal of Public Administration* (Winter, 1957), pp. 359–71; Sterling D. Spero, *Labor Relations in British Nationalized Industry* (New York: New York University Press, 1955).

leaders were accustomed to being militant and aggressive toward management. During the emergency of World War II the official side asked the staff for help in solving problems previously considered to be matters of management prerogative. The result has been a maturing of Whitley institutions into vehicles of genuine collaboration.[5] A start toward Whitleyism was made in Canada in 1944 through establishment of the National Joint Council.[6]

British Whitleyism has been referred to as genuine collective bargaining within the limitations postulated by the sovereignty of the employer.[7] Institutions similar to Whitleyism are needed in the United States for the purpose of federating the many independent unions so that they can put up a united front in their negotiations with management. It seems reasonable that American public personnel administration will meet the need for similar institutions before long. Indeed, a precedent already exists in the Tennessee Valley Trades and Labor Council.

LEGAL CONSIDERATIONS AND THE RIGHT TO STRIKE

Discussions of collective bargaining in the public service are often approached with considerable emotion, usually triggered by the word "strike." Visions of administrative chaos arise upon mere mention of unions or collective bargaining. The idea of public employees going on strike is so contrary to the average legislator's notion of what is proper that it colors his entire approach. This attitude has in turn affected the law, which has been far from friendly to the introduction of the industrial pattern of unionism in public administration. Such an attitude flows from two basic precepts of the law: (1) the sovereign nature of the employer, and (2) the sovereign as protector of the public safety and public welfare. The former springs from the source long responsible for the exemption of government from tort liability—immunity of the sovereign. "The king can do no wrong." As sovereign he is the repository of the police power, and therefore a strike would be a threat to public order and safety.

Legal Prohibitions. Most legal statements on the subject accept the right of employees to join organizations of their own choosing. Federal unions were prohibited by administrative order from lobbying before Congress until 1912, when the Lloyd-La Follette Act repealed the restrictions.[8] The right to strike, however, is universally denied by the

---

[5] Cagan, "Recent Transformation in Civil Service Whitleyism."
[6] Taylor Cole, *The Canadian Bureaucracy* (Durham, N.C.: Duke University Press, 1949), pp. 123–33.
[7] Cagan, "Recent Transformation in Civil Service Whitleyism," p. 30.
[8] Spero, *Government as Employer*, p. 142.

courts, and such prohibitions are firmly fixed in the law.[9] Civil service employees who have been dismissed for unauthorized absence caused by strikes are not likely to be reinstated by the courts, although there are not many specific legal precedents on this point. There is some tendency for the law to be more lenient with employees of proprietary functions, such as street railways, than with governmental activities such as police and fire. Collective bargaining that results in a binding contract is not legal, but there is a move toward negotiation which ends in a gentlemen's agreement, an initialed memorandum, and in some cases a city ordinance. The union shop is regarded as illegal, but there is some official sanction of the checkoff of dues.

Thus the letter of our law frowns upon the application of industrial patterns of employee relations to public personnel administration. Even so great a friend of labor as Franklin D. Roosevelt wrote to Luther C. Steward that "the process of collective bargaining, as usually understood, cannot be transplanted into the public service. . . . The very nature and purposes of government make it impossible for administrative officials to represent or bind the employer in mutual discussions with government employee organizations."[10] Legislatures have reflected a similar opinion in enacting drastic antistrike laws such as the New York Condon-Wadlin Act or the federal Taft-Hartley Law. These laws usually provided that an employee who has participated in a strike automatically forfeits his job.[11]

Strikes in the Public Service. Students of human behavior are well aware that behavior patterns having deep cultural roots cannot be prohibited or altered by legislation. This is equally true in the area of employee relations. Strikes do occur among government employees, frequently among those doing blue-collar work at the municipal level, and spasmodically among school teachers and policemen.[12] The relative absence of strikes at the federal level can probably be attributed to the area wage boards which keep the pay in shipyards and arsenals on a par with that of private employers. Most of the strikes in recent years have been by such workers as street railway and bus drivers and garbage

[9] Reviews of the legal aspects can be found in Charles S. Rhyne, *Labor Unions and Municipal Employee Law* (Washington, D.C.: National Institute of Municipal Law Officers, 1946); H. Eliot Kaplan, "Legal Aspects of Public Employee Relations," **10**, *Public Personnel Review* (January, 1949), pp. 40–43, and in Kaplan's "Concepts of Public Employee Relations," **1**, *Industrial and Labor Relations Review* (January, 1948), pp. 206–30.

[10] Cited in Paul P. Van Riper, *History of the United States Civil Service* (Evanston, Ill.: Row, Peterson and Co., 1958), p. 350 ff.

[11] See discussion of these laws by Leonard D. White, "Strikes in the Public Service," **14**, *Public Personnel Review* (January, 1949), pp. 3–10.

[12] David Ziskind, *One Thousand Strikes of Government Employees* (New York: Columbia University Press, 1940).

handlers. One reason for this is that these workers are usually organized by union officials whose experience has been with unions in private industry. They bring to public employment the cultural beliefs and behavior patterns characteristic of industry. These clash violently with those of municipal officials who tend to be socially conservative and antiunion in outlook. Furthermore the persons employed at this occupational level have a set of cultural values which differs from those of the white-collar world. They are conditioned to intermittent employment with the result that job loss may not be a calamity; nor do they have the white-collar person's horror of a blot on his employment record.

It is more difficult to explain the reason for strikes by school teachers and policemen, who tend to have a white-collar stereotype about labor unions.[13] Teachers, especially, regard themselves as professional people. It is difficult for them to become militant as a group, with the result that they have rebelled against employment conditions only under extreme provocation. The last epidemic of teacher strikes came in the post-World War II period when pay schedules lagged far behind the inflation spiral. Strikes occurred in Buffalo, Minneapolis, Chicago, and elsewhere. In New York City, recently, an unofficial strike occurred among high school teachers. Their cause could usually be traced to two sources: (1) stubborn refusal by the community authorities to meet the wage problem realistically, and (2) an accumulation of grievances, many of which were long standing. School boards and school authorities have fostered an authoritarian personnel policy which has shut off upward communication. Too often the teacher has been treated as an automaton rather than as a professional person. Public personnel administration has in general lacked the means of forcing the communication of day-to-day grievances up the administrative hierarchy. Employee morale suffers accordingly. As we have seen earlier, the value of catharsis through sounding off cannot be overestimated. The National Civil Service League was correct when it said that the establishment of the industrial-type grievance system would prevent strikes.[14]

GRIEVANCE PROCEDURES IN GOVERNMENT

A universal aspect of hierarchies is their tendency to stifle upward communication. Persons in positions of leadership are especially annoyed when they have to listen to the complaints of subordinates. Even those who loudly proclaim that they maintain an "open door," accessible at any time to employees on all levels, display discomfort at the expression of discontent. Executives are human in that they do not like bad news.

[13] Spero, *Government as Employer*, pp. 245–337.
[14] **68**, *Good Government* (May–June, 1951), pp. 29–30.

Employee complaints are especially disturbing because in a certain sense they imply a criticism of management. They seem to suggest that the boss is not the wisest, most humane, most beloved, and cleverest supervisor in the organization. This naturally pricks his ego, for man made into a supervisor often sees himself as infallible. He wants others to confirm this picture of himself and becomes irritated when they fail to do so.

Industrial Precedent. The industrial grievance system has institutionalized upward communication by opening up the channels and furnishing pushers in the form of union business agents and shop stewards. The shop steward, shop committeeman, or chapel chairman, as he is known in the printing trade, is the lowest official in the union hierarchy —a sort of noncom. He differs from other officials in that he is a full-time employee, not of the union but of management. He is merely a fellow worker who has been elected by his colleagues to represent union interests at the shop or office level. Many contracts provide that he may devote a certain amount of company-paid time to union business, perhaps an hour a day. The supervisor is expected to deal with the steward on all grievances; indeed, an alert steward will often initiate grievance claims. Management sometimes complains that stewards go around manufacturing grievances on company time. However, like other humans, stewards vary a great deal in their militancy or docility, and certain managements have fostered training courses for them because of their failure to put forth much effort on behalf of employees.[15]

Applying Industrial Grievance Procedures to Government. Similarities in problems and procedures between industry and government are detectable in many kinds of grievances. Here again the lessons of industry could be applied to public service. The typical industrial grievance system provides a hierarchy of appeals. Whenever possible, grievances are settled between the employee, the steward, and the immediate supervisor. When informal negotiations of this kind fail, the grievance is put in writing. The matter is then taken up with the next higher supervisor, and if not settled, usually goes to a formally constituted tribunal where trial procedure prevails, with witnesses and recording of testimony. The head of the company is usually the final resort, but sometimes there is provision for arbitration. The majority of grievances have to do with job evaluation and job rating of individual employees. It is idle to say that this type of grievance procedure is not needed in public personnel administration. One has only to contemplate the spectacle of

---

[15] On the relationships between foremen and stewards, see Glenn Gardiner, *When Foreman and Steward Bargain* (New York: McGraw-Hill Book Co., Inc., 1945), pp. 131–32; Lloyd G. Reynolds, *Labor Economics and Labor Relations* (Englewood Cliffs, N. J.: Prentice-Hall, Inc., 1949), pp. 50–51; and Benjamin M. Selekman, *Labor Relations and Human Relations* (New York: McGraw-Hill Book Co., Inc., 1947), pp. 51–52.

the traffic of a large metropolitan area paralyzed for several days because of a dispute over split shifts on the part of a handful of municipal streetcar men, or a walkout by teachers protesting inadequate wages.

Federal practice in the last decade, especially in the defense agencies, has embraced a grievance system based upon the industrial pattern. The difference is that such systems usually are not operated under conditions of collective bargaining, with the union officials taking an aggressive part. The result undoubtedly is that utilization of this machinery varies considerably from place to place, depending upon the attitudes of the man in command.

Many federal grievances, such as veterans' appeals, classification of positions, and security actions, must go through the U.S. Civil Service Commission instead of being heard by the departmental grievance system. In pondering the following figures, it should be remembered that these would probably be combined in an industrial grievance system. In 1957–58 the Air Force processed 429 civilian appeals at all levels. During the same period 600 Air Force employees appealed various adverse actions to the Civil Service Commission.[16] In each case the employee was upheld in 20 to 25 per cent of the appeals.

The old notion that civil service legal protection gave the employee an adequate outlet for his grievances has been giving way in the face of growing unionization. Unions of governmental employees are beginning to operate at the production level, looking out for the personal feelings of the individual worker. This is in addition to their former preoccupation with lobbying for the legislative interests of their members. The shop steward function is beginning to emerge, although often under a different title. Indeed, public personnel administration is gradually acquiring many of the activities and some of the atmosphere of industrial labor relations. This fact is apparent in the character of disciplinary practices such as dismissal, in which the public employee benefits both from the psychological support of his union or employee association and from a well-established removal procedure.

Removal Procedure. There is a widely held belief that civil servants can neither be disciplined nor dismissed. A joke current in 1958 was that the unsuccessful Vanguard Rocket had been renamed the Civil Servant "because it won't work and you can't fire it."[17] This is another example of a myth that has become a guide for thought and action, not because it is true but because individuals, including government supervisors, believe it to be true. As a matter of fact, it is quite possible to remove

[16] Letter from John A. Watts, Director of Civilian Personnel, dated October 8, 1958.

[17] "How to Get Better Public Servants," *Harper's Magazine* (September, 1958).

government employees, but the procedure required is often prolonged and embarrassing. A kind of due process has been built up which provides employees a necessary safeguard against arbitrary removal, but it is widely viewed as leaning too far in that direction. As a result, removal is difficult though possible.

Obstacles to Dismissal. Governmental supervisors hesitate to dismiss an unsatisfactory employee chiefly because of the unpleasantness involved. Those who criticize government supervisors on this point should keep in mind that in industry too this task is not relished; it is avoided as long as possible. The difference in industry is that individual productivity becomes a survival factor sooner than in government. In those governmental agencies where the dismissed employee has no right to appeal for reinstatement, the supervisor hesitates to take action because of pressures that are brought to bear on him. These are the telephoned inquiries of a Congressman, the pressure of influential friends, the displeasure of fellow employees, whether organized or unorganized, and the possible repercussions among social and fraternal organizations such as the employee's lodge, church, or the service men's club. But the governmental supervisor is most reluctant and apprehensive about appearing before a civil service dismissal hearing.

A hearing on appeal from a disciplinary action is always a trying experience. It has to be public in order to satisfy the requirements of due process, and it has to meet the rudimentary demands of legal procedure because the transcript of the evidence may become the basis for a court decision. Many law suits are brought by employees dissatisfied with civil service decisions, and in states like New York, a large volume of such litigation occurs. This tendency to turn to the law illustrates again the legal flavor of public administration. In the larger jurisdictions one or more full-time attorneys advise the civil service commission. Indeed, some public personnel agencies have had to hire full-time examiners or referees to hear evidence because it would be impossible for the commissioners themselves to handle the volume.

The Hearing Procedure. Let us picture briefly what goes on at a typical civil service hearing. Assume that this is a state or local jurisdiction where the commissioners, lay business or professional people, hear all the evidence themselves. The commissioners, with the director of personnel and a stenographer, are grouped on one side of the conference table. On the other is the deputy attorney who handles the case for the employer; farther down the table sits the dismissed employee or his representative, either an attorney or a union agent, or both. Witnesses are sworn in as in a court of law, and every word is recorded. Witnesses for the employer are called first. Each is questioned by the lawyer for the city or state and then by the employee's attorney. The latter is ordinarily more accustomed to the rigor of jury trial rules of evidence and, if an aggressive type, will try to confuse witnesses who are unfavorable to his client. The chairman of the commission may become irritated at such tactics and admonish the attorney that this is not a court of law but an administrative tribunal where considerable informality is permissible.

During the testimony of the employer's witnesses, there is often an atmosphere of tension. The first witnesses are usually supervisors who have participated in the dismissal. The employee's lawyer may try to induce them to reveal personal animosity toward the discharged employee. The employee's lawyer loses no opportunity to embarrass the supervisors and fellow employees who are the complainant's witnesses. He tries to make it appear that the supervisor responsible for the dismissal is a tyrant who habitually practices favoritism. This impugning of the supervisor's motives has led to the cliché that dismissal hearings frequently result in the trial of the supervisor instead of the employee. Civil service commissioners often reveal a certain sentimentality toward employees which they would not condone in their private affairs. They frequently seem to believe that their duty is to protect the employee rather than to render an objective judgment.

A Sound Approach. Public jurisdictions need to be conditioned to deal humanely, yet firmly and courageously, with people who for a number of reasons are not making their proper contribution. The counseling process will be able to assist some of these misfits, but others will require disciplinary treatment. The tone of an organization can be seriously impaired if the supervisory staff is under the impression (held by some governmental organizations) that no one can be fired. There is a tendency for the supervisor to compare his position unfavorably with that of a supervisor in private industry. This is an escape mechanism, for supervisors in unionized plants have been known to cause strikes merely by disciplining an employee. Furthermore, disciplinary actions in industry can also be appealed through a hierarchy of grievance committees, arbitration tribunals, labor relation boards, up to the Supreme Court.

In the area of disciplinary action, civil service jurisdictions will have to undergo a cultural change involving the following steps:

1. Civil service commissioners and hearing officers must attend training conferences where they will be exposed to management viewpoints.
2. Top executives must adopt a policy of supporting supervisors who have the courage to discipline workers.

3. Supervisory training should include the preparation of discipline cases. This training would involve:
   a. Keeping disciplinary records.
   b. Preparing evidence.
   c. Learning counseling methods, including how to handle maladjusted persons.
   d. Learning to deal with employees who appear to have political protection or sponsorship.
4. Civil service laws interfering with disciplinary action must be amended.

COLLECTIVE BARGAINING IN THE PUBLIC SERVICE

Government agencies that employ skilled craftsmen, particularly the building trades, tend to follow the pattern of employee relations generally characteristic of that section of industry. This has happened in the Tennessee Valley Authority, the Bonneville Power Administration, the Atomic Energy plants, and in some municipally owned utilities. The unions involved include a dozen or more crafts, all within the traditional craft setup of the American Federation of Labor, but each having considerable autonomy. For purposes of bargaining, the several unions have entered a federation which at TVA is called the Tennessee Valley Trades and Labor Council; and at Bonneville, the Columbia Power Trades Council. This type of federation parallels the building trades bargaining structure in metropolitan areas.

TVA and Bonneville. Early in its history (1935), the Tennessee Valley Authority issued an "Employee Relationship Policy" which emphatically declared in favor of collective bargaining, subject to such limitations as might apply to a government agency. It gave the employees the right to organize into unions of their own choosing. The personnel department was authorized to hold elections in cases of disputed jurisdiction. The adjustment of grievances, the classification of jobs, hours of work, and standard rates of pay were designated as proper subjects for collective bargaining. White-collar employees at TVA have also been encouraged to take advantage of collective bargaining opportunities. From its very beginning, the Authority has had a reputation for fostering progressive personnel practices, in many respects a model for other government units. It is noteworthy that TVA has not been under the jurisdiction of the Civil Service Commission, being autonomous in its own personnel practices.

The Bonneville Power Administration (1937) employs craftsmen of the same type as those at TVA. During the first few years of its existence, labor conditions were not so good as those of workmen for the private power companies in the area. The rigidity of the civil service system, the absence of benefits such as overtime pay, and the failure of the government personnel system to react quickly to on-the-job gripes—all led to the adoption of an agreement with the Columbia Power Trade Council in 1945. The result has been a gradual improvement in labor relations, but it has involved the incorporation of building trade practices into the orthodox civil service setup. The improvement of the lot of craftsmen has been so obvious that white-collar unions have received a stimulus. This pattern of labor relations now prevails throughout the Bureau of Reclamation's electric power generation and distribution operations. A survey of the history of personnel administration at Bonneville is a good antidote for those who uncritically assume that traditional civil service is the acme of perfection, that it automatically ensures the best possible personnel relationships.[18]

The type of collective bargaining at TVA and Bonneville is duplicated in many municipal civil service jurisdictions for employees in the utilities and public works departments. In these instances it is not based upon firm legal foundations because city attorneys have sometimes ruled that collective bargaining is illegal. What happens is that the union has demonstrated its right to speak by signing up a majority of the garbage handlers or the bus drivers. The business agent has convinced the city council and the civil service commission that this is so, perhaps through the realities of a strike. He then demands the right to be consulted in the future before decisions are made relative to wages and working conditions. There gradually evolves a pattern of union-management consultation. The employer representatives protest, at first, that they are not in a position to sign a contract, but the business agent may ask for a memo or for minutes of the meeting setting forth the concensus of understanding and initialed by both sides. In these areas a stage is perhaps being reached where folkways are different from the formal declaration of law. The latter still declare, rather finally, that collective bargaining is not legal, but the folkways are gradually evolving a practice that belies this. In another generation today's folkways may become law.

Collective Bargaining in Canadian Cities. Trade unionism and the practice of collective bargaining have become well-established features of municipal government in Canada. In general these statutes recognize the right of municipal employees to organize themselves into unions or associations of their own choice and to bargain collectively with their municipal employers. Formal procedures are provided for the certifica-

[18] Senate Committee on Labor and Public Welfare, Senate Report 192, 82d Cong., 1st sess. *Labor-Management Relations in the Bonneville Power Administration* (Washington, D.C.: U.S. Government Printing Office, 1951); U. J. Gendron, "Labor Management Cooperation in Government," 18, *Public Personnel Review* (January, 1957), pp. 45–47; Harry L. Case, *Personnel Policy in a Public Agency* (New York: Harper & Bros., 1957), p. 44 ff.

tion of a trade union or employee association as the recognized bargaining agent for a specific group of workers. In most provinces only policemen and firemen are denied the right to strike; however, in lieu of the denial of this right, compulsory arbitration is usually stipulated when disputes involving these workers cannot be resolved through the normal collective bargaining process.[19]

New Pattern in United States Cities. Two of this country's largest cities, New York and Philadelphia, have set a pattern for municipal industrial relations that may be the model for the second half of the twentieth century. In 1958 each city formalized its procedures very much along the lines of familiar practices in industry, following the majority bargaining agent feature of the National Labor Relations Act.

On March 31, 1958, Robert F. Wagner, mayor of New York City, issued Executive Order No. 49 which set forth the policy of collective bargaining with groups representing a majority of employees in their units. This was followed on June 23, 1958, by the city labor commissioner's announcement of the procedure to be followed in the handling of requests to be certified as a collective bargaining agent. The commissioner is given discretionary power to make a finding that an organization does represent a majority of the employees in a "unit or grouping." This finding may be based upon the number authorizing check-off of union dues from payroll, the presentation of union membership cards, or by secret ballot.

In those cases where an organization is not able to establish a clearcut majority but can present evidence that it represents at least 30 per cent of the employees of a grouping, it may call for a secret ballot election. If a majority of the employees then designate the organization as their bargaining agent, it will be certified as such. Administrative safeguards with opportunity for adequate hearing are provided to protect the interest of opposing organizations.

On February 20, 1958, the City of Philadelphia entered into a collective bargaining agreement with the American Federation of State, County, and Municipal Employees, AFL-CIO, under which the latter became the sole and exclusive bargaining agent for all public employees except the uniformed forces, supervisors, and professional personnel. The fact of representation was determined by the number of employees who had authorized check-off of dues. Apparently the dominance of this particular union was such that no jurisdictional conflicts have arisen.

The contract deals with the items now covered in most civil service rules and regulations, including pay, time off, seniority, sick leave, and

[19] Thomas J. Plunkett, "Collective Bargaining and the Municipal Personnel Offices," **16,** *Public Personnel Review* (July, 1955), p. 139.

working conditions. It also provides for a grievance procedure, the final step of which calls for mediation by a board consisting of three union representatives and three other members appointed by the personnel director. Undoubtedly many civil service jurisdictions are now dealing informally with union representatives in much the same manner. The distinctive aspect of the Philadelphia venture is that the union is given formal status plus security as a negotiator. The mechanics of civil service are not overthrown or superseded; they are merely incorporated in the contract, thus perhaps providing a certain amount of face saving.

Need for Change. It is the authors' view that the old rationale of hiding behind the cloak of sovereignty is just as unrealistic in labor relations as in the law of tort liability, where traditional doctrine is being rapidly abandoned. Public personnel administration cannot hope to compete successfully with private employers if its policies and procedures do not compare favorably with those of industry. There may have been a time when civil service employment offered more advantages than private industry. But two factors in recent years have swung the balance in the other direction: the advantages accruing to labor through widespread unionization, and comparatively full employment since 1941. The former has brought labor many of the fringe benefits formerly enjoyed only by government employees, such as paid holidays, more generous paid vacations, sick leave, and pensions. The latter has reduced the advantage of security formerly enjoyed by government employees. A good mechanic has usually been able to get a job in industry often at better wages than under civil service.

Moreover the historic argument that government employees are more closely identified with the public safety is open to question. Is the delivery of mail, for example, any more important than the delivery of milk? We agree that the distinctions between union and nonunion occupations should be made upon the basis of the usual practice in the trade rather than on the basis of government or nongovernment vocation.[20] The strike has led to an emotional clouding of the issue. It has been demonstrated in countless cases that public employees will defy a no-strike law when the conditions of employment are no longer tolerable. This matter can be handled by restricting the right to strike in exceptionally critical occupations such as law enforcement without unduly restricting the bargaining area for industrial-type employees.

The preceding chapter pointed out that the industrial-type worker in federal establishments has his compensation set by area wage boards. Inasmuch as 90 per cent of such workers are in defense or ordnance establishments, the procedure followed by the Navy may be taken as

[20] White, "*Strikes in the Public Service.*"

typical. The commanding officers of establishments in an area designate representatives to an Area Wage Survey Committee which gathers wage data from private employers in that area. These data are sent to Washington for review by a Navy Wage Committee consisting of five members, two of whom are from unions. The presidents of the Metal Trade Department of the American Federation of Labor, and of District No. 44, International Association of Machinists, nominate one member each. The recommendations of this group, based upon the area surveys, are presented to the Secretary of the Navy who makes the final determination.[21] This procedure involves collective bargaining because the two union representatives, even though a minority on the board, are actually in a strategic position to exert very great influence.

FOSTERING EMPLOYEE COOPERATION

One of the biggest problems in employee relations is how to stimulate employees to become production-minded or to see production problems from a management viewpoint. Employees, whether organized or unorganized, have traditionally failed to be as industrious as executives expect. Indeed, they rather generally set their own work pace and rate of production, and in so doing, they defy the theoretical productivity standards which management has in mind. The engineering logic of management has assumed that workers should think and react the same as management on these matters. The logic of management has assumed further that: (1) ever-increasing productivity is a desirable goal, (2) financial incentives dominate all people, and (3) measured production is the basis for financial reward. Recent social science research, as we have seen, has shown that these assumptions are only partially true; workers have a logic of their own.

Some Avenues of Cooperation. Several means have been tried to secure the cooperation of workers in improving and maintaining productivity—in other words, to induce them to expend optimum effort. Particularly, attempts have been made to encourage the worker to identify himself with the organization. Modern social science research recognizes that the worker has to "identify" with the enterprise; that is, he must feel that he "belongs," that he is a part of things. One of the major difficulties in accomplishing this is that traditional management lore has assumed that people on the workaday levels should be order-takers with no part in the "idea" process, and that it was management's exclusive responsibility to do the thinking for the organization. Furthermore, lower supervisors have tended to reflect this viewpoint by stifling

21 "Policies and Procedures Governing Wage Administration for Navy Wage Board Occupations" (Mimeographed, undated).

the ideas of subordinates who want to improve production methods. They have failed to give credit because they feared that higher supervisors would censure them for not thinking of the improvements themselves.

In general there are two broad approaches to stimulating rank-and-file employees to suggest improved methods. One is the formalized suggestion system; the other consists of developing a climate that will encourage supervisors to listen to the ideas of subordinates. Many private establishments and government agencies use the formalized suggestion system wherein employees write out their ideas for improvement and submit them through boxes conveniently located at the work area. These ideas are usually reviewed by a staff or committee, and those that are adopted receive a cash award. In private organizations this is usually a percentage of the estimated saving.

There is another viewpoint which holds that a proper environment would encourage employees to offer their suggestions without the lure of financial reward. If employees become identified as members of the enterprise, they will participate voluntarily. As a matter of fact, people like to contribute toward the improvement of methods and procedures when they know that they can do so with impunity. The Tennessee Valley Authority has been particularly successful in securing this type of cooperation through its collective bargaining machinery. At the beginning of World War II, the unions suggested that they would like to cooperate with management in devising ways and means to increase productivity to advance the war effort. The result was a system of cooperative committees representing both management and employees. They dealt with a wide range of matters outside the area usually included in contract negotiation. Suggestions for improving methods were considered by these committees, but there were no cash awards. Emphasis was placed instead upon group discussion of ideas and upon suggestions as a part of the normal course of management. The arrangement continued after the war, and in a recent fiscal year, the committees received an average of eleven suggestions per one hundred employees. What was started as a wartime measure to meet a national emergency has now become a normal operating feature.[22]

BIBLIOGRAPHY

AVERY, ROBERT S. *Experiment in Management: Personnel Decentralization in the Tennessee Valley Authority.* Knoxville, Tenn.: 1954.
BIBLIOGRAPHY. "Collective Bargaining in the Public Service—U.S. and Canadian Experience," **19**, *Public Personnel Review* (April, 1958), pp. 160–64.

[22] Thelma Iles Dodd, "Teamwork Approach to Productivity," **15**, *Personnel Administration* (January, 1952), pp. 1–9.

CORNELL, HERBERT W. "Civil Service Benchmark Court Decisions," 17, *Public Personnel Review* (October, 1956), pp. 215–24.

DUBIN, ROBERT. *Working Union-Management Relationships.* Englewood Cliffs, New Jersey: 1958.

GOMBERG, WILLIAM. "The Use of Psychology in Industry: a Trade Union Point of View," 3, *Management Science* (July, 1957), pp. 348–70.

KRAMER, L. "Reflections on Whitleyism in English Local Government," 36, *Journal of the Royal Institute of Public Administration* (Spring, 1958), pp. 47–69.

NADWORNY, MILTON J. *Scientific Management and the Unions.* Cambridge: 1955.

PICTON, GLYN. "Whitley Councils in the Health Service," 35, *Journal of the Royal Institute of Public Administration* (Winter, 1957), pp. 359–71.

POSEY, ROLLIN B. "Employee Organization in the United States Public Service," 17, *Public Personnel Review* (October, 1956), pp. 238–45.

SCARROW, HOWARD A. "Employer-Employee Relationships in the Civil Services of Canadian Provinces," 35, *Journal of the Royal Institute of Public Administration* (Spring, 1957), pp. 65–76.

SPERO, STERLING. *Government as Employer.* New York: 1948.

——. *Labor Relations in British Nationalized Industry.* New York: 1955.

STAFF REPORT, INTERNATIONAL ASSOCIATION OF CHIEFS OF POLICE. *Police Unions.* Rev. ed.; Washington, D.C.: 1958.

VAN RIPER, PAUL P. *History of the United States Civil Service.* Evanston, Ill.: 1958.

CHAPTER 19

Developmental Personnel Administration

We now turn to the problem of finding, developing, and keeping outstanding individuals in the public service. Government's new role in economic stabilization and international affairs has brought a fresh emphasis to this need. Devotion is no longer enough; in addition the bureaucracy now requires exceptional competence. In western Europe, where political systems and the range of government services are roughly similar to ours, the public service is an honored craft that attracts the best talents of society. In the United States, however, the indifferent status of the public service has meant that competent people have often turned to other fields.[1] There are, of course, exceptions to this generalization. During the Depression years, for example, highly skilled individuals flowed into government service, pushed by economic necessity and attracted by the dynamic social program of the New Deal. In the main, however, the difficulty of attracting and retaining outstanding people has been a persistent and often discouraging aspect of our public service.

THE HIGHER CIVIL SERVICE—SOME CULTURAL FACTORS

A basic disagreement exists in our universities regarding the proper education and training of higher executives. Roughly, the division is between those who advocate highly specialized, vocational training and those who have been impressed by the success of British liberal educa-

---

[1] Prestige studies have shown quite consistently that governmental employment is decidedly not the first preference for Americans. During the 1930's a higher percentage of educated men entered public employment, but a poll of physicists in the late 1950's showed a very definite aversion toward federal employment as compared to working for industry or a university career. George A. Peters, "Scientists and Their Employment Preferences," **20**, *Personnel Administration* (November–December, 1957), pp. 10–15; however, a more recent study suggests a marked increase in the prestige of public employment, unfortunately not shared by university graduates from middle and upper classes; see M. Janowitz, Deil Wright, and William Delany, *Public Administration and the Public-Perspectives Toward Government in a Metropolitan Community* (Ann Arbor: University of Michigan, Governmental Studies, 1958).

tion in preparing individuals for service in the higher civil service. In order to provide a background for our consideration of these views, we must consider briefly the civil service traditions and selection practices in western Europe and Britain.

British Administrative Class. It is still customary in this country, as well as in Britain, to view the British administrative class as an elite, open only to those who have graduated with highest honors at Oxford and Cambridge. That this is a false picture can be seen by the fact that in the mid-1950's, half its members had entered the class by promotion.[2] Furthermore the supposedly aristocratic character of the service is being dissipated by the facts that Oxford graduates from lower social classes are now gaining entry and that there is increasing recruitment from the provincial universities. Moreover the new alternative method of selection based upon stress interviews is bringing in persons from a wider social spectrum.

What tasks and duties are performed by the British administrative class? One is struck by the fact that most accounts of their duties center around intellectual and literary processes. Their work consists mainly of processing policy reports which often bear upon parliamentary discussion. Almost from the beginning of their careers, they are involved in reading files and writing reports on whether Wiltshire should have a new town hall, how much revenue a one-penny tax on tobacco imports would raise, and in phrasing a reply for a minister to an irate constituent. These officials, who have been trained to be gentlemen and scholars, are past masters at avoiding trouble for ministers. Some of them become permanent department heads under the transitory political ministers. One gets the impression that administrative officials are advisers on policy rather than managers, although as hierarchical leaders they must also devote considerable time to the servicing and control of their respective organizations in personnel, fiscal, and organizing matters.[3]

It was pointed out above that the rigid distinction between the administrative and executive classes in Britain is breaking down. This is partly due to democratic trends, and it is certainly influenced by the political power of labor. The administrative class has always been a social as well as an administrative institution, just as the House of Com-

[2] Frank Dunnill, *The Civil Service: Some Aspects* (London: Geo. Allen & Unwin, Ltd., 1956), pp. 9–22.

[3] Descriptions of the duties of typical persons in the administrative class are contained in R. K. Kelsall, *Higher Civil Servants in Great Britain* (London: Routledge, Kegal Paul, Ltd., 1955), chap. x; *Posts in the Civil Service for University Graduates* (London: H. M. Stationary Office, 1951), pp. 5 ff; the influence of post-war conditions on recruitment in the British service is outlined in Arthur H. M. Hillis, "The British Civil Servant of Tomorrow," 11, *Public Administration Review* (Summer, 1951), pp. 173–79.

mons was once dubbed London's finest club. The aristocratic nature of the higher civil service lingered on for several decades after the democratization of the House of Commons, but now it seems that leveling forces are at work in both areas. This raises the question as to whether traditional educational values will also be altered.

The American View. The nature of a liberal education provokes considerable argument at home and abroad. There is no question but that our higher civil servants should be broad-gauged and cultured persons. But when we say this, we do not equate our statement exactly with the European practice. Higher education in the rest of the world, whether European or Asiatic, has usually meant a rather formal study of classical literature, history of the civilizations of the past, ancient and modern languages, literature, and philosophy. American higher education in the liberal arts has departed rather widely from this emphasis, even in the more conservative institutions of the Atlantic seaboard. Harvard's Charles W. Eliot provided much of the impetus for innovation by sponsoring the elective system. And even the University of Chicago, with its emphasis on philosophic values, was more interested in the world of today than in traditional classical subjects.

There remains in America, however, a gulf between those who advocate a broad general liberal arts education and those who favor a vocational approach. One, it is said, wants to educate for life, the other for making a living. On every hand there is much deploring of vocational trends, coupled with appeals to return to philosophy, the humanities, and the classics. Those on the antivocational side sometimes find John Dewey and progressive education convenient whipping boys. University schools of education are often criticized for emphasizing methodology at the expense of content. It is sometimes said that we are raising a generation of teachers who know how to teach but not what to teach. The attainment of American school children, and even college graduates, is compared unfavorably with those in the equivalent European grades, particularly on the continent. A French child in his early teens, it is generally agreed, is much more mature in mathematics, history, and languages than his American contemporary. A British graduate of Oxford or Cambridge is likely to be a better linguist, a better speaker, have more social poise, and know a great deal more about what happened in the world prior to 1900. He can also best the American graduate at a variety of other things, such as discussing poetry and philosophy and quoting from the classics.

Although we admire the members of the British administrative class and wish that America could produce more officials with similar qualities, we do not believe that America could or should copy British practice.

Pervasive cultural differences in educational philosophy, occupational status, class distinction, and social mobility make a similar development here impossible. Moreover we feel that our higher civil service has a representative function which is eased by a broad base of recruitment. There should be several avenues of entry into the higher bureaucracy. A huge national bureaucracy needs leaders with highly diversified talents. Furthermore it is inconsistent with the American interpretation of democracy to establish an elite that is closely bound up with educational achievement. Criticisms of the administration of the State Department, for example, often center upon the social stratification of the foreign service, one of our foremost civilian elites.[4] Recent reorganization of the foreign service was in part directed toward meeting this criticism.

Problem of an Elite. What are some of the belief systems and behavior patterns of an elite? In the first place, members have a powerful in-group feeling. Although they may disagree among themselves, they quickly close ranks against external threats. They tend to be intolerant of lay opinion, often resenting any questioning of their behavior by outsiders. This group self-consciousness sometimes becomes so strong that members avoid contact with outsiders, building their entire social life within the group. From the administrative standpoint, they place so high a value on their special competence that coordination is impeded. In their view administration is a rather low order of human activity in which only men who enjoy record keeping and detail could possibly become interested. Obviously, beliefs such as these aggravate the natural tendency of subunits to seek autonomy in big organizations.

C. Wright Mills specifically excludes the American higher civil service in his categories of *The Power Elite*. He states flatly, "The civilian government of the United States never has had and does not now have a genuine bureaucracy."[5] By "a genuine bureaucracy," Mills means a permanent, career corps that gives impartial advice on policy matters to the political heads of a government; it seems clear that he is thinking of the British higher service. Nevertheless we do have groups working in our civil service who meet several of the criteria for an elite, as set down above. The foreign service and the professional military officer class are examples. In military industrial establishments such as ship-

---

[4] But see James L. McCamy, *The Administration of Foreign Affairs* (New York: Alfred A. Knopf, Inc., 1950), chap. viii, who shows that the education, training, and experience of foreign service officers varies rather broadly. It is also true that members of our professional military academies are drawn from diversified socioeconomic backgrounds. What happens to an individual once he becomes part of an elite remains a suggestive question. See staff study, Senate Committee on Foreign Relations, 85th Cong., 2d sess., Doc. No. 91, *Recruitment and Training for the Foreign Service* (Washington, D.C.: U.S. Government Printing Office, 1958).

[5] *The Power Elite* (New York: Oxford University Press, 1956), p. 237.

yards and aircraft repair centers, members of the officer class are rotated in positions of leadership within the local civilian hierarchy. Similarity of training, function, and social attitude tend to bind them together in a self-conscious alliance.[6]

An administrative problem here is that such officers, who are often specialists, have little understanding, experience, or sympathy for the problems with which they must deal when placed at the head of an organization. Foreign service officers rarely have had experience in hierarchical relationships; they have been concerned with specialist work on the Far East, South Africa, or western Europe. Coordinating and motivating hundreds of workers is not only foreign to them but often distasteful. While the military officer has had hierarchical experience, his natural interests tend toward directing soldiers in the field, navigating ships, or flying airplanes. When placed in charge of organizations that include a large number of civilians, who are skilled technicians in their own right, he often takes refuge in the satisfactions and understandings offered by the elite, military in-group.[7]

THE NEED FOR CONTINUITY AND EXPERTISE

Regardless of any problems raised by permanent elite groups in the civil service, the crucial need remains for continuity in administration and for impartial, expert guidance for temporary political leaders in their efforts to carry out major policy. Several recommendations have been made for some kind of official corps that will provide these requirements. In England and France, as seen in Chapter 4, continuity and expertise are provided by the higher civil service. In the United States the politicization of the bureaucracy and the turnover and specialization of the higher service have resulted in a lack of confidence by political figures in the top levels of the system. However, these officials comprise such a reservoir of experience, administrative skill, and (perhaps most important) effectiveness in dealing with Congress that it is impossible to do without them. As former Governor Harriman of New York insists, "This places the United States in a perilous position. Our most urgent need is vigorous and imaginative political leadership. But to be effective it must be combined with an equally vigorous and im-

[6] Among others, see Arthur K. Davis, "Bureaucratic Patterns in the Navy Officer Corps," in R. K. Merton, *et al.* (eds.), *Reader in Bureaucracy* (Glencoe, Ill.: The Free Press, 1952), pp. 380–95; R. L. Warren, "The Naval Reserve Officer: A Study in Assimilation," 11, *American Sociological Review* (1946), pp. 202–11; S. Stouffer, "Barriers to Understanding Between Officers and Men," in Merton, *Reader in Bureaucracy*, pp. 265–72.

[7] The Navy has recognized this problem by establishing a management school for its officers at Monterey, California.

aginative civil service which can carry the leaders' plans through to completion."[8] Among recent efforts to meet this problem was the second Hoover Commission's recommendation for a senior civil service. This plan and the reactions to it deserve careful analysis.

Senior Civil Service. The Commission's recommendation included the following points: The proposed senior civil service was to be administered by a Senior Civil Service Board. Members of the senior civil service would be nominated by department and agency heads and appointed by the Board to positions approved by it with the consent of the President.[9] They would have rank status rather than job status and would be expected to be politically neutral. In the words of the Commission, this would achieve the following important result: "The primary objective is to have always at hand in the Government a designated group of highly qualified administrators whose confidence, integrity, and faithfulness have been amply demonstrated; who will make it easier for non-career executives to discharge their responsibility; and who will add to the smoothness, effectiveness and economy of governmental operations. A secondary but related objective is to make the civil service more attractive as a career to able men and women." Compensation would begin at present General Service Grade 15 ($13,770–$13,970) and go on up to the equivalent of secretaries.

A corollary of this recommendation was that a clear distinction should be made between noncareer and career people at the top levels. Much was made of the distinction between policy and nonpolicy positions. In general, career administrators were not to make final policy decisions or to appear before the public as advocates in matters involving public policy; however, the Commission did not go on to solve the vexing problem of defining policy. It did say that the distinction between policy jobs and career jobs has not been clearly demarcated in the past. As was indicated, the Eisenhower administration attempted to meet this situation in 1953 by setting up a Schedule C category of political appointments.

In the federal service we have not yet learned how to meet the problem of career officials who are regarded as unacceptable to an incoming administration. Both the British and the Continental civil ser-

---

[8] "How to Get Better Civil Servants," *Harper's Magazine* (September, 1958); the need for a corps of excellent higher officials is underscored by Herbert Hoover's comment that, if he were permitted to chose only *one* of the 314 Commission recommendations for implementation, he would unhesitatingly choose the one for the senior civil service. N. Macneil and H. W. Metz, *The Hoover Report, 1953–55* (New York: The Macmillan Co., 1956), p. 29.

[9] Commission on Organization of the Executive Branch of the Government, *Personnel and Civil Service* (Washington, D.C.: U.S. Government Printing Office, 1955), p. 39.

vice systems have no difficulty in solving this because their tradition ensures that the civil servant remains through changes of administration. The Hoover Commission sought to meet this situation by having a senior civil servant continue to draw his basic salary "for a time." At the end of six months, if he was still unassigned, he could be continued on full salary for six months, put on half-salary for six months, or retired.

The proposal for a senior civil service did not meet the approval that might have been expected, especially in view of the distinguished membership of the task force, including President Harold Dodds of Princeton as chairman. The opposition came from three sources: (1) career employees, (2) Congressmen, and (3) some professors of political science. The reaction of many career servants centered around their specialist role and the fear of becoming too political.[10] A large proportion of the administrative jobs in the federal service is filled by persons who are specialists first and administrators second, including engineers, foresters, economists, and scientists. These people did not want to become generalists and subject to transfer to departments other than those in which they had grown up and to which they had become accustomed. This feeling was so general in the federal service that the proposal for a senior civil service[11] had virtually no spokesman among the federal bureaucrats. As one of them insisted: "The U.S. government does not have need for a system which gives special rewards and recognition to just a part of its senior career executives, just because they happen to choose administrative functions instead of line specialties and, therefore, can be used in more places. Such a system would be a discriminatory kick in the teeth to the men who carry the bulk of the load of making the federal government work."[12] (Parenthetically, it should be noted that this statement documents the self-consciousness of specialists which we have stressed in several chapters.) Apparently, part of the opposition of career employees was also based upon their reluctance to be moved about from one department to another, as the plan proposed, again in line with British practice.

Sociologically speaking, the reaction to the proposal signifies a deep-seated *aversion to change* that is part of organizational dynamics. Well-established systems of behavior are comfortable, and countless patterns of accommodation and interest develop around them, making change threatening. Three specific factors have worried career officials.[13]

[10] Among others, see Earl H. DeLong, "Who Are the Career Executives," **19**, *Public Administration Review* (Spring, 1959), pp. 108–13.

[11] *The Hoover Report.*

[12] DeLong, "Who Are the Career Executives," p. 113.

[13] These are summarized in William Pincus, "The Opposition to the Senior Civil Service," **18**, *Public Administration Review* (Autumn, 1958), pp. 324–31.

1. Concern that many top officials would not be covered into the SCS.
2. The fear that they would be asked to change jobs and perhaps be rotated to regional offices.
3. Anxiety about the proposed method of nominating individuals to the SCS, namely, nomination by one's agency head. (Apparently self-nomination has been regarded as an acceptable alternative.)[14]

The objection of some professors to the concept of the senior civil service is indicated by two men who have served as administrators in the federal service, Wallace S. Sayre and Herman M. Somers.[15] They insist that it would be impossible to make a clear demarcation between politics and administration, as the Commission's recommendations seemed to assume. Sayre believes that there is "nothing so characteristic of twentieth century legislation as the amount of discretion it confers upon the administrative branch."[16] Somers says, "to identify good management in the civil service as indifferent to the objectives of management and unconcerned with the social consequences of policy is to make of public administration a barren, if not nihilistic, affair which seems unlikely to attract the kind of imaginative competence which the report hopes for."[17]

The other major point of emphasis by these observers reflects the fact that each formerly held administrative posts in the federal government. They would not like to see the federal bureaucracy sealed off in a watertight compartment to which there would not be lateral entry from business and the universities. They would like to see competent people, who are not strongly identified politically, move in and out of the federal service at rather high levels. They believe that this would strengthen the federal administrative arm by establishing a desirable turnover and the transfusion of new blood and ideas. It would also help, they argue, preserve the democratic nature of our culture by keeping the bureaucracy in touch with popular sentiment by ensuring an influx of individuals who have had recent contact with the public.

How valid and relevant are these judgments? First, in regard to the politics-administrative issue, the academic opponents seem to have underestimated the success of the British administrative class from which the SCS idea comes. Obviously no precise line can be drawn between political and administrative activities. Indeed, as we saw in Chapter 8, the high-level, permanent official in the federal service is usually more astute "politically" (that is, at dealing with Congress and interest groups)

---

[14] Report of Society for Personnel Administration's Executive Development Conference, (1955), 19, *Personnel Administration* (January–February, 1956).

[15] Wallace S. Sayre, "The Public Service Staff: Its Future Status," *Democracy in Federal Administration* (Washington, D.C.: Department of Agriculture Graduate School, 1955), pp. 65–73; Herman S. Somers, "Some Reservations about the Senior Civil Service," 19, *Personnel Administration* (January–February, 1956), pp. 10–18.

[16] Sayre, "The Public Service Staff: Its Future Status," p. 67.

[17] Somers, "Some Reservations About the Senior Civil Service," p. 11.

than his political superior. British administrative class servants make political decisions; they play both political and administrative roles. The important thing is *impartiality*: that their policy advice to their political masters is not colored by personal preferences. They have been able to do this under administrations that have *real* policy differences. Thus one may argue that in the United States, where parties have no substantial policy differences, the senior civil servant's problem would be far simpler. Everyone recognizes that a career service requires neutrality and impartiality among higher civil servants; in our society, in which consensus about most things seems the rule, such conditions should be obtained easier than in Britain.

Thus the central point in the posture of academic critics seems to be ". . . opposition to the whole idea of divorcing politics from the higher civil service."[18] But the cost of political commitment on the part of career servants is the kind of suspicion and turnover seen during the Eisenhower administration. A more significant dysfunction is the waste of administrative and "political" (read negotiatory) skill of the higher civil service; and its resulting inability to provide continuity and expertise to *successive* administrations.

The other central theme in the opposition argument is the fear of creating an elite and thereby shutting out talent from business and government. Certainly there is no doubt but that fresh talents and points of view can help vitalize the federal bureaucracy, although of late this help seems to have been most needed and received from *scientific and technical* people, not from administrative generalists with whom the SCS program is concerned. At the generalist level, one finds two serious problems that limit the value of such transfer. First is the lack of continuity that accompanies this practice. As we saw in Chapter 8, low pay, fear of losing out in the competitive race in one's own permanent organization, and diffused authority and responsibility are responsible for the great turnover and reluctance of private executives to take federal appointments. Given the size and scope of federal programs, continuity and experience are probably of greater value than the drive and skill that private executives presumably bring in from the outside world.

The second problem is simply that *government is different*. Added to the need for energy and administrative ability is the capacity for negotiation with many diverse interests. The scale and character of government operations mean that responsibilities and authority for any given program overlap several agencies; decisions therefore become collective, and the role of any one executive is necessarily less significant. This aspect of government work is frustrating and novel for many executives

---

[18] Pincus, "The Opposition to the Senior Civil Service," p. 329.

brought in from private spheres. While they often come from large, complex organizations, their experience has not included dealing with reluctant Congressmen, other organizations as large as their own, or interest groups who have direct access to policy determination. Recommendations for lateral entry must keep these conditions in mind.

Despite the opposition from some sources, President Eisenhower issued an Executive Order in March, 1958, providing for the establishment of a career executive board, for the selection of members of the SCS. Although the order was worded rather flexibly, it did permit the first steps toward implementing the concept of a senior civil service. In November, 1958, the Board appointed its first Executive Secretary, and presumably was ready for business. However, by late 1959, there were signs that some big agencies were not prepared to support the program in their budgets. Further developments remain to be seen.

QUALITIES OF ADMINISTRATIVE LEADERSHIP

Regardless of conflict over the institutional arrangements made to provide it, everyone agrees that leadership is required in the higher civil service. Since we have seen that leadership is *situational,* that is, that its quality and methods differ according to the particular social setting in which it occurs, we can expect that bureaucratic leaders will have to possess certain discrete skills and attitudes. Among these are the ability to work in a highly political environment, which requires flexibility and skill in interpersonal negotiation. Hence the effectiveness of executives will vary considerably. As we have seen in the case of the U.S. Information Services, George V. Allen was much more effective than his predecessor in dealing with Congress and the press. Another recent example was the difficulties experienced by Professor Bernard Schwartz during his role as chief counsel of the House Subcommittee on Legislative Oversight. Although Schwartz had studied the independent regulatory commissions for years and had written articles and books about them, he was apparently shocked to find that their operations were highly political. In his case, however, his unorthodox methods and righteous indignation brought results—as seen in the Miami Channel 10 television and the Adams-Goldfine cases.[19] However, in the long run, it seems that certain other, less dramatic qualities are more functional. What, then, are some of these qualities?

The Art of Generalization. Paul Appleby has suggested three qualities desirable in high-level civil servants. The first is the quality of philosophy, which he describes as the "capacity to see public policy

[19] Bernard Schwartz, *The Professor and the Commissions* (New York: Alfred A. Knopf, Inc., 1959).

in terms of thousands of different actions and to relate these actions to each other in terms of public and governmental interest."[20] The second is "governmental sense, the ingrained disposition to put the public interest first and thus to recognize the great, essential, and pervasive difference that distinguishes public administration from the management of private enterprise." The third is public relations or political sense. Appleby goes on to list six more qualities desirable in a political department head such as a cabinet member on the federal level. He should, first of all, operate on his proper level, by which is meant roughly that he should not make decisions in the province of the bureau chief or the section supervisor. He should seek coordinated teamwork by horizontal clearance and communication. He should organize by "building into the structure of the agency a central core of authority reaching all levels." He should decentralize, but he cannot do so until he has already centralized, that is, established the hard core of authority mentioned above. He should be an active leader, motivating the agency so as to avoid the "tendency of all organizations to petrify." Lastly, he should exemplify democratic leadership in his everyday actions and conduct.[21]

Both Culture and Expertise. An American civil servant needs two qualities or skills which complement those suggested above. He should be "civilized" and he should possess the skills which make him a good organizer and manager. By being "civilized" we do not necessarily imply being "cultured" in the European sense, but this latter quality is not excluded; indeed, it is desirable. It is difficult to say what constitutes a "civilized" person. Certainly such a person has a sensitivity to the public interest, he has the tolerance that comes from a humanistic education, and he recognizes that personal needs and desires are an integral part of work behavior. He need not be a colorless person; we want our bureaucrat to speak up when the occasion demands. This retiring quality, moreover, is hardly a prominent characteristic of high level executives. His influence upon policy decisions should be based upon knowledge, research, and mastery of all available facts, and he should present them forcefully when necessary. He should therefore be a social scientist, not a research specialist in a narrow field but a person with a grasp of the social sciences. For example, he should know about the anthropologist's concept of race, the work of experimental psychologists, the basic approach to clinical psychology, the reasons why Keynes became a whipping boy in economics, and the relation of the culture concept to Ameri-

---

[20] Paul H. Appleby, *Big Democracy* (New York: Alfred A. Knopf, Inc., 1945), p. 43; John M. Gaus has also stressed this generalizing ability, in Gaus *et al., Frontiers of Public Administration* (Chicago: University of Chicago Press, 1936), pp. 104–5.

[21] Appleby, *Big Democracy*, pp. 44–47.

ca's place in the world. He should have some feel for the philosophy of history, know something about the decline and fall of governments, and have at least a passing acquaintance with the political philosophers. Is this too much to expect? Perhaps. Certainly it requires a broad education, but it is a splendid target nevertheless.

EDUCATION FOR LEADERSHIP

College courses in public administration have been offered almost exclusively in departments of political science. This was quite natural because the interest was there; political scientists have always wanted to improve the administration of government. It was equally natural that the first courses in social work should have originated in departments of sociology, just as business administration started in the economics curricula. However, in the latter instances the professional curricula have become largely divorced from the academic departments. Indeed, they are often separated by an ideological gulf which leads to sharp criticism of one another. Why did this occur, and will it happen to political science and public administration? We are not able to answer the latter question, but an attempt to analyze the first may throw light on both.

Liberal Arts Versus Specialization. Liberal arts or "academic" departments often have an antivocational point of view. Academic faculties are primarily concerned with the philosophical and historical aspects of their subjects. They tend to avoid the vocational and operating phases of their disciplines. An economist, for example, is likely to be immersed in the theory of the incidence of taxation, while a tax specialist in the department of commerce normally directs his attention to accounting phases of current tax laws. Similarly a sociologist will be inclined to study the general causes of poverty, while the social worker will probably be more interested in how to rehabilitate a particular family of indigents.

The issues involved here have been widely discussed in both professional and lay circles in recent years. One side indicts vocationalism for producing narrow specialists when, in fact, society needs leaders with a broad general education. The other replies that we are living in a world where we can no longer afford to educate people merely to be gentlemen. They argue that the graduates of our school system must be trained to do useful work. It is also maintained that this objective need not be inconsistent with producing a well-rounded personality with a basic understanding of human affairs, equipped to become a useful citizen in a democracy.

Of course the move for the autonomy of vocational curricula springs partly from empire building on the part of leaders who have been frustrated by their academic colleagues. It has also been influenced by disenchanted alumni who protest that they were handicapped by not being taught certain professional courses. A great deal of the vocationalizing of curricula results from pressures outside the university, often aided by professors with special interests. Pressures of this kind will undoubtedly be brought upon departments of political science to expand their curricula in at least two directions. One will be toward more courses of the practical management type; the other, toward teaching and research in the social aspects of organization. The former will be inclined toward industrial management, the latter toward the methodology and concepts of psychology, sociology, and anthropology.

At the same time, the development of public administration curricula has not yet reached the stage where an attempt at national standardization is desirable.[22] One point, however, on which practically everyone agrees is that the *undergraduate curricula* should not be vocationalized. This does not mean that it is improper to have a few courses in the general aspects of public administration. But specialization should probably be confined to the graduate level. Experimentation and variety should be encouraged at this stage. Perhaps some institutions should develop the scholars and idea men and permit others to turn out the technicians. Perhaps there should be a very few specialized institutes in areas such as governmental accounting, logistics and supply, work-load analysis, training and motivation, and statistics. Certainly the administration of huge government agencies will suffer unless there is an adequate supply of such specialists.

FUNCTIONAL SPECIALIST AS ADMINISTRATOR

People often ask what graduates of public administration do, what kinds of jobs they get. Administration has been popularly associated with the functional specialty which is being administered, and quite properly so. Thus a physicist administers a research laboratory, a forester manages a forest, an engineer superintends a factory, and an educator serves as superintendent of schools. Natural and logical as this may be, it nevertheless gives rise to certain difficulties, one of which is that persons who are competent in their specialties are often not good administrators. There are at least two possible ways of meeting this problem. One is to include courses in administration in the curricula of professional schools. The other is to place administrative generalists alongside the

---

[22] Beginning about 1958, the heads of special public administration programs began meeting with a view toward establishing a national organization.

specialists. Attempts to teach the art of administration in professional schools have been limited because they have not been convinced of its efficacy. The pressure for introducing new professional courses in the curricula has been so strong that proposals to bring in administration subjects have been coolly received. In some instances the need is being met by special courses such as those in hospital administration, but these are attended mostly by nonmedical students. The administration of hospitals has for the most part been turned over to laymen.

Limitations of Specialists as Administrators. What are some of the shortcomings of professional specialists as administrators? In the first place, they frequently seem to dislike administration and administrators. This is not always the case, of course, and the mere fact that an individual is a good physicist does not mean that he cannot also have a broad understanding of contemporary affairs and a cooperative nature. And yet, specialists often view administrators as their natural enemies. Administrators are always cutting the budget, refusing upward reclassification, demanding reports, and pressing for immediate results.[23] By virtue of their specialized training, professional persons are often highly individualistic. They tend to build little empires which the administrator finds difficult to coordinate. They resent attempts to evaluate their work, taking refuge in the unanswerable defense that creative effort cannot be measured in terms of day-to-day production. They are impatient of the internal checks that weld hierarchies together and synthesize collective effort.[24]

The problem of introducing good administrative practices into scientific organizations is not new, nor is there a pat answer to the problems posed.[25] The following avenues, however, seem to be open:

1. Introducing the specialized graduate curriculum. There are now several schools for hospital administrators attended by both M.D.'s and laymen.
2. Detailing specialists to graduate schools of public administration.
3. Integrating public administration graduates into the scientific hierarchy, where they become administrative assistants, management consultants, personnel directors, budget directors, executive officers, and even lay directors or managers.[26]

[23] There is now evidence that this prevails among industrial research establishments; see Robert N. Anthony *et al.*, *Management Controls in Industrial Research Organizations* (Boston: Harvard School of Business Administration, 1952), p. 57.

[24] Peter Drucker, "Management and the Professional Employee," 30, *Harvard Business Review* (May–June, 1952), pp. 84–90.

[25] Norman Kaplan, "The Role of the Research Administrator," 4, *Administrative Science Quarterly* (June, 1959), pp. 20–42.

[26] This is happening in public health. See "Report on Educational and Experience Qualifications of Administrative Personnel (Non-Medical) in Public Health Agencies," 41, *American Journal of Public Health* (April, 1951).

POST-ENTRY TRAINING

One of the most successful devices in developing effective administrators has been the post-entry training program. Post-entry training takes a variety of forms such as after-hours university classes, weekly sessions conducted by the training department on the premises, short courses on the premises, and more prolonged staff colleges, as per the British prototype. Internship has also become a widely accepted device for management development of younger recruits from college.

After-hours university classes are to be found most often in metropolitan centers, such as American and George Washington Universities at Washington, D.C., Syracuse and New York Universities have a jointly administered curriculum for New York State employees at Albany.[27] Other programs for state employees include those offered by the University of Minnesota, Wayne State University, and Sacramento State College. New ventures along this line are about to be inaugurated by the University of Wisconsin and the University of Oregon; indeed, the movement is gathering such momentum that an up-to-date listing would have to be based on more recent data than are now available.[28]

Internship. Internships are designed to furnish practical contact with administration for the recent college graduate. The impetus to this movement was given by the former National Institute of Public Affairs, a privately financed venture which induced college men to come to Washington for internships during the 1930's and 1940's. Although the NIPA no longer exists, its work is being carried on by the U.S. Civil Service Commission and agency personnel units, and internships are available for those appointed from the Federal Service Entry Examination.

One of the most interesting current ventures along this line is offered by the Southern Regional Training Program, jointly sponsored by the Universities of Alabama, Kentucky, and Tennessee.[29] It offers "compen' sated internship in a public agency—federal, state, or local—in the Southern region followed by course work for nine months at the three member universities. Upon successful completion of both the internship and the courses, fellows are given a certificate in public administration, conferred jointly by the three universities. Their course credits are sufficient to qualify for a Master's degree if supplemented by a Master's thesis. The

[27] Luther Gulick *et al., State Sponsored Education in Public Administration* (New York: Institute of Public Administration, 1958).

[28] One of the oldest, if not the oldest, after-hours university program is that conducted since 1929 by the University of Southern California at its Civic Center Division. The California State Colleges at Los Angeles, Sacramento, San Diego, Long Beach, San Francisco, San Jose, and Fresno now have similar programs.

[29] Gladys M. Kammerer, *Thirteen Years of Achievement* (University, Ala.: University of Alabama, Bureau of Public Administration, 1958).

thesis, however, is done under the supervision of one of the three universities chosen by the fellow, and the Master's degree is conferred by that institution alone."[30]

Administrative internships for recent graduates are also maintained by some state and local governments. The International City Managers' Association has long maintained a placement service for interns in city managers' offices, and many members of the profession have been inducted in that manner. The University of Pennsylvania and University of Kansas have special programs devoted to developing city managers through internships combined with classroom work.[31]

Staff College. The term "staff college" is used here as a generic designation for programs with the following characteristics: (1) participants are high- or middle-level personnel with administrative responsibilities; (2) they are relieved of all job duties; (3) participants live together in dormitories or a hotel, at a site physically removed from job contacts; (4) they devote full time to the study of the generalist approach to administration. The idea of the staff college probably springs from the military, where the more specialized service schools have long been an established factor in the development of officers.

The current civilian prototype is offered by the British Administrative Staff College at Henley-on-Thames, which is attended by civil servants although intended primarily for industrial personnel.[32] In the United States, government employees have attended similar-type programs conducted by the American Management Association and the Harvard and Cornell Business Schools. The Brookings Institution has also inaugurated a staff college experiment, which has attracted much interest.

The staff college idea has not met with universal approval; there has been some apprehension that a staff college would compete with, and to a certain extent substitute for, the universities. This feeling has perhaps been reinforced by concern that staff college training would emphasize management techniques at the expense of broad background. It is interesting to note in this connection the growth of short college courses for industrial executives, composed entirely of liberal arts content. It seems safe to predict that there will be more and more experiment with management development programs which take executives away from the job and relieve them of operating duties for a period. Industry has set the example, which will surely be followed by government.[33] A major obstacle

[30] *Ibid.*, p. 3.

[31] Committee Report, *City Management—a Growing Profession* (Chicago: International City Managers' Association, 1957), pp. 59–66.

[32] Marshall E. Dimock, "Executive Development after Ten Years," 18, *Public Administration Review* (Spring, 1958), pp. 91–97.

[33] See *Proposal for a Federal Administrative Staff College* (Washington, D.C.: Society for Personnel Administration, 1953).

to federal programs has been the lack of legal authority (excepting the military) for individuals to attend on pay and at government expense. Happily, this restriction was removed by Congress in 1958, and the Civil Service Commission and the agencies are presently making plans to get the program under way.

A PROPOSED PROGRAM

At the present time the problem of training civil servants is not amenable to any single solution. A huge bureaucracy needs a tremendous variety of skills, backgrounds, and professional preparation. Considerable research is needed before it can be concluded that this or that is the proper path to be taken in developing the required skills. Sufficient experience is available, however, to indicate that the following combination of approaches may be fruitful:

1. *Preservice Undergraduate*
    a. Undergraduate training should probably emphasize the liberal arts and general education approach. There should be a small core of orientation courses in public administration offered in the department of political science. A social science major, including at least one course in statistics, is particularly desirable for those intending to become administrative generalists.
    b. Courses in administration should be required in professional schools such as engineering and forestry.
2. *Preservice Graduate*
    a. The traditional M.A. and Ph.D. should continue to give students a broad philosophical, historical, and cultural background, and enable them to take their place among the "civilized" bureaucrats referred to above.
    b. The future will require more social scientists trained in empirical methodology: persons who can design studies involving the gathering of large-scale data and carry through to interpretation of results.
    c. The specialized degrees of M.S. in Public Administration and Doctor of Public Administration should continue to develop persons skilled in processes of organization and management.[34]
3. *In-service Collegiate*
    a. Metropolitan universities should offer evening courses on the collegiate level.
    b. Programs like that of the Graduate School of the Department of Agriculture should be encouraged.[35]

[34] The experiments now being conducted by the Brookings Institution should be watched closely.

[35] This program, begun in 1921, is perhaps the best example of its kind. Its program is at a graduate level and its faculty includes several distinguished members. For a summary of its work and organization, see V. E. Jensen, "A Training Center for Federal Employees," *Adult Education* (Spring, 1955).

  c. Special "institutes" should be offered by qualified universities for officials detailed for full-time study. The Harvard Graduate School of Business, for example, has conducted courses for the military in areas such as accounting and supply.

4. *Other In-service*

  a. A variety of full-time concentrated schools in the various fields of management and administration should be developed. These might be patterned after the military staff schools which have been very successful in developing leadership.

  b. There should be a sustained management development program in public agencies, tied in with continuous research in motivation, leadership, and administrative planning.

BIBLIOGRAPHY

BERNSTEIN, MARVER H. *The Job of the Federal Executive.* Washington, D.C.: 1958.

COMMITTEE REPORT, INTERNATIONAL CITY MANAGERS' ASSOCIATION. *City Management—a Growing Profession.* Chicago: 1957.

KAMMERER, GLADYS M. *Thirteen Years of Achievement: The Southern Regional Training Program.* University, Alabama: 1958.

KATZELL, RAYMOND A. "Reflections on Educating Executives," **19,** *Public Administration Review* (Spring, 1959), pp. 1–6.

KAUFMAN, HERBERT. "The Next Step in Case Studies," **18,** *Public Administration Review* (Winter 1958), pp. 52–59.

NELSON, CHARLES A. "The Liberal Arts in Management," **36,** *Harvard Business Review* (May–June, 1958), pp. 91–99.

PERKINS, JOHN A. "Higher Education and Training for Administrative Careers," **18,** *Public Administration Review* (Winter, 1958), pp. 14–20.

PERLOFF, HARVEY S. *The Urban Administrator: Education for Service in Metropolitan Communities.* Maryland: 1958.

REYNOLDS, HARRY W., JR. "Developing Middle Management," **19,** *Public Personnel Review* (October, 1958), pp. 279–84.

STENE, EDWIN O. "Some Notes on Case Writing and Teaching," **1,** *Philippine Journal of Public Administration* (October, 1957), pp. 335–41.

SWEENEY, STEPHEN B. (ed.). *Education for Administrative Careers in Government Service.* Philadelphia: 1958.

SYMPOSIUM. "Educating Executives: Social Science, Self-Study, or Socrates?" **18,** *Public Administration Review* (Autumn, 1958), pp. 275–305.

ULLMANN, CHARLES A., and BAYEN, WALTER F. *Management Intern Programs—A Tool for Developing Better Managers,* U.S. Civil Service Commission Management Series No. 11. Washington, D.C.: 1957.

Part V

FINANCIAL ADMINISTRATION

CHAPTER 20

What Is Financial Administration?

Students of administration often regard financial administration as a difficult and forbidding subject, to be avoided whenever possible. This attitude exists partly because financial administration in the past has been associated almost entirely with accounting and applied economics; it has been somewhat removed from the human side of administration, which is more attractive to both the citizen and the scholar. This attitude also reflects the distaste for mathematics characteristic of students of government. But the terms "budgeting" and "financial administration" comprise much more than accounts and figures. They are concerned with many basic social and political values, and, in fact, lie at the heart of administration.

THE IMPORTANCE OF BUDGETING

The budgetary process is central to administration because control of the purse is perhaps the most effective tool of coordination; the scope and nature of the entire governmental operation is determined by the allocation of appropriations to the various big programs, such as defense and social services. In this sense, budgeting is the generalist's sphere of action par excellence. His role is not limited merely to preparing estimates in a routine way; instead he must understand and evaluate proposed expenditures in a variety of areas, particularly if he is in a central staff agency. He is thus a management expert, often called upon to work closely with the chief executive, the governor, or the mayor, as well as to testify before legislative appropriation committees. When not occupied with such work, the budget man often engages in administrative surveys of operating departments, which provides him further insight into the program side of administration. In these ways the budget process touches upon the whole spectrum of public affairs and human behavior.

As defined here, financial administration is composed of three broad elements which will be examined in greater detail in subsequent chapters. The most basic of these is fiscal policy determination, which concerns the role of the political leaders in hammering out the broad outlines of programs and in authorizing the appropriations necessary to carry them out. This aspect ordinarily includes problems of employment, taxation and revenue, deficit financing, etc., matters that require more extensive discussion than can be given here. Instead we shall assume that a given amount of revenues are available and that the initial problem is for legislatures and chief executives to allocate them among several program areas. A second element in financial administration is the broad problem of accountability, that is, of ensuring that money is spent wisely and honestly by political leaders and their administrative aides. Finally, there is the management element, which includes recommended fiscal organization; various financial officers and their duties; and the budget process.

FISCAL POLICY DETERMINATION

Although fiscal policy is obviously of signal importance, it is usually viewed as the province of political executives and legislators. American budget agencies have for the most part given little consideration to the impact of government finance upon the entire economy. Their primary concern has been to find new sources of revenue to meet the ever-growing demands of the spending agencies. Thus municipal budget agencies have at times made studies of such matters as service-fee charges for sewers, business licensing, and distribution of gasoline taxes. But these have all had a single objective, namely, increasing municipal revenues. They have not been concerned with those issues that interest the professional economist when he deals with taxes. Instead of asking who will ultimately pay the taxes and whether he can afford it, the main question has been how to get more revenue with the least cost and fewest protests.

American budgeting is very young, the major federal act coming as late as 1921. As in every young enterprise, the approach has been pragmatic rather than scientific and theoretical. The first budget agencies were staffed by pragmatists with little previous experience. As a matter of fact there was no previous American experience to build upon. We had gone along for a century and a half with governmental surpluses, except during the Civil War. Although state and municipal finances were not well administered for the most part, crises did not appear until the 1920's. If one had to designate causes in an area where causation flows from a variety of influences, it would not be too far wrong to attribute the rise of budgeting to three things: government deficits caused by war; the automobile; and unemployment. In the nineteenth century when life was simple, the economy could absorb small government without strain. When the governments on all levels take one-third of the national income in taxes, as they do at mid-twentieth century, pragmatism must make room for planning.

It seems probable that the budget staffs of the future will give more attention to the relation of government expenditure to the economy as a whole. Certainly this is desirable. One difficulty lies in the fact that here the economist is dealing with such controversial material. The British economist John Maynard Keynes was perhaps most responsible for our greater sophistication regarding the role of government in the national economy.[1] Keynes not only challenged the conventional economic wisdom, he urged on government a positive role in shaping the economy, particularly the use of deficit financing to combat depression and unemployment. Needless to say, such viewpoints were very controversial. When the President's Council of Economic Advisers was established in 1946 there was widespread feeling that the advice of the council would reflect the underlying social philosophy of the administration in power rather than "sound" economic doctrine.[2] Indeed, the resignation of one of the original members was motivated by his dissatisfaction with such a state of affairs. Although there certainly is a place for the trained economist in the budgetary process, the science of economics is so inextricably bound up with conflicting value judgments regarding the proper role of government in the economy that such disagreements are bound to occur. This points up again the difficult problem of harnessing scientific techniques to social values. This problem of financial or fiscal policy, so vital in providing the framework for the budget process, will be treated more fully in Chapter 21.

ACCOUNTABILITY

Perhaps the most important value pressing upon the whole budgetary process is the concept of accountability. Here we are mainly concerned with its political and cultural origins, leaving for later chapters the institutional and mechanical checks which try to achieve it.

Who is accountable to whom, and for what? In a certain sense everyone is accountable to someone, but we are concerned here with financial accountability for both money and property. Such accountability applies not only to high-status officials but also to the rank and file. This problem of accountability pervades all organizations where funds and property are involved, whether a church, a family store, a giant corporation, or a government bureau. The journeyman is accountable to his supervisor

[1] R. F. Harrod, *The Life of John Maynard Keynes* (New York: Harcourt, Brace & Co., 1951).

[2] Among others, see Edwin G. Nourse, *Economics in the Public Service: Administrative Aspects of the Employment Act* (New York: Harcourt, Brace & Co., 1953).

for the proper use and custody of tools; the hospital pharmacist must at all times account for his supply of narcotics; the cashier must balance his cash; the store manager must see that his inventory conforms to the records of income and outgo.

Accountability is accomplished by a system of internal checks based upon record keeping. Thus when the journeyman checks out a diamond drill, he receives an order signed by his supervisor showing that he is authorized to use it. He presents the order to the toolkeeper who requires him to sign a receipt. Thus the supervisor knows who was authorized to use the valuable instrument, and the toolkeeper is under constant audit by an equipment control unit. This is the red tape so often decried by the critics of bureaucracy. A great deal of this criticism is unfair because private organizations have these same internal checks. There is a tremendous amount of record keeping in all large businesses. Indeed, as we have seen, red tape is a function of size rather than of ownership. Many small government units such as cities, counties, and school districts have rather elementary records. A Harvard Business School study indicates that manufacturing businesses emerge from one-man personal control into control by record (red tape) when they have more than a hundred and fifty or two hundred employees.[3]

It is probably true, however, that the government environment requires and tolerates more record keeping than business. Perhaps the primary reason is that government is more accountable to the public for the details of its operations. The public business is everybody's business, whereas private business has been permitted a considerable degree of internal autonomy. However, one should hasten to add that this situation is changing very rapidly; the income tax, combined with increasing government regulation, is making private business more and more accountable to the public for the details of its operations. Nevertheless the tendencies toward red tape are probably greater in government than in business. Several reasons explain this: (1) many government records are required by law rather than by the needs of management; (2) there may be more record keeping for its own sake in government because of stratification and hierarchy, which in turn cause resistance to change; (3) one often senses a clerico-legal accounting stereotype that makes government record keeping a holy rite. Because the rite has the sanction of time and was approved by the forefathers, only the sacrilegious would suggest its abolition; (4) a vested interest in record keeping may be easier to defend in government.

But the prime purpose of fiscal accountability is to ensure democratic responsibility to the public at large. The public official has two types of

[3] Paul F. Lawler, *Records for the Control of Growing Manufacturing Enterprises* (Boston: Harvard School of Business Administration, 1947), p. 12.

such accountability: (1) fiduciary accountability and (2) accountability for the exercise of wisdom and judgment in making fiscal decisions. "Fiduciary" refers to faith, trust, confidence; it is the kind of quality expected of bankers, trustees, and treasurers. Fiduciary accountability looms largest in those areas where custodianship predominates: the work of treasurers and cashiers, investment of trust funds, and warehousing. Loss in these areas is fairly well guarded against by traditional bonding, auditing, record keeping, reporting, and regulation by law. The other type of accountability involves more discretion; it goes further than custody and stewardship and enlists the dynamic policy-determining qualities of management. The decisions required during the budget process are illustrative. Should we hire a hundred more police or should the money go toward building a juvenile detention building? Would money be saved by consolidating the park and recreation departments? Should the Veterans Administration be required to abandon its own warehouses and use those of the General Services Administration? In other words, this kind of accountability asks whether fiscal officers are "good managers."

Myths of Accountability. It has long been an American myth that the way to control malpractice in government is to divide power among many independent officers. Students of political science know that this myth gained support through the writings of de Montesquieu and his description of mid-eighteenth century British practice. Present-day observers believe that de Montesquieu misinterpreted the British system of checks and balances, and that the present constitutional pattern of accountability had not evolved and matured at that time. While we cannot speak for all students of government, it can be said that many students of political thought believe the extreme American interpretation of separation of powers to be dysfunctional, primarily because it diffuses leadership and prevents the assignment of responsibility (accountability).[4]

In the area of financial administration this interpretation of the separation of powers has led to several abuses and weaknesses. In the first place, it has led to the choosing of the chief fiscal officers by popular election on the state and local level. This has often resulted in the selection of unqualified persons who have struggled to set up feudal domains rather than instrumentalities of fiscal coordination and control. In the second place, it has led to an irrational division of functions between the legislative and executive branches, best illustrated by the perennial controversy over the federal Comptroller General, discussed in the following

---

[4] For the typical viewpoint of such scholars, see Charles McKinley, "Federal Administrative Pathology and the Separation of Powers," 11, *Public Administration Review* (Winter, 1951), pp. 17–25.

chapter. In brief, this officer exercises powers of control of an executive rather than a legislative nature. The same can be said of many elective state comptrollers and municipal auditors.

In the third place, this situation has militated against the inauguration of modern systems of budgetary and accounting control because of the dispersion of power and authority. Even when power existed, effective accounting systems have not been installed largely because those responsible were not technically qualified to do so. In order to shield their own inadequacies, they have laid down smokescreens of petty attention to auditing detail. Thus they have been able to build up reputations as fiscal watchdogs and have often gained the approbation of the legislature and public. This posture is the product of a frontier philosophy of democratic administration, which had some validity in the days when fiduciary accountability was a very real problem. But the opportunity for loss today is not in the custodial or fiduciary realm where the holes have been plugged by gradual maturing of the banking and trust laws. Today the leaks are more likely to occur as the result of poor administration. Although the honesty of men is always a matter of concern, governmental costs are now more sensitive to management ineptitude than to defalcation. Indeed, good management is the best antidote and preventive for dishonesty. Today the costs of government can be traced to overstaffing, incompetent personnel practices, poor motivation, unwise spending, poor accounting practices, unimaginative leadership, and pork-barrel appropriations. Yet the cure-all too often advanced for these ills is negative prescriptions backed up by a paralyzing division of authority. The proper therapy, of course, lies in placing responsibility in dynamic and constructive administrative leadership and holding it responsible.

Perhaps the greatest need in this whole area of accountability lies in the area of standards. What are people to be held accountable for? The answer may seem obvious: for doing a good job. But what constitutes a good job? The answer is not obvious at all because we do not know the proper standard of performance in most activities. The heart of scientific management, which worked so effectively in American industry, is measured production. Yet in government a kind of defeatism has thwarted most efforts to develop standards. The current watchword of the administrative reformers is "performance budgeting."[5] Time alone will tell whether it is a fad or a substantial contribution to management; but it cannot be put into effect without some form of work measurement. It is based upon budgeting units of work rather than things to be bought and paid for, such as paper and personnel services. The theory is that the taxpayer can hold the bureaucrat more accountable when it is known

[5] See Clarence E. Ridley and Herbert A. Simon, *Measuring Municipal Activities* (Chicago: International City Managers' Association, 1938).

that a given amount of money should buy x miles of street sweeping or y acres of soil conservation. The objective "performance" or program budget is laudable, and one hopes that it will lead to a renaissance of the standards movement of a quarter-century ago. Much more will be said about it in subsequent chapters.

FINANCIAL FUNCTIONS

The Comptroller Function. The comptroller function is really that of the chief accounting officer, although some industrial comptrollers are much more than heads of accounting departments. A good comptroller, in addition to being a Certified Public Accountant, is a member of top management and the most influential person relative to financial policy. Public administration has not developed the comptroller function as a unified entity, the state and municipal director of finance perhaps being the nearest approach. Indeed, government has in general failed to develop a unified approach to accounting. Nevertheless, accounting is basic to all other fiscal activities. That is why it is mentioned first in this inventory, rather than budgeting which is of much more interest to the generalist. There are certain accounting activities that have to be performed, and one need not be a CPA to know whether they are being accomplished. The quality of the accounting process is indicative of the tone of financial administration.

The chief accounting officer keeps the accounts necessary to render a report on current status of funds and to maintain control. From a general administration standpoint, his most important operation is maintaining the appropriation and revenue control ledgers that reflect how money going out compares with money available. He also supervises the decentralized accounting systems maintained in other agencies; he has power to make them comply with over-all policies and to conform to uniform accounting practices. His relationship to the other agencies, as with all other financial officers, is one of functional supervision rather than line-of-command control. Nevertheless his latent authority is such as to require compliance when necessary. The accounting function in the department is performed by accounting officers reporting to department heads.

The accounting office maintains budgetary control accounts that furnish the program chiefs with up-to-date reports on the status of expenditure accounts. Proposals for expenditure are invariably routed to the accounting office to see whether money is available—a process widely known as the preaudit. This office also conducts the administrative audit, which is to be distinguished from the outside or legislative audit.

It is perfectly proper to have both an inside and outside audit; most industrial concerns find both necessary. Hence the chief accounting office usually has a corps of traveling auditors who examine the agency's accounts periodically—another example of the internal checks which accompany tight financial management. It is similar to the inspection function in decentralized personnel administration. The chief accounting officer also examines and certifies all payments into and out of the treasury, usually evidenced by a paper called a "warrant." In federal practice a warrant is a blanket instrument covering many millions; when signed by the Comptroller General, it legalizes the transfer of funds from the Treasury to the disbursing officer or from a collection agency into the Treasury. In local government a warrant is merely a check upon a bank.

The Budget Bureau. The financial agency that has most appeal to the public administration generalist is undoubtedly the budget office. It reports directly to the chief executive or his director of finance, and acts as his financial staff arm. If it enjoys competent and imaginative leadership, the budget bureau can become the very heart of day-to-day management. Through the power to allocate money, it possesses tremendous coordinative influence. Instead of being a mere fiscal unit, it often acts as a catalyst for management improvement. Its principal function is the preparation of the annual budget which the President, governor, or mayor presents to the legislature. During the period of annual budget preparation, most budget agencies work under pressure, putting in much overtime. But in the off-budget season the staff members often engage in management improvement surveys. Indeed, it is now recognized that the budget agency should take a lead in stimulating the program departments to adopt better management practices. Experience in a budget agency is a valuable item on an employment record, not only because it affords personal contact with influential officials but also because it offers training in the art of coordination, which is the primary skill of the administrative generalist.

Revenue and Custody. The office of treasurer is no longer so important as in the days of debased coinage, wildcat banking, and unstable currency. Then the treasurer had the responsibility of guarding against a variety of losses that do not confront him today. (The chief danger is now inflation, about which the treasurer can do little.) The duties of treasurer today are for the most part composed of routine compliance with law. His responsibilities as a custodian are transferred to the banks, the soundness of which is guarded by such agencies as the Federal Reserve Board, the Comptroller of the Currency, and the Federal Deposit Insurance Corporation.

In essence, the treasurer of a governmental jurisdiction is the official and legal possessor of the bank books and deposit slips. To be sure, he may have important fiduciary functions as investor of surplus and administrator of the public debt. But the really important revenue functions today relate to the assessment and collection of taxes. A quarter-century ago books on this subject would have been concerned mainly with the assessment of property for state and local jurisdictions and with the customs for the federal system. Today the administration of the income and sales taxes requires a virtual army of people whose supervision constitutes an administrative problem of great proportion. In American public administration there is a tendency for separate agencies to be set up for the collection of each new tax. The best administrative thought, however, favors combining all revenue activities into an integrated revenue unit.

The flow of money into and out of the Treasury is subject to internal checks somewhat as follows: the revenue agency collects the taxes, the comptroller audits receipts, and if he finds them correct, he "covers" them into the Treasury. The money is usually deposited in a bank while these official checks are going on because large sums of cash are not ordinarily kept on hand. When an obligation has been duly incurred by a spending agency, payment is made by warrant drawn on the treasurer but countersigned by the comptroller. In the federal government the vastness of operations requires an additional step: the warrants are issued in lump sum to disbursing officers who make the detailed payments.

Auditing. The term "auditor" has often been misused in American financial administration because of the tendency to regard this officer as the chief accountant. This is particularly true in state and local governments, but confusion has also prevailed on the federal level, as evidenced by the functions of the Comptroller General, who is an auditor rather than a comptroller. Strictly speaking, an auditor keeps no books of accounts because it is his primary duty to examine the books of others. Every organization requires two types of audit, the current inside audit and the outside post-audit. The latter is regarded as a legislative function. Current administrative thought favors attaching an auditing office to the legislature. However, it should be noted that the office of "legislative auditor," which has arisen in some states and cities, is a different kind of agency. It operates in fact as a staff agency, advising the legislature on fiscal policy and expenditures and actually doing little or none of the detailed examination of books traditionally associated with auditing.

INTEGRATED FINANCIAL STRUCTURE

Expert opinion favors the integration of financial functions in state and local government under a director of finance who reports directly to the chief administrative officer.[6] At the federal level, however, integration finds less favor. The task force report of the first Hoover Commission, written by A. E. Buck, recommended the transfer of the Bureau of the Budget to the Treasury Department and the establishment of a General Accountant in the Treasury. This would have made the department the focal point of federal financial administration. This recommendation was not accepted by the Commission. The coordination of federal finance administration is in fact being achieved through the Joint Accounting Committee representing the Comptroller General, the Secretary of the Treasury, and the Director of the Bureau of the Budget.

The principal argument for fiscal integration is that it makes for better management. Budgeting, accounting, and supply, along with personnel, constitute the cardinal management control activities. If these are well managed, the program activities are also likely to be well run. In other words, program accomplishments correlate highly with the quality of administration. The chief function of administration is coordination, which in turn depends on budgeting, accounting, personnel, and supply. Personnel is mentioned here because certain personnel activities will inevitably impinge on financial decisions, whether they are placed in a department of finance or not. In the past there was some advocacy of a bureau of personnel under the department of finance, but there is now little trend in that direction. Many budget agencies, however, are in charge of wage analysis and salary administration. Moreover, Congressional pressure for reduction of staffs has stimulated the Budget Bureau to inaugurate programs that motivate employees to be more productive. The administration of such personnel activities is not ordinarily under a finance officer.

The latter will usually supervise four or five bureaus corresponding to the financial activities discussed above. These include budgeting, accounting, taxation and revenue, treasury, and auxiliary services. There is some question as to whether the budget director should not report directly to the chief political executive without going through the director of finance. Originally the federal Bureau of the Budget was in the Treasury but was removed by Presidential reorganization order. In states and cities there has been some favorable experience with the director of finance appointed by the governor, mayor, or manager. These officers tend, for all practical purposes, to exercise preponderant influ-

[6] Perhaps the most consistent advocate has been A. E. Buck, whose writings are cited in the Bibliography. Integration is advocated in the Model City Charter and Model State Constitution of the National Municipal League; in *Municipal Finance Administration* (Chicago: International City Managers' Association, 1949), pp. 58 ff.; and by the Fiscal Task Force of the Hoover Commission.

ence over the chief's budget decisions. Indeed, where the office of director of finance exists and where it has been given adequate power, it tends to become quite influential.[7]

THE BUDGET PROCESS

Although financial administration is mainly concerned with the functions mentioned above, we have defined it broadly to include the wide policy framework within which the budget process is carried on. This broad treatment helps dramatize the fact that budgeting is much more than a technical exercise. It is always affected by high-level political decisions; these will be considered at length in the next chapter under the heading of fiscal policy determination. Such decisions involve the process of allocating money in line with the major political objectives of the government. Once this policy framework has been provided, we can turn directly to the budget process, which includes the following major phases:

1. *Agency preparation of estimates for program* activities. At this point the budget is sometimes defined as "a device for securing money from a legislature."[8] But budget preparation involves much more than justifying an agency's requests for money. It is also a fiscal plan of their operations; a way of coordinating work throughout the entire organization; and an inducement to better administrative practices, such as increased cost-consciousness and better program evaluation.[9]

2. *Legislative authorization of the appropriations requests of the agencies.* This is a most critical phase in the budgetary process, since it determines how well the agency's program is to be supported by public funds. Its outcome is anxiously watched by agency employees, since the legislature's reaction is the best index of its opinion of the agency and its program. Here the agency's higher executives must enter the political arena, and often their expertise is not enough to save them from rough treatment by legislators who are disenchanted with the agency for several possible reasons.

3. *The final and less "political" phase in budgeting is the execution stage.* Here the big decisions have been made, and the main question becomes one of spending the money according to a rational plan. The official is helped at this stage by numerous controls which require among other things that money appropriated for one purpose not be spent for another or that the money in one account be expended according to a schedule which prevents exhaustion of the account before the fiscal year is over.

---

[7] For an article that touches upon the budget director's role in New York State, see Frederick C. Mosher, "The Executive Budget, Empire State Style," 12, *Public Administration Review* (Spring, 1952), pp. 73–84.

[8] Jesse Burkhead, *Government Budgeting* (New York: John Wiley & Sons, Inc., 1956), p. 246.

[9] *Ibid.*

BIBLIOGRAPHY

Burkhead, Jesse. *Government Budgeting*. New York: 1956.

Garvey, Neil F. *Government and Administration of Illinois*. New York: 1959.

Gaus, John M., and Wolcott, Leon O. *Public Administration and the United States Department of Agriculture*. Chicago: 1940.

Hoover Report, First. Commission on Organization of the Executive Branch of the Government. *Budgeting and Accounting*. Washington, D.C.: 1949.

Hoover Report, First. Task Force Report. *Fiscal, Budgeting and Accounting Activities*. Washington, D.C.: 1949.

Hoover Report, Second. Commission on Organization of the Executive Branch of the Government. *Budget and Accounting*. Washington, D.C.: 1955.

Hoover Report, Second. Task Force Report. *Budget and Accounting*. Washington, D.C.: 1955.

Institute for Training in Municipal Administration. *Municipal Finance Administration*. 5th ed. Chicago: 1955.

Nolting, Orin F. (ed.). "Municipal Finance," *Municipal Year Book*. Chicago: Consult current edition.

President's Committee on Administrative Management (Brownlow). *Report with Special Studies*. Washington, D.C.: 1937.

Seckler-Hudson, Catheryn. "Performance Budgeting in Government," **18**, *Advanced Management* (March, 1953), pp. 5 ff.

Smithies, Arthur. *The Budgetary Process in the United States*. New York: 1955.

Winnifrith, A. J. D. "Treasury Control of Establishments Work," **36**, *Public Administration*, British (Spring, 1958), pp. 9–17.

CHAPTER 21

Fiscal Policy
Determination

The budget process flows within a larger framework of national fiscal policy. Such policy, which is determined in the main by political leaders (although higher civil servants are vital, too), is the result of a compromise among many factors. Such factors include the so-called objective conditions of national security, the state of the national economy, the availability of revenues for public programs, the sunk costs which the government already has in existing programs, and the demand for new programs. Allied with such "objective" factors are a complex of influences that are essentially normative. They include the economic philosophy of the political leaders and their top advisers, their attitudes toward the "proper" role of government in our mixed economy, the demands of interest groups, and the weight assigned to their respective demands by legislators and chief executives. Both kinds of factors impinge upon every major policy question. In this chapter we shall attempt to show how these decisions are made and how they provide the framework for the budget process that implements them. This requires a brief introductory essay on political dynamics.

ROLE OF POLITICAL PARTIES

The big questions such as tax policy, foreign policy, and government's role vis-à-vis business are defined, debated, and incorporated into their platforms by the major political parties. When the victorious party assumes control of the government following an election, these policies provide the broad guidelines for the programs of the new administration. As we have seen, party leaders attempt to ensure that such policies are carried out by placing members of the party in strategic, policy-determining positions throughout the administrative hierarchy.[1] These high political aides, in turn, are heavily dependent upon the career civil servant

---

[1] Congress, of course, is similarly organized to ensure control by the majority party of committees, bills to be introduced, debate, etc.

for advice and administrative skill. In this way, theoretically at least, popular control of the government's activities is maintained through periodic elections which permit the citizen to accept or reject the policies and programs of the two parties.

However, the system does not work quite like this, and the reasons it does not have important implications for national financial policy and for the role of the bureaucracy in it. First, the differences in substantive policy between the two major parties are rarely significant enough to give the voter a real choice. Hence the competition between our parties is mainly for office and control of the government, rather than one among competing policies. However, this competition for office is carried on in the rhetoric of policy which tends to obscure the main locus of party motivation.[2] This condition reflects the consensus that Americans have about major aspects of our social system: our form of government; the economic system; and foreign policy (here, perhaps, "lack of interest" is a more accurate symbol than consensus). Our relatively high standard of living also helps us escape the tension based on the sharp economic disparities existing in many parts of the world. This condition also reflects a less happy attitude; namely, the combination of cynicism and indifference with which many Americans view government and politics, despite our reliance upon government for many vital services. The lack of party discipline, which would permit party leaders to make good their campaign promises, is a related factor. As Woodrow Wilson said,

This indifference of the country to what is said in Congress, pointing, as it obviously does, to the fact that, though the Committees lead in legislation, they lead without concert or responsibility, and lead nobody in particular, that is, no compact and organized party force which can be made accountable for its policy, has also a further signifiance with regard to the opportunities and capacities of the constituencies. The doubt and confusion of thought which must necessarily exist in the minds of the vast majority of voters as to the best way of exerting their will in influencing the action of an assembly whose organization is so complex, whose acts are apparently so haphazard, and in which responsibility is spread so thin, throws constituencies into the hands of local politicians who are more visible and tangible than are the leaders of Congress, and generates, the while, a profound distrust of Congress as a body whose actions cannot be reckoned beforehand by any standard of promises made at elections or any programmes announced by conventions.[3]

As a result, our party system is not one in which the voter has a real political choice between parties having real policy differences, nor can he be sure that the victorious party will carry out its announced policies.

[2] See R. V. Presthus and L. V. Blankenship, "Dixon-Yates: A Study in Political Behavior" (unpublished ms., Cornell University, 1960).

[3] W. Wilson, Congressional Government: A Study in American Politics (New York: Meridian Books, Inc., 1956), pp. 128–29.

Given these conditions, another factor shaping national fiscal policy becomes even more important, namely, that the government's huge program commitments prohibit any radical change in its character, scope, and role. This fact is dramatically illustrated by the experience of President Eisenhower's administration, which came into office pledged to balance the budget by reducing the scale of government operations. Federal expenditures were to be cut and government was to be taken out of economic areas where it "competed" with private interests. These policies were evident in the natural resource field (particularly in the area of hydroelectric power), in efforts to discontinue the postal savings system, to cut the size of the federal civil service, etc. However, the record shows that the administration was able to accomplish few, if any, of these major policy objectives. In 1959 the President was obliged to ask Congress to raise the ceiling on the national debt in order to permit his programs to continue. Indeed, under the Eisenhower administration a new high was reached in peace-time federal budgets.

In economic terms, these results were a reflection of the huge "sunk costs" of modern government, which create financial and political commitments that are impossible to discontinue. One significant implication of this situation is the resulting importance of the bureaucracy's role in providing continuity for these programs, which tend to go on, not much changed, despite the rhetoric and mock combat of the political branches. This central role is apparent in the fact that today something over half of all the legislative measures proposed to Congress come from the departments and agencies and affiliated interest groups. Congress must finally authorize these measures and the appropriations that they require, but political realities have brought a gradual but fundamental change in the legislator's role at every level of government. He has become less and less an initiator of policy, and more and more an instrument for criticizing and synthesizing legislative proposals that come from the executive branch and the great interest groups.

THE PRESIDENT'S ROLE

These qualifications must be kept in mind as we trace the process and instruments by which fiscal policy is determined and enunciated. While our examples are from the federal level, a similar process goes on at the state and local levels, although at the local level administrators are apparently much more concerned with the revenue side of the budgetary process than they are elsewhere.[4] The President now exercises fiscal policy leadership, not only because of the executive budget which enables

[4] A. M. Hillhouse, *Capital Programming and Budgeting in Government* (In preparation).

him to go to Congress with a comprehensive, well-documented financial plan for federal programs but also because he is the political leader of the party in power and is thus officially responsible for carrying out its policies. In the next chapter we shall examine the staff services which strengthen his hand in financial policy determination. In the main, the President's role is expressed through two major speeches, the Budget Message and the Economic Report,[5] although he will exercise day-to-day influence over policy through his meetings with the Cabinet and other officials concerned with broad financial affairs.

The Budget Message. One of the major ways that the President can exercise his responsibility for national leadership and counteract the atomistic effect of interest group and sectional politics upon the budget is through his annual budget message, which defines and defends his major policies. However, everything that is said here must be qualified by the recognition that the President is not master of his own administrative house; his Cabinet aides and their bureau chiefs are all inclined to rationalize the budget in terms of the needs and demands of the substantive interests with which they are most closely identified. Federal financial determination is in no sense a matter of a united executive branch preparing a synthesized budget or program for presentation to Congress. Despite the improvements made since the Budget and Accounting Acts of 1921 and 1950, which provided the chief executive with the Bureau of the Budget and other aids, much remains to be done before the budget becomes as effective as observers believe it can be.[6]

In any event, the budget message provides the President an opportunity to present his recommended budget to Congress and the country. In it, he outlines the final administrative result of some eighteen months of examination, analysis, and compromise among the departments and agencies of the entire federal bureaucracy. The following example illustrates the administration's major objectives and economic philosophy regarding federal spending as enunciated by President Eisenhower on January 16, 1957:

To the Congress of the United States:

I am presenting with this message my recommended budget for the United States Government for the fiscal year 1958, which begins next July 1. This is the fourth budget which I have transmitted to the Congress. In my first budget message—that for the fiscal year 1955—I emphasized the administration's deter-

[5] The President's State of the Union message is not included here, since it covers much the same ground as the Budget Message and the Economic Report.

[6] Perhaps the most authoritative work on the federal budget, written in a most readable style and covering every major question, is Arthur Smithies, *The Budgetary Process in the United States* (New York: McGraw-Hill Book Co., Inc., 1955). This entire section relies heavily upon this analysis.

mination to chart a course toward two important fiscal goals—balanced budgets and tax reductions. Reductions in spending evidenced in the 1955 budget made possible a large tax reduction and tax reform program.

The 1956 budget was balanced.

The 1957 budget will be balanced.

A balanced budget is proposed for 1958.

I believe this policy of fiscal integrity has contributed significantly to the soundness of our Nation's economic growth and that it will continue to do so during the coming fiscal year.[7]

The President then went on to enumerate the "national objectives" which had guided him in his financial planning. These included peace, justice and freedom; powerful armed forces; a healthy and growing economy; wise conservation and development of natural resources; fiscal integrity; a well-balanced choice of programs; and increased international trade and investment.[8]

The President's statement of budget policy made it clear that a balanced federal budget was among his highest normative assumptions in constructing the 1958 budget.[9] Among the ways this was to be accomplished was a reduction in federal employees, to continue "efforts which have resulted in a net reduction of approximately 240,000 in the civilian work force during the past four years."[10] This goal was reiterated by reference to "balanced budgets in 1956, 1957 and 1958," and to the fact that the current proposals provided for expenditures which were "279 million dollars less than estimated budget receipts."[11] Tax policy was adumbrated by the President's words, "it is my firm belief that tax rates are still too high and that we should look forward to further tax reductions . . ."[12] Still, the defense program was clearly the highest priority, accounting for 63 per cent of the entire budget.[13]

The message also included a section on the administration's legislative program, outlining the major proposals to be submitted to Congress during "the next few months." These included federal aid for school construction, extended social security, aid to small business, placing the post office on a pay-as-you-go basis, modifications of the farm subsidy program, admission of Hawaii as a state, authorization to the President to reward outstanding civilian achievement and to establish a Federal Advisory Commission on the Arts.

[7] "Budget Message of the President," *Budget of the United States Government* (Washington, D.C.: U.S. Government Printing Office, 1957), p. 5.

[8] *Ibid.*

[9] *Ibid.*

[10] *Ibid.*, p. M7.

[11] *Ibid.* This optimistic forecast for 1958 was premature; fiscal 1958 ended with a deficit of nearly $3 billion.

[12] *Ibid.*

[13] *Ibid.*, p. M12.

The priorities assigned by the administration to these various programs and proposals is quite obvious, particularly if the amounts requested to carry them out are used as the criterion. The important objectives include adequate defense, reducing nonmilitary federal expenditures, and balancing the budget. Legislative proposals such as federal aid to school construction and aid to small business may safely be regarded as secondary goals. For budgetary purposes, the vital thing is that these major goals have provided the terms of reference for the Bureau of the Budget during their eighteen-month effort to hammer out the executive budget for presentation to Congress. Since these objectives inevitably conflict with those of various departments and bureaus, each of which has political support in some measure, the resulting budget is a compromise measure.[14] While it represents a great advance over practices of some twenty years ago, much remains to be done, as will be shown in subsequent chapters.

The President's Economic Report. Among its provisions the Employment Act of 1946 required that the President submit an annual report on the state of the economy. Although the report comprises information and recommendations from the major departments and agencies, it is mainly the result of work by the Council of Economic Advisors, also established under the Employment Act. The reports are much more than a detached statement of economic conditions; they also provide the raw materials for the interpretation of economic trends and policies, and it is this aspect of the reports which strengthens the President's hand in guiding federal financial policy. For example, in his Economic Report in 1959, after tracing the course of the economic decline during 1957 and 1958, the President drew the following conclusions and recommendations from this experience:

In many respects the most important lesson taught by the recent recession is that a competitive economic system has remarkable power to resist contractive pressures and, without an extended interruption of growth, to stage a good recovery.[15]

As for recommendations based upon this judgment, the President added:[16]

---

[14] For a survey of the kinds of policy conflict that occur among the executive, legislative, and administrative branches, see S. M. Cohen, "Economic Policy and the Federal Budget," 9, *Federal Accountant* (September, 1959), pp. 00-00; see also, Committee for Economic Development, *The Budget and Economic Growth* (New York: April, 1959); Lewis H. Kimmel, *Federal Budget and Fiscal Policy 1789–1958* (Washington, D.C.: Brookings Institution, 1959).

[15] Economic Report of the President (Washington, D.C.: U.S. Government Printing Office, 1959), pp. 1–2.

[16] *Ibid.*, pp. 2–3.

These features of our economy . . . have certain implications for public policy that are worthy of special note. First, the capacity of our economy to withstand contractive influences provides time for regenerative processes to make the adjustments needed for sound recovery, and for the counteractive measures taken by Government, jointly with factors making for long term growth, to make their effects felt. Where necessary, efforts should be made to strengthen these features of our economic system.

Second, the major emphasis of federal countercyclical policy should be placed on measures that will result in prompt action to help promote a shift in the balance of economic forces from contraction to recovery and growth. . . .

Third, in contrast to large-scale public works, monetary and credit policy used vigorously, can produce prompt and significantly helpful results. . . . Finally, the capacity to resist short-term fluctuations can be increased by government actions to strengthen the factors that make for long-term economic growth—vigorously competitive markets, research and development activity, and heightened incentives for all Americans to work, save, and invest.

These conclusions and recommendations are statements of administration fiscal policy and economic philosophy. They make clear to Congress and the bureaucracy the broad terms of reference within which budgetary determinations will be made. They outline to the nation the administration's achievements and its aspirations as indicated by Chapters 3 and 4 of the Report which "summarize the government actions that helped shorten the decline," and "propose a program for promoting economic growth on a sustained inflation-free basis."[17]

However, it must be said that there is considerable disagreement about the assumptions and the conclusions set down so concretely in the President's economic report and in his budget message. Since Keynes and Hansen, the balanced budget under all circumstances is no longer accepted as the *sine qua non* of federal budget policy.[18] Indeed, majority opinion among economists probably accepts the idea of countercyclical budget policy. Similarly, it is a moot point whether monetary and credit policy are capable "promptly" of reversing economic decline.[19] But the most important criticism of these economic assumptions is their view that it is enough merely to maintain national economic growth at the existing level, particularly in the face of the rapid economic growth of Russia and the increase of our own population. Goods and services lost during a period of "contractive pressures" can never be regained, as suggested by the comparative figures in 1957 and 1958 for Gross

[17] *Ibid.*, p. 1.

[18] J. M. Keynes, *General Theory of Employment, Interest and Money* (New York: Harcourt, Brace & Co., 1936); A. Hansen, *Fiscal Policy and Business Cycles* (New York: W. W. Norton Co., 1941).

[19] Among others, see Paul S. Samuelson, *Economics* (New York: McGraw-Hill Book Co., Inc., 1956), pp. 316–17.

National Product.[20] Finally, there is the social implication of the administration's policy of "waiting out" a decline until "regenerative processes" take effect: While this policy may be economically feasible, it is less acceptable politically in terms of the strain and hardship by attending unemployment. As Senator Humphrey said in criticizing this policy, "Let's balance people, not budgets." The normative element in federal fiscal policy is suggested by these observations.

THE ROLE OF THE TREASURY AND THE FEDERAL RESERVE SYSTEM

Even a brief survey of federal fiscal policy must include some mention of the Treasury's role, both in terms of its impact on debt policy and its regulation of credit and the volume of money available for investment exercised mainly through the Federal Reserve System. The Federal Reserve System's influence over the money supply has been outlined; for example, assuming that the government wishes to contract the money supply and raise interest rates, it may take the following steps:[21]

1. Most important are its *open market operations*, whereby selling securities, federal reserve notes, and member bank reserves may contract available money as much as fivefold.
2. It can raise reserve requirements.
3. It can raise the rediscount rate, raising the discount or interest rate on acceptances, etc.
4. The government can use moral pressure, urging the banks to tighten up their lending operations. Margin requirements for buying stocks on credit can also be raised to curtail installment buying in the stock market.

The administration's activities during 1956–58 are suggested by the President's statement in the Economic Report: "During the past 18 months, monetary and credit policy was directed successively to moderating the rate of credit expansion, helping to reverse economic contraction, and encouraging a steady and balanced recovery and growth."[22] The availability of capital for industrial and business investment immediately before the 1957 downturn was limited by the Federal Reserve Board's policy of limiting the reserve funds to member banks to levels that would meet only the ordinary demands of seasonal shifts in economic activity, as distinct from the sharp demands just before the

[20] GNP in 1957 was 407 billion; by 1958 it had fallen to 399 billion; more disturbing was the recent trend, in which annual increases before 1958 had been: 1952, 353 billion; 1953, 369 billion; 1954, 363 billion; 1955, 392 billion; 1956, 402 billion (all figures in constant dollars); *U.S. Income and Output,* Department of Commerce (November, 1959), p. 119.

[21] Samuelson, *Economics,* p. 310.

[22] *Ibid.,* p. 33.

downturn. Interest rates rose to the highest point in almost thirty years. Once the 1957 recession began, these and related techniques were reversed in an effort to stimulate economic activity. Housing and home financing activities were among those which showed most clearly the impact of these policies. The building industry had been on the downturn for two years before 1957, but by late 1957 private housing starts had begun to stabilize, and by February, 1958, they had begun a sharp increase.[23]

The Treasury Department's major influence on economic activity comes through its control of the borrowing of the huge amounts needed for federal programs, including the management of the federal debt. By correlating its issues, and their interest rates, with the supply and demand for private capital, the Treasury can also counterbalance economic trends of inflation and deflation.[24] Nevertheless the continuing imbalance between federal receipts and expenditures amounted to almost thirteen billion dollars by mid-1959, adding a built-in inflationary quality to the economy.

Here again, both economists and politicians disagree about these policies. The Federal Reserve System's policy of tightening up reserves and thus forcing private borrowers into the private capital markets, with a resulting increase in interest rates and a scarcity of money, has been regarded as favoring financial lending institutions while limiting the ability of small business, such as those in the construction industry, to maintain a high level of activity. Some individuals have urged that the "tight money" policy of the administration aggravated the downturn beginning in the last half of 1957. Also, the failure of the administration to balance the budget as promised, particularly in a period of high economic activity, has been criticized. Hence the administration has been the target of both its "conservative" supporters and those who advocate a more liberal money policy. These observations again suggest the subjective aspects of federal fiscal policy and its underlying economic philosophy.

CONGRESS' ROLE IN FISCAL POLICY

Congress is not quite a full-fledged partner in fiscal policy determination. The President comes to Congress with a prepared, rationalized budget, which gives him leadership in fiscal policy determination. Still, one of the main criteria in the preparation of the executive budget has been the President's judgment as to Congressional reactions to its proposals. Congressional committees scrutinize the budget, and the records

[23] *Ibid.*, pp. 37–39.
[24] *Ibid.*, pp. 44–47.

of their hearings are voluminous. Thus, to borrow a phrase from Justice Holmes, Congress is a "brooding omnipresence" throughout the eighteen-month period of budget preparation. While no legislative consensus exists, its attitudes toward specific programs are well known by the agencies concerned; and its view of proper fiscal policy during a given period is made known through several media, to which we now turn. Of course final authorizing must come from Congress.

The Joint Economic Committee. Among the provisions of the Employment Act of 1946 was the establishment of a joint Congressional committee responsible for analyzing the President's annual Economic Report and presenting its views to the entire Congress. The kind of scrutiny and influence that this responsibility gives Congress is suggested by some examples from the Committee's hearings in 1959. The range of issues covered in the hearings is apparent from the following questions put to the Council of Economic Advisers:[25]

1. What are the levels of employment, production and purchasing power needed in 1959 to carry out the objectives of the Employment Act?
2. What are the current and foreseeable trends in employment, production, and purchasing power?
3. What assumptions with respect to prices, national income, personal income, corporate profits, and the like underlie the President's Economic Report? Are these assumptions consistent with those upon which the budget is based? Are these assumptions consistent with the attainment of the Employment Act objectives in calendar 1959?
4. In discussing the economic outlook for 1959 and in formulating its recommendations, does the Economic Report take account of likely developments with respect to the broad outlines of monetary and credit policy to be expected this year? . . .
5. With the advantages of hindsight, do you now think different public policies should have been adopted after mid-1957? If so, what changes would you have made?

The answers to these questions were requested from Council members Saulnier, Brandt, and McCracken. While one suspects that this is an unusual situation, the resulting testimony was not at all one between bureaucratic experts and legislative laymen, mainly because the Chairman of the Joint Economic Committee was Senator Paul H. Douglas, an eminent economist. The Council came in for some sharp probing:[26]

THE CHAIRMAN: Now, as it turns out, the deficit for fiscal 1958 was almost $3 billion and the deficit for 1959 almost $13 billion, and the corporate profits for 1958 fell off so that the total receipts of the Government, instead of being the $73 or $74 billion which the President had estimated, it is

[25] Joint Economic Committee, 79th Cong., 1st sess., *Hearings*, "Economic Report of the President" (Washington, D.C.: U.S. Government Printing Office, 1959), p. 1.
[26] *Ibid.*, p. 8.

believed will fall to $68 billion. And this required the administration to come to the Congress and ask for an increase in the debt limit.

MR. SAULNIER: Yes.

THE CHAIRMAN: I am not interested in scoring points on you. But I do want to point out that last year when you were optimistic about the budgetary figures and I was pessimistic about the figures events have proved me to be right and proved you to be wrong. And, therefore, I wonder if this past experience shouldn't make you a little bit more cautious in your estimates of this year.

Another set of questions, addressed to the Director of the Bureau of the Budget similarly illustrates the nature of the Committee's inquiry:[27]

1. What are the major changes in expenditures and revenues contemplated in the President's budget for fiscal year 1960?
2. What assumptions with regard to prices, national income, personal income, corporate profits, and the like, underlie the President's budget?
3. In preparing the budget how have the objectives of the Employment Act of 1946 been taken into account; how is the budget expected to contribute to their achievement?
4. What effect are changes in the budget estimated to have on the gross national product and on Federal revenues?

Criticism of the administration's efforts to keep expenditures down by cutting nondefense programs illustrates disagreement as to the best way of meeting the rising costs of government. Like many economists who point to the slowdown in national economic growth as reflected in GNP, Senator O'Mahoney advocated the expansion rather than the restriction of federal programs on the assumption that this policy will stimulate more private economic activity and increased tax revenues. The following exchange between Senator O'Mahoney and the Director of the Bureau of the Budget illustrates this basic conflict in economic policy; it follows a colloquy in which the Senator had deplored the administration's 1959 budget cutback on natural resource development:[28]

SENATOR O'MAHONEY: Well, sir, if Soviet Russia is concentrating ... on a drive to increase the utilization of the water that is running to waste in Russia and in Siberia, and we are stopping conservation of that water, doesn't that bring about a rather surprising situation?

MR. STANS: Senator, I dislike very much differing with you on this; but I don't believe we are stopping the conservation of water. Of course, I am not familiar with what the Soviets are doing. But I am sure the gentleman will agree that they started out very much behind us; and perhaps they have much more to do, too.

SENATOR O'MAHONEY: Oh, there is no doubt about that. But isn't it known to the Bureau of the Budget that we are engaged in a cold war with Soviet Russia?

[27] *Ibid.*, p. 1.
[28] *Ibid.*, p. 59.

MR. STANS: Certainly it is.

SENATOR O'MAHONEY: An economic war?

MR. STANS: Certainly it is.

SENATOR O'MAHONEY: Isn't it known to the Bureau of the Budget that the interest on the national debt for 1960 will be greater than ever before?

MR. STANS: Yes, it is.

SENATOR O'MAHONEY: Isn't it known to the Bureau of the Budget that the public debt as set forth in the budget for 1960 will be higher than ever before?

MR. STANS: Yes. And it will require an increase in the debt ceiling again.

SENATOR O'MAHONEY: Well, if it be true, as you have just said, that the public debt is getting greater, that the interest on the public debt is getting greater, and that we are finding it more difficult to balance the budget, doesn't it follow that we ought to have a policy that would direct the expenditure of budgetary funds to the development of new opportunities to increase production and increase the receipts of domestic industry?

In addition to government officials, the Committee heard testimony from bankers, university professors, farm, business and labor union representatives, and staff members of private research organizations such as the Committee for Economic Development. The resulting 787 pages of testimony and illustrative materials would seem to ensure that the Committee members receive a broad and authoritative critique of the administration's economic assumptions and policies and the rationality of its budgetary efforts to carry them out. Yet, we shall see in Chapter 23 that Congressional review and authorization of the huge federal budget has many shortcomings and that legislative "control" of the budget is tenuous.

CONGRESSIONAL REVIEW OF MILITARY POLICY

In view of the vast amounts now being spent for armaments and the maintenance of armed forces around the world, a special look at Congress' role in fiscal policy determination in this area seems warranted. In 1959, 46 billion dollars were obligated for major national security programs; this amounted to 63 per cent of the entire federal budget.[29] The Department of Defense's total personnel strength, civilian and military, was 3,600,000.[30] In the military sector, Congress' posture had changed radically since the early 1930's when defense spending was treated on a year-by-year, piecemeal basis. A position of relative isolation even amid growing international tension and the depressed economic conditions which persisted until World War II contributed to its earlier attitude. During World War II, of course, Congress authorized anything the military requested, on the ground that national survival was at stake

[29] *Ibid.*, p. 703.
[30] *Ibid.*, p. 704.

and rational expenditures and civilian control were secondary. Only toward the end of the war did Congressional criticism begin to appear, mainly through Senator Truman's Special Committee to Investigate the National Defense Program. By mid-1943, Truman could declare that the military forces "know how to waste money better than any other organization I have ever had anything to do with. . . . I could stand here all afternoon and give example after example showing that tremendous sums of money are simply being thrown away with a scoop shovel.[31]

However, during the four years following World War II, Congress did limit military spending to amounts ranging from fourteen billion dollars in 1947 to twelve billion dollars in 1950. However, this level was still some twelve times higher than peace-time spending in 1939. By 1951, however, the cold war psychology had been generally accepted by Congress, and military spending began to climb at a phenomenal rate. Congress' posture now became less one of initiative and direction of military policy than one of fearful reaction to a succession of world events that were beyond its control; such factors included the Korean War, the Russian development of atomic and hydrogen bombs, the advance of communism in many parts of the world, and Russia's military and industrial progress so dramatically symbolized by the sputnik. In addition, questions of global military strategy, weapons development, and preparedness had become increasingly technical, involving issues that Congressmen were unable to scrutinize incisively. Equally important, many Congressmen were not prepared to accept the responsibility for limiting the preparedness of the military forces in the face of Russian and Chinese power. For example, in 1947, Styles Bridges, chairman of the Senate Appropriations Committee, said:

I would not wish to have on my conscience or on my shoulders the responsibility that we here in the Senate of the United States did not take the necessary steps to develop and modernize the great striking air force which must be the spearhead of defense and offense in any action in which we may become involved.[32]

Senator O'Daniel said similarly, "I don't think this is the time to quibble regarding the amount of money necessary to furnish airplanes and all the other weapons we need . . .[33]

In 1946 this psychology resulted in Congress overruling the President, who had recommended a 55-group air arm, in favor of the 70-group air establishment requested by the Air Force. In this case, even the Com-

[31] *Congressional Record*, 89 (June 29, 1943), p. 6706; cited in Elias Huzar, *The Purse and the Sword* (Ithaca: Cornell University Press, 1950), p. 163.

[32] *Congressional Record*, 94 (May 6, 1948), pp. 5402–5403; cited in Huzar, *The Purse and the Sword*, p. 181.

[33] *Ibid.*, pp. 5404–5.

mander-in-Chief was unable to carry out his military policy. For our purpose the major policy implication here was the legislators' decision to build up one arm of the services, the Air Force, vis-à-vis the traditional services. Since the latter also had a claim to roughly one-third of the military pie, this meant an over-all increase in military appropriations. Moreover, when the Air Force was so favored, the Navy, which also had its air arm, was also provided a logical basis for larger requests for its air units. Thus, while Congressmen publicly criticized military policy and administration, they continued during the late 1940's to authorize appropriations for defense.[34] Their much vaunted theme of "economy and efficiency" became even less relevant in the face of international realities.

In recent years, the military budget has become the "single most important contact between the military and Congress." We are told that it affords Congress the opportunity to consider and lay down the broad lines of military policy and to review in exhaustive detail military procedure and administration.[35] While this judgment seems somewhat overdrawn, as the subsequent discussion suggests, certainly the question of national defense and military spending have become the most important fiscal policy issues faced by Congress. Evaluation of these issues is carried out through the committees on armed services and the committees on appropriations, in both Houses of Congress. The work of these committees will now be considered.

The House Armed Services Committee. The working philosophy of the House Armed Services Committee is explicit in the following comment by its venerable chairman, Carl Vinson:

Where do we look mainly in this country for the best judgment on what is needed for an adequate national defense? The ultimate responsibility for the executive branch rests, of course, with the President. But his is not the expert military view. It can never be so, nor does our system so intend. Our top source for military judgment is the Joint Chiefs of Staff who, under the law, are charged among other things with the Nation's strategic and logistic planning. It is these men, who have risen to the top in the Nation's armed forces after a generation of experience and effort in military life, to whom we must look and to whom the President must look, for the most authoritative advice on our national-defense requirements.[36]

This being so, the Chairman tends to set the President's recommendations against those of the Joint Chiefs of Staff and to recommend a figure

---

[34] Huzar, *The Purse and the Sword*, pp. 199–206.

[35] Samuel P. Huntington, *The Soldier and the State: The Theory and Politics of Civil-Military Relations* (Cambridge: Harvard University Press, 1957), p. 407.

[36] *Congressional Record*, **95** (March 30, 1949), p. 3540; cited in Huntington, *The Soldier and the State*, pp. 415–16.

somewhere between. Vinson's reliance upon military judgments suggests the common tendency for alliances to develop between substantive committees and their administrative agencies.[37] In the military appropriations process, unlike those in most other substantive areas, the appropriations committees are permitted to make substantial changes in the policy set down by the armed services committees.[38] While some critics feel that the appropriations committee have used this freedom only to evaluate administrative details, Huntington argues that "Congress also gives considered and effective attention to the major issues of military policy involved in the budget."[39] The following analysis should be set against this judgment.

A look at hearings before the House Armed Services Committee suggests the character of its inquiry and the sources of its information. The following remarks of Chairman Vinson suggest the rapport between him and military leaders, built up over his long service as chairman of the Committee. In a session on the general posture of the military defense system, he opened the hearing and welcomed the Secretary of Defense as follows:[40]

Now, after discussion with some of my colleagues [*sic*] in the Department of Defense . . . I have reached the decision that the proper way to commence it [the hearing] will be first to permit Secretary McElroy to present his views, publicly, and then we will go into executive [secret] session. Then we will have the views of General Twining. And then later on, we will go back into public session to question Secretary McElroy. Now, with that understanding we will proceed. Members of the committee, all of you know our distinguished Secretary of the Department of Defense, Mr. McElroy. . . . The committee welcomes this opportunity for you to present to the committee and the public your views with reference to our military posture, the defense of the nation.

The Secretary then outlined the "basic policy" of the Department of Defense as follows:[41]

1. Protecting the ability of this country to retaliate with large weapons in case of an outbreak of general war;
2. Providing a capacity to apply military force promptly in various local conflict areas of the free world similar to Lebanon and Taiwan of the past year; and
3. To seek these objectives without in any way overlooking the need of continental air defense and for maintenance of open sea lanes.

[37] Huntington cites Vinson as one of a House group who "support stronger military forces in general and who oppose executive cuts in any defense budget," *ibid.*, p. 419.

[38] *Ibid.*, p. 407.

[39] *Ibid.*, p. 407.

[40] House Armed Services Committee, 86th Cong., 1st sess., *Hearings* (Washington, D.C.: U.S. Government Printing Office, 1959).

[41] *Ibid.*

In some eleven pages of prepared testimony, the Secretary next reviewed strategy and military weapons being used and developed to achieve these ends. He concluded with the declaration: "Our forces are fully capable of carrying out their assigned missions and will continue to have this capability during the foreseeable future."[42] Among his important policy statements was the military's continued reliance upon manned bombers because, "they . . . will continue to be an important element of our retaliatory forces for some years to come."[43] An air-to-ground missile, with the unlikely name of Hound Dog, would permit bombers to remain "hundreds of miles away from the target and deliver a weapon with a very large destructive power."[44] The Atlas missile, was "moving ahead even faster than originally expected."[45] A Polaris submarine would be at sea, ready to fire, in the latter part of 1960.[46]

Following Mr. McElroy's statement, the Committee raised (among others) the following questions on military policy and budget:

1. The Committee was concerned about the new budgeting requirement that the military submit their requests in broad "program" terms, principally with the fact that this could mean that appropriations would no longer continue to be made to each of the armed services, but instead that the Appropriations Committee would be authorized to make appropriations directly to the Department of Defense. (The Committee was assured by the Secretary that no such change would occur.)
2. The Chairman noted that whereas the Congress had recommended that the regular army be maintained at "not less than 900,000 men during the fiscal year 1959," the Secretary of Defense had reduced the size of ground forces to 870,000 men. (The Secretary explained that there are ". . . two groups in Government to which the Secretary of Defense is responsive. One of them is the Congress and the other is the President." In this case the instructions of the President to reduce the forces had been "overriding.")
3. The Committee was concerned about the large "administrative tail" in our Army whereby of some 870,000 men, 394,000 were engaged in noncombatant, supporting jobs of various kinds. (The Secretary assured the Committee that Defense was working on this problem.)
4. Several Committee members were concerned with missile development and our comparative position with Russia in the missile race. (Here, the Secretary reassured the Committee that ". . . our best defensive posture in the deterrence of general war is one in which we have a combination of a variety of delivery systems for large weapons. . . .")
5. Congressman Gavin was worried about the true influence of Congress' wishes upon military policy as revealed by the following comments:[47]

[42] *Ibid.*, p. 801.
[43] *Ibid.*, p. 792.
[44] *Ibid.*
[45] *Ibid.*, p. 793.
[46] *Ibid.*
[47] *Ibid.*, p. 814–15.

MR. GAVIN: Mr. Secretary, it seems to me that this cutback on the Army is quite drastic. Congress has spoken and indicated to the Department of Defense that they wanted the Army maintained at a strength of around 900,000. Now some of us, like our Chairman, have been around here a long time. And what I am trying to determine [is]: What is the use of us sitting around here debating on these problems of national defense, and when we reach a conclusion and we make a suggestion or recommendations, that one or two or three men over there can change the whole setup and say, "You can't have it. You are going back to 870,000." Now, what I am trying to find out is: Do your people over there respect the wishes and the will of Congress concerning matters of national defense . . . ?

SECRETARY McELROY: I am sure there is no question, Mr. Gavin, about the respect of the people in the Defense Department for the people in the Armed Services Committees and throughout Congress. . . . This decision was taken . . . by the President, with full justification, in my opinion, out of the rights of the Commander in Chief to set the size of the forces.

The Committee also raised related questions about Congress' military policy role vis-à-vis the chief executive, with several of the Congressmen expressing the view that they had delegated too much authority to the President, his political aides, and professional military leaders.[48] Representative Hardy, for example, made the following comments to the Secretary of Defense:[49]

MR. HARDY: You have the responsibility for operating the Department. I don't think the Congress wants to take that responsibility. But I am a little concerned about the extent to which the Department is trying to take over the responsibility of the Congress to legislate. . . . I have listened with a great deal of interest to your words of reassurance based on your judgments and I respect your judgments, but I don't think they can take the place of the judgments which we are charged with performing ourselves on behalf of the American people. . . . I look back a few years to the period immediately preceding Korea and I recall that we had another Secretary of Defense up here reassuring Congress. His name was Mr. Louis Johnson, in another administration. And I recall that he sat out there, in that same chair that you are occupying, and he wasn't going to hurt the Department of Defense. He was just going to cut the fat out. And he had us in one miserable situation when Korea broke out. I am not at all sure you aren't getting us unwittingly into the same sort of situation. I think we have a responsibility for exercising some judgment and a reasonable basis to hope that the judgments that we exercise as representatives of the people may be carried out. I am a little disturbed by the discussion . . . yesterday in connection with the extent to which the Department may or may not ignore the mandate of Congress. . . .

To sum up, the Armed Services Committee seemed divided both as to its satisfaction with and its knowledge of military policy as outlined by the Secretary of Defense. Some members appeared to be blissfully con-

[48] *Ibid.*, pp. 827–36; 861–67.
[49] *Ibid.*, pp. 861–62.

fident of the judgments made by the President, the Secretary of Defense, and his military aides. Others seemed to feel that the problems of technical judgment and the drastic costs of inadequate preparation dictated a reluctant acceptance of military judgment and huge appropriations. At several points the Secretary of Defense reminded them, as did Chairman Vinson, that their questions raised delicate issues, that they could only be discussed in the executive session, that, after all, security was expensive, all of which added to this aura of mystery and commitment. The quality of Committee questions ranged widely, from incisive probing into the administration's uncertain missile program and the problem of reaching an appropriate balance between military and executive initiative and Congressional control, to vacuous generalizations about the need for "team" play and mutual self-congratulations about patriotism, political impartiality, and good intentions.[50]

While some major policy issues were touched upon, such as manpower ratios of the various services, the missile program, the rationality of our reliance upon foreign air bases, problems of legislative participation in military policy, and the possible effects of the administration's economy program, no definitive answers were reached. And there seemed an undercurrent of frustration on the Committee's part because of its limited role and the difficulty of making judgments and proposals that would make good their responsibility to the public. On the positive side, even though the initiative clearly remained in the administration's hands, the Secretary of Defense was surely made aware of Congressional opinion on these matters.

The Appropriations Committees. The other major instrument of Congressional inquiry and control of military policy is the appropriations committees of the House and Senate, which we are told, have more latitude with requests from the military establishment than with those of other substantive programs. As we have seen, since World War II the

---

[50] *Ibid.*, pp. 822–23:

MR. RIVERS: Well, politics has never had any part on this committee and I don't believe you are going to let political considerations distort your judgment in the Department of Defense.

SECRETARY MCELROY: On this kind of thing—this is my country as well as it is yours.

MR. RIVERS: That is right.

SECRETARY MCELROY: And I am pretty much interested in it.

MR. RIVERS: Absolutely. And on the battlefield we are all the same.

SECRETARY MCELROY: Yes.

MR. RIVERS: And I want to congratulate you for that statement, and for the job you have done, and I hope you live a long time.

SECRETARY MCELROY: I hope you do, too, Mr. Rivers.

Air Force has received generous appropriations in recognition of Congress' belief that it was the most essential element in contemporary military strategy, making possible the swift delivery of atomic weapons over tremendous distances.[51]

For this reason we shall illustrate legislative policy influence from hearings on the Air Force appropriations. Here again, the following analysis can only be random, since the subject covers an immense range of military activities carried on by all branches of the military establishment. Chairman Mahon began with the usual Congressional obeisance to economy and efficiency: "As all of you know there is a great demand in and out of Congress for increased efficiency in government, and for reduced spending wherever reduced spending can be safely achieved. Our emphasis will be on ways and means of reducing the defense budget without impairing our defense program."[52]

Preceding this hearing, Secretary of the Air Force Quarles and General Nathan Twining, Chief of Staff, U.S. Air Force, had outlined for the Committee the Air Force programs and the underlying assumptions. Testimony was begun by Mr. Lyle S. Garlock, Assistant Secretary of the Air Force for Financial Management, who gave the Committee a summary of the major program categories in the Air Force budget. These included such elements as the purchases of new aircraft, overprogramming (a kind of reserve fund budgeted at 363 million dollars, to meet unexpected contingencies in the Air Force's procurement program), research and development, operation and maintenance of aircraft and installations, payroll for civilian personnel, and unforeseen events such as the Hungarian airlift in 1957, military personnel, reserve personnel, air national guard, the two warning systems SAGE and DEW, family housing, and management improvement.[53]

To carry through these and related programs for 1958 Assistant Secretary Garlock requested nearly 16½ billion dollars, which, as he put it, "we estimate as the minimum with which we can perform our mission . . . and can continuously increase the effectiveness of our airpower, while concurrently maintaining operational readiness at all times."[54] Garlock

---

[51] As Representative Clarence Cannon, Chairman of the House Appropriations put it, "The only way to avoid war is to have available at any instant the means of striking swiftly and surely and effectively at any distance. And the atomic bomb serviced by land-based bombers is the only weapon which can insure that protection. As long as we have both we can and will maintain the peace of the world," cited in Huzar, *The Purse and the Sword*, p. 189.

[52] House Subcommittee of the Committee on Appropriations, 85th Cong., 1st sess., *Hearings*, "Department of the Air Force, Appropriations for 1958" (Washington, D.C.: U.S. Government Printing Office, 1957), p. 1. (As it turned out, the Air Force asked for $16,481 million for 1958, and the final appropriation was raised to $17,383 million).

[53] *Ibid.*, pp. 3–19.

[54] *Ibid.*, p. 2.

was followed by several other individuals, all concerned with budget and programming in the Chief of Staff's Office, who discussed various aspects of the programs listed above. For example, developments in financial management were outlined by the Deputy Chief of Staff, Comptroller; the Director of Budget explained the steps involved in preparing the budget, which was presented in broad program terms. Charts and graphs were liberally used by these specialists, most of whom were military officers of general's rank.

Committee members raised some pointed questions on the "overprogramming" policy, whereby appropriations which were not spent might be "recouped" and then spent for other programs than those initially authorized by Congress:[55]

MR. MAHON: Does not this overprogramming proposal represent a confession on the part of the Air Force that you are not able to budget with sufficient accuracy for items required?

MR. GARLOCK: I don't consider it that, sir. . . . I consider it good budgeting practice. The difficulty is in the research and development and production people being unable to forecast their state of the art 18 to 24 months in advance.

Referring to the fact that the Air Force had carried over from the previous four years some four and one-half billion dollars, one Committee member said:[56]

MR. WHITTEN: When you reach away back to these open-end appropriations, as you might say, or carryovers, it is actually recoupment. It is a matter of recouping for new use money that was appropriated for an entirely different purpose sometime prior to that time; is that correct?

MR. GARLOCK: That is not true. . . . On a big contract there always tends to be something left over when you finally clean it up. So, you clear it out and say . . . there was $1 million or $5 million left . . . you deobligate that, and it is still used for the same general purpose, and it is specifically justified before this Committee before it is again used.

Another member raised questions about the accuracy of estimates:[57]

MR. SCRIVNER: Reprogramming, of course, we see year after year. Still it is a little hard to explain and sometimes it is a little hard to understand because you will come in here . . . and say, "This is how much we have asked for and this is the number of planes of this type we will buy." There is never any doubt expressed about it. Perhaps six months or a year later you come in and say, "Yes, I know we said that but we will not do it." That has been going on for years. . . . After you serve on the Committee a long time sometimes you do get a little skeptical about how factual some of the presentations are.

55 *Ibid.*, p. 58.
56 *Ibid.*, p. 65.
57 *Ibid.*, p. 73.

In the main, a survey of the hearing gives the impression that the Committee members confine themselves to procedure and management rather than to policy questions. There was little questioning as to the need for a given program, and when there was, the Congressmen were no match for the military specialists who justified and explained it. When questions are raised, they are often put in a somewhat defensive tone, usually accompanied by the admonition that the legislator doesn't want to do anything that will impair national defense.[58] This posture is suggested in the following examples: Mr. Mahon had written the Assistant Secretary of Defense raising questions about the costs of shipping servicemen's automobiles overseas, amounting in 1956 to $16,490,249 for the three services. In his reply, the Assistant Secretary concluded that any change was unfeasible because "the automobile is part of the American way of life"; any alternative would result in "unreasonable hardship to individuals"; and "the automobile becomes even more meaningful in our overseas bases where the transportation systems are inadequate, erratic, and nonexistent" (sic).[59]

Pursuing his interest in this phase of budget policy, the Chairman asked:[60]

MR. MAHON: The attitude of the Air Force is that the present system should be continued?
GENERAL LIGON: That is correct.
MR. MAHON: Does the Air Force have any possible recommendation as to some slight improvement? There is hardly anything that cannot be improved.
MAJOR RICE: We know of no way it can better be handled.
GENERAL LIGON: I think it is the American standard of living. . . .

Similar questions were raised, with similar results, about the cost of shipping household effects of servicemen abroad, estimated for 1958 at $40,238,000 for the Air Force alone.

Conclusions on Congress' Role. In generalizing from these examples of legislative participation in military policy, one must conclude with Chairman Vinson that it is to the President and the top military leaders that we look for "the best judgment on what is needed for an adequate national defense." While the legislators are given rather complete briefings on military policy and the resulting programs and appropriations needs, the context of this legislative scrutiny is so prestructured that their

[58] *Ibid.*, p. 75. As one member said, "I questioned some of them [changes from the original estimates] when they were first presented and I was told that elimination of them would almost wreck the Air Force. . . . Anything you do means it will be detrimental to national defense, and after all the years I have put in on this I surely would not do anything knowing that it would do that. Yet that is always the charge we run up against."
[59] *Ibid.*, pp. 511–13.
[60] *Ibid.*, pp. 514–15.

examinations and recommendations can only be of limited effectiveness. It is true that this picture of Congressional weakness seems peculiar to questions of defense, which are different from ordinary programs in order of magnitude, legislative competence, the vast stakes at issue, and the terrible penalty of inadequacy. Nonetheless, since defense costs represent so large a part of the federal budget, the uniqueness of the military defense complex is of little consolation; indeed, the need for understanding, control, and the assumption of responsibility on the legislator's part becomes even greater than with more traditional programs. Additional data on this problem will be presented in Chapter 23 on the budget authorization phase.

BIBLIOGRAPHY

BURKHEAD, JESSE. "Informing Government with Economics," 18, *Public Administration Review* (Autumn, 1958), pp. 340–49.

COMMITTEE FOR ECONOMIC DEVELOPMENT. *Control of Federal Government Expenditures.* New York: 1955.

KIMMEL, LEWIS H. *Federal Budget and Fiscal Policy 1789–1958.* Washington, D.C.: 1959.

MARTIN, ROSCOE C. *From Forest to Front Page.* University, Alabama: 1956.

NATIONAL MUNICIPAL LEAGUE. *Model State Constitution.* Rev. ed. New York: 1941. (Watch for new edition.)

RATCHFORD, B. U. *Public Expenditures in Australia.* Durham, N.C.: 1959.

RIDLEY, C. E. *The Role of the City Manager in Policy Determination.* Chicago: 1958.

SMITHIES, ARTHUR. *The Budgetary Process in the United States.* New York: 1955.

WILBERN, YORK. "Administration in State Governments," in *The Forty-eight States: Their Tasks as Policy Makers and Administrators.* New York: 1955, pp. 111–37.

CHAPTER 22

The Budgetary Process: Preparation

In this chapter we turn to the preparation of the executive budget by the administrative branch for presentation to the legislature for authorization. Although the process is similar at all levels of government, we shall focus mainly on the federal system, since it is probably the most advanced in this area and it deals with problems on so vast a scale, even in comparison with big states such as New York and California. In the federal government, as in advanced state and local systems, a special office, the Bureau of the Budget, has the responsibility for preparing a coherent financial program for the President, who presents it to Congress. Coordinating the disparate requests of many departments and agencies in such an office requires centralization to ensure that the combined requests remain within estimated revenue and that they reflect generally the political preferences of the chief executive. This policy of presenting a synthesized executive budget is comparatively recent, and for this reason we turn first to a brief account of its development and main features.

THE REORGANIZATION MOVEMENT

Beginning about 1920, efforts were made to centralize federal fiscal planning by structural and procedural innovations. Before this time each of several departments and legislative committees proposed legislation that required appropriations. There was no single office to coordinate these appropriations and weigh them against demands of either politics or revenue.

Another unhappy factor was the *absence of budgetary accounting,* a process designed to gather and assimilate information upon which administrative decisions could be based. In the first decades of this century most governmental accounting systems failed to do this. At best they gave an accurate report of how much cash had been taken in or paid out, but they often failed to achieve even this rudimentary objective.

On the state and local level, accounting activities were under an officer who had been elected without reference to vocational qualifications. Nor were things much better at the national level. Indeed, federal government budgetary accounting is just now beginning to achieve maturity.

No one was charged with the responsibility of pulling the expenditures together into a coordinated statement or report, let alone a plan. Under this system of legislative anarchy, there was no curb on the lobbyists, the seekers of pork-barrel appropriations, or the pleaders for special interests. Everyone except the public was represented. There was no one to take an over-all view and say, "While this proposal for expenditure has its merits, the current condition of the Treasury does not justify it in the light of other obligations." It was this weakness that the budgetary reforms of the 1920's sought to remedy through a system of structural and procedural changes.

The Executive Budget. Since the most serious weakness had been the absence of any collective financial plan, the major reform proposed an executive budget in which the chief executive would be called upon to submit annually an all-inclusive budget plan to the legislature. This plan was to be submitted to the legislature early enough so that it could be scrutinized and authorized before the beginning of the coming fiscal year. The proposed executive budget was to include estimates for both revenues and expenditures, and in principle at least, these were to balance. If deficits were to be incurred, they were to be planned for, and means of financing them were to be recommended by the chief executive.

Integrated Financial Structure. The second proposal for overcoming existing inadequacies was the establishment of an integrated financial structure in which financial activities were to be placed under a single director of finance. This was a reaction against the extreme diffusion of the financial function, which was often shared by several independent, elected officials. The department of finance would include bureaus dealing with: (1) budget planning; (2) accounting; (3) treasury functions, including tax collection; (4) purchase and supply, and (5) assessment.[1]

Although the concept of an integrated department of finance had influential advocates, and still commands favor, the widespread resistance to appointing comptrollers, auditors, and treasurers soon refocused reformist efforts toward achieving integration within the existing structure.[2] As a result, improvement in financial administration during the last two decades has resulted more from improved coordination than from in-

[1] *Model City Charter* (New York: National Municipal League, 1941), Art. VI.
[2] The progress of financial reorganization in the states is outlined in *Reorganizing State Government* (Chicago: Council of State Governments, 1950), pp. 110–22.

tegrated structure. Great progress has been made in establishing budget agencies under the chief executive, but the *accounting function* has often remained under some independent agency or has been divided between several agencies with ill-defined jurisdictional boundaries. An example of this is the situation in the federal government where (again because of the cultural myths of the wisdom of a separation of powers) some accounting functions are placed in an agency responsible to Congress, the General Accounting Office, and others in the Treasury Department. Because neither of these agencies developed an effective accounting system, the Bureau of the Budget had to get into the act. This it did by tactfully organizing a committee of the three agencies, which over a period of years has developed a coordinated approach to budgetary accounting. This device has recently been recognized by Congress, which placed the responsibility for developing budgetary accounting throughout the federal government in the Bureau of the Budget.

THE BUREAU OF THE BUDGET

At the federal level, the staff agency for achieving the major objectives of the reformers is the Bureau of the Budget, established in 1921 under the Budget and Accounting Act. Located in the Executive Office of the President, the Bureau has two principal functions: to prepare the President's annual budget for presentation at the beginning of each session of Congress and to encourage the entire administrative branch to improve its management practices. Under its first director the Bureau had a rather limited view of its function, restricting itself in the main to technical questions of economy and efficiency. As Director Dawes said, "the Bureau of the Budget is concerned only with the humbler and routine business of government."[3] After 1937, however, the Bureau's role began to be more broadly conceived as a staff arm of the President, charged with the review of the substantive programs of the departments and agencies. Since then it has increased in both size and influence, as an analysis of its reorganization in 1952 and its role in program review will show.[4]

The Bureau's Reorganization in 1952. In 1952 a functional division of activities was set up to bring about coordination and consultation between the "offices" and "divisions" of the bureau. The "divisions" are charged with broad general purpose functions: International, Military, Resources and Civil Works, Commerce and Finance, and Labor and

[3] Charles G. Dawes, *The First Year of the Budget of the United States* (New York: Harper & Bros., 1923), p. xi.

[4] For a review of the Bureau's history and organization, see Jesse Burkhead, *Government Budgeting* (New York: John Wiley & Sons, Inc., 1956), pp. 288–304.

Welfare. The "offices" are set up to deal with the "process" activities of Legislative Reference, Management and Organization, Budget Review, and Statistical Standards. The Office of Accounting was added in 1956.

The Legislative Reference Office reflects the importance of the bureaucracy in the legislative process. It was originally set up to prevent the executive agencies from dealing directly with Congress without the President's knowledge or consent. Today it "reviews and coordinates" the views of the executive agencies on legislative matters and maintains liaison between Congress and the President on most legislative items. It also coordinates the preparation and presentation of bureau testimony before Congressional committees. The key words in the job descriptions for each of the offices are "coordinate" and "review." Thus the Office of Budget Review "coordinates the review of annual, supplemental and deficiency estimates." The Office of Management and Organization assists the director in the formulation and coordination of programs for improving management and organization in the Executive Branch. The Office of Statistical Standards coordinates the statistical activities of the government by reviewing questionnaires and statistical procedures.

Bureau's New Prestige. The Task Force of the first Hoover Commission, under the leadership of A. E. Buck, criticized the Bureau of the Budget. Among other things, it was accused of poor relationships with Congress, departure from its role of neutrality in advocating partisan White House objectives, general bureaucratic inertia, and lack of leadership. Whatever may have been the justice of these criticisms, the fact seems to be that the Bureau has now achieved an added prestige, as reflected by the leadership thrust upon it in carrying out the budgeting and accounting recommendations of the two Hoover reports. In the executive branch reorganizations of 1950 and 1956, Congress gave the Bureau a key role in bringing about the desired improvements. This new legislation called upon the head of each executive agency, in consultation with the Director of the Bureau of the Budget, to take whatever action would be necessary to accomplish the following objectives:

1. Achieve consistency in accounting and budget classifications.
2. Bring about synchronization between accounting and budget classifications and organizational structure.
3. Provide information on performance and program costs to justify budget requests.

Agency heads were also instructed by this law to cause, as soon as practicable and in accordance with principles and standards prescribed by the Comptroller General, their accounts "to be maintained on an accrual basis to show the resources, liabilities, and costs of operation

. . . with a view toward facilitating the preparation of cost-based budgets. . . ."

In the fall of 1956 the Bureau of the Budget issued its Bulletin No. 57–5 designed to carry out the above instructions by Congress.[5] Legislation was enacted in 1956 that set the base for implementing the recommendations of the second Hoover Commission. But the most significant development was the emerging role of the Bureau of the Budget.

Budget Bureau Leadership. The Bureau of the Budget is becoming the management staff arm of the federal government, both by default and by general consent. While the Bureau has long had an office of Management and Organization, it has tended to regard its modus operandi as purely staff in nature. This was partly due to the venerable historical status of the Treasury (the Hamilton-Mellon myth, etc.), and it also reflected the fact that the Budget and Accounting Act of 1921 specifically charged the General Accounting Office with supervision of accounting. The Bureau has always been hesitant about seeming to encroach upon the historical functions of these two agencies. Nevertheless it has gradually been realized that the federal government did not have an effective system of budgetary accounting and reporting, as pointed out by the task force of the first Hoover Commission.

The findings of the Commission confirmed the criticisms of its task force; the Commission pointed out that responsibility for accounting was dispersed among three agencies: (1) the Treasury, responsible for the fiscal accounts; (2) the Comptroller General, with over-all responsibility for administrative accounts; and (3) the departments, almost autonomous in respect to accounting. Thus the Commission recommended that an Accountant General be established under the Secretary of the Treasury with authority to prescribe general accounting methods and to enforce accounting procedures, subject to the approval of the Comptroller General, within the powers conferred upon him by Congress. The Accountant General would take data from agency accounts and prepare reports for the President and Congress which would reflect the government's current financial condition.

The second Hoover Commission reemphasized these points but recommended that the Bureau of the Budget be given responsibility for budgetary accounting and reporting. The amendment to the Budget and Accounting Act in 1956 recognized the primacy of the Bureau while still retaining the Comptroller General's function of approving systems. That the Congress has accepted (although reluctantly) the Bureau's leadership is suggested by reports of the committees dealing with these mat-

---

[5] Bureau of the Budget, *Improvement of Financial Administration in the Federal Government*, (Washington, D.C.: U.S. Government Printing Office, 1956).

ters.[6] In line with the second Hoover Commission's recommendations, an Office of Accounting has been established in the Bureau of the Budget, and an assistant director (a professional accountant) has been brought in from a firm specializing in industrial practice.

PREPARING THE EXECUTIVE BUDGET

Now that the organization and the main functions of the Budget Bureau have been outlined, we can turn to the major interest of this chapter, the construction of the President's annual budget. While leadership is exercised by the President through the Bureau, the various departmental budgetary offices are equally concerned with this process.

The Call for Estimates. While there is considerable variation from department to department, the federal budgetary cycle usually takes place over an eighteen-month period, beginning about June of each year, with the completed budget being submitted to Congress in January of the second year following. At the beginning of the cycle, the Budget Bureau sends out a request for budget estimates from the many departments and agencies. This obviously requires advance planning, since the federal agencies are expected to have their estimates for 1963 in the Bureau's hands by September 15, 1961. Thus their planning begins almost two years before the close of the current budget year. Agency estimates are prepared on standard forms, known as the "green sheets," which contain vertical columns showing the figures for the last completed fiscal year, the estimated amounts to be spent during the current year, and the amounts requested for the coming year.

The method of computing the estimates varies. In the large "holding-company" departments such as the Treasury or Health, Education and Welfare, decentralization will go at least as far down as the bureaus—especially in those departments where bureaus enjoy considerable autonomy. Budget planning in some agencies will be decentralized to the regional offices and from there to the field stations. The more decentralized agencies set upper limits of expenditure for field units and ask them to develop plans within the stated amounts. In the centralized agencies the detailed planning will go on almost entirely in Washington. In general, even though the existence of work-load standards in many federal agencies may facilitate budgetary decentralization, Washington is egocentric, and consequently the dominant pulls are toward centralization.

[6] See particularly a Staff Report, Committee on Government Operations, *The Budget Process in the Federal Government*, H. R., 85th Cong., 1st sess. (Washington, D.C.: U.S. Government Printing Office, 1957).

The bureaus and departments have their own fiscal and budget agencies which do the staff work for their chiefs. One of the best known of these is the Office of Budget and Finance of the Department of Agriculture, long headed by the late William A. Jump, a highly respected career civil servant. One of its subunits is the Division of Estimates and Allotments which "analyzes and evaluates agency budget requests and program proposals . . ."[7] Apparently in 1949 most other federal departments did not match Agriculture in this respect, in the opinion of the first Hoover Commission's task force, which complained that the "weakest link in the present budgetary structure of the government . . . is the departmental and agency budget offices."[8] As a matter of fact, comparatively little is known about what goes on in departmental budget planning. The literature of public administration needs more studies of budgeting at the departmental level.[9]

To see how agencies prepare their budget estimates, the Air Force example that follows is instructive.

PREPARING AIR FORCE ESTIMATES. In this department, according to its budget director, the preparation of the annual budget begins with the "call for estimates," which is sent out to major commands in January of each year for the fiscal year beginning eighteen months later.[10] The initial call outlines budget policies and assumptions and cites program information that may be helpful to the budget officers. Estimates from the field come in six months later and are then reviewed by the respective USAF headquarters elements and by the director of the budget. They are reviewed with the following criteria in mind:

1. Air Force policies and attending program guides.
2. Validity of the formulas used in determining command requirements and in converting these into dollar form.
3. Consistency with the object of "optimum economy."
4. Elimination of duplication.

[7] For a description of how this was done in Jump's day, see Verne B. Lewis, *Budgetary Administration in the United States Department of Agriculture* (Chicago: Public Administration Service, 1941), reprinted from John M. Gaus and Leon Wolcott, *Public Administration in the United States Department of Agriculture* (Chicago: Public Administration Service, 1940).

[8] Commission on Organization of the Executive Branch of the Government, *Task Force Report on Fiscal, Budgeting, and Accounting Activities* (Washington, D.C.: U.S. Government Printing Office, 1949), Appendix F, p. 67.

[9] For an excellent example dealing with the military establishment, see Frederick C. Mosher, *Program Budgeting: Theory and Practice* (Chicago: Public Administration Service, 1954).

[10] Subcommittee of the Committee on Appropriations, 85th Cong., 1st sess., *Hearings*, "Department of the Air Force, Appropriations for 1958," (Washington, D.C.: U.S. Government Printing Office, 1957), pp. 22–24; for a detailed analysis of the preparation of military estimates, see Mosher, *Program Budgeting*, pp. 140–65.

The resulting recommendations are then presented for review to the Budget Advisory Committee, chaired by the budget director and including representatives from the major staff units, with the Assistant Secretary for Financial Management sitting in as adviser.[11] "This assures balance among the several financial programs." By the time the estimates reach this Committee, certain refinements have been made in the initial program data upon which the field commands have made their estimates. These adjustments and new information mean that the appropriation requests that go to Congress are based upon different and more current information than those prepared by the field. This facet of the budget preparation process illustrates one of its main characteristics, namely, the revision of estimates at higher levels and the changing premises of preparation as policy modifications come down from the President and the Bureau of the Budget. This is not only unavoidable, but it is good budgetary practice. As Burkhead says, "the budget cycle in any government should be characterized by a flow-up and a flow-back of decisions. Certain kinds of decisions will be made at the operating level and will move up the organizational hierarchy to influence decisions there. At the same time, policy and program decisions will be made at the higher levels, to move down to the operating levels."[12]

The recommendations of the Budget Advisory Council are submitted to the Air Force Council, an advisory body to the Chief of Staff on policy matters. This group includes the Vice Chief of Staff, the five Deputy Chiefs, and the Air Inspector General. Upon occasion, Assistant Chiefs of Staff will also be called in. From this point the estimates go to the Chief of Staff and the Secretary of the Air Force for final approval. The Chief of Staff exercises the final *military* judgment; and at the Secretary level, *fiscal* considerations are "taken into account . . . in greater measure than in the preceding steps in the process." At each successive step, however, the make-up of the committees provides for an "increasingly broader perspective."

At the Secretary's level, a Bureau of the Budget officer enters the picture and reviews the estimates, since "their size and complexity virtually preclude separate reviews in the time remaining to prepare the estimates in final form for review by the President." According to Mosher, this joint review is the most "important and effectual" part of the whole military review system, for the following reasons:[13]

1. It is the first stage at which the budget is viewed in the broad dimension of government financial policy and capability.

[11] For details on military review, see Mosher, *Program Budgeting*, pp. 165–85.
[12] Burkhead, *Government Budgeting*, p. 89.
[13] Mosher, *Program Budgeting*, pp. 183–84.

2. It is the first point at which the operating assumptions and policy of the military are really challenged.
3. The review is detailed and thorough.
4. This is the first complete review by civilians, under civilian authority.

Although these are impressive considerations, the question arises, however, whether this examination does not occur at a stage when the major policies and expenditures are so structured that the Secretary and the Budget Bureau are, like the Congressional committees, hard put to criticize or to make any substantial change in them.

The Budget Bureau's Role. At the same time that the agencies are doing their work, the Budget Bureau is going through its own cycle.[14] In June its officials talk with departmental and agency heads about their money needs for the coming year, thereby giving the Bureau a general picture of major demands. During this time the Director of the Bureau confers with the President and outlines the emerging shape of the entire budget. Clearances for major programs may be requested. Meanwhile the Bureau gets estimates of revenue from various sources such as the Treasury, the Council of Economic Advisors, and the Department of Commerce, which forecasts anticipated federal revenues. A kind of counterpoint goes on between the agencies, the Bureau, and the President and his White House staff. "This is how the 'President's program' is formulated—it emerges and crystallizes as decisions are made; it does not spring full-blown from a planning staff that outlines it in advance."[15]

On the basis of the kind of information acquired from these sources, the Bureau next sends out a policy letter to all agency heads, outlining the economic assumptions upon which their estimates should be based. We can assume that these are a preview, in more detailed terms, of the objectives that will emerge as the President's Economic Report. Specific kinds of programs may be mentioned as falling within these terms; that is, the agency is told that it may expect approval of certain kinds of public programs that the administration feels are warranted in line with its policy and the general economic outlook. The policy letter also includes appropriation ceilings for the major agencies and departments. Like the policy directives and estimations of expected federal revenues, these ceilings are subject to change as new trends appear, particularly in the international sphere. As the director of the Air Force budget concluded, "in the course of the Office, Secretary of Defense–Bureau of the Budget review . . . evaluations are in the light of policies, assumptions, planning factors, economic estimates, et cetera, as they then exist rather than as

[14] The following chronology is mainly from Burkhead, *Government Budgeting,* pp. 88–96.
[15] *Ibid.,* p. 91.

they existed earlier in the budget preparation cycle. . . . Obviously, all the steps involved in the process . . . alter materially the character and the magnitude of the estimates, so that what appears in the President's budget will differ substantially from what is initially prepared by our major commands."[16]

While the departmental budget officers are working out their respective estimates, Bureau specialists in their substantive field are available for consultation. Within the departments, hearings are held, and revisions are made in the light of changes both from the policy level above and from departmental sources. In the big holding-company departments, which have many discrete functions and bureaus, one sees political and power struggles that are different only in scale from those that characterize budget preparation for the entire bureaucracy. It is quite clear from the legislative hearings on appropriations that interest group and legislative friends have often been alerted by a given agency to raise questions about its treatment in the proposed budget. Those who prepare the Executive budget are well aware of the relative political strength of the agencies, and this awareness becomes part of the assumptions that guide them during the budget construction phase. Occasionally, the President may go to bat for agencies, such as the U.S. Information Services, which have little political support; but as events have shown, even his active support cannot overcome their strategic and political weakness.[17]

Returning to the Budget Bureau's activities, we find that the departmental estimates begin to come in during early September. They are carefully reviewed by examiners who have special training and experience in the program area concerned; soon after this, the Bureau begins its own hearings with the major financial officers of the agencies who come in to explain their budgets. Usually the Bureau has already sent a memorandum to these officials, outlining the main questions that will be raised about their estimates.[18] What happens here is a sort of preliminary bout for the main event, the hearings before the legislative committees, with the important difference that Bureau representatives are usually not involved in the latter phase. In any event, the operating officials must justify their requests before the Bureau in the light of Presidential policy. While the operating people and the Bureau examiners aim at consensus, major differences sometimes arise, and these are referred to higher levels. However, the two groups are not obliged to agree on the final amounts for a given agency or its major programs; in the military establishment, for example, "there have been, in each year, im-

---

[16] *Hearings,* "Department of the Air Force Appropriations for 1958," p. 23.
[17] See Chapter 8 for an outline of the Information Services' debacle in 1958.
[18] Burkhead, *Government Budgeting,* p. 93.

portant and sizable differences totaling some billions of dollars. In the majority of such instances, the Bureau's figures are lower."[19]

The Bureau examiner's recommendations are finally reviewed by a committee, organized for that purpose, of members from the several Bureau divisions and from the Director's staff. At this point the operating agency officials may ask for a reappraisal of their rejected or modified requests, and those with grievances may even appeal to the President to reverse the Bureau's decision. Finally, the President reviews the budget and from it prepares his annual budget message, which is given to the departments and agencies during November. Latest revenue estimates are brought in by the Treasurer and the Council of Economic Advisers, and these may result in last-minute changes in the appropriation authorizations by the President and the Bureau.

The President's Budget. In the last stage of the budget's preparation, the Bureau pulls together the multitude of estimates and supporting documents into final form for printing and for eventual presentation in late January to Congress and the legislative committees. The resulting volume is awe-inspiring: In 1958, for example, it consisted of some 1,200 pages of policies, programs, and their dollar indexes, amounting to 73 billion dollars. The President's budget message comprises the first section of the document. In the message he outlines his analysis of the major aspects of the budget such as national defense, commerce, housing, and natural resource development. In each major program area he sets down his recommendations and a brief explanation of the assumptions underlying them. Relatively little consideration is given to revenues; the President focuses on programs and attending expenditures. Little is said about tax policy; in the 1958 budget only two pages were devoted to "revenue policy," prefaced by the President's highly generalized judgment that "tax rates are still too high and that we should look forward to further tax reductions as soon as they can be accomplished within a sound budget policy."[20]

EVALUATIONS OF THE PRESIDENT'S BUDGET. In comparison with the chaotic situation existing during the reform movement beginning about 1910, the present Executive budget is a miracle of precision and progress, enabling the President to exercise major policy leadership, as he must in our system if leadership is to occur. This condition reflects the lack of party discipline, the traditional separatism and conflict between Executive and legislature, the lack of strong central direction in our political parties, and the fact that the President is, after all, the only nationally elected political leader. The Executive budget gives the President a

[19] Mosher, *Program Budgeting*, p. 182.
[20] Budget of the United States (1958) "Message of the President," p. M8.

great psychological and strategic advantage in fulfilling this necessary leadership role. It enables him to present a coherent, well-worked-out political and financial program that Congress finds difficult to set aside. It enables him to maintain some degree of order in his own administrative house, to coordinate the big federal programs within the framework of larger national objectives.

Despite these impressive gains, some observers are very critical of the Executive budget as it now operates. Arthur Smithies, for example, raises questions in terms of "the organization and structure of the Government which seems to require an undue element of arbitrariness in major decisions concerning the defense budget."[21] He finds that the departmental approach to federal budgeting "interferes in important instances with effective programming at the Presidential level."[22] He advocates instead increased reliance on a program budget whereby the President would be given appropriations on a program basis which he could then allocate to the departments. This, however, would require extensive regrouping of functions among departments to avoid duplication and overlapping. In the natural resource field, for example, he argues that "there is almost complete agreement by everyone concerned that no substantial change . . . is likely without drastic organizational changes in the Executive Branch."[23] Here, of course, one runs into the problem of the "politics of reorganization," whereby the departments concerned and their legislative and interest group supporters have made reorganization extremely difficult in certain areas.

An interesting criticism, which appears to conflict with the program budget recommendation just mentioned, is the view that "the increase in the program emphasis in the budget has meant that the budget has become less useful for reviewing efficiency of administration."[24] Moreover, under the program budget each activity is still broken down into "objects" such as personal services and travel equipment, existing alongside the broad program classifications. But in reality the problem is one of weighing the obvious advantages of the "program" system in increased simplicity and Congressional understanding against the loss of detailed information that enables the legislators to raise questions of administrative detail, which it seems, is their major function under the present system.

Smithies also feels that the President's budget lacks the information necessary for an appraisal of the reasonableness of the appropriations

---

[21] Arthur Smithies, *The Budgetary Process in the United States* (New York: McGraw-Hill Book Co., Inc., 1955), p. 129.

[22] *Ibid.*, p. 106.

[23] *Ibid.*, p. 353.

[24] *Ibid.*, p. 107.

requests. "There is rarely any attempt to explain the cost factors underlying the estimates or the President's reasons for recommending an increase or decrease in the scale of the program."[25] He adds that the chief executive's statements in support of his recommendations are "perfunctory and formal," sometimes consisting only of mentioning the statutory basis for the program. The "time-consuming" estimates process, he adds, has not done much for economy and efficiency. The system has proved too rigid for the demands brought by emergency. The President often has to set rigid ceilings, particularly in defense spending, that are arbitrary and unduly restrictive for the agencies concerned. Finally, Smithies maintains, the "expenditure and revenue sides of the budget have not been related to effective programming or to adequate consideration of the economic impact of the budget."[26]

Despite these and other criticisms such as those raised by the two Hoover Commissions, the President's budget does give order to an immensely complicated process, and perhaps more important, it gives the President a reasonably effective instrument of policy leadership. Moreover, changes that will result in continuing improvement have been made. Although it is true that increased rationality in the budget preparation process itself has not resulted in any lessening of spending in such areas as national defense, this is in good part more a function of Congress's role in authorizing such expenditures, a subject to which we now turn.

BIBLIOGRAPHY

BRITISH TREASURY, Organization and Methods Divisions. *The Practice of O & M.* London: 1955.

BURKHEAD, JESSE. *Government Budgeting.* New York: 1956.

DAVIES, ROBERT W. *The Development of the Soviet Budgetary System.* Cambridge, England: 1958.

JACOBY, NEIL H. *Can Prosperity Be Sustained?* New York: 1956.

JOINT STATEMENT, National Planning Association. *The Need for Further Budget Reform.* Washington, D.C.: 1955.

KAMMERER, GLADYS M. *Program Budgeting: an Aid to Understanding.* Gainsville, Florida: 1959.

MARTIN, ROSCOE C. (ed.). *TVA: The First Twenty Years.* University, Alabama: 1956.

MOREY, LLOYD, and HACKETT, ROBERT P. 2d ed. *Fundamentals of Governmental Accounting.* New York: 1951.

MOSHER, FREDERICK C. *Program Budgeting: Theory and Practice.* Chicago: 1954.

TENNER, IRVING. 3d ed. *Municipal and Governmental Accounting.* Englewood Cliffs, New Jersey: 1955.

TICKTON, SIDNEY G. *The Budget in Transition.* Washington, D.C.: 1955.

[25] *Ibid.,* p. 108; see also, Mosher, *Program Budgeting,* pp. 183–85.
[26] Smithies, *The Budgetary Process in the United States,* pp. 129–30.

CHAPTER 23

The Budgetary Process: Authorization

As Congressmen delight in pointing out, the Constitution in Article I gives them the major role in fiscal matters. Money bills must originate there, tax bills must be approved by them, and they alone can authorize the borrowing and the spending of money. In theory at least, the only limitation upon Congress's authorization power is that the period of military appropriation can be for no more than two years. The manner in which Congress is organized to handle these functions in regard to the annual budget is the subject of this chapter. We have already suggested that Congressional review of the huge Executive budget is a superhuman task, and this problem will be touched upon here. We shall see that one of the main reasons for incomplete and sporadic legislative review is the diffusion of financial responsibility within Congress. We shall also find that the authorization phase of budget making is intensely political and that the authorization power is a means of implementing legislative values about particular programs. It seems well to begin by outlining some of these political factors.

THE LEGISLATIVE MIND

In considering the President's budget, legislators are buffeted by two opposing forces, one a highly articulated desire for economy and efficiency; the other, the pressure of special interests for appropriations. A member of the House Appropriations Committee has stated that for "every member of Congress there are scores of pressure groups and lobbyists, including the government agencies, with conflicting objectives, eager to make a Congressman's life easier by making his decisions for him."[1] There is little question but that some legislators genuinely desire limited expenditures. On the other hand, the legislator is keenly sensitive

[1] John Phillips, "The Hadacol of the Budget Makers," 4, *National Tax Journal* (September, 1951), p. 255; also Paul H. Douglas, *Economy in the National Government* (Chicago: University of Chicago Press, 1952).

to appropriations for his own district. Thus if the Navy proposes to shut down the Pismo Beach Shipyard, the local Congressman is immediately bombarded by telegrams, letters, special delegations, and phone calls. His success as a Congressman may be largely judged by whether he is able to keep the shipyard open.

In order to understand the legislative phase of budgeting, we must know something about the behavior and sentiments of legislators. They have certain reactions which, within limits, are predictable. In other words, a stereotyped legislative belief system exists. This stereotype is vocational in nature; that is, it is molded and conditioned by environment. The legislator reacts as he does because he is conditioned by American cultural influences. What are the components of this legislative belief system?

Parochialism. Perhaps the most powerful legislative characteristic is parochialism; if the legislator is to stay in office, he must be something of a ward heeler. Let a professor write a book on political theory in which he decries the influence of sectionalism and advocates national, as against local, interests. Then let the same professor be elected to Congress and sit on an appropriations subcommittee which threatens to cut out a half-million dollars for dredging the harbor in his home town. Will he tell the Chamber of Commerce that it is unethical for him to take a personal interest in the matter? Another conditioning factor is the functional pressure group. If the legislator is from a seaport fishing constituency and the fishing fleet is idle and cannery workers are unemployed, how will he vote on a tariff on fish imports? Suppose he is a Ph.D., with a major in economics and a minor in political science. He has been conditioned by study and research to believe that international trade barriers are bad; yet his choice will often be to vote for the fish tariff or return to the classroom.

In addition the American legislator is an individualist; he is under little party discipline. To be sure, he must gain seniority if he is to have influence among his colleagues, but he cannot be easily disciplined for failure to follow party leaders. Political scientists have long decried our lack of a genuine two-party system that ensures responsibility.[2] For example, during most of the Roosevelt-Truman period, the principal committees were often chaired by conservative southern Democrats who were openly opposed to Presidential policy. This situation is often contrasted unfavorably with the British situation, where individual members of Parliament are under rigorous party discipline. If the House rejects a

[2] Committee on Political Parties of the American Political Science Association, *Toward A More Responsible Two-Party System* (Washington, D.C.: U.S. Government Printing Office, Committee Print, Committee on Expenditures for the Executive Departments, 1951), pp. 24 ff.

government bill designated as a matter of policy, the House is dissolved and members must seek reelection.

Antipathy Toward the Executive Branch. This suggests another facet of the American legislative mind: a critical attitude toward the President even if he is a member of one's own party. Legislators want to get publicity and praise for noteworthy deeds instead of having the kudos go to the President, governor, or mayor. They have perhaps greater than normal egotism and personal ambition. They are not content to take a passive role. A legislative body also constitutes a social club and an in-group; members may quarrel among themselves, but they will take collective offense at any criticism of the institution itself.[3]

Perhaps the most disruptive trait of the legislative mind is its intuitive mistrust of bureaucrats and experts. This attitude toward bureaucrats flows partly from the fact that bureaucrats are allied with the executive branch and are therefore considered henchmen of the chief executive. But bureaucrats are also to be classed with experts, and Americans have always been apprehensive of giving experts governmental power. Our institutions are based upon an implied assumption that there is a superior lay wisdom which should supersede expertise in the determination of public policy. Also present is Jacksonian egalitarianism, the idea that one man is as good as another. The legislator may lose face if he admits his own lack of knowledge or incompetence. This ties in with an ego drive which makes the legislator want to run things instead of merely engage in passive deliberation or review, as demanded by the authorization process.

THE DILEMMAS OF REFORM

Political Values Versus Expertise. What has this discussion of the legislative mind to do with budgeting? Observers have tended to feel that legislative parochialism can be modified by internal reorganization of the legislature. All the reforms advocated in recent years by the Hoover Commissions, the National Planning Association,[4] and the Committee on Political Parties of the American Political Science Association[5] have some bearing on the appropriation process. The first Hoover report recommended performance budgeting that would necessitate simplifica-

---

[3] See William S. White, *The Citadel* (New York: Harper & Bros., 1957); H. Wilson, *Congress: Corruption and Compromise* (New York: Rinehart & Co., Inc., 1951).

[4] Robert Heller, *Strengthening the Congress* (Washington, D.C.: National Planning Association, 1945).

[5] Committee on Political Parties of the American Political Science Association, *Toward A More Responsible Two-Party System.*

tion of the appropriation structure.[6] The Heller report stated that, "Congress should place more emphasis on major policy and less emphasis on detail." The Legislative Reorganization Act of 1946 actually took steps to put some of the Heller recommendations into practice. Political scientists advocated reorganization of Congress in order to enhance party responsibility and ensure that a committee chairman would be in sympathy with his party's program.[7]

Some of these recommendations have been adopted by Congress only to be honored in the breach. Thus the Legislative Reorganization Act of 1946 required that the members of the House and Senate revenue and appropriations committees meet, consider the President's budget recommendations and prepare a report to Congress, which would set ceilings "fixing the maximum amount to be appropriated for expenditure in each year."[8] This was tried for one year and then allowed to lapse, largely because the time schedule and the uncertainty of world affairs would not permit accurate prediction. The single-package appropriation bill was also tried for one year and then abandoned. It provided for substituting one appropriation bill for the dozen or so normally passed. In the year in which it was tried, the appropriations were not passed until August 4, long after the beginning of the budget year. Chairman McKellar of the Senate Committee complained that the single package placed an unbearable burden on a few key persons.

Policy Determination or Managerial Control? The conclusion to be drawn is that the mere enactment of reform will not change legislative behavior and thought patterns. The essence of reform proposals lies in the proposition that legislatures should avoid the consideration of detail and concentrate on matters of broad policy. Thus the principal theory underlying performance budgeting now holds that the legislature should be told that it costs $1.19 per unit to provide police patrol. One hundred thousand units would cost so much and two hundred thousand units so much more. The legislature would determine what level of law enforcement it wanted to buy and forget about the cost of patrol cars, gasoline, jail food, and printing. The trouble is that the average legislator wants to know the details. Members of Congress do not agree with the theoretical concept that their role is that of deliberation on large policy issues. They want a hand in actually running things. As one observer concluded:

[6] Commission on Organization of the Executive Branch of the Government, *Budgeting and Accounting* (Washington, D.C.: U.S. Government Printing Office, 1949), pp. 12 ff.

[7] Committee on Political Parties of the American Political Science Association, *Toward A More Responsible Two-Party System*, pp. 56–70.

[8] Phillips, "The Hadacol of the Budget Makers," p. 256.

Congress does not view the budget as a means of effecting a rational distribution of funds among alternatives. Instead, Congress sees the budget as an instrument for exerting managerial control over the executive and ... as a means of establishing the supremacy of private and local interests over the national interest.[9]

It is significant that the second Hoover Commission pursued two main themes: the need for better accounting and the "Restoration of Congressional Control of the Purse."[10] The devices proposed as the means for obtaining greater administrative accountability to Congress, and also to the President, were essentially of a technical accounting nature, yet understandable by the layman. They aimed to produce *information* that the average Congressman could use to evaluate administration. On the second point, establishing Congressional control of the purse, the Commission made the following proposals:

1. Continued effort toward changeover from an object to a performance type of budget.
2. Revamping of the structure and format of the budget document and appropriation acts so as to reflect expenditures (instead of obligations) by programs.
3. Accrual accounting that will reflect the resources available at the beginning of the year, goods and services received, use of resources in relation to work performed, and liabilities at the end of the year.
4. The adoption of the cost or "business" type of accounting wherever applicable.

As the following review indicates, some progress has been made toward these goals. Nevertheless, Congress remains perplexed about its inability to control expenditures. Its appropriation procedure has been studied by both its own committees and outsiders. The Legislative Reorganization Act of 1946 has proved to be largely abortive because Congress has found its provisions for a legislative budget completely unworkable. To understand the reasons for this situation, let us examine the existing organization for control and authorization of the President's budget.

THE AUTHORIZATION PROCESS

The most striking thing about the budget authorization phase is that there is no *over-all* review of the budget by any committee or by either

---

[9] Edward C. Banfield, "Congress and the Budget: A Planner's Criticism," **43**, *American Political Science Review* (December, 1949), pp. 1220.

[10] Quotation is chapter heading IV in: Commission on Organization of the Executive Branch of the Government, *Budgeting and Accounting* (Washington, D.C.: U.S. Government Printing Office, 1955), p. 17.

of the Houses.[11] There is no formal debate in Congress on the whole budget nor is there joint consideration by the powerful appropriations and revenue committees. This condition reflects the dispersion of authority among several Congressional committees and subcommittees, which are usually organized on the basis of substantive interest and expertise. Hence, in each house there is a Ways and Means Committee (called Finance Committee in the Senate) that is responsible for finding the sources of revenue; an Appropriations Committee which reviews and recommends appropriations; a Committee on Government Operations that has the authority to oversee Executive management practices; a Joint Committee on Reduction of Nonessential Expenditures (which, parenthetically, must be among the most frustrated of legislative agencies, since it has worked hard over the years to promote economy and efficiency without much headway); a Joint Committee on the Economic Report, whose work was outlined in the last chapter; and a Joint Committee on Internal Revenue Taxation.[12]

The Appropriations Committee. Our major concern is with the Appropriations Committees and their various subcommittees, each of which handles a particular aspect of the federal program such as Army, Air Force, or Agriculture. Although the Constitution provides that revenue bills must originate in the House, appropriations as well as revenue measures have come to originate there. A kind of rough division of labor occurs between the House and Senate Committees: The former initiates such measures and the latter reviews them.

A brief description of the House Appropriations Committee and its work may be useful at this point. The House Committee has fifty members, divided by the Committee into several subcommittees with from three to six members each. The Chairman, who serves ex officio on all subcommittees, also schedules the hearings for the subcommittees and, as would be expected, is a powerful influence on them. About fourteen appropriations bills are considered each year, and each subcommittee is responsible for reviewing one or two of them. Since members remain on the committees indefinitely, they may build up considerable experience and knowledge in their respective program areas. The subcommittee hearings are not open to the public and are restricted to members of the government. The work of the subcommittee is usually definitive, since the Appropriations Committee accepts its decision as binding.

---

[11] Thus in recent years the Congressman who would appraise the entire budget has had to read some 25,000 pages of subcommittee hearings. See Arthur Smithies, *The Budgetary Process in the United States* (New York: McGraw-Hill Book Co., Inc., 1955), p. 131.

[12] *Ibid.*, p. 131–33.

Another relevant facet of the authorization process, as mentioned earlier, is that the departments and agencies present their own budgets to the committees without any participation by the Bureau of the Budget. Moreover, relations between Congress and the Bureau have been somewhat strained in recent years. Even a brief view of the hearings will reveal that Congress has serious misgivings about the Bureau and its powerful role in budgetary affairs. Referring to the Bureau's practice of apportioning money to the departments after it has been appropriated by Congress, a House Appropriations Subcommittee member remarked:[13]

MR. FLOOD: I see the language "The general apportionment was enacted on July 2; the Bureau of Budget apportionments were made on August 1." What does that mean? . . .

MR. KING: I would like to explain what happens to July 2. We initiate our apportionments . . . for the Bureau of the Budget.

MR. FLOOD: Describe that for us. You pick up your briefcases and you take General Lawton [Director of Army Budget] and everybody down, and you go to the Bureau of the Budget with your hat in hand. Why?

MR. KING: We have to rejustify to the Bureau of the Budget the requirement for the moneys appropriated on July 2.

MR. FLOOD: Do you hear that, Mr. Chairman? Now after Congress has enacted constitutionally, and the President has signed the law, the Army must now get out its retinue of chauffeurs, automobiles, and the parade goes to the Bureau of the Budget. They go to the Taj Mahal where . . . they must rejustify what they have just done with the legislative branch of the Government.

In sum, the legislators regard the Bureau as a competitor that strengthens the President's part in budgetary preparation and control, such as the impounding of funds for projects that the President deems unessential, by actions that seem to cut into the legislative power of authorization.[14]

Subcommittee Hearings. Budget hearings before the subcommittees usually begin with a prepared statement by the department head outlining his program, its major assumptions, the money needed to carry it out, and the reasons for significant changes from the previous year. Once this has been done the department head will often call upon his budget and financial aides to present specific parts of the proposed budget. These men often know the subcommittee members well, and their introductory remarks often refer to their pleasure at appearing before the subcommittee again. The subcommittee's work and assistance

---

[13] Subcommittee of the Committee on Appropriations, 85th Cong., 1st sess., *Hearings,* "Department of the Air Force, Appropriations for 1958" (Washington, D.C.: U.S. Government Printing Office, 1957), pp. 50–51.

[14] See, for example, J. D. Williams, *The Impounding of Funds by the Bureau of the Budget* (University, Alabama: University of Alabama Press, 1955).

is usually acknowledged by such officials, and often their compliments are returned by the subcommittee members who commend them on the detailed and comprehensive information given to the committee. Such officials, in sum, combine technical skill with experience and political acumen.

It is generally agreed that once the prepared statement is read by the department head, the hearings become highly random and the questioning may lead anywhere. As Smithies remarks, "each subcommittee member has the right to question each department witness, and the questioning frequently fluctuates violently from basic policy issues to the most trivial detail."[15] Although the legislators' are helped by their continuing service on a given committee, it is extremely difficult for them to get a rounded view of the whole budget. Only rarely do they raise questions about the size and rationality of the whole budget; and such questions occur most frequently in the Senate, where, for example, Paul Douglas has from time to time questioned the defense budget.[16] Apparently the failure to debate the budget as a whole on the floor of Congress leads to "frustration and cynicism on the part of members of Congress who are not directly involved in the appropriations process."[17]

As is understandable, the subcommittees take a specialized view of their authorization role; they are not inclined to accept reductions in order that some other element in the budget can receive more money. Thus they resist the coordinating efforts of the Bureau and the President. The legislators become members of committees on the basis of their own experience, interest, and the dominant economic character of the region they represent. It is well known, for example, that members on the agricultural committees are from the major agricultural states. This condition, plus the difficulty of gaining any insight into the budget as a whole, results in a piecemeal approach to authorization on the part of Congress. Although there is a subcommittee on Full Defense which considers the military budget en bloc, there are also subcommittees for the three services, each of which has its advocates. The following comment of the Chairman of the House subcommittee on Army appropriations suggests the affinity between the members and their related service:[18]

MR. SIKES: We recognize the fact that we have a very serious responsibility this year in that there is a general demand for a more searching analysis of all budget requests. However, there is a belief that the Army has been cut more substantially in previous budgets than have other branches of the Ser-

---

[15] Smithies, *The Budgeting Process in the United States*, p. 133.

[16] For a summary of Douglas' experiences in this context, see *Economy in the National Government* (Chicago: University of Chicago Press, 1952).

[17] Smithies, *The Budgeting Process in the United States*, p. 135.

[18] *Hearings*, "Department of the Army Appropriations for 1958," p. 1.

vice. We recognize the fact, too, that the Army has a very important job to do in the national defense . . . we must be careful that we do not cripple its effectiveness.

After the various subcommittees have reviewed the requests, they prepare recommendations and a report covering the rationale for their actions. These documents are then sent on to the Appropriations Committees of the House and Senate, where they are rarely considered in detail. The subcommittees' decisions become binding in most cases; this policy is the result of necessity, tradition, and the pressure of time. The consideration of the President's budget on the floor of Congress is perfunctory, and the result is usually authorization of a budget figure that is very close to that recommended initially by him. The bill finally goes on to the President for his signature, and since his requests are usually accepted, he rarely vetoes an appropriation bill.[19]

One result of this authorization procedure is that Congress rarely cuts the President's budget; even a 5 per cent cut is the exception rather than the rule.[20] The House, which gets the appropriations bills first, often makes a substantial cut, but this is usually restored by the Senate, and the ensuing conference committee meeting between the two Houses usually compromises on a figure very close to the President's original request. In sum, "at the appropriation stage, it is fair to state that the President is in a stronger position than the committees. This strength results in part from the fact that the committees are handicapped by lack of information. Neither the President's budget nor the extensive hearings provide them with a reasonable basis for differing from the President on major terms."[21]

IMPROVING CONGRESSIONAL REVIEW

The preceding survey indicates that legislative authorization is based on incomplete information reflecting the size and complexity of the budget, its failure to provide the information needed for effective debate, and the organization and procedures that characterize Congressional review.

One must conclude that Congress as a whole and its subcommittees exercise only a limited control and scrutiny over the budget. We are told by Smithies that the full House Appropriations Committee considers

[19] However Franklin D. Roosevelt, when governor of New York, once vetoed an entire appropriation bill of $52,000,000, which in 1929 was a substantial sum. See James M. Burns, Roosevelt: The Lion and the Fox (New York: Harcourt, Brace & Co., 1956), pp. 110–11.

[20] Smithies, The Budgetary Process in the United States, p. 140.

[21] Ibid., pp. 140–41; see also pp. 163–67 for a summary of defects in both Congressional and Presidential budgetary activities.

the budget prepared by the various subcommittees for only about an hour and then sends it on to the Senate unchanged. While debate of broad policy matters is Congress's proper role, it is too often occupied with questions of administrative detail or isolated aspects of the program in which members have some special interest or knowledge. In scanning the hearings, one gets a sense of frustration and resignation on the part of some committee members. This frustration is manifest in the contentious way that minor questions are sometimes raised, and in the general posture of the members who, as noted earlier, are often defensive about their questions. This is especially true in the military sphere, where Congressmen do not usually have the expertise that they may have in labor or agriculture.

As Mosher concludes with respect to the military budget, "The Defense Department, the Budget Bureau, and the committees of Congress may bring about individual economies here and there on the basis of specific studies; they may prod the military agencies into changing their methods of handling individual problems. But the occasional penetration of a few persons into an operation which expends more than 10 billion dollars a year [note that this judgment was written in 1951; today, of course, the figure has been raised to over 40 billion] can hardly cover more than a tiny fraction of its processes, and even in that tiny fraction their effect may be very small."[22]

During the past decade many attempts have been made to improve this situation. Congress itself has set up investigating committees, legislation has been passed seeking improved methods, the Budget Bureau has been reorganized, citizen's groups such as the Hoover Commission have made intensive studies, and so have individuals. It seems worthwhile at this point to outline the major recommendations that have resulted from this combined effort.[23]

Recommended Elements in Budgetary Procedure. Although there are wide differences about budgetary matters, most experts in the field would probably agree on several general objectives. However, it must be said that they are not acceptable to everyone, and particularly not to legislators because the objectives would somewhat restrict legislators' ability

[22] Frederick C. Mosher, *Program Budgeting: Theory and Practice* (Chicago: Public Administration Service, 1954), p. 235.

[23] Many of the problems of federal budgeting and some of their solutions may be found in *Hearings*, "Improving Federal Budgeting and Appropriations," Subcommittee of the Committee on Government Operations, 85th Cong., 1st sess. (Washington, D.C.: U.S. Government Printing Office, 1957); Smithies, *The Budgetary Process in the United States*, pp. 163–74; 175–97; 198–225; Frederick C. Mosher, *Program Budgeting: Theory and Practice* (Chicago: Public Administration Service, 1954), pp. 230–49; Jesse Burkhead, *Government Budgeting* (New York: John Wiley & Sons, Inc., 1956), pp. 326–38.

to criticize executive management by confining legislative review to broad policy questions. In any event, these objectives include:

1. *Planning*. The principle of democratic long-term planning must be accepted as being consistent with a limited private enterprise economy.

2. *Research*. Such planning should be based upon an infinite variety of information on all phases of national and world economy. The world is becoming ever smaller as a result of technology, war, and cultural interdependence. What happens to Australian wool or Bolivian tin has profound and immediate repercussions in New York, London, and Des Moines. The budget planner for a national economy needs to have all possible data relative to these economic processes. Hence, much of the budget planning of the future will flow from statistical machines that constantly tabulate the flow of information from the remote corners of the world. Some of this information is already gathered through both governmental and private sources.

3. *Balanced Budget*. The President should present a balanced budget plan to Congress. The term "balanced budget" is used here not in the sense that there will be no deficits but that deficits, if they do occur, will be planned in advance. The budget message will state the reason for planned deficits.

4. *Appropriation Procedure*. Congress should organize its appropriation procedure so as to minimize the harmful effects of both regional and occupational pressures. Various means of accomplishing this purpose have been suggested in this section.

5. *Post-audit*. The current tendency of the General Accounting Office toward post-audit, as against the pre-audit of the past, should be encouraged.

6. *Flexible Control*. The President should exercise through the Bureau of the Budget the same type of flexible control of expenditures as the British Treasury. In other words he should have the power to withhold and grant the right to spend, subject of course to the limits established by Congress in the general appropriation bills.

7. *Appropriations*. These should be made in lump sum instead of in detail by object. Appropriations should be by function or general purpose based upon work programs, which are in turn built up from performance work-load standards.

8. *Management Analysis*. Budget work in the agencies should be intimately tied in with constant work-load analysis aimed at establishing productivity standards. The Bureau of the Budget should exert leadership in this campaign in order to counteract the frustration, inertia, and resistance that is usually met. It must propagate the idea that meaningful standards can be established, even for those areas where measurement is difficult.

9. *Decisions Made on Program*. The legislature should confine itself to large policy matters and refrain from assuming administrative control. It should have available all the detailed information it desires, but its determinations should be on the basis of the amount of program work units it wishes to buy. It should refrain from making decisions on an object breakdown of expenditures. The legislative function should be mainly that of making program value judgments.

10. *Annuality*. The principle of annuality should apply to all expenditures. Budgetary planning is decidedly limited in flexibility by virtue of the fact that about three-quarters of the expenditures are now provided by permanent appropriations. The authority to spend exists regardless of current budgetary allotment. Such expenditures should be made subject to annual budgetary review.

11. *Long-Term Planning.* Budget planning should be projected over a period of years, especially planning for capital expenditures.[24] One of the defects of federal public works budgeting lies in the fact that local pressure groups can secure approval of a huge project through the authorization of a small initial appropriation. What is needed is an accounting system that will reflect not only current charges but also future obligations and maintenance costs as well as capital outlays. More coordination is needed between authorization and appropriation.

Although these elements of budgetary procedure would require considerable self-restraint on the part of legislatures, particularly in relinquishing their demands for detailed information on expenditures, considerable progress has been made toward incorporating them into public budgeting. Nevertheless, it seems well to conclude on the point that the big questions that underlie government finance and budgeting are *political,* and necessarily so. While improved methods of accounting and information gathering are important management objectives, they have little impact on the decisions to increase, or not to increase, expenditures for the costly programs that governments have now assumed. In a word, it is politics, not administration, that is responsible for the huge public budgets of today.

BIBLIOGRAPHY

BEER, SAMUEL H. *Treasury Control: the Coordination of Financial and Economic Policy in Great Britain.* Oxford: 1956.

CHUBB, BASAL. *The Control of Public Expenditures; Financial Committees of the House of Commons.* Oxford: 1952.

DUE, JOHN F. *Government Finance, an Economic Analysis.* Rev. ed.; Homewood, Illinois: 1959.

GROVES, HAROLD M. *Financing Government.* 5th ed.; New York: 1958.

HARVEY, GEORGE Y. "Contract Authorization in Federal Budget Procedure," **17,** *Public Administration Review* (Spring, 1957), pp. 117–24.

KIMMEL, LEWIS HENRY. *Federal Budget and Fiscal Policy, 1789–1958.* Washington, D.C.: 1959.

LEWIS, EDWARD G. "Parliamentary Control of Nationalized Industry in France," **51,** *American Political Science Review* (September, 1957), pp. 669–83.

LIVINGSTON, WILLIAM S. "Congressional Control of the Budget," **3,** *Midwest Journal of Political Science* (May, 1959), pp. 151–67.

MOSHER, FREDERICK C. *Program Budgeting: Theory and Practice.* Chicago: 1954.

SMITHIES, ARTHUR. *The Budgetary Process in the United States.* New York: 1955.

WILLIAMS, J. D. *The Impounding of Funds by the Bureau of the Budget.* ICP Case No. 28. University, Alabama: 1955.

[24] Banfield, "Congress and the Budget," pp. 1217–28; and Phillips, "The Hadacol of the Budget Makers," pp. 255–68.

CHAPTER 24

The Budgetary Process: Execution

We now turn to the final and somewhat more prosaic phase of budgeting: execution and control. On the one hand this phase can be defined negatively to mean the process whereby the chief executive and the legislature keep the departments honest. On the other, execution can be defined as the phase in which the money needed to carry out programs is made available in the most positive and flexible way possible. Both aspects will be considered here because both can be seen at work in most agencies. We must also say at the outset that execution is not a discrete phase in the budget process but is closely interwoven with both the preparation and appropriation phases, particularly with the latter, which often includes specific measures for controlling expenditures. Execution and control are carried out at three fairly distinct levels, Presidential, legislative, and departmental. Each will be considered separately, after a review of the major objectives of execution.

THE OBJECTIVES OF EXECUTION

Most commentators believe that the execution stage should aim for a nice balance between legislative intent and administrative flexibility.[1] From what we have seen, however, the budget is more an index of Executive than legislative intent, which suggests that this concept ought to be added to the traditional aim. However that may be, it is clear enough that the legislature has participated in the defining of budgetary objectives and that these same objectives, whether they were initiated by the legislature or, as seems more likely, merely endorsed by it, should remain paramount during the final stage. No doubt the President is affected by his impressions of legislative wishes, both in the preparation and appropriation phases; moreover he must return to the legislature for

[1] These objectives are set down in detail in Jesse Burkhead, *Government Budgeting* (New York: John Wiley & Sons, Inc., 1956), pp. 342–48.

426

authorizations the succeeding year. Thus we may assume that he will not deliberately flaunt their will.

An even more traditional objective of execution is the observance of financial limitations set down by the legislature. This objective falls within the "control" context mentioned above. Today the acceptance of deficiency, or supplemental, appropriations is quite general, and indeed, they are regarded as necessary and proper when they are the result of emergencies, such as the Korean War. There was a time when it was felt that deficiency appropriations were acceptable only when they were planned for, but this view has also been challenged. Smithies, for example, argues that deficiency appropriations "can strengthen rather than weaken Congressional control."[2] This is because, assuming that deficiencies were prohibited, regular appropriations would have to be more "liberal" than at present; also the burden of proof is shifted to the executive branch to show that it really needs a supplemental grant.[3] One less acceptable aspect of deficiencies, however, is their use to conceal major increases in the President's initial budget.[4]

The final objective is in maintaining flexibility so that the administration can meet the demands of change and emergency. As Burkhead says, "the ability of a budget execution system to cope with these changes depends in large measure on the way in which budget authorizations are written by the legislature.[5] An exceptional but instructive example occurred in 1943 when an appropriations measure included a provision that funds of any act of Congress were not to be used to pay the salaries of Messrs. Lovett, Watson, and Dodd, three employees who had been accused of subversive activities.[6] Efforts to limit deficiencies, to prescribe the number of personnel specialists per X number of federal employees, to fix the total amount of money that may be spent during any given fiscal year—all have been tried without much success. Apparently, if the expenditures are to remain within initially authorized limits, it is the administrative branch that must do it.

The problem of achieving flexibility is that it must overcome deep-seated tensions between legislature and executive; it is hard for legislatures to make lump sum grants and permit the departments to transfer, to spend, or not to spend funds. As the hearings cited in the preceding chapter suggest, legislators' regard such latitude as a violation of their constitutional right to authorize spending. American budget history

[2] Arthur Smithies, *The Budgetary Process in the United States* (New York: The McGraw-Hill Book Co., Inc., 1955), p. 149.
[3] *Ibid.*
[4] *Ibid.*
[5] Burkhead, *Government Budgeting*, p. 345.
[6] *United States* v. *Lovett* (328 U.S. 303, 1946).

is replete with examples of legislative efforts to control spending by
line-item appropriations and restrictions against deficiency appropriations.[7] Despite this, the trend is definitely toward increased autonomy for
the executive branch, particularly at the federal level where the Bureau
of the Budget provides the President with expert and continuous staff
services.

PRESIDENTIAL ROLE IN EXECUTION

Apportionment. The major instrument of Presidential control is the
right to apportion the rate at which appropriated funds are spent. In
addition, if the need arises, the President can require the departments
to withhold unneeded funds as reserves. The President assumed this
power under the Budget and Accounting Act of 1921, and in 1950 the
General Appropriation Act specifically confirmed his legal authority to
do so. Perhaps the most dramatic use of this power in recent times
occurred in 1947 when President Truman impounded an 875 million
dollar appropriation for the Air Force which provided for a 70-group air
arm when he had recommended a 55-group arm.

As Mosher says, "the apportionments may be considered the first stage
of budget execution."[8] This process of setting up the schedule and the
amounts to be spent for given programs is also sometimes called funding
or financial planning. The main distinction between this process and
the initial budget is that funding involves the *operational aspects* of the
budget, that is, it "provide[s] an operating plan for the execution of the
budget."[9] The initial budget is a statement of "requirements," while
funding is concerned with "capabilities."

An outline of apportionment in the Defense Department suggests the
character of this aspect of execution and Presidential influence over it,
usually exercised through his political aides at the secretarial level.
The President gets into this act through the Budget Bureau, which holds
hearings on the apportionment requests of the military departments.
Representatives of the Secretary of Defense's Office attend such hearings,
after which "advices of apportionment" are issued by the Budget Bureau,
"usually authorizing the obligation of funds for each of the first three
quarters of the fiscal year within each appropriation."[10] Before these
apportionment authorizations go to the three services heads, they are
reviewed and certified by the Secretary of Defense, who can limit or

---

[7] See L. Wilmerding, Jr., *The Spending Power* (New Haven: Yale University Press,
1943).

[8] Frederick C. Mosher, *Program Budgeting: Theory and Practice* (Chicago: Public
Administration Service, 1954), p. 185.

[9] *Ibid.*, p. 186.

[10] *Ibid.*

reserve the use of funds. In important matters, he will do this at the direction of the President, as the following exchange suggests:[11]

MR. VINSON: Now, my question, Mr. Secretary, is how can you justify a reduction of force in view of the conference report setting forth the belief and intent of the Congress?

MR. McELROY: . . . In this instance the instruction of the Commander in Chief with respect to the size of forces was in my opinion overriding and it was on that instruction . . . that I took the action of instructing that the size of the Army be reduced to 870,000, June 30, 1959, and 175,000 in the Marines June 30, 1959.

It should be noted that apportionment is also a mechanism for *internal* department control by the various agency heads. This aspect will be mentioned subsequently when this level of execution is outlined.

The Budget Bureau. Another useful instrument of Presidential control is through the divisions of the Budget Bureau that are concerned with improving management practices throughout the federal government.[12] Although this division has never quite achieved the active influence that was hoped for, the Bureau's influence has increased during the past few years, mainly as a result of the Hoover Commission recommendations and increased acceptance of the Bureau's role by Congress.

The Joint Accounting Program illustrates the way in which the Bureau has become more important in financial matters. For many years, accounting functions in the federal government were spread about among several agencies, including the Comptroller General who was regarded as the watchdog of Congress. However, during World War II, the Comptroller, the Budget Bureau, and the Treasury began informal cooperation, largely on the basis of personal rapport among their top officials. In 1950 Congress formalized this arrangement in the Budget and Accounting Act, which was amended in 1956 to further shift the balance of power and initiative from the General Accounting Office to the Bureau.

In all this there has been a gradual change from defining accounting as a negative control instrument to one of positive administrative direction. In this case the new program charged the Comptroller General with encouraging the development of better accounting, disbursement, collection, and reporting practices. The extent of the changes is suggested by the fact that the General Accounting Office has decentralized accounting functions to the departments and agencies almost completely. It no longer

[11] Hearings, *Military Posture Briefing*, p. 806, see also, p. 832.

[12] Functions that are quite similar to those of the Budget Bureau are carried out in Russia by the Supervision and Inspection Department, which is empowered to impose fines of up to three months wages and in extreme cases to initiate criminal proceedings against department heads and others for "violations of financial discipline," R. W. Davies, *The Development of the Soviet Budgetary System* (Cambridge: Cambridge University Press, 1958), pp. 271–72.

has any central accounting functions; its main role is to encourage the operating agencies to improve their own practices.

Insofar as complete reporting is essential to Presidential control, the recommendations of the second Hoover Commission were most important. The Commission proposed that the Bureau be empowered to require annual "performance" reports from the heads of all operating agencies, which in turn would permit the President to make an annual report on administrative performance in the executive branch. When set alongside the Commission's recommendations for central financial reporting, this suggests a trend toward accepting the need to centralize leadership for management improvement in some central agency. However, the Bureau itself was reluctant to add to existing demands for reports from the operating agencies, and suggested that for the present it would confine itself to developing central reports on financial matters.[13] While declaring its "firm intention to take all possible measures to bring Bureau staff into closer contact with agency operations and employees . . . ," the Bureau suggested that the trend toward reducing its staff while constantly adding new functions ought to be reversed.[14]

President's Fund for Management Improvement. The federal budget contains a small appropriation of about $400,000 which may be used for "expenses necessary to assist the President in improving the management of executive agencies and in obtaining greater economy and efficiency through the establishment of more efficient business methods in Government operations . . ."[15] This enables the Executive to bring in consultants or to have the agencies themselves survey their methods under general Budget Bureau direction. Here again, the President has an opportunity to control financial practices and to improve them.

In sum, the President through the Budget Bureau and his political control of department heads can exert important controls during the execution process. However, the authority and responsibility for long-run management effectiveness must rest elsewhere. Most authorities believe that improved performance in execution must devolve upon the departments and the agencies themselves; neither the President nor the Congress can exercise a continuous and detailed scrutiny of their programs in day-to-day terms. Fortunately the current trend is clearly in the direction of understanding the limitations of both Executive and Congressional controls, with more emphasis upon ways and means of encouraging administrative improvement by the departments themselves.[16] Frequently

---

[13] Bureau of the Budget, *Improvement of Financial Management in the Federal Government* (Washington, D.C.: U.S. Government Printing Office, 1956), pp. 25–26.

[14] *Ibid.*, p. 28.

[15] U.S. Budget for 1958, pp. 73–74.

[16] Smithies, *Budgetary Process in the United States*, p. 153.

recommended is the requirement of annual reports to the President by the departments; yet as we have seen, Budget Bureau officials are not sanguine about this method. In order to give both Congress and the President more information on performance, periodic management audits have also been recommended by groups such as the Committee for Economic Development.[17] This brings us to the question of legislative control during the execution phase.

LEGISLATIVE OVERSIGHT

Control by Appropriation. The close relationship between the three major budgetary phases is suggested by the fact that the main legislative control is through appropriations, by which legislatures often try to limit the discretion of the executive agencies. Examples include specific provisions against the transfer of funds from the appropriated account to some other program. This proscription is, quite common among state legislatures and occurs also in many city governments. In the federal government, as Burkhead concludes, "the tradition has long been to permit no transfer among agencies and very little within agencies, except on specific occasions and for specific purposes, as stated in annual appropriation acts; for example, a department might be permitted to transfer 5 per cent from one title to another."[18] Legislators are very reluctant to grant transfer authority to the agencies; yet, the trend is clearly in this direction as indicated by the lump sum appropriations that now characterize the federal budget.

Another traditional instrument of control was the line-item appropriation, which made it difficult to transfer money from one item to another and resulted in a rigidity that most observers deplore.[19] Line-item appropriations control expenditure by a line in the budget document, such as X typist clerks at $3,000 per year or X automobile tires at $27,000. A related example of Congressional efforts to control expenditures is the Whitten amendment to the Supplemental Appropriations Act of 1952, which attempted to prevent expansion of the federal payroll during emergencies, with resulting strains and hardships when people were let go following the emergency.[20] Limitations were placed on promotions and the opportunities for people to gain civil service tenure. Most federal personnel officers opposed the amendment, and even the Civil Service Commission was accused of dragging its feet in supporting it. This seem-

[17] Committee for Economic Development, *Control of Federal Government Expenditures* (New York: January, 1955).
[18] Burkhead, *Government Budgeting*, p. 349.
[19] *Ibid.*, pp. 128, 355.
[20] *Report of the Committee on Post Office and Civil Service*, 84th Cong., 2d sess., House Report No. 1855 (March 1, 1956), p. 11.

ingly inherent tendency of bureaucracies to expand has been delightfully caricatured by Professor Parkinson, who showed among other things that the smaller the number of capital ships in the British Navy, the larger the number of civilian personnel in the Naval Establishment.[21] Legislators everywhere suspect that Parkinson's so-called "law" is valid, and some of them, like Senator Byrd, have spent decades trying unsuccessfully to curtail the growth of the federal bureaucracy.[22]

It is easy to understand the tendency of the legislator to control expenditures by such means as "ceilings" on personnel and limiting the number of budget items and determining their costs. Here it seems is something definite to which the legislator can hold the official. By contrast, the program budgeting concept seems strange, and as we have seen, it does limit the legislator's ability to evaluate administrative practices by limiting detailed information. This posture is also encouraged by the fact that most legislators are small-town lawyers or businessmen with little experience in big organizations where cost-centered approaches to accountability have been more common. Gradually, however, Congress is learning that its efforts to check details has weakened its ability to scrutinize and to control the larger issues of fiscal policy.

The Comptroller General's Role. Since the comptroller general is often regarded as a servant of Congress, it seems appropriate to review his activities here. The Budget and Accounting Act of 1921 established the office of Comptroller General as head of the new General Accounting Office. The position is filled through appointment by the President, with Senate approval, for a term of fifteen years, no incumbent being allowed to succeed himself. The following powers and duties were imposed: (1) devising and installing improved accounting procedures, (2) covering monies into and out of the treasury by signing payment and covering warrants, (3) auditing of accounts, and (4) acting as financial adviser to Congress. Out of this assignment has developed the practice of rendering opinions in advance on whether certain types of obligations would be approved for the final settlement. The innumerable decisions thus resulting have in a sense become the common law of federal financial transactions.

An example suggests the role of the Comptroller General as the "watchdog" of Congress. In mid-1959, at the same time that appropriations for the administration's foreign aid program were being considered

---

[21] C. Northcote Parkinson, *Parkinson's Law* (New York: Harper & Bros., 1957), p. 33.

[22] The Byrd committee published a ten-year trend report covering 1949–1958. *Additional Report of the Joint Committee on Reduction of Nonessential Federal Expenditures*, 85th Cong., 2d sess. (Washington, D.C.: U.S. Government Printing Office, 1958).

in Congress, the Comptroller General testified before a House Appropriations subcommittee that waste, inefficiency, and lax administration "runs throughout the entire complex" of the foreign aid program.[23] Specifically he referred to programs in Korea and Pakistan where "serious deficiencies" existed. United States aid to Pakistan, he insisted, had been beyond Pakistan's "technical and financial capacity," while in Korea vast stores of military supplies were lying about unused. The Comptroller General criticized both the Defense Department and the International Cooperation Administration for keeping records secret from his agency. It is well known that Congress is hostile to the foreign aid program, and in this case the Comptroller General's testimony provided reinforcement for this position.

The Office of the Comptroller has been controversial almost from the start, largely because of the negative interpretation of his role by the first Comptroller General, J. R. McCarl.[24] He saw the unit as the wielder of the big stick against bureaucrats who sought to get more than their share of government money. Through his authority to approve the final settlement of claims, he began demanding the return to the Treasury of monies which in thirty years have added up to about seven hundred million dollars. It is this authority that makes responsible officers turn to the Comptroller General for decisions before undertaking obligations. As we have seen, this role of the autonomous finance officer as guardian of tax revenues is a popular one in American folklore. Many a city manager has had the experience of being thwarted in attempts to install financial management by an elected auditor, treasurer, or clerk. Americans seem to prefer the external checks of untrained laymen to the internal management checks of professionals.

Critics of the office have also said that it failed to fulfill the injunction to install uniform accounting systems. Its auditing procedure was said to be archaic, especially as applied to government corporations such as the Tennessee Valley Authority, which required a business-type audit of resources and assets rather than the traditional paper audit for fidelity. The Comptroller General was said to have become an adviser of Congress in only the most perfunctory sort of way. But the main criticism of the office concerns the proper allocation of legislative and administrative activities.

Since the first Hoover Commission report, criticism of the Comptroller General has subsided. The second Hoover report even went so far as to commend his office for being "an inspiring and constructive influence in developing consciousness of the need for accounting reforms in the ex-

[23] *New York Times,* July 24, 1959, pp. 1, 6.
[24] A critical treatment of the McCarl regime is contained in Harvey C. Mansfield, *The Comptroller General* (New Haven: Yale University Press, 1939), pp. 1–22.

ecutive agencies."[25] The third Comptroller General, Joseph Campbell, the first to have a professional accounting background, generally pursued a policy of cooperation toward better accountability rather than behaving as a gadfly, although, as his foreign aid testimony shows, vestiges of the traditional role remain. Constructive trends in the operations of the GAO may be summarized as follows:

1. A greater emphasis upon reporting to Congress relative to the effectiveness of agency operations.
2. Continued participation in the Joint Accounting Program with Treasury and Budget.
3. The abandonment of detailed claims auditing in favor of decentralized internal auditing by the agencies themselves, followed by sample checks by the General Accounting Office. In addition, the latter conducts "business-type" audits aimed at evaluating over-all effectiveness.[26]
4. Acceptance of the Bureau of the Budget's role of leadership within the Executive branch for those aspects of accounting which provide management information and facilitate budgetary control and feedback.

The Need for More Information. Congress' main problem in the execution phase has been a lack of information that would provide a basis for adequate review. Several developments suggest that improved Congressional participation can occur, and we shall now outline some of the recommendations made by students of budgeting. Arthur Smithies has suggested that Congress's role will not be much improved until a distinction is made between the policy program side and the management performance side of the federal budget.[27] To improve program evaluation, he recommends first that the reports made by the Appropriations Committees to Congress should include judgments as to what effects the appropriation legislation will have on "the controllability of the budget." Second, he suggests that the Committees be given power to propose amendments to such legislation if it thinks this will bring better balance to the entire budget. In these ways, attempts to bypass the appropriations stage by using some other means of financing, such as by enacting contract authorizations or the use of public-debt transactions,[28] would be made known to Congress.

On the performance side, Smithies recommends several ways of digging out information that would help Congress determine how effec-

[25] Commission on Organization of the Executive Branch of the Government, *Budgeting and Accounting*, p. 59.

[26] Committee on Government Operations, 84th Cong., 2d sess., Union Calendar No. 852, House Report No. 2264, *The General Accounting Office* (Washington, D.C.: U.S. Government Printing Office, 1956).

[27] *Budgeting Process in the United States*, pp. 175–78.

[28] Contract authorizations commit Congress automatically once the initial program is begun; public-debt transactions enable the agencies to borrow from the Treasury, thereby avoiding legislative scrutiny.

tively public funds have been used. More joint committee action is recommended; the Committees of Government Operations and the Appropriations Committees, for example, should "review the economy and efficiency of government operations."[29] He believes, as did the second Hoover Commission, that Congress should require periodic reports on departmental and agency performance and on ways of improving their effectiveness. He urges that these committees become more concerned with major management issues and that they be staffed to carry out complete studies. The Committee on Economic Development has offered similar suggestions for improving federal administration.[30]

PERFORMANCE BUDGETING

We are living today in a scientific culture in which complex and versatile machines make possible the collection of data on an unprecedented scale. We have been thrust into a bureaucratically organized society so rapidly that we have not yet developed yardsticks with which to evaluate our huge institutions. We often try to deny that they exist, to revert to attitudes and thinking characteristic of a simpler nineteenth-century environment while demanding the services which only a bureaucratic society can bring us. However, as we gradually assimilate this change, we shall attack the real problem: The need for social control of bureaucracy through modern instruments designed for that purpose. Performance budgeting is one device that attempts to do this.[31]

Performance budgeting stresses the gathering of statistical information, such as man-hours worked or number of miles flown. While the first Hoover Commission (1949) popularized the concept of performance budgeting, the second Hoover Commission (1955) emphasized the need for more accounting information. Particular emphasis was placed upon what the Commission dubbed "accrual accounting," a term that needs some explanation because the Commission seemed to use it synonymously with "annuality of appropriations"; at least much of the opposition encountered in Congress flowed from this interpretation. Perhaps a discussion of the matter should be preceded by a note on commercial accounting.

Business Type of Accounting. The Eisenhower Administration brought into its councils many business men with an affinity for corporate business practices. Although this trend toward the introduction of business accounting to government has been subject to controversy, there was a

[29] Smithies, *The Budgetary Process in the United States,* p. 178.
[30] *Control of Federal Government Expenditures,* pp. 20–23.
[31] Floyd Mann and Howard Baumgartel, *The Supervisor's Concern with Costs in an Electric Power Company* (Ann Arbor: Survey Research Center, 1953).

certain timeliness in its revival during the 1950's. Corporate business had in general vastly improved its own accounting practices by then. The urgent need for up-to-date procedures had been brought home to industry by the Ford Motor Company's recent experience in the late 1940's, widely reported in the business press. In the Ford case a financial crisis was precipitated largely because the only information available on its financial condition at that time was the balances in the numerous bank accounts which the senior Henry Ford had established. When these began to get alarmingly low, his grandson had been forced to reorganize both management and accounting in order to provide the information needed to pinpoint weaknesses.[32]

This example is mentioned in a discussion of legislative control to illustrate the following points: First, the practice of accounting and the availability of information has increased vastly in recent years. Second, there is a resistance to the introduction of new accounting procedures, even from top management itself. Third, this maturation of the theory and practice of accounting calls for a reevaluation of its applicability to government. Finally, the new emphasis on program budgeting calls for a new type of accounting information.

Until now governmental accounting has been mainly concerned with accountability for cash, with maintaining fidelity and probity. While business accounting is also interested in keeping people honest, it has been more concerned with providing information that management could use in *making* decisions and in evaluating management results. There is no inherent conflict between fidelity accounting and this approach. Indeed, the best way to keep people honest is to create a record of all transactions. The business type of accounting provides more meaningful records than a mere accounting of cash receipts and disbursements. It calls for information about the results of operations, supported by data related to such results. The main evaluation document in a business enterprise is the profit and loss statement; and the fact that this datum does not apply to government has led to the assumption that business accounting practices are also inapplicable. But certain aspects of business accounting apply to government, especially those activities that are amenable to performance budgeting.

Accrual Accounting. The distinction between accrual and cash accounting lies in the fact that under the latter, accumulated totals can be supplied only for cash paid out or taken in. Accrual accounting, on the other hand, can tell one how much cash is due and what obligations

---

[32] William B. Harris, "Ford's Fight for First," **50**, *Fortune* (September, 1954), pp. 123, 126; for an account by a Ford official, see R. E. Roberts, "Ford's Reorganization: the Management Story," **19**, *Advanced Management* (May, 1954), pp. 9–12.

have been incurred but not yet paid for. Accrual accounting is not new, having been advocated by budget specialists for many decades; indeed, it has been practiced in progressive agencies for some time.

The second Hoover Commission's recommendations for accrual accounting were concerned with the same principle but with a slightly different application. Expenditures for many government projects such as flood control or military airplane procurement often extend over more than a single fiscal year. The result is that money appropriated for a particular year will not be "spent" until two or three years later. Hence it becomes impossible to furnish a budgetary statement that will show at any particular time the true status of expenditures because bills accumulated from prior years are always being paid.

The Hoover Commission sought to correct this situation by requiring the appropriations for each long-term project to be reappropriated in each annual budget. Thus the annual budget would show not only the "new" spending for that year but also the obligations from previous years which were expected to be spent during that year. Appropriation accounts could thus reflect at any time an accurate report on current expenditures as well as the status of "accrued" obligations. This would ensure an accurate picture of the status of appropriations and expenditures.[33]

In 1958, after long hearings, Congress passed a watered-down amendment to the Budget and Accounting Act of 1921[34] authorizing the President to take steps in this direction, but only time will tell whether the full intent of the Hoover Commission will be achieved.

EXECUTION AND CONTROL IN THE DEPARTMENTS

We have seen that the major burden for effective execution rests within the individual departments and agencies. What are the ways used by operating officials to carry out and control the spending phase? At this point we touch upon the traditional "control" instruments that ensure honesty and regularity in financial practices. Within the broad framework of administration policy, the agency head has considerable freedom of action. He has the responsibility for setting up effective internal systems of accounting and reporting. Generally his guide is the objectives set down in the Budgeting and Accounting Act of 1950, as amended in 1956, which include: full disclosure of financial activities; providing information that will encourage management improvement;

[33] Committee on Organization of the Executive Branch of the Government, *Budget and Accounting* (Washington, D.C.: U.S. Government Printing Office, 1955), pp. 22 ff; House Committee on Government Operations, *The Budget Process in the Federal Government* (Washington, D.C.: U.S. Government Printing Office, 1957), 101–2.
[34] USC 11; 42 Stat. 20.

maintaining effective control over assets; providing adequate budgetary information; and achieving integration with the accounting system of the Treasury.[35]

Internal Controls. The performance budget concept is helpful here also, for it enables the agency to operate by a financial plan built from estimates of the costs of the various elements in the agency program.[36] Because the budget is stated in terms of anticipated accomplishments during the coming fiscal year, it provides a standard against which the agency can measure its progress over time. Since performance budgeting involves relating costs to work-load information, all costs of a particular program must appear in the reports that the operating official uses to make decisions. As a result, there is a trend toward organizing all operations into "cost centers," that is, organizational units to which personnel, tasks, goals, and activities have been assigned so that program costs can be worked out. This need for precise cost figures has led to a renaissance of the "standards movement," signalized by Ridley and Simon's early work in municipal performance measurement.[37]

Central financial agencies, both within and outside the department, also require periodic reports that condition internal management. Such reports serve as instruments of self-evaluation that periodically oblige the operating units to scrutinize their operations; as noted above, if they have a performance type of budget, they have a built-in plan against which to check their efforts.

The need to get accurate and up-to-date information is thus the basis for the current interest in better accounting methods. It also underlies the growing reliance on data processing machines. For, while electronic data processing will not, of course, solve value-laden problems or struggles for power among the departments, it will make more information available in a much shorter time than before. It will also improve accountability by requiring that individuals maintain better records of their operations.

Spending Controls. Certain controls exercised both by higher levels within the departmental hierarchy and by central fiscal agencies such as the Bureau of the Budget, the GAO, and the Treasury also affect *internal* execution and control. An example of a very significant external control is the requirement that all departmental deficiency or "supplemental" appropriations must be approved by the President before they

---

[35] Section 113(A).

[36] For a detailed analysis and illustration of performance budgeting, see Mosher, *Program Budgeting*, pp. 78–123. However, Mosher concludes that by 1952, although the military services were clearly working *toward* performance budgets, many difficulties remained to be overcome before they would achieve such a budget.

[37] C. E. Ridley and Herbert A. Simon, *Measuring Municipal Activities* (Chicago: International City Managers' Association, 1938).

can be submitted to Congress for authorization. Since such appropriations always occur in response to emergencies of one kind or another, and since an agency may otherwise be inclined to exhaust its appropriation before the end of the fiscal year, central control is an important factor in execution within the departments.

Transfers of funds appropriated for one item to another are another area in which agency discretion is circumscribed by the Budget Bureau and the President, and even their authority is limited in this sphere. The President has only the authority specifically granted to him in the appropriations act for the program concerned. Sometimes the act will set a percentage figure, usually 5 or 10 per cent, within which the Executive may transfer funds from one kind of expenditure to another. Congress is very jealous of its authorization power and resists Executive transfer of funds. However, as noted, in 1950 Congress authorized the President to establish reserves in appropriations for unexpected developments, to curtail agency spending for unnecessary programs, and control spending by more effective operations within the departments. However, it is a moot point how far the President will go in changing legislative authorizations for a given department or agency; certainly he will consider the potential political repercussions before doing so, especially since he must go back to Congress in the succeeding year to gain authorization for his budget.

BIBLIOGRAPHY

HEIN, CLARENCE J. *State Supervision of County and City Expenditures in Kansas* Lawrence: 1957.

HOUSE COMMITTEE ON GOVERNMENT OPERATIONS. *The General Accounting Office,* 84th Cong., 2d sess. Union Calendar 852, H.Rept. 2264. Washington, D.C.: 1956.

KOHLER, ERIC L., and WRIGHT, HOWARD W. *Accounting in the Federal Government.* Englewood Cliffs, New Jersey: 1956.

MANDEL, BENJAMIN J., *et al.* "Work Sampling in a Nationwide Field Organization," 18, *Public Administration Review* (Summer, 1958), pp. 201–7.

MUNICIPAL FINANCE OFFICERS ASSOCIATION. Committee Report. *Bibliography on Performance Budgeting.* Chicago: 1954.

MUSOLF, LLOYD DARYL. *Public Ownership and Accountability: the Canadian Experience.* Cambridge (U.S.A.): 1959.

NATIONAL MUNICIPAL LEAGUE. *Model Accrual Budget Law. Model Cash Basis Law.* New York: Look for latest revision.

PARKINSON, C. NORTHCOTE. *Parkinson's Law.* Boston: 1957.

SCHULSINGER, GERALD G. *The General Accounting Office: Two Glimpses,* Inter-university Case No. 35. University, Ala.: 1956.

SHERWOOD, FRANK. *The Management Approach to Budgeting.* Brussels: 1954.

SIMON, HERBERT A., *et al. Centralization vs. Decentralization in Organizing the Controller's Department.* New York: 1954.

STANS, MAURICE H. "Financial Reorganization in the U.S. Post Office," *Journal of Accountancy* (June–July, 1957).

SYMPOSIUM. "Municipal Accounting and Financial Reporting," 31, *Municipal Finance* (November, 1958). [Entire issue.]

WINNIFRETH, A. J. D. "Treasury Control of Establishments Work," 36, *Journal of the Royal Institute of Public Administration* (Spring, 1958), pp. 9–17.

Part VI

ADMINISTRATIVE LAW
AND REGULATION

CHAPTER 25

Administration
and the Law

Industrialization, urbanization, economic depression, and two world wars have transformed public administration during the past century. Public opinion generally favored more government intervention in the economy, and many problems once left largely to private discretion came under the aegis of the state. Atomic energy, health, welfare, labor relations, agricultural production, investment practices, and the rates charged by public utilities were among such areas. As public supervision and control increased, administrative authority and discretion also increased. A large body of rules and regulations appeared, made and enforced by administrators, under powers delegated to them by legislatures unable to meet the demands of an industrial society for expertise and flexibility. This body of sublegislation, adjudication, and procedure is known as administrative law and includes the following elements:

1. The constitutions, statutes, compacts, charters, ordinances, and resolutions defining the powers and duties of administrative agencies.
2. The rules and regulations made by administrative agencies.
3. The decisions, directives, and orders issued by administrative officers.
4. The investigations and hearings conducted by administrative officers.
5. The judicial decisions and precedents relating to all of the foregoing.

HISTORICAL LIMITATIONS ON
ADMINISTRATIVE DISCRETION

The expansion of administrative power and the breakdown of the separation-of-powers principle did not go unchallenged. The Anglo-Saxon tradition of constitutional government demanded the limitation of executive power. Hence the separation-of-powers theory, the myth of rugged individualism, and the "rule of law" principle were evoked to oppose the trend toward expanded administrative discretion. Bureaucracy, as noted previously, functions within a carefully defined legal framework. Lawyers are central figures in administration which must always conform to the "brooding omnipresence" of the law. The resulting struggle between administrative power and those who fought to limit it meant that public administration became immersed in legal issues. While the need for more administrative discretion was gradually recognized and met, the safeguarding of individual rights was also emphasized. In this context a survey of the constitutional theory that guides public administration is in order.

English Traditions of the Limited Executive. Administrative discretion involves the power of an official to select alternative courses of action in line with the law, agency policy, program objectives, and his own conscience. An examination of Anglo-Saxon political institutions reveals that such discretion has existed for centuries. Before Magna Carta, no problem existed, for the power of the king was almost unlimited. With the crumbling of feudalism, however, English constitutionalism became concerned with the struggle to limit royal prerogatives. The dominant theme of three hundred years of history became the struggle between royal absolutism and the rule of law expressed through legislatures on the one hand and the courts on the other. The barons who wrested Magna Carta from King John in 1215 demanded concessions similar to those embodied in the Bill of Rights signed by William and Mary over four centuries later. In each case the idea of a contract was paramount (the Crown was recognized in exchange for the acceptance of specific restrictions), and the supremacy of law was explicit. Parliament was to be called into session annually; no taxes were to be levied without its consent. Arbitrary imprisonment was proscribed, and no man was to be judged guilty of a crime without trial. Men were to be secure in their homes against arbitrary search and seizure; and the king's officers were bound to observe the privileges and immunities guaranteed by law.

Supremacy of the Law. Our constitutional heritage is most clearly expressed in the supremacy of law concept. In practice, this means that all officials from the President downward are subject to certain rules and precedents that limit their discretion. Law in turn is expressed in statutes and constitutions, as interpreted and enforced by courts. In theory such laws are not subject to executive interpretation but are administered in line with the "letter of the law." Such a neat separation, as we have seen, is not possible in practice. And yet, broadly, the separation of powers between executive, legislative, and judicial branches does mean that the *major* activity of each branch is confined to its basic constitutional function.

An important part of the supremacy of law doctrine is procedural due process. The Fifth and Fourteenth Amendments to the Constitution provide that no persons shall be deprived of life, liberty, or property without due process of law. This means that certain procedures must be followed in applying the law to a particular instance. The rights of persons accused of crime provide an example. They are guaranteed a fair trial before an impartial jury, representation by counsel, cross-examination of witnesses, and similar protections. Another pillar in the supremacy of law doctrine is the independent judiciary. The independence and impartiality of judges are guarded by both law and custom. Contempt of court citations for those attempting to influence the judgment of the court attest to this. Similarly, life tenure and adequate pay for judges is a safeguard of judicial independence. Broadly speaking, the power of public opinion has supported judicial integrity; many Americans believe, for example, in the sanctity of the Supreme Court as a body above politics. This view is less strongly held today, partially as a result of the 1937 struggle over the Court and political controversies of the past few decades.

Such traditions mean that public administration is everywhere subject to the rule of law. The doctrine of *ultra vires,* for example, provides a means of obtaining judicial review on the basis that an official has exceeded his power. As a result officials are inclined to be very sure of their legal position before taking action. The courts, moreover, tend to restrict the scope of official authority to those powers clearly assigned or logically derived from those assigned. This negative legal context is among the principal distinctions between public and private administration. It explains the frustration often experienced by private executives who become public servants. In private management one assumes that he can do anything not specifically forbidden. In public administration, on the other hand, discretion is limited by a great number of laws, rules, and regulations.

Administrative regulation and discretion are sensitive matters because they concern the individual's freedom and his pocketbook. The issue is often one between individual rights and public necessity. When the Interstate Commerce Commission, for example, orders a railroad to install automatic controls to increase public safety, it is exercising discretion, under a statutory mandate and its own rules and regulations. The stockholders are disadvantaged by increased operating expenses and the consequent reduction of dividends. But the public will travel in greater safety. Similarly a city fire inspector is exercising discretion when he decides that a night club must be closed because it is a fire hazard. The owners and entertainers are clearly injured, but public safety is increased. Administrative officials exercise discretion in thousands of similar ways. In a democratic society, it is essential that their discretion be exercised in a responsible way.

Supremacy of Lawyers. The legal context of public administration means that lawyers play a vital role. Legislation must be drafted, hearings must be held, legal opinions must be prepared, and litigation must be conducted. Lawyers also prepare legal documents of many kinds, including administrative orders and rules, contracts and leases, regulations and notices, and the like. The lawyer affects policy-making and he often has a controlling voice in the major issues of his agency, particularly in interpreting the statutes which it administers. Agencies must know what is legally possible. In this context some executives apparently maintain both "hot-running" and "cold-running" lawyers—that is, one group that usually concludes that a thing can be done, and another that always insists that any proposed innovation is impossible.[1] This practice suggests some basic controversies in administrative law.

CONFLICTING INTERPRETATIONS OF THE LAW

Many lawyers and students of public administration are at odds concerning the legality and propriety of administrative discretion in the administrative process. Lawyers often deny the right of administrative agencies to exercise judicial functions such as rate determination. They also question whether the individual's property and personal rights can be adequately protected under the quasijudicial procedures of such agencies. This conflict in part reflects different values. Public administration specialists tend to accept in principle the priority of the community interest and the regulation of private interests to achieve it. The lawyer, on the other hand, tends to define the problem in terms of protecting individual rights against a government which he has been taught to believe is often arbitrary. As Louis L. Jaffe, an eminent legal specialist in administrative law, says in a thoughtful discussion of such differences:

Lawyers come to think of administrative law and the administrative process as significant and worthy of study only in those areas where private interests think it worth their while to demand protection. As a consequence lawyers seeking for their clients elaborate procedural protection modeled on the judicial process may, in an excess of generalizing zeal, induce legislators, administrative agencies, and courts to extend such procedures into areas where they are alien and inappropriate.[2]

---

[1] Albert Lepawsky, *Administration: The Art and Science of Organization and Management* (New York: Alfred A. Knopf, Inc., 1949), p. 591.

[2] Louis L. Jaffe, *Administrative Law* (Boston: Little, Brown and Co., 1954), p. 3, pp. 3–9 *passim.* Other lawyers are less well-balanced; for a polemical and prolix attack, which somehow found its way into the pages of the *American Political Science Review*, on the way that public administration experts have interpreted administrative law, see K. C. Davis, "Reflection of a Law Professor on Instruction and Research in Public Administration," **47,** *American Political Science Review* (September, 1953) pp. 728–52; for rebuttals pointing out the exaggerated character of this article, see **48,**

Broadly speaking, two major interpretations of the nature of law and the judicial process exist. One view, stemming from Roman jurisprudence, is that law represents a body of fundamental and unchanging principles deeply rooted in the nature of things. Such law is self-contained and independent of human judgment. Lawyers and judges are therefore regarded as mere instruments of the law. No individual discretion is involved in the judicial process. The judges merely discover the law and apply it to individual cases. As Justice Roberts said in *U.S. v. Butler:*

> When an act of Congress is appropriately challenged in the Courts as not conforming to the constitutional mandate the judicial branch has only one duty—to lay the article of the Constitution which is invoked beside the statute which is challenged and to decide whether the latter squares with the former. All the court does, or can do, is to announce its considered judgment upon the question.

In this view, the law tends to regard occasional specific hardships arising from the immutability of the law as less important than preserving the authority of legal precedent. Those who have supported the supremacy of law doctrine throughout Western history have often been politically conservative. The great English petitions were not products of radical revolt. It was the feudal nobility who wrested Magna Carta from King John in 1215. It was the aristocracy again who brought about the eclipse of the Stuarts and the signing of the Bill of Rights in 1689. Nor were the great names on the American Constitution representative of the artisan, agrarian, mechanic, and debtor classes. As Charles A. Beard has shown, they were to a considerable extent men of property who created a document which provided safeguards against the excesses of democracy.[3] The view that the best government is that which governs least followed.

The other major theory may be called the sociological interpretation of the law. It maintains that law is conventional, the product of changing social demands. This theory holds that judges do in fact make law. As Oliver Wendell Holmes once said, "We are under a Constitution, but the Constitution is what the judges say it is." In view of past judicial

---

American Political Science Review (March, 1954), pp. 174–85; for the question of individual opportunity for recourse against state action and the conclusions of the Franks Committee, which studied the organization and procedures of British administrative tribunals, particularly those involved in hearings in which individuals object to the compulsory purchase of land, see William A. Robson, "Administrative Justice and Injustice: a Commentary on the Franks Report," *Public Law* (Spring, 1958), pp. 12–31; and Robert V. Presthus, "British Town and Country Planning: Local Participation," **45**, *American Political Science Review* (September, 1951), pp. 756–69.

[3] Charles A. Beard, *An Economic Interpretation of the Constitution of the United States* (New York: The Macmillan Co., 1913); also Madison's *Federalist Paper No. 10.*

experience, this seems a reasonable proposition. Congress has greatly expanded the powers of the federal government, and these powers have been upheld by the Supreme Court in almost every instance. The great constitutional issues of the 1930's, including federal regulation of labor relations, agricultural production, and investment policy, were all covered under the same Constitution that long restricted government to a negative role. Although this theory of judicial realism supported administrative regulation and discretion, the principal reason for its rise was not judicial invention but, as shown in Chapter 2, social change.

EXPANSION OF ADMINISTRATIVE DISCRETION

The Industrial Revolution and Social Change. Adam Smith's economic theory and James Watt's steam engine appeared about the same time. The engine produced a series of events that challenged the doctrine of laissez faire, seriously modifying it. The machine transferred production from the home and the shop to the large factory. This brought workers together and culminated in the urbanization of England and the United States. Unprecedented problems of housing, transportation, sanitation, health, welfare, and crime followed, and soon came into conflict with legal tradition. Social reform demanded the transformation of legal thought.

The American legal system adapted itself to social change rather slowly. Conservatives used the symbols of constitutional liberty in the struggle against social change. The separation-of-powers and the supremacy-of-law doctrines were the principal weapons. In almost every case where social legislation was enacted, additional administrative apparatus was necessary to administer it. Officials and agencies, moreover, had to be entrusted with a certain measure of discretion to provide flexibility. In exercising this discretion, which included both legislative and judicial power, it was claimed that they were violating the separation of powers principle. During the early days of the New Deal, the Supreme Court briefly stemmed such developments by nullifying several regulatory programs. However, after the election of 1936 and Franklin D. Roosevelt's efforts to reorganize the Court, its attitude suddenly changed. Since that time, every important piece of social legislation has been approved. In substance, this meant the approval of increased administrative discretion, for it is impossible to add new social legislation without increasing the scope of administrative power.

The problem is to adjust social institutions and legal theory without altering the rule of law insofar as individual rights are concerned. What is needed is a nice balance between the supremacy of law in the historic sense of preserving individual liberty against arbitrary official action and the development of administrative discretion. This is different from using that doctrine as a means of thwarting necessary social change. The problem is one of ensuring that government's new increments of power are used according to the rule of law.

Rise of Regulatory Agencies. Social change requires organizational change. In administration the principal means has been to give agencies the power to regulate the activities of private individuals, corporations, and agencies. Workmen's compensation commissions illustrate this practice. Under common law an injured worker was compelled to sue his employer in a court of law to obtain damages. In addition to the expense of a lawyer and drawn-out court proceedings, he had the cards stacked against him by certain legal technicalities. There was the assumption of risk doctrine whereby the individual accepted at his own risk and expense the hazards of personal injury on the job. The contributory negligence rule also existed, under which the employer could escape liability if he could prove that the worker's negligence contributed in any way to the accident. Still another factor was the fellow-servant doctrine which also absolved the employer who could show that the injury resulted from the negligence of a fellow worker. The injured workman had little chance of recovery in the great majority of cases.

Under the new workmen's compensation laws, however, industrial accident commissions were authorized to make decisions. In so doing the commissions exercise discretionary power, both judicial and legislative. As a result the law now protects those least able to protect themselves because majority public opinion demands that industrial accidents be regarded as the responsibility of society in general.

Regulatory agencies are now common.[4] At the federal level, a venerable example is the Interstate Commerce Commission, the oldest of the independent regulatory commissions, established in 1887. Federal commissions with independent status include the Federal Trade Commission, the Federal Power Commission, the Securities Exchange Commission, the National Labor Relations Board, as well as several others. That regulatory power is also vested in many federal departments should not be overlooked. Indeed, some of the most important administrative law cases before the Supreme Court have involved the Secretary of Agriculture. In the Department of Commerce one finds regulatory activities in the Bureau of Marine Inspection and Navigation and in the Civil Aeronautics Board. But not all regulatory authority occurs at the federal level; the early social legislation programs were directed largely by the states. Examples of state regulatory agencies are public utility com-

[4] See Robert E. Cushman, *The Independent Regulatory Commissions* (New York: Oxford University Press, 1941).

missions, industrial accident commissions, banking commissioners, and insurance commissioners, as well as the boards which license professions and vocations.

Students of administrative law sometimes overlook the fact that considerable regulation of private business, property, and individual activity is also carried on by municipal governments. A conspicuous example is the administration of building codes. In most cities one can no longer build as he chooses. Not only must he get a building permit, but the structure is inspected in accord with certain standards and specifications during the course of construction. City health departments regulate the serving of food and the sanitation of all types of establishments. The fire department inspects private buildings to ensure that they meet safety standards established by municipal ordinances. Certain types of business, such as pawnshops, are regulated by the police department through the licensing power. Another common form of regulatory activity has been the control of land use through zoning.

Limitations of the Judicial Process. The question now arises: Why were such regulatory functions not assigned to ordinary courts of law? One reason was the belief that precedent could not and should not rule in the technical areas being supervised. Regulation in such fields as agricultural production, investment practices, and public utility rates, it was felt, required a great deal of flexibility. No background of experience was available to crystallize regulatory action into a body of law. As a result administrative agencies were obliged to establish precedent as the needs of the moment required. The desire to avoid the delays and red tape of legal procedure was another reason for using administrative tribunals rather than courts. Proceedings before most administrative agencies have, until recently, been rather informal. Although attorneys are often present, there are few questions about the competency of witnesses or the admission of evidence. Witnesses testify in an informal manner, frequently without interruption.

Demand for Expertise. Administrative regulation, in addition, makes possible the use of experts for investigation and analysis in a particular field. Judges, on the other hand, are not suited by training or experience to decide on technical questions of great complexity such as those involved in public utility regulation, banking and insurance, or radio and television. Nor can courts exercise any continuous surveillance of the important economic sectors that require regulation. Administrative tribunals, however, can provide both expert technicians and intelligent laymen toward this end. As Robert E. Cushman has shown, the desire to provide such expert, independent bodies was an important objective of Congress in establishing the commissions.[5] This theory has not always worked in practice, largely because of the practice of appointing mediocre persons on a political basis, but this does not alter this objective of the commission device.

Another distinction between courts of law and the regulatory commissions is the fact that the latter are not expected to be neutral arbiters but instead are commonly viewed as guardians of the public interest. Judges, of course, are supposed to be merely impartial umpires between two contesting parties. In legal terms a lawsuit is known as the *lis inter partes*—a controversy between two parties, the plaintiff who complains and the defendant who answers. To be a party in a lawsuit, one must have a legal interest, and such an interest is defined as one which involves the possibility of being injured in one's person or property. One does not have a legal interest if he has only the desire to be of benefit to the community or if he has a mere curiosity in the outcome. His interest must be personal, direct, and substantial. In administrative tribunals, however, the situation is rather different. Such tribunals are required by law to be guardians of the public interest, as opposed to the limited interest of private persons. Furthermore, one need not have a legal interest to appear before an administrative tribunal. Any interested citizen can be heard.

LEGAL ISSUES IN ADMINISTRATIVE REGULATION

The expansion of administrative power during the New Deal period was met with widespread criticism by lawyers, economists, businessmen, and a few political scientists. The American Bar Association was particularly active in attacks upon the administrative citadel, being primarily responsible for the drastic Walter-Logan Bill, passed by Congress in 1944 but vetoed by President Roosevelt. The ABA was also among the principal supporters of the Administrative Procedure Act of 1946. Much of this opposition was based upon a sincere apprehension of the effect of administrative discretion upon individual liberties. With the impact of war and the expansion of executive power which continued in the post-war period, however, the earlier issues lost much of their immediacy. The legal profession slowly accepted increased administrative discretion as a corollary of big government and shifted its efforts from substantive opposition to controlling the procedures whereby regulation was carried out. The major issues that now provide the basis for attacks upon the regulatory process are the merging of agency functions, the requirements of procedural due process, and the opportunity for judicial review.

[5] *Ibid.*, chap. iii.

Unlawful Delegation of Legislative and Judicial Power. As we have seen, the separation-of-powers theme is a basic element in American constitutional theory. Both the arbitrary policies of George III and the activities of early state legislatures ensured a healthy respect among the founding fathers for Montesquieu's dictum, "power must be checked with power." They sought limited government by a separation of legislative, executive, and judicial power. Certain checks and balances as well as specific restraints upon Congress in several areas, notably civil liberties, were also established. This theory also maintained that no sector could lawfully delegate its principal function to another. However, in issuing rules, regulations, and orders under broad grants of power from legislatures, administrative agencies are in fact exercising *legislative* power. Moreover, in deciding the rights and interests of contesting parties through administrative adjudication, administrative officials often act as judges. Such quasijudicial and quasilegislative activities have alienated many observers who maintain a strict interpretation of the separation-of-powers principle.

Judicial Review. Although the Constitution does not mention the right of judicial review, the federal courts soon assumed the power to challenge executive and legislative actions held contrary to the Constitution. Judicial review became a curb upon the executive and legislative arms of government and a means of safeguarding individual rights of person and property. It also became a useful device for restricting the expansion of public power. Until 1937, for example, much of the early New Deal legislation was negated by the Supreme Court. Since that time, as pointed out above, a sympathetic Court has been an equally effective means of expanding public power. The Constitution is indeed what the judges say it is.

The delegation of legislative power to administrative agencies and particularly their regulation of great economic interests were attacked as violations of the separation-of-powers principle. In time, however, the attack was gradually modified to demand instead that adequate procedural standards be included in regulatory laws to guide and to limit administrative discretion. As a result, during the 1930's, several parts of the recovery program were invalidated by the Supreme Court on the ground that standards were so general that delegation had "run riot."[6]

The Due-Process Requirement. Another major limitation on administrative discretion has been the due-process clause. While the separation-of-powers barrier has largely been overcome, the due-process require-

[6] *Panama Refining Co.* v. Ryan (293 U.S. 388, 1935); *Schechter Poultry Corporation* v. *U.S.* (295 U.S. 495, 1935).

ment remains at the center of administrative law. As contained in the Fifth and Fourteenth Amendments to the Constitution, due process says in effect that no person shall be deprived of life, liberty, or property without due process of law. It includes two broad concepts: procedural and substantive due process. Insofar as agencies are concerned, procedural due process requires that individuals affected by their action must be given prior notice, fair hearing, opportunity for judicial review, and the like. Substantive due process asks the question: Is the objective of a law reasonable? Does a statute, by itself, amount to an arbitrary deprivation of life, liberty, or property? Some observers maintain that this criterion permits the judges to apply their own notions of what public policy should be as substitutes for the more representative decisions of the chief executive and the legislature. The substantive criterion, however, has gradually been abandoned, largely because of changing public opinion and the reluctance of the courts to substitute their judgment for that of the "political" branches.

Procedural due process, on the other hand, has provided the framework for many attacks on the activities of regulatory agencies. Among them is the charge that due process is violated because administrative agencies in handling controversies act both as prosecutor and judge. This merging of functions is held to increase the vulnerability of agencies to pressure from Congress, the President, and private groups. The informal procedures of the commissions have also been attacked. Such practices allegedly create an unsuitable atmosphere for the adjudication of individual rights. Criticisms of this kind led eventually to a successful demand for change.

JUDICIALIZATION OF THE ADMINISTRATIVE PROCESS

The objections of the American Bar Association to the New Deal's expansion of regulatory activities led to the creation of its administrative law committee which introduced legislation in 1939. The Walter-Logan Bill, as the measure was known, included the following provisions: (1) Administrative rules issued under a basic statute would be drawn up only after formal public hearings, and would be subject to judicial review by any person "substantially interested" in the matter. (2) Any person having a complaint against an administrative decision could demand quasi-judicial hearings before three-man boards, set up in all administrative agencies except the so-called independent regulatory commissions. (3) Finally, judicial review of all administrative orders would be greatly expanded and systematized. Congress exempted several agencies from these measures, recognizing perhaps that they would make effective administration difficult. In December of 1940, however, the bill was vetoed by President Roosevelt with the comment that it would place the "Government at the mercy of never-ending law suits and subject all administrative acts and processes to the control of the judiciary."

The Attorney General's Committee. The Supreme Court's interest in administrative procedures and the criticism of private parties resulted next in a distinguished committee whose recommendations became the basis for the Administrative Procedure Act of 1946.[7] The Attorney General's Report of 1941 contained the following majority recommendations, most of which were sympathetic to the needs of administrative agencies:

1. An office of Federal Administrative Procedure to be established to make studies and improve existing operating procedures.
2. Agency policies and procedures to be published, and the agencies to be required to issue interpretive declaratory judgments that would be subject to judicial review.
3. Hearing commissioners to be appointed to several agencies.
4. Rule making to be somewhat formalized to include conferences with affected interests but not to the degree recommended in the Walter-Logan Bill.
5. Informal and voluntary means to be used whenever possible to settle disputes.
6. The existing arrangements for judicial review to be left unchanged.

Insofar as the dual role of agencies as prosecutor and judge was concerned, bias could be avoided by careful internal segregation of investigation and adjudication at the operating level, rather than by a complete separation of these activities. The latter, it was believed, would cause undue policy uncertainty and conflict.

The minority report of three members, on the other hand, urged more stringent requirements, many of which appeared in the Administrative Procedure Act. These included the external separation of judicial from other functions, a uniform administrative procedures code, and a greatly expanded scope for judicial review. A general statutory provision for judicial review and review standards was recommended. Finally, it was urged that the practice whereby agency findings were sustained by isolated bits of "substantial evidence" should be modified to require that such evidence appear *throughout* the record.

The Administrative Procedure Act. In 1946, several of these recommendations, including those of the minority, were embodied in a law which has been called both the Magna Carta and the saboteur of the

---

[7] *Administrative Procedure in Government Agencies; Final Report of Attorney General's Committee on Administrative Procedure,* Senate Doc. No. 8, 77th Cong., 1st sess. (Washington, D.C.: U.S. Government Printing Office, 1941).

administrative process, depending upon the values of the observer.[8] The Civil Service Commission rather than the recommended Office of Administrative Procedure is charged with recruiting and supervising hearing officers or "trial examiners" who preside at cases involving conflicting interests. Although the Commission's initial attempts to carry out this responsibility resulted in a controversy with the American Bar Association,[9] the position of the hearing officer as the central figure in the system of separated investigative and judicial functions seems well established. In a recent case the Supreme Court reaffirmed the need to overcome "the evils from the commingling of functions. . . ."[10] The Taft-Hartley amendments to the National Labor Relations Act also vested independent authority in the General Counsel for the issuance and prosecution of complaints of unfair labor practices. However, the disagreement between the Counsel and the Labor Board on basic policy appears to confirm the belief of the Attorney General's committee that confusion would result from separation.[11]

[8] Public Law 404, 79th Cong., 2d sess. (1946). The range of view which apparently reasonable men can have about the same subject is indicated in the following comments. The first is from the foreword to the act written by its principal sponsor, Senator McCarran:

"The Administrative Procedure Act is a strongly marked, long sought, and widely heralded advance in democratic government. It embarks upon a new field of legislation of broad application in the 'administrative' area of government lying between the traditional legislative and fundamental judicial processes on the one hand and authorized executive functions on the other. Although it is brief, it is a comprehensive charter of private liberty and a solemn undertaking of official fairness. It is intended as a guide to him who seeks fair play and equal rights under law, as well as to those invested with executive authority. It upholds the law and yet lightens the burden of those on whom the law may impinge. It enunciates and emphasizes the tripartite form of our democracy and brings into relief the ever essential declaration that this is a government of law rather than of men."

Frederick F. Blachly and Miriam E. Oatman, on the other hand, are less sanguine about the effect and intent of the law: "The act in no way solves the major difficulties of the federal administrative process: the fact that hundreds of statutes deal in slightly different ways with identical situations; the fact that there has been a failure to develop three or four standardized procedures to meet similar legal situations; the fact that some one hundred courts and tribunals rather than one high administrative court now pass upon administrative action. . . . Impartial and constructive changes should take the place of the destructive and malicious policies of the present act, adopted with the purpose of impeding and confusing administration and thus weakening important governmental controls and adding to the incomes of the lawyers sponsoring it through the American Bar Association." "Sabotage of the Administrative Process," 7, *Public Administration Review* (Summer, 1946), p. 227.

[9] Ralph F. Fuchs, "The Hearing Examiner Fiasco under the Administrative Procedure Act," **63**, *Harvard Law Review* (March, 1950), pp. 737–68.

[10] *Wong Yang Sung v. McCarthy* (339 U.S. 33,46, 1950).

[11] For an analysis of such issues, see Nathanial L. Nathanson, "Central Issues of American Administrative Law," **45**, *American Political Science Review* (June, 1951), pp. 348–85.

Minority Recommendations Adopted. The Administrative Procedure Act provided for a code of administrative standards for federal agencies. In general, however, it appears that little was added beyond the usual notice and hearing demanded by the courts in line with procedural due process. The statute is so general that its meaning must be deduced largely from specific court cases. It seems clear, moreover, that the myriad of special and changing situations which led to extensive administrative discretion do not lend themselves to treatment under a general code. In the area of judicial review, the act seems to have brought a slowing down of government action. The provision that "any person suffering legal wrong because of any agency action, or adversely affected or aggrieved by such action within the meaning of any relevant statute, shall be entitled to judicial review," expands greatly the scope of review, and speed of decisions has been reduced as a result. The act also removes hearing officials from their position as administrative authorities and gives them the status of judicial officers. The hearing officer, however, does not make the final decision; he secures the information upon which the responsible agency heads will finally recommend a decision. The act also assumes that all administrative hearings are judicial, which is true in only a minority of the cases; namely, when cease and desist orders are issued, licenses are suspended or revoked, or a reparations award is made.[12]

"Rules" and "orders," moreover, are given a much broader definition than previously. The distinction between the former as measures of general application and the latter as specific sanctions against a particular person is blurred. Although this was done in an effort at simplification, it has proved confusing while extending greatly the scope of judicial review.

Several commentators feel that the act has had an unfortunate effect on administrative action. Blachly and Oatman conclude that only two "rays of hope shine through this darkness": That Congress will recognize the inadequacy of the law and either repeal it or make drastic amendments, and that the courts will adhere to the distinctions which they have always regarded as controlling in taking or refusing jurisdiction.[13] Another observer concludes, "On balance, despite some desirable results, it is in tone and intent an unfortunate piece of legislation. . . . There is little question that the act is basically anachronistic in spirit and intent, if not in effect."[14]

[12] Blachly and Oatman, "Sabotage of the Administrative Process," pp. 213–27.
[13] *Ibid.*, pp. 226–27.
[14] V. M. Barnett, Jr., "Judicialization of the Administrative Process," **8**, *Public Administration Review* (Spring, 1948), p. 133.

State Action. Meanwhile, although there is no general agreement that such codes are effective, there has been a trend toward establishing procedural codes for regulatory agencies at the state level.[15] Here again the American Bar Association has been active, through its sponsorship of the Model State Administrative Procedure Act which has provided a pattern for action in several states. The state codes deal with the three major areas of administrative procedure, rule making, administrative adjudication, and judicial review. In rule making, the main emphasis has been upon proper notice and the means of putting rules into effect. Fortunately, no rigid scheme has been introduced for the formulation, modification, and repeal of rules. The California provisions are examples of current practice. Notice of proposed rules must be published thirty days in advance and mailed to every "interested person," which includes all those who have filed a request for notice. The latter have an opportunity to present, either orally or in writing, arguments which the agency must consider before the rule is adopted. Emergency rules and regulations are exempted from these requirements.

Administrative adjudication in contested cases has apparently not been much changed by the new codes. Procedural requirements have been regularized somewhat, but the principal effect has been educational rather than revisionary.[16] The usual requirements are emphasized: notice, clearly specified issues, rules as to the types of permissible evidence, opportunity for cross-examination of witnesses, and subpoena power to compel testimony at hearings. Although the federal act emphasizes the role of the hearing officer, and the ABA has recommended standards of appointment for trial examiners (including several years of legal practice), the Model Act and most state acts say little about it. The California statute, however, provides for unusually detailed requirements. The State Personnel Board determines general qualifications, and all hearing officers must be lawyers possessing at least five years' experience in California. A Division of Administrative Procedure maintains a staff of qualified officers who are assigned to various agencies. However, agencies requiring full-time hearing officers may appoint their own officers, subject to the requirements listed above. The powers of the hearing officer are impressive. He presides at hearings, decides on the admission of evidence, and advises the agency on matters of law. There is in addition a move under way to extend the hearing officer's power by compelling the agency to accept his decision if the agency itself did not hold the hearing.

[15] Ferrel Heady, "State Administrative Procedure Laws," 12, *Public Administration Review* (Winter, 1952), pp. 10–20; and his *Administrative Procedure Legislation in the States* (Ann Arbor: University of Michigan Press, 1952).

[16] Heady, "State Administrative Procedure Laws," p. 14.

In Missouri, Michigan, and to a lesser extent in California, there has been an effort to separate completely prosecuting and judging functions and to judicialize the rules of evidence before administrative tribunals.[17] In Michigan, for example, a Citizen's Advisory Committee has proposed a complete denial to the regulatory body of the power to review or alter the decision of the hearing officer. This would practically abolish the process of agency adjudication and review for policy consistency. It would give the major responsibility for implementing a regulatory statute to the hearing officer, reducing the agency's role to that of initial investigation and decision, subjecting even its expert findings on matters of fact to overrule by the independent hearing officer.

Expansion of Judicial Review. Judicial review has also been broadened in scope, although the methods of review have apparently been little changed, with the exception of the "sufficiency of evidence" required by the courts to uphold an administrative decision. "Substantial evidence" must be found throughout the *entire record* of the case and not merely anywhere in the record as supporting evidence for the agency's decision. This change will probably have the effect, which it has had at the federal level,[18] of broadening the authority of the courts and somewhat overemphasizing judicial review.

In sum, while the states that have adopted procedural codes have sometimes been motivated by distrust of the administrative process, and while the organized legal profession has had an active interest in promoting such laws, the total effect is hard to determine. Such codes may be a prelude to more drastic action that could seriously impair the effectiveness of administrative procedures. The problem is that legislation by itself can only set minimum standards and cure patent deficiencies; it is ill-suited to the requirements of expertness, reasonable speed, and the quasi-judicial procedures that make them possible.[19]

BIBLIOGRAPHY

BROWN, ESTHER L. *Lawyers, Law Schools and the Public Service.* New York: 1948.
CARLSTON, KENNETH S. *Law and the Structures of Social Action.* New York: 1956.

[17] *Ibid.*, pp. 15–16.

[18] At the federal level, Nathanson concludes, ". . . there can be little doubt that the findings of the Labor Board in particular, and to some extent of administrative agencies in general, will fare somewhat more roughly than before in the federal courts. The judgment of the expert is still to be respected, but only to the extent that it does not shock the common sense of the judiciary," "Central Issues of American Administrative Law," p. 359.

[19] For a review of recent developments and a plea for procedures that recognize the administrative need for flexibility, see Ferrel Heady, "The New Reform Movement in Regulatory Administration," **19**, *Public Administration Review* (Spring, 1959), pp. 89–100.

DICKINSON, JOHN. *Administrative Justice and the Supremacy of Law.* Cambridge: 1927.

FREUND, ERNST M. *Administrative Powers Over Persons and Property.* Chicago: 1928.

HART, JAMES. *An Introduction to Administrative Law.* New York: 1940.

HEADY, FERREL. *Administrative Procedure Legislation in the States.* Ann Arbor: 1952.

MENDLSON, WALLACE. "Mr. Justice Frankfurter on Administrative Law," *Journal of Politics* (August, 1957).

MEYERS, LEWIS. *The American Legal System: The Administration of Justice in the United States by Judicial Administrative Military and Arbitral Tribunals.* New York: 1955.

PARKER, REGINALD. "The Execution of Administrative Acts," *University of Chicago Law Review* (Winter, 1957).

PENNOCK, J. RONALD. *Administration and the Rule of Law.* New York: 1941.

REDFORD, E. S. *Administration of National Economic Control.* New York: 1952.

CHAPTER 26

The Regulatory
Commissions

Our analysis of regulatory agencies will be devoted mainly to the federal independent regulatory commissions. Although somewhat restrictive, since considerable regulation also occurs at state and local levels, this focus is understandable when one considers the broad jurisdiction, the volume and importance of business, and the extensive public interests affected by the federal commissions. They now employ some twelve thousand persons, and their annual cost of operation is about sixty million dollars. One of the most important, the Federal Trade Commission, spent $5,516,000 in 1957. Another, the Federal Communications Commission, spent about $8,000,000. In the total of federal expenditures such amounts are small, but the significance of the commissions lies in the fact that they regulate the main elements of the economy, including trade practices, transportation, labor, securities, electric power, credit, and banking. Beginning with the ICC in 1887, they were created to encourage the orderly development of important economic activities, to provide a sustained and expert surveillance of their operations, and to carry on adjudication between the regulated interests and the public.

COMMISSION STRUCTURE AND PERSONNEL

In order to carry out these functions, the commissions have a special type of organization. Their relationship with the three great branches of government has been unique, and they have been given special means of action to ensure that their policies are carried out. They are different from the great departments in other ways. They are headed by boards whose principal function is to make policy. Their responsibility is shared between Congress and the President. They do not carry out service functions that require a great number of employees, like the Post Office or the Department of Agriculture. They are for this reason rather small; the ICC, the largest, has only about twenty-five hundred employees.

Regulatory agencies of a similar kind are found at the state level. In fact, the first regulatory commissions were those established in the mid-western states in order to remedy the abuses of railroad and warehouse interests. Most of the economic interests regulated in their interstate activities at the federal level are also supervised within each state by special agencies. Public utility commissions and state securities commissions are common examples. Considerable regulatory power is also vested in local government officials, although they rarely use the independent commission form, with the exception of city planning commissions and boards of zoning appeal. But it is the federal regulatory commissions whose experiences and problems best illustrate the character and basic issues of regulation at every level. Although Congress has never developed a consistent theoretical basis for the structure and position of the federal commission, it did adopt a fairly consistent pattern in establishing the commissions up through 1936.[1] Plural membership has been used to increase the independence of the commissions and ensure that several points of view will influence the determination of regulatory policy. In order to remove the commissions from executive domination, they have been placed outside the great departments. Another reason for placing them there is that they have legislative, judicial, and executive powers, and consequently (according to the separation-of-powers theory) should not be located in any single branch. This argument, however, is not very strong. As Robert E. Cushman notes, the important thing about a commission is not its structural location in the federal system but the character of its job.[2] In addition, as we have seen, several executive departments also exercise both legislative and judicial powers. The fact that the commissions were to perform an expert and specific task which could not very well be distributed among several agencies also influenced Congress in its effort to make the commissions independent.[3]

As far as personnel is concerned, it was assumed in 1887 when the first agency, the Interstate Commerce Commission, was established that the commissions must be directed by men of high caliber and that high salaries were required to secure them. The salary of ICC members was fixed at $7,500, an amount then exceeded only by that of Supreme Court

[1] There are now eleven regulatory commissions including:

Interstate Commerce Commission	Federal Communications Commission
Federal Power Commission	Civil Aeronautics Board
Federal Trade Commission	Federal Reserve Board
U.S. Maritime Board	National Labor Relations Board
U.S. Tariff Commission	Federal Aviation Agency
Securities and Exchange Commission	

[2] Robert E. Cushman, *The Independent Regulatory Commissions* (New York: Oxford University Press, 1941), p. 444.

[3] *Ibid.*, pp. 58–59.

justices. Since that time salaries have been increased in line with rising prices, and the present salary of most commissioners is $25,000 per year. The use of bipartisanship as a means of promoting impartiality was agreed upon from the start, a policy that may have enhanced the consistency of regulatory policy by enlisting the support of minority parties. Members may not have a financial interest in the sector of the economy with which they are concerned. Members are appointed by the President with the consent of the Senate and serve overlapping terms, ranging from five to fourteen years, depending on the agency. Such a practice is believed to promote independence by ensuring that no President will normally appoint a majority of the commission members. Finally, insofar as independence is concerned, the members are subject to removal in most cases only for specific cause. Inefficiency, neglect of duty, or malfeasance is the usual ground for removal.

FUNCTION OF THE COMMISSIONS

The commissions exercise three main functions: to inform industry and other regulated groups as to the objectives of public policy insofar as regulation and development are concerned; to discover and promulgate the rules and regulations that will effect this policy; and to enforce such regulations either by adjudicating controversies arising between the public and the interest regulated or by prosecuting acts that violate policy. These functions are closely interrelated. The content of basic policy, for example, is immediately influenced by the practical results of adjudication and prosecution. Policies that are ill conceived are soon revealed in the light of experience. In addition the dynamic nature of our economy means that the regulatory process will require continuous modification in response to changing circumstances. For these reasons the suggestion that the various functions of the commissions be externally separated is open to serious question. Instead, full consultation among all sections is required. The suggested separation is based too much on the concept of regulation as prevention rather than as a positive guide to a mutually satisfying social policy.

At bottom, the function of the commissions is to construct broad social policy and enforce it while planning for the orderly development of the activities under their aegis. The more dramatic aspects of their work, such as formal adjudication and prosecution, are in a sense the by-products of failure to arrive at policies that are feasible in practice. To avoid such failures, the commissions establish policy only after extensive consultation with affected interests and careful analysis of the problems concerned. Neither the basic law nor the rules and orders stemming from it are products of a single, limited view but are compromise measures that attempt to strike a judicious balance between governmental necessity and individual liberty. Needless to say, there are conflicts of interest between regulation in the public interest and the objectives of private interest. The objective of regulation, however, is to achieve a balance among them. Here again the differences between theory and practice are substantial.

PROBLEM OF INTERNAL ORGANIZATION

The basic problem here is one of securing unity and communication between the commissioners at the top and the staff members upon whom they must depend for the expert advice and judgments necessary to make their determinations meaningful. The customary separation of the staff into various technical specialties compounds the problem. Legal, accounting, and engineering divisions understandably approach issues with different frames of reference, and their scrutiny of a case may result in opposing recommendations. Consultation between commissioners and staff eases some of these difficulties, but the divergent points of view that reflect different backgrounds are not easily overcome. More important, in rendering a final decision, the commissioners often rely entirely upon written memoranda from the staff. They may thus decide without seeing either their staff or hearing the witnesses in the case at issue. Again, administration in the commissions has suffered from the tendency to equate technical expertise with administrative ability. This results in the appointment of men of technical skill as division heads. But such persons, by virtue of their analytical outlook and preoccupation with detail, often have limited success in organizing work, dealing with others, and generally maintaining the smooth flow of paper necessary to avoid delay.

Another charge often levied against the commissions is that the staff is inadequately supervised. This is partially a reflection upon the ability of commissioners, who as Cushman concluded, have often been appointed for personal and political reasons rather than for the ability to administer, to judge, or to plan.[4] But the lack of adequate direction is also due to the gulf that separates the lay commissioner from the expert staff member. The relationship of internal organization to the effective transmission of information to the commissioners received special emphasis from the task force of the first Hoover Commission, which recommended several administrative changes. In view of the inadequacy of staff supervision, the task force urged that the commission chairman be ". . . specifically designated as the person responsible for administration within

[4] Cushman, *The Independent Regulatory Commissions*, pp. 731–32.

the commission."[5] This function should not be discharged by the chairman personally but by an executive officer. Broad questions of policy or substance, however, should remain the prerogative of the entire commission.

The present practice of dividing the staff on a professional basis into areas of law, engineering, accounting, and the like was believed to hamper coordination and diffuse responsibility. The task force recommended, instead, organization on a functional basis in which each bureau would assume responsibility for a certain task and would be assigned the various types of necessary management aids. Better supervision and administration were believed obtainable in this way. The Securities and Exchange Commission has used this type of organization with considerable success. Finally, the task force recommended improvements in operating procedures, particularly with regard to informal negotiation carried out through the conference method.

THE PROBLEM OF INDEPENDENCE

As we have seen, the federal regulatory commissions are often called "independent," and several institutional devices are used to promote this condition. Independence has usually meant freedom from immediate control by Congress and the President. As Cushman notes, however, in the case of the original federal commission (the ICC) this requirement actually meant freedom from partisan, political control rather than independence from Congress.[6] As time passed and the commissions' powers were extended, "independence" came to mean also freedom from the private groups that they regulate. This freedom is generally held to be necessary if the public interest is to be served. Thus "independence" has meant different things to different people, illustrating again the semantic problem resulting from the diverse meanings often assigned to the same word.

The President and the Commissions. In theory at least, "independence" includes either a complete freedom or substantial measure of freedom from President and Congress. In actual fact, of course, complete independence of the commissions is a myth. The President, Congress, and the courts have certain powers and functions that circumscribe the commissions. Although it is true that the commissions arrive at decisions without consultation with the President, decisions which he may not modify or revoke, their members are appointed by him. And this means

[5] Commission on Organization of the Executive Branch Government, *Task Force Report on Regulatory Commissions* (Washington, D.C.: U.S. Government Printing Office, 1949), pp. 39–55.
[6] Cushman, *The Independent Regulatory Commissions*, pp. 61–62.

that he can greatly shape their regulatory policy by the caliber and values of those appointed. In view of the fact that two terms appears to have become the common Presidential tenure of office, he is often able to appoint several commissioners.

The President has, moreover, a broad general power of removal. Although there are limits on this power, the President has always been able to remove purely executive officers. In the celebrated Myers case, it was established that Congress could not constitutionally restrict the President's power to remove a first-class postmaster appointed by him and confirmed by the Senate.[7] Plaintiff had claimed that since the Senate's participation was required for appointment, it should also be required for removal. In rejecting this view, the Court relied on both historical and constitutional claims. It was shown that a time-honored precedent of unlimited Presidential removal power over executive officers existed. Discretionary removal was held, in addition, to be an inherent part of the Executive power given him in Article II of the Constitution, as well as of his obligation to ensure that "the laws be faithfully executed." Judicial infringement upon this power would, the Court held, violate the separation-of-powers doctrine.

LIMITATIONS: THE HUMPHREY DOCTRINE. The principal limitation on Presidential removal power is illuminated by the Humphrey case, arising from Franklin D. Roosevelt's removal of a Federal Trade Commissioner in 1933 for a cause not among those prescribed in the statute.[8] The President fired Humphrey on the basis that their views as to the proper function of the FTC were directly opposed. Humphrey held the Wilsonian view that the commission should function mainly as "an indispensable instrument of information and publicity." The President, on the other hand, felt that the agency had an overriding regulatory obligation. Humphrey, it should be added, was the most conservative member of the commission and had recently been reappointed to a second five-year term. In a somewhat ambiguous opinion, the Court held that he could be removed only in accord with statutory provisions. The FTC's functions were not only part of the executive branch but also involved legislative and quasijudicial activities. The Myers case, which the decision seemed to contravene, involved "purely executive officers," who were clearly subject to Presidential removal. Although, as Cushman points out, there is probably no such thing as a "purely executive officer," there are, on the other hand, substantial differences between the "administrative" functions of a postmaster and a Federal Trade Commissioner.

[7] 272 U.S. 52 (1926).
[8] 295 U.S. 602 (1935).

The President's removal power, however, is very broad. If there is no specific statutory restriction, he may remove any and all executive officers. This is implied from his constitutional power of appointment. Moreover his general authority to remove commission members for "inefficiency, neglect of duty, or malfeasance in office" is held to include the authority to require, under penalty of removal, reasonable efficiency, effective management, immunity to improper pressure, integrity, proper conduct, and in general, competent performance. He may, apparently, also force the commissioners to comply, in the absence of specific legislative requirements to the contrary, with Executive orders of general application, under pain of dismissal for refusing to do so. The commissions may also be directed to undertake investigations at the direction of the President.[9] Indeed, his authority in the area of removal is so broad that Cushman recommends that Congress make more definite the extent of his powers.[10]

Congress and the Commissions. Congress, however, has the most far-reaching power over the commissions. It creates them, determines their functions and powers, can investigate them and even abolish them. It is also clear that Congress can pass legislation and resolutions that will directly influence commission policy. The Hock-Smith Resolution (1925), for example, directed the ICC to consider sympathetically the interests of agriculture in setting freight rates. Its power of the purse is equally important. Congress, as we have seen, rewards its friends and punishes its enemies through appropriations. Congressional disapproval incurred by commission policies and procedures will be reflected in quantitative terms when budget requests are considered. In addition Congress may direct that appropriated funds not be spent for certain purposes, as in the case of the Federal Trade Commission which was instructed in 1945 not to use funds for certain investigations of trade practices.

Congress, understandably, tends to regard the commissions as "arms of Congress," meaning that their primary responsibility is to the legislative rather than the executive branch.[11] According to this view, their regulatory functions are delegated to them by Congress, which retains final jurisdiction. Cushman, however, regards this view as wrong. He notes that the commissions perform several functions which Congress could not constitutionally perform; namely, issuing cease-and-desist orders, and executive activities involved in enforcing basic acts. As Cushman observes, "it is clear that the arms of Congress do things which

---

[9] Cushman, *The Independent Regulatory Commissions*, pp. 464–65.

[10] *Ibid.*, p. 465.

[11] It is interesting to note that the courts have on occasion regarded the commissions as "an agency of the judiciary." In the Humphrey case—*Humphrey's Executor v. U.S.* (295 U.S. 602, 1935)—Justice Sutherland so referred to the Federal Trade Commission.

Congress cannot do." The desire of Congress, nevertheless, to exercise more control over the commissions was indicated by Senator E. C. Johnson's proposition that the appointing power should be given to the Speaker of the House, subject to confirmation by the Senate. As C. Herman Pritchett remarks, however, this is a ". . . proposal not the least of whose defects is its unconstitutionality."[12] The appointing power, of course, rests with the President. But the Senate may refuse to approve his nominations, as the case of Leland Olds illustrates. It should be recognized that the approval power has a larger effect than that indicated by such refusals; the number of persons not appointed because of the Senate's prior indication of disapproval is probably significant.

LEGISLATIVE INVESTIGATION. Congressional influence upon the commissions is dramatically illustrated by its investigatory power, which enables it to focus national interest upon the commissions and to mold public opinion as to their honesty and effectiveness. During 1957–58, for example, a special House Subcommittee on Legislative Oversight held a series of hearings and employed a professional staff of investigators which revealed numerous instances of unusual behavior on the part of commissioners, private interests regulated by the commissions, and highly placed officials, including Sherman Adams of the White House staff.[13] The following were some of the activities of commissioners revealed by the Committee:[14]

1. Certain FCC commissioners had received full expenses for themselves and their wives to attend industry conventions and had also had various other expenses paid for by regulated industries while attending such conventions.
2. Commissioners had engaged "in constant fraternization" with individuals and corporations who appear as litigants before the Commission.
3. Commissioners had *ex parte* discussions with industry representatives about cases pending before the agency. As the House Committee noted, "it is almost self-evident that such discussions between a quasi-judicial officer and a litigant are wholly improper."

When such activities are given national publicity, it may be assumed that some change in the methods of the Commissions results, although the extent and nature of such changes are not always predictable.

[12] C. Herman Pritchett, "The Regulatory Commissions Revisited," 43, *American Political Science Review* (October, 1949), p. 988.

[13] The *New York Times* carried complete and often verbatim reports of the investigations and the hearings; for an example of a summary of the Committee's memorandum on the Federal Communications Commission, see the *New York Times*, January 28, 1958, p. 14.

[14] *Ibid*; for a dramatic account of the 1958 investigation, see Bernard Schwartz, *The Professor and the Commissions* (New York: Alfred A. Knopf, Inc., 1959).

Insofar as larger policy questions were concerned, the House Committee noted the following "disturbing factors":[15]

1. The traditional criterion of "local ownership" as a basic guide in granting licenses for radio and television franchises had been "distorted" by a commission policy that looked to the residence of the principal officers rather than to that of the stockholder-owners as the basis for determining residence. Also, in a number of cases, the Commission had "held against local owners," and preferred applicants who represented wholly owned outside interests.

2. In the area of integration of ownership and management, another basic aim of traditional policy, there had been "a tendency where corporate applicants are concerned for the commission to look to the integration not of the corporation stockholders but of its principal officers in the management of the proposed television station."

3. With regard to the established criterion of avoiding monopoly control of the mass media, both by Congress and the Commission, "in a number of recent decisions . . . the commission appears to have been minimizing the importance of the diversification criterion, emphasizing in its stead the factor of broadcasting experience."

The Committee also questioned the FCC for its failure to inquire into the antitrust aspects of concentrated ownership, and indeed, noted that it had granted licenses to some applicants who had been convicted of antitrust violations outside the mass media field.

In sum, the Committee found, in the case of one important commission that both the conduct of its commissioners and their administration of Congressional policy through their determinations in license applications left a great deal to be desired. It now remained for the President to use his appointing and removal power and the Congress to use its financial and legislative power to correct the inadequacies.*

Interest Groups and the Commissions. In terms of economic power and sustained attention, it can be argued that private interests have the greatest influence upon the regulatory commissions. Yet the commissions are charged with protecting and advancing the public interest by controlling the activities of powerful economic groups. Frequently this objective may require a denial of certain specific interests of the groups regulated. There is at times, for instance, a conflict of interest between the general welfare and that of producer groups. The "public interest" is often far removed from the clear and limited interest of any special group.[16] It is not surprising, therefore, that such groups spend considerable time and effort in keeping regulation as harmless as possible. Pro-

---

[15] *Ibid.*

* The hearings did result in the removal or resignation of some Commissioners, and will probably inspire prudent behavior among the remaining members, at least in the immediate future.

[16] An attempt to consider the "public interest" more critically is made in our chapters on Administrative Responsibility.

ducer groups pay the most sustained attention to regulation. They are directly affected by regulatory policy and are often brought into the determination of that policy. The public, on the other hand, usually because of apathy and preoccupation with the routine business of making a living, exercises no vigilant scrutiny of commission activity. The average citizen, it seems fair to say, knows only vaguely about the existence of the commissions, much less about their policy and procedures.

Thus, as Senator Douglas has pointed out, there is a ". . . tendency of independent regulatory agencies to surrender their regulatory zeal as they age, and to become more and more the protagonists of a clientele industry, and less and less the vigilant defenders of the welfare of the consumers or the general public. All too often, those who are supposedly being regulated, actually regulate their nominal regulators."[17] This suggests why a basic need of modern democratic government is the clear definition and assignment of responsibility so that the ordinary citizen can more easily identify those at fault if his interests are allowed to languish. It explains why many political scientists call for integration of the commissions in the departments, under the more direct control of the chief executive. In this way alone, they feel, can regulation be made subject to political control in accord with majority public opinion.

THE LELAND OLDS CASE. Of the various parties concerned, producer groups have the most compelling motivation to enter the regulatory arena. It is their ox that is being gored. Moreover, to carry the figure along, ownership of the ox is not widely distributed, so the injury is sharply felt. The general public, on the other hand, is affected in a relatively painless way by regulation favorable to producer groups. The injury is so widely distributed that the pain experienced by each individual is often insignificant. The outcry is correspondingly less in volume and duration.

A case that illustrates producer interest in regulatory agencies is that of Leland Olds, former chairman of the Federal Power Commission, which (at that time, at least) was thought to have jurisdiction over natural gas rates.[18] His reappointement was ". . . vigorously opposed by

---

[17] Paul H. Douglas, "Improvement of Ethical Standards in the Federal Government," 280, *Annals of the American Academy of Political and Social Science* (March, 1952), p. 154.

[18] The influence on the FPC of Senator Kerr, sponsor of the bill to remove natural gas from FPC regulation, is suggested in the following reply of Commissioner Harrington Wimberly to the implication that he is "Senator Kerr's man": "I don't know whether I am Senator Kerr's man or whether he's my man. But it is well known that I am for Bob Kerr first, last, and all the time." John Osborne, "Natural Gas and the Authoritarian Liberals," *Fortune* (May, 1952), p. 190. According to Osborne, "Wimberly is a small town newspaper publisher and Democratic politician in Oklahoma, and he readily acknowledges that his appointment to the FPC in 1945 was a straight piece of patronage."

the oil and natural gas interests."[19] Members of Congress from the south-western gas-producing areas spearheaded the attack. Olds was supported by consumer groups and several students of the public utilities field. Thus the stage was set for a battle of opposing interests; as Morris Cooke said:

> Clearly the battle over the confirmation of Leland Olds as a member of the Federal Power Commission is a battle between the great body of people who are consumers, on the one side, and the monopolistic power and oil-gas interests on the other. It is a part of the battle which has been going on for years to bring these vital interests under some measure of public control. This battle must go on if democracy itself is to survive.[20]

The tactics of interest groups are well shown in this case. Of the fifteen witnesses opposing Olds, ". . . all came from gas-providing areas, and all were directly or indirectly connected with the gas industry."[21] The battle was not entirely a party affair, since Senator Morse, Oregon Republican, strongly defended Olds in Senate debate. In the end, Olds' appointment was rejected by the Senate. The real issue was not his radical writings during the 1920's, or the unbased charges of communism but ". . . federal regulation of the price of natural gas." Consequently "his rejection was a victory for the gas and oil interests."[22] It is perhaps significant that the FPC, in opposition to the recommendations of its staff, found some two years later that the regulation of natural gas prices was not within the commission's jurisdiction.[23]

The Federal Trade Commission. The most widespread criticism, however, has been directed against the Federal Trade Commission, mainly for its failure to try seriously to achieve the antitrust objectives of the Sherman and Clayton Acts and its confused and inconsistent statements of policy in the antitrust field. The first Hoover Commission, for example, concluded rather mildly, "Over the years, the Commission has engaged mainly in activities contributing little toward accomplishing the primary Congressional objectives of assuring widespread effective competition." Another observer, who holds no positive or "liberal" view of the Commission's trustbusting responsibilities, maintained that "the consensus of informed people . . . is that the Federal Trade Commission

[19] Joseph P. Harris, "Senatorial Rejection of Leland Olds: A Case Study," **45**, *American Political Science Review* (September, 1951), p. 677.

[20] Subcommittee of the Senate Committee on Interstate Commerce, 78th Cong., 2d sess., *Hearings*, "Leland Olds' Reappointment to Federal Power Commission," (Washington, D.C.: U.S. Government Printing Office, 1948), p. 187.

[21] Harris, "Senatorial Rejection of Leland Olds," p. 685.

[22] *Ibid.*, p. 691. For an opposing view, see John Osborne, "Natural Gas and the Authoritarian Liberals," p. 124, *passim*.

[23] *In the matter of the Phillips Petroleum Company*, Federal Power Commission, Opinion No. 217, Doc. No. G-1148, August 16, 1951.

has utterly failed in its intended purpose."[24] It had failed to inform the business community of its obligations. It had failed to enforce a consistent and reasonable antitrust policy and had, indeed, brought great confusion to this area by contradictory decisions and public statements, particularly in regard to the legality of the basing-point system of pricing.

Dean Landis, formerly a FTC Commissioner, commented recently about the "noticeable decline in the quality of the personnel of the top level of bureaucracy that has the responsibility for administrative regulation. This fact was commented on again and again in the reports of the Hoover Commission. . . . Secondly reference must be made to what I would call the utter bankruptcy of the Federal Trade Commission."[25] The House Subcommittee on Legislative Oversight also trained its guns on the FTC in 1958, particularly in the area of influence apparently exercised upon the Commission by the White House on behalf of a Boston textile and real estate operator with far-flung connections with high-level state and federal officials. While the burden of the Committee's attention focused on the White House's role, it was clear that the FTC had responded with alacrity to requests for satisfactory negotiations with the textile operator who had been cited for mislabeling of cloth produced in mills in which he had a major interest.[26] Such activities are relatively insignificant in the context of the FTC's major statutory obligation to maintain competition by discouraging the concentration of ownership in commerce and industry, but here too it has been singularly ineffectual. Admittedly, in a "free enterprise" economy, the FTC has not had an enviable task. The generality of the complaints that are directed toward it signalizes the problem of regulatory agencies which are closely bound up with important interest groups. The problem here may be one of a fundamental ambivalence in our national attitude toward competition as a way of economic life. It is not at all certain that the competition sought by the Sherman and Clayton acts is favored by either the business community or the general public.

COOPERATION OR CONTROL? The dependence of the commissions upon support from the areas regulated, and in turn the influence that such interests enjoy, is clear. The problem, of course, is how to achieve a just compromise between the public and the private interest. It is adequately clear that the cooperation of affected interests is an essential requisite of regulation and that the positive planning role of the commissions must be kept in view. But is the price for such cooperation too high? Although

[24] W. Simon, "The Case Against the Federal Trade Commission," 19, *University of Chicago Law Review* (Winter, 1952), pp. 297–338; see also, Subcommittee of Select Committee on Small Business, *Hearings*, pt. I.

[25] Cited in Simon, "The Case Against the Federal Trade Commission," p. 329.

[26] See *New York Times*, June and July, 1958.

it is obvious that the public interest and the private interest are not always or necessarily at odds, the historical circumstances of the establishment of regulatory agencies suggest that conflict between them often exists. The ICC came into being following an agrarian and business protest against railroad rate discriminations; the FTC followed crude monopolistic practices during the formative years of American capitalism; the FCC appeared after a chaotic condition in radio transmission during the 1920's; the SEC followed the stock market boom and collapse of 1929.

The organic statute of every commission establishes in one way or another its "public interest" obligation. The problem revolves around the conflicting interpretations of this standard. The critics of regulation often proceed on the assumption that government regulation curtails the free enterprise system which has brought America's high standard of living and great international power. The advocates of regulation, on the other hand, tend toward a positive theory of government in which public power not only redresses the imbalance between organized and unorganized political power but also makes the great decisions concerning investment policy, labor relations, and the like with the aid of agencies such as the Council of Economic Advisers. Although our mixed enterprise system is accepted, and its contributions to national wealth are freely recognized, there is a tendency to value more highly the government's role as a positive factor in social and economic life. There is also a tendency to define the public interest as the consumer or majority interest. Both groups (and the many shades of opinion they include), it seems fair to say, seek the "public interest" in general terms of full employment and high standards of life, but the means to this end, especially insofar as government is concerned, are a matter of grave controversy.

From this it is clear that the regulatory commissions' lot, like that of the policeman, is not a happy one. If they act in the consumer interest, they incur the enmity of the producer groups who scrutinize their activities and upon whose cooperation successful regulatory administration often depends. If they are too sedulous a guardian of producer interest, they may expect an articulate, however fleeting, protest from the "liberal" columnists and those organized groups such as the CIO, Americans for Democratic Action, the Farmers' Union, and cooperative associations that tend to reflect consumer opinion.

The Courts and the Commissions. Finally, although the scope of judicial review over the commissions' actions is not well defined, it is clear that the courts feel free to step in whenever individual rights are infringed upon by official action. It must be said, however, that with few exceptions, the "individuals" being regulated are corporate entities who have long enjoyed a somewhat anomalous benefit from their artificial classification as "persons" under the due-process clauses of the Constitution. Although the extent of judicial power has receded considerably from the earlier period when the Federal Trade Commission's determinations were virtually emasculated, the administrative discretion of the late 1930's again seems to be in the process of restriction. The commissions will apparently enjoy less freedom from judicial surveillance of their expert findings. The subject of judicial review will be considered in some detail in a subsequent chapter. Here it is enough to note that the independence of the regulatory commissions is circumscribed by court action and the possibility of such action.

CRITICISMS AND RECOMMENDATIONS

There has been considerable dissatisfaction with both the structure and role of the commissions and their procedures. Such criticism was reflected in the President's Committee on Administrative Management (1937) which handed down some rather extreme recommendations. The location of the commissions, which the committee viewed as a "headless fourth branch of government," seemed to make virtually impossible an effective over-all management by the President. Thus the committee suggested placing the commissions into executive departments having "functions . . . that are neutral with respect to the regulatory duties of the commission rather than 'promotional' or 'otherwise biased.'" A second proposal recommended that the executive and judicial functions of the commission be externally segregated. In this way judicial impartiality and independence would be achieved while routine administrative and policy-determining functions would remain responsible to the secretary and the President.

Most of the agencies concerned took exception to these proposals. Congress exempted the commissions in the reorganization acts of 1939 and 1945, which authorized the President to reorganize the Executive branch. The majority report of the Attorney General's Committee, as we have seen, opposed a complete separation of judicial and prosecutory functions on the ground that the resulting multiplication of agencies would be unsatisfactory and that duplication and confusion of policy would result. Political scientists have not usually been so worried about the problem of impartiality, or at least, this objective has had a lesser priority than that of maintaining effective and powerful administrative procedures. The recommendations of the President's committee may have been based on the assumption that value judgments can be avoided by organizational measures.[27] This is similar to the Congressional belief

[27] President's Committee on Administrative Management, *Report with Special Studies* (Washington, D.C.: U.S. Government Printing Office, 1937), p. 229.

that bipartisan membership on the commissions would assure political impartiality. It is now clear that this practice tends instead to ensure that political activity is a prerequisite for appointment, thereby making the commissions more, rather than less, political.

But regulatory policy in any case is essentially a political matter, reflecting the policies of the President and the party in power. The attempt "to take politics out of politics" is based on a fear of government and a distrust of public servants, if not of majority rule. Regulation of the economy is in fact *political*, brought into existence by public demand for the protection of the consumer interest. It is vital, therefore, that regulation remain politically controlled by the majority acting through their representatives, preferably the President, who represents the national interest and is alone responsible for and capable of synthesizing national policy.

The First Hoover Task Force Proposals. In contrast to the over-all view of the President's committee, the Hoover Commission undertook through its task force a detailed study of the administration of the regulatory commissions as well as external matters of policy.[28] While recognizing the important role of the commissions in our society, the Commission concluded that their original purpose had not been "adequately fulfilled." The caliber of members was sometimes below standard because of inadequate salaries and the failure of the President to recognize the importance of appointing outstanding men.[29] Administrative duties that had been imposed upon the commission interfered with their regulatory obligations. The direction of such work was not adequately assigned; chairmen were frequently merely presiding officers at meetings rather than executive directors of commission affairs. The neglect of broad-gauged planning for the development of the fields which they regulated was a principal failure of the commission. The provisions for tenure and removal varied considerably among commissions. Perhaps most important, administratively speaking, coordination between the several commissions and the executive departments was either casual or entirely absent.

Insofar as the question of poor coordination was concerned, the task force recognized that the "independent" status of the commissions raises special problems. However, it was felt that adequate coordination could

[28] Commission on Organization of the Executive Branch of the Government, *Task Force Report on the Regulatory Commissions* (Washington, D.C.: U.S. Government Printing Office, 1949), Appendix N; Pritchett, "The Regulatory Commissions Revisited," pp. 978–89.

[29] This is in contrast to Great Britain where the Franks Committee recently concluded that the quality of members of English tribunals had been satisfactory; William A. Robson, "Administrative Justice and Injustice: A Commentary on the Franks Report," *Public Law* (Spring, 1958), p. 21.

be assured through the President's power of appointment, his influence on commission policy through the Bureau of the Budget, and his power to name chairmen in some commissions. The task force was not convinced that more than limited Executive control was desirable or necessary. Placing the commissions in the great departments in an effort to increase Executive influence and general coordination with the executive branch was unnecessary. An influential and vigorous President could influence the commissions as he does Congress, by making widely known his views in regard to regulatory policy, thereby ensuring public support. The commissions, like the courts, were not immune to public opinion.

The administrative performance of the commissions, on the other hand, was viewed with less satisfaction. It was recommended that the administration of purely executive functions be transferred to the regular departments. Only if the relationship of regulatory and operating functions was so intimate that separation would cause confusion and conflicting jurisdiction should the latter remain in the commissions. The commissions' plural leadership, it was maintained, results in all the traditional shortcomings of the board type of organization. Diffusion of authority, haphazard planning, casual supervision of the staff, and consequent lack of clear responsibility have characterized the commissions. The task force recommended therefore an executive officer to assist the chairman. But it immediately warned against the creation of a general manager who would report to the entire commission, with the accompanying unfortunate tendency to segregate commissioners and staff.

In its study the Commission's task force examined several characteristics that are usually regarded as the major advantage of the commission device.[30] The ability to resist pressure has been a basic advantage of the independent commission. Collective policy formation has been held a guaranty of more rational decisions. The commissions have been able to devote a sustained and expert direction in their respective fields. Finally, continuity of policy has been ensured by the commissions' knowledge of the problems and needs of the industries they regulate. In general the task force's investigations upheld these several advantages while recognizing several areas that needed improvement.

The First Hoover Commission Recommendations. With only two important exceptions, the Hoover Commission endorsed the recommendations of its task force. Presidential designation of commission chairmen was not mentioned, suggesting that the Commission did not wish to increase executive responsibility. Also, the proposal that regulatory functions dealing with transportation (then discharged by the ICC, the CAB,

[30] Commission on Organization of the Executive Branch of the Government, *Task Force Report on the Regulatory Commissions*, p. 982.

and the Maritime Board) be consolidated into one commission was not endorsed, principally because the commissions involved were held to be overworked already and the problems of regulation in the areas concerned were too different. Administrative responsibility, however, was to be centered in the chairman; routine matters should be increasingly delegated to the staff; operating procedures, particularly those concerned with hearings, appeals, and records, should be simplified. Administrative justice, the Commission held, did not have the necessary economy and dispatch. Finally, the Commission recommended that certain executive functions be transferred from the Federal Power Commission, the then Maritime Commission, the Interstate Commerce Commission, and the Civil Aeronautics Board to the departments.

ACTION ON THE COMMISSION'S RECOMMENDATIONS. The Hoover Commission's recommendations for the regulating commissions included no startling changes. Internal opposition arose, however, in the government and in the commissions themselves, mainly in the Federal Trade Commission, which viewed with alarm the centering of administrative responsibility in the chairman. The FTC evidently felt that this change as well as the designation of the chairman by the President would place the agency too much under his control. The Commission and its task force appeared to differ basically as to the proper relationship of the commissions to the President and Congress. The Commission seemed to favor the status quo, with a leaning toward the concept of Congressional control, a view shared by several of the regulatory commissions. The professional task force, on the other hand, favored Executive direction, within limits. The President's hand was to be strengthened by his designation of the chairman, although his power to discipline members was to be limited to removal for cause. The task force recommended that the three agencies not now protected under this sanction be covered. Thus the task force moved somewhat in the direction of increased recognition of the Executive relationship with the commissions.

Of the twelve specific recommendations of the first Hoover Commission concerning the commissions, six required legislation, five required only the President's approval under his general reorganization authority, and one could be carried out by administrative action.[31] The Reorganization Act of 1949 enables the President to recommend changes in the structure and function of the Executive branch; such proposals are sent to Congress for approval. Scattered agencies can be brought under one head, duplication of functions can be reduced, and generally more effective administration can be achieved. When sent to Congress such reorganization plans are referred to the House and Senate Committees on

[31] Pritchett, "The Regulatory Commissions Revisited," p. 986.

Expenditures in the Executive departments. Unless a majority of the total membership in either house disapproves, the plans become law sixty days after submission. Congress votes on reorganization plans only if a member introduces a resolution of disapproval. Once a plan is approved, the responsibility for pushing it through devolves upon the department or agency head affected. Some forty-two reorganization plans were submitted by President Truman, of which thirty had been approved by January, 1953.

Several plans affected the regulatory commissions. On March 13, 1950, Plans 7, 8, 9, and 10, affecting the ICC, FTC, FPC, and SEC, respectively, were submitted, authorizing the President to designate the chairmen and to transfer responsibility to them for routine administrative affairs. Plan 7 was disapproved, but the others were accepted. Meanwhile, three additional plans (11, 12, and 13), affecting the FCC, and NLRB, and the CAB, were introduced. These would transfer responsibility to the chairmen for routine administration. Of these, only Plan 13, covering the Civil Aeronautics Board, was accepted. Finally, Plan 21, providing for a complete reorganization of the much criticized Maritime Commission, was submitted and accepted.

Direct legislative action on the commissions, as distinct from reorganization plans, had been proposed by the Hoover Commission in June, 1949. In the main, however, very little was done because the changes that Congress was prepared to accept had already been made through reorganization plans.[32] In 1949 Public Law 359 made it possible to increase commission salaries. In 1950 Public Law 858 authorized the CAA administrator to delegate certain functions. An omnibus bill (S. 1139) was introduced in the 82d Congress to meet the remaining recommendations of the Hoover Commission. But Congressmen, as well as the commissions concerned, remained fearful that Executive control of regulation would become too great if the President were allowed to appoint chairmen who, in turn, could control personnel appointments, commission business, and the execution of agency policy. A Senate report maintained, "the issue . . . was whether the vesting of administrative powers in the chairman would impair the independence of the regulatory agencies as quasi-judicial arms of the legislative branch."[33] As we have seen, this "arms of Congress" claim is without much foundation. The bill itself was passed on April 9, 1952, but only after sharp modification, and it died in the House Committee on Expenditures in the Executive Departments.

[32] Committee on Government Operations, *Senate Action on Hoover Commission Reports* (Washington, D.C.: U.S. Government Printing Office, January 9, 1953), pp. 18–19, 65–67.

[33] *Ibid.*, p. 66.

Second Hoover Commission Recommendations (1955). The second Commission's task force report covered the whole gamut of problems raised by the "quasi" functions of the regulatory commissions.[34] Both the task force and the Commission were unsympathetic to the needs of the regulatory commissions. Among the Commission's most important recommendations was that several important judicial functions be transferred to the courts. To ensure the independence of the hearing examiners, it recommended that an Office of Hearing Commissioners be made responsible for the selection and supervision of the hearing examiners in all agencies. To further ensure their autonomy, the examiners (to be renamed "commissioners") were to be appointed by the President, confirmed by the Senate, and given twelve-year terms. The Commission also insisted that the regulatory agencies should separate in all instances their investigatory and adjudicatory functions. It was autocratic and a threat to freedom, the Commission believed, to give one agency or individual the role of both prosecutor and judge.

The second Hoover Commission recommended further extension of the right of judicial review. Here the Commission mentioned the gains made under the Administrative Procedures Act of 1946 but felt that much more remained to be done. For example, it recommended that judicial functions of the agencies that could not be transferred to regular courts should be handled by an Administrative Court, which should handle taxation, trade regulation, and labor relations, with a section of the Court being responsible for each area. This would remove from such agencies as the FTC, FCC, the Department of Agriculture, and the Food and Drug Administration their responsibilities for regulating trade practices. In sum, the Commission aimed at "re-establishing the supremacy of the rule of law throughout the administrative agencies and the Government." In the words of one observer, however, the Commission's recommendations ". . . reached the high point of proposals for the restriction of the regulatory process."[35]

What were the concrete results of the second Hoover Commission's recommendations for the regulatory commissions? An important general provision was the extension of the Reorganization Act of 1949, which permits the President to reorganize agencies by executive order, to June 1, 1959, at which time it was extended again by amendment. The only other law affecting the agencies was 72 Stat. 810 (Aug., 1958) which

[34] Commission on Organization of the Executive Branch of the Government, *Legal Services and Procedures, A Report to the Congress* (Washington, D.C.: U.S. Government Printing Office, March, 1955).

[35] R. F. Fuchs, "The American Bar Association and the Hoover Task Force Administrative Code Proposals," 23, *I. C. C. Practitioners Journal* (1956), cited in Heady, "The New Reform Movement in Regulatory Administration," p. 93.

established the Federal Aviation Agency having power to regulate commercial and military aviation.[36] The Commission's findings about the administrative process within the regulatory agencies also encouraged further efforts to judicialize their internal procedure, culminating in 1956 in the ABA's stringent administrative code. The effects of this Code upon agency adjudication and the opportunity for judicial review will be discussed in the next two chapters.

THE PRICE OF INDEPENDENCE

In view of the opposing ideas regarding the location of the primary responsibility of the regulatory commissions, it may be well to consider the problem further. A fairly strong case can be made for expanding the President's control of the commissions. Robert E. Cushman has shown that the commissions' work is primarily executive, or at least, that they are not properly regarded as "arms of Congress." But a more basic consideration is involved—the question of the best way of implementing the commissions' obligation to further the public interest. It seems clear that the public interest is not attained through a satisfaction of the interests of powerful minority groups. There is evidence also that such groups prefer the "independent" commission device. Not only is there less prospect of vigorous regulation but the opportunities for representations and litigation are more numerous than under regulation administered by an executive department.[37]

On the other hand, the President, by virtue of his status and the fact that he alone is elected by all the people, is in a better position to resist particular interests and provide strong policy leadership in the public interest. He formulates issues and Congress must accept them. It has been shown again and again that the President has more freedom to promote the general welfare because, unlike the Congressman, he is less susceptible to the appeals or the discipline of any given interest

[36] For a complete summary of Congressional and Executive action, see Report, *Action by the 85th Congress on the Second Hoover Commission Reports*, Senate Committee on Government Operations, 86th Cong., 1st sess., subcommittee on Reorganization and International Organization (Washington, D.C.: U.S. Government Printing Office, March 23, 1959); and Report, *Action by the Congress and the Executive Branch of the Government on the Second Hoover Commission Reports, 1955–57*, 85th Congress, 2nd. sess., Senate Committee on Government Operations, subcommittee on Reorganization (Washington, D.C.: U.S. Government Printing Office, February 13, 1958).

[37] Among others, see S. Huntington, "The Marasmus of the ICC: The Commission, the Railroads, and the Public Interest," **61**, Yale Law Journal (April, 1952), pp. 473–92; and James Fesler, "Independent Regulatory Commissions," in Fritz Morstein Marx (ed.), *Elements of Public Administration* (Englewood Cliffs, N.J.: Prentice-Hall, Inc., 1946); James W. Fesler, *The Independence of State Regulatory Agencies* (Chicago: University of Chicago Press, 1942).

group. If this is true, if regulatory policy is a political matter, and if responsible government is a worth-while end, it would appear that the President should have the means of bringing commission policy into line with the policy of his party. If he cannot do this, the public interest may go by default. Like the Supreme Court, the commissions must, it would seem, take due cognizance of the election returns. If democratic majority control is to be preserved, the "independence" of the commissions must be limited.

Dangers of Independence. The great dangers of true independence are these: inertia, lack of policy planning, and irresponsibility (or at least a diffusion of responsibility). The ICC's lethargy with respect to southern and western freight rate inequities and the rates of pipe lines, its "railroad mindedness," Humphrey's view that the FTC was a service agency for the business community, the FPC and the Kerr bill, the recent revelations about the FCC, the FTC, and the SEC's relations with private interests—all suggest that the price of independence may be too high. Democratic government requires policy coordination and determination at the Presidential level.

As always, however, there is another side of the coin. Executive control can be only as democratic and effective as the individual exercising it. An incompetent Chief Executive could abuse his increased power, just as a weak President could fail to exercise it in the public interest. Also, regulatory policy would fluctuate more than at present, resulting in undue uncertainty for the interests regulated. Finally, the judicial functions of the commission could become excessively vulnerable to the influence of the Chief Executive.

Need for Presidential Control. And yet, when the alternatives to Presidential control are considered, one must conclude that such control seems preferable. In the last analysis, regulatory policy is a "political" matter, properly amenable to "political" direction in the representative sense of the word. Changing public opinion is most clearly reflected in the President, who alone has a national constituency. Judicial control is clearly unsuited to the needs of the regulatory process. Congress also suffers from inherent disadvantages: it is already overburdened, its view is often parochial rather than national, its supervision and interest are necessarily spasmodic. As Cushman concludes, "Congress has little chance to reach an informed judgment on how efficiently the commissions are doing their work."[38]

The first Hoover Commission task force must have had these considerations in mind when it concluded that both nonpolitical regulation and

[38] Cushman, *The Independent Regulatory Commissions*, p. 678.

Presidential control were possible.[39] As we have seen, however, other commentators are less hopeful about the possibility of the commissions' maintaining so delicate a balance between independence and responsibility. Here again one's evaluation of the "proper" administrative position and function of the commissions reflects his value premises. Those who fear Executive control and strong government will press for the "arm of Congress" interpretation, while those who want a more responsible, politically controlled administration will place the commissions within the departments where they will be more amenable to Executive control.

BIBLIOGRAPHY

BERNSTEIN, M. *Regulating Business by Independent Commission.* Princeton, N.J.: 1955.

CUSHMAN, ROBERT E. *The Independent Regulatory Commissions.* New York: 1941.

FESLER, JAMES W. *The Independent Regulatory Agencies.* Chicago: 1942.

HARRIS, JOSEPH P. "Senatorial Rejection of Leland Olds: A Case Study," **45**, *American Political Science Review* (September, 1951).

HOOVER COMMISSION, *Task Force Report on the Regulatory Commissions.* Appendix N. Washington, D.C.: 1949.

HUNTINGTON, S. P. "The Marasmus of the ICC: The Commission, The Railroads, and the Public Interest," **61**, *Yale Law Journal* (April, 1952).

LANDIS, JAMES E. *Monopoly and Free Enterprise.* New York: 1951.

OSBORNE, JOHN. "Natural Gas and the Authoritarian Liberals," **45**, *Fortune* (May, 1952).

SALOMON, L. I. (ed.). *The Independent Federal Regulatory Agencies.* New York: 1959.

SCHWARTZ, B. *The Professor and the Commissions.* New York: 1959.

SIMON, W. R. "The Case Against the Federal Trade Commission," **19**, *University of Chicago Law Review* (Winter, 1952).

[39] Pritchett, "The Regulatory Commissions Revisited," y. 686.

CHAPTER 27

The Regulatory Process

We can now turn to the methods by which administrative agencies carry out their regulatory powers. As noted previously, such methods are extremely important because they touch upon the central political question; the rights of the individual vis-à-vis those of the state. But where does individual liberty end in deference to the larger good of the community? It is clear that individual freedom cannot be absolute. Instead, wherever men live in groups, government of one kind or another must exist. In this sense a great number of private organizations are also governing bodies that control individual and group behavior to achieve stability and consistency. The range of individual interests covered by such organizations is often as broad and immediate as that exercised by public government. Private corporations, unions, professional organizations, and academic institutions all have an apparatus of control that both extends and restricts individual liberty.

Many observers argue, however, that final power must rest in public government in order that the more specialized interests of private governments can be limited in the public interest. The use of regulatory power is of particular interest because it is concerned with maintaining public supremacy. The problem is how to achieve this majority supremacy without abrogating individual rights through arbitrary or unfair action. In this chapter we shall consider this problem, noting the way that individual interests are safeguarded without losing sight of the larger social objects of regulation.

TYPES OF ADMINISTRATIVE ACTION

Administrative agencies use broadly three kinds of regulatory action.[1] These include administrative adjudication, or case-by-case determinations of individual rights arising in controversies between parties who are aggrieved by the prices or the services of enterprises subject to

[1] Among others, see *Hearings, The Organization and Procedures of the Federal Regulatory Commissions and Agencies and Their Effects on Small Business*, Subcommittee of the Select Committee on Small Business (H.R.), 84th Cong., 1st sess. (Washington, D.C.: U.S. Government Printing Office, 1955).

regulation in the public interest. A second form of administrative action is rule making, which involves the promulgation of rules and regulations governing the future activity of regulated interests. Such measures are known as sublegislation because they are created under broad grants of power which legislatures have been obliged to delegate in order that regulation may be flexible, expert, and expeditious. Finally, there is a broad category of action whose method is basically educational, with the prospect of negative sanctions should noncoercive means fail. This last group includes inspection, conferences with private interests, and regulation through example.

Administrative Objectives. The administrative process has at least four distinct objectives, in each of which procedures are necessarily different. There is the regulatory function in which the government attempts to gain information as a basis for action in the "public interest." At other times the agency acts as a disciplinary authority that secures evidence against offenders through a courtlike procedure and which may issue orders that are judicially enforceable. When it decides a case between two private parties, the administrative tribunal acts as an impartial arbiter or judge. Finally, the agency passes upon broad questions of public policy, granting certificates of public interest, necessity, and convenience.

We have seen that the transition of America from a rural, agrarian society to an urban-industrial culture put new demands upon government. Many of these demands required the regulation of individual and group conduct in the larger public interest. Admittedly, it is difficult to define the public interest, but it does seem clear that the concept involves something more than the mere satisfaction of numerous competing special interests. The delegation of legislative power to administrative agencies, for example, charges them with making concrete such vague prescriptions as "reasonable protection" for employees, "fair" practices in trade, "just" and "equitable" rates, and the like. These standards are directed primarily toward the protection of the consumer public and competing interests. What are the principal methods of achieving these ends?

ADMINISTRATIVE ADJUDICATION PROCEDURE

Two types of administrative adjudication exist. In the first, the agency acts as a partisan charged with protecting the public interest and with acting upon a complaint which the agency formally initiates. The agency drafts the complaint, notifies the offender, holds the hearing, and finally decides whether to issue an order. This order may be positive, as in the case of an individual directed by the Board of Tax appeals to pay a certain amount, or negative, as in the case of a cease-and-desist order of the Federal Trade Commission directing a firm to refrain from certain unfair trade practices. As noted previously, it was this combination of agency functions that aroused the criticism of businessmen and the American Bar Association.

The second type of administrative adjudication is rather different in that the regulatory agency usually decides the rights of individuals but does not itself take the initial action, which is brought instead by some private person. The agency in this case is applying the law between a plaintiff and a defendant, such as an aggrieved shipper and a railroad. Such proceedings have not been subject to widespread criticism, mainly because the agency is acting only as an impartial arbiter. The proceedings may result in reparations orders, such as those by the ICC directing that unreasonable shipping rates be adjusted. The awards made by a workmen's compensation commission also fall in this category.

In the discussion that follows we shall be primarily concerned with the first type of adjudication, in which the tribunal acts both as prosecutor and judge, handing down orders of legal effect that direct private interests to act in a certain manner. Administrative adjudication and the orders resulting from it are remedial in nature; they seek to correct previous actions against the public interest.

The Complaint. A case before a regulatory body may originate in several ways. An informal complaint from an individual by telephone, letter, or personal appearance is often sufficient. The Federal Trade Commission, for example, upon receiving a letter stating the principal facts, will initiate an investigation which may result in formal action if the evidence warrants it. In other instances, particularly in rate cases before state public utility commissions, a formal complaint may be required in the form of a petition signed by a certain number of consumers. The National Labor Relations Board, similarly, requires that charges of unfair labor practices be in writing. Finally, the regulatory agency itself may initiate proceedings. This is generally preceded by a preliminary investigation that establishes the need for action.

Here the agency obviously functions somewhat as a prosecutor and judge, although it is incorrect to equate a trial examiner with a judge or a regulatory tribunal with a court. A complaint is issued in the name of the commission, charging an individual or a firm with a violation of the law and stating the specific charges. Advance notice to parties concerned is required in line with traditional due process. The Administrative Procedure Act, Section 5(a), sets down general requirements which ensure that interested parties learn the principal issues involved. In fixing the time and place of hearings, for example, "due regard shall be had for the convenience and necessities of the parties and their representatives."

The Hearing. The hearing that follows is roughly similar to the proceedings in an ordinary court of law. A basic difference, however, is that the judge in ordinary courts usually hears the evidence personally. The opposite is often true in regulatory procedure in which an agency will have a panel of hearing officers who preside at hearings and formulate findings of fact and law, which the commissioners or the department head, as the case may be, will ultimately review and sign. In effect an "institutional" decision results in which agency members, when determining facts, must rely upon memoranda of the record prepared by staff assistants. The evidence is thus reweighed by the commissioners. The second Hoover Commission suggested a way of overcoming this "reweighing" problem[2] by recommending that the hearing officers' findings of fact could not be set aside by the commissioners "unless clearly erroneous on the whole record."[3] A Michigan University Law School study concluded that this recommendation was practical,[4] and that it would ease the problem now arising from the fact that the members presently decide without seeing or hearing the witnesses. In effect, the hearing officer's role would be strengthened. However, as we shall see below, this argument reflects the lawyer's assumption that the hearing officer and the agency's adjudication are, or can be made, analogous to that of the regular courts. Most public administration specialists, as well as some lawyers, are unwilling to accept this assumption. However, this is not true of most lawyers.[5]

In the past the role of the hearing officer was largely advisory to his superiors, although he did in some cases both recommend and make the final decision. Under the Administrative Procedure Act, however, he enjoys greater power. The system of internal separation of prosecutory and judicial functions provided for in the Act makes him a pivotal figure.[6] The requirement is now that hearing officers must make initial or recommended decisions to their superiors. The provision for special recruitment of hearing officers through the Civil Service Commission

[2] Commission on Organization of the Executive Branch of the Government, *Legal Services and Procedures, A Report to the Congress* (Washington, D.C.: U.S. Government Printing Office, March, 1955), Secs. 38, 48, 49, pp. 170–72, 201–6.

[3] *Ibid.*, ¶ 1107(d).

[4] Frank E. Cooper, "Administrative Law: the Process of Decision," 44, *A.B.A. Journal* (March, 1958), p. 133.

[5] For an example of the A.B.A.'s efforts to further strengthen the trial examiner's role and his independence from the regulatory agency, see V. B. Deale, "A Major Reform: The Administrative Practice Reorganization Act," 44, *A.B.A. Journal* (February, 1958).

[6] Nathaniel L. Nathanson, "Central Issues of American Administrative Law," 45, *American Political Science Review* (June, 1951), p. 350.

suggests again the importance of their role. Section 8(a) of the act specifically requires that when an agency head has not presided at a hearing, the hearing officer shall initially decide the case or the agency head shall require that the entire record be certified to the agency for initial decision. Furthermore, when such officer makes the initial decision and no appeal is made to the agency, his decision shall become the final decision of the agency.

Evidence. As noted previously, the rules of evidence and cross-examination have been liberal in administrative hearings. Hearsay evidence is permitted, and other types of evidence not allowed in regular courts are accepted. It is felt that the hearing officers and the commissioners are experts who can determine important facts without resorting to the traditional rules governing evidence. The Administrative Procedure Act did not change this situation, other than to reinforce the probability that all evidence will find expression. Thus "any oral or documentary evidence may be received. . . ."[7] The scope of cross-examination is broadened by the provision that "every party shall have the right to present his case or defense by oral or documentary evidence, to submit rebuttal evidence, and to conduct cross-examination as may be required for a full and true disclosure of the facts."[8] The statute thus attempts to obviate the claim that the restriction of cross-examination results in an unfair hearing.

Another requirement is that "substantial evidence" must be found throughout the entire record to support administrative action. "Substantial evidence" was held by Chief Justice Hughes to mean ". . . such relevant evidence as a reasonable mind might accept as adequate to support a conclusion."[9] Prior to the Administrative Procedure Act, the general practice of the courts had been to sustain agency findings if adequate evidence could be found *anywhere* in the record. The Taft-Hartley Act, similarly, in amending the Wagner Act, provides that findings must be supported by substantial evidence throughout the record. The Supreme Court in the Universal Camera–NLRB case held that both statutes had intended by such language to extend the scope of judicial review over administrative action. Although some authorities disagree with the Court's interpretation, the scope of review has apparently been expanded.

IMPACT OF THE ADMINISTRATIVE PROCEDURE ACT. The "substantial evidence" requirement means that instead of proceeding on a positive assumption toward an agency's establishment of its case, the courts

---

[7] *Legal Services and Procedures, A Report to the Congress,* Sec. 7(c).
[8] *Ibid.*
[9] *Consolidated Edison Co.* v. *NLRB* (305 U.S. 197, 1938).

now tend to require a fuller demonstration of such evidence. As Justice Frankfurter said in the Universal Camera case, "Congress expressed a mood in the Taft-Hartley and Administrative Procedure Acts. . . . As legislation that mood must be respected, even though it can only serve as a standard for judgment and not as a body of rigid rules assuring sameness of application."[10] Although evidence must now appear throughout the record, this apparently does not mean that the entire record must be read but refers to the "attitudes of judgment."[11] That is, the *weight of the evidence* must now clearly support administrative findings rather than the less demanding earlier requirement. In a summary of the new requirements of evidence, however, Louis L. Jaffe cautions, "it would be a drastic and unwarranted conclusion to read either act as impairing the long standing doctrine that there are valid areas of administrative discretion and that judgment within these areas will be set aside only if unreasonable or arbitrary.[12] As we have seen, other observers are less optimistic.

THE SECOND HOOVER COMMISSION RECOMMENDATIONS

This Commission went considerably further than its predecessor in recommending changes in regulatory procedures. Perhaps the main point was the Commission's effort to supplement the Administrative Procedure Act with an entirely new administrative code, which was drafted by the Commission's task force. This code was too drastic even for the ABA, whose special committee proposed similar but less far-reaching changes. According to one authority, both the Commission's and the ABA's recommendations are based upon two assumptions, neither of which has "any widespread public support."[13] These assumptions are (1) that the judicialization of the administrative process is essential to prevent abuses and protect private rights, and (2) that the role of the courts in administrative determinations must be enlarged by broadening judicial review and by permitting the courts a wider latitude in that review.

More specifically the Commission's code included the following recommendations:

1. "Rule making" should be redefined to include only matters of general applicability and future effect. Under the Administrative Procedure Act it had included also matters of *particular* applicability. Some very tech-

---

[10] *Universal Camera Corp.* v. *NLRB* (340 U.S., 1951).

[11] Louis L. Jaffe, "Judicial Review: Substantial Evidence on the Whole Record," 64, *Harvard Law Review* (June, 1951), p. 1239.

[12] *Ibid.*, p. 1260.

[13] S. Thomas, "The Proposed Code of Federal Administrative Procedure," 25, *I.C.C. Practitioners' Journal* (February, 1958), pp. 518–24.

nical matters of definition and interpretation would, of course, be introduced by such a change.

2. Hearing officers should be required to render an initial decision in all formal proceedings where the agency had not presided at the hearing. This would tend to delay adjudication and limit the influence of the commissioners.

3. Pleadings in formal adjudication should follow the practice required in federal district courts unless the agency finds this "impractical" and provides other rules. Here again the effect of such a provision hinges upon the word "impractical," and litigation would often be required to determine its meaning in a specific instance.

4. The agency's role should, in effect, be reduced to the determination of broad findings of fact, whereas the hearing officer should have final authority in matters of "evidentiary fact" subject to limited review by the agency.

Most of these prescriptions add to the burden of the agency and would surely hinder the speed with which it can function. At this time, however, the fate of these recommendations cannot be predicted.

In sum, one observer, whose position brings him into contact with the ICC, believes the proposed code would: (1) "seriously impair the effectiveness of these independent regulatory agencies. . . . [which] deal with highly complex and rapidly changing economic problems and . . . [whose] procedures must be flexible," (2) create new uncertainties when already those created by the Administrative Procedure Act are still being litigated; and (3) tend to force the commissions into a "procedural mold" even though those who practice before the agencies are generally satisfied with their procedures.[14]

FORMAL ADJUDICATION: THE FTC EXAMPLE

A brief summary of how the Federal Trade Commission issues a cease-and-desist order illustrates the process of formal administrative adjudication. The FTC commonly initiates a preliminary investigation on the basis of a complaint from a consumer, a competitor, or some other public source. It may, however, undertake the investigation on its own initiative. The attorney entrusted with the informal examination of the facts either makes a recommendation to the commission for further action or suggests that the case be closed for lack of evidence. It is important to note here that investigation or prosecutory functions and so-called judicial functions are internally separated in the FTC. The former are carried on by a special investigative board, while the latter are administered by a panel of trial examiners. Assuming that the commission decides that formal action is necessary, a complaint is issued naming the respondent and the violation charged. The individual who brought the

[14] *Ibid.*, p. 519.

original charge is not a party to the complaint; here the commission itself is acting in the public interest to prevent unfair methods of competition and other practices prohibited by the Federal Trade Commision Act, the Export Trade Act, and the Clayton Act, as amended by the Robinson-Patman Act.

Within a certain time the respondent must admit the charges or announce his intention to contest the complaint. If he fails to reply to the charges within the twenty-day period allowed, the commission is authorized to issue a cease-and-desist order against further violation. If the case is contested, hearings are held before a trial examiner. The commission and the respondents are represented by counsel. Witnesses are called and the proceedings follow generally the practices of judicial courts, except for greater informality with regard to rules of evidence, cross-examination, and the interest of persons appearing. Under the Administrative Procedure Act every party can present his case orally or by documentary evidence and can conduct cross-examination.[15] However, the needs and objectives of the administrative process are recognized in the provision that "every agency shall as a matter of policy provide for the exclusion of irrelevant, immaterial or unduly repetitious evidence. . . ."[16] After both sides have presented their case, the trial examiner or hearing officer prepares a report of the evidence for the commission and the lawyers of the respondent. Exceptions to the trial examiner's report are included in the record. The trial examiner recommends in addition an initial decision to the commission, and his interpretation of facts must be given due weight by the commission.

Within a certain time after the trial examiner's report is made, briefs are filed by the contestants, and the scene is set for final hearing before the commission, which then decides whether the original complaint has been sustained. If so, the commission will issue a cease-and-desist order requiring the offending individual or company to mend its ways. The respondent, of course, still has access to the regular courts of law for appeal against the commission's ruling. In fact, FTC cease-and-desist orders require confirmation by the Circuit Court of Appeals before becoming operative. The court may modify, set aside, or affirm such orders. Once an order is upheld, however, the respondent must comply or become liable to a civil penalty of not more than $5,000 for each violation.

The FTC and the Book-of-the-Month Club. An interesting example of the FTC's activity occurred when the Commission ordered the Book-of-the-Month Club, Inc., to stop using the word "free" in its advertising

[15] Sec. 7(c).
[16] *Ibid.*

and promotional literature. In upholding the decision of its trial examiner, the Commission maintained that the word was misleading because the "free" book was "free" only if a member bought four of the club's books. If not, the "free" book had to be paid for. In this instance the Commission took action under the statutory obligation to prevent unfair or misleading advertising. The Book-of-the-Month Club indicated that it would appeal further to the Circuit Court of Appeals, basing its case largely on the comments of the lone dissenting commissioner, Mason. Mason's statements are worth repeating because they indicate the diversity of opinion on the commission and the point of view that commissioners may hold regarding the regulatory process. After suggesting that the Commission's decision was based upon the "urge to tell someone off," Mason concluded that "people bought things to get something else free—a dangerous tendency liable to stimulate trade, palliate unemployment, and eradicate bankruptcy in the book business. Something had to be done to a merchandising plan that was so simple and so plain it could be explained in twenty-five words—a plan that was selling millions of books and spreading education, culture and knowledge, along with a not unreasonable amount of tripe to the public."[17]

INFORMAL ADJUDICATION

This summary of formal adjudication should not obscure the fact that the great majority of administrative adjudication is carried out informally. As the Attorney General's Committee remarked, "informal procedures constitute the great bulk of administrative adjudication and are truly the lifeblood of the administrative process." In most cases formal safeguards are not available in the original instance when administrative action occurs. The Selective Service Administration inducted millions of men into the armed forces without formal classification proceedings, except in cases of appeal. Agencies such as the Veterans Administration and the Social Security Board handle thousands of cases, with only infrequent resort to formal procedures. The Federal Trade Commission concludes more cases by informal stipulation, in which respondents agree informally to cease and desist, than by the formal process described previously.[18] The Bureau of Internal Revenue, similarly, uses correspondence and personal conferences, both locally and

---

[17] *New York Times*, May 16, 1952.

[18] A recent annual report of the FTC indicates that the Commission has issued about 4,770 cease-and-desist orders since its inception in 1914 as against 8,800 stipulations in the last thirty years to discontinue unlawful practices; FTC *Annual Report*, (Washington, D.C.: U.S. Government Printing Office, 1956), p. 55, 65. All the regulatory agencies issue similar annual reports which describe clearly and briefly their legal basis and major activities.

in the office of the technical staff division where the final decision will be made, for persons whose tax returns are suspect.

Advantages of Informal Procedures. The informal aspects of administrative adjudication have been strangely neglected in view of their overwhelming frequency as compared with formal proceedings. The Administrative Procedure Act, for example, says nothing about the subject, while the Attorney General's Committee considered it only briefly. The fact of the matter is that administrative regulation does not lend itself best to formal procedures. Nor do formal hearings necessarily provide the best protection to the individual; "it is the [informal] conference with its give and take of ideas and information, with its possibilities of detailed exploration of minor points and hidden corners which stirs the mind to action."[19] This comment suggests why informality is so necessary a part of administrative regulation. Experiences of the ICC are germane. Railroad valuation, for example, is a time-consuming and difficult process, necessary to determine equitable rate charges and other matters involving the sale and combination of railroad companies. As the Attorney General's committee reported, one such series of formal hearings lasted 137 days and amassed a record of 12,518 pages, with 462 exhibits! The director of the ICC's Bureau of Valuations therefore experimented with breaking up the hearings into separate conferences, for engineers, land appraisers, accountants, and the like. Furthermore, lawyers were prohibited from attending the conferences because "it was found that the participants . . . could come to agreement with much greater facility without the assistance of legal talent."[20]

A similar practice developed in the Commission's experience with disputes involving charges levied against consignees who retained freight cars an undue length of time. The facts were disputed in only about 15 per cent of the cases. The ICC settled the disputes by informal proceedings in all but five of the thirty-five hundred cases, illustrating again the efficacy of informal adjudication in achieving speedy agreement between contesting parties.

ADMINISTRATIVE RULE MAKING

Whereas administrative orders are directed to particular cases and are used to correct existing inequities or infractions, rules and regulations are general and are designed to meet probable future needs. They

[19] A. H. Feller, "Administrative Law Investigation Comes of Age," 41, *Columbia Law Review*, (January, 1941), p. 596.

[20] *Administrative Procedure in Government Agencies*, Final Report of the Attorney General's Committee on Administrative Procedure, Sen. Doc. No. 8, 77th Cong., 1st sess. (Washington, D.C.: U.S. Government Printing Office, 1941), p. 52.

stem mainly from statutes and seek to establish modes of behavior for certain classes of persons or property. A brief enumeration of their advantages over statutes as regulatory media indicates again the advantages of the administrative process.[21] First, since rules are easily amended, as compared with statutes, they permit rapid adjustment to the changing conditions that characterize our complex industrial society. The administrator is free from the restrictions that come from freezing regulatory details into law. Delegation enables the administrator, when he becomes acquainted with the needs of regulation in a particular area, to promulgate the rules needed to carry out regulation effectively. Delegation also permits the legislature to restrict itself to that activity for which it is best fitted: the blocking out of large policy, leaving to administrators the "filling in of details."

Another essential distinction between rules and orders is that orders are *judicial* in nature, whereas rules are *legislative* prescriptions based on authority delegated to administrators by legislators. Although administrative legislation is often internal, such as the rules established by the Civil Service Commission to govern the removal of incompetent employees, we are primarily interested in rule making that touches immediately on the interests of private individuals. Something over a hundred federal agencies now exercise rule-making power. As noted above, procedures whereby rules are drafted and enforced have been severely criticized, and the Administrative Procedure Act lays new demands upon administrators in an effort to ensure standardized treatment.

The act divides all rules and regulations into two classes: those requiring only administrative procedures and those requiring adjudicatory procedures. All agency action that is not defined as rule making is left in the adjudication category. Licensing is included in this category. This is one of the most confusing parts of the act. The internal separation of functions which the act now requires for adjudicatory proceedings is not required for rule making. A problem arises here because it is difficult to define all administrative actions as *either* rules or orders. Rules now require notice, hearing, reference to the agency involved, the terms of the proposed rule, and a description of the subject or issues involved. Interested parties, moreover, must be given an opportunity to participate in rule making. This complicates the administrative process by applying to rules and regulations the judicial-type procedures which formerly applied only to orders and to those categories of rules in which the statute itself called for hearings before rules could be made. Although some exceptions exist, the result is to judicialize the rule making process beyond anything previously required. The matter of deciding

[21] James Hart, *An Introduction to Administrative Law* (New York: Appleton-Century-Crofts, Inc., 1940), pp. 153–55.

when a hearing shall be required is also thrown into the courts because many statutes do not specifically state whether hearings are required or not.

PROCEDURAL SAFEGUARDS IN
ADMINISTRATIVE RULE MAKING

The delegation of legislative authority involved in administrative rule making has been attacked on two grounds: that it violates the separation of powers by improperly vesting legislative functions in the executive branch; and that the way in which rules and regulations are made and enforced violates procedural due process. In general, for delegation to be acceptable, the following requirements have been laid down by the courts: The legislature must in the first place have power to regulate the subject concerned; delegation must be limited by a precise definition of the subject and the provision of standards to guide the administrative agency; the agency must, moreover, make a specific finding that the general conditions set down by the legislature under which regulation could be put into effect did in fact exist; delegation must be to public bodies and not to private persons; and finally, any penal sanction for violation must be prescribed by the legislature.[22]

Proper Standards of Delegation. When Congress delegates power to an administrative agency, it must lay down certain standards to control the exercise of such power in order not to violate the separation-of-powers theory of the federal Constitution. This general rule is one of those legal dictums to which lip service is frequently paid but which is not easy to apply in specific situations. In practice, it is difficult to provide standards that are concrete; consequently they often take the form of a broad declaration of policy, framed in terms of "public interest, convenience, or necessity." However, two general theories of delegating legislative authority to an administrative official or agency have been sanctioned by the Supreme Court. For convenience these have been designated as "primary standard" and "contingent effect."

PRIMARY STANDARD. In delegating some of its legislative authority under the first prescription, the legislature fixes by statute the boundaries or standards within which administrative action must be confined. An illustration of the primary standard theory is found in *Schechter Poultry Corporation* v. *United States*.[23] The President had been authorized under Section 3 of the National Industrial Recovery Act of 1933 to approve "codes of fair competition." As a condition of approval, he could "impose such conditions including the requirement of reports and keeping of accounts for the protection of consumers, competitors, employees. . . ."

[22] *Ibid.*, p. 165.
[23] 295 U.S. 495 (1935).

Furthermore, where such a code had not been approved, the President could prescribe one, either on his own motion or on a complaint. Violation of the code was made a misdemeanor. In the Schechter case, the defendants, indicted for violation of the "Live Poultry Code," contended that the code was unconstitutional because no standard was set by Congress to control the code-making power given the President. The Supreme Court agreed that "fair competition" was not a sufficient standard. Congress, therefore, cannot delegate legislative power to the President to exercise unlimited discretion to make whatever laws he thinks may be needed for the rehabilitation of trade or industry.[24]

CONTINGENT EFFECT. Under the theory of contingent effect, the authority to determine the conditions under which an existing statute is to be invoked is delegated to an administrative official or commission; that is, Congress will define only generally the circumstances under which a contingent statute shall be brought into operation by an administrative authority. Such delegation is especially broad in the area of foreign affairs and includes: empowering the President to adjust tariff rates in order to equalize them and protect domestic manufacturers and permitting him to declare an embargo under the provision of the Neutrality Act. A joint resolution of Congress on May 28, 1934, provided, for example:

... if the President finds that the prohibition of the sale of arms and munitions of war in the United States to those countries now engaged in armed conflict in the Chaco may contribute to the reestablishment of peace between those countries, and if after consultation with the governments of other American Republics and with their cooperation, as well as that of such other governments as he may deem necessary, he makes proclamation to that effect, it shall be unlawful to sell, except under such limitations and exceptions as the President prescribes, any arms or munitions of war in any place in the United States to the countries now engaged in that armed conflict, or to any person, company, or association acting in the interest of either country, until otherwise ordered by the President or by Congress.

In refuting the claim that the resolution was an unconstitutional delegation of power, the Court stated:

When the President is to be authorized by legislation to act in respect of a matter intended to affect a situation in foreign territory, the legislator properly bears in mind the important consideration that the form of the President's action—or, indeed, whether he shall act at all—may well depend, among other things, upon the nature of the confidential information which he has or may thereafter receive, or upon the effect which his action may have upon our foreign relations. This consideration ... discloses the unwisdom of requiring Congress in this field of governmental power to lay down narrowly definite standards by which the President is to be governed.[25]

[24] See also *Panama Refining Co. v. Ryan* (293 U.S. 388, 1935).
[25] *U.S. v. Curtiss-Wright Export Corporation* (299 U.S. 304, 1936).

Prenatal Consultation. Another important safeguard provides for consultation between an agency and affected interests before administrative rules become law. Several methods are used to bring about cooperation of this kind. Advisory committees are widely used in regulating western grazing lands. Some agencies serve notice upon the parties affected and hold a formal hearing before issuing rules and regulations. While judicial-type hearings are not always required in the making of rules and regulations, the device of notice and hearing is often used in order to secure information and promote public acceptance in advance. Thus industrial accident commissions usually notify the industries concerned, labor leaders, and welfare groups relative to proposed rules affecting working conditions.

Such consultation often includes informal conferences with the groups affected. Although there is danger that this practice may result in undue intimacy between officials and those who have special axes to grind, there seems to be no way of preventing it. If properly utilized, of course, such a procedure is desirable. Successful regulation depends upon the support of the interests regulated. The county committees of the Production Marketing Administration, which handles farm production allotments for subsidy purposes, are an example of the way in which consultation can draw upon the interest and experience of those regulated.

Post-natal Publication. It has long been the practice to publish the laws enacted in legislative sessions. While it has been British practice for many years to publish administrative rules and regulations, it was not until 1935 that similar provisions were made by our federal government. In that year an act was passed establishing a Division of the Federal Registrar. The division publishes the *Federal Register* which includes Presidential proclamations, Executive orders, and any order, regulation, rule, certificate, license, notice, or similar document which has general applicability and regulatory effect. A rule or regulation is not valid until filed with the Federal Registrar Division and made available for public inspection. The contents of the *Federal Register* are required by law to be judicially noticed, which means that the courts are authorized to take notice of their existence even when they have not been cited or pleaded in court proceedings.

Legislative Review. Attempts have been made to establish a cross-check on administrative legislation for a given period, usually sixty days, as is the case with federal reorganization acts. The regulations become effective only after they have been before Congress for the designated period, provided, of course, that Congress has not voted adversely on them during the interim. In some of the major transfers of administrative agencies in 1939 and 1940, resolutions were enacted in both Houses approving the President's action, although this was probably not required. The procedure in England often provides that regulations shall become effective at once, except that if either House objects, the document may be annulled without prejudicing the validity of anything done under it. In order to achieve a more effective scrutiny of the flood of delegated legislation (an approximate annual average of two thousand executive rules has appeared during the past decade) which Parliament must theoretically approve, a Select Committee on Statutory Instruments was created in June, 1944.[26] The Committee has no power to consider the merits of any executive rule but merely brings such rules to the attention of the House of Commons, indicating their effect, any unjustifiable delay in placing them before the House, and any unusual feature which, in the opinion of the Committee, is worthy of special legislative consideration. Even when this has been done, however, there is no assurance that the House will discuss the matter. Before this can occur, a member must raise the question specifically. In those instances when the committee has made representations to Parliament, only something over half have actually been brought up for discussion. In addition the Committee's functions relate only to delegated legislation which must by law be laid before Parliament. The majority of such legislation does not have to be so treated. In 1944, for example, only "291 instruments, out of a total of 1,483 registered, were subject or liable to parliamentary proceedings," and henceforth, to the scrutiny of the Select Committee.[27] In 1945, 1946, and 1947, the percentages so handled were 22, 43, and 37. However, as Robson notes, Parliament has never paid any real attention to the problem of administrative adjudication.[28]

In sum, while such committees represent a valuable and more effective check on delegated legislation, they do emphasize again the fact that external controls are of limited efficacy in modern public administration. In individual matters of great importance, they are clearly effective, but insofar as daily, routine matters (which play so large a role in molding policy) are concerned, we must rely to a great extent on the ethics and professional standards of the administrator.

INSPECTION AND LICENSING

Inspection. In descending the scale of administrative powers, one next encounters inspection. Inspection is a method of controlling behavior in

---

26 K. C. Wheare, "Controlling Delegated Legislation: A British Experiment," 11, *Journal of Politics* (November, 1949).

27 *Ibid.*, p. 751.

28 William A. Robson, "Administrative Justice and Injustice: A Commentary on the Franks Report," *Public Law* (Spring, 1958), p. 15.

the public interest. It uses definite sanctions such as revocation, fine, and even imprisonment for those who attempt to operate without authorization or fail to honor the conditions explicit in the granting of the license. Inspection is probably the most common of public regulatory activities. In America it dates back over a century to the inspection of New England town markets, where the principal objective appears to have been the preservation of the good name of the markets concerned. The growth of the inspection function was correlated with the rise of our urban-industry society and the scientific advances that assisted its growth. Both the demand for inspection in the public interest and the development of systematic and scientific criteria for evaluating products and processes were made possible by this development.

THE EDUCATIONAL OBJECTIVE OF INSPECTION. Effective public regulation probably depends mainly upon exhortation. Appeals to self-interest, good citizenship, and community spirit provide important motivation at every level. Conferences, inspiration by example, mediation, and publicity provide the techniques. In a word, public policy is sought through education. Although minimum standards and sanctions are available in most areas of inspection, these represent only the starting point of policy. Instruction concerning the benefits of preventive or corrective action is the principal means of securing compliance. Inspection has as its long-range objective the positive end of achieving cooperation from those whose activities are regulated. The inspector is actually a teacher who will apply the sanctions available to him only as a last resort.

The Administrative Procedure Act, it should be noted, formalizes this concept of inspection into law. According to Section 9, licenses may not be revoked, "except in cases of willfulness or where public health, interest or safety requires otherwise . . . until the parties have been given in writing an opportunity to demonstrate or achieve compliance." Although this clause provides considerable latitude for the administrative agency concerned, it also provides additional opportunities for judicial review as to whether these conditions actually existed, and it also gives regulated interests an apparently indefinite time to get around to complying with the conditions required for licensing.[29] Here again the act seems to lean over backward in the direction of safeguarding private interests even though federal inspection has always been characterized by an educational approach.

Inspection is often a prelude to the issuance of a license. It is the method of control of which the license is often the formal notification of approval. Thus innumerable activities and occupations for which

[29] Ashley Fellers, "Adjudication by Federal Agencies Under the Administrative Procedure Act," in G. Warren (ed.), *Federal Administrative Procedure Act and the Administrative Agencies* (New York: New York University Press, 1947), pp. 540–42.

licenses are required involve inspection. Individuals who operate auto-mobiles, trucks, airplanes, ships, and racing cars must have them in-spected prior to licensing. In most states about thirty occupations, rang-ing from bankers to barbers, taxidermists to truckers, require inspection and/or examination in order to determine that licensing conditions are being met. In every case the state seeks control of private activity by establishing minimum conditions of entry and performance.

OTHER OBJECTIVES OF INSPECTION. Although the basic objective of inspection is the control of private activity in order to ensure public health, safety, and morals, it is also a preventive measure seeking to detect and remedy dangerous conditions which could result in serious harm. Inspection, for example, protects public health by enforcing standards for the food and drug products that the public consumes. The U.S. Food and Drug Administration, under the several food and drug acts, maintains a corps of inspectors who carry on a continuous scrutiny of manufactured products to ensure that they meet proper standards of health and safety. Railroad safety equipment and locomotives are regularly inspected by the Interstate Commerce Commission. The Atomic Energy Commission, which has the sole responsibility for the ownership and manufacture of fissionable materials, grants licenses that govern the manufacture, use, and export of such materials.

It is interesting that the volume of inspectoral services increases as one descends the governmental scale. At the national level, inspection is largely a twentieth-century phenomenon and is still relatively in-frequent in comparison to that at the state level. At the city level, in-spection flourishes, centering about the following areas: building, hous-ing, plumbing, elevators, health, ventilation, foods, weights and measures; in addition there are examining boards for various trades.[30] The various areas are usually under the jurisdiction of separate agencies without much central supervision. Achieving coordination between overlapping supervisional areas is correspondingly difficult.

Licensing. Licensing is not only a method in itself. It may be viewed also as the formal certification of a method—inspection. Despite the necessity of periodic renewal, licensing often follows some demonstrated ability or compliance ascertained through inspection, examination or hearing, and adjudication. It also provides a sanction for continuing regulation. Minimum requirements are demanded, not only before a license is issued but also in order that it may be retained. A license may be defined as an official grant of permission to engage in a certain pro-fession or activity. The legal basis for most licensing is found in the

[30] Chicago Budget Survey Committee, *Report on the Regulatory Inspectional Serv-ices of the City of Chicago* (Chicago: The Committee, 1945).

police power, based on the maxim that "the safety of the people is the highest law."

The police power permits the states to take any steps necessary to promote the health, safety, welfare, and morals of the community.[31] As a result, those professions or activities that are of compelling public importance, such as medicine, teaching, law (as well as a plethora of lesser occupations) have been made subject to licensing. Here again a compromise between governmental necessity and individual rights is sought. The police power, however, has been very liberally interpreted by the courts and has been among the principal bases for the extension of regulation.

Although legislative standards are theoretically required in order to prevent arbitrary discretion by licensing authorities, in actual practice a great deal of latitude exists. The courts have been most liberal, for example, in assuming the need for considerable administrative freedom regarding the personal qualifications required for various occupations. Detailed legislative specifications of personal fitness have not usually been demanded. Moreover, when standards are not expressed, the courts have interpreted this as a legislative intention to vest discretionary power in the administrative agency concerned. From this it is clear that licensing is different from rule making in point of greater administrative discretion, and it is consequently more open to abuse because precise standards and judicialized procedures are not always required.[32] Review is limited therefore to those cases in which an agency appears to have exercised unreasonable discretion in denying, suspending, or revoking a license. Notice and hearing, however, are required in certain instances, depending mainly upon the importance of the privilege involved. Revocation usually requires notice. When the granting agency has discretion, as distinguished from purely routine grants such as automobile licenses, denial must be accompanied by a hearing. Revocation of licenses in which the individual has a property or occupational right, such as in the practice of law or medicine, always requires a hearing. Licenses that involve a privilege (such as the sale of liquor or the operation of a public hall) can, however, be revoked without a formal hearing. But beyond this point few generalizations are possible, and prediction is possible only in the context of a particular jurisdiction.[33]

LICENSING AS REGULATION: THE FEDERAL AVIATION AGENCY. Licensing provides a means of regulation (and of endorsing inspection which is a means of regulation) in a great variety of instances. The Federal Avia-

[31] Malcolm B. Parsons, *The Use of the Licensing Power by the City of Chicago* (Bloomington: University of Indiana Press, 1952).
[32] Hart, *An Introduction to Administrative Law*, p. 176.
[33] *Ibid.*, chap. ix.

tion Agency, for example, inspects and licenses both aircraft and the personnel who operate them. Certification following examination is required for pilots, flight engineers, navigators, dispatchers, mechanics, traffic-control operators, and parachute technicians. A plethora of regulations exists covering preflight action, right of way, distress procedures, landing conditions, altitude requirements, clearance procedures, radio communications, instrument approaches, foreign and domestic operations, and so on.

Elaborate regulations exist for the operation and maintenance of commercial planes. The physical fitness of pilots is checked regularly to ensure sight proficiency, muscular coordination, and depth perception. This is a continuing inspection function exercised in the public interest. An indication of the thoroughness of physical examinations given pilots is indicated in the FAA's Civil Air Regulations, "Physical Standards for Airmen." In regard to vision, for example, applicants must have a "visual acuity of at least 20/20 in each eye separately without correction." "An average depth perception of 30 millimeters . . . is required." Again, "no diplopia in any meridian within 35 degrees from the point of visual fixation" is permitted! This last requirement suggests again the complexity of modern public administration and the variety of skills needed to carry out regulation.

IMPETUS FOR LICENSING. The question may arise as to the reasons for the tremendous increase of licensing. While the public interest, safety, and convenience are the major objects, it seems clear that the desire for revenue is also involved. The search at every government level for additional income to meet increased costs and expanded services has contributed substantially to the trend. Indeed, regulation in some major cities has become extreme; the maintenance of order and safety sometimes appears to be of secondary importance. The huge revenue in fines resulting from assiduous enforcement of traffic regulations is suggestive. The revenue objective is probably more important at the city level, where the greatest pressure for additional funds exists.

Considerable impetus for the extension of licensing also comes from various occupations and professions that seek to obtain a monopoly, or at least to limit entry, by expanding their requirements. Most vocational groups are characterized by a certain cohesion of interest, reflected in many practices that seek to increase their income and status. Licensing provides an official, and in most cases, a socially approved medium for attaining these ends. The legal standards for entry into most professions are promulgated by associations representing these groups. Such standards are endorsed by state legislatures and administered by officials under the watchful supervision of the professions involved. An important characteristic of public administration is reflected here: the commingling of government and private groups to the extent that the two are often indistinguishable. In this context it is clear that the popular view of government as "they"—as a thing apart from everyday private interests and activities—is out of focus.

Accountants, dentists, insurance agents, lawyers, optometrists, pharmacists, doctors, teachers, undertakers, and veterinarians are the groups most frequently licensed in every state. As far as the most vital professions are concerned, licensing has often been demanded by the public to ensure that practitioners are in fact competent. Thus a certain minimum period of training and achievement in recognized institutions (accredited by the professional association concerned) is required as a prerequisite to licensing in established professions such as law, teaching, and medicine. Such action also serves a useful professional purpose by discouraging entry, preventing malpractice, and keeping incompetence to a minimum. More positive benefits are derived in terms of relative economic equality and effective relations with the public.

But licensing has long since spread to many other types of activity, including many trades in which protection of the public can hardly be the objective. McKean's study of political pressure in New Jersey, for example, noted efforts in a single session of the legislature to require licensing for beauty shops, florists, photographers, cleaners and dyers, and bait-fishing boats.[34] In some of these cases the limitation of competition by the groups concerned and the revenues obtained by the state are probably the essential motivations.

BIBLIOGRAPHY

BLACHLY, FREDERICK, and OATMAN, MIRIAM E. *Federal Regulatory Action and Control.* Washington, D.C.: 1940.

FAINSOD, M. "Some Reflections on the Nature of the Regulatory Process," in Carl J. Friedrich and Edward A. Mason (eds.), *Public Policy.* Cambridge: 1940.

HEADY, FERREL. "The New Reform Movement in Regulatory Administration," **19**, *Public Administration Review* (Spring, 1959).

LANDIS, JAMES M. *The Administrative Process.* New Haven: 1938.

McKEAN, D. D. *Pressures on the Legislature of New Jersey.* New York: 1938.

PARSONS, MALCOLM B. *The Use of the Licensing Power by the City of Chicago.* Bloomington, Ill.: 1952.

SCHWARTZ, BERNARD. "Legislative Control of Administrative Rules and Regulations: The American Experience," **30**, *New York University Law Review* (1953).

SHNIDERMAN, HARRY L. "Federal Trade Commission Orders Under the Robinson-Patman Act, **65**, *Harvard Law Review* (March, 1952).

[34] D. D. McKean, *Pressures on the Legislature of New Jersey* (New York: Columbia University Press, 1938), pp. 56–57.

UNITED STATES COMMISSION ON ORGANIZATION OF THE EXECUTIVE BRANCH OF THE GOVERNMENT. *Task Force Report on Legal Services and Procedures.* Washington, D.C.: 1955.

UNITED STATES CONGRESS, HOUSE COMMITTEE ON GOVERNMENT OPERATIONS. *Executive Orders and Proclamation: A Study of the Use of Presidential Powers.* Washington, D.C.: December, 1957.

WARREN, G. (ed.). *The Federal Administrative Procedure Act and the Administrative Agencies.* New York: 1947.

CHAPTER 28

Judicial Review of Administrative Action

In the United States there is in theory almost no limit upon the right of courts to review the decisions of administrative tribunals. Our doctrine of constitutional limitations is such that the judiciary can question almost every administrative act. Occasionally legislatures insulate administration against judicial review by including in statutes clauses designed to prevent review. Even if a state constitution did set up an administrative commission whose acts were not reviewable by the state courts, judicial review could probably be accomplished in the federal courts under the due-process clause of the Fourteenth Amendment. Speaking very generally and subject to many exceptions, one may summarize the situation as follows: (1) The courts may in theory review to the extent they deem desirable; (2) there is no method of determining whether they will or will not review in individual cases; and (3) administrative decisions are to some undefined extent final.

FINALITY OF ADMINISTRATIVE DECISIONS

The Supreme Court has been content to permit a large degree of administrative finality in old and tested fields where accepted principles and techniques of regulation prevail, and it has been responsible for the acquisition of certain new powers by the regulatory commissions.[1] Nevertheless it maintains a watchful eye even on such venerable agencies as the Interstate Commerce Commission. Thus the Court has consistently upheld administrative determinations in the tried and tested area of railroad regulation,[2] but it has reversed a commission order in the relatively new field of truck transportation on the ground of in-

---

[1] "The Function of the Supreme Court in the Development and Acquisition of Power by Administrative Agencies," 42, *Minnesota Law Review* (December, 1957), pp. 271–91.

[2] *Chicago, P.M.&O. Ry.* v. *U.S.* (322 U.S. 1, 1944); *Interstate Commerce Commission* v. *Jersey City* (322 U.S. 503, 1944).

adequacy of record and proof.[3] Students of administrative procedures agree, however, that there are certain areas of discretion and fact in which the courts should grant considerable leeway to the regulatory agencies. As one observer notes, "the courts have long recognized the importance of the specialized experience and technical competence of these administrative bodies and the need for uniformity of regulation."[4] Another concludes that the courts should ". . . be most reluctant to substitute their judgment for that of the body of seasoned experts."[5]

On the whole the courts, especially the federal judiciary, welcome the relief afforded by the growth of administrative adjudication in the last few years. Without this aid their dockets would have been so crowded that some other solution would have been required. Here, New York State's experience with judicial review of administrative decisions under its civil service law is illustrative. In 1903 the court held that classifications of civil servants were quasi-judicial, and therefore reviewable by certiorari rather than by mandamus, which is customarily used against administrative determinations.[6] Three years of experience under this rationale, however, indicated that the court had in effect assumed the functions of the civil service commission; every decision challenging the commission was brought into the courts as a question of law. The court thereupon reversed its earlier decision and limited the scope of its review of such decisions to matters properly reviewable in actions begun by mandamus.[7] The court concluded:

Where the position is one . . . [in] which there is a fair and reasonable ground for difference of opinion among intelligent and conscientious officials, the action of the commission should stand, even though the courts may differ from the commission as to the wisdom of the classification.[8]

The courts have nevertheless been reluctant to relinquish their right to a final review of administrative action. The Administrative Procedure Act expanded the scope of judicial review. The subsequent paragraphs will consider the present status of review of administrative action, with particular emphasis on the changes introduced by the 1946 act, those recommended by the second Hoover Commission, and the resulting American Bar Association proposal for a new administrative code.

Exhausting Administrative Remedies. An individual cannot ordinarily resort to the courts until he has exhausted all administrative remedies.

[3] *Eastern Central Assn.* v. *U.S.* (321 U.S. 194, 1944).

[4] S. Thomas, "The Proposed Code of Federal Administrative Procedure," *I.C.C. Practitioners' Journal*, **25**, (February, 1958), p. 523.

[5] V. S. Netterville, "The Administrative Procedure Act: A Study in Interpretation," **20**, *George Washington Law Review* (October, 1951), p. 86.

[6] *People ex rel. Sims* v. *Collier* (175 N.Y. 196, 67 N.E. 309).

[7] *People ex rel. Schau* v. *McWilliams* (185 N.Y. 92, 77 N.E. 785).

[8] *Ibid.*, p. 99.

This is quite proper since to have earlier recourse to the courts would soon deprive the administrative process of the speed which is one of its major virtues. Section 10 of the Administrative Procedure Act, however, has a provision for "interim relief" which apparently aims at undercutting this doctrine of the exhaustion of administrative remedies. To avoid "irreparable harm," every reviewing court is authorized to issue all orders necessary to postpone the effective date of agency action or to preserve status or rights until the review proceedings are ended. This places a new emphasis upon review by making it easier for individuals to go to the courts for declaratory judgments or orders before exhausting the remedies available through administrative action.

The American Bar Association's proposed code would further increase the scope of judicial review by substituting for the present "substantial evidence" test the standard now used by the U.S. Courts of Appeal in reviewing findings of fact by district courts. This change would encourage the courts to substitute their own judgment for that of the agency in determining the validity of facts in a given case.[9] It would substitute judicial judgment for administrative judgment. The proposed code would also allow the courts to reverse agency action that seems a "clearly unwarranted exercise of discretion," even though Section 10(e) of the Administrative Procedure Act already guards against the abuse of administrative discretion. This change would also permit injunctions to be sought at any stage of the agency proceeding and would therefore undercut the rule that all administrative remedies must be exhausted before the individual turns to the courts. In commenting upon these and other proposed changes, the General Attorney of the Atchison, Topeka and Santa Fe Railway Company concludes, "this represents a complete departure from the philosophy of regulation that has evolved through experience over the course of the last fifty years . . . [the] existing relationship between the courts and the independent regulatory commissions in this field is in a reasonably satisfactory state of balance."[10]

Questions of Law and of Fact. Courts have usually not examined questions of fact unless they also involve questions of law or questions of constitutional authority.[11] In sum, when a hearing is held, it is the responsibility of the agency to determine the facts upon which the

---

[9] Thomas, "The Proposed Code of Federal Administrative Procedure," p. 523.
[10] *Ibid.*, pp. 523, 524.
[11] L. J. Jaffe, "Judicial Review: Question of Law," 70, *Harvard Law Review* (1955), p. 239. For a general analysis, see Louis L. Jaffe, "Judicial Review: Question of Law," 69, *Harvard Law Review* (1955); "Judicial Review: Question of Fact," 69, *ibid.*, (1956); "Judicial Review: Constitutional and Jurisdictional Fact," 70, *ibid.*, (1957); Frederick F. Blachly and Miriam E. Oatman, *Federal Regulatory Action and Control* (Washington, D.C.: The Brookings Institution, 1940), pp. 121–22.

agency's decision rests. Judicial control is limited to whether there is substantial evidence. Under the provisions of the Johnson Act,[12] for example, a federal district court is denied the power to issue an injunction against a state administrative order when such an order (1) affects rates chargeable by a public utility, (2) does not interfere with interstate commerce, (3) has been made after reasonable notice and hearing, and (4) where a plain, speedy, and efficient remedy may be had at law or in equity in the courts of such state.[13] As applied to judicial review of tax errors, where there has been a failure to resort to administrative remedies, this doctrine has tended to expand administrative finality.[14] This is due to the judicial tendency to refuse the right to attack tax administrators through the courts for mere irregularities. There must be a showing of fraud to merit a judicial remedy.

As a general rule, then, courts have attempted to distinguish between questions of law and fact and have reviewed the former but not the latter. The notable exceptions to this rule are rate-fixing cases in which confiscation is alleged; there the Supreme Court has stated that the appellate courts will grant a trial *de novo*.[15] In findings of fact, however, the rule prevails that there must be evidence sufficient to support the decision. This provision actually vitiates the hypothesis. In deciding whether a given set of facts is sufficient to support administrative findings, the court is establishing a precedent that will guide future cases, since such a decision formulates a given set of facts into a legal measure of the sufficiency of evidence. Under such conditions the distinction between questions of law and questions of fact breaks down. As John Dickinson put it, matters "of law grow downward into roots of fact, and matters of fact reach upward, without a break, into matters of law."[16]

The distinction between fact and law therefore provides little guidance toward a rule as to when the courts will review. This generalization is reinforced by the Administrative Procedure Act, which clearly extends the power of the courts to matters of fact insofar as they bear upon questions of agency jurisdiction. The "substantial evidence" requirement also brings the courts into the area of administrative fact finding. The Supreme Court, moreover, has long held that findings necessary to determine the *jurisdiction* of the administrative authority or

[12] 48 Stat. 775, 28 U.S.C.A. (May 14, 1934).
[13] "The Johnson Act—A Return to State Independence," 30, *Illinois Law Review* (1935), p. 215; "Limitation of Lower Federal Courts' Jurisdiction Over Public Utility Rate Cases," 44, *Yale Law Journal* (November, 1934), p. 119.
[14] *Dobson* v. *Commissioner* (320 U.S. 489, 1943).
[15] *Ohio Valley Water Co.* v. *Ben Avon Borough* (253 U.S. 287, 1920); *St. Joseph Stock Yards Co.* v. *U.S.* (298 U.S. 38, 1936).
[16] John Dickinson, *Administrative Justice and the Supremacy of the Law* (Cambridge: Harvard University Press, 1927), p. 38.

the *constitutionality* of its decisions must be reviewed *de novo* by the courts. Dickinson's conclusion is still useful: "When the courts are unwilling to review, they are tempted to explain by the easy device of calling the question one of 'fact'; and when otherwise disposed, they say that it is a question of 'law'."[17]

Jurisdictional Facts. Here we find another difficulty in attempting to distinguish between law and fact. The decision in a celebrated Supreme Court case[18] presents the doctrine of "jurisdictional fact," also referred to as a basic or constitutional fact. Briefly this doctrine states that when a fact is the constitutional basis for the exercise of administrative power, the court itself must make a finding as to the fact.[19] A federal statute gives the U.S. Employees' Compensation Commission authority to make awards to certain persons. However, among other things, the relation of employer and employee must exist before the commission has jurisdiction to make an award. Since the fact of the employer-employee relation is the one that determines the jurisdiction or power of the Commission to act, it is referred to as a jurisdictional fact, which raises a question of law.

In this case the Commission decided that such a relation existed and made an award to the injured employee. The employer appealed and the Supreme Court held that the Commission had no authority to make an award unless the injured party actually was an employee. Since the fact was a jurisdictional one, the Commission should not be permitted to decide unilaterally, for to do so would be to allow the Commission to decide for itself whether it had jurisdiction. The court, in deciding against the Commission, held that the person seeking the award was not in fact an employee, and hence its ruling prevented enforcement of the award. In spite of the vigorous dissent of Justice Brandeis, the majority of the court held that the question of the existence of the jurisdictional fact must be determined by evidence presented in a court of law.

The practical result of the doctrine of jurisdictional fact is to permit a complete judicial reexamination, or trial *de novo*, of facts that otherwise would have been conclusively determined by the administrative agency. Yet, a decision of the Interstate Commerce Commission, made after a formal hearing and protected by procedural safeguards, should be con-

---

[17] *Ibid.*, p. 55.

[18] *Crowell* v. *Benson* (285 U.S. 22, 1932); and see *Producers Transportation Co.* v. *Railroad Commission* (176 Cal. 499; 169 Pac. 59, 1917), and *People* v. *Lang Transportation Company* (217 Cal. 166; 17 Pac. (2d) 721, 1932); "Finality of Administrative Findings of Fact Since Crowell vs. Benson," 24, *Virginia Law Review* (January, 1933), p. 478.

[19] Jaffe, "Judicial Review: Constitutional and Jurisdictional Fact," p. 953.

sidered differently from a decision of fact made by a meat inspector that impure food must be destroyed. In the former case the doctrine of jurisdictional fact does not have the strong reasons for its application. Where a case can be tried again on new evidence before another tribunal and thus delay the final settlement, the result is to deprive the administrative authority of its advantage of speed. It also tends to make the administrative agency appear ineffectual. Yet the *Crowell* v. *Benson* doctrine has never been specifically abandoned by the Supreme Court, although subsequent decisions have restricted its scope.[20]

Other Factors Affecting Administrative Finality. The adequacy or even the existence of an administrative hearing also determines whether the courts will review. If there has been no hearing, the courts frequently review, since hearing is essential to due process.[21] Adequacy is also tied up with the question of whether the hearing satisfies due process. Although the courts will normally refuse to interfere with immigration orders for deportation, they will set aside such orders if they are based on an arbitrary hearing. In general, procedural due process has been emphasized to the extent that a full hearing is usually required, and the administrative process moves more slowly as a result.[22]

Probably the safest guide as to whether the courts will review is the nature of the subject matter. In this respect it is necessary to distinguish between a legal right that is a privilege and a legal right that is not so clearly a privilege. In the former instance, including mainly cases where an individual has sought some gratuity or benefit from the government, such as grants of public land, the courts have been reluctant to review. Similarly the courts have usually refused to reverse Post Office Department fraud orders because, here also, the government is performing a business service to individuals on favorable terms. However, this distinction is not a very useful one because of the difficulty in distinguishing between "rights" and "privileges."[23]

Even these very tentative generalizations have been challenged by recent developments in which judicial review of administrative action has been concerned with the requirements of due process in cases involving personal freedom, foreign travel, personal security, military discharge, immigration, and deportation.[24] In several cases, for example, doctors who refused to sign loyalty oaths were inducted as privates

[20] B. Schwartz, "Does the Ghost of Crowell v. Benson Still Walk?" **98**, *University of Pennsylvania Law Review* (December, 1949), pp. 163–82.

[21] "Judicial Review of Administrative Adjudicatory Action Taken Without a Hearing," **70**, *Harvard Law Review* (February, 1957), pp. 698, 698–708.

[22] N. L. Nathanson, "Law and the Future: Administrative Law," **51**, *Northwestern University Law Review* (May–June, 1956), p. 174.

[23] C. F. *Slochower* v. *Board of Higher Education* (24 U.S.L. Week 4178, 1956).

[24] Nathanson, "Law and the Future."

under a law permitting the drafting of physicians and dentists. They were granted review, and following an amendment to the law, the lower courts held that the army could not retain them in a noncommissioned status.[25] The view that "privileges" fare less well in the courts than "rights" has also been challenged. For example, after a New York City school teacher had been discharged solely for pleading the Fifth Amendment before an investigating committee, the Supreme Court held that the discharge was arbitrary and therefore void.[26] Thus, although there is no constitutionally guaranteed right to be a school teacher, the court has seen fit to ensure that even "privileged occupations" may not be taken away without due process.

The federal and state "loyalty-security" programs have been similarly regarded by the Supreme Court. Thus a state law holding that membership in a proscribed organization had the effect of barring individuals from public employment was held to violate due process, since there was no requirement that the individual had to have been aware of the subversive purposes of the organization.[27] At the federal level, the Supreme Court in the *Peters*[28] case found that the action of the Loyalty Review Board in removing Peters, a physician in the Department of Health, Education and Welfare, exceeded the authority of Executive Order No. 9835, President Truman's original "loyalty" order of March, 1947. It held the board's action properly belonged to the Secretary of Health, Education and Welfare, to whom Peters was responsible. In the *Cole*[29] case the Court found that Executive Order No. 10450, which extended the basic "security" act of 1950 (64 Stat. 476 5 U.S.C.A.) to all civilian employees of the federal government, was *ultra vires*. The Court held that the 1950 statute related only to "sensitive" jobs, whereas the security order attempted to cover *all* employees.[30]

Another area in which judicial review has checkmated administrative power is in the issuance of passports, which the Secretary of State has denied to persons whose political views and associations would allegedly make foreign travel inimical to the national interest. This issue was treated by the Circuit Court in *Briehl* v. *Dulles*,[31] where the Secretary's power to deny the passport was upheld because Briehl, a psychiatrist who wanted to attend professional conferences in Geneva and Istanbul,

[25] *Nelson* v. *Peckham* (210 F. 2 & 574; 4th Cir., 1954); *Levin* v. *Gillespie* (121 F., Supp. 239; N. D. Cal. 1954).

[26] *Slochower* v. *Board of Education* (350 U.S. 551, 1956).

[27] *Wieman* v. *Updegraff* (344 U.S. 183, 1952).

[28] *Peters* v. *Hobby* (349 U.S. 331, 338; June, 1955).

[29] *Cole* v. *Young* (351 U.S. 536, 1956).

[30] For an analysis of judicial review of Presidential action affecting the civil service, see Glendon A. Schubert, Jr., *The Presidency in the Courts* (Minneapolis: University of Minnesota Press, 1957), chap. ii.

[31] 248 F. 2 & 561 (D. C. Cir. 1957).

refused to sign an affidavit concerning present and/or past membership in the Communist party. While this power is traditional and is based upon the inherent power of the executive branch to act independently in foreign affairs, the courts have begun to question it on the ground of due process and on the premise that foreign travel is a fundamental personal liberty.[32] Thus it has been held that a "quasi-judicial" hearing is required when a passport is denied, that certain grounds of refusal are subject to judicial review, and that passport issuances are not solely a matter of executive discretion.[33]

The Due-Process Clause. In administrative action, then, the due-process clauses of the Fourteenth and the Fifth Amendments frequently enter to question or nullify the administrative acts of the states. One of the fundamental elements of due process is representation by counsel, and this applies to administrative proceedings as well as to judicial, after it has been determined that there is a right to a hearing. The doctrine here has been stated as follows: "The rule generally formulated is that a formal hearing, presumably including the right to counsel, is necessary to satisfy due process requirements when the agency is acting in an adjudicatory (quasi-judicial) capacity, and when the interest involved is regarded as a substantive right and not as a mere privilege."[34] There are three bases upon which right to counsel rests: by *statute,* in which legislation, such as the Administrative Procedure Act, Section 6(a), guarantees the right; by *implication,* in which the right to a hearing subsumes representation; and by *constitutional* right.[35]

Our courts sometimes interpret due process to include matters of substantive law as well as procedure. It is under the guise of due process that the courts sometimes express disapproval of new social and economic concepts by reading their own philosophy into a section of the Constitution originally designed to protect freed Negro slaves. As noted earlier, the section of the Fourteenth Amendment which says that no state shall "deprive any person of life, liberty, or property, without due process of law" has been interpreted as a bar to arbitrary government in general. Toward the end of the nineteenth century the Supreme Court began to use this clause to nullify administrative acts and legisla-

[32] "Authority of the Secretary of State to Deny Passports," **106**, *University of Pennsylvania Law Review* (January, 1958), p. 420–36.

[33] *Schachtman* v. *Dulles* (225 F. 2 & 983; D. C. Cir. 1955); *Dulles* v. *Nathan* (225 F. 2 & 29; D. C. Cir. 1955); *Boudin* v. *Dulles* (136 F. Supp. 218; D. D. C. 1955); *Bauer* v. *Acheson* (106 Supp. 445; D. D. C. 1951); "Passports—The Executive's Discretion over Foreign Affairs As a Basis for Passport Denial," **19**, *University of Pittsburgh Law Review* (Spring, 1958), pp. 661–66.

[34] "Representation By Counsel in Administrative Proceedings," **58**, *Columbia Law Review* (March, 1958), pp. 396–97.

[35] *Ibid.,* pp. 403–7.

tion which seemed to it contrary to "good" social, economic, and political policy. Judicial review under this clause has had a widespread effect on administrative practice and findings.[36]

Other Avenues of Appeal. There are several ways whereby an administrative action may be brought before a court for review. An aggrieved party may bring an action for damages. Sometimes, as in the case of the Federal Trade Commission, the administrative agency must resort to the courts to enforce its orders. The so-called extraordinary writs also serve to bring administrative acts before the regular courts. These include certiorari, prohibition, mandamus, injunction, quo warranto, and habeas corpus. Then there are express statutory provisions for appeal; for instance, the provision allowing appeal from the California Railroad Commission direct to the state supreme court. Another opportunity for judicial review occurs when an agency is permitted by statute to sue for the expense of executing an order after its nonobservance. The question of the validity of the order may be raised in such a suit.

As noted previously, under our system of law courts have the power to review administrative acts to the extent that they deem desirable. There are no ironclad rules, however, that will enable one to forecast with accuracy how far a court will review in a given case. James M. Landis would determine the basis of judicial review or administrative finality upon such factors as competence and expertness. He would leave questions involving strictly legal interpretation to the courts, whereas matters of technology would rest with administrative officials who were experts in that field. Difficulties have arisen in the past because the courts have been prone to cloak themselves in an aura of expertness "in matters of industrial health, utility engineering, railroad management, even bread making."[37] The courts, according to Landis, should retreat from fields of expertness in which they have no claim to fitness and leave final determination of such problems to administrators.

CRIMINAL JURISDICTION AND ADMINSTRATIVE ADJUDICATION

It is the general rule that administrative agencies cannot exercise criminal jurisdiction. Ordinarily, due process includes the right of trial

[36] The due-process clause of the Fifth Amendment has had a similar application to federal legislation and administrative agencies, although much more limited in practice. See A. H. Feller, "Administrative Procedure and the Public Interest—The Results of Due Process," **25**, *Washington University Law Quarterly* (April, 1940), p. 308; and Henry W. Bikle, "Safeguarding Private Interest in Administrative Procedure," *ibid.*, p. 321.

[37] James M. Landis, *The Administrative Process* (New Haven: Yale University Press, 1938), p. 155.

in a court of law before one can be deprived of life, liberty, or property; and it has been decided that only regular courts and legislative bodies have the power to punish summarily for contempt. Nevertheless, deportation procedures of the national government, although essentially criminal in nature, are carried on for the most part without many of the safeguards of judicial process. Sentence of deportation is executed entirely by administrative process unless the defendant appeals to the courts. However, there is recent evidence that the Court, under the influence of the Administrative Procedure Act, is exceptionally sensitive to the injustice possible in this practice.

In *Wong Yan Sung* v. *McGrath* it was held that deportation proceedings must conform to the Administrative Procedure Act insofar as the separation of functions requirement in Section 5 is concerned.[38] Justice Jackson, speaking for the majority, concluded, "nothing in the nature of the parties or proceedings suggests that we should strain to exempt deportation proceedings from reforms in administrative procedure applicable generally to federal agencies." The government had contended that Section 5 did not apply to deportation proceedings because hearing was not required by the statute authorizing deportation. But the Court rejected this interpretation, holding that Section 5 applied whenever a hearing was required, whether by the basic law or by implication from the due-process clause of the Constitution. It must be added, however, that Congress, in a supplemental appropriation act of September, 1950, declared that the proceedings of the Immigration Service need not comply with the act. On the other hand, Congress about the same time provided that the proceedings of loyalty cases arising under the Internal Security Act of 1950 should conform to the new requirements.

The Administrative Procedure Act was also held to apply in another deportation case, *Shaughnessy* v. *Pedreiro*,[39] where six members of the Supreme Court held that Section 10 of the Act provided for judicial review of a deportation order against an alien. The decision specifically overruled the Immigration and Nationality Act of 1952, which provided that deportation orders should be final. It is significant here that the Court again commented upon the "basic policy" of the act to "facilitate court review of administrative action."

The Power of Contempt. The question of contempt of an administrative body sometimes arises. Most of the cases have occurred where the defendant has refused to testify or has failed to heed agency efforts to reach an informal compromise. There have been some decisions upholding the administrative use of the contempt power under these circumstances. However, there is a general assumption that the contempt

[38] 339 U.S. 33 (1950), p. 46.
[39] 349 U.S. 48, S Ct 591 (1955).

power is not inherent in administrative bodies because of the separation-of-powers doctrine.[40] Although the enforcement of contempt proceedings is generally regarded as an inherent right of the judiciary, administrative agencies sometimes have the power to punish contempt in support of their administrative functions. Examples include giving a milk control board the power to fine and/or imprison a dealer who refuses to abide by an order issued after notice and hearing. Constitutional provisions giving similar powers to the California Railroad Commission have been upheld. Although use of the contempt power seems never to have been permitted under federal statutes, it may be inferred that the administrative contempt power is both reasonable and constitutional, and that it may begin to appear in statutes.

In general the courts have gradually granted more latitude to administrative agencies in the areas of subpoenas and orders.[41] The rule is that subpoenas must carefully describe what is relevant to the inquiry and must not be unduly burdensome.[42] Orders are more drastic and are the final product of the agency procedure; hence the courts have often given full review of all the issues when the agency applies for the enforcement of an order. Two criteria are used: Are the agency's findings based on substantial evidence? Is the order reasonable in the light of its object of preventing future violations?[43] Apparently, the main limitation of the present procedure is the "easy opportunity" given for delaying tactics.[44]

The states, for example, have been granting the contempt power to their administrative agencies with increasing frequency. This trend emphasizes again the pressing need of such agencies for adequate powers to carry out their functions.[45] The California Railroad Commission and

[40] Penfield Co. v. SEC (330 U.S. 585, 1947), (dissenting opinion); Interstate Commerce Commission v. Brimson (154 U.S. 447, 1893). See also R. John Tresolini, "The Use of Summary Contempt Powers by Administrative Agencies," 54, Dickinson Law Review (June, 1950), pp. 395–405. R. Parker, "Contempt Procedure in the Enforcement of Administrative Orders," 40, Illinois Law Review (January–February, 1946), pp. 344–54; "Power of Administrative Agencies to Commit for Contempt," 35, Columbia Law Review (April, 1935), p. 578–91: cases unholding contempt power for refusal to testify, notes, p. 585; cases holding invalid use of contempt power for refusal to testify, notes, p. 585; citations holding that contempt power is not inherent in administrative bodies, note 37, p. 584.

[41] "Use of Contempt Power to Enforce Subpoenas and Orders of Administrative Agencies," 71, Harvard Law Review (June, 1958), p. 1541.

[42] Ibid.

[43] Ibid., p. 1544.

[44] Ibid., p. 1546.

[45] Observers have long urged a similar development at the federal level, especially for the older tribunals which, it is held, will exercise the contempt power with due regard for individual rights. W. Pillsbury, "Administrative Tribunals," 36, Harvard Law Review (February–March, 1923), pp. 405–25, 583–92; E. Albertsworth, "Administrative Contempt Powers, A Problem in Technique," 25, American Bar Association Journal (November, 1939), pp. 954–58.

the Workmen's Compensation Commission have the power to punish for contempt upon failure to comply with their orders. The Railroad Commission, after a hearing in one case, found that the defendant was operating as a common carrier without a certificate of public convenience and necessity and ordered him to cease such operation. For refusing to comply with the order, the defendant was found guilty of contempt by the Commission, which imposed a fine of five hundred dollars and five days' imprisonment. The state supreme court and the United States District Court upheld the decision, and the defendant paid the fine and served the sentence.[46]

THE ADMINISTRATIVE PROCEDURE ACT AND AFTER

The act put a new emphasis upon judicial review in order to ensure that administrative discretion would not override individual rights. Not only has any person suffering "legal wrong" properly been given the right to review, but the scope of review is dilated by the guaranty of review to any person "adversely affected or aggrieved" by administrative action. Although the meaning of such terms can only be found in specific cases, it suggests that the courts may scrutinize all regulations that harm any special interest. Also, the new definitions of rules and orders, and licensing broaden the scope of review and bring under judicial supervision many activities not hitherto covered. These include such matters as railroad valuations, licenses issued by the Department of Agriculture and the Secretary of the Treasury, and actions by the Veterans Administration, the Civil Service Commission, and the Tennessee Valley Authority. In fact only two areas are exempted from review: cases in which the statute specifically prohibits review (as in veterans' pensions) and those in which the issue is by law a matter of agency discretion.

This preoccupation with judicial review is somewhat surprising in view of the Attorney General's committee report which found, after the most extensive study of administrative procedures yet made, "few instances of indifference on the part of the agencies to the basic values which underlie a fair hearing," but instead "a healthy self-criticism and considerable alertness to fulfill not only the letter of the judicial pronouncements but the basic implications of fairness in hearing." Indeed both the Attorney General's committee and the first Hoover Commission

---

[46] Public Utilities Act of the State of California, Statutes 1915, ch. 91, p. 115 secs. 54, 81. *Rice Transportation Company v. John Betts Transportation Company,* 36 California Railroad Commission 840 (1931), C. R. C. Dec. No. 26334, Case No. 2994 (September 11, 1933); *Re John H. Betts for Writ of Habeas Corpus,* Crim. No. 3631, California Supreme Court (January 12, 1933); *John H. Betts v. Railroad Commission,* in Equity No. 2-6C, District Court of the United States, Central Division, California (September 5, 1933).

agreed that the administrative agencies were too judicial, slow, and detailed in their procedures.

Extending the Scope of Review. Despite this, the Administrative Procedure Act enlarged the scope of review. Questions of fact, which previously were given a large measure of finality by the courts, are now to be set aside unless supported by "substantial evidence throughout the record." In the past the "substantial evidence" rule had been an index of administrative independence, meaning that the courts were obliged to uphold administrative findings when substantial evidence existed. The Supreme Court had declined to review the inferences drawn from facts by some agencies, particularly the Labor Board.[47] Now the courts are admonished to "review the whole record or such portions thereof as may be cited by any one party and due account shall be taken of the rule of prejudicial error."[48] The change from a positive to a negative approach is borne out again by the requirement that the "proponent of a rule or order shall have the burden of proof."[49] In some cases, such as cease-and-desist orders or deportation proceedings, everyone will agree that the burden of proof properly rests upon the government. In broader areas involving determinations of public policy, the requirement seems ill-suited.

NLRB v. Pittsburgh S. S. Co. That reading the entire record and requiring substantial evidence throughout the record is a new departure is suggested by Justice Frankfurter's comment in *NLRB* v. *Pittsburgh S. S. Co.* Referring to court practice in an earlier case, he said:

One of them, if I may intervene, is a decision . . . [where] this court said, "since upon an examination of the record we cannot say that the finding of fact of the Board is without support in the evidence" . . . that means if I find *something in the evidence* which supports it, my case is at an end. That is what I thought I had been doing.[50]

As far as reading the entire record is concerned, it is well established that ". . . not even judges reviewing on 'the weight of the evidence' habitually read the whole record."[51] Despite these precedents, the Supreme Court has declared that both the Administrative Procedure Act and the Taft-Hartley Act broaden the scope of judicial review over administrative determination in these very areas.[52] In *NLRB* v.

[47] *NLRB* v. *Bradford Dyeing Association* (310 U.S. 318, 1940).
[48] Sec. 10(e).
[49] Sec. 7(c).
[50] 340 U.S. 498 (1951); italics added.
[51] Louis L. Jaffe, "Judicial Review: Substantial Evidence on the Whole Record," **64**, *Harvard Law Review* (June, 1951), p. 1238.
[52] *Universal Camera Corp.* v. *NLRB* (340 U.S. 474, 1951) and *NLRB* v. *Pittsburgh S. S. Co.* (340 U.S. 498, 1951); Jaffe, "Judicial Review: Substantial Evidence on the Whole Record," pp. 1233–61.

Pittsburgh, the changed view is especially clear.[53] There the Court remanded the case to the Court of Appeals on the ground that the trial examiner's findings did not in fact reveal prejudice; the lower court then decided that the statutes had so broadened the scope of review that under the new test, the *whole* record did not sustain the NLRB's order. The Supreme Court then upheld this decision. These cases are vital because the meaning of the general language of the Administrative Procedure Act is a matter for judicial interpretation. At present, at least, it appears that the tradition upholding a legitimate area of administrative discretion has been somewhat undermined.

Presumption Now in Favor of Review. This interpretation, based upon Section 19(c) of the Administrative Procedure Act, which requires judicial determination of all questions of law, is supported by eminent authority.[54] However, the extent of judicial invasion into administrative territory will be determined by specific tests. The statute provides new opportunities for such an extension; it now remains to be seen how the courts will use their new latitude. The distinction between questions of law and fact, the problem of determining the proper jurisdiction of an agency, and the question of agency impartiality can be determined only in the context of particular cases.

The Act not only covers all existing instances of review assured by special statutes but extends the scope of review by a provision which makes reviewable "every final agency action for which there is no other adequate remedy in any court."[55] In the past some doubt has existed as to whether review was permissible in those instances where no mention of review was made in the statute. In the Switchmen's Union case,[56] for example, the Supreme Court held that findings of the mediation board were not subject to review in a situation involving the right of a union to be the representative of employees under the Railway Labor Act. At present, if the statute does not specifically forbid review, the act seems to say that the courts are free to interpret whether or not Congress meant to exclude review. A presumption in favor of review is thus created. "Properly construed the new statute does make a change . . . and broadens in both instances (errors of law and fact and prejudicial error) the scope and measure of the review which the Federal courts are

[53] Nathaniel Nathanson, "Central Issues of American Administrative Law," **45**, *American Political Science Review* (June, 1951), pp. 358–59.

[54] John Dickinson, "Judicial Review Provisions of the Federal Administrative Procedure Act, Background and Effect," in G. Warren (ed.), *Federal Administrative Procedure Act and the Administrative Agencies* (New York: New York University Press, 1947), pp. 584–85.

[55] Section 10(e).

[56] *Switchmen's Union of North America* v. *National Mediation Board* (320 U.S. 297, 1943).

henceforth required to make of administrative action in cases where such action is reviewable at all."[57]

This conclusion is advanced after an analysis of the sections of the law aimed at preventing the recurrence of earlier decisions in which the court had declined to substitute its own judgment for that of the agency in matters of legal conclusions drawn from facts.[58] As noted above, the dichotomy between "fact" and "law" is at best a tenuous one. Section 19(3) insists that the reviewing court "shall interpret constitutional and statutory provisions" and also "decide all relevant questions of law." Moreover the court is directed to "determine the meaning and applicability of the terms of any agency action." These statements are followed by several specific conditions under which agency actions are henceforth to be found unlawful. In sum, as Nathanson concludes, "whatever the exact formulations or explanations may be, there can be little doubt that the findings of the Labor Board in particular, and to some extent of administrative agencies in general, will fare somewhat more roughly than before in the federal courts."[59]

The second Hoover Commission's recommendations, as noted earlier, resulted in 1956 in the promulgation of a new and even more stringent administrative code by the American Bar Association. With respect to judicial review, the ABA code proposed in part:

a) that the scope of judicial review of agency determination of facts in formal proceedings be equivalent to the scope of review by the U.S. Courts of Appeals of determinations of fact by the U.S. District Courts in civil non-jury cases.

b) . . .

c) extending the scope of judicial review of the exercise of administrative discretion by authorizing judicial review where agency action constitutes an abuse or clearly unwarranted exercise of discretion.

d) authorizing reviewing courts, subject to appropriate safeguards and upon a showing of irreparable damage, to enjoin at any stage of an agency proceeding agency action clearly in excess of constitutional or statutory authority.

While many lawyers will support these prescriptions, there are other lawyers who have practiced before the regulatory commissions who deplore them on the ground that the expertise of the commissions will be undercut, their speed and effectiveness reduced, and the administrative process "judicialized" in a way that defeats its essential purpose. A. J. G. Priest, for example, concludes, "paragraphs a) and c) clearly

[57] Dickinson, "Judicial Review Provisions of the Federal Administrative Procedure Act, Background and Effect," p. 581.

[58] C. F. Dobson v. Commissioner (320 U.S. 489, 1943).

[59] Nathanson, "Central Issues of American Administrative Law," p. 359.

contemplate taking the long established 'expertise' doctrine by the throat and strangling it. . . ."[60]

He concludes that "this may be the place to confess that, after years of struggle with them, the writer has the most wholesome respect for the staffs of the regulatory tribunals before which he has appeared."[61] (Note here that a distinction is made between the civil service staff of the commissions and the commissioners, who are often appointed on a political basis.) We saw earlier that S. Thomas, who also practiced before the agencies, shared this view. Here again we must conclude that different value judgments are at work, with those who favor the principle of regulation in the public interest in favor of a maximum of agency discretion, and those who tend to be more concerned with the possible dangers to individual rights tending to advocate added restrictions upon the agencies.

AN ALTERNATIVE TO JUDICIAL REVIEW

Often suggested as an alternative to ordinary judicial review is a system of administrative courts, patterned after the French, Italian, Swiss, German, and Turkish systems in which two mutually independent systems coexist; one the ordinary judiciary, and the other the administrative. In France, an independent Tribunal of Conflicts determines the appropriate jurisdiction when necessary. Although some observers have criticized the French courts on the ground that they give the government official a privileged position, there is a substantial opinion which believes that they offer both expertise and adequate protection of individual rights.[62] Perhaps the basic reason for the administrative court system is French acceptance of state responsibility for private damages arising from its torts or those of its agents. In England and America, although change has been rapid during the past decade, the concept of liability has been by comparison relatively limited.

The cases that come before Continental administrative courts include tort liability, violation of contracts, controversies arising out of rank, salary, and pension awards in the civil service and the military, and *ultra vires* proceedings. French *droit administratif* is case law, developed mainly during the last half-century. Although the Third Republic was characterized by a loosely written constitution and a very powerful executive and legislative branch, the Council of State (the supreme

[60] "The Independent Regulatory Agencies," 24, *I.C.C. Practitioners' Journal* (May, 1957), pp. 796–806.

[61] *Ibid.*

[62] Lord Hewart, *The New Despotism* (London: Ernest Benn, Ltd., 1929), p. 39; F. J. Port, *Administrative Law* (London: Longmans, Green & Co., Inc., 1929), pp. 296–326.

administrative court) could nullify the acts of the executive. Although it could not declare statutes unconstitutional, it could nullify administrative ordinances that were legislative in character; even the decrees of the President could be voided. In sum, the French system provides forceful, expert, and yet judicial review of administrative actions. The problems arising in America from the conflict between administrators and lawyers, and the difficulty of obtaining a sympathetic review of administrative action, have led observers to recommend a similar system here.[63]

Administrative Courts for the United States. In the earlier edition of this text we said, "although the Administrative Procedure Act marks a temporary reversal, there is some indication that we are moving toward a system of administrative courts." It is therefore interesting to report that both the second Hoover Commission and the ABA have recently (1956) recommended the establishment of federal administrative courts to handle the swiftly growing volume of work in this area. The ABA proposes to establish these new administrative courts of original jurisdiction: The present tax court would become part of the judicial branch; the jurisdiction now vested in the National Labor Relations Board would be given to a new Labor Court; and the jurisdiction now held by the FTC and several other regulatory agencies would be assumed by a Trade Court, also a specialized court within the judicial branch. This proposal suggests again that the ABA is intent on further judicialization of the administrative process.[64] However, here again, many lawyers as well as students of public administration have reacted adversely. It is not surprising either that the members of the regulatory agencies themselves should oppose this proposal.[65]

BIBLIOGRAPHY

CARR, R. K. *The Supreme Court and Judicial Review.* New York: 1942.

GELLHORN, W. K., and BYSE, C. *Administrative Law: Cases and Comments.* Brooklyn: 1954.

JAFFE, L. L. "The Right to Judicial Review," **71**, *Harvard Law Review* (January and March, 1958), pp. 401–37, 769–814.

[63] S. Risenfeld, "The French System of Administrative Justice: A Model for American Law?" **18**, *Boston University Law Review* (January, April, November, 1938), pp. 48–82, 400–32, 715–48; Fritz Morstein Marx, "Comparative Administrative Law: The Continental Alternative," **91**, *University of Pennsylvania Law Review* (October, 1942), pp. 118–36.

[64] For a statement of the ABA's rationale by the chairman of the Special Committee which prepared the proposals, see A. Sellers, "The A. B. A.'s Legislative Proposals Respecting Legal Services and Procedures," **24**, *I.C.C. Practitioners' Journal* (September, 1957), pp. 1115–28.

[65] Among others, see R. W. Minar, "The Administrative Court—Here It Comes Again," **24**, *I.C.C. Practitioners' Journal* (May, 1957), pp. 807–15.

————. "Judicial Review: Constitutional and Jurisdictional Fact," **70**, *Harvard Law Review* (April, 1957), pp. 953–85.

DEVELOPMENTS IN THE LAW. "Remedies Against Government Officers, Agencies, and Corporations," **70**, *Harvard Law Review* (March, 1957), pp. 827–38.

MUSOLF, L. D. *Federal Examiners and the Conflict of Law and Administration.* Baltimore: 1953.

NOTE. "Judicial Review of Administrative Action Taken Without a Hearing," **70**, *Harvard Law Review* (February, 1957), pp. 698–707.

NOTE. "Judicial Review of Discharge Classifications Determined in Military Proceedings," *ibid.* (January, 1957), pp. 535–45.

SCHUBERT, JR., G. A. *The Presidency in the Courts.* Minneapolis: 1957.

————. "The Steel Case: Presidential Responsibility and Judicial Irresponsibility," **6**, *Western Political Quarterly* (March, 1953).

SEAVEY, W. A. "Dismissal of Students: 'Due Process,'" **70**, *Harvard Law Review* (June, 1957), pp. 1406–10.

Part VII

ADMINISTRATIVE
RESPONSIBILITY

CHAPTER 29

Legislative Control of Administration

The means of controlling administration, as briefly indicated in earlier chapters, are vested in the legislature, the executive, and the judiciary. The role of the courts was discussed in Chapter 28 in connection with administrative law, and the formal executive controls will be dealt with in Chapter 30. The present discussion will be focused on the instrumentalities of legislative control.

The legislature is probably the chief instrument of control, defining the broad objectives of administration and providing the funds necessary to achieve them. Routine activities of the bureaucracy are also open to legislative scrutiny through committee hearings. At other times, individual legislators may develop an exhaustive interest in a particular agency, seeking evidence of official dereliction. Such excursions are often of value and appear to have become an accepted part of legislative activity. It should not be forgotten, moreover, that the mere possibility of legislative intervention has a restraining influence on administrative behavior.

LEGISLATIVE CONTROLS

Basically, of course, legislatures determine the great objectives of administration. That the chief executive and the bureaucracy participate in policy making and that both define and expand policy does not alter the fact that legislatures provide the laws and the money which make administration possible. Legislatures also determine the structure of agencies and sometimes concern themselves with the minutiae of their internal operations. This is obviously important for the functioning of administration. Had Congress, for example, refused to accept the executive recommendations that the TVA be designed as a public corporation, enjoying certain freedoms which departments do not possess, it could not have earned international acclaim in the areas of regional planning, power development, and personnel policy. On the other hand, official discretion can be limited and routine decisions controlled through detailed legislative prescriptions such as the allocation of International Cooperation Administration funds and the limiting of Presential discretion in reciprocal tariff agreements.

Legislatures, in sum, have final control over administration through the powers of appropriation and law making. They may, as they occasionally do, abolish an agency or cripple it through limiting the funds necessary to support its programs. They can check the achievements and routine work of agencies through hearings before which officials appear. Investigation often reveals how well the bureaucracy is carrying out its legal obligations. Legislatures also participate in the appointment of public officials, and thus shape the character of administration through their powers of confirmation and rejection. Each of these measures will now be considered.

The Appropriation Process. Legislatures control the purse strings and hence, it would seem, the very existence of the bureaucracy. It is generally agreed that appropriation committees are the main instrument of legislative scrutiny and control of administration. In issues of striking importance or in instances where the lawmakers' wrath has been stirred by official misbehavior, legislatures can and do punish offenders by slashing their appropriations. But in many cases legislatures (especially Congress, given the huge sums and programs involved) are not competent to evaluate administrative requests for funds. In the first place, executive budgets have grown to huge proportions. The annual federal budget, for example, now totals about seventy billion dollars, set down in some fourteen hundred pages. Congress does not have the time to analyze this huge budget, partially because of the late date at which it is received. Congressmen, moreover, are laymen; they cannot be expected to have the technical knowledge or experience required to evaluate the requests of scores of agencies charged with a bewildering variety of programs. They must rely on the experts, the bureaucracy.

Not only is careful appropriations analysis beyond the technical competence of Congressmen; they have, for reasons which are not very clear, failed to provide themselves with the staff necessary to give them the specific information without which control of governmental functions is extremely difficult. The dilemma of Congress here is explicit in the words of Senator Paul Douglas, a well-known economist: "I shall never forget my gasp of surprise when I discovered that the Senate Appropriations Committee had only *one* professional man to help evaluate a $61 billion appropriation bill for the Department of Defense."[1]

---

[1] Paul H. Douglas, *Economy in the National Government* (Chicago: University of Chicago Press, 1952), p. 68.

The words of Congressman Meader, member of a House subcommittee on military appropriations, are even more impressive:

> The Committee and the House are dealing with this huge and difficult task without adequate tools. Seven men almost with their bare hands are standing up to a huge organization with thousands of officials, both civilian and military, devoting their full time to the presentation of self-serving statements and documents, and inundating the committee with a plethora of testimony and charts and statistics which the committee is unable to digest, to say nothing of challenging. The Congress is at the mercy of the executive . . . What if they had asked for eighty billion instead of fifty-six billion? Would the committee have been able to challenge and resist the request?[2]

The problem is aggravated, moreover, by the fact that the budget estimates are distributed among several subcommittees of the appropriations committees; each proceeds independently with little communication with the others. Although it is true that the recommendations of each subcommittee are reviewed by the parent committee, little time is left for careful analysis, and the expertise which the subcommittees develop in their given areas means that their decisions have great influence. Committee members may also become too sympathetic toward the programs with which they are concerned. Some observers do not agree that Congress does not handle appropriations analysis adequately, but the weight of opinion supports this conclusion.[3] One must be impressed by the experiences of Senator Douglas, who fought hard to reduce federal expenditures and was admirably equipped for the task, yet whose accomplishments were infinitesimal, in the light of the huge appropriation bills passed during the last few years. This being so, it seems fair to conclude that although Congress' potential control over administration through the appropriations process is great, it has usually been obliged to accept the Executive budget without much change.

Committee Hearings. Committee hearings on appropriations requests provide a reasonably effective medium through which legislators can acquaint administrators with their values and objectives. Committee

---

[2] Cited in "Has Congress Failed?" *Fortune* (February, 1952), p. 222.

[3] Among others see, George B. Galloway, *Congress at the Crossroad* (New York: Thomas Y. Crowell Co., 1946); and Roland Young, *This is Congress* (New York: Alfred A. Knopf, Inc., 1943). Charles A. Beard, speaking of legislative consideration of the Executive budget says: "the result is not unity but prolonged, piecemeal action," *American Government and Politics* (New York: The Macmillan Co., 1949), p. 308. Elias Huzar says of legislative control of military appropriations, "the estimates about which members of the subcommittees on military appropriations ask the most and the best-informed questions are not necessarily those most important from the standpoint of national defense. Rather, they are those which fall within the experience, the competence, and the interest of the subcommittees' members. The basic difficulty is their sheer inability with limited time and means at their disposal, to review thoroughly all parts of the budget for the Military Establishment." *The Purse and the Sword* (Ithaca: Cornell University Press, 1950), p. 84.

members and the officials who appear before them often retain their respective posts over a long period of time, which means that each will come to know the other's mind. At times, legislators will single out a certain agency for criticism, making the appearance of its officials a trying experience. At the same time, of course, there are agencies such as the Federal Bureau of Investigation, the Army Corps of Engineers, and the Passport Division of the State Department, which enjoy the full confidence of Congress.

Legislative control is most dramatically illustrated in the case of agencies that have incurred legislative wrath. The State Department, for example, came under sharp attack following World War II, mainly as a result of Congressional disapproval of Administration policy in Europe and the Far East, the removal of a very few "disloyal" officials through Loyalty Board proceedings, the discovery of some individuals of questionable moral character, and the resulting public criticism of the department. Although the department may have brought some of this criticism upon itself through unsatisfactory public relations, the criticism was basically "political," reflecting opposing beliefs as to the "proper" role of the United States in world affairs. In any event, a climate of opinion resulted in which the department suffered and its requests for funds were unsympathetically received. Legislative disapproval was quantitatively reflected in the department's appropriation for fiscal 1953. State requested an increase of some eighty million dollars over 1952, which was pared down to even less than the 1952 budget.[4]

THE LEGISLATURE SPEAKS

Legislative Inquiries. Congressional attitudes and the type of detailed influence exerted through committee hearings are suggested by the following testimony before a Senate subcommittee on government operations concerning a bill to regulate the outside employment of civil servants. The major basis for the discussion was a report by the General Accounting Office showing that certain employees involved in map making had formed dummy corporations to carry out contracts with federal agencies. In its investigation the GAO found that 125 federal employees had worked for local map making companies during the period 1953–56, and that some of them had financial interests in the companies. The report also revealed that only four of these 125 employees had informed their superiors that they were engaged in outside work. Another background datum is that all the government agencies appearing before the committee opposed the proposed legislation on the basis that

[4] Comparable figures were: 1952, $262,232,661, and 28,518 positions; 1953, $237,-659,174, and 27,692 positions.

they already had sufficient authority to control personnel activities. The inquiry was initiated by Senator George D. Aiken of Vermont on the basis of complaints received from one of his constituents. As the Senator remarked before the subcommittee, "I want to tell you why this bill, S. 2259, has been introduced by me. It was drafted to end abuses which first came to my attention approximately 4 years ago. Between 1954 and 1957 I received repeated complaints from The National Survey, a map-making concern located at Chester, Vt. These complaints alleged that much of the Government map-making work was being done by fly-by-night companies located in the Washington metropolitan area. The president of The National Survey told me that these companies were hiring Government employees in their spare time to do map work under Government contracts to local concerns, and that bidding was done by Government employees on Government contracts through strawmen or dummy companies. The National Survey is widely recognized as one of the Nation's outstanding map-producing firms . . ."[5]

The following colloquy between Senator Thurmond, chairman of the subcommittee and Captain W. N. Price, Deputy Chief, Industrial Relations Branch, Department of the Navy, is suggestive. Captain Price had just read a prepared statement indicating the Department of Defense' opposition to the proposed bill.

SENATOR THURMOND: In what way do you think it could have undesirable effects?

CAPTAIN PRICE: It creates an additional administrative workload, additional reports; and the "prior approval" concept, Mr. Chairman, is going to be a little bit difficult to carry out.

SENATOR THURMOND: If evidence is brought out here that the present system permits abuses to exist, then do you think this bill ought to be passed?

CAPTAIN PRICE: We are certainly in accord with the spirit of the bill, sir.

SENATOR THURMOND: I am not talking about the spirit of the bill now. I am talking about enacting the bill.

CAPTAIN PRICE: If in the judgment of the committee, sir, the bill is necessary, after it has received all the evidence, we will certainly support it; but our feeling now is that it is unnecessary and would just create more reports and more of an administrative workload without really doing substantial good.

SENATOR THURMOND: Do you think it would be much trouble for the man who is working with the Government who wants to do some outside work or hold outside employment, to get approval of the head of the agency under whom he is working? . . . You have regulations on the subject now, as I understand it.

CAPTAIN PRICE: Yes, sir.

[5] *Hearings, On A Bill To Regulate Outside Employment of Federal Employees,* Subcommittee of the Senate Committee on Government Operations, 85th Cong., 2d sess. (Washington, D.C.: U.S. Government Printing Office, 1958), p. 7. It should be noted that the initiation of this inquiry actually came from the public, in the form of the president of The National Survey.

SENATOR THURMOND: How effective have your regulations been on this question?

CAPTAIN PRICE: Although we do not have any comprehensive survey, we feel they have been fairly effective, sir. This is only an opinion.

SENATOR THURMOND: How do you know if you have not made any survey?

CAPTAIN PRICE: Merely by those instances that have come to our attention. Even if the law were passed, sir—

SENATOR THURMOND: How would they come to your attention unless you did make a survey? . . . Have you seen the Comptroller General's report?

CAPTAIN PRICE: Yes, I saw it yesterday. I have read it.

SENATOR THURMOND: You are familiar, then, with the fact that the GAO report shows that under the Department of Defense, the Army Map Service reported 30 people who hold part-time employment, one employee doing subcontract work, and 6 who worked on Government contracts?

CAPTAIN PRICE: Yes, sir.

SENATOR THURMOND: And that in the Navy Hydrographic Office, [there are] 16 part-time employees of private map makers, of whom 14 worked on Government contracts?

CAPTAIN PRICE: Yes, sir. . . .[6]

The kind of probing of administrative policy and the expression of legislative attitudes toward policy made possible through hearings is again suggested by the following exchange between Senator Morse of Oregon and Mr. R. R. Rubottom, Assistant Secretary of State for Inter-American Affairs, relative to the use of ICA military aid assistance in Cuba:

SENATOR MORSE: I want to ask a question or two about Cuba. Mr. Secretary, can you say categorically that United States military aid is not being used by Batista against the Cuban rebels?

MR. RUBOTTOM: No, sir; I cannot say that categorically, Senator.

SENATOR MORSE: Do you think it is?

MR. RUBOTTOM: I think that there is evidence to believe that some of it may have certainly brought to their attention their responsibilities under the Mutual Assistance Act, under their agreement with us.

SENATOR MORSE: What would be your reaction if this committee should decide to send a fact-finding mission to Cuba to determine whether or not our arms aid to Cuba is in the interests of our country? Do you think it would create problems between the State Department and Cuba if this committee decided to send a special mission to take a look at the situation?

MR. RUBOTTOM: I think in the present context of events there that it probably would, Senator. I am going to answer your question directly. I have always taken advantage of your recommendations and have found them to be constructive and helpful. I think I recognize the spirit which motivates your question, but I feel in the present circumstances there that that would be played up by many of the Cubans as unwarranted intervention in their internal affairs.

SENATOR MORSE: Mr. Secretary, I have in my hand a memorandum which you may have seen, to the Members of the United States Congress from Cuban

[6] *Ibid.*, pp. 17–18.

Congressmen in exile dealing with the Batista situation. I will pass it over to you. You may want to file a statement on it later. It is not very pleasant reading, and leaves me with the impression that if these Congressmen, who were once democratically elected in Cuba and then have had to go into exile because of the Batista totalitarian state, are right in some of their observations, this committee had better take a long, hard look at any appropriations in the mutual security program for military assistance to Cuba. I wondered if you were familiar with that document.

MR. RUBOTTOM: I have not seen this document until now. We may or may not have received a copy of it in the Department. I see you received it here in the committee on March 29. We are very, very aware of the seriousness of this problem, and I do not think that there is anything, Mr. Chairman and Senator, that has occupied more of the mind as well as the heart of all of us who are working with Latin America than the situation in Cuba. . . .

SENATOR MORSE: I have been receiving a terrific amount of mail in regard to this Cuban situation in recent weeks and it disturbs me very much. Mr. Secretary, I see you propose [deleted]. That is what I do not understand. Why should we be pouring more money into a totalitarian government by way of military assistance?

MR. RUBOTTOM: I think it is fair to say that we are giving very, very careful consideration to the matter of arms shipments, both under the agreement and on arms that Cuba may purchase from the United States for that country.

We are consulting with the appropriate Cuban officials and we, I think, recognize fully our responsibilities in this connection. I do not know what the [deleted] contemplated for fiscal year 1959 consists of. . . .

SENATOR MORSE: I will be very glad to have the colonel or anyone else break it [military aid] down. Mr. Chairman, let me say quite frankly that I would have to have much more data on Cuba than we have gotten before this committee yet to justify my voting [deleted] military aid for what I think is one of the most dangerous totalitarian states under Batista in all Latin America. [Deleted.] . . .

COLONEL HANFORD: Mr. Senator, if I may bring forth one more thing, the bilateral agreement signed with Cuba was with a government prior to the government in being right now, and our international agreements that we do keep in the areas are in the security interests of the United States and the hemisphere as a whole.

SENATOR MORSE: That is your assumption. I do not share your assumption. That is the assumption you military make. You come through with a bilateral agreement that was made at some time with a democratic regime, and after there has been a complete change in the organization of the country you say it is in our interests to continue that agreement. Well, we had better take a look at what the effect of it is going to be.

COLONEL HANFORD: May I add one more thing, sir. By participating in these bilateral agreements with these countries and the military defense of the hemisphere, we do have some direction in the use of the equipment.

As borne out by the past experience with the 12 countries with whom we do have military agreements, there have been very few violations.

SENATOR MORSE: I would like to take a look at it, may I say, Colonel, by way of a Senate investigation.

I have long since lost confidence in the reports I get from the military on these matters, may I say quite frankly. I think we had better take a look at what is happening to this equipment.

I would like, Mr. Chairman, to make a request officially that we have a detailed breakdown submitted to us as to where every one of these [deleted] funds for Cuban military aid are going to go. I want to know what is going to go in planes, what is going to get into small arms, what is going to go into any pay assistance. I want a justification for each one of these [deleted] over and above what we have in this table in front of us.[6a]

While this example reveals the detail into which legislators may go in questioning administrative officials, and also the kind of information they receive from interested individuals and organizations, one gets the impression that the legislators are rather frustrated by their lack of knowledge of administrative policy and action. The time available to cover the vast scope of administrative operations is also limited, and as the following comments suggest, there is some evidence that legislators find it difficult to attend hearings:

MR. BADER (President U.S. Arab-Asian Institute, Inc.): Mr. Chairman, good morning. It looks like again this year it is you and I. May I ask the name of the other Senator present?

CHAIRMAN (Senator T. F. Green, R. I.): Will you please respond?

SENATOR AIKEN: My name is George Aiken.

MR. BADER: Mr. Aiken, I am glad to know you.

THE CHAIRMAN: We are both from New England.

MR. BADER: I see. I regret that there are no more Senators present because several of them expressed the desire and the promise that they would be here.

CHAIRMAN: Well. It is their loss.

MR. BADER: But it might be Easter week, and perhaps they have all gone home for the Easter holidays.

SENATOR AIKEN: I think we have to make a little correction here. I think most of them are in other committee meetings, because I have other committee meetings myself. I find it impossible to be in more than one place at a time, so we just have to divide ourselves up. I think the others are nearly all on the job.

MR. BADER: I am glad to hear that.

CHAIRMAN: Since the subject has come up, I am sorry to say I will have to leave before you have finished your statement.

MR. BADER: Is that so? Well, anyhow I have submitted a 20-page statement, Mr. Chairman, and I hope you will have the time to read it. I hope the other Senators will have the time to read it because there are a lot of provoking and challenging statements there.

CHAIRMAN: I hope they are not too provoking.

MR. BADER: Sometimes you have to provoke people to get them to do something.[7]

Such hearings can be used to implement legislative control in still another way. They provide Congress an opportunity to give directions to

6a *Ibid.*, pp. 443, 444, 448–50.
7 *Ibid.*, p. 608.

officials concerning specific legislation. The effectiveness of this technique can be seen in the comments by former Senator McCarran in regard to security measures:

> I will tell you something coming from the heart of the Chairman. If the policy of the State Department would be to carry out the spirit and intent of the internal Security Act, you will get a lot of sympathy from one member of this committee. I would like to see it carried out more rigidly and more emphatically than I think it has been carried out . . .[8]

LIMITED EFFECTIVENESS OF HEARINGS. As seen from the foregoing discussion, committee hearings on legislative proposals also enable Congress to influence administrative behavior. The social attitudes of committee members and their interpretation of the objectives of a particular bill are often made patent. When the bill becomes law and an agency becomes responsible for its implementation, the officials concerned will be fully aware of the legislature's will and can make this will known through directives and general supervision. Hearings, in sum, provide a means of inquiry into proposed measures, the reasons for their introduction, the bases of their support, and the objectives their sponsors seek. But here again their effectiveness as a control measure is limited. They are often of a partisan character in which witnesses are usually "for" or "against" the measure and present only selected data supporting their point of view. In many cases, moreover, committee members themselves do not bring an open mind to the hearing. They have already decided whether or not they favor a particular bill and will often bend the questions and testimony to justify their preconceptions. More effective and impartial hearing procedures could do much to help the legislature recapture policy leadership.

Special Investigation Committees. A distinction exists between the legislative inquiries of regular standing committees and the special investigations of select committees. Although the use of such committees can degenerate into a scramble for publicity, some of these investigations have been valuable, and if properly used, could be a necessary means of administrative control. During the 1920's Congressional investigations focused attention upon corruption in the Harding administration; during the 1930's the Temporary National Economic Committee carried out a broad-gauged inquiry into the growing concentration of economic power in the United States. The evidence and recommendations of the TNEC had considerable impact. Certainly the differences between economic theory and practice in our economy were dramatized.

---

[8] *Hearings,* On the Appropriation for the Department of State, Subcommittee of the Senate Committee on Appropriations, 82d Cong., 2d sess. (Washington, D.C.: U.S. Government Printing Office, 1952), pp. 36–37.

During the New Deal the scope of the investigatory power to control administration was expanded by its use to dramatize the need for social change. Investigations were nicely timed to coincide with Presidential recommendations for important legislation. The inquiry into lobbying in 1935, for example, opened the way for laws restraining utility holding companies, while the enactment of the Securities and Exchange Act of 1935 was undoubtedly made easier by committee revelations of questionable practices in stock exchanges and banking which had contributed to the 1929 debacle.[9] During the 1940's major investigations of war expenditures carried on by the Truman Committee were very effective in encouraging agencies to adopt improved procedures. The Committee's methods were exemplary. A bipartisan approach promoted objectivity, witnesses were well treated, and responsible officials were allowed to read and evaluate the committee's reports before their release. During the post-war period, the scrutiny of military expenditures has been continued by several Congressional committees which have revealed some instances of maladministration. Perhaps the most effective has been Senator E. C. Johnson's preparedness subcommittee and that of Congressman Hardy, who after an on-the-scene investigation branded the North African air base construction program a "fiasco" in which some fifty million dollars had been wasted. In 1957–58, a subcommittee on legislative oversight made some important revelations about the policies and practices of the regulatory commissions. No one can doubt the value of such investigations.

Senate Confirmation of Appointments. In major positions, the President's appointing power is shared with the Senate, which enables it to participate directly in selecting high officials who play an important role in directing the bureaucracy. Appointments have an immediate effect on the implementation of legislation. The Senate's rejection of Leland Olds as chairman of the Federal Power Commission is an example of this stratagem.[10] Even when the Senate confirms an appointee, the hearing gives members an opportunity to influence administration by expressing their values and expectations in regard to the operation of the agency concerned. This aspect of control was illustrated in the nomination of Wayne Coy to the Federal Communications Commission:

SENATOR TOBEY: You are familiar with the Communications Act largely authored by Senator Wallace White years ago?

MR. COY: Yes, sir.

SENATOR TOBEY: You have read it?

---

[9] M. N. McGeary, *Developments of Congressional Investigation Power* (New York: Columbia University Press, 1940), pp. 37–45; J. K. Galbraith, *The Big Crash,* 1929 (Boston: Houghton Mifflin Co., 1955).

[10] See Chapter 26 for a detailed consideration of the Olds case.

MR. COY: Yes, sir.

SENATOR TOBEY: What stands out in your mind as the most important single sentence or clause in that law?

MR. COY: It would be very difficult for me to pick the single clause—

SENATOR TOBEY: It ought not to be.

MR. COY: Of course, public convenience and necessity—

SENATOR TOBEY: May I remind you of the important clause—

MR. COY: I was just going to say that the general overriding provision, and not a detailed one, is public convenience and necessity.

SENATOR TOBEY: And public interest?

MR. COY: Public interest, yes.

SENATOR TOBEY: Is that close to your heart?

MR. COY: It is, sir.

SENATOR TOBEY: Will it be during your term of office?

MR. COY: I intend it to be.

SENATOR TOBEY: Will it be so much so that the long arm of powerful radio interests reaching out in this country, as it does, into this Commission many, many times, will be stopped on their heels when they try to approach the Commission in anything else than the public interest, as far as you are concerned?

MR. COY: Yes, sir, as far as I am concerned.

SENATOR TOBEY: Your first devotion in your post will be to the public?

MR. COY: Yes, sir.

SENATOR TOBEY: You won't be amenable to this long arm and these powerful interests, which operate very cleverly down here in Washington in matters of communications?

MR. COY: I trust I will not.[11]

Senate confirmation has long been a means of promoting legislative control over foreign policy. From Washington's administration onward, the Senate has used this instrument in order to advance its views on foreign affairs.[12] In 1809 nonconfirmation was used as a means of denying the need for foreign missions. By a refusal to confirm two nominees of President Jefferson, William Short and John Quincy Adams, as envoys to Russia, the Senate expressed its disapproval of the President's policy of representation. In neither case was the character of the nominee questioned. Although the Senate's role in controlling foreign policy through the confirming power has steadily diminished, new demands for greater participation occurred after World War II, signalized by Senate power to confirm all appointments to the various European Aid missions. A related example was the refusal of a Senate subcommittee to confirm Philip C. Jessup as United States representative to the General Assembly

[11] *Hearing*, Senate Committee on Interstate and Foreign Commerce, "Nominations of Wayne Coy and George E. Sterling to the Federal Communications Commission" (Washington, D.C.: U.S. Government Printing Office, 1948), pp. 1–2. One of the problems of the federal civil service is suggested by the fact that shortly thereafter Mr. Coy became associated with one of the major networks.

[12] Felix A. Nigro, "Senate Confirmation and Foreign Policy," 14, *Journal of Politics* (May, 1952), p. 283.

of the United Nations, mainly because some committee members felt that he was "soft" toward communism and the fact that he had been a member of several groups which later came to be classified as "un-American" by the Attorney-General.[13] In July, 1959, the Senate refused to confirm Lewis Strauss as Secretary of Commerce, mainly because of his role in the Dixon-Yates case and his strained personal relations with several members of the Senate. Among the latter was Senator Clinton Anderson of New Mexico, who had been chairman of the Joint Committee on Atomic Energy, which had experienced considerable difficulty in getting complete information on the contract from Mr. Strauss during its hearings on the Dixon-Yates contract.

Other Media of Legislative Control. In the past few years Congress has turned increasingly to statutory devices and committee activities to make or control administrative policy.[14] Three measures have been used: concurrent resolutions, simple resolutions, and committee action; for example, the requirement that the actions of federal executives be reported to Congress or to one of its committees *before* the proposed action takes effect.[15] For students of administration the most interesting use of the concurrent resolution concerns the reorganization proposals of the President. The Reorganization Acts of 1939, 1945, and 1949, gave Congress the power to nullify such proposals. Shortly after the 1949 Act was passed, Congress used this power to reject President Truman's proposal for a Department of Welfare. The resolution may also be used to terminate executive actions in international agreements, such as the Greek-Turkish Aid pact (1947) and the Mutual Defense Assistance Act (1949). Another interesting use is intervention in Executive appointments; for example, in the case of the TVA, board members may be removed by a concurrent resolution of the House and Senate.[16]

The requirement of "prior approval" by legislative committees of administrative actions is illustrated in a law (H. R. 4914) concerning naval and military installations, whereby the Secretaries of the Navy, Army, and Air Force must "come into agreement" with the Senate and House Armed Services Committees with respect to the purchase, transfer, or lease of land for such purposes. The Atomic Energy Act (1946)

---

[13] *Hearings*, Subcommittee of Senate Committee on Foreign Relations, The Sixth General Assembly of the United Nations (Washington, D.C.: U.S. Government Printing Office, 1951).

[14] See Roger H. Jones, "Congressional Control of Administration" (unpublished seminar paper), Cornell University, June, 1959.

[15] Robert Ginnane, "The Control of Federal Administration by Congressional Resolutions and Committees," **66**, *Harvard Law Review* (February, 1953), pp. 569–611.

[16] Jones, "Congressional Control of Administration," p. 8.

also requires Congressional approval of administrative actions; for example, the Atomic Energy Commission is required to report all contractual arrangements with private and public agencies to the Joint Committee on Atomic Energy, which has a thirty-day period in which to scrutinize them. While one may question such legislative intervention, it is well to remember that in some cases, notably the Dixon-Yates affair, it was this requirement that led to the termination of a contract which was clearly against the public interest. At the same time, for administrators to argue that such interventions violate the separation-of-powers principle seems somewhat strained, since this "principle" is no longer relevant insofar as political and administrative realities are concerned.

APPRAISAL OF LEGISLATIVE CONTROL

On the surface it appears that Congress has adequate means of controlling administration through its powers of lawmaking, appropriation, and investigation. Yet, as we have seen, its policy-making power is now broadly shared with the administrative branch. Largely in response to the demands of constituents for service, interest group activity, and the complexity of modern legislation, Congress' role has shifted from one of policy initiation to the screening, sifting, and referending of policy laid before it by others. Congress, moreover, has extreme difficulty in exercising an incisive review of appropriations. Finally, the investigatory instrument has inherent defects. Thus for several reasons, most of which spring from the atomization of legislative time and energy, legislative control is of limited effectiveness.

The evidence in support of this conclusion is convincing. Senator Paul Douglas has shown that Congress is almost helpless in considering the validity of Department of Defense budget requests, which represent by far the largest share of present expenditures: "Because of the technical knowledge of military men, we are reluctant to criticize them or their budget."[17] Robert E. Cushman says, moreover:

The conclusion seems inevitable that legislative bodies are not capable of exercising effective control over administration or even over their own special agencies, the independent regulatory commissions, except the general, sporadic control which has been described. One must further conclude that there may be real danger in encouraging a type of Congressional supervision which lies beyond the capacity of Congress. The temptation to indulge in sniping and various other forms of ulterior pressure is always present, and much of the Congressional activity aimed at the control of the independent commissions in the past has been vicious and misdirected. Congress is fully competent to tell the independent regulatory commissions what they are to do. It is not

[17] Douglas, *Economy in the National Government*, p. 140.

competent, and is never likely to become competent, to hold them accountable in any effective way for the efficiency of their performance.[18]

Improving Legislative Scrutiny. The means to improve legislative control are well known, but they fly in the face of constitutional prescription, the weight of tradition, and the demands of political survival. Party responsibility is a basic requirement, but given the separation-of-powers system, the localism, and divided loyalty which accompany our method of electing United States legislatures, party responsibility is extremely difficult to achieve. Improving the committee system by curbing committee autonomy and abolishing seniority as the basis for appointment and influence are widely recommended, but here again political realities have usually been an insurmountable barrier. Although not everywhere accepted as desirable, the provision of more staff aid for Congressional committees is often recommended and is slowly being followed. Certainly Senator Douglas' experiences lend weight to the recommendation. Meanwhile the legislator's time will continue to be devoted mainly to the requirements of political success: political fence building and constituents' demands. Politics is a vocation in which priorities must be carefully assigned to ensure survival. Although the means to more adequate control are no secret, rational solutions are not always applicable in the political arena. The impact of "facts" and the admonitions of experts is limited by conflicting social and political interests.

BIBLIOGRAPHY

BAILEY, S. K., and SAMUEL, H. D. *Congress at Work.* New York: 1952.
CROSSKEY, W. W. *Politics and the Constitution in the History of the United States.* Chicago: 1953.
DOUGLAS, PAUL, *Economy in the National Government.* Chicago: 1952.
GALLOWAY, G. B. *The Legislative Process in Congress.* New York: 1953.
JOHNSEN, J. B. *The Investigating Powers of Congress.* New York: 1951.
KEATON, G. W. *The Passing of Parliament.* London: 1952.
KEFAUVER, E., and LEVIN, J. *A Twentieth-Century Congress.* New York: 1947.
MACLEAN, J. C. (ed.). *President and Congress: the Conflict of Powers.* New York: 1955.
WHITE, W. S. *Citadel: the Story of the U.S. Senate.* New York: 1957.

[18] Robert E. Cushman, *The Independent Regulatory Commissions* (New York: Oxford University Press, 1941), p. 679.

CHAPTER 30

Executive Control of Administration

Effective control of administration by higher executives is a central requisite of democratic government. Under our party system these executives have a major responsibility for designing and carrying out public policy. If this responsibility is to be made good, they must be able to control the bureaucracy that is charged with carrying out their policy. The President especially needs authority and assistance which are more equal to the responsibilities of his office. Although new measures are undoubtedly required, executives do have several ways of controlling and influencing the administrative branch. This aspect of responsible administration has not always been adequately emphasized, perhaps because we tend to define the bureaucracy as an instrument for achieving public policy, forgetting that it is sometimes an impediment. The civil service, as we have seen, develops precedents which sometimes make the acceptance of new policy and programs difficult. During the New Deal, for example, party leaders were obliged to bypass old line agencies in order to push through their programs. The British Labour government after 1945 met some resistance from a conservative administrative class, and the counterrevolutionary role of the German civil service during the Weimar Republic is well known. It is well, therefore, to note that chief executives have several means of controlling a reluctant bureaucracy.

MEDIA OF EXECUTIVE CONTROL

Achieving executive control of the vast administrative systems now existing in national, state, and many local governments is a herculean task. The number and size of agencies are awe-inspiring, and the various elements of the machine are often in conflict. They seek to strengthen their position vis-à-vis the executive by alliances with legislatures and pressure groups, as well as by appeals to the general public. They develop vested interests not only in program areas but also in established ways of doing things which enhance their power and strategic position. Change

537

threatens this equilibrium and is often resisted. For these reasons the bureaucracy, although it is often an aggressive contender for new power, is also a conservative force.[1]

The issue of adequate control of the civil service was dramatized during the Eisenhower administration. It is clear that many department heads under Eisenhower did not feel able to carry out their policies with personnel who had served under the Roosevelt and Truman administrations; yet most of the department staffs, including top personnel had civil service tenure. At least one department head found even his number two man under civil service.[2] As a result Eisenhower directed the Civil Service Commission to reexamine all classified jobs with a view to removing from civil service protection those "of a confidential or policy-determining character." This Schedule C category illustrates well the control instruments available to the chief executive. Apparently its intended impact has been considerably less than anticipated, since by the end of January 1954, only 879 positions had been approved by the Commission, which rejected 929 agency requests for Schedule C positions.[3] Whether "confidential or policy-making" positions can be defined accurately, and whether the bad impact on civil service morale, of such orders outweigh the benefits, are moot points.[4] They do show that Presidential efforts at control can also have unhappy effects. Certainly, when government's role is critical and expanding, and excellence is required in the public service, the suspicion, high turnover, and low morale that has characterized the federal service during the past decade can only make its task more difficult.

Power of Appointment. The President relies mainly upon high-level, politically appointed officials to give direction and inspiration to the civil service.[5] These officials influence the broad outlines of public policy, the general objectives of the bureaucracy, and they also guide the implementation of such policy. The power of appointment rests upon the Constitutional mandate which charges the President with responsibility to ensure "that the laws be faithfully executed."[6] Almost all members of the public service are appointed. In the case of major officials, such as department heads, members of the regulatory commissions, Supreme

---

[1] See Chapter 3 for a detailed analysis of bureaucracy.

[2] Herman M. Somers, "The Federal Bureaucracy and the Change of Administration," **53**, *American Political Science Review* (March, 1954), p. 141.

[3] *Ibid.*, p. 143.

[4] For example, in 1953 the Under Secretary of the Interior stated publicly that he had kicked out "a group of Ph.D.'s from Harvard and Columbia," *Washington Post,* Sept. 29, 1953.

[5] Although this chapter relates primarily to Presidential controls, the observations apply in most cases to governors and mayors as well.

[6] Edward S. Corwin, *The President: Office and Powers* (New York: New York University Press, 1948), pp. 82–83; chap. xxxi, *passim.*

Court justices, ambassadors, ministers, and consuls, the President's appointing power is shared with the Senate. In practice the appointing power is also shared with special interest groups. Groups that have real political power, such as the Farm Bureau Federation, the AFL–CIO, the National Association of Manufacturers, and the Air Force Association, play an active role in the appointment of top officials in their respective areas. The President cannot avoid being influenced by them. Often their influence is exerted through the Senate, which can sometimes be prevailed upon to reject "controversial" nominations.

The practice of "senatorial courtesy," whereby appointments to positions in a state are in effect made by the Congressmen from that state, is another limitation on the President's power. The appointment of "inferior" officials, however, is usually vested entirely in the President, the courts of law, and department heads. At the state and local levels, the appointing power of the chief executive is much more limited. In many states, for example, almost all top-level executive positions are elective. In these cases, officials are virtually independent of the chief executive and develop political machines of their own which give them independence and extended tenure.

The removal power is bound up with the executive and the appointive powers. The problem of delineating the scope of this power brought about the first major Constitutional debate in our history, centering about a bill that originally authorized the President to remove the Secretary of "Foreign Affairs" without the concurrence of the Senate. The controversy ended in a narrow victory for the advocates of unrestricted Presidential removal power over department heads.[7] This power permits the President to discipline important officials who fail to carry out their duties properly, as defined by him. It is clear that, insofar as executive officials are concerned, his removal power is not subject to judicial review.[8] Because removals often appear in the guise of "resignations," the significance of the removal power tends to be underestimated. In point of fact, high officials are often removed as a result of inadequate performance or as a concession to unfavorable public opinion. Examples are plentiful. Since John Adams removed his Secretary of State, Timothy Pickering, when that official's opposition to the President's second French mission and other policies made further association impossible, Presidents have not hesitated to remove their subordinates. During Jackson's war on the Bank of the United States, which he regarded as both unsafe and undemocratic, he ordered his Secretary of the Treasury, William J. Duane, to remove all federal funds from the Bank. Duane refused and

[7] Leonard D. White, *The Federalists* (New York: The Macmillan Co., 1948), pp. 17–25.

[8] *Myers* v. *U.S.* (302 U.S. 379).

was immediately removed; his successor, Roger B. Taney, carried out the President's order. Franklin D. Roosevelt removed Arthur E. Morgan as Chairman of the TVA, and Harry Truman fired Secretary of Commerce Wallace in 1946 following a speech in which the Secretary took sharp issue with the administration's foreign policy. Eisenhower removed Secretary of the Air Force Talbot when the latter used his official position to promote business for his own company. He also removed Arthur Larsen as Director of the U.S. Information Agency when Larsen revealed a lack of political acumen in working with Congress.

Presidential Law Making. The extension of administration into technical areas and the need for prompt action have resulted in the increasing delegation of law-making power to the President by Congress. He, in turn, subdelegates much of this power to his administrative aides. The orders, rules, and regulations by which this is done provide the President with an important means of controlling and coordinating the sprawling administrative structure. Such powers must in every case be vested in the executive by the Constitution, treaties, or statutes. Increasingly, however, Congress has been content to set down its objectives in very broad terms, permitting the President to "fill in the details" through sublegislation.

Through sublegislation, the President can issue directions concerning the implementation of legislation, the action of officials in specific cases, and the powers of particular agencies. The Defense Production Act of 1950, for example, authorizes the President to allocate materials in any way considered necessary to promote national defense.[9] He is given power (Section 704) to ". . . make such rules, regulations, and orders as he deems necessary or appropriate to carry out the provisions of this Act." The statute enumerates various officials, departments, and agencies to whom the President may delegate his authority under the act, according to conditions which the President sets down and may modify or withdraw as he sees fit. The Board of Governors of the Federal Reserve System is empowered (Section 606) to regulate consumer credit controls "until such time as the President determines that the exercise of such controls is no longer necessary." The President, moreover, can create new agencies, appoint their principal officers (with Senate consent), and set their pay without regard to existing compensation law.

Another use of executive law-making power to control administration is seen in Truman's Executive Order 9835, the "Loyalty Order" of March 21, 1947, which provided for the removal of civil servants about whose loyalty "reasonable grounds" for question were found by a Loyalty Review Board. The proceedings included scrutiny by the Loyalty Board of the defendant's agency and the Federal Loyalty Review Board. Al-

---

[9] Public Law No. 774, 81st Cong., 2d sess., September 8, 1950.

though proceedings under it were widely criticized,[10] the immediate significance of the order is that it gave the President a most severe disciplinary instrument covering the entire civil service.

Control over Official Information. The power of the President over administration in the higher bureaucracy is not confined to appointment and sublegislation. Specific directions to officials are often used to obtain desired behavior. While it is well known that officials reveal information by indirection before committee hearings and "leak" information to the press, the information they release is subject to some control by the President. The 1947 loyalty order provides an example. In March, 1948, President Truman issued an order forbidding all departments and agencies to furnish information concerning the loyalty of any employee to Congressional committees or to the courts. This move followed demands of the House Un-American Activities Committee that Secretary of Commerce Harriman surrender an FBI report on Dr. Edward Condon who the Committee termed "one of the weakest links in our atomic security" program. By direct order of the President, Harriman refused to comply. Rather than cite the Secretary for contempt, which logically it should have done,[11] the Committee waited for reinforcement which soon came in the form of a House resolution ordering the President to release the Condon file. The President's "freeze order" of March 15 followed. During subsequent appropriations hearings, a State Department official, complying with the order, refused to disclose certain information concerning persons handled under the department's loyalty proceedings.

SENATOR McCARTHY: Who were the other 11?

MR. HUMELSINE: The other 11 cases, Senator, I could not give. I could not answer that.

SENATOR McCARTHY: On what theory can you not give them—under the Presidential order?

MR. HUMELSINE: Under the Presidential order.[12]

Such measures, of course, are not limited to the President but are available to governors and mayors as well. In 1952, for example, Mayor Impellitteri of New York City found the new president of the council,

---

[10] "The procedures of the loyalty program obviously fall far short of what has been established in this country as due process of law." From Allan Barth, *The Loyalty of Free Men* (New York: The Viking Press, Inc., 1951), p. 110, chap. v. *passim*; also letters of Professors Chafee, Griswold, Katz, and Scott in the *New York Times*, April 13, 1947; H. S. Commager, "Who Is Loyal to America," **195**, *Harper's Magazine* (September, 1947); see pp. 292–94.

[11] Corwin, *The President: Office and Powers*, p. 142.

[12] *Hearings,* on the Appropriation for the Department of State, Subcommittee of the Senate Committee on Appropriations, 82d Cong., 2d sess. (Washington, D.C.: U.S. Government Printing Office, 1952), pp. 404–5.

Rudolph Halley, assuming too vigorous a role in supervising city administration, particularly in regard to contract awards to private firms.[13] Although it was reported that Halley's efforts to obtain information from the official family had not "met with spectacular success," the mayor, on September 18, 1952, served notice on all heads of city departments and agencies "not to answer the telephone when the president of the council calls up." Officials were further admonished to "ask him to put in writing any requests he may make for information."

CARRYING OUT EXECUTIVE CONTROL

In part because of the recommendations of students of public administration, the President has been provided with numerous staff aids which help him check on the huge administrative machine for which he is constitutionally accountable. His staff provides eyes and ears with which the President can maintain a certain surveillance of official activity. It can also be used to galvanize particular agencies into action in response to the demands of policy and politics.

Staff Aids. The President's Committee on Administration Management in 1937, and the Commissions on Organization of the Executive Branch in 1949 and 1955, joined in advocating more help for the President, upon whom "falls the crushing burden of bringing all the units of the executive branch into harmony . . ."[14] His main staff agency is the Executive Office of the President, comprising the White House Office, (including a special assistant to the President), the Bureau of the Budget, the Council of Economic Advisors, the National Security Council, the National Security Resources Board, and the Office of Defense and Civilian Mobilization. Of these, the Bureau of the Budget is perhaps the most important, enabling the President to act as chief fiscal planner for all public activity. The Bureau also acts as the President's agent in coordinating policy and in improving the management practices of the entire federal administrative operation. To do this, the Bureau relies principally upon the budget estimates process, which permits a broad overview of the Executive program, gained primarily through discussions between the Bureau's estimates and fiscal units and the budget officers of the various departments.[15] Subsequently the director of the Bureau meets with Cabinet officers and the heads of the independent agencies to discuss their pro-

---

[13] New York Times, September 19, 1952.

[14] Commission on Organization of the Executive Branch of the Government, General Management of the Executive Branch (Washington, D.C.: U.S. Government Printing Office, 1949), p. 11.

[15] For a survey of the role of the bureaucracy in presidential policy planning, see Richard E. Neustadt, "Presidency and Legislation: Planning the President's Program," 49, American Political Science Review (December, 1955), pp. 980–1021.

posed programs and set them in the framework of Presidential policy.[16] Detailed budgets are then submitted by the departments and agencies and justified before Bureau examiners. Finally, the President and the director meet, review the broad outlines of agency programs and policies, and make decisions as to the appropriation figures that will finally be presented to Congress.

The terms of reference of this fiscal evaluation include a broad estimate of tax revenues, the economic outlook, the urgency and level of defense preparations, and the main elements of the President's legislative program.[17] The policies and programs of the bureaucracy are fitted into these larger objectives and expressed in quantitative terms. Thus the Bureau of the Budget has the unpopular task of keeping proposed agency expenditures in line with the larger policy of the chief executive.

The Budget Bureau also attempts to coordinate nonfiscal legislation originating in the executive branch by requiring Bureau advice on all proposed measures. Although measures opposed by the President are sometimes sent to Congress, independent agency action is discouraged by the Bureau's close association with the President and its power of recommending approval or disapproval of bills before the President signs them.[18] All these instruments obviously facilitate Presidential management, but the record shows that the size and scope of federal administration, as well as that of state and big city governments, make sustained control by the chief executive virtually impossible. The job is too big; too many individuals and too many activities are involved.

WARTIME EXPERIENCE. In 1943 under the pressure of wartime needs, the President created the Office of War Mobilization. Sixteen months later Congress, looking forward to peace time, extended the powers of the agency and renamed it the Office of War Mobilization and Reconversion. This superagency, which had great authority over the domestic phases of government, provided a new chapter in the history of Presidential administrative control. It sought primarily to give the President an instrument for coordination of the whole administrative arm. An "assistant president" was created to head the agency and to have easy access to the President. Possessing the President's complete support, he was to have the independence necessary to remain above departmental rivalries as well as the stature required to make his decisions effective.

[16] For a dramatic example of the Bureau's role in carrying out Presidential policy, see Robert V. Presthus and L. Vaughn Blankenship, "Dixon-Yates: A Study in Political Behavior" (Unpublished ms., Cornell University, 1960).

[17] Paul H. Douglas, *Economy in the National Government* (Chicago: University of Chicago Press, 1952), p. 48.

[18] "The FBI Retirement Bill," in Harold Stein (ed.), *Public Administration and Policy Development* (New York: Harcourt, Brace & Co., Inc., 1952), pp. 651–60.

The office's role covered three main areas: the allocation of material resources, the coordination of manpower programs, and the reconversion of industry. The ramifications of these several areas cut across the entire span of administrative activity and required not only institutional innovation but an unusual capacity for leadership, synthesis, and diplomacy on the part of the agency's director. Here again the informal aspect of administration is emphasized. There is complete agreement that the success of OWMR was largely due to the political skill and personal attributes of its directors, particularly former Senators Byrnes and Vinson, who had the confidence of Congress and the administrative officials with whom they dealt. Like the Presidency itself, the agency was highly personalized. Although the agency's successor, the Office of Defense Mobilization, played an active role in the federal establishment, its powers were not comparable to those of the OWMR.[19]

This wartime experience is suggestive in its potential value as a peacetime instrument that could assist an overworked President by improving routine policy and program coordination.[20] Since World War II, government has assumed new and sweeping functions, including the production and control of atomic energy, responsibility for full employment, and global foreign aid programs, all of which cut across agency lines and require coordination at the Presidential level. Several staff agencies have been established since the war to help the President, but these are not enough. Some observers endorse the addition of a "chief of staff" or a program coordinator to the President's staff, who will push administrative programs and iron out conflicts among the agencies.[21] The need is not for new instruments of administrative management or fiscal control but for "an office for central control, review, and reconciliation of the myriad particular programs and aspects of programs pursued by individual agencies to keep them consistent with the broad policies of the administration."[22]

Since World War II, largely because of huge armament expenditures and the need for central planning to ensure better management in government, two important agencies have been added to the President's executive staff. These are the Council of Economic Advisers and the

---

[19] This office has since been merged with the Civil Defense Agency and made a part of the Executive Office of the President.

[20] H. M. Somers, *Presidential Agency* (Cambridge: Harvard University Press, 1950), pp. 2–3, chaps. iii, vii, *passim.*

[21] Among others, Don K. Price, "Staffing the Presidency," 40, *American Political Science Review* (December, 1946), pp. 1154–68; John M. Gaus, *Reflections on Public Administration* (University, Ala.: University of Alabama Press, 1947), pp. 46–51; William Y. Elliot, *Hearings,* Joint Committee on the Organization of Congress, 1945, p. 963.

[22] Cited in Somers, *Presidential Agency,* p. 220.

National Security Council. In brief, the Council seeks to assist the President in forming national economic policy by providing expert analyses of economic developments which provide the basis for his annual Economic Report. The Security Council has broader terms of reference; it seeks to ". . . advise the President with respect to the integration of domestic, foreign, and military sources and the other departments and agencies of the Government to cooperate more effectively in matters involving the national security." Perhaps the most significant use of the Security Council arose in connection with the President's decision to send American troops into Korea in 1950.[23]

Despite these new aids, Executive control remains inadequate. Within the Executive Office itself a lack of unity and communication persists between the various specialist staffs. The integration that ensures a collective intelligence is lacking.[24] Externally the office has been unable to accomplish the difficult task of cutting through the federal hierarchy to achieve sustained contact with other agencies, particularly staff agencies.

Reorganization Power. Insofar as Executive control is increased by coherent organization and a rational division of authority and responsibility in an agency, the President's reorganization power is an important instrument. Beginning with the Reorganization Acts of 1939 and 1949 (as amended), he has been given power to submit reorganization schemes to Congress. While Congressional exemption of certain agencies has restricted such action, the most recent statute (1949) included no exemptions and extended somewhat the two-year time limit during which the President can act. Under this statute, President Truman submitted some forty reorganization plans in an effort, in his words, "to achieve a more responsible and efficient administration of Federal programs." The vast majority of these plans, which go into effect automatically in sixty days if not negated by a majority of House or Senate, were accepted by Congress.[25]

President Eisenhower has continued to use the reorganization power, as suggested by his letter accompanying Reorganization Plan No. 1 of 1958, which merged the civil defense establishment with the office of defense mobilization: "I transmit herewith Reorganization Plan No. 1 of 1958, prepared in accordance with the Reorganization Act of 1949, as

[23]Richard N. Snyder, "The U.S. Decision to Resist Aggression in Korea," 3, *Administrative Science Quarterly* (December, 1958), pp. 341–78.

[24] George Graham, "The Presidency and the Executive Office of the Presidency," 12, *Journal of Politics* (November, 1950), pp. 599–621.

[25] Senate Committee on Expenditures in the Executive Departments, 82d Cong., 2d sess., *Reorganization of the Federal Government* (Washington, D.C.: U.S. Government Printing Office, 1952).

amended. The reorganization plan provides new arrangements for the conduct of Federal defense mobilization and civil defense functions. In formulating Reorganization Plan No. 1, I have had the benefit of several studies made by the Executive Branch as well as those conducted by the Congress."

The principal effects of the reorganization were to transfer to the President the functions of the Civil Defense Administration and the Office of Defense Mobilization, establishing a single agency for the two somewhat related functions. A new Office of Defense and Civilian Mobilization was set up in the Executive Office of the President. The main reasons for the President's action are suggested by his concluding statement:

> The taking effect of the reorganizations included in Reorganization Plan No. 1 of 1958 will immediately reduce the number of Federal agencies by one and, by providing sounder organizational arrangements for the administration of the affected functions, should promote the increased economy and effectiveness of the Federal expenditures concerned. It is, however, impracticable to itemize at this time the reduction of expenditures which it is probable will be brought about by such taking effect. I urge that the Congress allow the reorganization plan to become effective.

The second Hoover Commission, reporting in 1955, brought public opinion to bear by its recommendations for further Executive reorganization. As the national chairman of its Citizens Committee put it, "a national ground swell of public sentiment for Federal economy and efficiency is gaining strength daily and is now close to the surface."[26] Since at about the same time the President was obliged to ask for an abrogation of the existing federal debt limit, those who emphasized the economy aspect of reorganization must have experienced some frustration. Nevertheless the Commission's record with Congress was impressive. In 1958 the House Government Affairs Committee reported that the second Hoover Commission had made 167 recommendations for reorganization that required legislative action. Of these, 55 were carried out by the 84th Congress, while the 85th Congress passed laws "consistent with 11 recommendations." By mid-1958 the Citizens Committee's major remaining objectives were as follows:

1. Reduce government competition with private enterprise.
2. Achieve "businesslike handling" of surplus property.
3. Eliminate the postal savings system.
4. Achieve unified procurement by the armed services.
5. Modernize federal personnel procedures, in part by the establishment of a nonpolitical "senior service" corps.
6. Coordinate federal medical services.

[26] Clarence Francis, *Congressional Quarterly*, April 4, 1958, p. 436.

Appeals to Public Opinion. By virtue of his position as political leader of his party, general manager of the executive branch, and commander in chief, the President enjoys great influence over public opinion. The Presidency provides a rostrum that enables its occupant to focus national attention upon great issues and to generate support for his policies. While this influence is most dramatically illustrated in Executive relations with a reluctant Congress, the President can also use his position to tune up the administrative machine. Despite the particularist forces which divide it, the bureaucracy performs a broadly representative function because its members share the dominant values of the community. It is well known that on various occasions, administrative agencies have offered greater resistance to special interests than have either the legislature or the courts. The public opinion that the President creates on policy issues not only defines more clearly for the agency the public interest insofar as it relates to these issues; it also helps the agency resist the claims of special groups. When faced with a particular issue, administrators often have difficulty in identifying the public interest. Presidential emphasis upon an issue, reinforced by the public discussion which follows, can provide both a criterion for administrative action and a base of support. The emphasis here upon the public interest and the tacit assumption that it can actually be identified are warranted by the fact that the issues upon which the President takes a stand usually involve interests that are broader than those of any single group or constellation of groups.

However, it is important to add that the effectiveness of appeals to public opinion is largely a function of the personality of the President and his conception of the office itself. In the case of Franklin D. Roosevelt, for example, the Presidency was used as a forum for vigorous leadership. President Eisenhower, on the other hand, has played a reluctant role, reflecting his conception of a legislatively dominated federal government.[27] Organizationally, such diverse conceptions are reflected in different degrees of dependence upon staff aides. Whereas both Truman and Roosevelt tended to act independently on vital issues, Eisenhower tends to delegate considerable authority to his immediate staff aides, such as the Assistant to the President.[28]

THREE VITAL SPEECHES. The most effective appeal to national opinion is through the statement of administrative policy in the three principal speeches made by the President each year. The State of the Union Message, for example, given at the opening session of each Congress, sets

---

[27] Among others, see Marian D. Irish, "The Organization Man in the Presidency," **20,** *Journal of Politics* (May, 1958).
[28] *Ibid.*

down very generally the main objectives of the administration. Cabinet members and key officials participate in drafting the message, indicating the major domestic and foreign problems and the general plan for attacking them. Thus the issues are placed before the nation, Congress, and the bureaucracy, and the responsibilities of all are clarified. The Economic Report, which consists of a detailed analysis of current economic problems and the prospect for the immediate future, provides another opportunity to formulate administrative policy and mobilize public support. Prepared with the aid of the Council of Economic Advisers, the report recommends legislation to meet existing or anticipated events. Finally, the President's Budget Message provides a means of planning and controlling administration by outlining the programs and financial requirements of the entire administration, as prepared by the Bureau of the Budget. Included in this message is a statement of the legislation (ranked in order of priority by the Legislative Reference Office of the Bureau) which the various agencies have requested.

These instruments of Presidential leadership and control are of great importance. They not only enable the President to focus public attention upon critical problems and his proposed solutions, but they also serve as a challenge to Congress and the bureaucracy. The President in effect says, "Here is my program; this is what I need in the way of legislation, money, administrative skill, and devotion." Given the representative character of the Presidency and the political independence the President enjoys because of his national constituency, this demand can have great weight. He possesses, moreover, a unity of intent and purpose, as well as a capacity for decisive action, which Congress by its very nature is unable to achieve. Unlike the individual administrator, who is hedged about by specific pressures and programs, the President has more freedom to speak in terms of the public interest. This combination of constitutional and strategic power gives him a peculiar advantage in focusing public opinion upon the bureaucracy, an opinion to which it will, as part of a democratic society, often respond.

CONCLUSION: CONTROL REMAINS INADEQUATE

The President, for several reasons, finds his control of the administrative arm less than adequate. The resistance of departments and agencies, each of which has its own external source of political strength, the sheer magnitude of the federal program, the opposition of Congress to measures strengthening Executive control—an important obstacle to federal reorganization, for example, has been the contest for power between the President and the Congress—and the peculiar position of the independent commissions, are the major factors that inhibit effective management by the Chief Administrator. He can, it is true, appoint his major aides and remove them. He can appeal to the nation, dramatizing issues which Congress and the bureaucracy must accept. By Executive Orders, directives to key officials, and reports from agencies he can guide administrative energy. The reorganization power, moreover, enables him to improve the structure and operation of the bureaucracy. His staff aids, particularly the Bureau of the Budget and the National Security Council, can also assist him in coordinating the economic and military resources of the nation.

But the task of supervising and controlling some seventy departments and agencies which report to the President is too great. The conflicting interests and loyalties of a competitive bureaucracy (which has been called the last vestige of free enterprise) create centripetal drives beyond the control of a single individual. While progress has been made through new staff aids, central planning, and reorganization, the President, like Congress, is still unable to comprehend and control the administrative branch. This emphasizes again a major theme in public administration: the necessity, given the size and discretion of the bureaucracy, of supplementing existing measures of control with a more positive instrument, namely, *an appeal to the ethical and professional sensibilities of the public servant,* to which we now turn.

BIBLIOGRAPHY

BARNARD, C. I. *The Functions of the Executive.* Cambridge: 1938.

BERNSTEIN, M. H. *The Job of the Federal Executive.* Washington, D.C.: 1958.

BINKLEY, W. E. *The Man in the White House.* Baltimore: 1959.

CORWIN, E. S. *The Presidency: Office and Powers.* New York: 1958.

FENNO, JR., R. F. *The President's Cabinet.* Cambridge: 1959.

MACMAHON, A. W. "Woodrow Wilson as Legislative Leader and Administrator," **50**, *American Political Science Review* (September, 1956).

NEUSTADT, R. S. "Presidency and Legislation: Planning the President's Program," **49**, *American Political Science Review* (December, 1955).

SCHUBERT, JR., G. S. *The Presidency in the Courts.* Minneapolis: 1956.

SOMERS, H. M. *OWMR: Presidential Agency.* Cambridge: 1952.

CHAPTER 31

Administrative Responsibility

The preceding two chapters have been concerned with the problem of making administration responsible. It is now clear that the public official both designs and executes public policy, because of his technical skill and the discretion which comes with increased governmental activity. But how can the community obtain a degree of control proportionate to the influence that administrators now possess? Lord Beveridge once said, "democracy, if it knows its business, has no need to fear bureaucracy." If administration is not to become arbitrary and complacent, however, the public must take steps to know its business. And this must somehow be done without denying the official the initiative he needs in a complex society. Some modification of the formal measures of control by executives, legislatures, and courts seems necessary. While such measures will continue to play their important role in making good the responsibility of the few to the many, responsible administration also depends upon the responsibility and skill of the administrator.

WHAT IS RESPONSIBILITY?

Some definition of the concept "responsibility" seems necessary. Although responsibility, like "the public interest,"[1] is a nebulous term, it is a basic democratic ideal, bound up with the idea of government's obligation to some external body or standard of behavior. For example, public administration is responsible to the rule of law doctrine, which provides a fairly effective standard for judging administrative decisions. Political responsibility is similarly involved with the idea of government's control by public opinion, political parties, and the community. Responsibility is also commonly used to denote the obligation of an individual to be-

[1] The lively role of values in public administration is clearly apparent in this chapter, which in discussing "the public interest" and the "proper" role of the official reflects the subjective preferences of the authors.

have according to certain standards of conduct. In public administration, responsibility often has a negative connotation: we are usually satisfied if the official is kept from wrong doing.

Responsibility and Accountability. "Responsibility" and "accountability" should be distinguished. Accountability refers to the formal or legal locus of responsibility. Responsibility on the other hand, has a highly personal, moral quality and is not necessarily related to formal status or power, although it is probably true that greater power brings greater responsibility. Thus a department head is accountable for the actions of all his subordinates, although in actual fact he is not "responsible" for their use of the power which he must of necessity delegate to them. Similarly in exercising discretion the official is morally responsible for his decisions, although he is often not legally accountable. In practice, responsibility must be shared; it percolates down throughout the entire administrative branch. On the other hand, accountability, which concerns the formal relationships between administration and the legislative and judicial branches, can never be shared. In general the bureaucracy is regarded as accountable to elected representatives and to the courts who give meaning to the rule of law doctrine. Within the Executive branch, accountability is sought through a hierarchy of offices and duties that makes possible a "line of command" from top to bottom. The chiefs of the various departments must answer to the President as general manager. Bureau, section, and division chiefs are legally accountable in turn to department heads. Upon the President falls the impossible task of coordinating and directing the entire executive branch. Under the Constitutional mandate that gives him "executive power" and directs him to ensure that "the laws are faithfully executed," he is accountable for the entire administrative branch.

This legal theory of accountability, however, is misleading. Actually, the President's control over the executive arm is limited by the vast size and conflicting loyalties of the bureaucracy, as well as by the diffusion of power in our system. He cannot hope to supervise or even be aware of the activities of the agencies for which he is constitutionally accountable. Executives at every level face a similar problem. As a result, legal accountability often becomes a mere façade, like the public interest rhetoric of a bureau chief who is in fact the captive of his most vocal clientele group. In such instances, the prestige of the state is bent to the service of private groups, and hence responsibility to the general public, the chief executive, and the department head is a myth. As we have seen, this situation is encouraged by the size and scope of governmental activity and by the diffusion of power in our political system.

Administrative Discretion. Responsibility is also bound up with discretion. When an official has no power to choose among alternatives, he cannot be held personally responsible because he has exercised no choice. If this situation *were* characteristic of administration, the head of an agency could be held *responsible* as well as *accountable* for everything its members did. In modern administration, however, it is clear that officials have considerable discretion. The locus of responsibility has shifted from the top and is now diffused throughout the entire bureaucracy. Responsibility is broadly shared, and the traditional measures of popular control suffer accordingly. At the same time the necessity of relying on the moral and professional ethics of the individual official becomes greater. Responsible administration is further complicated by the fact that the decision maker is often not only unaccountable, but also anonymous. In practice, this means that the legally accountable chief must often assume a burden of moral responsibility that properly belongs to his subordinates. Thus the President may be held responsible for unethical conduct anywhere in the civil service. This suggests why many executives are reluctant to delegate. If a subordinate errs, they are accountable.

These factors mean that traditional concepts of administrative responsibility tend to be unrealistic and vastly oversimplified. They fail to recognize the highly institutionalized nature of administrative behavior in which decisions are a joint product of many minds. The increase of official discretion that follows the failure of our political parties to provide clear guidelines of public policy is hardly recognized. A power vacuum is created into which administrators, interest groups, and other wielders of informal power move. The psychological differences that cause one official to grasp authority while his colleague shrinks from power also tend to be overlooked. The broad range of official reactions to community expectations is often minimized. Too often, in an effort to rationalize democratic theory, officials are viewed as mere automatons who passively follow the dictates of higher reason, presumably supplied by legislatures.

RESPONSIBILITY TO WHOM?

Despite these complexities, there are a few rough standards that help determine the true locus of administrative responsibility. One criterion is the location of an agency's ultimate loyalty: To whom does an agency answer? Whose objectives and values does its program tend to reflect? It is not enough to say that agencies are responsible to the people at large through their elected representatives. One must analyze particular agencies in particular situations and build generalizations about their concept of responsibility. It is clear that an agency must often compromise between numerous interests, but by checking its decisions and policies over time in selected cases where the issues are fairly well defined, it is possible to determine where its responsibility lies.

The various publics influenced by an agency will, of course, have different points of view about its "proper" role. Interest groups sometimes regard regulatory agencies as service units. Consumers, on the other hand, may regard them as defenders of the majority interest over against such groups. But this does not prevent the careful observer from discovering an agency's locus of responsibility.[2]

An administrator's loci of responsibility probably include the following:

1. Responsibility to some normative standard such as the "public interest."
2. Responsibility to the ethical and technical standards of his professional group.
3. Responsibility to his agency's most powerful and vocal clientele group.

What are the advantages and limitations of these criteria? Certainly it is easy to demolish the "public interest" as an operational concept, except in the broad and vital sense that it binds the community together by its very abstractness. Perhaps, like the platforms of our political parties, the strength of the public interest concept lies in its very vagueness.

A Hierarchy of Values. In considering the values that influence the official, it seems worthwhile to pose the idea of a hierarchy of values. This recognizes that many values affect the administrator's behavior but assumes that these values are assigned different weights in the administrator's calculus of behavior in a given situation. We have suggested three possible elements in this hierarchy: the official's professional standards; the values of his dominant clientele group; and his conception of the public interest. (In many cases his decisions will be based upon an amalgam of these values.) While the administrator will no doubt weigh all these factors in making up his mind, we can assume that he will not weigh them all equally. The problem, of course, is that one cannot generalize as to how administrators will weight such values in given cases, since this will vary in terms of the situation, the administrator's personality, the prestige and independence of his agency, the power and status of the individual or group whose interest is at issue, and several other factors.[3] We can only generalize that in the decision-making process, the

[2] A well-documented analysis of administrative responsibility to a particular interest is available in Arthur Maass, *Muddy Waters* (Cambridge: Harvard University Press, 1951).

[3] For a thoughtful analysis of the many problems affecting a given decision, see Wayne, A. R. Leys, *Ethics for Policy Decisions* (Englewood Cliffs, N.J.: Prentice-Hall, Inc., 1952), chaps. xix, xx, xxi.

administrator will consider several variables and that these will be assigned different weights according to his personality and the peculiar conditions impinging upon the given situation. In many cases the "public interest" will have the highest priority; in others, the welfare of the official's major client groups; sometimes, his professional standards will carry more weight.

As we saw in the chapter on decision making, careful studies of representative decisions are required in order to determine the procedure and the substantive characteristics that affect decision making. It may be possible eventually to predict results as certain categories of decisions are analyzed. But at present we cannot do much more than emphasize the complexity and the variability of decisions. However, we have enough empirical evidence from statements of civil servants, politicians, and students of administration to conclude safely that such values as professionalization, the public interest, and clientele interests do press upon the administrator when he exercises discretion.[4]

Role of Value Judgments. Normatively speaking, we shall argue that the public interest "should" be paramount among these criteria. The demand for responsible administration requires some standard as to what in fact constitutes responsible administration. To whom is responsibility due? The answer to this question involves value judgments; as an "ought" question it is not subject to scientific validation, but it is worth discussing. Should an administrative agency be responsible to those groups most intimately affected by its activities, to the agency's idea of the public interest, to the professional sense of expertise which the agency brings to its task, or to some amalgam of these alternatives? The answer hinges on one's definition of "the public interest." Although the concept is purely normative, it is our belief that the primary allegiance of the administrator should be to the public interest, defined as the majority and usually the consumer interest.[5]

Setting aside for the moment the considerations that oppose such a conclusion, let us develop this theme.

IMPACT OF DEMOCRATIC THEORY. The public official cannot avoid being influenced in some measure by the dominant political thought of the

---

[4] Among others, see A. Maass, *Muddy Waters*; E. Pendelton Herring, *Public Administration and the Public Interest* (New York: McGraw-Hill Book Co., Inc., 1936); P. Appleby, *Big Democracy* (New York: Alfred A. Knopf, Inc., 1948); W. J. Gore, "Decision Making in a Federal Field Office," **16**, *Public Administration Review* (Autumn, 1956), pp. 281–91.

[5] Even Adam Smith maintained that "consumption is the sole end and purpose of all production; and the interest of the producer ought to be attended to, only so far as it may be necessary for promoting that of the consumer. The maxim is so perfectly self-evident, that it would be absurd to attempt to prove it." *The Wealth of Nations,* edited with Introduction and Notes by Edwin Cannan (London: Methuen & Co., Ltd., [1930]), Book 4, chap. viii, p. 159.

society in which he lives. In this century, such thought strongly reflects a majoritarian emphasis as shown by our survey of democratic theory in Chapter 2. The official knows (or at the very least he often wants to believe) that final political authority rests in all the people. The authority to act must necessarily be delegated to elected representatives and appointed officials—to legislatures and chief executives, and to the administrative branch that reflects and molds their policy. But this imperative does not change the fact that popular sovereignty and majority rule are the essential ideals of American government.

In the liberal democratic view, moreover, the state is now widely regarded as a means of extending and guaranteeing both individual and community freedom, rather than as an instrument for curbing an arbitrary majority. Government is no longer, as Madison would have it, devoted mainly to the preservation of that "diversity in the faculties of men from which the rights of property originate." Instead, government is often regarded as a means of preventing economic dislocation and ensuring social, economic, and political equality. This view of government has deep roots in democratic theory and has been increasingly realized in practice in democratic countries during the twentieth century.[6] In the process an inversion of government's historic role has occurred. As Carl Becker says:

In the eighteenth century the most obvious oppressions from which men suffered derived from governmental restraints on the free activity of the individual. Liberty was therefore naturally conceived in terms of the emancipation of the individual from such restraints. In the economic realm this meant the elimination of governmental restraints on the individual in choosing his occupation, in contracting for the acquisition and disposal of property, and the purchase and sale of personal services. But in our time, as a result of the growing complexities of a technological society, the emancipation of the individual from governmental restraint in his economic activities has created new oppressions, so that for the majority of men liberty can be achieved only by an extension of governmental regulation of competitive business enterprise.[7]

EXTENDING INDIVIDUAL OPPORTUNITY. In the United States, despite some rather articulate mythology to the contrary, the main political drift is thus toward majoritarian government. It seems impossible, moreover, to separate individual gains from community gain; to insist, in effect, that a majority-oriented government must necessarily deny or harm individual rights or minority interest in order to achieve community ends. Instead, contemporary democracy has usually sought to extend privilege beyond a limited group, thereby adding to the sum of indi-

[6] Alpheus Thomas Mason, "American Individualism: Fact and Fiction," 46, *American Political Science Review* (March, 1952), pp. 1–18.

[7] Carl Becker, *Modern Democracy* (New Haven: Yale University Press, 1941), p. 34.

vidual opportunity and freedom. It should not be forgotten that the strength of liberal democracy in the eighteenth and nineteenth centuries came from its devotion to freedoms which transcended class lines —freedom of speech and religion, and freedom from oppressive administration. Economic freedom alone, on the other hand, can never command such widespread support because of the conflict between the economic interests of social groups.

In this sense the public interest is bound up with the majority or the community interest. Aristotle made the need for such a community feeling clear in his claim that any form of government was acceptable, provided the rules aimed at the good of all rather than at the good of certain classes. Lord Bryce, similarly, in describing democracy said, "the average citizen . . . will try to comprehend the main issues of policy, bringing to them an independent and impartial mind, which thinks first not of its own but the general interest." This "general interest" theme runs throughout western democratic political theory. At the same time, of course, individual liberty has been a constant factor, and since World War II we are all aware of how government action can threaten individual freedom. However, as Leslie Lipson maintains, ". . . to the modern mass electorate, equality has the same significance that liberty had for the middle class a century ago, because equality is more likely than liberty to promote the economic and social security which the mass of people desire."[8]

SEEKING THE PUBLIC INTEREST

We now turn to some opposing considerations. Despite the ethical impact of democratic theory and the evidence that the public interest is essentially a majoritarian ethic, the official often finds that "the public interest" is a tenuous guide for his behavior. Like many of our democratic ideals, the public interest as a concept remains almost as vague as it was during the eighteenth century when Rousseau defined it as "the general will." In Machiavellian terms, its strategic usefulness is probably the most obvious quality of the public interest. On every hand it is eulogized by legislators, officials, and pressure groups. Individuals and groups (including at times, one suspects, administrative agencies) often justify their limited objectives in terms of the public interest, seeking thereby to broaden their base of popular support by associating themselves with an honorific symbol. But no one defines the public interest precisely, and few attempt to rationalize it as an operational standard for administrative action.

[8] Leslie Lipson, "The Prospects of Representative Democracy," 11, *Journal of Politics* (August, 1949), p. 563.

Glendon Schubert, Jr., who has tried to operationalize the concept, has concluded that we must forget about the substantive side of the public interest and devote ourselves to its *procedural* implications, either establishing via systematic research the relationship between the "public interest" and official behavior or else ceasing to mislead students by writing about something that doesn't exist.[9] This somewhat immaculate view fails, however, to appreciate I. W. Thomas' comment, "If things are defined as real, they are real in their consequences." If an administrator defines his own view of what ought to be done as "the public interest" and enjoys whatever impetus in morale and energy this claim gives, the consequences are "real," they are an important variable both in his conduct and in the research spectrum of the observer. Many powerful motivations and beliefs that affect administration are not presently subject to precise analysis and validation because of the complexity of human behavior and the variability of the situations in which decisions are made. No one doubts that it would be highly satisfying to be able to demonstrate scientifically the character and impact of the "public interest" in a series of instances, but the pressure of events prevents us from remaining immobilized until that time arrives. In sum, the present normative, majoritarian public interest isn't much, but it's all we've got. Certainly the idea that the public interest is what remains when all affected parties are satisfied enough to stop fighting is not much of a substitute.[10] The "group process" view that there is no public interest other than the resulting balance among the claims of special interests is equally unsatisfactory except as a description (or a legitimation) of what too often occurs in administration.[11]

Group Basis of Political Behavior. The analysis of responsible administration and the public interest is complicated by the pluralism of American society. As Arthur E. Bentley showed some time ago, ours is a political system in which infinitely varied groups and associations compete and cooperate to attain their ends. Most of them, moreover, rationalize these ends in terms of the public interest. They usually seek to gain popular approval by identifying with approved values. Labor

[9] Glendon A. Schubert, Jr., "The Public Interest in Administrative Decision-Making," 51, *American Political Science Review* (June, 1957), pp. 346, 346–68.

[10] Avery Leiserson, *Administrative Regulation* (Chicago: University of Chicago Press, 1942), p. 14.

[11] As one observer concludes, in "the public interest as a balance of interests, the public interest ceases to be either 'public' or 'interest.' It ceases, furthermore, to be a prior standard by which we might evaluate the claims of competing interests . . . since it does not exist until after the group struggle is lost and won, it can provide no benchmark for policy formation. . . . all public policy is *ipso facto* in the public interest"; Frank J. Sorauf, "The Public Interest Reconsidered," *Journal of Politics* (November, 1957), pp. 629–30.

unions, corporations, governments, and universities, however oligarchic, strive to achieve deference by structural and procedural concessions to the democratic way. Such efforts illustrate the *practical significance* of value propositions such as the public interest.

Faced by the confusion and ethical devaluation attending this competition for respectability, some observers have come to hold that no national interest distinct from the interests of such groups exists.[12] This group thesis of politics is very suggestive, for clearly individual objectives in our complex society are usually attained through group action, and the great influence of interest groups in our system is well established. However, the thesis leads to the following questionable proposition: that public administration should be responsible primarily to organized client groups, since they are part of the public interest and are the only groups which systematically make their wishes known.[13] In a word, agencies are responsible if they meet the demands of their client groups through negotiation, consultation, and the securing of adequate support for their programs from interested publics.[14] But is this not the very criterion that has motivated the FCC and the FTC and has brought them under Congressional investigation for unethical practices and subordination to the interests they are presumed to regulate?[15]

[12] Others, however, who accept the group character of political action, maintain that there is a larger interest; E. H. Carr, for example, says "every modern state has intervened, first, to protect employers against trade unions, and, later, to protect the rights of the unions. If we wish to get a correct picture of the structure of the modern world, we must think not of a number of individuals . . . but of a number of large and powerful groups, sometimes competing, sometimes cooperating, in the pursuit of their group interests, and of a state constantly impelled to increase the strength and scope of its authority in order to maintain the necessary minimum of cohesion in the social fabric. . . . The issue is whether to allow social action to depend on the haphazard outcome of a struggle between interest groups or to control and coordinate the activities of these groups in the interest of the community." *The Conditions of Peace* (New York: The Macmillan Co., 1942), pp. 74–75. The student who seeks to understand contemporary society, and particularly the reinterpretation of nineteenth-century "liberty" into twentieth-century "equality" should read this book.

[13] The "functional representation" theory is expressed in C. M. Wiltse, "The Representative Function of Bureaucracy," 35, *American Political Science Review* (June, 1941), pp. 510–15.

[14] Among others, see Arthur Maass and L. I. Radway, "Gauging Administrative Responsibility," 9, *Public Administration Review* (Summer, 1945), p. 184: "an administrative agency should be responsible to pressure groups as far as necessary to equalize opportunities for safeguarding interests, to acquire specialized knowledge, and to secure consent for its own program."

[15] While his statements seem overdrawn and no doubt reflect the circumstances surrounding his removal by the House Subcommittee on Legislative Oversight, the conclusions of Bernard Schwartz, chief counsel for the subcommittee, are germane:

1. That "the evidence brought to light at last week's hearings has shown shocking improprieties on the part of the chairman of the Federal Communications Commission."

2. That "members of the subcommittee [are] . . . suppressing the investigation for

Undoubtedly this criterion meets the demands of organizational survival in our system, but its relevance to responsibility and the public interest is less apparent. Indeed, one could argue that an agency's resistance to client group demands provides a better index of its responsibility, since, in the case of the regulatory agencies, at least, its obligation is to enhance the *public* interest, convenience, and necessity.

Under the theory of functional representation, moreover, the bureaucracy presumably becomes a passive agent that merely referends the power of organized groups. Administrative behavior becomes only a reflection of the existing distribution of economic and social power. Finally, the group thesis seems to accept the mechanistic notion that competition among special interests culminates in the general interest. In this sense it is a philosophy of frustration that leaves little place for the community objectives which government in a politically sophisticated society must seek. Democratic government survives by its ability to compromise special interests, not merely among themselves but in the larger public interest. But as we have seen, the public interest cannot be systematically defined.

Operational Significance of the Public Interest. The public interest is not systematically defined because it is usually impossible to identify in any specific instance. It would, of course, be most helpful if the executive faced with a vital decision could determine objectively the public interest and act accordingly. However, even if such a reality existed in a given case, it is not possible to isolate it. Definition of the public interest, therefore, is largely a matter of the values of the particular individual or group defining it.

Why, then, our concern with the public interest? *Simply because it is a powerful social myth which exerts a sustained influence on administrative behavior.* Actually we are not speaking of *the* public interest, but rather of the conception of the public interest that some administrators have as members of a democratic community. For example, it is often maintained that there is some inherent opposition between special interests and the general interest. Whether this is objectively true or not, many individuals *believe* it to be true and act accordingly. This suggests again the majoritarian nature of the public interest. In a democracy, majority is, over time and with many aberrations, the best criterion. The public official will be conditioned by majority values. He may believe, for

---

fear lest evidence obtained of improper White House influence be made public."

3. That "the majority of the subcommittee ... [is] firing me knowing that I have evidence of the payment of money to a Federal Communications Commissioner in a competitive television case." *New York Times*, February 12, 1957, p. 20.

example, that it is "right" for the government to assume a major role in reducing the disparity between democratic theory and practice, as, for example, in the case of guaranteeing political rights of the Negro. He may believe that "the public interest is not the mere sum of the special interests, and it is certainly not the sum of the organized special interests. Nor is it an automatic consequence of the struggle of the special interests. . . ."[16] Operationally, then, the public interest may be defined as a normative standard that assists the official in achieving a working compromise between the claims of various publics, without sacrificing the interest of the inarticulate, unorganized majority.

REPRESENTATIVE ROLE OF BUREAUCRACY

Given the strategic role of administrators in compromising group claims, it is clear that the bureaucracy has a representative function. In the case of regulatory activity, for example, administrators give meaning to broad legislative declarations of social policy by their decisions in specific cases. In advancing the social objectives of the community, they sometimes develop a rough index of the public interest which is applied when decisions are made. The bureaucracy shares with the legislature the task of ensuring that the community receives a reasonable amount of justice in the distribution of public resources. Moreover, by virtue of a recruitment policy that gathers individuals with socio-economic backgrounds far more varied than those of Congress, the bureaucracy may be viewed as a truer cross-section of the nation, providing a necessary supplement to the incomplete representation which Congress offers.[17] Although this thesis violates traditional democratic theory, the hard facts of administrative policy determination and the official's role in compromising group demands suggest that orthodox interpretations require some modification.

In selecting among alternative policies, in extending or withdrawing consent, the official necessarily works in a value context. The various factors impinging upon a particular decision are isolated and assigned relative weights in accord with what the official thinks is "right." In many cases, the "public interest" will be an element in this process. This criterion is neither scientific nor quantitative. It is not necessarily based upon majority will because this will cannot be known, concerned with, or in many cases affected by the particular issue at hand. It is often not clearly rationalized in the official's mind in the sense that it is a conscious

---

[16] E. E. Schattschneider, "Political Parties and the Public Interest," 280, *Annals of the American Academy of Political and Social Science* (March, 1952), p. 22.

[17] For this point of view, see Norton E. Long, "Bureaucracy and Constitutionalism," 46, *American Political Science Review* (September, 1952), pp. 808–18.

influence. Rather his feeling for the public interest is an emotive force, bound up with the administrator's personal code of values, which will often in turn reflect the equalitarian values of our society.

Positive Role of Administration. In the modern democratic state, government does more than merely adjudicate the claims of organized groups. Public policy can no longer be allowed to reflect haphazard shifts in power relations among such groups. Instead, the state has been given a moral sanction to act as arbiter. As Reinhold Niebuhr maintains:

Social life, when not consciously managed and manipulated, does not develop perfect equilibria of power. Its capricious disproportions of power generate various forms of domination and enslavement. Human society therefore requires a conscious control and manipulation of the various equilibria which exist in it. There must be an organizing centre within a given field of social vitalities. This centre must arbitrate conflicts from a more impartial perspective than is available to any party of a given conflict; it must manage and manipulate the processes of mutual support so that the tensions inherent in them will not erupt into conflict; it must coerce submission to the social process by superior power whenever the instruments of arbitrating and composing conflicts do not suffice; and finally it must seek to redress the disproportions of power by conscious shifts of the balances whenever they make for injustice.[18]

The bureaucracy shares this responsibility.

This view of the official's role is sometimes challenged on the basis that it allows the official to "play God," to assume that he *knows* what the public interest is in any particular instance. The presumed neutrality of the public service is violated. But this is not the point. Delegated legislation and the institutionalized decisions that occur in our complex government have made policy leadership and choices by administrators inevitable. These decisions are not made in a vacuum. The official must act, and his actions will reflect certain assumptions about the public interest. How he arrives at a definition of that interest is an infinitely complex process, reflecting his social and political preferences, educational background, personal security, the nature of his agency's program, and the election returns. His loyalty to professional standards of competence also conditions his reaction to demands for preferential treatment; that is, his decisions will often be governed by the objective "law of the situation," rather than by personal or "political" considerations. The failure to recognize the role which the official plays in tempering particularist claims is one of the inadequacies of the group analysis of the political process.[19]

[18] Reinhold Niebuhr, *The Nature and Destiny of Man,* Vol. II (New York: Charles Scribner's Sons, 1948), p. 266.

[19] Merle Fainsod, "Some Reflections on the Nature of the Regulatory Process," in C. J. Friedrich and E. S. Mason (eds.), *Public Policy* (Cambridge: Harvard University Press, 1940), p. 298.

It is worth noting, moreover, that unorganized publics need the special attention of the administrator. Their interests will not be satisfied unless he is able to reconcile the disparities in power that exist in modern society. This is simply because "in the struggle between concentrated private interest and the diffused public interest, the former usually wins. For the decisions have to be made on individual items and not on great and glowing general principles. The special interests are organized on each of these individual items, but the public is uninformed and comparatively indifferent."[20] Certainly, competing groups must exist in a democracy, and their objectives are not necessarily in conflict with the public interest, but organized groups often distort public power to achieve limited objectives. The administrator, meanwhile, cannot avoid speculation about the results of his decisions for the various groups affected. These speculations will often include the unorganized consumer interest. This feeling for the public interest is a subjective and political aspect of administrative behavior which (like most value processes) is difficult to describe and perhaps impossible to quantify. No one can doubt, however, its influence on administrative decision making.

BIBLIOGRAPHY

Dotson, Arch. "Fundamental Approaches to Administrative Responsibility," *Western Political Quarterly* (September, 1957).

Forman, Howard I. "The Role of Courts in Effecting Administrative Responsibility," **22**, *Temple Law Quarterly* (January, 1949).

Leys, W. A. R. "Ethics and Administrative Discretion," **3**, *Public Administrative Review* (Winter, 1943).

——, *Ethics and Social Policy*. Englewood Cliffs, N.J.: 1941.

Leys, W. A. R., and Perry, C. M. *Philosophy and the Public Interest*. Chicago: 1959.

Moneypenny, Philip, "A Code of Ethics as a Means of Controlling Administrative Conduct," **13**, *Public Administration Review* (Spring, 1953).

Odegard, Peter H. "Toward a Responsible Bureaucracy," *Annals of the American Academy of Political and Social Science*, **292**, (March, 1954).

Schubert, Jr., Glendon A. "The Public Interest in Administrative Decision Making: Theorem, Theosophy, or Theory?" *American Political Science Review* (June, 1957).

Sixth American Assembly. *The Federal Government Service: Its Character, Prestige and Problems*. New York: 1954.

Sorauf, Frank J. "The Public Interest Reconsidered." *Journal of Politics* (November, 1957).

---

[20] Paul H. Douglas, *Economy in the National Government* (Chicago: University of Chicago Press, 1952), p. 220.

Index